FIFTH EDITION

NEWS REPORTING
AND WRITING

THE MISSOURI GROUP

Brian S. Brooks

George Kennedy

Daryl R. Moen

Don Ranly

School of Journalism
University of Missouri at Columbia

NEWS REPORTING
AND WRITING

St. Martin's Press
New York

Sponsoring editor: Suzanne Phelps Weir
Development editor: Sylvia L. Weber
Managing editor: Patricia Mansfield Phelan
Project editor: Diana Puglisi
Production supervisor: Joe Ford
Art director and cover designer: Lucy Krikorian
Text design: Dorothy Bungert, EriBen Graphics
Graphics: Accurate Art
Photo research: Eloise Marion
Cover art: Ralph Mercer Photography

Library of Congress Catalog Card Number: 95-67062

Manufactured in the United States of America.

0 9 8 7 6
f e d c b a

For information, write:
St. Martin's Press, Inc.
175 Fifth Avenue
New York, NY 10010

ISBN: 0-312-11718-3

Acknowledgments

Acknowledgments and copyrights are continued at the back of the book on pages
542–543, which constitute an extension of the copyright page.

Pp. 47 and 75. Excerpts from "Backhoe hits overpass, then kills two in vehicle" by Alison
Boggs, staff writer, *The* (Spokane, Wash.) *Spokesman-Review*, May 20, 1994, reprinted
courtesy of *The Spokesman-Review*.
Pp. 64-65. Article by Robert Rankin, *Detroit Free Press*, reprinted courtesy of Knight Ridder.
Pp. 73, 91. Linda Keene, *The Seattle Times*, excerpt from pp. 1 & 3. Copyright © March 11,
1993. Reprinted with permission.
P. 217. Excerpt from "To dazed L.A. . . ." by Paul Pringle, reprinted courtesy of Copley
News Service.
Pp. 228-230. "Chicago-Bound Plane Crashes; 68 Are Killed" by Flynn McRoberts and
George Papajohn, Nov. 1, 1994, © Copyrighted Chicago Tribune Company. All rights re-
served. Used with permission.
Pp. 230-231. "68 Die in Indiana Crash" by Jerry Bonkowski and Gary Fields, Nov. 1, 1994,
Copyright 1994, *USA Today*. Reprinted with permission.

CONTENTS

PART **TWO**

BASIC SKILLS

PART **THREE**

BASIC STORIES

PART **FOUR**

BEAT REPORTING

14 *Covering a Beat 292*

PART FIVE

SPECIALIZED TECHNIQUES

PART **SIX**

RIGHTS AND RESPONSIBILITIES

21 *Press Law 444*

PREFACE

For the prospective journalists of the 21st century, the one constant is change. News-gathering is changing. News distribution is changing. News audiences are changing. News rooms are changing. Even definitions of news are changing. Those changes are reflected and demonstrated in this fifth edition of *News Reporting and Writing*.

Organization of the Text

We begin where the craft of journalism begins—with consideration of what news is, who audiences are and what principles guide journalists in their efforts to supply readers, listeners and viewers with the news they need and want. The first chapter sets the tone for the entire book. It is written in clear journalistic style. It links theory to practice. It is packed with real examples drawn from the best work of journalists who are thriving in the world of constant change.

Chapter 1 also introduces ethics—a topic that runs throughout *News Reporting and Writing*. As teachers and practitioners, we believe that the toughest and most important ethical issues can be understood only in the context of the realities of journalism. So we return repeatedly to those issues in preparation for the detailed discussion, which we think is the most useful available in any reporting textbook, in Chapter 22.

From news we move to news rooms. In Chapter 2 we show you how news rooms and the journalists who work in them are changing to adapt to a multimedia world. We compare structures and functions of newspaper and television news rooms. We introduce you to the state-of-the-art on-line journalism that is rapidly becoming both a tool for reporting and a medium for reaching computer-literate audiences.

Then, in Part Two, you get down to work. Through example, explanation and exercise, you will learn the fundamental skills of reporting and storytelling. You'll start with the classic inverted pyramid, as alive today in on-line communication as it was on the newspaper pages of 50 years ago. You'll learn the importance of good writing and how to improve your own writing. You'll learn and practice interviewing skills. You'll learn how to capture the words people speak and how to put those quotes to good use. And you'll learn how to go beyond interviewing to locate information in documentary sources on the printed page and the computer screen. As you become familiar with the Internet and learn how to search electronic databases, you will have an opportunity to apply modern technology to achieve the traditional aims of journalism.

Next, in Part Three, comes the application of the basic skills to the basic stories—obituaries, rewriting news releases, speeches and meetings, accidents and disasters, crime and court proceedings, even follows.

In Part Four, you move from the basics, just as many professional reporters do, to the coverage of major beats ranging from local government to business to sports. Building on what you have learned, in Part Five you explore alternatives to the inverted pyramid, applying the tools of social science to reporting and to the most demanding form of journalism: investigative reporting. You'll also learn how to prepare copy for delivery on radio and television newscasts.

The two chapters in Part Six provide detailed discussions of law and ethics. Throughout the skills chapters, you will have encountered practical problems involving both. These last two chapters are resources that may be consulted any time legal and ethical issues arise.

What's New?

First page to last, this edition of *News Reporting and Writing* has been revised and updated to reflect the freshest thinking and incorporate the most relevant examples to prepare you for the changes sweeping the practice and the content of journalism. In "On the Job" boxes featured in every chapter, you'll hear from real working journalists who are grappling with those changes. One change is the growing importance of numeracy (literacy in numbers). You'll find examples and exercises giving you practice in reporting on and writing about numbers throughout the book and in the *Workbook*. Finally, this edition's fresh new design, reflecting a newspaper or magazine layout, features notes and quotes in the margin to summarize and amplify the text.

Ancillaries

The *Instructor's Manual* and the *Workbook* have also been expanded and updated. Supplementing the activities at the end of the chapters in the text, the *Workbook* contains approximately one hundred new exercises. Challenge exercises in every chapter provide a chance to develop your journalistic skills at a higher level. Special attention is paid to practice in the use of numbers and statistics and in accessing information from electronic sources. Another new source in the fifth edition of the *Workbook* is a city directory. City directories, which provide addresses and occupations along with phone numbers, are basic tools that professional reporters use every day. Now you have one, too. To increase your comfort with computerized journalism even more, exercises are provided on disk as well as in the *Workbook*. Additional grammar and style software, *The St. Martin's Wire Service Hotline*, is also available to adopters of the text.

One more thing: We hope that *News Reporting and Writing* will give you a sense of the importance and excitement of journalism. Those qualities are what make the work worthwhile.

Acknowledgments

We want to thank our colleagues for their contributions to this edition. Dr. Sandra Scott, an attorney who is on the Missouri journalism faculty, has updated her chapter on journalists and the law. Janine Latus, who teaches business reporting at Missouri, revised the chapter on that topic. Dan Kelly, a journalist on the staff of New Directions for News, a newspaper think tank, provided advice and examples dealing with numbers. Mike McKean, a broadcast journalist and colleague at the University of Missouri, helped with information about his field. We are grateful, too, to colleagues across the country who provided helpful comments and suggestions for this fifth edition: Paul H. Anderson, University of Tennessee at Martin; Dave Bennett, Indiana State University; Jean L. Brodey, Temple University; Wallace B. Eberhard, University of Georgia; Susanne C. Havlic, William Rainey Harper College; Napoleon Johnson, Houston Community College; George LaTour, Rhode Island College; Carol S. Lomicky, University of Nebraska at Kearney; Jack Lule, Lehigh University; John McClelland, Roosevelt University; David C. Nelson, Southwest Texas State University; Robert M. Ours, West Virginia University; Mary-jo Popovici, Monroe Community College; Chris Ransick, Arapahoe Community College; Carl Sessions Stepp, University of Maryland; and Jodell D. Strauch, Northwest Missouri State University.

The St. Martin's staff guided us, pulled us and cheered us through the extensive revisions. Thanks to Suzanne Phelps Weir, editor; Sylvia L. Weber, development editor; Diana Puglisi, project editor; Joe Ford, production supervisor; and Lucy Krikorian, art director.

We thank our students past and present whose work we've used to illustrate the principles of good journalism and from whom we've learned. And as always, we are grateful for the help of our spouses, who have been full partners in this project.

Brian S. Brooks
George Kennedy
Daryl R. Moen
Don Ranly

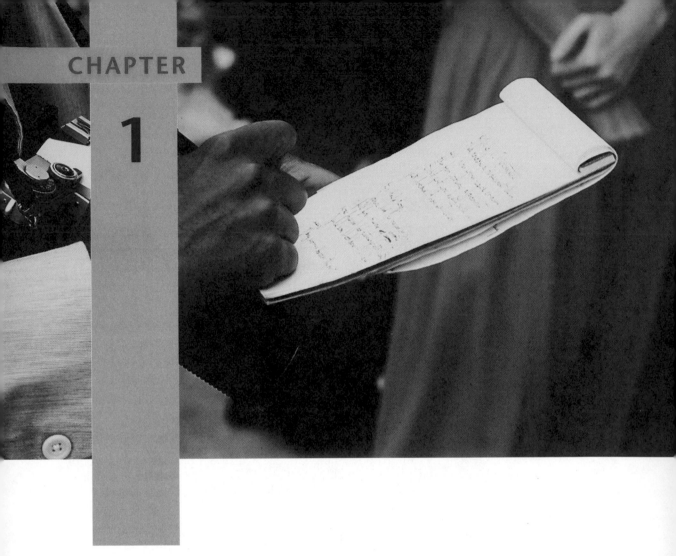

THE NATURE
OF NEWS

Imagine yourself as a reporter in the not-so-distant future. You're headed for a public forum your newspaper is sponsoring to help local residents organize to combat neighborhood crime. You pause to review your instructions.

When you get to the meeting room, you'll set up the video camera to record both pictures and sound. Then you'll find a seat on the aisle where you can take notes on your laptop computer and still move around to check the names of any speakers you'll want to quote.

Back at the office, you'll feed the video recording into the news-room computer, where it will be edited and displayed on the video and audio on-line services for those who want instant access to the news via computer or telephone. Then you'll sit down at a PC to write your story. First, you'll write a summary paragraph for the on-line bulletin board. Last but not least will come the story for tomorrow's paper. In it, you'll include the background and context that will add meaning even for those readers who have already learned the outcome from another medium.

It's all in a day's work.

At least, it's likely to be all in a day's work for the 21st-century reporter. Already, news organizations such as the Raleigh (N.C.) News and Observer, *the* Kansas City Star *and the* San Jose (Calif.) Mercury News *are looking to the future by taking advantage of new technology for gathering and reporting the news.*

Even the news itself is changing. You'll notice that as a future reporter you were covering an event sponsored by your employer. That's no fantasy. Newspapers, radio and television stations—sometimes working together—already are becoming participants in public affairs. A movement called "public journalism" is a response to the recognition that journalism and democracy must work together if both are to survive. "Public journalists" seek to help the democratic process work rather than merely stand back and report on its failures. Not all journalists agree completely with the philosophy of public journalism, but nearly all do agree that the journalist's proper role in the '90s and beyond is more than passive.

Changes in society and journalism's response are summed up well in the words of Gregory Favre, speaking as president of the American Society of Newspaper Editors (ASNE):

> Never before have we been needed as much as we are needed today. We are living in a time when communities as we have known them are breaking up, public places are becoming scarce, values are disappearing and newspapers are probably the last hope to keep people together.
>
> No other business can contribute more to the overall strength, vitality and conscience of a community. . . .
>
> We have to continue to find ways to meet readers' needs and expectations, to produce newspapers that are both educational and pleasurable, to embrace change as our readers are doing it in their own lives.

Columnist Ellen Goodman introduced an ASNE report on the future by identifying its theme in a phrase that could also serve as the theme for all of journalism near the turn of the 21st century—"permanent change."

Amid this change, some things remain the same. One is the central role of journalism in a democratic society. Another is the importance of accuracy and fairness in filling that role. A third is the continuing need for all who would be journalists to master the basic skills of reporting and writing—no matter what tools you use or how your reports reach the public.

What News Is

Webster's Unabridged Dictionary defines news as:

1. New information about anything . . .
2. recent happenings . . .
3. reports of such events, collectively.
4. a newspaper.

That definition raises more questions than it answers. Read your local newspaper, listen to a radio newscast, watch the evening news on any network. Clearly, not just "anything" is reported. Nor are all "recent happenings." And there are differences among what you see, hear and read. So how do journalists decide which pieces of new information, which recent happenings, are worth reporting?

The criteria used by professional reporters and editors can be summarized in three words:

Relevance
Usefulness
Interest

Those criteria apply generally, but each journalist and each news organization uses them in a specific context that gives them particular meaning. That context is supplied by *the audience.*

Let's look at an example:

The Springfield Police Department spends more money on drug enforcement than does the Lincoln County Sheriff's Department, but you wouldn't know that from the numbers of arrests and amount of drugs seized.

The two departments have different philosophies on how to keep drugs off the street.

The sheriff's department concentrates on arresting people who supply large quantities of drugs. The city police do not think the quantities are important.

"If we find drugs on them, they go to jail," said Springfield police Deputy Chief Dennis Veach. "We don't wait around until they have a large quantity."

Detective Ken Kreigh, supervisor of the sheriff's two-man drug enforcement unit, disagrees. "If I wanted to focus on small-time dealers, we could get a high arrest number that might be a good-looking statistic, but one bust of 20 kilos is worth a hundred little busts."

The story continues with details and examples. Consider its value to its audience. The *relevance* is obvious. The struggle to control drug trafficking concerns policy-makers, police and citizens in every community. This is a *useful* story because it explores and explains an important difference in the ways this community's law enforcement agencies approach this central—and controversial—duty. It's also useful because it explains how readers' tax money is being spent. The story draws no conclusions about which is the wiser or more effective policy. It's up to the citizens and their elected representatives to draw those conclusions. This story provides the information they need. The combination of relevance and usefulness add up to a high degree of reader *interest*.

You've been looking at a story that appeared in a newspaper. The same kind of story could have been reported for radio, television or the new computer-based media. The presentation would be different in each medium, but the news values that make it important and the reporting skills required to tell it would be the same. Later chapters will help you learn those skills. For now, let's look a little more deeply at news values, the criteria journalists use to decide which stories are worth telling.

Relevance, *usefulness* and *interest* are the broad guidelines for judging the news value of any event, issue or personality. Within those broad standards, journalists look for more specific elements in each potential story. The most important are these:

*Important elements
in a news story*

Impact
Conflict
Novelty
Prominence
Proximity
Timeliness

Impact—This is another way of measuring relevance and usefulness. How many people are affected by an event or idea? How seriously does it affect them?

Conflict—This is a recurring theme in all storytelling, whether the stories told are journalism, literature or drama. Struggles between people, among nations or with natural forces make fascinating reading. Conflict is such a basic element of life that journalists must resist the temptation to overdramatize or oversimplify it.

Novelty—This is another element common to journalism and other kinds of stories. People or events may be interesting and therefore newsworthy just because they are unusual or bizarre.

Prominence—Names make news. The bigger the name, the bigger the news. Ordinary people have always been intrigued by the doings of the rich and famous.

Proximity—Generally, people are more interested in and concerned about what happens close to home. When they read or listen to national or international news, they often want to know how it relates to their own community.

Timeliness—News is supposed to be new. If news is to be relevant and useful, it must be timely. For example, it is more useful to write about an issue facing the city council before it is decided than afterward. Timely reporting gives people a chance to be participants in public affairs rather than mere spectators.

Notice that this list suggests two important things about news. First, not all news is serious, life-and-death stuff. Journalism has been described as "a culture's conversation with itself." The conversation that holds a culture together includes talk of crime, politics and world affairs, of course; but it also includes talk of everyday life. It includes humor and gossip. All of that can be news. Second, news is more than just collections of facts. Telling the news usually means telling stories. The narrative, the humanity, the drama of storytelling is the art of journalism. To gather the facts for their stories, journalists use many of the same techniques used by sociologists, political scientists and historians. To tell their stories so that those facts can be understood, journalists often use the techniques of other storytellers, such as novelists and screenwriters.

Changing Audiences, Changing Journalism

The best judges of what is important and which stories are worth telling are the consumers of journalism, the audiences. Those audiences are changing, and so are the demands on journalists. The technology of gathering and distributing the news is changing, too.

One of the most important changes that the new media bring to you as a consumer is the ability to choose your news where and when you want it. Today, with a computer and modem, you don't have to wait for the nightly news on television or the delivery of the morning paper. You can call up the resources of an on-line source at any time of the day or night. You can seek out as much depth and detail as you want, or you can choose to ignore broad subjects altogether. The new computer-based media, in other words, put consumers in charge of their news. You'll find out more about that in Chapter 2. Let's look now at the consumers of journalism and what they want and need.

The American Society of Newspaper Editors sponsored a research project intended to create a newspaper for the year 2000. Here's a summary of what the researchers concluded about wants and needs:

- Readers want news in their newspapers.
- Readers want news to be relevant and to focus on them and their community.
- Readers do not want their newspapers to ignore what is going on elsewhere in the nation and the world.
- Readers are not fooled by gimmicks or fancy designs. They will accept them only if they seem relevant to stories, make the newspaper easier to use or make the information easier to grasp. If the gimmicks are self-conscious or the designs radical, readers will reject them for interfering with their ease of readership.
- Readers want practical and useful information that helps them

live their lives. They want tips and advice. As the lifestyles of readers change, editors must produce newspapers that focus on how they live. . . .

With just a few changes in wording, this list of wants and needs could apply to consumers of broadcast news, too. The new emphasis on keeping up with the changing needs of changing audiences arises from one of those changes—the tremendous increase in competition for the time and attention of people who every day have more demands on both. Just consider for a moment the sources of information and entertainment available to you. There are newspapers, of course. There are magazines and books. There are dozens of channels of cable television. If you have access to a computer and modem, there are worldwide interlocking networks to explore.

Journalists traditionally have been "gatekeepers" who sorted through multiple sources of information, discarded much and let some through onto pages or screens. In the future, that role is more likely to be one of "navigator." Journalists will continue to organize and explain, but their audiences will expect and need more than will fit on a newspaper page or television screen. People who are pressed for time don't have much to waste on irrelevant or useless materials. And when they need to know more, they need to know it now. Already, journalists are tapping sources such as computer databases and on-line references for their own work, and pointing readers and viewers in the same direction.

When you consider what soon will be widely available, journalists today stand where seafarers stood 500 years ago—on the edge of the unknown. Just as those navigators mapped the way for the less adventurous, so will journalists have to learn the information highways and byways and then lead audiences toward the information resources they'll need.

The New Audiences

And just who are those audiences, anyway? New Directions for News, a think tank for newspapers, has taken a fresh look and discovered what it calls "the new USA." The population of this new USA will consist of:

- 51 percent women
- 30 percent young adults, between ages 18 and 34
- 25 percent ethnic minorities and immigrant groups
- 21 percent adults over 50
- 15 percent aged 5-17.

Teams of futurists working with New Directions for News came up with prototype publications aimed at meeting the needs of the new USA. The prototype for women was called *The New News* (see Figure 1.1). Its features included:

"(On television) Superficiality is not just built into the lack of time. It's that we spend a lot of time not on the phone, not in the library, but trying to show visually what we're talking about."

— Sam Donaldson, ABC News correspondent

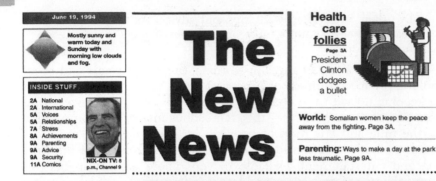

June 19, 1994

Mostly sunny and warm today and Sunday with morning low clouds and fog.

INSIDE STUFF

2A National
2A International
5A Voices
5A Relationships
7A Stress
8A Achievements
9A Parenting
9A Advice
9A Security
11A Comics

NIX-ON TV: 6 p.m., Channel 9

The New News

Health care follies
Page 3A
President Clinton dodges a bullet

World: Somalian women keep the peace away from the fighting. Page 3A.

Parenting: Ways to make a day at the park less traumatic. Page 9A.

NO WAY: Mai Chin didn't stand by while her home was "legally" taken away. She fought back — and won.

Don Juan in Court

Would reviving seduction suits keep lovers honest?

By Jim Warren
New News Staff

Cynthia, a 33-year-old Chicago lawyer, said "I felt like someone had stabbed me with a knife" after she was dumped by a 43-year-old divorced biotech executive who had lied and not let on to his simultaneous dating of a divorcee and an ex-live-in girlfriend. Well, how about taking him to court? If Jane Larson, an associate professor at Northwestern University School of Law, has her way, it would be possible: She's arguing for bringing back the 19th

Mr. Don Juan

Century cause of action (a 'tort' in legalese) of seduction, which was used mainly by Victorian women who became social pariahs after bearing children out of wedlock. An updated version would emphasize loss of trust and control, anger and violation of bodily integrity that come from being sexually exploited, Larson says. "The injury here is having
Turn to DON JUAN, Page 2A

Folks hurl trash back at council

By Stacy Wasserman
New News Staff

The city council's attempt to force citizens to keep their garbage longer ran amok when one homeowner hurled a ripe red tomato at the city leaders.

"Keep it yourself," shouted a middle-aged woman, breathing heavily as she took careful aim at the commissioners. She missed her mark – barely – but eluded police and escaped into the dark night. The law had its hands full suppressing the uproar that erupted in the packed and steaming council chambers.

The melee lasted 10 minutes. Before it was over,
See MAD, Page 2A

What the council did:
Voted (4-3) last night to space out garbage collection schedules so that collections will be made every nine days, rather than weekly.

By Seymore Jefferson
New News Staff

Mai Chin stood in front of her brick bungalow on Wilson Avenue and looked at the For Sale sign that a superior court judge ordered removed yesterday.

The action in the civil case brought on Chin's behalf by the Neighborhood Legal Action League came one day after the district attorney announced the indictment of three mortgage brokers and two lawyers.

Authorities said the brokers, and the lawyers working for them, cheated Chin and more than a dozen other recent widows out of their homes.

"It sounded good, like I needed the help," Chin said. "But they were not helping me. They should go to jail."

The For Sale sign was still in front of Chin's home, but First National Bank said the home was no longer on the market.

Instead of enforcing the terms of the second mortgage whose payments Chin could not meet, the bank said it would end foreclosure proceedings and reinstate the mortgage on which Chin and her late husband had made more than 18 years of payments. Chin said she and her family could meet those payments.

No charges were filed against First National or its employees. The bank had provided funds to the mortgage companies for the loans and purchased the second mortgages from them after they were signed.

Assistant District Attorney Maria Cartanini, the prosecutor in the criminal case, said the second mortgages which Chin and the other women had signed violated state consumer protection and banking statutes.

The two owners of Sunset Mortgage and the owner of Lifelong Mortgage were charged with 14 criminal counts including fraud and felony theft. The two lawyers who represented the mortgage companies at closings each face four felony charges of criminal misrepresentation.

It was Chin's complaints, first to the city's Consumer Services
Please see CHIN, Page 2A

One woman said no

'I was not going to lose my house. They should have known that.'
– Mai Chin

Inside Stress: How to tell your boss where to go, losing your job, nasty children and never-ending seminars ...   Page 3B

Figure 1.1.
The New News, *a prototype newspaper of the future designed for women, features articles by and about women and a personalized writing style intended to appeal to this major market segment.*

The audiences of the 21st century

▪ *By 2050, one-fifth of the U.S. population will be Hispanic.*

▪ *By 2010, married couples will no longer make up a majority of households.*

▪ *By 2025, Americans over 64 will outnumber teenagers 2-1.*

▪ *In the 1990s, people entering the work force will work for an average of five different companies and will work in 10 different jobs before they retire.*

▪ *By 2000, nearly two-thirds of new workers will be women.*

▪ *By 2000, one-third of all school-age children will be from racial or ethnic minorities or immigrant populations.*

All from Undercovered: The New USA, *published by New Directions for News*

▪ smaller pages, designed to be more comfortable for women to hold;
▪ women depicted in a variety of roles, not merely as victims;
▪ issues important to women, from the "everyday" struggles of balancing family and career, to public policy problems such as crime and politics, to success stories of role models;
▪ women's presence in stories written from a personal viewpoint and containing the detail and description women regularly find in magazines; and
▪ women as sources and as subjects, and women writers on all topics.

For young adults, a group that is reluctant to read traditional newspapers, the futurists came up with *Power* (see Figure 1.2). The "windows" on the front of this prototype could serve as gateways to stories on the inside of the paper or even to further information available on-line. The prototype's theme is empowerment. Its goal is to encourage and to help young adults understand and master their world. A glance at the topics shows less from such traditional sources as capitals and city halls, and more from young people themselves with relevant, useful stories to tell.

Richard Saul Wurman has written a book every journalist should read and read again. It is called *Information Anxiety*. In it, Wurman says that most news could be divided into three categories: hope, absurdity and catastrophe. Journalists typically emphasize absurdity and catastrophe. Audiences hunger for hope. You'll notice that the prototypes for new newspapers include a lot more news of hope than most traditional papers or news programs usually offer. Another term for the journalism of hope is "solution" journalism. Instead of merely pointing out problems, which can increase feelings of detachment and despair, journalists can identify possible solutions to those problems, provide examples of such solutions and tell audiences where to go for further information or how to get involved.

Wurman makes another point that journalists are beginning to grasp: Mere information is not the most valuable product. Understanding is essential to effective communication. As journalists concentrate on telling stories that are relevant and useful, they are more likely to convey understanding. Without that, audiences drift, and sometimes drown, in the ever-deepening sea of information.

"The computer is an icon for our age, but reason and imagination, which yield understanding, are yet to be programmable."
— *Richard Saul Wurman*

The New Journalism

When journalism has been done well, it always has been a demanding craft. Gathering information, organizing it coherently, placing it in context and writing it clearly—that is work that has tested the intelligence, skill and stamina of practitioners since Daniel Defoe wrote his *Journal of a Plague Year*. Now, in some ways, the demands are becoming even greater. Let's consider why.

Figure 1.2.
Power *is a prototype of a future newspaper for young adults. The layout is designed to appeal to an audience reared on computers, and the content focuses on readers as the subject of news.*

First, the tools journalists use are becoming more powerful and more sophisticated. In later chapters you will be introduced to the most important of these tools—the computer. You will see how you can—and must—move beyond the keyboard to use the computer for such tasks as checking background information in the reference library, conducting database searches that extend reporting beyond the interview, even performing analyses of budget data and surveys. With better tools, you'll be expected to produce better stories.

Second, the requirement to report and write stories that are relevant, useful and interesting means that the days of the reporter-as-recorder are numbered. Not so long ago, most reporters and editors were content with, for example, a story about a city council meeting that accurately recorded who said what to whom. Today, and tomorrow even more, a reporter who covers such a meeting is expected to tell her or his readers not only what was said but what the discussion means to the readers. Busy people don't have the time or inclination to read stories of no apparent relevance to them, so reporters must have the ability to spot significance and explain it. This kind of journalism—you might call it reporting in contrast to recording—requires an in-depth understanding of topics and a high level of writing skill.

Third, the steadily lengthening list of legitimate subjects of news stories requires of reporters both broader knowledge than ever before and an ability to seek out and use new kinds of sources.

Newspapers, more than the other traditional news media, are redirecting their efforts to meet these challenges. (This probably doesn't mean that the newspaper industry is any wiser than the broadcast industry. It does mean that the threat to newspapers from loss of readers—and therefore possible loss of advertising and revenue—is more immediate. Necessity inspires change.)

Beginning with the *Orange County* (Calif.) *Register* in the early '90s, many news rooms have abandoned traditional reporting beats in favor of teams whose efforts are focused on covering the issues most relevant to readers' lives. At the *Register*, for instance, the newly assigned topics include relationships, commuting and shopping malls.

Across the continent, at the *Norfolk* (Va.) *Virginian-Pilot*, a "public life" team not only covers local government but seeks actively to involve the citizenry in that coverage. Public life reporters regularly convene groups of residents for discussions of issues and conduct scientific polls to sample public attitudes reliably rather than just accepting the assessments of a few spokespersons. The newspaper also regularly asks its community to assess how well its coverage is meeting community needs.

Some papers are going even further. Pioneering public journalism projects in Charlotte, N.C., Wichita, Kan., Akron, Ohio, and elsewhere have seen newspapers taking the lead in generating public discussion of important issues ranging from politics to race. These newspapers are seeking not just to report on the problems of democracy but also to grapple with those problems and try to increase citizen involvement in public policy-making. Public journalism's critics, most of them more traditional journalists, worry about possible losses of independence. Its advocates insist that the decay of democratic institutions, from Congress to city hall, is too critical to permit a continued policy of detachment.

This redefining of news and re-examining of roles is not, of course, news to the '90s. Rather, the direction was established tentatively more than 20 years earlier, when journalists began having to learn how to cover the social and political movements that were changing American life. Probably the first of these was the civil rights movement of the 1960s. Then came the emergence as powerful forces of women, the young, consumers, environmentalists, gays and others. The agendas and tactics of these movements differed, but collectively they forced journalists away from their traditional reliance on elected officials, government bureaucrats and business leaders as the sources of news. Martin Luther King Jr., Gloria Steinem, Ralph Nader, Cesar Chavez, Barry Commoner—none of them held political office or occupied a position of economic power, but they and dozens like them captured the attention and the headlines of America. Journalists had to learn how to find, deal with and evaluate newsmakers who lacked the traditional kinds of "official" credentials and who, in many cases, were highly suspicious of mainstream journalists.

You will have to do the same thing. You can't cover relationships by interviewing the mayor (unless, of course, you're writing about her or his relationships, but that's another story). You won't make sense of shopping malls by talking to a press officer at the U.S. Department of Commerce. To track down these new kinds of news, reporters must as never before draw on broad interests and broad educations.

The journalists of the 1990s and beyond need to know more than earlier generations about a growing number of issues, including biology (AIDS isn't going away), sociology (minorities are becoming the majority), statistics (it's a quantitative world out there) and the other disciplines that help explain an increasingly complicated and interrelated world. You are only beginning a learning process that, if you make your career in journalism, must be a continuing commitment.

Accuracy, Fairness and the Problem of Objectivity

Amidst all the changes that are sweeping American journalism as the 20th century draws to a close, two traditions remain central. The first is the *professional ethic* that demands accuracy and fairness of every journalist. The second, more difficult to explain and easier to attack, is the tradition of objectivity. The two come together when we try to

More than Just the Printed Word

Nancy Tracewell's career provides a one-woman guide to the rapidly changing world of journalism. In her mid-30s, she was named a vice president of the *Kansas City Star*, in charge of electronic media. That isn't at all what she started out to be.

In journalism school, she emphasized science and technology writing. But she didn't turn out to be a science writer. Instead, she began as most new journalism school graduates do, with a series of reporting jobs on small newspapers in West Virginia and New York state. She covered everything from rural life to cops.

Then she switched to specialty publications, serving as writer, editor and corporate trainer for a chain of business journals. Promising as it was, that didn't turn out to be her career, either.

She and her husband

were, as she says, "bitten by an entrepreneurial bug." They bought a monthly lifestyles magazine. Like most shoestring magazines, this one was undercapitalized. The couple sold out in less than a year. And the changes continued.

Nancy was hired by the *Star* as an assistant city editor. However, within six months the afternoon paper for which she worked was folded and the staff combined with the morning edition. At the time, the *Star* was also joining the industry-wide exploration of new media—audio reports on telephone lines and on-line news for computer users.

She began developing news-room content for both. She "led the charge to use audio to update news, to invite reader interaction and to offer audio elements of the news—like interview excerpts or music—integrated with printed news stories."

For the news room, she says, the new media represent "big cultural change." For herself, the new grad who started out covering rural West Virginia says, "I tell reporters to get used to thinking of more than just the printed word."

She hasn't lost touch with her journalistic roots. "We're not changing the essence of the business."

sum up what it is that reporters and editors are trying to do with their work.

Accuracy and Fairness

The goal toward which most journalists strive has seldom been expressed any better than in a phrase used by Bob Woodward, a reporter, author and editor at *The Washington Post*. Woodward was defending in court an investigative story published by the *Post*. The story, he said, was "the best obtainable version of the truth."

A grander-sounding goal would be "the truth," unmodified. But Woodward's phrase, while paying homage to the ideal, recognizes the realities of life and the limitations of journalism. After centuries of argument, philosophers and theologians have been unable to agree on just what truth is. Even if there were agreement on that basic question, how likely is it that the Roman Catholic Church and the Planned Parenthood organization would agree on the "truth" about abortion, or that a president and his challenger would agree on the "truth" about the state of the American economy?

In American daily journalism, that kind of dispute is left to be fought out among the partisans on all sides, on the editorial pages and in commentaries. The reporter's usual role is simply to find and write the facts. The trouble is, that turns out often to be not so simple.

Sometimes it's hard to get the facts. The committee searching for a new university president announces that the field of candidates has been narrowed to five, but the names of the five are not released. Committee members are sworn to secrecy. What can you do to get the names? Should you try?

Sometimes it's hard to tell what the facts mean. The state supreme court refuses to hear a case in which legislators are questioning the constitutionality of a state spending limit. The court says only that there is no "justiciable controversy." What does that mean? Who won? Is the ruling good news or bad news, and for whom?

Sometimes it's even hard to tell what is a fact. A presidential commission, after a yearlong study, says there is no widespread hunger in America. Is the conclusion a fact? Or is the fact only that the commission said it? And how can you determine whether the commission is correct?

Daily journalism presents still more complications. Usually, as a reporter you have only a few hours, at most a few days, to try to learn as many facts as possible. Then, even in such a limited time, you may accumulate information enough for a story of 2,000 words, only to be told that there is space or time enough for 1,000 or fewer. The new media offer more space but no more time for reporting.

When you take into account all these realities and limitations, you can see that just to reach the best obtainable version of the truth is challenge enough for any journalist.

How can you tell when the goal has been reached? Seldom, if ever, is there a definitive answer. But there are two questions every responsible journalist should ask about every story before being satisfied: Is it accurate? Is it fair?

Accuracy is the most important characteristic of any story, great or small, long or short. Accuracy is essential in every detail. Every name must be spelled correctly; every quote must be just what was said; every set of numbers must add up. And that still isn't good enough. You can get the details right and still mislead unless you are accurate with context, too. The same statement may have widely different meanings depending on the circumstances in which it was uttered and the tone in which it was spoken. Circumstances and intent affect the meaning of actions, as well. You will never have the best obtainable version of the truth unless your version is built on accurate reporting of detail and context.

Nor can you approach the truth without being fair. Accuracy and fairness are related, but they are not the same. The relationship and the difference show clearly in this analogy from the world of sports:

The umpire in a baseball game is similar, in some ways, to a reporter. Each is supposed to be an impartial observer, calling developments as he or she sees them. (Of course, the umpire's job is to make judgments on those developments, while the reporter's is just to describe them.) Television has brought to sports the instant replay, in which a key development, say a close call at first base, can be examined again and again, often from an angle different from the umpire's view. Sometimes the replay shows an apparent outcome different from the one the umpire called. A runner who was ruled to be out may appear to have been safe instead. The difference may be due to human error on the umpire's part, or it may be due to the differences in angle and in viewpoint. Umpires recognize this problem. They try to deal with it by obtaining the best possible view of every play and by conferring with their colleagues on some close calls. Still, every umpire knows that an occasional mistake will be made. That is unavoidable. What can, and must, be avoided is unfairness. Umpires must be fair, and both players and fans must believe they are fair. Otherwise, umpires' judgments will not be accepted; they will not be trusted.

With news, too, there are different viewpoints from which every event or issue can be observed. Each viewpoint may yield a different interpretation of what is occurring and of what it means. There is also, in journalism as in sport, the possibility of human error, even by the most careful reporters.

Fairness requires that you as a reporter try to find every viewpoint on a story. Hardly ever will there be just one; often there are more than two. Fairness requires that you allow ample opportunity for response to anyone who is being attacked or whose integrity is being questioned in a story. Fairness requires, above all, that you make every effort to avoid following your own biases in your reporting and your writing.

Objectivity

These rules that mainstream journalists follow in attempting to arrive at the best obtainable version of the truth are commonly summarized as objectivity. Objectivity has been and still is accepted as a working credo by many, perhaps most, American journalists, students and teachers of journalism. It has been exalted by leaders of the profession as an essential, if unattainable, ideal. Its critics, by contrast, have attacked objectivity as, in the phrase of sociologist Gaye Tuchman, a "strategic ritual" that conceals a multitude of professional sins while producing superficial and often misleading coverage.

Michael Schudson, in his classic *Discovering the News*, traces the rise of objectivity to the post-World War I period, when scholars and journalists alike turned to the methods and the language of science in an attempt to make sense of a world that was being turned upside down by the influence of Freud and Marx, the emergence of new economic forces and the erosion of traditional values. Objectivity was a reliance on observable facts, but it was also a methodology for freeing factual reporting from the biases and values of source, writer or reader. It was itself a value, an ideal.

Schudson wrote, "Journalists came to believe in objectivity, to the extent that they did, because they wanted to, needed to, were forced by ordinary human aspiration to seek escape from their own deep convictions of doubt and drift."

Schudson and Robert Karl Manoff, editors of *Reading the News*, an important collection of essays, describe the conflict between the ideal of journalistic objectivity and the way journalism really works:

> The reporter not only relates stories but makes them.
> This, of course, is heresy within the world of journalism. You report, you do not manufacture. You ask your who, what, when, where, why, and how, get the answers; and come on home. But how . . . does the reporter know when to ask the basic journalistic questions, and who to ask them of? How does the reporter know when the questions have been answered? Who counts as a newsworthy "who"? What facts or events qualify as reportable responses to the question "what"? Even with the apparently simplest questions of all, "when" and "where," how does the reporter know if the answer is really sufficient? . . .
> In short, the apparently simple commandment questions of journalism presuppose a platform for inquiry, a framework for interpreting answers, a set of rules about who to ask what about what. . . .

The best journalists keep in mind these questions and limitations, even if they are seldom articulated in news rooms. Ideally, your study of the craft will give you a critical understanding of its platform, framework and rules. You need to understand them whether in the end you choose to pursue the kind of mainstream, "objective" journalism practiced in most American news rooms or another of the many possible channels for expression.

In 1947 the Hutchins Commission on freedom of the press concluded that what a free society needs from journalists is "a truthful, comprehensive and intelligent account of the day's events in a context which gives them meaning." The goal of this chapter is to show you how the journalists of today and tomorrow understand that need, how they are trying to meet it, and the complexity of the task. The rest of the book will help you develop the skills you'll need to take up the challenge. There are few challenges so important or so rewarding.

> *"You go into journalism because you can do good, have fun and learn."*
>
> *—Molly Ivins, Reporter and columnist*

Suggested Readings

Journalism Reviews: Any issue of the *Columbia Journalism Review*, the *Washington Journalism Review*, the *Quill* or the *American Editor*, bulletin of the American Society of Newspaper Editors, offers reports and analyses of the most important issues of contemporary journalism.

Manoff, Robert Karl and Schudson, Michael, eds. *Reading the News*. New York: Pantheon Books, 1986. A stimulating collection of essays that challenges the most important conventions of journalism.

New Directions for News. *Undercovered: The New USA*. Columbia, Mo.: New Directions for News, 1994. A thought-provoking summary of research into underserved audiences. Includes suggestions for improvement.

Schudson, Michael. *Discovering the News*. New York: Basic Books, 1978. Subtitled *A Social History of American Newspapers*, this well-written study traces the development of objectivity in American journalism.

Willis, Jim. *The Age of Multimedia and Turbonews*. Westport, Conn.: Praeger, 1994. A clearly written survey of the new information sources and outlets.

Wurman, Richard Saul. *Information Anxiety*. New York: Doubleday, 1990. This guide for consumers of information can also serve as a guide for journalists as they seek to provide understanding.

Exercises

1. Get copies of today's issue of your local newspaper, a paper from a city at least 50 miles away and a paper of national circulation, such as *USA Today* or *The Wall Street Journal*. Analyze the front page according to the criteria discussed in this chapter.

   What can you tell about the editors' understanding of each paper's audience by looking at the selection of stories?

   If you find stories on the same topic on two or more front pages, determine if they are written differently for different audiences. Are there any attempts to localize national stories? Suggest any possibilities you can think of.

   On the basis of what you've learned in this chapter, do you agree or disagree with the editors' news judgments? Why?

2. Go to your library and look at both a recent issue of *The New York Times* and an issue from the same date 20 years ago. Describe the differences you find in subjects and sources of stories.

3. As a class project, visit or invite in the editor of your

local paper and the news director of a local television station. Study their products ahead of time and interview them about how they decide the value of news stories, how they assess the reliability of sources and how they try to ensure accuracy.

4. Take a cruise on the information superhighway. Sample some of the sources you find. Describe briefly at least five sources of information you can use as a journalist and at least five sources of news you can use as a consumer.

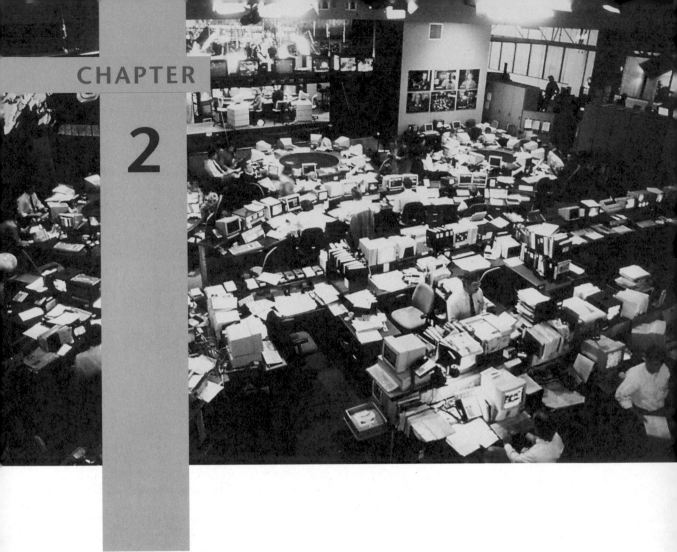

NEWS ROOMS AND THE CHANGING MEDIA

*T*he media landscape is changing, and it is changing more rapidly and in more uncertain ways than at any point in history. It's only natural, then, for you as an aspiring journalist to ask: What does the future hold as I prepare for a career in the media industry?

No one can answer that question with any certainty. The existing media appear to be threatened to some degree by the so-called **new media**, a term that refers to computer-based news and information delivery systems. Many pundits, in fact, expect an eventual melding of newspapers, magazines, radio and television into a new information medium of the future. Just how fast that will happen, and when, is anyone's guess. That means you face a challenge as you plan your media career. Not only must you prepare for a job in one of today's media, you also must be ready to work in the information media of the future. You may work in jobs that will disappear, but you may also work in jobs that have yet to be invented. Through it all, one certainty remains: Regardless of the medium, there will continue to be a demand for news practitioners who report well, write well, edit well and communicate well visually.

To understand the changes about to take place, consider these facts, published by the Newspaper Association of America, the newspaper industry's leading trade organization:

 ▪ The newspaper industry is shrinking. There were 1,538 daily newspapers in the United States at the end of 1994, compared to 1,745 as recently as 1980. During the same period, the number of weekly newspapers declined from 7,954 to 7,176.
 ▪ In 1970, 78 percent of the nation's adults read a newspaper daily, but by 1994 that percentage had declined to 61.5. Worse, survey after survey has revealed that the biggest decline is among readers 34 and younger, which sounds an ominous note for the future; as older readers die, there is no one to replace them. Research suggests that those who fail to develop the newspaper reading habit early will not acquire it later in life.

But if the newspaper industry is dying, as some argue, it is far from dead. Consider that:

 ▪ Newspapers remain one of the most profitable industries around, helped in large part by their near-monopoly situation in most cities.
 ▪ Daily newspapers continue to capture the largest share of the U.S. advertising dollar, edging out broadcast television 22.8 percent to 20.8 percent (see Figure 2.1). And newspapers usually dominate the local news and advertising markets.

Newspapers' competitors have their own problems. Network television, the main competitor both for advertising dollars and audience, has experienced tough financial times. The creation of a fourth major U.S. network (Fox) has fragmented audiences, and the proliferation of cable

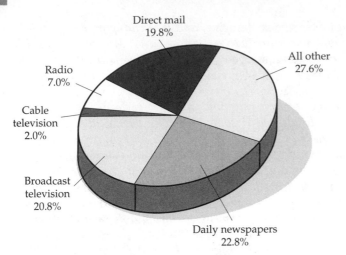

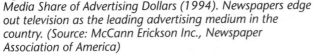

Figure 2.1.
Media Share of Advertising Dollars (1994). Newspapers edge out television as the leading advertising medium in the country. (Source: McCann Erickson Inc., Newspaper Association of America)

television channels has divided those audiences into even smaller segments. The cable channels are worrisome indeed for the broadcast industry; unlike the networks, they are ideally positioned to deliver targeted audiences to advertisers because of their focus on specific areas of information (sports, health and fitness, children, etc.). Like newspapers, network television is best able to deliver mass audiences, not the cohesive audiences that many advertisers covet. Radio does a better job of targeting specific audiences, but its impact on the media industry is minuscule.

Magazines, like radio and cable television, deliver target audiences to advertisers, but they do so at a rapidly increasing cost. In the long term, like newspapers, magazines are threatened by rising production costs, and their distribution relies heavily upon escalating postal rates.

Many media experts conclude that the future lies in a new computer-delivered medium capable of combining the best features of television with the best of newspapers. Many of those pundits believe we are now witnessing the leading edge of a major change in the media landscape. Nicholas Negroponte, founder and director of the Media Lab at Massachusetts Institute of Technology, describes the infomedium of the 21st century as a home computer system capable of searching vast on-line data banks and displaying its results in text, audio or video form. Thus, the primary advantages of television—color, eye appeal, immediacy and low distribution costs—can be combined with the advantages of the print media—depth, interpretation and portability.

The Growth of Multimedia Organizations

Traditional media companies are scrambling to be part of the new media mix, as are telephone companies, the cable television industry and entertainment conglomerates. Some examples:

- Henry Luce created an empire around *Time* magazine. His successors added other successful magazines, including *Fortune* and *Sports Illustrated*. Now, the magazine division is a small part of a colossal company with entertainment, book publishing, magazine and cable television interests.
- The Walt Disney Co. owns Capital Cities Communications and the ABC television network. But it also owns newspapers such as the *Fort Worth Star-Telegram* and the *Kansas City Star*, which are offering audiotext and computer-based news services.
- Cox Enterprises began as a newspaper group. With headquarters in Atlanta, Ga., it now owns broadcast and cable television properties, and it is a national leader in experimenting with computer-based news services. Led by the flagship *Atlanta Journal and Constitution*, Cox operates Access Atlanta, arguably the most successful newspaper venture into new media, on Prodigy (see Figure 2.2).
- At a lab in Boulder, Colo., Knight-Ridder, one of the largest media

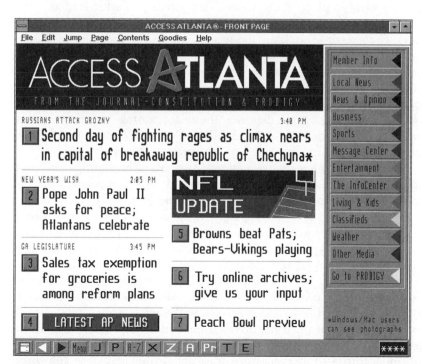

Figure 2.2.
Access Atlanta, a service of the Atlanta Journal and Constitution, *is probably the most successful newspaper venture into new media to date.*

companies in the country, is developing a computerized newspaper delivered by electronic tablet. One of Knight-Ridder's largest newspapers, the *San Jose Mercury News*, can be found on America On-line, where you'll also find the *Chicago Tribune*.

- *Skiing* magazine is available on CD-ROM. Click on an icon and you can examine video of the slopes. Click another and get price information. Click yet another to make travel and hotel arrangements or buy a lift ticket. Similarly, *Newsweek* offers a CD-ROM edition, and *Time* is available in limited form on the Internet, the growing network of computer systems now estimated to link more than 30 million people worldwide.

- Corporations as diverse as IBM and Sears own Prodigy, and both Apple Computer and Microsoft, the software giant, have started their own on-line information services. Turner Broadcasting, the parent company of cable television's CNN and TNT, is a major owner of movie rights and covets a television network. Mergers and buyouts in the movie industry abound as companies try to increase their ability to deliver all forms of information—both news and entertainment. Content, it is said, is the key to the future.

All of these examples show how dramatically the media landscape is changing as corporations try to position themselves for a role in the media marketplace of the future. And, while no one knows the exact form the medium of the future will take, or how it will be delivered, everyone wants a piece of the action. The potential market is huge.

Because corporate structures are changing, so, too, are news rooms. For example, at *USA Today*'s suburban Washington headquarters, staff members work to create CD-ROMs that can be sold to document the paper's coverage of momentous events—war in the Middle East, a famine in Africa, the Olympics. At NBC's New York headquarters, a new breed of journalist takes stories from the network's news rooms and digitizes them for storage in a computer. These stories form the basis of NBC Desktop News, a video-on-demand system being marketed to corporations nationwide.

Part of the new-media mix are the emerging computer-based public information utilities, which include CompuServe, Prodigy, America Online, Delphi, GEnie, eWorld, The Microsoft Network and others (see Figure 2.3). Increasingly, they are filled with advertising. Even the Internet, once an arcane collection of computers understood only by a few academicians and computer scientists, is becoming a carrier for commercial advertising in targeted audience segments.

That leads us to an observation that few newspeople like to hear: Advertising, not news, drives the media marketplace. To understand shifts in the media industry, follow the advertising dollar. Trends show more and more of the advertising dollar flowing into nontraditional media—direct mail, cable television and computer-based information systems—and away from traditional media such as television and newspapers. So far, that shift is slight, but advertising experts expect it to accelerate as the search continues for the best way to find target audiences. While there is no clear picture of where the industry

Typical of the new-media conglomerate is The Walt Disney Co., which in mid-1995 gobbled up Capital Cities/ABC. The media giant now owns:

- *Walt Disney Studios.*
- *The Walt Disney amusement parks.*
- *The ABC television network.*
- *Several local radio and television stations.*
- *ABC Distribution, a company that distributes ABC programming worldwide.*
- *Buena Vista Home Video, Buena Vista Television, Buena Vista Pictures Distribution and Buena Vista International.*
- *The Disney Store Inc.*
- *The Disney Channel.*
- *Partial interest in several other cable television channels, including ESPN, Arts & Entertainment and Lifetime.*
- *Partial interest in several European television channels.*
- *Fidelity Television.*
- *A multimedia group that is exploring all sorts of new-media ventures.*
- *Several newspapers, including the* Kansas City Star *and the* Fort Worth Star-Telegram.
- *Specialized publications, including the largest business publishing group in Mexico; Chilton Enterprises, which focuses on specialized publications for various industries; and* Los Angeles, *a city magazine.*
- *Fairchild Publications, publisher of* W.
- *Capital Cities Capital, a unit that exchanges advertising time and space for equity interest in growing companies.*

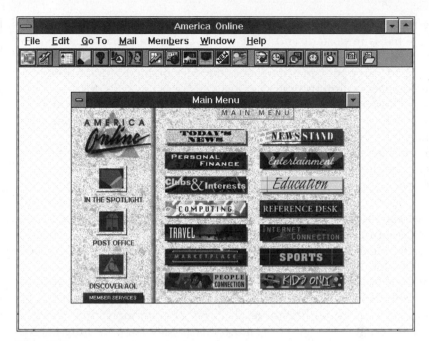

Figure 2.3.
The front page of America Online, one of the nation's leading public information utilities.

"Paper won't disappear [in the future], but paperless media will soak up more of our time. We will eventually become paperless the same way we once became horseless. Horses are still around, but they are ridden by hobbyists, not consumers."
—Paul Saffo,
Institute for the Future

is headed, one certainty is that the next few years will bring accelerating change to the media mix.

As that media mix changes, so does the definition of news. As we learned in Chapter 1, traditional definitions of news don't work as well as they once did. Moreover, the definition of news is changing in ways that many news practitioners never imagined. The proliferation of computer-based information services and electronic mail has enabled people from throughout the world to meet electronically. There they share their knowledge and report the latest developments about thousands of topics. Without exception, the most-used parts of those systems are the so-called bulletin boards, where those electronic exchanges take place. Users get information on topics about which they are keenly interested. To them, that information is every bit as much "news" as the information provided by the mass media.

That raises the question of whether we are entering an era in which the agenda-setting role of the media will diminish. Traditionally, the media have decided what the public needed to know about a given event. Further, the media have set the public agenda by ranking the relative importance of those items—by headline size and placement or by placement in the broadcast. In addition, by serving as gatekeepers to information, the media have helped to decide which news events get exposure at all. With the advent of computer-based media, all that is changing. Increasingly, the public will have the ability to sort through massive amounts of information and decide for itself what is important and what is not. Unlike newspapers, television and even magazines, computer-based media have virtually unlimited space to carry information. Thus, the role of media practitioners as gatekeepers is diminishing.

Those changes will require an adjustment in the role of the journalist. How that adjustment will affect our society is far from clear. Many futurists believe the media will continue to play an important role in agenda-setting if not in gatekeeping. Journalists will have to help people sort through the mass of information and tell consumers what is important. Few will have the time to do that for themselves.

There will be plenty of jobs for journalists. After all, someone still must gather the news and organize it into a useful, easily consumable package. But the new-media services will require of the journalist a broader range of skills. While some journalists, just as now, may be able to focus on writing, they will have to display a richer appreciation of how photos, charts, graphs and maps—and even full-motion video—can complement their articles. That's because the journalist of the future will have to be literate in all forms of communication, visual as well as verbal. Many news organizations already are preaching that reality as they attempt to get reporters to think more visually and photographers and videographers to think more verbally. To provide those skills, journalism and communications schools are revamping their curricula to make it easier for students to get the necessary exposure to all media forms. Yet despite that shift, most young journalists in the next few years will enter the industry in more traditional positions.

So here's the challenge as you plan your media career: Not only must you prepare for a job in one of today's media, you also must prepare for a period of wrenching change. But while change presents problems, it also brings hope. You have a chance to participate in a media transition that is sure to open many doors of opportunity.

Newspapers

The popular misconception that newspapers are dying contradicts reality. As measured by the U.S. government, newspapers continue to rank among the top 10 manufacturing industries in total employment. While the industry appears to be shrinking, it is far from dead, as the existence of more than 1,500 dailies and 7,100 weeklies will attest.

Those newspapers appeal to diverse audiences. In the New York area alone, one finds not only the *New York Times*, the *New York Post*, the *New York Daily News* and *Newsday* but also the ethnic dailies, such as the *New Amsterdam News*, *El Diario* and the *Jewish Daily Forward*. For various other audiences, there are the *Wall Street Journal*, the *American Banker* and *Variety*. That diversity is mirrored elsewhere on a smaller scale. Because of the industry's size, it is difficult to gen-

tencing of an armed robber in a Florida Keys courthouse ended with the man stripping down to his underwear, then running out the door. After a manhunt involving helicopters, the local police, the sheriff and divers, the man was still at large at deadline.

Later, as an intern at the *Wall Street Journal*, Robichaux learned not to brush off unsolicited tips. After taking a call from a man in Florida whom his editor believed to be a crank, Robichaux wound up with a national story about a defective flea spray that was killing kittens and dogs.

Robichaux has this advice for new reporters: Hone a healthy skepticism toward sources, but beware of falling into the trap of knee-jerk cynicism. He lists two important criteria in reporting and assessing every story: Is it accurate? Is it fair?

The most difficult thing for a journalist, he says, is to close the gap between what's in your head and what you put on the computer screen. Clear writing is clear thinking.

eralize about the internal organization of newspapers. Still, a few organizational characteristics are commonplace.

Newspaper Organization

The top managers of newspapers usually are known as the **publisher** and **general manager**. The publisher is the owner or, in the case of newspaper *chains* or *groups*, the top-ranking local executive. The publisher typically presides over business operations and leaves editorial operations to the editors. The general manager directs day-to-day business operations and is primarily responsible for advertising, circulation and production. The general manager, however, works with the top editors to determine the editorial department budget.

Top managers in the editorial department are the **editor** (or editor-in-chief), the **editorial page editor**, the **managing editor** and possibly one or more *assistant managing editors*. The editor is the top editorial executive and is responsible for all editorial content. Under that editor are the editorial page editor, who, as the name implies, directs the editorial page, and the managing editor, who has primary responsibility for news-gathering operations. Often, the managing editor makes major decisions about news coverage and the placement of stories. The managing editor also oversees the news room budget.

Under the managing editor may be one or more assistant managing editors. These positions often are created to help the managing editor supervise various parts of the news operation. For example, there may be an assistant managing editor for news, an assistant managing editor for features and an assistant managing editor for photos and graphics.

The news department itself probably will have other levels of managers. The **city editor** (or *metropolitan editor*) handles local news coverage, while the **news editor** oversees the copy desk and regional, national and international news. Larger newspapers may have separate *regional*, *national* and *international editors*, each supervising both a news-gathering operation and its own copy desk. Large newspapers also are likely to have remote bureaus in Washington, the state capital or suburban areas, each managed by a **bureau chief**, who functions as a city editor for those reporters who work there. Increasingly, larger newspapers are separating the design function from the copy desk. When that occurs, design desks often are supervised by an *assistant managing editor for design*.

At larger papers, a **graphics editor** often supervises the production of maps, charts and other graphic devices that go into the newspaper. A **photo editor** supervises the photo staff. Specialized departments such as business, sports and lifestyle have their own editors and often their own copy desks. And, as we have seen, new-media ventures may necessitate the creation of other layers of management. The size of the newspaper, more than any other factor, affects the newspaper's organization (see Figures 2.4, 2.5 and 2.6).

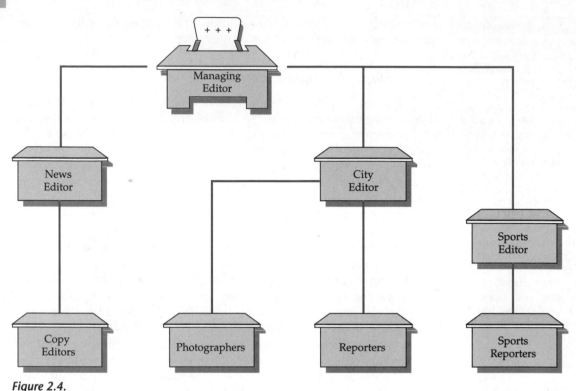

Figure 2.4.
Typical News Room Organization of a Small Daily Newspaper

Increasingly, innovative editors are breaking the mold of news room organization in an effort to do a better job of gathering and packaging the news. The reporting staff historically has been organized by beats (see Chapter 14), but traditional beats such as fire, police and city government are being joined by beats such as neighbors. On that beat, the reporter covers zoning disputes and neighborhood associations, taking reporting into areas that readers care most about—their own neighborhoods. Attempting to connect better with readers is today's most important trend in news coverage, and to do that journalists must understand what interests readers. If that happens to be neighborhood news, that's what the newspaper covers. And because the definitions of news are changing, as we learned in Chapter 1, staff organization must change to keep pace.

Similarly, today's editors seek to improve ways of presenting the news. In the past, it was common for a reporter to finish a story before photographers or graphic designers were brought in to illustrate the piece. When that occurred, too often it was too late for the visual experts to do their best work. On major stories today, teams of reporters, photographers, graphic designers and editors are assigned from the outset. As a result, the best way to present various parts of

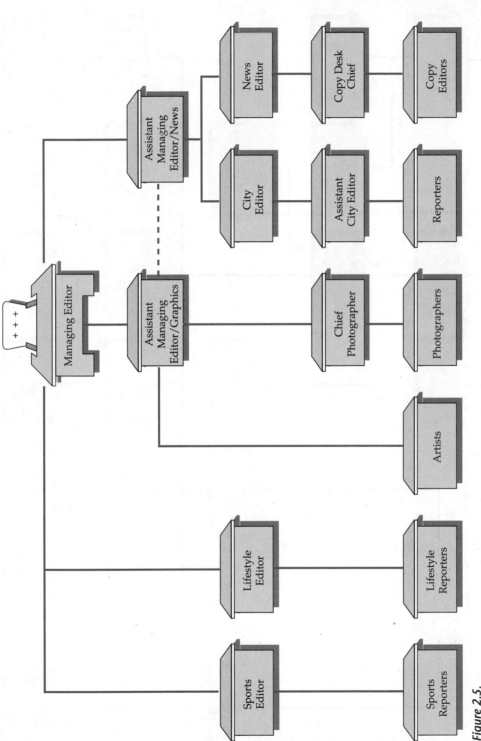

Figure 2.5.
Typical News Room Organization of a Medium-Sized Daily Newspaper

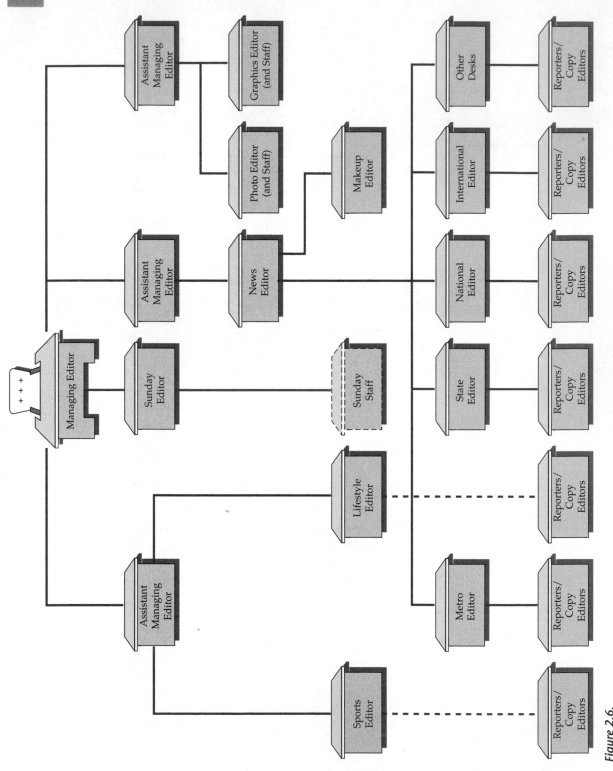

Figure 2.6.
Typical News Room Organization of a Metropolitan Daily Newspaper

the story is determined in a team setting. The team leader is sometimes called a **maestro**, someone who leads a reporting team just as a conductor leads an orchestra in the quest for the best possible result.

Newspaper Job Prospects

Typically, newcomers are hired in newspaper editorial departments as **reporters**, who work directly for the city editor; as *copy editors*, who work for the news editor; or as *photographers*, who work for the photo editor. Some beginners now start as **page designers**, *graphics reporters* or as *new-media editors*. Entry-level jobs also exist at weekly newspapers, where journalists may well be expected to report, write, edit, take pictures and design pages.

Fewer than 10 percent of journalism and communications graduates went directly to work for newspapers in the mid-1990s, down from more than 11 percent as recently as 1989. But it is important to remember that only about 13 percent of students in such programs are news-editorial majors.

Winning your first job is a first step. Continued employment prospects will relate directly to your job performance. But other factors may contribute. One journalism graduate wrote a former professor and urged that his school spend more time discussing what he called "news room politics." He wrote:

> Human behavior is not a hands-off topic for classroom discussion. Reporters need to be taught that news room politics is not just a game of favoritism. If favoritism exists, it is earned.

The message was clear: Work hard, do a good job, and sooner or later you will be rewarded with the best assignments. In the meantime, expect to be tested. You also can expect periodic reviews of your performance, offered either orally or in writing by your supervisor. Increasingly, newspapers are formalizing annual evaluations (see Figure 2.7).

Newspaper Production

Once you've landed that first job, ask for a thorough tour of the newspaper. The **editorial department** is just one of several departments that must work in close coordination if the newspaper is to be successful. If the **advertising department** fails to sell enough advertising, the news hole is small, and your department's ability to provide a comprehensive news report is adversely affected. If your department misses its deadlines, the **production** and **circulation departments** could spend thousands of dollars in overtime pay, and subscribers may not receive their newspapers on time. It's important to learn how you and your department fit into the picture. To do so, you must fully understand the role of the other departments—advertising, business, circulation, production and perhaps others (see Figure 2.8). A newspaper is a product, and you must learn the role of each department in producing it.

The Seattle Times
REPORTER
PERFORMANCE REVIEW

Date _____

Employee _____

Job Title_____

Classification_____

Period Reviewed_____

Evaluated By_____

Department Manager Review_____

PERFORMANCE-REVIEW
GUIDELINES

Each employee is reviewed annually. This form is designed to help the supervisor assess the employee's performance over the past year and to help the supervisor and the employee set goals for growth and development over the next year. It is also an opportunity for the employee to express his or her thoughts on the performance of the supervisor and of the newspaper, and to lay out longer-term career objectives.

The evaluation and self-evaluation sections of the review form should be filled out independently by the employee and the supervisor. After exchanging those sections, the employee and supervisor should together write the development plan. Each can also offer additional thoughts in the commentary section.

Figure 2.7.
These performance review guidelines reflect the changing notions of the responsibilities and skills required of reporters.

JOB DESCRIPTION: REPORTER

The following attributes and responsibilities are expected of every Seattle Times reporter. Additional responsibilities might be part of a specific job assignment. This list is meant as a guide and not as a grading grid; the employee and supervisor should decide which items deserve the most attention.

PROFESSIONAL SKILLS:

- Seeks out and acts quickly on story opportunities.
- Aggressively follows through on stories.
- Gathers facts carefully and accurately.
- Seeks a variety of sources in covering a story, and effectively develops sources of continuing stories.
- Uses documents effectively.
- Handles a variety of stories and writing approaches.
- Writes clear, well-focused and well-organized stories.
- Writes effective, appropriate leads.
- Writes with authority based on clear understanding of the topic or beat.
- Produces stories that are fair and balanced.
- Self-edits for crisper, cleaner copy.
- Works well under pressure and meets deadlines.
- Maintains a steady flow of ideas and stories.

WORK HABITS:

- Knows and effectively uses library and computer systems.
- Understands how the newsroom operates, and works effectively within it.
- Works effectively as a member of a team, including with other reporters, photographers, artists and editors.
- Responds well to direction, suggestions, criticism.
- Keeps appropriate people informed of schedules, work in progress, problems, changes.
- Works in a cooperative spirit in accepting, discussing or proposing changes in assignments.
- Keeps well-informed about news in general and assigned specialties by reading The Times and other publications.
- Organizes time well, and can work on more than one task at a time when necessary.
- Is punctual for staff meetings and time commitments.
- Maintains good staff communications and relationships.
- Shares knowledge and ideas with less-experienced workers.
- Seeks diversity in coverage.

ENTERPRISE SKILLS:

- Demonstrates willingness to perform routine but necessary duties such as digest items, etc.
- Consistently suggests ideas for stories, photographs and illustrations.
- Produces enterprise stories.
- Seeks fresh ideas and approaches in reporting and writing.
- Stays ahead of stories by anticipating or uncovering developments.
- Is willing to travel, make calls from home and work unusual schedules when the coverage requires it.
- Is willing to take leadership of a story or project.
- Offers suggestions for improving the newspaper.
- Takes on new challenges.

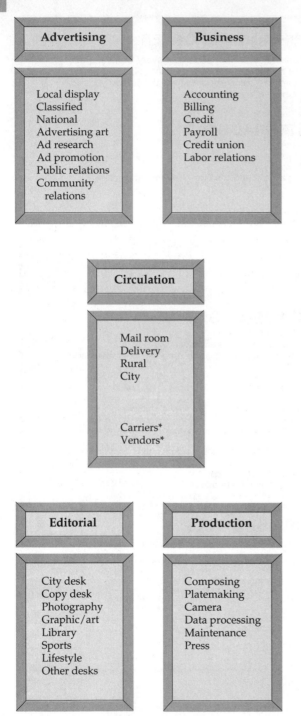

Advertising

Local display
Classified
National
Advertising art
Ad research
Ad promotion
Public relations
Community
   relations

Business

Accounting
Billing
Credit
Payroll
Credit union
Labor relations

Circulation

Mail room
Delivery
Rural
City

Carriers*
Vendors*

Editorial

City desk
Copy desk
Photography
Graphic/art
Library
Sports
Lifestyle
Other desks

Production

Composing
Platemaking
Camera
Data processing
Maintenance
Press

*Outside contractors not employed by newspaper.

Figure 2.8.
Major Departments of a Typical Newspaper and Their Subsections

Working in a Team

If learning how your newspaper is produced is important, even more important is learning how the news room works. Just as the various departments of the newspaper work as a team, so do the individuals in the news room. You must learn to function as part of that team, and you must know what happens to a story as it makes its way through the news room production process.

At today's newspaper, the reporter must be much more than a gatherer of facts. If you hope to be a reporter, you must learn the best way to tell a story. That means knowing the roles of photography, illustration and information graphics as well as the role of words, and being able to use the inverted pyramid—the classic news storytelling format—and other story forms. That also means breaking out into lists information readers can use.

The image of the reporter as the Lone Ranger is yesterday's picture. Today the reporter is a member of a team. Reporters work with photographers to tell stories. Photojournalists tell stories with pictures. Sometimes photographers illustrate the story; sometimes reporters complement the pictures.

Reporters work with graphics reporters to tell stories. Graphics reporters tell stories with numbers in *information graphics*. They show trends and relationships among numbers. They can make writing easier for you as a reporter by allowing you to concentrate on the meaning of the numbers rather than getting bogged down in the details. They can show biographical data visually by creating a chart called a *dateline*. That allows you to concentrate on the narrative rather than the dates. They can create maps to show location or the distribution of numbers.

It is not enough for you to know that these story forms exist. You must recognize their strengths and weaknesses so you can help choose the best approach. Parts of your story may appear in pictures, parts in information graphics.

As a member of a team, it is the reporter's responsibility to get photographers and graphics reporters involved early in the storytelling process. Don't expect photographers and graphics reporters to become involved hours or days after you have started a story. You need to recognize their expertise, and they need to be involved as early as possible. The packages the team produces will always be better than the work of the individuals. And the readers will be the winners.

Working with the Editor

Once the package is prepared, editors polish it for publication. At first glance, the flow of copy through an editorial department seems simple enough (see Figure 2.9 on page 34). You write your story and transfer it to the city desk queue, the electronic equivalent

Information Graphics

What is an information graphic?

An information graphic is a visual representation of data.

How do people read information graphics?

People read charts on two levels. One is the visual, a quick scan that picks up trends or relationships. The second level of readership comes from those who examine the graphic closely and look at the numbers, the trends and the second and third levels of information.

What do we know about readership?

From a variety of studies, we know:

- Readers comprehend data better in graphics than in text.

- Readers are more likely to read and remember data in graphics than in stories.

- Information graphics attract slightly higher levels of readership than do stories.

- Readers have a low threshold for "chartjunk," the artwork some artists build into the data lines. The art sometimes distorts or obscures the data.

- Charts allow readers to grasp trends among numbers quickly, but comprehension of the numbers in tables is higher than that in charts.

Why do reporters need to be knowledgeable about information graphics?

The reporter's job is to ask the question, "What is the best way to tell the story?" The answer will come back in various ways: inverted pyramid, narration, lists, sidebars. Often the story, or at least parts of it, are told most effectively in pictures, in information graphics, in illustrations, in maps. And there are all kinds of maps, ranging from a locator map to a topographical map.

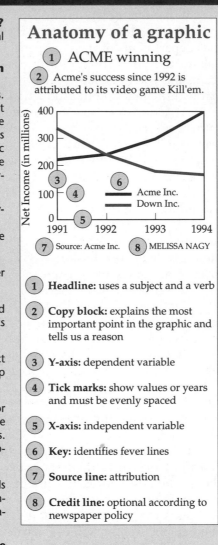

Anatomy of a graphic

(1) ACME winning

(2) Acme's success since 1992 is attributed to its video game Kill'em.

(Line graph: Y-axis labeled "Net Income (in millions)" from 0 to 400; X-axis years 1991, 1992, 1993, 1994. Key: Acme Inc., Down Inc. Markers 3, 4, 5, 6 placed on axes and key.)

(7) Source: Acme Inc.   **(8)** MELISSA NAGY

(1) Headline: uses a subject and a verb

(2) Copy block: explains the most important point in the graphic and tells us a reason

(3) Y-axis: dependent variable

(4) Tick marks: show values or years and must be evenly spaced

(5) X-axis: independent variable

(6) Key: identifies fever lines

(7) Source line: attribution

(8) Credit line: optional according to newspaper policy

What do I need to know about information graphics?

You must know the different kinds of information graphics and know the kind of information you must gather for them. You must also appreciate that readers can understand numbers better in information graphics. This realization helps you as a writer: You can get some of the numbers out of your story. You can concentrate on the meaning of the numbers.

Information Graphics

What kind of information graphics are there?

The three most common information graphics:

1. Line or fever charts. Think of them as video. They show motion. Lines rise or fall. They emphasize trends.
2. Bar charts. Think of them as a still picture. They freeze the numbers so we can look at comparisons. They can show trends, but they are most useful to compare numbers at a given moment.
3. Tables. Tables help organize lots of data that do not necessarily have a mathematical relationship. A voting chart showing how the people in each precinct or ward voted for all the candidates would be a table. So would a chart showing the levels of various nutrients in fruit or breakfast cereals.

What is the reporter's role in creating information graphics?

In most situations, it's your job to gather the information for the graphic. It comes from the same people and paper sources that you will be using to do your story anyway. By gathering the data, you will do a better job of reporting your story. You should understand the numbers better. If numbers are important to your story, it is essential that you understand them so that you can explain them clearly to the reader. Write the story with the knowledge of what the information graphic will contain. You don't have to repeat all the numbers. And help the graphic reporter to understand what is important. The headline and copy block in the information graphic should emphasize the key points in the numbers.

What do I need to understand about the data?

First, understand that numbers don't mean much until they are compared to something else. For instance, if you are doing a story about the SAT scores at your local high schools, you need to compare them to something, just as a graphics reporter would. That means you probably need the scores for the schools over five or 10 years. But you also should compare them to state or national figures over the same period. Getting all the numbers for each of the years is not something a reporter normally would do. But you can't create a chart without them. And it may change the focus of your story. Your superintendent may brag about the scores, but when you start comparing, perhaps you find out that all the kids may be above average in Lake Woebegon but they are below average compared to other cities.

Second, get the right numbers. If you are doing a story about felonies in your local area, you should look at the numbers over a period of time. You should be sure to ask if either the record-keeping process or the legal definition of felonies has changed during that time. Then you should start looking at other cities for comparisons.

Can you compare local data only to comparable data for other cities of a similar size? Not if you use *rates* instead of the numbers. You can compare felonies per capita. The right numbers, then, are translated to per capita so you are comparing apples and apples.

Third, if you are dealing with money, understand the impact of inflation. Most reporters don't, and we mishandle numbers badly as a result. For instance, in the recent debate about the minimum wage, few journalists, if any, adjusted the minimum wage for inflation. The debate was about the impact on businesses of raising the minimum wage. If journalists had adjusted the wage for inflation, the public would have discovered that the minimum wage was lower in real terms than it had been 20 years earlier.

How do the pros regard information graphics?

Information graphics are a widely used device because they're effective.

Information Graphics

Reporters may refer to them familiarly as "infographics," but don't ever call them "informational graphics." The term "information graphics" is a compound noun. If we used the adjective "informational," we would be saying that some graphics aren't. That may be true, but if so, the story and the information graphic need some heavy editing.

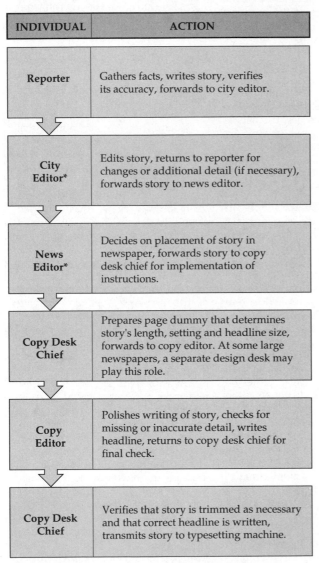

INDIVIDUAL	ACTION
Reporter	Gathers facts, writes story, verifies its accuracy, forwards to city editor.
City Editor*	Edits story, returns to reporter for changes or additional detail (if necessary), forwards story to news editor.
News Editor*	Decides on placement of story in newspaper, forwards story to copy desk chief for implementation of instructions.
Copy Desk Chief	Prepares page dummy that determines story's length, setting and headline size, forwards to copy editor. At some large newspapers, a separate design desk may play this role.
Copy Editor	Polishes writing of story, checks for missing or inaccurate detail, writes headline, returns to copy desk chief for final check.
Copy Desk Chief	Verifies that story is trimmed as necessary and that correct headline is written, transmits story to typesetting machine.

* Or assistant

Note: At any point in the process, a story may be returned to an earlier editor for clarification, amplification or rewriting.

Figure 2.9.
Typical News Room Copy Flow Pattern

of an in-basket. There the city editor reads it and makes necessary changes. Then it is sent electronically to the copy desk, where it is edited again. The story is assigned a position in the newspaper, and a headline is written. Finally, an editor presses a key on the computer keyboard to send your story to a typesetting machine in the composing room. This simple copy flow pattern exists at most newspapers, whether the newspaper uses computers or still does things the old-fashioned way with typewriters and paper copy. Indeed, electronic copy flow patterns in most cases merely duplicate the pre-computer copy flow patterns of newspapers. Despite the seeming simplicity of the pattern, many decisions can be made along the way that make the process much more complicated than it appears at first glance.

When the city editor receives your copy, that editor must read it and make some initial decisions: Is information missing? Does the story need to be developed? Does it need more background? Are there enough quotes? Are the quotes worth using? Does the lead, or opening, need to be polished? Have you chosen the right lead or should another angle be emphasized? Is the story important? Is it useful, interesting or entertaining? Is there, in fact, some reason for publishing it? If it is important, should the managing editor and news editor be alerted that a potential Page One story is forthcoming? Each time a city editor reads a story for the first time, these questions and more come up. The city editor is expected to answer them quickly; there is no time for delay.

After making those initial decisions, the city editor confers with you and gives directions on changes to be made. If the changes are minor ones, simply rewriting a section of the story or inserting additional information will suffice. If the changes are more substantial, involving additional interviews with sources or major rewriting, your job is more difficult.

When those changes are made, you resubmit your story to the city editor, who reads the revised version and edits it more carefully. Your work may be finished after you answer a few remaining minor questions. Or, if the city editor is still unhappy with it, another rewrite may be ordered.

You can expect frustration in the process. Often an assistant city editor reads your story first and gives instructions on how it is to be revised. When your rewrite is submitted, the city editor or another assistant may do the editing, resulting in the need for more changes and yet another rewrite. This can be discouraging, but such a system has its merits. Generally, a story is improved when more than one editor handles it. Each sees gaps to be filled, and a better story results.

Working with the Copy Editor

The copy editor asks many of the same questions about your story that the city editor asks. Have you selected the right lead? Does the writing need to be polished? Have you chosen the correct words? Primarily, though, the copy editor checks for misspelled words, adherence to style, grammatical errors, ambiguities and errors of fact. The copy editor reworks a phrase here or there to clarify your meaning but is expected to avoid major changes. If major changes are necessary, the copy editor calls that to the attention of the news editor. If the news editor agrees, the story is returned to the city editor, and perhaps to you, for yet another revision.

When the copy editor is satisfied with the story, work begins on the headline. The size of the headline ordered by the copy desk chief determines how many characters or letters can be used in writing it. Headline writing is an art. Those who are able to convey the meaning of a story in a limited number of words are valuable members of the staff. The quality of the copy editor's work can have a significant impact on the number of readers who will be attracted to your story. If the headline is dull and lifeless, few will; if it sparkles, the story's exposure will be increased.

The copy editor also may write the **cutline**, or caption, that accompanies the picture. At some newspapers, however, this is done by the photographer, by the reporter or at the city desk. Large newspapers may have a photo desk to handle cutlines as well as picture cropping and sizing.

When finished, the copy editor transfers the story to the copy desk chief, who must approve the headline and may check the editing changes made by the copy editor. When the desk chief is satisfied, the story and headline are transferred to the composing room, where the creative effort of writers and editors is transformed into type. The picture is sent to another section of the production department for processing.

The size of the newspaper may alter this copy flow pattern substantially. At a small newspaper the jobs of news editor, copy desk chief and copy editor may be performed by one person. Some small dailies require the city editor or an assistant to perform all the tasks normally handled by the copy desk.

News room copy flow patterns have been designed with redundancy in mind. Built into the system is the goal of having not one editor, but several, check your work. Through repeated checking, editors hope to detect more errors—in fact and in writing style—to make the finished product a better one.

In this sense editors work as gatekeepers. They determine whether your work measures up to their standards. Only when it does is the gate opened, allowing your story to take the next step in the newspaper production process.

Magazines

The magazine industry is vast, and generalizations about magazine publishers are difficult to make. Publishers range from conglomerates like Time Warner, whose mass-audience magazines include *Time*, *Peo-*

graduate's resumé. He won an internship at AT&T and discovered he liked working in corporate communications. AT&T hired Hong for what he considered a good salary when he graduated.

At AT&T Network Systems in Morristown, N.J., Hong is a writer for the internal newsletter and magazine.

Like thousands of his colleagues in corporate communications, Hong believes his news courses have served him well. "There is an immediacy to the issues and events that we cover even within a corporation such as AT&T that demands someone who can take complicated information and tell readers what they need to know quickly.

"News-writing skills do not just serve the 'news rooms' of major metropolitan newspapers," Hong says. "They are essential to the success of any organization that thrives on information and the ability of its communicators to get that information out quickly, accurately and concisely."

ple and *Sports Illustrated*, to companies as diverse as International Harvester and Texaco, which publish magazines written and designed for employees or customers or both. Many also are published by not-for-profit organizations like the Girl Scouts.

Most magazines, even those that are commercially published, do not target mass audiences, as *Time* does, but instead target smaller audiences with a passion for the subject matter. Those include such titles as *Popular Mechanics, Boating, PC Magazine* and *Skiing*. Even more prevalent are company magazines, which usually are written and edited by corporate communications departments. Smaller magazines, those published by corporations or nonprofit organizations, often are put together by tiny staffs. Editors often write the stories, design the pages and even arrange for printing by outside vendors.

Magazine Organization

Magazines are organized much like newspapers, their print cousins. Among the various departments, only the circulation department will differ much from that of newspapers. That's because the method of distribution is dramatically different. Most magazines, on the one hand, depend heavily on the mail and on newsstand sales for distribution; daily newspapers, on the other hand, are distributed primarily by carriers. For most newspapers, mail service and newsstand sales are secondary.

In magazine and newspaper news rooms, most of the titles and job functions are the same. Still, a few titles are unique to the magazine industry. Major magazines are likely to have **senior editors** and **senior writers**. Senior editors usually edit a particular section of the magazine. At *Time*, for example, senior editors direct the International, Arts and other sections. Senior writers, as the name implies, are the magazine's best and most experienced writers. At *Time*, they may seldom leave the office but instead take information from numerous reporters in the field and meld their reports into a well-written, coherent story.

Some magazines also have **contributing editors**. Typically, these are columnists or reporters whose work is purchased for publication. They are not employed by the magazine, and sometimes their work will appear in several industry-related magazines each month.

Magazine Job Prospects

Few journalism and communications graduates go directly to work for large national magazines such as *Time, Newsweek* or *Sports Illustrated*. More likely, those who pursue magazine careers start elsewhere, get some experience and then market their reporting and writing skills to magazine editors. Or they start in corporate communications, where the job market is much larger and the pay is relatively good.

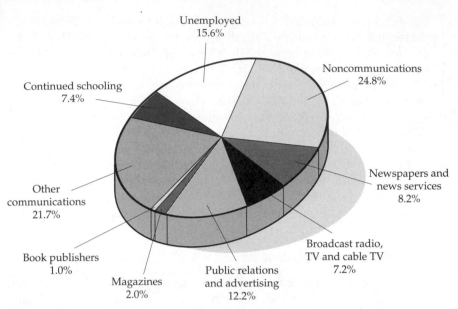

Figure 2.10.
Where Journalism Graduates Went to Work (1993). (Source: Ohio State University School of Journalism)

About 2 percent of journalism graduates go to work for magazines directly out of school (see Figure 2.10). But that statistic may be misleading. Those who go to work in public relations or "other communications" jobs often find themselves writing or editing magazines.

Magazine Production

To those used to the fast-paced world of daily newspapers, the magazine production cycle looks terribly appealing from a distance. But looks can be deceiving. The deadline pressures that face magazine writers and editors are just as intense; they merely are spread over longer time periods. Still, magazine writers and editors have more time to produce their work, and as a result there is more pressure to produce a near-perfect product.

The tight deadlines of newspapers often result in less-than-perfect writing, typographical errors and similar gaffes. Those mistakes are not tolerated at the best magazines, where longer deadlines mean there is more time to strive for perfection. Additional time also allows magazine editors to expend more effort on fact-checking and polishing of writing and design.

Magazine editors also spend much more time on writing to fit. Articles often are meticulously edited to fill an exact number of typeset lines in a magazine layout. Similarly, photo captions are fine-tuned so that all lines are completely filled. Such niceties often are dismissed at newspapers, where time is more precious. The result is that most magazines have a more polished look than newspapers. That's true not only because they are printed on higher quality paper but also because they are more meticulously edited. Unfortunately, at low-budget magazine operations those conditions may not exist.

Broadcasting

Broadcast stations play a major role in the way the public receives its news. Increasingly, so do cable television channels like Cable News Network, C-SPAN and CNBC, which we'll include in this section despite the fact that their programming is not really "broadcast." Radio, once a major player in news distribution, now is relegated to a second tier of service except for a few all-news stations in major cities and National Public Radio. Radio is used as a news medium primarily by those driving to and from work, and little of its reporting is original. Most radio news operations rely heavily on wire services for their news.

Broadcast Organization

The news room is only one part of the overall operation of a radio station, a network or a local television station. Other departments include *programming, sales, promotion* and *engineering*. At the local level, the news room is the station's biggest profit center.

A small-market television news operation may employ fewer than 20 people. In a large market, such as New York or Chicago, that number may be 100 or more. Network news divisions generally employ several hundred journalists each, even after big cutbacks in the late 1980s and early 1990s. Radio news rooms are invariably much smaller, and today few journalism graduates find their way to radio jobs.

The top news executive at a local television station typically is the **news director** or, at some group-owned stations, the *vice president for news*. The news director is responsible for managing news room personnel and resources and for setting news room policies. Often, the news director does not deal with details of daily news coverage. Instead, that responsibility is delegated to an *assistant news director* or *managing editor*.

The other key management role in a television news room is that of **executive producer**. The producer determines the overall look of the station's newscasts. This includes the use of video, graphics and animation; the length and placement of stories; whether a reporter or anchor is seen delivering the story; and how upcoming stories are "teased" going into a commercial break. Most stations also hire **show producers**, who report to the executive producer and are responsible for individual newscasts.

"Nowhere is the impact of the new media on the old more visible than in television broadcasting. Over-the-air television is under siege these days, largely because its audiences (and its revenues) are being increasingly preempted by cable television and home video-cassette recorders."
— **Wilson Dizard Jr., Old Media, New Media**

Producing requires an ability to see the "big picture" under the extreme pressure of broadcast deadlines. It is a high-stress, high-turnover job. It also is the position most in demand in local television news.

Television news, of course, requires reporters. In addition to gathering and writing the news, broadcast reporters must know how to present it in a lively and personable fashion. To be successful in large markets or at the network level, reporters must have a distinctive style and personality. In fact, **network correspondents** often do little original reporting themselves, leaving the news-gathering to **field producers** or **off-camera reporters**.

Anchors also are critical to a successful television news operation. In important ways they represent the persona of the news broadcast. Viewers know and have strong opinions about news anchors, even when they can't remember the call letters or channel of the station for which the anchors work.

Videographers play a key role in the television news room as well. TV news lives and dies by pictures. Creative videographers add to the look that often separates the top station in a market from its competitors.

In larger markets, **desk assistants** serve at the entry-level position in the television news room. They keep watch on material from the wire services, make routine beat calls, monitor fire and police scanners, and take in satellite feeds from networks or regional cooperatives.

Broadcast Job Prospects

Most broadcast news graduates who seek employment in television news take their first job in a small- or medium-sized market. Students have historically aspired to reach the ranks of a network correspondent or anchor. But network cutbacks, along with the growth and increasing sophistication of local television news, have altered the dreams of many prospective broadcast journalists.

As noted earlier, radio news jobs are few and far between. But they do exist, and a few graduates manage to find them. Except in large cities, radio news departments often are one-person operations. Where that situation exists, reporters depend heavily on wire services and do most of the rest of their reporting by telephone.

About 6 percent of journalism graduates found jobs in broadcasting or cable television in the mid-1990s. That was down from almost 10 percent in 1989. Overall, broadcast majors account for slightly more than 10 percent of journalism and communications students.

Broadcast News Production

Viewers use television news in a fundamentally different way than they do newspapers or magazines. The audience expects and demands immediacy, so local stations program several newscasts a day and put a premium on live reporting of newsworthy events.

and after graduation worked as a general assignment reporter and fill-in anchor for three-and-a half years at WLOS-TV in Asheville, N.C. Now she's an education reporter at NewsChannel 5 in Nashville, Tenn.

"It's my second year here," she says, "and I'm having a ball. It's often said this fast-paced, hectic business that's riddled with deadlines is one that will burn out a person. It can happen to some reporters, but I'm not feeling it yet. Good pacing, I guess."

Eaton has a few words for "reporters-in-the-making":

1. If you really want to be in the news business, keep at it. Don't let the "there-are-no-jobs" comments slow you down.
2. Constantly work to improve your writing.
3. It's OK to know you do good work; just don't let your head get so huge you can't make it through the news room door.
4. Remember, someone helped you get to where you are, so reach back and help others.

The frequent deadlines of broadcast news force reporters, videographers and producers to think quickly on their feet, to boil down a story to its most easily understood elements and to get on to the next assignment as quickly as possible. Broadcast journalists often find themselves "working without a net," making split-second decisions without the benefit of editors or time for reflection.

Broadcast reports are almost always team efforts. A reporter on assignment is accompanied by a videographer. Together, they collect the material that will form the basis of the report. When they finish collecting the material, they return to the station to edit it into the final form that will appear on the air. Or they edit their report in a mobile van capable of transmitting it back to the station by satellite or microwave. Editors and producers weave their material and that of other broadcast teams into the newscasts with which all are familiar.

By necessity, broadcast news focuses more on process than completeness. While radio and television journalism are capable of great depth, analysis and perspective, those qualities are more often demanded of newspapers and magazines. (For more on broadcast news, see Chapter 20.)

New Media

Fewer than five years ago, no one would have thought of including a section on new media in a textbook of this type. But the burgeoning growth of new-media services makes such a section necessary. Today, people consume news and other forms of information in unconventional ways, and most of them involve the home computer.

The most prevalent of new-media services are the public information utilities—CompuServe, America Online, Prodigy, Delphi, GEnie, The Microsoft Network, eWorld and others. All PIUs carry news and other forms of information, including stories from the Associated Press and other wire services. America is tuning in. News consumers can get the news as soon as it happens; they don't have to wait for the newspaper to arrive. Nor must they wait for the nightly newscast. The public information utilities offer news on demand, 24 hours a day.

New-Media Organization

To think of such services as simply new ways to transmit wire-service news is a mistake. Each of the services maintains a news room, where at least some original material is created. Further, each buys free-lance material and repackages other forms of information such as airline schedules, restaurant reviews and stock market quotations. Most allow users to download full-color pictures and sound clips.

Without a doubt, the most popular function of PIUs is to serve as public bulletin boards, where users with a passion for a particular

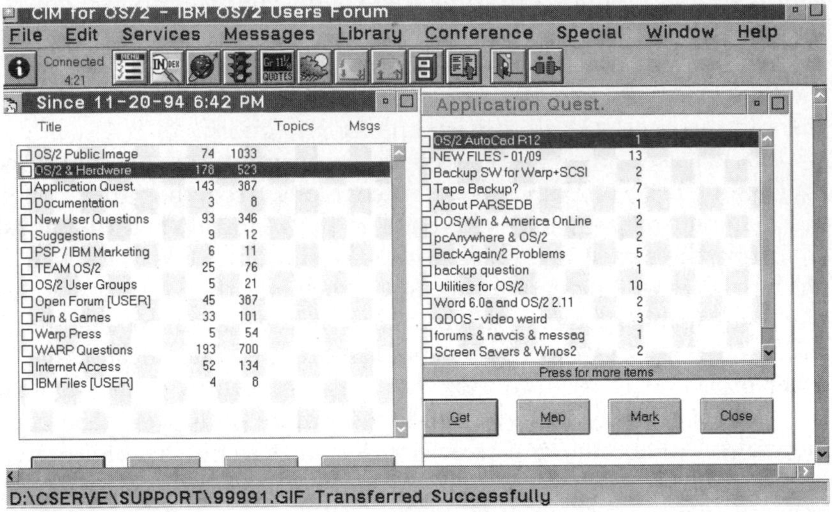

Figure 2.11.
Electronic bulletin boards, such as this one on CompuServe, are America's new meeting places—and a new place to get information.

topic can exchange ideas and information (see Figure 2.11). Interested in tracing your ancestry? You can get plenty of help from those who share that passion on bulletin boards pegged to that interest. Want to know more about the latest IBM computers than was printed in your local newspaper? Go to the public information utilities, where you'll find detailed information posted by the company, the full text of its news releases, complete technical specifications and a full-fledged discussion about the pros and cons of the new models. Exchanges range from irrational "flames," emotion-laden messages with little evidence of forethought or civility, to eloquent treatises on the virtues of multitasking computer operating systems.

To be sure, the public information utilities are far from being traditional media. Indeed, they are so diverse and operate so differently that it is almost impossible to create a typical organization chart. But the products they produce contain plenty of news, and computer users see them as ideal sources for the news they want. Now that an estimated 30 percent of American homes have computers and that percentage is climbing monthly, journalists cannot afford to dismiss the PIUs as insignificant.

Also worth noting is the rapid move toward commercialization of the Internet, the worldwide collection of computer networks that now has an estimated 30 million users. Once an exclusive terrain for academics and government employees, the Internet has grown into what could arguably be called the world's largest news medium. It carries unconventional as well as conventional forms of news, but its significance cannot be dismissed. Dozens of newspapers and magazines have begun experimenting with Internet-based supplements to their more traditional products. Increasingly, they are moving toward commercialization of these new products as the Internet becomes a more hospitable environment for business.

Finally, there are the various wire services and electronic information services. For years, the Associated Press, United Press International, Reuters and others have been viewed mainly as wholesalers of information to newspapers and broadcast stations. Through on-line services, their products are now going directly to consumers. More focused offspring such as Dow Jones News Retrieval and Bloomberg Business News are expanding rapidly. All of them represent new ways of delivering news into the home through the computer.

New-Media Job Prospects

Charles Hammer went to journalism school with the intention of preparing for a newspaper job. Like many who end up with jobs unlike those they imagined, he got sidetracked. University of Missouri researchers, who were seeking ways to arrest the downturn in newspaper readership among young people, decided to see if a computer-delivered, electronic newspaper would be more appealing to that audience than the printed newspaper. Hammer got involved in that successful experiment, and his involvement led directly to a job as an editor at Access Atlanta, the *Atlanta Journal and Constitution* product delivered on Prodigy. He now works for Delphi, one of the public information utilities.

Similarly, Jane Singer started out as a newspaper journalist but made her way to New York, where she played a key role in starting the Prodigy news room. Almost exclusively, the people she hired came from newspapers.

The stories of both of these individuals highlight the existence of journalistic jobs in the new media. The number of new-media jobs is growing rapidly. Newspapers, magazines and broadcast stations all are creating a computer-based electronic presence. As they do so, they are looking for young journalists with computer skills. Today, only a handful of journalism and communications programs attempt to train students for such jobs. But that number is steadily increasing as administrators become aware of the increase in demand. To prepare for such jobs, computer training is essential, as are visual and verbal skills.

New-Media Production

Few newcomers are hired as new-media *reporters*; instead, journalists are hired as new-media *editors*. That's because the strength of the new media lies not in the creation of new content but in the repackaging of existing content in a form that is more immediate and easier to use. That difference also helps one understand how new-media news rooms are organized. They are, in many ways, like one huge copy desk employing editors with multiple talents—computer skills, word skills and visual skills. Think of those editors as multimedia journalists.

Most new-media news rooms are filled with editors with titles not unlike those found at newspapers. Editors take responsibility for certain sections of the on-line service—news, sports, features and others. Content is gathered from both traditional and nontraditional sources. Graphic displays are designed for maximum appeal on computer screens. Immediacy is paramount.

Unlike editors at a newspaper or magazine, new-media editors must have skills that more closely resemble those of the broadcast journalist. It's not good enough to be a word editor for the new media; one must also have a good sense of visual design. That's because the new media, like television, depend on attractive screen presentation for impact. Journalists who work in the new media must be competent in writing, editing and design. Increasingly, they also will need audio and video skills; most of the new media are moving to incorporate audio and video clips into their services.

Like wire-service journalists, new-media journalists are constantly on deadline. Twenty-four hours a day, users dial in to get the latest news and information. Thus, producing news for the new media requires journalists who thrive on deadline pressure, who have strong computer skills, who understand both written and visual communication and who are interested in pioneering a new medium. Those who can meet these requirements should have little trouble finding jobs.

Other Career Opportunities

Journalism training is in many ways ideal training for almost any profession. The skills of writing, editing and visual communication are in great demand worldwide. The broad applications of journalism training account for the large number of journalism graduates who find themselves in jobs quite different from those they imagined.

In this chapter, we outlined the most common routes for those with journalism training to find jobs as reporters and writers of news. But there are many others, including public relations, corporate communications, advertising, ethnic newspapers, professional periodicals, union and trade publications and virtually any areas that require the skills of writing, editing or visual communication. Nationwide, the most popular majors among journalism and mass communication students are advertising and public relations. Many who receive degrees in news-editorial programs end up in other jobs, including public relations, corporate communications and new media. More than one journalism graduate has parlayed an interest in computers and journalism into a job as a newspaper systems manager. Others have found jobs training journalists to use new computer systems; vendors have learned that an understanding of how journalists work speeds that process.

Others have gone into publications work for nonprofit organizations such as the Girl Scouts and the American Heart Association. Still others who started at newspapers have moved to television or vice versa. Because journalism and mass communications accrediting standards emphasize the importance of a broad liberal arts education, students often get the ideal mix of practical training and the ability to think. That, more than any specific skill, is the mark of a well-trained journalist.

Suggested Readings

Czech-Beckerman, Elizabeth S. *Managing Electronic Media*. Boston: Focal Press, 1991. A contemporary discussion of broadcast management.

"Digital Media." Media, Pa.: Seybold Publications. An expensive but useful monthly newsletter that stays abreast of the latest new-media developments.

Dizard, Wilson, Jr. *Old Media, New Media*. New York: Longman, 1994. A good overview of the developing new-media landscape.

Giles, Robert H. *Newsroom Management: A Guide to Theory and Practice*. Detroit: Media Management Books, 1991. The best and most current discussion of newspaper management and organization.

Online Access. Chicago: Chicago Fine Print. A magazine published 10 times a year that covers on-line access to information.

Randall, Neil. *Teach Yourself the Internet—Around the World in 21 Days*. New York: Sams Publishing, 1994. One of the better primers on Internet access.

Exercises

1. Visit either your school newspaper or the local daily or weekly newspaper. Talk with staff members about how the staff is organized. Once you understand the system, draw an organization chart for the news department.

2. Draw a copy flow chart that shows how copy moves from reporters to the production department at the newspaper you chose for exercise 1.

3. Visit a local television station and interview the news director about how the news room is organized. Produce an organization chart that explains the operation.

4. Using the Internet or one of the public information utilities, locate information on the most recent U.S. census and report the following:

   a. The population of your state.
   b. The population of your city.
   c. The range of income levels and percentages of population that fall within those income levels in your city.
   d. The demographic breakdown of your city by race.

5. Compare the news offerings of CompuServe and America Online or any of the other public information utilities to which you have access. Describe differences in those offerings and explain which one you prefer. Why?

6. Make a list of at least 10 sources of information available on the Internet that would be good resources for journalists. Explain why.

FINAL EDITION UCLA, MEMPHIS, GEORGETOWN ALL WIN AT THE BUZZER, 1C

THE LATEST NEWS & SPORTS

The Evening Sun.

MONDAY, MARCH 20, 1995   HOME DELIVERY: 25¢ (in most areas) • NEWSSTAND: 50¢   BALTIMORE, MARYLAND

Lewis did use drugs, friend is quoted

A Baltimore man has told The Wall Street Journal that he used cocaine with pro basketball star Reggie Lewis on several occasions, including five days before the Boston Celtics captain collapsed during a 1993 playoff game.

Reggie Lewis later died from a scarred heart, and the cause of his death is still being questioned. A recent Journal article hinted of drug use, which has been denied by Reggie Lewis' family and critics officials, who have threatened a $100 million lawsuit.

Derrick Lewis, no kin to the National Basketball Association player, grew up with Reggie Lewis here and played basketball with him at recreation centers and at Northeastern University in Boston. He remained a close friend after Mr. Lewis attained NBA stardom. Derrick Lewis told the Journal that Reggie Lewis was "with me, an experimental user of cocaine like a lot of people from executives to college students, who try it once in a while. Reggie was addicted to basketball not drugs.

In college, Derrick Lewis said he and Reggie Lewis did a lot of "heavy partying, mostly with marijuana. There was a lot of partying on the team."

Reggie Lewis' wife, Donna Harris-Lewis, has maintained that her husband never used drugs. Derrick Lewis said it is possible she never knew if her husband's involvement. Derrick Lewis told the newspaper he has not used drugs since his friend died.

Infant girl is found abandoned

Left outside store in North Point

By Richard Irwin
Sun staff writer

A newborn girl was found abandoned outside a convenience store in North Point early today, Baltimore County police said.

The child, police said, was found inside a box at the High's dairy store in the 4000 block of North Point Blvd. Her mother's identity was still not known.

A police spokesman said someone found the child about 5:30 a.m. and carried her inside. A store employee called police.

A Fire Department ambulance was dispatched and it took the girl to Bayview Medical Center. The infant's condition was not immediately available.

Police were canvassing the area seeking anyone having information about the girl, who abandoned her. Anyone having such information was urged to call police commissioners at 887-2194 or the North Point Precinct at 887-7320.

Weather
Rain possible tonight, low of 46 degrees. Showers tomorrow, high 62, low 39. 10B

Terrorists hit Tokyo subway system

Nerve gas spews through train cars: at least 6 killed, thousands stricken

Associated Press

TOKYO — One of the world's busiest subway systems turned into a deathtrap today when nerve gas spewed through cars during morning rush hour, killing six people and sickening thousands. Authorities were treating it as a terror attack.

No motive was immediately apparent and no group claimed responsibility.

All over central Tokyo, subway passengers fainted, vomited and went into convulsions as the fumes spread. Some of those stricken foamed at the mouth and bled from the nose, witnesses said. Nearly 1,300 people were admitted to hospitals for treatment or observation.

Police said the toxic agent was sarin, a nerve gas that can be fatal even in small doses. Japanese news reports cited authorities as saying the substance was planted in wrapped containers to at least five subway cars on three train lines.

Sarin was blamed for seven deaths in June at houses in the central Japan town of Matsumoto. The source was never identified, and there were no arrests.

Authorities refused to discuss suspects — either individuals or groups — and would not say whether they included Aum Shinri Kyo, a religious cult that has been accused of making sarin.

The group, which has been linked

by news reports to several unsolved kidnappings, denied any involvement in today's poisonings and threatened in a statement to sue anyone who suggested there was a link.

Two unexplained incidents earlier this month could yield clues. On March 15, three mysterious attaché cases were discovered at a Tokyo subway station, each containing three tanks with an unknown liquid, small motorized fans, a vent, and a battery. One was giving off a vapor.

Ten days before that, 19 train riders in Yokohama, a port city near Tokyo, were taken to hospitals complaining of eye and respiratory pain from an unknown source of fumes.

Hospitals in central Tokyo were inundated today. Doctors and nurses rushed frantically to administer CPR, give oxygen and hook up intravenous drips.

Officials estimated that thousands of others had lesser symptoms, including coughing and dizziness and did not obtain treatment.

"When I got to the hospital, I couldn't move my hands enough to write my name and I could barely speak," said commuter Masashi Horiuchi.

The poisoning struck at a crowded national institution. Tokyo's clean and efficient subway network. The trains run on precise schedules carrying 2.7 million passengers.

See JAPAN, 4A

Associated Press

Subway passengers felled by toxic fumes receive medical attention at St. Luke's Hospital.

Supreme Court backs Maryland inventor

Associated Press

WASHINGTON — Chrysler lost a Supreme Court bid today to overturn an $18.7 million award won by a Maryland inventor who said the automaker stole his design for intermittent windshield wipers.

The court, without comment, turned down Chrysler's argument that it was improperly barred from introducing evidence of other previously existing intermittent wiper systems.

Virtually all cars sold in the United States now have intermittent wipers, as standard or optional equipment.

Robert W. Kearns of Queenstown, received several patents for his design in 1967. He shopped it around to various automakers but did not reach a licensing deal.

He sued Ford in 1978 and Chrysler in 1982, claiming patent infringement.

The Ford case went to trial first. A jury decided that Mr. Kearns' patents were valid and enforceable and ordered Ford to pay $5.2 million plus interest. Ford later agreed to pay $10.2 million and to drop all appeals.

Chrysler officials had promised to rely on the Ford jury's decision on whether the patents were valid and enforceable. But in 1991, Chrysler

unsuccessfully tried to convince a trial judge that it should be allowed to challenge the finding because Ford did not appeal it.

In the appeal acted on today, Chrysler's lawyers said federal judges should be required to allow evidence aimed at clarifying what aspects of a patented invention's design already were in the public domain.

Mr. Kearns, representing himself, said the appeals court ruled correctly on that issue.

The cases are Chrysler Corp. vs. Kearns, 94-1131, and Kearns vs. Chrysler Corp. 94-1269.

30 vehicles crash in fog, causing fiery pileup in Ala.

Collisions on Mobile Bay span

Associated Press

MOBILE, Ala. — Thirty cars and trucks collided in fog on a bridge across Mobile Bay today, creating a fiery pileup that left some cars hanging off the span, police and witnesses said.

Traffic was halted in both directions on the Interstate 10 bridge. It was not immediately known if anyone was injured.

The crashes began about 7 a.m. as a wall of fog made visibility difficult. There also were accidents reported on a two-lane causeway that roughly parallels the newer interstate bridge.

Massacre of 17 in Burundi sparks ethnic clashes

Tutsis and Hutus ignore peace plea

Reuters

BUJUMBURA, Burundi — At least 17 people, including three Belgians, were massacred by gunmen in Burundi, sparking clashes in the capital today in which another four people were killed.

Witnesses said members of the Hutu majority were taken hostage today in the central market.

The witnesses counted four dead after stone-throwing gangs of Tutsi and Hutu youths clashed outside the market as news of yesterday's massacre spread.

The youths ignored Prime Minister Antoine Nduwayo's appeal for peace today after the massacre at Wasesstandert, seven miles southeast of Bujumbura. Police said 17 people were killed on the main road.

Security sources said Tutsi youths were heading today for Nyamasandert, where they might take revenge for Tutsis, on a "punitive mission" in revenge for the attack blamed on Hutu gunmen.

The slain Belgians were a woman, her daughter and a man. His fiancée was among three Belgian wounded taken to hospital.

In Brussels, the Foreign Ministry condemned the killings and a spokesman appealed to the 850 Belgians living in Burundi to take extra security measures. The spokesman said the ambush took place about 7.30 p.m. yesterday, a half-hour after a curfew began in Bujumbura.

"They were traveling back from a sports meeting outside the capital when apparently they had tire problems and had to stop. An armed group then attacked them," the spokesman said.

The Belgian Foreign Ministry said no evacuation plan was being prepared. Burundi is a former Belgian protectorate.

"We are looking at this as an isolated incident. Burundi nationals were with the Belgians, so we do not think the attack was targeted at Belgians," the spokesman added.

Burundi has the same volatile ethnic mix as neighboring Rwanda, where up to 1 million Tutsis and allies Hutus were put to death by Hutus in last year's genocide.

Van fire on I-68

Sam Kriedel of Youngstown, Ohio, watches as the van he was driving burns along Interstate 68 near Frostburg, Md. Mr. Kriedel said he was trying to restart the engine by putting drops of gasoline in the carburetor when the fuel ignited. Police said there were various flammable substances in the van.

Associated Press

In court appearances, trend among defendants is come-as-you-are

Etiquette deteriorating, some say

By Robert Guy Matthews
Sun staff writer

Not long ago, people dressed for court the way they dressed for church. Now they dress for court the way they dress for a ballgame.

Throughout Baltimore County's District Courts, defendants in dingy gym jeans, T-shirts, baseball caps, tattered sweat pants and sunglasses wait for judges to decide their guilt or innocence. With even warmer weather on the way, tank tops, cutoff shorts and flip-flops will be much in evidence.

Many judges, defense attorneys and prosecutors call the new mode of dress outrageous but no longer surprising. They say it's symptomatic of the degeneration of courtroom etiquette during the past five

years. They also say that not much can be done to change it. Chief District Judge Robert F. Sweeney has no dress code in his court and encourages judges to tolerate diversity in attire. Still many jurists lament the long gone, unwritten rule that went to court what you wore to church.

Consider the defendant in a September drunken driving case who asked a Towson judge for lenience — standing before the bench in a Budweiser T-shirt and Jack Daniels belt buckle. Or the case of the man who pleaded not guilty to a drug possession charge before a Dundalk judge in December. On his denim jacket was a marijuana plant emblem.

Both were found guilty.

Columbia graphic artist Aaron Lynch wore to Essex District Court what he wore to a beer bash the night before — gray sweat pants and a purple shirt he had slept in the previous night.

"I don't see why I should dress

up for a judge," said the man who was found guilty of bad check and battery charges in November. "Who cares what I look like?"

Judges do, defense attorneys say. Although no one keeps statistics on attire and length of sentence, veteran lawyers believe that a client's dress can affect the severity of punishment.

Baltimore defense attorney Roland Walker tells his clients that

See ETIQUETTE, 6A

THE INVERTED PYRAMID

*S*pecialized news delivered to customers' desks—one of the hottest new services in the 1990s—relies on the **inverted pyramid**, one of the most traditional story forms.

So do newspapers, despite many editors' emphasis on encouraging new writing forms. So do radio, television stations and newsletters. Business executives often use the inverted pyramid in company memos so their bosses don't have to read to the end to find the main point.

Frequently misdiagnosed as dying, the inverted pyramid has more lives than a cat. Perhaps it is because the more people try to speed up the dissemination of information, the more valuable the inverted pyramid becomes. This is happening because in the inverted pyramid, the information is arranged from most important to least important. The king in *Alice in Wonderland* would never succeed in the electronic news service business. When asked where to start a story, he replied, "Begin at the beginning and go on till you come to the end; then stop." Reporters, however, often begin a story at its end. Subscribers to Dow Jones News Retrieval, Reuters and Bloomberg, for instance, react instantly to news about the financial markets to get an edge. They don't want narration; they want the news.

So do many newspaper readers, who, on average, spend 15 to 20 minutes a day reading the paper. Many have time to read only a few paragraphs of most stories. If a reporter were to write an account of a car accident by starting when the driver left the house, many readers would never stay with the story long enough to find out that the driver was killed. Instead, such a story starts with its climax:

> Two people died Thursday when a backhoe fell off a truck's flatbed and sliced the top off an oncoming vehicle near Fairchild Air Force Base.

The inverted pyramid was fairly common by the turn of this century. Before then, reporters were less direct. In 1869, the New York Herald *sent Henry Morton Stanley to Africa to find the famous explorer-missionary David Livingstone. Stanley's famous account of the meeting began:*

> Only two months gone, and what a change in my feelings! But two months ago, what a peevish, fretful soul was mine! What a hopeless prospect presented itself before your correspondent!

After several similar sentences, the writer reports, "And the only answer to it all is (that) Livingstone, the hero traveler, is alongside of me."

Stanley reported the most important information so casually that today's subscriber probably would not have read far enough into the story to learn that Livingstone had been found. Today's reporter would probably begin the story like this:

Dr. David Livingstone, the missionary-explorer missing for six years, has been found working in an African village on the shores of Lake Tanganyika.

The inverted pyramid saves readers time and editors space. Time *by allowing readers to get the most important part of the story first—the climax of the event, the theme of a speech, the key finding in an investigation. Space by allowing editors to shorten stories by whacking from the bottom. That's less important for electronic news services than newspapers, where space is limited. But if an editor had cut Stanley's story from the bottom we would never have had these now famous lines, which end the story:*

"Dr. Livingstone, I presume?"
And he says, "Yes."

The inverted pyramid lead is presented as simply and clearly as possible. It sets the tone. It advertises what is coming in the rest of the story, and it conveys the most important information in the story.

The lead sits atop paragraphs arranged in descending order of importance. These paragraphs explain and provide evidence to support the lead. That's why editors can quickly shorten a story; the paragraphs at the bottom are the least important. The need to produce multiple newspaper editions with the same story running different lengths in each one makes it important that stories can be shortened quickly. The inverted pyramid serves that need well.

In Part Three, where basic story types are discussed, we will see some examples of stories that are more effectively written in less traditional forms than the inverted pyramid, and in Chapter 17, we will discuss other ways to organize a news story.

The inverted pyramid does have some shortcomings. Although it delivers the important news first, it does not encourage people to read the entire story. Stories stop; they don't end. There is no suspense. In a Poynter Media Institute study, researchers found that of the 25 percent who started a story, half of them dropped out midway through the story. Interest in an inverted pyramid story diminishes as the story progresses. But the way people use it attests to its value as a quick form of information delivery. Readers can leave whenever their needs are met, not when a writer finishes a story. In an age when time is golden, the inverted pyramid still offers value.

The day when the inverted pyramid is relegated to journalism history is not yet here and probably never will be. Perhaps 80 percent of the stories in today's newspapers and almost 100 percent of the stories on news services for target audiences such as the financial community are written in the inverted pyramid form. The trend is changing—as it should be—but it's changing slowly. Some of the new media will require other forms. For instance, tailored stories for news-on-demand services that will reach a general audience need not use the inverted pyramid. Still, as long as newspaper, electronic and broadcast journalists continue to emphasize the quick, direct, simple ap-

"Because a story is important, it doesn't follow that it must be long."

— Stanley Walker,
City Editor

proach to communications, the inverted pyramid and modifications of it will have a role.

Every journalist should master its form. Those who do will have mastered the art of making news judgments. The inverted pyramid requires you to identify and rank the most newsworthy elements in each story. That is important work. No matter what kind of stories you write—whether obituaries, accidents, speeches, press conferences, fires or meetings—you will be required to use the skills you learn here.

How to Write Leads

To write a **lead**—a simple, clear statement consisting of the first paragraph or two of a story—you must first recognize what goes into one. As you read in Chapter 1, you begin by determining the story's *relevance, usefulness* and *interest* among readers. One way to measure those standards is to ask "so what?" or "who cares?" So what if there's a car accident downtown? If it's one of hundreds a month, it may not be news. Any holdup in a community of 5,000 may be news because the so-what is that holdups are uncommon. Residents probably know the person working at the store. Neither newspapers nor broadcast stations may report the holdup in a metropolitan area because holdups are so common. But if the holdup appears to be part of a pattern or if someone is killed, the story becomes more significant. One holdup may not be news, but a holdup that authorities believe is one of many committed by the same person may be news. The so-what is that if the police catch this robber, they have stopped a crime spree. To determine the so-what, you have to answer six basic questions. They are: *who, what, when, where, why, and how?*

The six basic questions

1. Who?
2. What?
3. When?
4. Where?
5. Why?
6. How?

William Caldwell, winner of a Pulitzer Prize in 1971, remembers the best lead he ever heard. He tells the story in an Associated Press Managing Editors "Writing" report:

> One summer afternoon in 1922, I was on my way home from school and my daily stint of work as editor of the village weekly, unhonored and unpaid. Like my father and two uncles, I was a newspaperman.
>
> My little brother came running to meet me at the foot of our street. He was white and crying. A telegram had come to my mother. "Pa drowned this morning in Lake George," he gasped, and I am ashamed to be remembering my inward response to that.
>
> Before I could begin to sense such elements as sorrow, despair, horror, loneliness, anger—before all the desolation of an abandoned kid would well up in me, I found myself observing that the sentence my brother had just uttered was the perfect lead. Noun, verb, predicate, period, and who-what-when-where to boot.

The information from every event you witness and every story you hear can be reduced to answers to these six questions. If they add up to a significant so-what, you have a story. Consider this example of an incoming call at fire headquarters.

FINAL EDITION

UCLA, Arkansas And Georgetown Win NCAA Thrillers, 1C

THE SUN

LATEST NEWS & SPORTS

MONDAY, MARCH 20, 1995   HOME DELIVERY: 25¢ *(in most areas)* • NEWSSTAND: 50¢   BALTIMORE, MARYLAND

Graduation prayer issue returns

Supreme Court expected to cure split in circuits

By Lyle Denniston
Washington Bureau of The Sun

WASHINGTON — It is just about voting, and high school seniors are beginning to count the days until graduation the constitutional lawyers, find courts are moving toward the accrual ritual of fighting over prayers at the students' commencement exercises.

At the Supreme Court, the justices are close to taking center stage themselves once more on the issue. They would have something to say as early as today.

The controversy over prayers in public schools, at any time of the year in any school setting, is never far from the court's docket. But prayer at graduation ceremonies has been one of the most heated points of dispute in recent years, and a new case on it is ready for the court. The question: It is unconstitutional for school officials to arrange for prayer at graduation, may students themselves do so?

Three years after the court's major decision banning many but perhaps not all graduation prayers, the issue still roils high schools. No one can be sure just what is to be not allowed, at least until the court acts again.

In Maryland where the state attorney general officially frowns on all student prayers at public school graduations, some students — as in Westminster — have been holding separate religious services at commencement earlier than fighting over religious expression at school sponsored ceremonies.

The justices' first step on the issue is due soon in a case from Idaho. They will decide whether to review the entire question of graduation prayer again. Because lower courts have been divided over it, the chances seem stronger that the court will agree to provide new constitutional guidance.

In Grangeville, Idaho, where the case began, School Superintendent Al Arizona Sias a meeting with his board of trustees this afternoon, and hopes the court has acted by then so he can tell them something. "This year, we haven't done anything previous or been kind of waiting to see what's going to happen."

For the time being, he said, he is prepared to leave matters as they have stood for years. The students will decide without interference from school officials, whether to invoke prayers in their commencement exercises at school — even though that very practice in Grangeville was ruled unconstitutional by a federal appeals court in November.

At Grangeville High School, the largest of three high schools in the local district in equal terms 130 in his graduation in that year's 79 se

See COURT, 4A

Gas poisons subway in Tokyo

6 die, 1,200 hospitalized after apparent attack

From Staff and Wire Reports

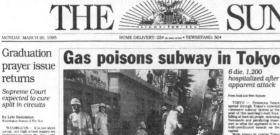

TOKYO — Poisonous fumes spread through Tokyo's crowded commuter subway system at the peak of this morning's rush hour, killing at least six people, sickening thousands and paralyzing transport in what the appeared to be a well-coordinated assault on the capital.

Main streets in central Tokyo were chaotic with emergency vehicles wailing and helicopters buzzing overhead. Hospitals were overwhelmed with people complaining of nausea, headaches and coughing. At least 1,200 were admitted for treatment or observation.

Government spokesman Kozo Igarashi called the poisonings a "random mass attack" and said that police were treating the case as a murder investigation. The authorities refused to say whether they had any suspect.

Police said it was "highly possible" that the gas was Sarin, an extremely toxic and volatile nerve gas developed by Nazi scientists in the 1930s. They said the attack, which was similar to an incident last year in central Japan, appeared to be an organized act of sabotage. But no group immediately took responsibility.

The fumes were detected at 18 stations on the Hibiya and Marunouchi lines, which slice through the heart of Tokyo. Both lines were closed, affecting 26 stations and paralyzing traffic into government, financial and retail districts.

Police confirmed six deaths. Hospital officials said at least 15 of those hospitalized were in critical condition.

The Tokyo Metropolitan Fire Department said the first report came about 8:15 a.m. from Tsukiji station, a crowded area near Tokyo's largest fish market.

Passengers reported that a man

See JAPAN, 8A

Subway passengers sickened by toxic fumes stretch on the ground outside Tokyo's Tsukiji station.

Major has earful for Clinton

British leader upset by visit by Sinn Fein's Adams

New York Times News Service

LONDON — After not accepting a telephone call from President Clinton for more than a week, Prime Minister John Major relented yesterday afternoon, and in a 25-minute conversation, promptly struck a tough stance on talks with Sinn Fein, the political wing of the Irish Republican Army.

Mr. Major insisted that Sinn Fein had not yet made a firm enough commitment to "decommission" the arms of the IRA to enter into high-level talks with the British government, according to an account of the conversation provided by the prime minister's office.

Up to now, in a slow-moving but methodical initiative for peace in Northern Ireland, Sinn Fein representatives have held only exploratory sessions with British civil servants.

The prime minister's office said he also expressed "concern" that Mr. Clinton had allowed Gerry Adams, the Sinn Fein president, to raise funds for his political party during a trip to Washington last week. The nationalist leader met the president twice, once at a luncheon given by the speaker of the House, Newt Gingrich, and later at a St. Patrick's Day dinner at the White House.

Mr. Major pointed out that there was a long history in the IRA purchasing arms with money raised in the United States and said it was vital that any funds raised not be used by the organization to replenish its arsenal.

Mr. Clinton, Mr. Major's office said, "acknowledged the importance of decommissioning of weapons" made it clear that the United States

See MAJOR, 3A

JORDAN AIRBORNE ONCE MORE

Chicago Bulls superstar's return elevates pro basketball

By Ken Rosenthal
Sun Columnist

INDIANAPOLIS — The Market Square Arena is where Elvis performed his last concert. How fitting that Michael Jordan began his comeback tour on the same stage.

Elvis is back, back wagging his tongue, back in long, baggy shorts. He didn't hit all of his high notes yesterday, but such was the excitement, hardly anyone noticed.

Jordan's return transformed a routine NBA game between the Chicago Bulls and Indiana Pacers into a nationally televised thriller, won by the Pacers in overtime, 103-96.

Just like that, the NBA is again the hottest attraction in sports. Did

Michael Jordan drives to the basket against the Indiana Pacers.

COMMENTARY

anyone watch the NCAA tournament yesterday? Does anyone still care about baseball and its silly strikes?

"Hey time you've got the best player coming back to play, that would rejuvenate any league," Pacers star Reggie Miller said. "That would be like Babe Ruth or Johnny Unitas coming back to play."

Jordan, 32, retired from basketball 17 months ago, then went on to baseball as a minor-league outfielder with the Chicago White Sox. His frustration with the game's 2-month-old strike helped bring him back to the NBA.

He announced his return Saturday by releasing a two-word statement through his agent, saying only, "I'm back." Reporters flew to Indianapolis from all over the country yesterday to catch this only attraction in sports.

"I love the game," Jordan said. "I tried to stay away as much as I could. The more active I was in other sports, it really kept my mind away from the game. When I was in baseball, I was a very far distance away.

"But when you love something for so long then try to walk away — I probably needed it mentally. But I missed my friends, I missed my teammates. I missed the atmosphere around a bit."

See JORDAN, 4A

Road warriors make deals at the wheel

Increasing numbers of business people work even in traffic

By Mark Guidera
Sun Staff Writer

William Woods, is a a high-tech road warrior. His weapons: a cellular phone, a laptop computer, a portable notebook and his Lincoln Town Car.

Mr. Woods, vice president of Xtron & Young in a startling growing number of business people who conduct a large slice of their work from behind the steering wheels of their cars.

This new breed of mobile worker zips from home to appointments to sales meetings packing virtual offices — laptop computers, cellular phones and facsimile machines — with hardly a pit stop at their home offices. Cyberspace mavens call them road warriors.

Traveling salespeople have known this perpatetic life for years. But what there is no limit to the possessions hitting the highways, portending what some predict will be a radical change in the not-too-distant future for offices as many have known them.

It's a trend driven by high technology, ever smaller, more efficient and cheaper telecommunications devices. And it's a work life that poses its own particular challenges, from maximizing relationships with colleagues to being road-wise.

"The main strategy to survive is know the traffic patterns," says Mr. Washecka, director of Ernst & Young's life sciences and high technology division in Washington. "You don't want to be on the wrong side of the bridge at rush hour."

As many as 4 million U.S. workers — out of the nation's total work force of 123 million — already qualify as road warriors by operating almost exclusively out of their vehicles, says Edward Kirk of Hunt Valley, co-founder of the National Telecommuting & Telework Association.

Road warriors intersect with their co-workers via portable phones or the modems of their laptop computers, the heart of their virtual offices.

See VIRTUAL, 4A

❝ *Today, you can work from virtually anywhere you happen to be in the world. Even poolside if that's where you want to be.* ❞

EDWARD ROBERTSON
Consultant to road warriors

In addition, some pack portable facsimile machines, CD ROM drives and even scanners to file documents to their computers.

The increased reliability, affordability and availability of these gadgets mean the need for actual offices is fast fading, says Edward Robertson, a consultant whose Bethesda company, NetaBesema Inc., helps equip clients to become road warriors.

"Today, you can work from virtually anywhere you happen to be in the world. Even poolside if that's

---

INDEX

New TV column
Beginning today The Sun's column of television highlights. "Today's TV," will include more local information. Staff writer Steve McKerrow will be compiling viewing tips tailored exclusively to the Baltimore market. Page 4D

Israelis attacked
Gunmen open fire on a busload of Jewish settlers, killing two and wounding at least five in the West Bank. Page 5A

Bridge	6D	Editorials	8A
Business	11C	Horoscope	7D
Classified	1E	Lottery	2B
Comics	7D	Movies	3D
Deaths	4B	Television	4D

Weather
Partly sunny.
High, 63; low, 48. Yesterday's high, 64; low, 47.
Details 8B

♻ Portions of The Sun are printed each day on recycled paper. The newsprint also is recyclable.

4 SECTIONS

In court appearances, trend is come-as-you-are

By Robert Guy Matthews
Sun Staff Writer

Not long ago, people dressed for court the way they dressed for church. Now they dress for court the way they dress for a ballgame.

Throughout Baltimore County's District Courts, defendants in flings, torn jeans, T-shirts, baseball caps, tattered sweat pants and sunglasses wait for judges to decide their guilt or innocence. With even warmer weather on the way, tank tops, cutoff shorts and flip-flops will be much in evidence.

Many judges, defense attorneys and prosecutors call the new mode of dress outrageous but no longer surprising. They say it a symptomatic of the degeneration of courtroom etiquette during the past five years.

They also say that not much can be done to change it. Chief District Judge Robert F. Sweeney

has no dress code in his court and encourages judges to tolerate diversity in attire. Still, many judges lament the long gone courtroom rule that you wear to court what you wear to church.

Consider the defendant in a September drunken-driving case who asked a Towson judge for leniency — standing before the bench in a Budweiser T-shirt and Jack Daniels belt buckle. Or the case of the man who pleaded not guilty to a drug possession charge while wearing a Dundalk judge in December. On his denim jacket was a marijuana plant emblem.

Both were found guilty.

Columbia graphic artist Aaron Lynch wore to Essex District Court what he wore to a beer bash the night before — gray sweat pants and a purple shirt he had slept in the previous night.

"I don't see why I should dress

See ETIQUETTE, 4A

Figure 3.1.

Note the differences on Page One of the Baltimore Sun *and* Evening Sun *for March 20, 1995, the day the Tokyo subway system was attacked with nerve gas. The cycle the newspaper publishes on—and the production cycle for broadcast news—affect the emphasis in the news.*

FINAL EDITION UCLA, MEMPHIS, GEORGETOWN ALL WIN AT THE BUZZER, 1C

THE LATEST NEWS & SPORTS

The Evening Sun.

MONDAY, MARCH 20, 1995   HOME DELIVERY: 25¢ (in most areas) • NEWSSTAND: 50¢   BALTIMORE, MARYLAND

Lewis did use drugs, friend is quoted

A Baltimore man has told *The Wall Street Journal* that he used cocaine with pro basketball star Reggie Lewis on several occasions, including five days before the Boston Celtics captain collapsed during a 1993 playoff game.

Reggie Lewis here died from a scarred heart, and the cause of his death is still being questioned. A recent *Journal* article hinted of drug use, which has been denied by Reggie Lewis' family and Celtics officials, who have threatened a $100 million lawsuit.

Derrick Lewis, no kin to the National Basketball Association player, grew up with Reggie Lewis here and played basketball with him at recreation centers and at Northeastern University in Boston. He remained a close friend after Mr. Lewis attained NBA stardom. Derrick Lewis told the *Journal* that Reggie Lewis was, "with me, an experimental user of cocaine like a lot of people, from curiosities to college students, who try it once in a while. Reggie was addicted to basketball not drugs."

In college, Derrick Lewis said he and Reggie Lewis did a lot of "heavy partying, mostly with marijuana. There was a lot of partying in the years" before his friend died.

Reggie Lewis' wife, Donna Harris-Lewis, has maintained that her husband never used drugs. Derrick Lewis said it is possible she never knew of her husband's involvement. Derrick Lewis said in the newspaper he has not used drugs since his friend died.

Infant girl is found abandoned

Left outside store in North Point

By Richard Irwin
Sun Staff Writer

A newborn girl was found abandoned outside a convenience store in North Point early today. Baltimore County police said.

The child, police said, was found inside a box at the High's dairy store in the 4000 block of North Point Road. Her umbilical cord was still attached.

A police spokesman said someone found the child about 5:30 a.m. and carried her inside. A store employee called police.

A Fire Department ambulance was dispatched, and it took the girl to Bayview Medical Center. The infant's condition was not immediately available.

Police were canvassing the area seeking anyone having information about the girl or the abandoned her.

Anyone having such information was urged to call police or contact a private at 887-2198 or the North Point Precinct at 887-7320.

INDEX

The return

Michael Jordan makes his encore to the NBA, but his Chicago Bulls can't handle the Indiana Pacers. Page 1C

Accent	1D	Metro	1B
Classified	5D	Movies	11C
Comics	7D	Movers	3D
Deaths	4B	People	2A
Editorials	8A	Sports	1C
Lotteries	10B	Television	4D

Weather

Past people tonight, low of 45 degrees. Showers to-morrow, high 62, low 35. 10B

Terrorists hit Tokyo subway system

Nerve gas spews through train cars: at least 6 killed, thousands stricken

Associated Press

Subway passengers felled by toxic fumes receive medical attention at St. Luke's Hospital.

TOKYO — One of the world's busiest subway systems turned into a deathtrap today when nerve gas spewed through cars during morning rush hour, killing six people and sickening thousands. Authorities were treating it as a terror attack.

No motive was immediately apparent and no group claimed responsibility.

All over central Tokyo, subway passengers fainted, vomited and went into convulsions as the fumes spread. Some of those stricken foamed at the mouth and bled from the nose, witnesses said. Nearly 1,300 people were admitted to hospitals for treatment or observation.

Police said the toxic agent was sarin, a nerve gas that can be fatal even in small doses. Japanese news reports cited authorities as saying the substance was planted in wrapped containers in at least five subway cars on three main lines.

Sarin was blamed for seven deaths in June at houses in the central Japan town of Matsumoto. The source was never identified, and there were no arrests.

Authorities refused to discuss suspects — either individuals or groups — and would not say whether they included Aum Shinri Kyo, a religious cult that has been accused of making sarin.

The group, which has been linked

by news reports to several unsolved kidnappings, denied any involvement in today's poisonings and threatened in a statement to sue anyone who suggested there was a link.

Two unexplained incidents earlier this month could yield clues. On March 15, three mysterious attaché cases were discovered at a Tokyo subway station, each containing three tanks with an unknown liquid, small motorized fans, a vent, and a battery. One was giving off a vapor.

Ten days before that, 19 train riders in Yokohama, a port city near Tokyo, were taken to hospitals complaining of eye and respiratory pain from an unknown source of fumes.

Hospitals in central Tokyo were inundated today. Doctors and nurses rushed frantically to administer CPR, give oxygen and hook up intravenous drips.

Officials estimated that thousands of others had lesser symptoms, including coughing and dim vision and did not obtain treatment.

"When I got to the hospital, I couldn't move my hands enough to write my name and I could barely speak," said commuter Masashi Ito.

The poisoning struck at a cherished national institution, Tokyo's clean and efficient subway network. The trains run on precise schedules, carrying 2.7 million passengers a

See JAPAN, 4A

Supreme Court backs Maryland inventor

Associated Press

WASHINGTON — Chrysler lost a Supreme Court bid today to overturn an $18.7 million award won by a Maryland inventor who said the automaker stole his design for intermittent windshield wipers.

The court, without comment, turned down Chrysler's argument that it was improperly barred from introducing evidence of other previously existing intermittent wiper systems.

Virtually all cars sold in the United States now have intermittent wipers as standard or optional equipment.

Robert W. Kearns, of Queenstown, received several patents for his design in 1967. He shopped it around to various automakers but did not reach a licensing deal.

He sued Ford in 1978 and Chrysler in 1982, claiming patent infringement.

The Ford case went to trial first. A jury decided that Mr. Kearns' patents were valid and enforceable and ordered Ford to pay $5.2 million plus interest. Ford later agreed to pay $10.2 million and to drop all appeals.

Chrysler officials had promised to rely on the Ford jury's decision on whether the patents were valid and enforceable. But in 1991, Chrysler

unsuccessfully tried to convince a trial judge that it should be allowed to challenge the finding because Ford did not appeal.

In the appeal aired on today, Chrysler's lawyers said federal judges should be required to allow evidence aimed at clarifying what aspects of a patented invention's design already were in the public domain.

Mr. Kearns, representing himself, said the appeals court ruled correctly on that issue.

The cases are Chrysler Corp. vs Kearns, 94-1131, and Kearns vs Chrysler Corp., 94-1268.

Massacre of 17 in Burundi sparks ethnic clashes

Tutsis and Hutus ignore peace plea

Reuters

BUJUMBURA, Burundi — At least 17 people, including three Belgians, were massacred by gunmen in Burundi, sparking clashes in the capital today in which another four people were killed.

Witnesses said members of the Hutu majority were taken hostage today in the central market.

The witnesses counted four dead after stone-throwing gangs of Tutsi and Hutu youths clashed outside the market as news of yesterday's massacre spread.

The youths ignored Prime Minister Antoine Nduwayo's appeal for peace today after the massacre at Nyamutobo, seven miles southeast of Bujumbura. Fifty-odd 17 people were killed on the main road.

Security sources said Tutsi youths were heading today for Nyamutobo, where most victims were Tutsis, on a "punitive mission" or revenge for the attack blamed on Hutu gunmen.

The slain Belgians were a woman, her daughter and a man. His fiancee was among three Belgian nationals wounded in the attack.

In Brussels, the Foreign Ministry condemned the killings and a spokesman appealed to the 850 Belgians living in Burundi to take extra security measures. The spokesman said the ambush took place about 7:30 p.m. yesterday, a half-hour after a curfew began in Bujumbura.

"They were traveling back from a sports meeting outside the capital when apparently they had tire problems and had to stop. An armed group then attacked them," the spokesman said.

The Belgian Foreign Ministry said its evacuation plan was being prepared. Burundi is a former Belgian protectorate.

"We are looking at this as an isolated incident. Burundi nationals were with the Belgians, so we do not make any attack was carried out on ethnic lines," the spokesman said.

Burundi has the same volatile ethnic mix as neighboring Rwanda, where up to 1 million Tutsis and allies were put to death by Hutu gunmen in last year's genocide.

30 vehicles crash in fog, causing fiery pileup in Ala.

Collisions on Mobile Bay span

Associated Press

MOBILE, Ala. — Thirty cars and trucks collided in fog on a bridge across Mobile Bay today, creating a fiery pileup that left some cars hanging off the span, troopers and witnesses said.

Traffic was halted in both directions on the Interstate 10 bridge. It was not immediately known if anyone was injured.

The crashes began about 7 a.m. as a wall of fog made visibility difficult. There also were accidents reported on a two-lane causeway that roughly parallels the nearer interstate bridge.

Van fire on I-68 Sam Kriedel of Youngstown, Ohio, watches as the van he was driving burns along Interstate 68 near Friesburg, Md. Mr. Kriedel said he was trying to restart the engine by putting drops of gasoline in the carburetor when the fuel ignited. Police said there were various flammable substances in the van.

In court appearances, trend among defendants is come-as-you-are

Etiquette deteriorating, some say

By Robert Guy Matthews
Sun Staff Writer

Not long ago, people dressed for court the way they dressed for church. Now they dress for court the way they dress for a ballgame.

Throughout Baltimore County's Dundalk Courts, defendants in district court jeans, T-shirts, baseball caps, tattered sweat pants and sun-

glasses wait for judges to decide their guilt or innocence. With even warmer weather on the way, tank tops, cutoff shorts and flip-flops will be much in evidence.

Many judges, defense attorneys and prosecutors call the new mode of dress outrageous but no longer surprising. They say it is symptomatic of the degeneration of courtroom etiquette during the past five

years. They also say that too much can be done to change it. Chief District Judge Robert F. Sweeney has no dress code in his court and encourages judges to tolerate diversity in attire. Still, many jurists lament the long gone, unwritten rule that one wore to court what you wore to church.

Consider the defendant in a September drunken-driving case who asked a Towson judge for leniency — standing before the bench in a Budweiser T-shirt and Jack Dan-

iels belt buckle. Or the case of the man who pleaded not guilty to a drug possession charge before a Dundalk judge in December. On his denim jacket was a marijuana plant emblem.

Both were found guilty.

Columbia graphic artist Aaron Lynch wore to Essex District Court what he wore to a beer bash the night before — gray sweat pants and a purple shirt he had slept in the previous night.

"I don't see why I should dress

up for a judge," said the man, who was found guilty of bad-check and battery charges in November. "Who cares what I look like?"

Judges do, defense attorneys say. Although no one keeps statistics on attire and length of sentence, veteran lawyers believe that a client's dress can affect the severity of punishment.

Baltimore defense attorney Roland Walker tells his clients that

See ETIQUETTE, 4A

"Fire Department," the dispatcher answers.

"Hello. At about 10 o'clock, I was lying on my bed watching TV and smoking," the voice says. "I must have fallen asleep about 10:30 because that's when the football game was over. Anyway, I woke up just now and my bedroom is on fire. . . ."

That dialogue isn't very informative or convincing. More likely our sleepy television viewer awoke in a smoke-filled room, crawled to the telephone and dialed frantically. The conversation at headquarters would more likely have gone like this:

"Fire Department."

"FIRE!" a voice at the other end yells.

"Where?" the dispatcher asks.

"At 1705 West Haven Street."

When fire is licking at their heels, even non-journalists know the lead. How the fire started is not important to the dispatcher; that a house is burning—and where that house is located—is.

The journalist must go through essentially the same process to determine the lead. Whereas the caller served himself and the fire department, reporters must serve their readers. What is most important to them?

After the fire is over, there is much information a reporter must gather. Among the questions a reporter would routinely ask are these:

- When did it start?
- When was it reported?
- Who reported it?
- How was it reported?
- How long did it take the fire department to respond?
- How long did it take to extinguish the fire?
- How many fires have been attributed to careless smokers this year?
- How does that compare to figures in previous years?
- Were there any injuries or deaths?
- What was the damage?
- Who owned the house?
- Did the occupant or owner have insurance on the house?
- Will charges be filed against the smoker?
- Was there anything unusual about this case?
- Who cares?

With this information in hand, you can begin to write the story.

Writing the Lead

Start looking over your notes.

The who? The owner, a smoker, Henry Smith, 29. The age is important. Along with other personal information, such as address and occupation, it differentiates him from other Henry Smiths in the readership area.

What? Fire caused damage estimated by the fire chief at $2,500. Where? 1705 W. Haven St.

When? The call was received at 10:55 p.m., Tuesday. Firefighters

ON THE JOB

Thinking in the Inverted Pyramid

For Kelley Carpenter, a 1993 journalism graduate, the inverted pyramid is a way of thinking as much as a way of writing.

"As a police reporter, I *think* in the inverted pyramid when I arrive at a hectic homicide, crime or fire scene," she says.

"I think who, what, where, when and how because sometimes when you are caught up catching the human element and capturing color, you forget the little things."

Carpenter, who worked on the police beat for the *Topeka* (Ks.) *Capital-Journal* and on city government for the *Independence* (Mo.) *Examiner*, has written

" *Writing is easy; all you do is sit staring at a blank sheet of paper until the drops of blood form on your forehead.*"
— *Gene Fowler, Author*

from Station 19 arrived at the scene at 11:04. The fire was extinguished at 11:30.

Why? The fire was started by carelessness on the part of Smith, according to Fire Chief Bill Malone.

How? Smith said he fell asleep in bed while he was smoking a cigarette.

If you had asked other questions, you might have also learned from the fire department that it was already the eighth fire this year caused by smoking in bed. All last year there had been four such fires. Smith said he had insurance. The fire chief said no charges will be filed against Smith. It was the first fire at this house. Smith was not injured. Have you figured out the so-what yet?

Assume your city editor has suggested you hold the story to about four paragraphs. Your first step is to rank the information in descending order of importance. There are lots of fires in this town, but eight this year have been caused by smoking in bed. Perhaps that's the most important thing about this story. You begin to type:

```
A fire started by a careless smoker caused an estimated
$2,500 in damage to a home.
```

Only 16 words. You should try to hold every lead to fewer than 25 words unless you use more than one sentence. Maybe it's too brief, though. Have you left anything out? Maybe you should include the time element—to give the story a sense of immediacy. You rewrite:

```
A Tuesday night fire started by a careless smoker caused an
estimated $2,500 in damage to a home at 1705 W. Haven St.
```

The reader would also want to know "where." Is it near my house? Is it someone I know? Besides, you still have only 23 words.

Just then the city editor walks by and glances over your shoulder. "Who said it was a careless smoker?" the editor asks. "Stay out of the story."

You realize you have committed a basic error in newswriting: You have allowed an unattributed opinion to slip into the story. You have two choices. You can attribute the "careless smoker" information to the fire chief in the lead or you can rewrite. You choose to rewrite by using the chief's exact words. You also realize that your sentence emphasizes the damage instead of the cause. You write:

```
Fire that caused an estimated $2,500 in damage to a home at
1705 W. Haven St. Tuesday was caused by smoking in bed, Fire
Chief Bill Malone said.
```

Now 28 words have answered the questions of "what" (a fire), "where" (1705 W. Haven St.), "when" (Tuesday) and "how" (smoking in bed). And it is attributed. But you have not answered "who" and "why." You continue, still ranking the information in descending order of importance. Compare this fire story with the approach in Figure 3.2.

```
    The owner of the home, Henry Smith, 29, said he fell asleep
in bed while smoking a cigarette. When he awoke about 30
minutes later, smoke filled the room.
    Firefighters arrived nine minutes after receiving the call.
It took them 26 minutes to extinguish the fire, which was
confined to the bedroom of the one-story house.
    According to Chief Malone, careless smokers have caused
eight fires this year.
    Smith, who was not injured, said the house was insured.
```

You take the story to the city editor, who reads through the copy

A four-vehicle accident on eastbound I-70 near Stadium Boulevard ended in two deaths on Sunday.

Barbara Jones, 41, of St. Louis died at the scene of the accident, and Juanita Doolan, 73, of St. Joseph died at University Hospital, according to a release from Springfield police. Two other people, William Doolan, 73, of St. Joseph and Theodore Amelung, 43, of Manchester, Mo., were injured in the accident.

Both lanes of traffic were closed on the eastbound side and limited to one lane on the westbound side as rescue workers cleared the scene.

Authorities said a westbound late-model Ford Taurus driven by Lan Wang of Springfield was traveling in the right lane, developed a tire problem and swerved into the passing lane. A Toyota pickup truck in the passing lane, driven by Jones, was forced over the grassy median along with the Taurus. The two vehicles entered eastbound traffic where the truck struck an Oldsmobile Delta 88, driven by Juanita Doolan, head on.

Wang and the one passenger in his car, Kenneth Kuo, 58, of Springfield, were not injured.

John Paul, a semi-tractor trailer driver on his way to Tennessee, said he had to swerve to miss the accident.

"I saw the red truck come across the median and hit the blue car," Paul said. "I just pulled over on the median and called 911."

Jones, who was wearing a seatbelt, died at the scene, Officer Stan Williams said. Amelung, a passenger who had been in the truck, was out of the vehicle when authorities arrived, but it was unknown whether he was thrown from the truck or was pulled out by someone else, Williams said.

No charges have been filed, but the investigation continues.

What
Where
When

Provides details

Impact

How

Eyewitness

What's next

Figure 3.2.
Note how this story, typical of the inverted pyramid structure, delivers the most important news in the lead and provides less essential details toward the end.

quickly. Then she checks the telephone book and the city directory. As you watch, she changes the lead to emphasize the so-what. The lead now reads:

```
A smoker who fell asleep in bed ignited a fire that caused
minor damage to his home on W. Haven Street Tuesday. Fire
Chief Bill Malone said it was the city's eighth fire caused by
smokers, twice as many as occurred all last year.
```

The lead is 44 words, but it is broken into two sentences, which makes it more readable. The importance of the so-what changed the direction of the story. The fire was minor; there were no injuries. However, the increase in the number of fires smokers caused may force the fire department to start a public safety campaign against careless smoking. The city editor continues:

```
The owner of the home, Henry Smith, 29, of 1705 W. Haven
St., said he fell asleep in bed while smoking a cigarette.
When he awoke about 30 minutes later, smoke filled the room.
```

This time, though, you have an even more serious problem. Both the telephone book and the city directory list the man who lives at 1705 W. Haven St. as Henry Smyth. S-m-y-t-h. City directories, like telephone books or any other sources, can be wrong. But at least they can alert you to possible errors. Confirm by going to original sources, in this case, Mr. Smyth.

Never put a name in a story without checking the spelling, even when the source tells you his name is Smith.

There are several lessons you can learn from this experience. They are:

- *Always* check names.
- Keep the lead short, usually fewer than 25 words, unless you use two sentences.
- Attribute opinion. (Smoking in bed is a fact. That it was careless is an opinion.)
- Find out the who, what, where, when, why and how. However, if any of these elements have no bearing on the story, they might not have to be included.
- Write a sentence or paragraph telling readers what the news means to them.
- Report information basic to the story even if it is routine. Not everything you learn is important enough to be reported, but you'll never know unless you gather the information.
- Write to the length discussed with your editor.

Too many numbers bog down a lead. Focus on the impact of the figures in the lead and provide details later in the story.

The late Harry Stapler of the University of Florida studied stories in 12 metropolitan newspapers. He found that the number of words per sentence in the first paragraph was significantly longer than in the rest of the paragraphs. The average was 26.1 words per sentence for the first paragraph and 21.1 in the rest of the sentences. He also found that almost 84 percent of the first paragraphs had only one sentence while 54 percent of the rest of the paragraphs had two or more.

The lesson in this research is that writers are trying to cram too much into one sentence in the lead. Remember, there is no rule against using two sentences in your first paragraph.

Alternate Leads

In the lead reporting the fire, the "what" (fire) is of secondary importance to how it started. A slightly different set of facts would affect the news value of the elements and, consequently, your lead. For instance, if Smyth turned out to have been a convicted arsonist, you probably would have emphasized that bizarre twist to the story:

> A convicted arsonist awoke Tuesday to find that his bedroom was filled with smoke. He escaped and later said that he had fallen asleep while smoking.
>
> Henry Smyth, 29, who served a three-year term for . . .

That lead emphasizes the news value of novelty. If Smyth were the mayor, you would emphasize prominence:

> Mayor Henry Smyth escaped injury Tuesday when he awoke to find his bedroom filled with smoke. Smyth said he had fallen asleep while smoking in bed.

The preceding examples also illustrate the so-what factor in news. A $2,500 fire is not news to enough people in large communities where there are dozens of fires daily. Even if you crafted a tightly written story about it, your editor probably would not want to print or broadcast it.

In small communities the story would have more impact because a larger proportion of the community is likely to know the victim and because there are fewer fires. The so-what factor grows more important as you add other information. If the fire occurred during a fire-safety campaign, the so-what would have been an example of the need for fire safety in a community where awareness of the problem had already been heightened. If the fire involved a convicted arsonist or the mayor, the so-what would be even stronger. Oddity or well-known people increase the value of a story. If someone had been injured or the damage had been $250,000 instead of $2,500, the so-what factor might have pushed the story even into the metropolitan press. Remember that when you have answered all six of the basic questions, ask yourself what it means to the reader. The answer is your so-what factor.

No journalist relies on formulas to write inverted pyramid leads, but you may find it useful, especially in the beginning, to learn some

"Selecting the quotes isn't so hard; it's presenting them that causes the trouble. And the worst place to present them is at the beginning. Quote leads deserve their terrible reputation. Yet they still appear regularly in both print and broadcast journalism.

"We can make three generalizations about quote leads. They're easy, lazy, and lousy. They have no context. The readers don't know who's speaking, why, or why it matters. Without context, even the best quotations are wasted."
— *Paula LaRocque,*
Assistant Managing Editor,
Dallas Morning News

" The lead should be a promise of great things to come, and the promise should be fulfilled."
— *Stanley Walker,*
City Editor

typical types of leads. The labels in the following sections are arbitrary, but the approaches are not.

Regardless of which of these leads you use, journalists are trying to emphasize the relevance of the news to the reader. One good way to highlight the relevance is to speak directly to the reader by using "you." This informal second-person lead allows the writer to tell readers why they should care. For instance:

> You will make more money buying Savings Bonds starting tomorrow.
>
> The Treasury boosted the semiannual interest rate on Series EE Savings Bonds to 5.92 percent from 4.7 percent effective Tuesday.

Readers want to know what's in it for them. The traditional approach is less direct:

> The Treasury boosted Savings Bonds interest Tuesday to the highest rate in three years.

The traditional third-person approach often sounds as if the readers were disinterested, or even worse, uninterested, parties. When the occasion arises—as it often does—to speak directly to the readers' interest, try it:

> You'll have to pay $50 more to buy season tickets to the Eagles' games next year.

Like any kind of lead, the "you" lead can be overdone. You don't need to write "You have another choice in the student president's race." Just tell readers who filed their candidacy.

Immediate-Identification Leads

In the **immediate-identification lead**, one of the most important facts is "who" or the prominence of the key actor. Reporters often use this approach when someone important or someone whose name is widely recognized is making news. Consider the following example:

> Vince Gill Won his second consecutive entertainer of the year award at the 28th Annual Country Music Association Awards.

Gill, who was also named the top male vocalist for the fourth consecutive year, is well-known, even among those who don't follow country music. His name is in the lead because many people will recognize it. When writing for your campus newspaper or your local newspaper, you would use names in the lead that are known, not necessarily nationally but locally. The name of your student body president, the chancellor, the city's mayor or an entertainer who has a local following would logically appear in the lead. None of them would be used in a newspaper 50 miles away.

As Andy Warhol said, people have their 15 minutes of fame. When Nicholas Daniloff, then Moscow correspondent for *U.S. News & World Report*, was imprisoned in what was then the Soviet Union on a charge of spying, his name immediately became recognizable because of the saturation coverage of the case. Today if he appeared on your campus as a speaker, you probably would use a delayed-identification lead such as this:

> A journalist who was held for three weeks on a spying charge in the Soviet Union will speak of his experiences at 7 p.m. Sunday in University Auditorium.

In any accident, the "who" may be important because it is someone well known by name or position:

> MADISON,   Wis. — Mayor John Jones was killed today in a two-car collision two blocks from his home.

In small communities the "who" in an accident may always be in the lead. In larger communities names are not as recognizable. As a rule, if the name is well-known, it should appear in the lead.

Delayed-Identification Leads

When a reporter uses a **delayed-identification lead**, usually it is because the person, persons or organization involved have little name recognition among the readers. John Jones, the mayor, is well-known; John Jones, the carpenter, is not. Thus, in fairly large cities an accident is usually reported like this:

> MADISON,   Wis. — A   39-year-old carpenter was killed today in a two-car collision two blocks from his home.
>   Dead is William Domonske of 205 W. Oak St. Injured in the accident and taken to Mercy Hospital were Mary Craig, 21, of 204 Maple Ave., and Rebecca Roets, 12, of 207 Maple Ave.

However, in a smaller community, names almost always make news. For instance, if Domonske lived in a city of 10,000, his name probably would be in the lead.

By the same token, most people know that IRS stands for Internal Revenue Service. But many don't know that AARP stands for the

American Association of Retired Persons. An Associated Press reporter used a delayed-identification lead in a story about AARP:

> The nation's largest senior citizens organization paid $135 million to settle a dispute with the IRS over the income it earns from royalties.
>
> However, the settlement leaves open the question of whether future income earned by the American Association of Retired Persons will be taxed, said the group's spokesman, Peter Ashkenaz.

Because so many people over 50 belong to AARP, you could have written the lead using "you":

> If you are one of 33 million members of the nation's largest senior citizens organization, you just settled a bill with the IRS.
>
> The American Association of Retired Persons has agreed to pay $135 million to settle a dispute with the IRS over the income it earns from royalties.
>
> AARP, which still has $19.6 million in cash reserves, says the settlement will not affect any of your services.

There are two other occasions when the reporter may choose to delay identification of the person involved in the story until the second paragraph. They are:

> When the person is not well-known but the person's position, occupation, title or achievements are important or interesting.
> When the lead is becoming too wordy.

O.J. Simpson's name was recognizable to many Americans as a football hero and TV personality. When he was charged with murder, his name appeared frequently in the lead of stories. In the following, the judge's name—less recognizable in the early stages of the case—is delayed, but Simpson's isn't:

> The judge in the O.J. Simpson murder trial denied defense attorneys on Tuesday the right to review a police detective's military records.

A name that would appear in the lead in one city would appear in the second paragraph in another. The mayor of Birmingham, Ala., would be identified by name in Birmingham and by title in Bridgewater, Conn.

Some titles are bulky: "Chairman of the Federal Communications Commission" assures you of clutter even before you add the name. "United Nations ambassador" takes away many options from the writer. When dealing with these types of positions, writers often choose to use the title and delay introducing the name until the second or third paragraph. While the name often is shorter, it is more important that the title be introduced first. Many people would not recognize the name of the chair of the FCC or the ambassador to the United Nations. Thus, stories about them might open:

> WASHINGTON—The U.S. ambassador to the United Nations today asked the nations of the world to join in a battle against hunger.

> WASHINGTON—The chairman of the Federal Communications Commission said today that networks must decrease the amount of sex and violence shown on television.

In both examples, the title of the person who made the statements is more important than the name. The use of the title gives the story credibility. The exception occurs when an individual in one of those positions becomes well-known because he or she is popular or controversial. For instance, not many people outside the business community can name the president of your local chamber of commerce. But if the chamber president is the former mayor or is using the position to run for mayor, the name will be recognizable by itself.

Summary Leads

Reporters dealing with several important elements may choose to sum up what happened in a **summary lead** rather than highlight a specific action. It is one of the few times that a general statement is preferable to specific action.

When Congress passed a bill providing family members with emergencies the right to unpaid leaves from work, the writer had to make a choice: Focus on the main provision or write a summary lead. The writer chose the latter:

> A bill requiring employers to give workers up to three months unpaid leave in family emergencies won Senate approval Thursday evening.

Several other provisions in the bill are explained later in the story: The unpaid leave can be for medical reasons or to care for a new child, and employers would have to continue health insurance benefits and restore employees to their previous jobs or equivalent positions.

You can also show the readers the so-what with the "you" lead:

> The Senate voted Thursday to allow you to take up to three months unpaid leave in family emergencies without losing your health benefits.

Likewise, if a city council rewrites the city ordinances, unless one of the changes is of overriding importance, most reporters will use a summary lead:

> MOLINE, Ill.—The City Council replaced the city's 75-year-old municipal code with a revised version Tuesday night.

Summary leads don't only appear in reports of board meetings. A Spokane, Wash., reporter used a summary lead to report a neighborhood dispute:

> An Idaho farmer's fence apparently was cut last week. It set off a chain of events Friday night that landed three people in the hospital, killed a cow and totaled a vehicle in the eastern Spokane Valley.

The basic question the reporter must answer is whether the whole of the action is more important than any of its parts. If the answer is yes, a summary lead is in order.

Multiple-Element Leads

In some stories, choosing one theme for the lead is too restrictive. In such cases the reporter can choose a **multiple-element lead** to work more information into the first paragraph. But you should write the lead within the confines of a clear, simple sentence or sentences. Consider this example:

> PORTLAND, Wash.—The City Council Tuesday ordered three department heads fired, established an administrative review board and said it would begin to monitor the work habits of administrators.

Notice that not only the actions but also the construction of the verb phrases within the sentence are parallel. Parallel structure also characterizes the following news extract, which presents a visual picture of the scene of a tragedy:

> BAY CITY, Mich.—A flash fire that swept through a landmark downtown hotel Saturday killed at least 12 persons, injured 60 more and forced scores of residents to leap from windows and the roof in near-zero cold.

In the last example, we are told where it happened, what happened, and how many were killed and injured.

Some multiple-element leads actually consist of two paragraphs. This occurs when the reporter decides that there are several elements that need prominent display. For example:

> The Board of Education Tuesday night voted to lower the tax rate 12 cents per $100 valuation. Members then approved a budget $150,000 less than last year's and instructed the superintendent to decrease the staff by 25 people.
>
> The board also approved a set of student conduct rules, which include a provision that students with three or more unexcused absences a year will be suspended for a week.

> **Other council action**
> In other action, the council:
> ✓Voted to repave Broadway Ave.
> ✓Rejected a new sign ordinance.
> ✓Hired four school crossing guards.
> ✓Expanded bus hours.

Figure 3.3.
*A summary box can take the place of a multiple-
element lead.*

This story, too, could emphasize the so-what while retaining the multiple elements:

> The Board of Education low-
> ered your real estate taxes Tues-
> day. Members also approved a
> budget $150,000 less than last
> year's and instructed the super-
> intendent to decrease the staff
> by 25 people.

Simpler leads are preferable. But a multiple-element lead is one of the reporter's options. Use it sparingly.

Many newspapers are using graphic devices to take the place of multiple-element leads in some cases. Summary boxes can be used to list other actions. Because the box appears under the headline in type larger than text, it serves as a graphic summary for the reader who is scanning the page. The box frees the writer from trying to jam too many details into the first few paragraphs (see Figure 3.3).

Another approach is to break the coverage of a single event into a main story and a shorter story or stories, called **sidebars**. This approach has the advantage of presenting the information in shorter, more palatable bites. It also allows the writer to elevate more actions into lead positions.

Both these methods of presentation have advantages over the more complicated multiple-element lead.

Leads with Flair

Although the inverted pyramid is designed to tell readers the news first and fast, not all stories begin with the most important statement. When the news value you want to emphasize is novelty, often the lead is unusual.

When a group of suspected drug dealers was arrested at a wedding, the Associated Press account focused on the novelty:

NARRAGANSETT, R.I. (AP)—The wedding guests included drug suspects, the social coordinator was a narcotics agent, the justice of the peace was a police chief, and 52 officers were party crashers.

For the unsuspecting bride and groom, the ceremony Friday night was truly unforgettable—a sting operation set up by state and local police that led to 30 arrests.

Not exactly your traditional wedding or your traditional lead. Yet, the essential information is contained within the first two paragraphs. A less imaginative writer would have written something like this:

Thirty suspected drug dealers, including a couple about to be married, were arrested at a wedding Friday night.

That approach is like slapping a generic label on a Mercedes-Benz. The inverted pyramid approach is not so rigid that it doesn't permit fun and flair.

The difference between the two-paragraph, multiple-element lead on the board of education and the two-step lead on the wedding story is that in the first, the reporter was dealing with several significant actions. In the second, the reporter was dealing with only one, so she used the first paragraph to set up the surprise in the second.

Here's another opening that adds flair by deviating slightly from the standard inverted pyramid approach. Knight-Ridder News Service used narration for a few paragraphs to emphasize the drama in a last-second launch shutdown:

CAPE CANAVERAL, Fla.—The crew braced for launch. The main engines ignited. The countdown clock ticked to 00:00:00. A cloud of vapor and exhaust rose. Space shuttle Endeavour strained at its hold-down clamps.

And then . . . a heart-stopping shutdown at the most hazardous moment of a shuttle mission.

Endeavour and its six astronauts flirted with catastrophe yesterday, coming within seconds—maybe milliseconds—of a flawed launch and a variety of disasters.

Blastoff was aborted at the last possible instant by an engine failure.

Though rattled, the crew was uninjured in this close call. Never before has a countdown clock reached zero and a shuttle not been launched.

The story reverts to the inverted pyramid to rank the information in the rest of the story in descending order of importance. The inverted pyramid structure is an outline, not a straitjacket.

Story Organization

Like the theater marquee, the lead is an attention-getter. Sometimes the movie doesn't fulfill the promises of the marquee; sometimes the story doesn't fulfill the promises of the lead. In either case the customer is dissatisfied.

The inverted pyramid is designed to help reporters put information in logical order. It forces the reporter to rank, in order of importance, the information to be presented.

Just as there is a checklist for writing the lead, there is also a checklist for assembling the rest of the inverted pyramid. Included on that checklist are the following:

- Introduce additional important information you were not able to include in the lead.
- If possible, indicate the significance or so-what factor.
- Elaborate on the information presented in the lead.
- Continue introducing new information in the order in which you have ranked it by importance.
- Develop the ideas in the same order in which you have introduced them.
- Generally, use only one new idea in each paragraph.

Let's see how the pros do it.

One-Subject Stories

Most newspaper stories concentrate on a single subject. The following articles, written by Robert Rankin of the *Detroit Free Press* and by the Associated Press, show that there is no one way to construct a story successfully.

By Robert Rankin
Free Press Washington staff

Immediate-identification lead with the resignation and the tie to the ethical violation.

WASHINGTON — Agriculture Secretary Mike Espy, under investigation for accepting free football tickets and other favors from companies doing business with his department, resigned Monday.

Espy's connection to the president broadens the so-what. Because of their friendship, the resignation has more impact.

Espy is one of President Bill Clinton's most faithful political supporters, but White House aides indicated to Espy that it was time to go as an ethics investigation of his conduct neared completion.

Denial of wrongdoing high in the story to be fair.

"I owe it to the president to allow his agenda to go through with a minimum of distraction," Espy said in announcing he would leave Dec. 31. Both Espy and his attorney said there was no evidence that any government practice or policy was affected by the trips or gifts given to Espy or his girlfriend.

"I was indeed careless in managing the details of my personal activities," Espy said.

President's reaction enlarges on information introduced in first two paragraphs.

Clinton accepted Espy's resignation "with regret."

In a statement released by the White House, Clinton added that "although Secretary Espy has said he has done nothing wrong, I am troubled by the appearance of some of these incidents and believe his decision to leave is appropriate."

A court-appointed independent counsel is investigating whether Espy violated rules governing contracts with companies that do business with the department.

Impact of the problem on the presidency is part of the so-what.

His resignation adds another ethical strain to the Clinton administration at a time when the president's widespread unpopularity endangers his Democratic Party's hold on Congress in next month's elections.

"The real context is Bill Clinton campaigned on the premise that he was not going to allow business-as-usual anymore. This is about as business-as-usual as you can get," said Alex Benes, a director at the Center for Public Integrity in Washington.

"I think the Clinton administration doesn't need yet another senior official who has behaved in a ethically questionable manner. That's why there is no one at the White House defending Espy," Benes added.

Background. This material has been printed and broadcast in previous days.

Espy reportedly accepted gifts such as free tickets and skybox seats for Dallas Cowboys games from Tyson Foods Inc., the nation's largest poultry producer and, as such, an object of regulation by Espy's department. . . .

Immediate-identification lead that emphasizes his reason for resigning. By inference, it includes the tie to the ethical violations. Includes his reaffirmation of innocence. Support for information in the lead.

WASHINGTON (AP)—Agriculture Secretary Mike Espy resigned Monday, saying an investigation into gifts he accepted from people and companies that do business with his department was too distracting for him to remain. He predicted that he would be exonerated.

"I owe it to the president to allow his agenda to go through with a minimum of distraction," Espy said in announcing he would step down effective Dec. 31.

President's reaction enlarges on the so-what factor. Introduces less-important violation.

President Bill Clinton accepted the resignation from Espy, one of his most ardent and loyal supporters. But a separate investigation by the White House turned up more damaging information: that Espy's girlfriend Patricia Dempsey had accepted a $1,200 scholarship from a foundation run by Arkansas-based Tyson Foods Inc. The company has longtime ties to Clinton.

"Although Secretary Espy has said he has done nothing wrong, I am troubled by the appearance of some of these incidents and believe his decision to leave is appropriate," Clinton said.

We have the news; this is what comes next. If Espy had not resigned, this probably would be the lead.

Clinton said he had asked Abner Mikva, the White House counsel, to continue his review of the case. An investigation by Donald C. Smaltz, a court-appointed independent counsel, also will continue.

Smaltz, a lawyer in Los Angeles, is investigating a range of conduct by Espy, including whether he violated rules governing contracts with Tyson and other companies that do business with the Agriculture Department.

Support for two previous paragraphs.

A senior White House official, speaking on the condition of anonymity, said that officials there had learned of the scholarship only last week and that Dempsey had returned the money. Some of Espy's transgressions were "more modest than others," the official said, but "we just felt that, when you added them all together, there were serious concerns."

Allow the accused to respond.

Both Espy and his attorney, Reid Weingarten, said there was no evidence that any government practice or policy had been affected by the gifts to Espy or Dempsey.

Background.

Questions have been raised about Espy's acceptance of tickets to sports events, travel and lodging from Tyson. Espy denied any wrongdoing and has repaid more than $7,600 in expenses. . . .

As you analyze the two stories, you will see that the *Free Press* story emphasizes the impact on the presidency while the Associated Press story strikes a more even-handed approach to the breaking news that Espy has resigned, the charges and Espy's response. This is not unusual. Newspapers with Washington correspondents often expect them to provide more explanation of events. The AP story emphasizes the news developments.

Multiple-Element Stories

Earlier in this chapter, we discussed multiple-element leads. They occur most often when you are reporting on councils, boards, commissions, legislatures and even the U.S. Supreme Court. These bodies act on numerous subjects in one sitting. Frequently, their actions are unrelated, and more than one action is often important enough to merit attention in the lead. You have three options:

Options for multi-element stories

- *More than one story*
- *A summary box*
- *A multi-element story*

You can write more than one story. That, of course, depends on permission from your editor. There may not be enough space.

You can write a summary box. It would be displayed along with the story. In it you would list the major actions taken by the council or decisions issued by the court.

You can write a multiple-element lead and story. Let's go back to the one we used earlier when discussing leads:

> The Board of Education Tuesday night voted to lower the tax rate 12 cents per $100 valuation. Members then approved a budget $150,000 less than last year's and instructed the superintendent to decrease the staff by 25 people.
>
> The board also approved a set of student conduct rules, which include a provision that students with three or more unexcused absences a year will be suspended for a week.

There are four newsworthy actions in these two paragraphs: establishing a tax rate, approving a budget, cutting staff and adopting conduct rules. In this and all stories that deal with several important elements, the writer highlights the most important. Sometimes there are several that can be equated, as in the school board example. Most of the time, one action stands out above the rest. When it does, it is important to summarize other actions after the lead. For instance, if you and your editor judged that establishing the tax rate was more important than anything else that happened at the school board meeting, you would approach it like this:

Lead	The Board of Education Tuesday night voted to lower the tax rate 12 cents per $100 valuation.
Support for lead	The new rate is $1.18 per $100 valuation. That means that if your property is assessed at $30,000, your school tax will be $354 next year.
Summary of other action	The board also approved a budget that is $150,000 less than last year's, instructed the superintendent to cut the staff by 25 and approved a set of rules governing student conduct.

Notice that the lead is followed by a paragraph that supports and enlarges upon the information in it before the summary paragraph appears. Whether you need a support paragraph before summarizing other action depends on how complete you are able to make the lead.

In all multiple-element stories, the first two or three paragraphs determine the order of the rest of the story. To maintain coherence in your story, you must then provide the details of the actions in the order in which you have introduced them. We see this technique used in an AP roundup of Supreme Court decisions:

Multiple-element story with a lead that focuses on one of the actions

WASHINGTON (AP)—Family members can be barred from ending the lives of persistently comatose relatives who have not made their wishes known conclusively, the Supreme Court ruled Monday in its first "right-to-die" decision.

Specifics to support the lead

By a 5-4 vote, the justices gave states broad power to keep such patients on life-support systems. Specifically, the court blocked the parents of a Missouri woman, Nancy Cruzan, from ordering removal of tubes that provide her with food and water.

Transition to the other action

Details to support this action

The court, clearing the way to end its term on Wednesday, decided another fundamental and emotional privacy issue by making it significantly more difficult for young girls to obtain legal abortions without first notifying their parents.

Introduces the second case

The court voted 6-3 to uphold an Ohio law that bans abortions for unmarried girls under 18 who are dependent on one or both parents unless one parent is notified.

And the court voted 5-4 to allow Minnesota to require notification of both parents as long as girls can avoid telling them by getting a judge's permission instead.

Transition back to the subject introduced in the lead

Monday's right-to-die ruling encourages supporters of "living will" laws because the court said the Constitution guarantees a competent person—as opposed to someone in a coma—a right to refuse medical treatment.

The most important thing to remember about multiple-element stories is that you must explain the elements in the same order in which they are introduced and provide transitions out of and back into your items.

Suggested Readings

Brooks, Brian S. and Pinson, James L. *Working with Words*, Second Edition. New York: St. Martin's Press, 1993. A must reference book for any journalist. Excellent coverage of grammar and word usage and strong chapter on "isms."

Walker, Stanley. *City Editor*. New York: Frederick A. Stokes Co., 1934. Out of print, the book may be difficult to find, but it's worth the search. Walker was city editor of the *New York Herald Tribune*. His tips about writing news are still valid today.

Exercises

1. Identify the who, what, where, when, why and how, if they are present, in the following:

    The United Jewish Appeal is sponsoring its first ever walk-a-thon this morning in Springfield to raise money for The Soup Kitchen, a place where the hungry can eat free.

2. Here are four versions of the same lead. Which of the four leads answers more of the six questions basic to all stories? Which questions does it answer?
    a. What began 12 years ago with a federal staff investigation and led to hearings and a court fight culminates today with a Federal Trade Commission rule to prevent funeral home rip-offs.
    b. The nation's funeral home directors are required to offer detailed cost statements starting today, a service they say they are now ready to provide despite nearly a dozen years of debate over the idea.
    c. A new disclosure law going into effect today will make it easier for us to determine the cost of a funeral.
    d. Twelve years after first being proposed, a federal regulation goes into effect Monday to require funeral homes to provide an itemized list of services and materials they offer, along with the cost of each item, before a person agrees to any arrangements.

3. Rewrite two of the leads in exercise 2 as "you" leads. Which are better, the third-person or second-person leads, and why?

4. From the following facts, write a lead.
    Who: a nuclear weapon with a yield equivalent to 150,000 tons of TNT
    What: detonated
    Where: 40 miles from a meeting of pacifists and 2,000 feet beneath the surface of Pahute Mesa in the Nevada desert
    When: Tuesday
    Why: to test the weapon
    How: not applicable
    Other information: Department of Energy officials are the source; 450 physicians and peace activists were gathered to protest continued nuclear testing by the United States.

5. From the following facts, write the first two paragraphs of a news article.
    Who: 7-year-old boy missing for three years
    What: found
    Where: in Brick Township, N.J.
    When: Monday night
    Why: not applicable
    How: A neighbor recognized the child's picture when it was shown after the NBC movie "Adam: The Song Continues" and called police.
    Other information: Police arrested the boy's mother, Ellen Lynn Conner, 27; she faces Alabama charges of kidnapping and interference with a custody warrant.

6. From the following facts, write the first two paragraphs of a news article.
    Who: 40 passengers
    What: evacuated from a Northwest Airlines jet, Flight 428
    Where: at the LaCrosse, Wis., Municipal Airport
    Why: A landing tower employee spotted smoke near the wheels.
    When: Monday following a flight from Minneapolis to LaCrosse
    How: not applicable
    Other information: There was no fire; the smoke was caused by hydraulic fluids leaking onto hot landing brakes, according to Bob Gibbons, a Northwest spokesman.

7. Describe picture and information-graphic possibilities for the story in exercise 6.

8. Cut out six leads from newspapers. Identify what questions are answered (Who . . .). Identify what is not answered. Identify the kind of lead (Summary . . .).

9. Using a database that includes several newspapers, find at least two versions of the same story. Analyze the similarities and differences between them and decide which of the two is preferable and why.

THE IMPORTANCE OF GOOD WRITING

*W*hether you are writing a newspaper story, a television script, a news release or an article for an electronic news service, good writing is most important. Many journalists are getting the message. That's why we see stories like this more often:

On a Monday afternoon, Dr. Glenn Billman pulled back from the autopsy he was performing on a dead girl and stared at the sight before him.

In his seven years at Children's Hospital, he had never seen anything like it. The girl's colon was severely hemorrhaged, ravaged by bacteria that normally lived in a cow's intestine.

Puzzled and quietly alarmed, Billman notified local health officials. It was the first indication that the lethal strain of bacteria, E. coli 0157:H7, was on the loose.

But Billman didn't make his discovery at Children's Hospital in Seattle. He made it at Children's Hospital in San Diego, and he made it three weeks before the E. coli epidemic struck the Northwest, killing three children and sickening about 500 people.

In December, San Diego was hit by a small E. coli outbreak that killed the 6-year-old girl and made at least seven other people sick.

It is now being linked to the Seattle outbreak, but in its early stages, San Diego health officials were slow to recognize the crisis, and they have been sharply criticized for failing to notify the public about the E. coli death and illnesses. . . .

However, both journalists and readers are complaining about the lack of writing skills displayed in today's journalism. Some readers are voting with their feet; they are abandoning newspapers. Editors are looking at clips more closely for clarity and creativity, not just in feature stories but also in news stories. "It's not that our long stories are too long," said teacher and former editor Carl Sessions Stepp. "Our short stories are too long." Adds another teacher and former editor, Stewart Haas, "You can't be sure anymore whether you're starting a news story or a novel. The narrative lead has become the rage." From Frank Denton, an editor, comes this pronouncement: "If we are relying on the inverted pyramid style, we are making a mistake."

There's even some research to support the idea that newspapers are not as easy to read as they should be. Using the Flesch Reading Ease formula, researchers at the University of Texas looked at a century of writing in novels and newspapers. They concluded that novels had become easier to read, and newspapers had become harder.

Readability is a measurement of such things as the number of words in a sentence, the number of syllables in a word and the number of ideas in a sentence. In general, the more of them, the harder the sentence is to understand. Can we blame readers, then, for reeling when they encounter this typical lead?

WASHINGTON—A 10-year study of an increasingly popular surgical technique used to correct poor distance vision shows that the method is reasonably safe and effective but that it might lead to an accelerated decline in the ability to see things up close, researchers said Wednesday.

> "There's nothing to writing. All you do is sit down at a typewriter and open a vein."
>
> — *Red Smith,*
> *Newspaper sports*
> *columnist*

That's 45 words. Hidden somewhere in the thicket is the main idea. In case the readers were still standing, the writer followed with a 47-word second sentence. If you are thinking that science is a complicated subject calling for complicated writing, how do you explain this lead on a government story?

Hoping to prevent a recurrence of the wrongdoing uncovered during a recent nine-month undercover investigation at one of its main work sites, the New Orleans Sewerage & Water Board plans to hire a chief of security and devise a plan to prevent crimes by employees.

Writing to inform and entertain is as important for journalists as it is for novelists. Just because newspapers and broadcast reports are done and gone in a day doesn't mean that we should accept a lower level of skill. Syndicated columnist James Kilpatrick, himself an expert writer, challenged writers:

If 99 percent of what we write is instantly blown away with the wind, well that is how the world is. I would suggest to you . . . if we write upon the sand, let us write as well as we can upon the sand before the waves come in.

If Kilpatrick's challenge to your pride is not enough, then the demands of readers and listeners and of editors and news directors who are hiring should be. Editors are looking for those unusual people who can combine reporting and writing talents. The journalist whose prose jerks around the page like a mouse trapped in a room with a cat has no future in the business. The days when a reporter could hide behind the talents of a rewrite desk are over. To emphasize that point, the American Society of Newspaper Editors has made improved writing one of its principal long-range goals. Each year, in cooperation with the Poynter Institute of St. Petersburg, Fla., it awards $1,000 to the winners in several categories of the writing competition it sponsors. The winning entries are published annually by the institute in a book series titled "Best Newspaper Writing."

Many well-known writers—among them Daniel Defoe, Mark Twain, Stephen Crane and Ernest Hemingway—began their careers as journalists. A more recent list would include the names John Hersey, Tom Wolfe and Gay Talese as well. The best-seller list is peppered with the names of journalists: Bob Woodward, Russell Baker, William Safire, Ellen Goodman, George Will, Anna Quindlen, Edna Buchanan. At newspapers around the country today, small but growing numbers of journalists are producing literature daily as they deal with everything from accidents to affairs of state. If you have a respect for the language, an artist's imagination and the dedication to learn how to combine them, you, too, may produce literature.

We should all attempt to bring quality writing, wit and knowledge to our work. If we succeed, our work will be not only informative, but also enjoyable; not only educational, but also entertaining; and not only bought, but also read.

Good Writing Begins with Good Reporting

Without the proper ingredients, the best chef is no better than a short-order cook. Without the proper use of participant accounts, personal observation and detail, the best writer's stories land with a thud. Good writing begins with good reporting. It was the reporting that allowed Linda Keene of the *Seattle Times* to open her story tracing the trail of E. coli bacteria from San Diego to Seattle with narration. When the pathologist does the autopsy, we know both his physical and intellectual reaction to his discovery. Instead of listening to the reporter relay the story, we are in the lab watching the doctor.

That story took some time to write, but reporters pressing for detail can do it on deadline, too. In Chapter 3 (page 47), we introduced you to this lead:

> Two people died Thursday when a backhoe fell off a truck's flatbed and sliced the top off an oncoming vehicle near Fairchild Air Force Base.

Now let's look at some of the detail writer Alison Boggs of *The* (Spokane, Wash.) *Spokesman-Review* collected by being there:

> The top of the Suburban, from about hood height, was shorn off by the backhoe's bucket. The front seats were forced backward, and the dashboard, roof and steering wheel were torn off.
>
> Parts of the car lay in a heap of crumpled metal and glass under the overpass. The silver Suburban was identifiable only by a 1983 owner's manual lying in the dirt nearby.
>
> Both victims wore seat belts, but in this case, that was irrelevant, [Sgt. Jeff] Sale said. Both suffered severe head injuries.
>
> Sleeping bags, a Coleman cooler and fishing equipment scattered on the highway and in the back of the Suburban suggested a camping trip. Unopened cans of Pepsi were jammed behind the front seat of the car.

The writer jammed detail into every sentence. Good reporting made good writing possible.

When you read writing brimming with detail, you can be sure that the reporter's notebook is full of it, too. Reporters who smell—and write it down—are doing their jobs. Reporters who touch—and write it down—are doing their jobs. So are those who note that someone's eyes roll and hands gesture—and write it down. Notebooks should contain not only facts and quotes; notebooks should also contain the results of reporting with all your senses.

Specific detail gathered by observant and questioning reporters always surpasses general description. It builds credibility and generates interest. One young reporter learned that the hard way. His assignment began when the city desk heard that an elderly victim of a crime committed a week earlier had died in the hospital that evening. The reporter was sent to interview the victim's neighbors, one of whom had seen a

Figure 4.1.
These reporters, celebrated for the literary quality of their writing, are also published authors of books. On this page, shown from the top left, are William Raspberry, Anna Quindlen and Edna Buchanan. The next page shows Russell Baker and Molly Ivins.

man carrying a television out of the victim's house the night she was injured. Suspicious, the neighbor had summoned police, who arrived in time to make the arrest. They found the beaten victim inside the house.

The reporter's first draft was a dry, straightforward account of the neighbor's reactions to the woman's death and the burglary. The story obviously deserved much more.

Did the victim live alone? What is the neighborhood like? Were there many break-ins in that area? Were the neighbors friendly to her? What was her house like? Nearly every question directed at the reporter required him to return to the scene. He had failed to do his reporting.

He wrote a second draft that the city editor was moments from approving. "By the way," the reporter mentioned, "did you know the television set that guy tried to steal didn't even work?" That's when he started writing this third version:

When 11-year-old Tracy Britt visited her neighbor Rose Shock in the small, one-story house just two doors off Providence Road, they just talked, mostly, because the television set was broken.

One week ago tonight, another neighbor, Al Zacher of 300 Wilkes Blvd., heard suspicious noises. Looking outside, he saw a man carrying the television set that didn't work from Mrs. Shock's home. As the man set the television down and headed for a green station wagon, Zacher called the police.

Inside lay Mrs. Shock, battered about the face.

Sunday in Springfield County Hospital, where she worked as a dietitian for many years before she retired in 1955, 85-year-old Rose Shock died.

If Mrs. Shock's relatives had their way, she would not have been living in the house with aluminum siding and paint peeling from its window frames at 302 Wilkes Blvd. After her house was burglarized last summer, her family tried to convince her to move.

"She didn't seem to be too alarmed to be living by herself," her sister, Ruth Tremaine of 306 Harley Court, said Monday. "She'd been living there 18 or 19 years, and she was happier there than she would have been anywhere else. We wanted her to go, but she just wanted to stay in her own home."

Widowed since 1948, Mrs. Shock, cane in hand, would walk around the yard and talk to her neighbors. Gladys and Paul Ray of 410 Wilkes Blvd. lived near her for several years. To them, she was a "nice, gentle, kind person."

Ruth Britt, who lived around the corner at 804 N. Fourth St., had been to Mrs. Shock's home a few times with her children.

"I didn't even know her last name," she said. "We just always called her Rosie."

"My children loved her, and, as old as she was, she was always glad to see them."

Mrs. Shock's home is located in a neighborhood caught between a spreading downtown commercial district and Business Loop 70. Before and after school, the unkempt city streets and sidewalks teem with students from Jefferson Junior High School and Hickman High School. When Mrs. Shock bought the house, Springfield had a population of about 30,000, and Providence Road was just being expanded from two lanes to four lanes. In those postwar baby boom years, the seeds for a changing neighborhood were being planted.

Now residents of the neighborhood are afraid.

ing down descriptions, smells, sounds. I also try to write down analogies as I think of them, out in the field or even in the car back to the office. It's easier and more accurate than trying to be clever in front of the computer."

She tries to avoid the temptation to overwrite.

"Don't commit journalism by using stuffy phrases or overloading your piece with qualifiers. Tell a story: Write with active words, use natural language, and tie everything together from beginning to end.

"After you finish your interviews, try to remember the anecdotes and facts you couldn't wait to tell your roommate or deskmate. Try to get as many of those in the story as you can, even if you thought they were asides or not the story you set out to get."

She also writes for the ear.

"Read your stuff out loud, at least your lead. Yes, you'll feel goofy, but it gives you a sense of pace and rhythm and tells you which sentences are too complex and wordy."

"When something like this happens close to you, you think about it more," said Mrs. Ray.

Some residents spoke bluntly about their fear of burglary and refused to give their names because they believed it increased their chances of being victimized. A woman who lives down the street from the Shock home says, "They ought to string a few of them up down at the courthouse. That might teach them a lesson."

Another neighbor also criticized the system.

"They're letting them get by too easy," said Dorothy Mustain of 304 Wilkes Blvd. "If they'd punish them more so they'd have to suffer like the ladies they're beating up, maybe that would put a stop to it."

David Herron, 45, of 207 Providence Walkway, is being held in lieu of $100,000 bond in connection with the incident. He is charged with assault with intent to kill, carrying a concealed weapon and first-degree robbery.

Prosecuting attorney Milt Harper said Monday he will meet with the medical examiner Thursday before deciding whether to file additional charges. He is waiting for results of autopsy tests.

Monday night, flashing red lights atop Springfield police cars once again lit up the Wilkes Boulevard neighborhood. Police were investigating a report of a burglary at Zacher's house.

We see dirty streets, hear crowds of students walking down the sidewalk in front of Rose Shock's house, see the aluminum siding and feel the peeling paint. We learn that Mrs. Shock died in the hospital where she worked for many years. We know, too, the sad irony that she was killed over a broken television set.

Figure 4.2.
If you were reporting on this flood for your hometown newspaper, what details would you emphasize to appeal to your readers' senses?

Elements of Good Writing

Good writing has five characteristics: precision, clarity, concreteness, sensory appeal and use of figures of speech. Let's look at each of these characteristics.

Precision

Words should be used precisely. They should mean exactly what you intend them to mean. You should never use "uninterested" when you mean "disinterested." Nor should you use "allude" for "refer," "presume" for "assume," "endeavor" for "try," "fewer" for "less," "farther" for "further." If you report that fire has destroyed a house, you mean it must be rebuilt, not repaired. If you say firefighters donned oxygen masks to enter a burning building, you are impugning either their intelligence or yours. Oxygen is dangerous around fire; firefighters use air tanks. You can make the mayor "say," "declare," "claim" or "growl"—but only one is accurate.

Avoiding Biased Language

Even when used innocently, sexist and racist language, in addition to being offensive and discriminatory, also is imprecise. Doctors aren't always "he," nor are nurses always "she." Much of our language assumes people are male unless it is shown they are female. Precise writers avoid "policeman" (police officer), "adman" (advertising representative), "assemblyman" (assembly member) and "postman" (postal worker).

Our language is bursting with derogatory racial terminology. You should avoid using terms such as "Chinaman," "Jap," "nigger" and "Indian giver" not only because they are offensive but also because they are imprecise. They rain inaccurate stereotypes on a class of people. To be precise, use Asian-American, black or African-American, and American Indian or Native American.

Some words, perfectly precise when used correctly, are imprecise when used in the improper context. "Boy" is not interchangeable with "young man," and "girl" is not interchangeable with "young woman." A young Native American is not a "young buck." Not all elderly women are "blue-haired," nor are all active retired persons "spry." In that context, "spry" implies that the writer is surprised to find an elderly person who is active. "Grandmotherly" fails when you describe people in their 30s who are grandmothers.

"Dumb" as in "deaf and dumb" is imprecise and derogatory. To

Good writing:

- *is precise.*
- *is clear.*
- *is concrete.*
- *appeals to the readers' senses.*
- *uses figures of speech.*

Six ways to avoid sexism:

- *Use a generic term (flight attendant, firefighters).*
- *Participate in the movement to drop feminine endings (comedian, hero, poet).*
- *Make the subject plural (Reporters must not form their judgments).*
- *Drop the sexist pronoun and replace it with an article (A reporter must not form a judgment).*
- *Rewrite to eliminate the gender (A reporter must not judge).*
- *Write the sentence in the second person (You should not form your judgment).*

be accurate, use "speech-impaired." When the terms are used in tandem, use "hearing-impaired and speech-impaired" for parallelism. Because alcoholism is a disease, use "recovering alcoholic" instead of "reformed alcoholic." "Handicapped" is imprecise; "disabled" is precise.

The *Los Angeles Times* uses "lesbian" unless the source prefers "gay woman." *Times* reporters also ask sources their preference for describing their "partner," "companion," "lover," etc. The Associated Press uses "homosexual" and "gay," but "dyke," "fruit," "fairy" and "queer" are not permitted.

Some dismiss this concern for language as being politically correct. That implies we are afraid to tell the truth. If someone is born unable to speak, is it true that this person is "dumb"? What is the truth in any ethnic slang?

The truth is that many words historically applied to groups of people were created in ignorance or hate or fear. During the world wars, American citizens of German descent were called "Krauts" to depersonalize them. Americans of Japanese descent were locked up in internment camps. Almost every ethnic group that immigrated to America and started at the bottom of the ladder was regarded as dumb or as a threat to the economic well-being of those already here. Over the years, pejorative terms have been applied to immigrants from Ireland, Poland, China and Africa. We see the same thing happening to more recent immigrants from Vietnam, Haiti and Mexico. The adjective "Muslim" is seldom seen or heard in news reports except to modify "terrorists" or "fundamentalists." As writers concerned with precision of the language, we should deal with people, not stereotypes.

Words are powerful weapons. They define cultures, create second-class citizens and reveal stereotypical thinking. They also change the way people think about and treat others. Writers have the freedom to choose precisely the right word. That freedom can be both exhilarating and dangerous.

Avoiding Carelessness in Word Choice

Freedom in word choice is exhilarating when the result is a well-turned phrase. Here's Rick Bragg of the *St. Petersburg* (Fla.) *Times*: "She was the one who shouldered the burden of our lives, who pretended not to notice that her own life was slipping through her fingers like water." Here's Julie Sullivan of the *Spokane* (Wash.) *Spokesman-Review*: "Hand him a soapbox, he'll hand you a homily."

However, freedom in word choice is dangerous when it results in nouns masquerading as verbs (prioritize, impact, maximize) or jargon masquerading as respectable English (input, output and throughput).

Precision, however, means more than knowing the etymology of a word; it means knowing precisely what you want to say. Instead of saying, "The City Council wants to locate the landfill three blocks from downtown," to be precise, you say, "Some members of the City Council . . . " Or better yet, "Five members of the City Council . . ."

Precision means writing in the conditional when discussing proposals:

Incorrect: The bill will make it illegal . . .
Correct: The bill would make it illegal . . .

The use of "will" is imprecise because the legislation has not been passed. By using "would," you are saying, "If the legislature passes the bill, it would . . ."

Precision means choosing the correct sentence structure to communicate explicitly what you mean. The following sentence is technically correct but imprecise:

```
The City Council passed the ordinance, and the 250
supporters cheered.
```

It is imprecise because the compound sentence gives equal importance to the two thoughts expressed. To show cause and effect, the writer should have used a complex sentence:

```
Because (or When) the City Council passed the ordinance, the
250 supporters cheered.
```

When you write implicitly, you force the reader to make inferences. Say what you are thinking.

Achieving Precision in the Use of Numbers

To many journalists and readers, numbers are a foreign language. It is our job to learn that language and to speak it so that our readers understand.

The most important way to increase comprehension is to compare numbers and sizes. Authorities may announce that forest fires have destroyed vegetation over 500 square miles. What does that mean to you? To your readers? One way to make it meaningful is to compare the numbers, the unknown, to something known. Even if you don't know the size of your community in square miles, you have a good idea of its size. Readers in California could have un-

> *"When your reporters feel the innovative impulse, suggest that they lie down until it goes away."*
>
> —*James Kilpatrick,* **syndicated columnist**

derstood how large an area that was if they had been told the forest fire destroyed an area four times the size of San Francisco. It was eight times the size of St. Louis and 15 times the size of Springfield, Mass.

You translate large budget numbers by expressing them as spending per student. You translate a tax increase by expressing it as cost per taxpayer. You translate the rate of crime by expressing it as the number of crimes each minute or hour or day in your city. One newspaper examining the lack of screening for teachers expressed the findings this way:

> Spokane cabbies and Nevada blackjack dealers face tougher screening through background checks than teachers in 42 states.

A percentage is the ratio of two numbers converted to a base of 100. This makes comparisons and interpretations easier. To figure a percentage, divide the smaller number by the total, then move the decimal point two places to the right. For example, if 21 of 234 teachers go on strike, what percent go on strike? (21 divided by 234 equals .089 or 8.9 percent.)

Precision in the use of numbers also requires that you ask the basic questions. Reporters frequently encounter percentages. If someone is giving you percentages, you must ask what *population* the figures are based on. For instance, a juvenile officer told a reporter that 70 percent of the juvenile offenders do not have to return to his program. The reporter's first question should be, "What was the population used to figure the percentage?" Is that all the juveniles in the program during the last calendar year? If so, perhaps the success rate is high because the period measured isn't long enough. And how are the juveniles who are old enough now to be certified as adults counted in the population? How does he account for juveniles who may have committed a crime in another jurisdiction?

His answer may be that the figure is based on a *sample* of the population in the program over 10 years. That is, using common statistical tables, someone drew a sample of the names of all juveniles who were in the program over 10 years and contacted them. From those contacts, they could determine the success rate. If the figure is based on a scientific sampling like the one just described, there would also be an error rate. It would be expressed as "plus or minus X points." If X were four, it would mean that the success rate was between 66 and 74 percent.

Similarly, when government agencies or other groups report economic statistics, they usually do so in terms of increase or decrease. For example, one might report, "Housing starts increased 6.9 percent in February . . ." But the reports don't always say what those statistics are being compared with—sometimes it is the previous month, other times the previous year.

Never use percentages without knowing their basis.

Math You Can Count On

Many journalists joke about their mathematical ineptitude. They suggest that fear of math is why they went into the profession. But even for those who are genuinely afraid of statistics, there is no avoiding numbers in journalism. Numbers are at the heart of reporting government, business, sports and investigative issues, and they can surface in areas as diverse as obituaries, food, religion and entertainment.

Journalists who have a fear of numbers these days had better learn to overcome it. That might mean learning some math. Before using figures in your writing, be sure you understand what they mean.

Say you want to describe the volume of a child's screaming. Would you say the child belted out "a 25-decibel roar"? (No. It's barely above a whisper.) Or, do you know how many centimeters are in a foot? (30.5.) Or how far it is from home plate to the pitcher's mound? (60 feet 6 inches.) It is vital to check reference books when such questions arise.

Even the most respected journalists can run afoul of numbers. When reporting a Supreme Court case in 1987, *The New York Times* and other media outlets reported that defendants charged in Georgia with killing whites were four times as likely to receive death sentences as were defendants charged with killing blacks. However, reporters—and the Supreme Court itself—confused "probability" and "odds."

Probability represents the likelihood something will happen. For example, the probability of getting a heads when flipping a coin is $\frac{1}{2}$ (one of two possible outcomes) or .5. Odds represent the likelihood that one thing will happen rather than another. The odds of getting a heads—figured as the likelihood of getting a heads vs. the likelihood of getting a tails—are .5/.5 (even money in betting terms) or 1.

The Georgia study concluded that the odds of a death sentence when a white was killed were 4.3 times greater than the odds when a black was killed. That doesn't mean the same thing as "four times as likely."

The lessons from the above example are that probability and odds are not synonymous and that math errors can creep into reporting even when your source is the Supreme Court.

Some guidelines for reporting numbers:

- *Cite sources for all statistics.*
- *Use numbers judiciously for maximum impact.*
- *Long lists of figures are difficult to read in paragraph form. Put them in charts and graphs when appropriate.*
- *Graphs sometimes include estimates. If you use figures from a graph, make sure they are precise.*
- *Round off large numbers in most cases. For example: $1.5 million rather than $1,489,789.*
- *Always double-check your math and any statistics a source gives you.*
- *Be especially careful with handwritten numbers. It is easy to drop or transpose figures in your notes. Write neatly; when you read your notes you'll want to be able to tell a "1" from a "7."*
- *If you don't understand the figures, get an explanation.*

Clarity

Before typing a single word, reporters should remind themselves of three simple guidelines: simplicity, correct grammar and punctuation, coherence. The result will be clear writing.

Keep It Simple

The readers of one newspaper once confronted the following one-sentence paragraph:

"Paradoxically, cancer-causing mutations often result from the repair of a cell by error-prone enzymes and not the 'carcinogenic' substance's damage to the cell," Abe Eisenstark, director of biological sciences at the university, said at a meeting of the Ad Hoc Council of Environmental Carcinogenesis Wednesday night at the Cancer Research Center.

Guidelines for clear writing:

- *Keep it simple.*
- *Use correct grammar and punctuation.*
- *Be coherent.*

To write clearly:

1. *Keep sentences short.*
2. *Keep to one idea a sentence.*
3. *Favor subject-verb-object sentences.*
4. *Avoid using more than three prepositional phrases in one sentence.*
5. *Avoid using more than three numbers in one sentence.*
6. *Use plain and simple words instead of jargon, journalese, or clichés.*

*— **Paula LaRocque,***
Assistant Managing Editor,
Dallas Morning News

"Short is beautiful. Short and simple is more beautiful. Short, simple and interesting is most beautiful."

*— **Don Gibb,***
educator

If there is a message in those 53 words, it would take a copy editor, a lexicologist and a Nobel Prize-winning scientist to decipher it. The message simply is not clear. Although the sentence is not typical of newspaper writing, it is not unusual either. Too much of what is written is mumbo jumbo. For instance:

> Approximately 2 billion tons of sediment from land erosion enter our nation's waters every year. While industrial waste and sewage treatment plants receive a great deal of attention, according to the Department of Agriculture the number one polluter of our waterways is "non-point" pollution.

The writer of that lead contributed some linguistic pollution of his own. The message may have been clear in his mind, but it is not clear in print.

One remedy for unclear writing is the short sentence. The following examples introduce the same subject:

> NEW YORK—From measurements with high-precision laser beams bounced off reflectors left at three lunar sites by Apollo astronauts, plus one atop an unmanned Soviet lunar vehicle, scientists believe that the moon is still wobbling from a colossal meteorite impact 800 years ago.

> NEW YORK—The moon may still be wobbling from a colossal meteorite impact 800 years ago.

The writer of the first example drags the reader through some prickly underbrush full of prepositional phrases; the writer of the second has cleared the brush to expose the flowers.

Use Correct Grammar and Punctuation

Far too often, grammar and punctuation errors obscure meaning. Consider this example:

```
The Senate Tuesday rejected another attempt to block
adoption of a budget-cutting proposal by weighing it down with
complicating amendments.
```

Because of the loose sentence structure, the reader cannot be sure whether the proponents or the opponents of the measure tried to defeat the proposal by attaching the amendments. The phrase "by weighing it down with complicating amendments" incorrectly modifies "The Senate." Because of its placement, some readers may assume it refers to the budget-cutting proposal. That assumption is also incorrect. The phrase is supposed to describe the action of "opponents," but that term does not even appear in the sentence. The sentence could be rewritten this way:

```
The Senate rejected another attempt Tuesday to cut the
budget. Opponents had tried to block the proposal by adding
amendments.
```

No one who aspires to be a writer will succeed without knowing the rules of grammar. Dangling participles, split infinitives, noun-verb disagreements, pronoun-antecedent disagreements and misplaced modifiers are like enemy troops: They attack your sentences and destroy their meaning. The best defense is to construct tight, strong sentences.

The personnel director of an Inglewood, Calif., aerospace company had to fill out a government survey form that asked, among other things, "How many employees do you have, broken down by sex?"

After considering the sentence for a few moments, she wrote, "Liquor is more of a problem with us."

Sentence modification was more of a problem with the writer of the survey. Here are some typical errors and ways to correct them:

Incorrect antecedent:	Each of the boys brought *their* sleeping bags.
Correct:	Each of the boys brought *his* sleeping bag.
Dangling participle:	The mayor told the taxpayer to submit a claim to the clerk, *bringing it to her* before noon.
Correct:	The mayor told the taxpayer to submit a claim to the clerk before noon.
Split infinitive:	The mayor agreed *to* promptly *submit* his resignation.
Correct:	The mayor agreed *to submit* his resignation promptly.
Misplaced modifier:	*Despite his size*, the coach said Jones would play forward.
Correct:	The coach said that Jones, *despite his size*, would play forward.

Improper punctuation creates ambiguities at best and inaccuracies at worst. For instance:

```
Giving birth to Cynthia five years earlier had been
difficult for Mrs. Davenport and the two parents decided they
were content with the family they had.
```

Without the required comma before "and," the reader misses the pause and sees this: ". . . had been difficult for Mrs. Davenport and the two parents . . ." That's a lot of people in the delivery room.

Be Coherent

A coherent story is one in which the information is logically connected. Coherence results when you create logical story structures, express the relationship between ideas properly, use transitions and think clearly.

"The real problem is that misplaced modifiers and similar glitches tend to distract readers. Introduce blunders to an otherwise smoothly flowing story and it's as though a drunk stumbled through a religious procession.

"What's more, while those errors due to carelessness may not permanently damage the language, they can damage a paper's credibility. Botching a small job sows mistrust about the larger enterprise."

—*Jack Cappon, Associated Press*

A story must have a beginning, middle and end. When put in a maze, rats make many mistakes before they find their way out. So do writers who start a story without knowing where it is going. Chronology is the most easily understood of story structures. You start at the beginning and go to the end. Journalists often don't have the luxury of readers' time or publication space to use chronology. That's why it is important to outline a story, even if the outline is merely the three or four points you expect to make. Here's a simple outline you might make for a council story:

1. Approved one-way streets.
2. Raised parking fines.
3. Bought snowplows.
4. Will study downtown parking.
5. Hired audit firm.

You've ranked the actions in order of importance. Now you decide whether to focus on one element or write a summary lead or multiple-element lead. Once you have done that, your outline gets more detailed:

1. Single-element lead
2. Summary of other actions
3. Support lead
   a. The vote; Jones quote; opposition
4. Support other actions in order introduced in second paragraph
   a. Raised parking fines
      Amount; reason; no opposition
   b. Buy snowplows
      Cost; when delivered
   c. Downtown parking
      Define problem; when study is due; who will do it; Dehaven quote; Chamber of Commerce request
   d. Audit firm
      Who will do it; cost; when due

Although outlining make take five minutes, it will save you much more time. The outline also creates a structure that flows logically from one idea to the next. Here's how you could start the story:

Lead:	The Springfield City Council voted Tuesday to make four streets in the downtown area one-way.
Summarize other action:	The council also raised parking fines to $5, voted to buy two snowplows, ordered a study of downtown parking facilities and hired a firm to audit the city.
Support lead:	Effective March 1, the four streets that will be one-way are . . .

Within each of those sentences, you must express the proper relationships between ideas. One way to do this is to choose the correct sentence structure. Simple sentences express one idea. Compound sentences express two or more ideas of equal importance. Complex sentences also subordinate one idea to another. Here are some examples:

Simple:	The mayor scolded the council.
Compound:	The mayor scolded the council, and she insisted on a vote. (Equates the two ideas.)
Complex:	After the mayor scolded the council, she insisted on a vote. (Subordinates the scolding and emphasizes the insistence on the vote.)

Similarly, compound sentences equate two or more ideas without commenting on them; complex sentences can show cause and effect:

Compound:	The council members were angry, and they rejected the proposal.
Complex:	Because the council members were angry, they rejected the proposal.

The meaning in the first is implicit; that is, the reader has to infer the relationship. The meaning in the second is explicit. Each of these sentences is correct, but the meaning changes as you move from one to the other. Complex sentences show other types of relationships. Subordinating conjunctions such as "if," "since," "while," "after" and "until" each carry a different and precise meaning.

You also protect coherence by carefully choosing the proper conjunction. Observe how the meaning changes with the conjunction:

```
    The mayor insisted that the council vote, and the members
ignored her.

    The mayor insisted that the council vote, but the members
ignored her.
```

The second example is clearer—and thus more coherent—because it expresses the council members' reaction more logically.

Transitions also show the logical progression of story structure and the ideas within the structure. Transitions are road signs directing traffic on the information highway. They can be words, phrases, sentences or paragraphs. The reference to "memory" directs us from the first to the second paragraph in this example:

```
    Mr. and Mrs. Lester Einbender are using their memory to
project life as it might have been.

    That memory centers around a son named Michael, a rheumatic
disease called lupus and a desire to honor one while
conquering the other.
```

The word "That" in "That memory" is a demonstrative adjective. Its use is subtle, but its impact is dramatic. If you write "A memory," you are not linking the reader to the memory already mentioned; if you write "The memory," you are being more specific; if you write "That memory," you are pointing directly at the memory in the preceding paragraph. Because it is good only for general references, "a" is called an indefinite modifier; because it is more specific, "the" is called a definite modifier; because it is most specific, "that" is called a demonstrative adjective. It demonstrates precisely the word or phrase to which you are referring.

These linkages help you achieve **coherence**, the logical connection of ideas. The linkages transfer you from one sentence to the next, from one paragraph to the next. The different types of linkages are called **transitions**. Writers unfamiliar with transitions merely stack paragraphs, like wood, atop one another. Transitions keep the story, if not the woodpile, from falling apart.

Repeating a word or phrase is one way to keep the story from falling apart. In the preceding example, the writer both used a demonstrative adjective (others include "this," "these" and "those") and also repeated a word.

Repetition of a phrase or of sentence construction, called **parallelism**, is another way to guide readers through a story. Writers frequently use parallelism to achieve coherence.

Writing about the complicated subject of nuclear-waste disposal in America, Donald Barlett and James Steele of the *Philadelphia Inquirer* relied on parallelism for coherence and emphasis:

> This assessment may prove overly optimistic. For perhaps in no other area of modern technology have so many experts in the government, industry and science been so wrong so many times over so many years as have those involved in radioactive waste.
>
> They said, repeatedly, that radioactive waste could be handled like any other industrial refuse. It cannot.
>
> They said that science had most of the answers, and was on the verge of getting the few it did not have, for dealing with radioactive waste permanently. It did not, and it does not.
>
> They said that some of it could be buried in the ground, like garbage in a landfill, and that it would pose no health hazard because it would never move. It moved.
>
> They said that liquid radioactive waste could be put in storage tanks, and that rigorous safety systems would immediately detect any leaks. The tanks leaked for weeks and no one noticed.

Chronology and references to time are other ways to tie a story together. Words and phrases such as "now," "since then" and "two days later" are invaluable in helping readers understand where they have been and where they are going. Chronology is important in everything from reports of automobile accidents (which car entered the intersection first?) to recaps of events that occurred over months or even years. For instance, Barlett and Steele's stories covered 35 years of efforts to store nuclear waste.

Transitions include but are not limited to "and," "but" and "however." A word, a phrase, a thought, like a road sign, leads the reader from one paragraph to the next.

And finally, coherence results when you figure out what you want to say and then express it positively. Enter this thicket of verbiage at your own risk:

> The Missouri Gaming Commission has 30 days to appeal a
> judge's temporary order reversing the commission's decision
> not to grant a gaming license to a firm that wanted to dock a
> riverboat casino in Jefferson City.

The writer is lost in a maze of reversals of negative findings. The lead tries to cover too much territory. Express it in the positive and strip it to its essential information:

> The state has 30 days to persuade a judge it should not have
> to license a firm that wants to open a riverboat casino in
> Jefferson City.

The writer of this sentence also failed to think clearly:

> Amtrak, formally the National Passenger Railroad Corp., was
> created in 1971 to preserve declining passenger train service.

Do you suppose Amtrak was *really* created to preserve "declining passenger train service"?

Concreteness

For lawyers, the devil may be in the details, but for writers, clarity is in the details. Echoing your bureaucratic sources, you can write of infrastructures or facilities or learning pods. Try touching any of them. By contrast, you ride on a highway, sit in an arena and learn in a reading group.

Be specific. The speaker is big (compared to what?). The speaker is loud (how loud?). Abstractions are ambiguous. To someone who is 6 feet tall, someone big may be 6 feet 6 inches tall. To someone who is 5 feet 2 inches tall, 6 feet is huge.

We can describe something as colorful, or we can paint the colors. We can say the garbage stinks, or we can sniff the rotting beef. Describing the motivation of an actor-director, Richard Dodds of the New Orleans *Times-Picayune* relied on concrete details (italics added):

> He was the king of *AM radio* in *New Orleans* when AM radio was king. But C.C. Courtney wanted more than a *disc jockey's career*, and in *1967* he left his good gig spinning the hits for *WNOE* and headed to *New York*, where he began a promising acting career. But Courtney wanted more, and after the success of his *rock musical "Salvation,"* he decided to become a *full-time writer*. But still he wanted more, and to get it, he went through *two master-of-fine-arts programs in theater at two universities*.
>
> It turns out that what Courtney wants is to do it all.

"There's a time to sow and a time to reap, but there's never a time for seasonal agricultural activities."

—Jack Cappon, Associated Press senior writer and writing coach

To be concrete, you must have facts. Things you can touch and examine. Lazy reporters create puffballs. Poke the stories and you'll

On a Monday afternoon, Dr. Glenn Billman pulled back from the autopsy he was performing on a dead girl and stared at the sight before him.

In his seven years at Children's Hospital, he had never seen anything like it. The girl's colon was severely hemorrhaged, ravaged by bacteria that normally lived in a cow's intestine.

Puzzled and quietly alarmed, Billman notified local health officials. It was the first indication that the lethal strain of bacteria, E. coli 0157:H7, was on the loose.

But Billman didn't make his discovery at Children's Hospital in Seattle. He made it at Children's Hospital in San Diego, and he made it three weeks before the E. coli epidemic struck the Northwest, killing three children and sickening about 500 people.

In December, San Diego was hit by a small E. coli outbreak that killed the 6-year-old girl and made at least seven other people sick.

It is now being linked to the Seattle outbreak, but in its early stages, San Diego health officials were slow to recognize the crisis, and they have been sharply criticized for failing to notify the public about the E. coli death and illnesses.

"I really believe we need to be safe and not sorry, and the fact is, a girl died in San Diego," said San Diego County Supervisor Dianne Jacob. "I was outraged. The only way I found out was by reading it in the newspaper" after the Northwest outbreak.

When the first Washington cases were reported in mid-January, authorities here immediately queried neighboring states, including California, but were not told about the E. coli death of the San Diego girl. That information would have alerted them about the bacteria's severity and might have pointed them sooner to the source of the contamination.

Like the patients here, the San Diego girl had eaten a hamburger at a Jack in the Box restaurant days before she got sick and died. The seven other E. coli patients had all eaten hamburgers at fast-food restaurants, among them Jack in the Box.

That information was available in early January, according to Dr. Michele Ginsberg, San Diego County epidemiologist. She would not say how many of the seven patients had eaten at Jack in the Box.

"A variety of restaurants were mentioned," she said. "Naming any one of them would create public reaction and perhaps avoidance of those restaurants."

That reticence angers Jacob, the San Diego County supervisor. "I had a follow-up meeting with county health officials, and I have to tell you, very honestly, I was not pleased with their attitude," she said. . . .

Figure 4.3.
Note how transitional words and phrases maintain the coherence of the story as it moves from one paragraph to the next.

stick your finger clear through them. Instead of saying "Some council members . . ." say "Five council members." Instead of writing that a business is "downsizing," report that 150 workers will lose their jobs. Avoid abstractions; covet the concrete detail.

Sensory Appeal

As you chauffeur the reader through the scenes in your story, you can drive down the road or over the green-laced, rolling hills of Kentucky. You can report that a car hit a skunk, or you can convey the nauseating smell. A word here, a phrase there, and you hear the plane ripping the tin roof off the house, smell the acrid tires burning on a flaming car, feel the boxing glove's leather rasp against the skin. Good writing appeals to one or more of our five senses: sight, hearing, smell, taste and touch.

Whether he was reporting or writing a novel, Ernest Hemingway appealed to the reader's senses. Reporting for *The New York Times* from Madrid during the Spanish Civil War, he wrote:

> There is a rifle fire all night long. The rifles go "tacrong, carong, craang, tacrong," and then a machine gun opens up. It has a bigger caliber and is much louder—"rong, cararibg, rong, rong."

Moving to another war and another writer, we get the same sense of detail. Reporting for the *Chicago Daily News*, Keyes Beech described his flight from Saigon during the panic of the American evacuation from that city in 1975:

> We were only men fighting for our lives, scratching, clawing, pushing ever closer to that wall. We were like animals. . . .
> I lay on a tin roof gasping for breath like a landed fish, then dropped to the ground. God bless the Marines; I was one myself in the last of the just wars.

Through Hemingway's ears, we listen not just to gunfire but also to "rong, cararibg, rong, rong." Through Beech's fingers we feel not just a roof but a tin roof, too.

Knowing when a detail enhances the story rather than just making it wordy is the skill of an accomplished writer. Some details are as out of place as white tennis shoes with a black business suit. If Beech had written, "Wearing blue denim jeans, white sneakers and a torn blue shirt, I lay on a tin roof gasping for breath like a landed fish . . . ," we would laugh instead of marvel at the description. What he was wearing was not important.

But what country music singer Tammy Wynette was wearing was important in a profile of her, and reporter Leola Floren captured the scene this way:

On stage, she is surrounded by musicians in green suits and cowboy boots. Stuck there in the middle, Tammy looks like one smooth pearl in a bucket of peas. Her wavy blond hair tumbles over bare shoulders to the middle of her back. Her black strapless gown is of the kind the slightly bad girls wore to the senior prom: slit up past the knees in the back, cut so low in front there isn't any decent place to pin a corsage. When she picks up her guitar, you think it ought to be a champagne glass, she looks so elegant.

Notice Julie Sullivan's power of observation in her profile of a resident of Spokane:

Joe Peak's smile has no teeth.

His dentures were stolen at the Norman Hotel, the last place he lived in downtown Spokane before moving to the Merlin two years ago.

Gumming food and fighting diabetes have shrunk the 54-year-old man's frame by 80 pounds. He is thin and weak and his mouth is sore.

Words create pictures. Picture Johnny Cash: "He moves with the grace of a little boy who has to go to the bathroom." A student reporter lets us listen in because she listened:

His voice has a thousand personalities. When he is trying to convince you of something, his voice is so low you have to lean forward to hear him. When he's mad, he spits his words out in growls. When he's happy, his voice elevates, sometimes going so high that you look behind him to see if a woman entered the room.

Another student writer used her hand to gather information: "After 40 years of working outside, his skin is as leathery as an alligator's." Did she actually touch him? "Yes," she says. "I kept looking at his skin. Finally, even though I was embarrassed, I asked him if I could touch his face. He laughed. 'You can tell I don't use no fancy lotions, can't you?'"

The writing is better because the reporters didn't just ask questions and record answers. They looked, they touched, they listened. Readers can see and feel along with the reporters.

Figures of Speech

Good writers also know how to use the literary device known as **figures of speech** along with other forms of analogy. Analogies permit writers to show similarities and contrasts. Similes and metaphors are common figures of speech. Similes show similarities by using the word "like" or "as": "Tammy looks like one smooth pearl in a bucket of peas." Describing a long-distance runner, another writer used this simile: "Her legs, so rubbery they wobbled like jelly, shook and then surrendered."

The metaphor is the first cousin of the simile. Where the simile compares one thing to another, a metaphor says one thing is another:

"Tammy is one smooth pearl in a bucket of peas." A metaphor is a stronger analogy than a simile. Sports columnist Jim Murray once described football coach John Robinson in metaphorical language: "He's the world's biggest Easter rabbit, a marshmallow sundae."

With similies and metaphors, writers draw word pictures. Reading about Tammy Wynette, you see white and green. You picture Robinson as pudgy, friendly, smiling. The techniques set the pages of a scrapbook of images turning in each reader's mind.

The technique of analogy is also important to every journalist trying to make dimensions and numbers meaningful. That's important whether you are writing about the national debt or the size of the offensive guard. You make numbers meaningful by translating them. Writing about the national debt, one college reporter pointed out it was enough to operate the university for decades. No number means much unless it is compared to something else.

Instead of writing that 75 percent of the people in the United States do not know that you are innocent until proven guilty, say that three of four people do not know. When the Associated Press reported a jury award, the writer used an analogy to translate the numbers:

> ALBUQUERQUE, N.M.— A woman who was scalded when her McDonald's coffee spilled won a jury award of nearly $2.9 million—or about two days' coffee sales for the fast-food chain.

Reporters become writers by the sweat of their brows. John Kenneth Galbraith, a best-selling author who is able to make economics understandable to the lay reader, commented on the difficulty of writing well:

> There are days when the result is so bad that no fewer than five revisions are required. In contrast, when I'm inspired, only four revisions are needed.

Trying the techniques discussed in this chapter is the first step. Mastering them is the result of trying them repeatedly.

Suggested Readings

Barzun, Jacques. *Simple and Direct*. New York: Harper & Row, 1975. An excellent rhetoric book that explains many of the details of sentence construction.

Bernstein, Theodore. *The Careful Writer*. Boston: Atheneum, 1975. An excellent desk book for people concerned with both grammar and the precision of their language.

Brooks, Brian S. and Pinson, James L. *Working With Words*. New York: St. Martin's Press, 1993. Like Strunk and White's *The Elements of Style*, this is an excellent handbook for every writer. It covers everything from grammar and punctuation to racism and sexism in language.

Kilpatrick, James J. *The Writer's Art*. Kansas City: Andrews, McMeel & Parker, 1984. An informative and entertaining discussion of writing.

Strunk, William and White, E.B. *The Elements of Style*, Third Edition. New York: Macmillan, 1979. This little book practices what it preaches. For the beginner it is a good primer; for the pro it is a good review of writing rules and the meaning of words.

Exercises

1. Choose precisely the right word:
   a. We need to (ensure, insure) a victory.
   b. Stop (aggravating, annoying) your friend.
   c. The attorney won because she (refuted, responded to) the allegations.
   d. The prisoner was able to produce (mitigating, militating) evidence.

2. Rewrite the story on page 89 to take out the parallelism. Which version, the original or yours, is better, and why?

3. Punctuate the following sentences:
   a. Government officials have come under a newly enacted censorship system and several foreign speakers have been denied permission to enter the country.
   b. It was a Monday night and for the next two days he teetered between life and death.
   c. The council approved the manager's proposals and rejected a tax increase.

4. Use an analogy to explain the following numbers: The student council's budget is $350,000. The university has 19,000 students. The local city budget is $3 million. The city has 70,000 residents.

5. In newspaper articles find examples of:
   a. Incorrect word usage. (Correct it.)
   b. Ambiguous wording. (Correct it.)
   c. Incorrect grammar. (Correct it.)
   d. Incorrect punctuation. (Correct it.)
   e. A nicely worded sentence or paragraph.
   f. Use of figures of speech.
   g. Analogies that help translate numbers.

6. Access a computer database that carries several newspapers and find at least three versions of the same news event written on the same day. Compare the sentence length. Look for transitions. Find figures of speech and analogies. Which, in your opinion, is the most readable? The least? Why?

7. Using software that uses the Flesch Reading Ease formula or a similar measurement of readability, compare a story you have written to ones from the *New York Times* and the Associated Press. What are the readability scores? Why?

INTERVIEWING

*W*hen Walt Harrington was doing a profile of Jack Anderson, the syndicated columnist, he spent hours interviewing and observing him. He even traveled with Anderson to his hometown of Salt Lake City, Utah. Anderson took Harrington to his boyhood home. Harrington opened his profile for the Washington Post Magazine with that visit. We pick up the story at the second paragraph:*

Always aggressive, quick to step across the little boundaries that deter other men, the man walks right through the front doorway of what is now someone else's home. The house is being renovated—its wallpaper is stripped, its patched plaster is unsanded, its doors are off their hinges. And for an instant, everything seems wrong. But wait, that crystal chandelier, it was here 45 years ago. He points to it with a kind of excitement, and it seems that nostalgia might sweep over him, but it passes, and he continues to walk slowly from room to room, commenting in the deadpan tone of a bored tour guide: "These were a couple of bedrooms. This was the kitchen." Then he stops, turns to his right and looks down a narrow, darkened stairway to the basement. His voice goes hollow and distant . . .

"And this is where *we* lived."

Writing about the experience later in his book, American Profiles, *Harrington said that he didn't realize the importance of what he was seeing and hearing.*

I sensed only a sudden edgy quiet in Anderson. I knew little about his stormy relationship with his father then. Only later did I realize what had gone on during our tour of his old home. Fortunately, the details and the mood of the moment were recorded.

"Fortunately, the details and the mood of the moment were recorded." To many journalists, interviewing is the art of asking questions and recording answers. That is important and difficult work. But interviewing is much more. As Harrington's experience shows, interviewing is the process of gathering information with your ears and eyes and nose. Harrington had the experience to record those observations even though he didn't realize their significance at the time.

Interviewing—having conversations with sources—is the key to most stories you will write. Your ability to make people comfortable with you is the difference between mediocre reporting and good reporting.

Although you already have experience interviewing someone, you probably haven't thought much about how or why you've been doing it. And you probably haven't had much experience trying to get information from someone who wants to withhold it. Those few times you've tried, you probably have been frustrated:

"Professor, why did I get a B in your course?"
"Because you didn't deserve an A."
"Why not?"
"Because."

Sooner or later, you stomp out of the office. Now you are a reporter and confronted by a similar situation:

"Mr. Mayor, why did you fire the police chief?"
"I don't want to discuss that because it's a personnel matter."

Because journalists should not go stomping out of the room when they are denied information, they must have other resources. The mayor may not want to discuss the firing; perhaps he never will. But a skillful questioner often can obtain information the source does not want to divulge or does not even realize he or she is giving. The reporter may ask, for instance, what qualities the mayor will be looking for in a new police chief. The answer may provide the clue to why he fired the last one.

Information is the merchandise of a journalist. While some of it is gathered from records and some from observation, most of it is gathered in person-to-person conversations. For that reason every journalist needs to develop interviewing skills.

Interviewing is an imperfect process. As in the city water-works, there is plenty of leakage. When the city pumps a million gallons of water, not all of it reaches the customers. Some evaporates, some leaks through decaying pipes. Some people illegally siphon some of the water.

Information leaks out, too, as it is passed from source to interviewer to editor to reader. The source may not want you to know everything. The source may be telling you everything, but you may not understand the subject. Unrecognized differences in cultural and ethnic backgrounds can influence meaning. When someone says "blue" to you, a color flashes in your mind's eye. However, it may not be the same shade of blue that is in the mind's eye of the speaker. Shades of meaning often leak out of the information pipeline.

In such an imperfect system of information gathering and transfer, we can reduce—though not eliminate—the leaks. Consequently, you must work hard to refine your skills. You simultaneously ask questions, digest responses, record answers, cajole the source, gauge reactions and look for details. This is no work for the unprepared.

Preparing for the Interview

When Julie Sullivan saw an AP story that South African leader Desmond Tutu was going to stop in Helena, Mont., she wondered why. It would be his only stop in the United States. So she and her editors at the *Spokesman-Review/Spokane Chronicle* decided she should find out who invited him. In an interview published in *Best Newspaper Writing 1991*, she told how she managed to get the four

Interviews are best used to solicit reactions and interpretations, not to gather facts. Good reporters do their fact-gathering before interviews.

people who were responsible to talk to her so openly when they had so little time to spend with her.

They don't want to spend a lot of time talking to you. I knew that was going to be the case. I had called every one of these guys the week before. It sounds very elementary, but in the week before I left Spokane, I rounded up enough biographical information so that I was not going to waste my time interviewing them, asking them where they went to school and so on.

By the time they met me in person, the ice had been broken over the phone, and I could concentrate on developing the next phase of the interview.

A reporter who begins an interview without the proper preparation is like a student taking a final exam without studying. Both may make it, but luck, rather than skill, may have more to do with it.

The success of the interview depends as much on what you do before you ask the first question as it does on the questioning and writing. You should research both the subject and your source. A.J. Liebling, a famous journalist, author and press critic, didn't know much about horse racing, but his first question in an interview with jockey Eddie Arcaro was, "How many holes longer do you keep your left stirrup than your right?" Arcaro responded enthusiastically to the knowledgeable question. Liebling's research gave him the key to open the interview. A source who thinks the reporter is knowledgeable about the subject of the interview is more likely to speak frankly and fully than one who must explain everything as the conversation progresses.

Liebling was able to overcome Arcaro's skepticism with a single question. Syl Jones had considerably more difficulty with William Shockley, who won a Nobel Prize for his work developing the transistor. Jones, however, wanted to talk to him for *Playboy* magazine about much more volatile topics: Shockley's theory of black genetic inferiority and his revelation that he had participated in a Nobel-laureate sperm bank. Burned many times by the press, Shockley was exceedingly cautious.

Shockley often turned down reporters' requests for interviews because he believed they didn't know enough about genetics. By phone, Shockley quizzed Jones, a science and medical writer, about genetics. The quizzes involved complicated mathematical analyses of statistics designed by Shockley in support of his theories. After hours of grilling, he agreed that Jones was competent enough to interview him.

But first Shockley wanted even more information. He asked for personal information, everything from where Jones was born to where he went to school. Jones told the rest of the story in *Playboy*:

Long before this point in the process, most other reporters had written Shockley off as a kook and had given up. I was tempted to do the same. But something intrigued me: Never once did he ask my race or make any kind of racist remark, and he had no idea I was black. I didn't tell him, because I was hoping for a confrontation. . . .

When a white photographer and I showed up at Stanford for the interview, Shockley instinctively reached to shake the photographer's hand with the greeting, "Hello, Mr. Jones." It was a wrong guess that seemed almost to stagger him. Obviously stunned by my blackness, he insisted that I submit to one final test, concocted on the spur of the moment, concerning the application of the Pythagorean theorem to some now long-forgotten part of his dysgenic thesis. Somehow, I came up with a satisfactory explanation, and Shockley had no choice but to grant me the interview.

Let's hope you never have to overcome those kinds of barriers.

Consideration of Story Type

How you prepare for the interview depends in part on what kind of a story you intend to write. You may be doing a news story, a personality profile or an investigative piece. In each case, you check the newspaper library and search on-line databases, talk to other reporters and, if there's enough time, read magazine articles and books.

To prepare for a **news story**, you pay more attention to clips about the subject of the story than to those about the personality of the individual to be interviewed. To prepare for a **profile**, you look for personality quirks and the subject's interests, family, friends, travels and habits. To prepare for an **investigative piece**, you want to know both your subject matter and the person you are interviewing. In all these stories, do not overlook other reporters and editors who know something about the person or subject. Let's look at each of these three types of stories more closely.

The News Story

One day Paul Leavitt made a routine telephone call to a law enforcement source. Leavitt, then assistant city editor for the *Des Moines* (Iowa) *Register*, was working on a story. He knew the source from his days as a county government and courts reporter for the *Register*.

He expected the story, and the interview, to be routine. Polk County was building a new jail. Leavitt wanted to find out about the progress on the new building. The source pleaded ignorance. He said, "Oh, Leavitt, I don't know. I haven't had time to keep up on that, what with all these meetings on the pope's visit."

Leavitt didn't say anything right away. A less astute reporter might have let the source know he was surprised. The pope in Des Moines? Are you kidding? Instead, Leavitt remembered a story he

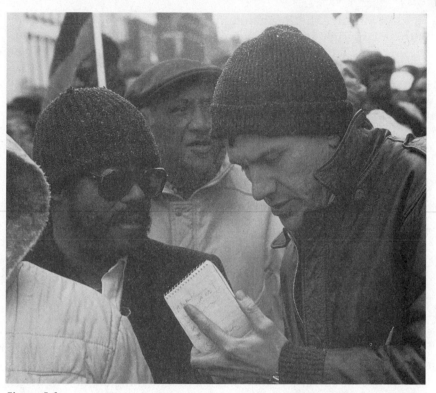

Figure 5.1.
This reporter dresses to fit in with the marchers he is interviewing; he gains their confidence by being friendly and attentive.

had read about an Iowan who had extended an invitation for John Paul II to stop in Iowa during his American visit. Leavitt didn't think the Iowan had much of a chance. When the Vatican had announced the pope's visit, people from every state were bartering for a chance to bask in the worldwide limelight.

Still, the source's slip of the tongue seemed genuine. Leavitt finally replied, "Oh, yeah, that's right. When's he coming, anyway?"

"October 4," the source said.

As the conversation progressed, Leavitt waved frantically to the *Register*'s managing editor. A major story was brewing.

"I started asking him some more questions," Leavitt recalls, "then it dawned on him that he probably wasn't supposed to be talking about this. But it was clear from what he said that the pope was definitely coming to Iowa. He even had the hours."

Before the conversation ended, Leavitt had learned of a meeting among the Secret Service, the Vatican, the U.S. State Department and Iowa law enforcement officials to discuss the trip. He also had learned when the pope would arrive, where he would arrive, where he would celebrate Mass and when he would leave.

As a result, the *Register* stunned its readers the next morning with a copyrighted story saying the pope would speak in Des Moines on Oct. 4. The story was printed three weeks before the Vatican released its official itinerary of the visit. Other area reporters scoffed at the story. One newspaper even printed a story poking fun at the thought of John Paul II hobnobbing in an Iowa cornfield.

Leavitt and the *Register* were vindicated. As scheduled, the pope arrived Oct. 4—and celebrated Mass in an Iowa cornfield.

Remembering his conversation with the source, and how a routine question turned into a bona fide scoop, Leavitt said, "I don't even remember what the original question was."

Leavitt probably would not have gotten the story had he not remembered the earlier story about the invitation and known something else about interviewing: When a source unwittingly gives you a scoop, sometimes it is best to act as if you already know it. That may encourage the source to give you more information.

The Profile

A reporter who decided to write a profile of a local free-lance writer prepared differently. Because the reporter had used the writer as a source in an earlier story, she knew something about the writer. But she needed to know more. So she looked in *Contemporary Authors* and found biographical information. She also asked the writer to send her copies of some of the articles she had written. Before the reporter went to see the free-lancer, she had read several of her articles. She also interviewed the editor at one of the magazines that bought the writer's material.

The reporter was prepared. Or so she thought. She had to pass one more test. The free-lance writer was an animal lover, and when the reporter arrived, she first had to make friends with a handful of dogs. Fortunately, she loved dogs. That immediately established rapport with the free-lancer. The resulting story was full of lively detail:

Joan Gilbert stretches lazily to soft sunbeams and chirping birds. She dresses casually in blue denim shorts and a plaid, short-sleeved blouse. She and her favorite work companions, five playful dogs, file out the door of her little white house to begin their day with a lazy walk in the surrounding woods. When she returns, she'll contentedly sit down at her typewriter. Such is work.

Joan Gilbert is a free-lance writer.

Walt Harrington of *The Washington Post* specializes in in-depth profiles. In his book, he talked about the time they take:

gate. She believed she would have a better chance of getting the interview if she could meet the man. Assuming she would be denied if she buzzed the couple's apartment, she waited until someone else opened the gate.

"As soon as I identified myself, his wife broke into sobs and begged him not to talk with me," Branch says. "But I figured he wanted to tell his story." She was right.

Branch agreed she wouldn't tell authorities where he was. The interview lasted 90 minutes. Several months later, authorities caught the man in a drug-smuggling sting in Guatemala.

Her degrees in journalism and Spanish have opened many doors for her. Her first journalism job was with the *Mexico City News*. Since joining the *Herald* in 1988, she has covered everything from Latino communities to the state legislature. She also covered such major international stories as the Zapatista rebels in Chiapas and the Mexican presidential elections.

Figure 5.2.
Barbara Walters has interviewed scores of celebrities from politicians to pop stars such as Sylvester Stallone.

Each took between one and three months to complete. All included many hours of conversation with the subjects. Most include days of tagging along as they did whatever they usually did. . . . With actress Kelly McGillis, I spent a hot August month traipsing to daily rehearsals and then back to Kelly's apartment, where she would analyze her day on stage. Most of these profiles also included numerous interviews with the subjects' family, friends, and enemies. For the George Bush and Carl Bernstein profiles, I did about eighty interviews each. Always there are also newspaper and magazine clippings, books, and documents to read.

Few journalists are afforded the luxury of three months to work on a profile, but whether you do eight or 80 interviews, the lessons are still the same: Be prepared. Be there.

The Investigative Piece

The casual atmosphere of the Gilbert interview is not always possible for the investigative reporter. Here, the adversary relationship determines both the preparation required and the atmosphere of the interview itself. An investigative reporter is like an attorney in a courtroom. Wise attorneys know what the answers to their questions will be. So do investigative reporters. Preparation is essential.

In the early stages of the investigation, you conduct some fishing-expedition interviews: Because you don't know how much the source knows, you cast around. Start with persons on the fringes. Gather as much as you can from them. Study the records. Only after you have most of the evidence do you confront your central character. You start with a large circle and gradually draw it smaller.

When Glenn Bunting, a reporter for the *San Jose* (Calif.) *Mercury News*, heard complaints about the low caliber of workers turned out by a government-funded training agency, he quietly did a little checking. Before he had gone too far, he had a friendly interview with the administrator, who did not know the real purpose of Bunting's inquiries.

Then Bunting went to work. He tracked the trail of money. He examined bank statements and canceled checks, government audit reports, purchase orders and weekly timecards—all public records because the agency got its money from the government. He interviewed counselors and job-training instructors, law officers and others who did business with the agency. By the time Bunting was ready to talk to the administrator again, he already had most of his story confirmed. This is how the story of the interview began:

> Robert Bernal was getting angry. Confronted with evidence of wrongdoing in Project DARE, his face turned red and his voice grew louder.
> "Why are you attacking me?" he asked. "You don't believe me, but everything I've told you is the truth. I haven't told you any barefaced lies."
> But he had.

Among other things, Bunting was able to show that Bernal had earned a "degree" not from Stanford as he claimed, but from San Quentin Prison. Confronted with the evidence, Bernal told Bunting, "You never lose the stigma of being in prison. You have a tendency to build up a facade, a degree of phoniness—even saying that you have a college degree."

Bunting was able to pierce the deceptions because he had drawn the circle around Bernal tighter and tighter before he went into the interview.

Getting the interview is sometimes as big a challenge as the interview itself. Sources who believe you are working on a story that will be critical of them or their friends often try to avoid you. Steve Weinberg, author of an unauthorized biography of industrialist Armand Hammer, had to overcome suspicion on the part of many former Hammer associates. Their former boss had told all of them not to talk to Weinberg. Instead of calling, Weinberg wrote letters.

"I sent letters, examples of my previous work, explained what I wanted to cover and why I was doing it without Hammer's blessing," Weinberg says.

He recommends that you use the letter to share some of what you know about the story that might surprise or impress the source. For instance, a reference such as "And last week, when I was checking all the land records . . ." would indicate the depth of your research.

In his letter to former Hammer assistants, Weinberg talked about how Hammer was one of the most important people in the his-

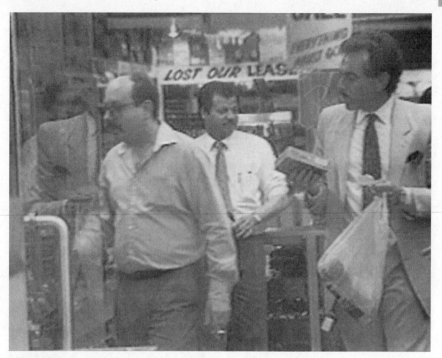

Figure 5.3.
Many local broadcast news organizations have consumer news reporters or ombudsmen. Their investigative interviews of unwilling subjects often result in dramatic news stories that attract viewer interest.

tory of business. The letters opened doors to all seven of Hammer's former executive assistants Weinberg contacted.

Weinberg, former director of Investigative Reporters and Editors, also offers to show the sources relevant portions of his manuscript as an accuracy check. He makes it clear in writing that he maintains control of the content.

Requesting an interview in writing can allow you to make your best case for getting it. And an offer to allow your sources to review the story assures them that you are serious about accuracy.

Other Preparatory Considerations

All this homework is important, but it may be something as trifling as your appearance that determines whether you will have a successful interview. You would hardly wear cutoff shorts into a university president's suite, and you wouldn't wear a three-piece suit to talk to underground revolutionaries. It is your right to wear your hair however you wish and to wear whatever clothes you want, but it is the source's prerogative to refuse to talk to you.

Rick Bragg of the *St. Petersburg* (Fla.) *Times* told the editors of

Best Newspaper Writing 1991 that his choice of clothing was important in establishing rapport with a man whose mother had died of injuries suffered 17 years earlier. Police were investigating the death as a homicide. "I think he (the son) was more than just a little put off with how brusque some of the other reporters had been," Bragg said, "and I showed up in a pair of jeans and a T-shirt because I knew where I was going, and I didn't see much point in hiding behind a Brooks Brothers suit."

Bragg chose to fit in with the environment. That environment, too, is important. You've already heard Harrington talk about visiting Salt Lake City with Jack Anderson and spending hours with actress Kelly McGillis at work and at her apartment. Most interviews are conducted in the source's office. Especially if the story is a profile or a feature, it usually is better to get the source away from his or her work. If you are doing a story about a rabbi's hobby of collecting butterflies, seek a setting appropriate to the topic. Suggest meeting in the rabbi's den or even outside.

In some interviews, it would be to your advantage to get the source on neutral territory. If you have some questions for the provost or a public official, suggest meeting in a coffee shop at a quiet time. A person has more power in his or her official surroundings.

It is important, too, to let the source know how much time you need and whether you expect to return for further information. And if you don't already know how the source might react to a tape recorder, ask when you are making the appointment.

You have now done the appropriate homework. You are properly attired. You have made an appointment and told the source how much time you need. Before you leave, you should write down a list of questions you want to ask. They will guide you through the interview and prevent you from missing important topics altogether. The best way to encourage a spontaneous conversation is to have your questions prepared. You'll be more relaxed. Barbara Walters once told a reporter that she writes as many as 500 questions on index cards, then selects the best ones for use during the interview. The thinking you must do to write the questions will help prepare you for the interview. Having questions prepared relieves you of the need to be mentally searching for the next question as the source is answering the last one. If you are trying to think of the next question, you will not be paying close attention to what is being said, and you might miss the most important part of the interview.

Preparing the questions for an interview is hard work, even for veterans. If you are writing for your campus newspaper, seek suggestions from other staff members. You will find ideas in the newspaper clips and your newspaper's or station's electronic database. If you anticipate a troublesome interview with the chancellor, you might want to seek advice from faculty members, too. What questions would they ask if they were you? Often, they have more background knowledge, or they might have heard some of the faculty talk around campus. Staff members are also valuable sources of information.

While you may ask all of your prepared questions in some interviews, in most, you probably will use only some of them. Still, you will have benefited from preparing the questions in two important ways. First, even when you don't use many, the work you did thinking of the questions helped prepare you for the interview. Second, sources who see that you have a prepared list often are impressed with your seriousness.

On the basis of the information you have gathered already, you know *what* you want to ask. Now you must be careful about *how* you ask the questions.

Phrasing Questions

Listen to an accomplished courtroom lawyer ask questions. How the questions are structured often determines whether the lawyer will win the case. Journalists face the same challenge. Reporters have missed many stories because they didn't know how to ask questions. Quantitative researchers have shown how just a slight wording change affects the results of a survey. If you want to know whether citizens favor a city plan to beautify the downtown area, you can ask the question in several ways:

- Do you favor the city council's plan to beautify the downtown area?
- The city council plans to spend $3 million beautifying the downtown area. Are you in favor of this?
- Do you think the downtown area needs physical changes?
- Which of the following actions do you favor?
  —Building a traffic loop around the downtown area.
  —Prohibiting all automobile traffic in an area bounded by Providence Road, Ash Street, College Avenue and Elm Street.
  —Having all the downtown storefronts remodeled to carry out a single theme and putting in brick streets, shrubbery and benches.
  —None of the above.

How you structure that question may affect the survey results by several percentage points. Similarly, how you ask questions in an interview may affect the response.

By the phrasing of the question, many reporters signal the response they expect or prejudices they have. For instance, a reporter who says, "Don't you think that the city council should allocate more money to the parks and recreation department?" is not only asking a question but also influencing the source or betraying bias. A neutral phrasing would be, "Do you think the city council should allocate more money to the parks and recreation department?" Another common way of asking a leading question is this: "Are you going to vote against this amendment like the other legislators I've talked to?"

If you have watched journalists interviewing people live on television, you have seen many examples of badly phrased questions. Many times they are not questions at all. The interviewers make statements and then put the microphone in front of the source: "You had a great game, Bill"; "Winning the election must be a great feeling." The source is expected to say something. What, precisely, do you want to know?

Sometimes a reporter unwittingly blocks a response by the phrasing of the question. A reporter who was investigating possible job discrimination against women conducted several interviews before she told her city editor she didn't think the women with whom she talked were being frank with her. "When I ask them if they have ever been discriminated against, they always tell me no. But three times now during the course of the interviews, they have said things that indicate they have been. How do I get them to tell me about it?" she asks.

"Perhaps it's the way you are asking the question," the city editor replies. "When you ask someone whether they have ever been discriminated against, you are forcing them to answer yes or no. Don't be so blunt. Ask them if others with the same qualifications at work have been advanced faster than they have. Ask if they are paid the same amount as men for the same work. Ask them what they think they would be doing today if they were male. Ask them if they know of any qualified women who were denied jobs."

The city editor was giving the reporter examples of both closed- and open-ended questions. Each has its specific strengths.

Open-Ended Questions

Open-ended questions allow the respondent some flexibility. Women may not respond frankly when asked whether they have ever been discriminated against. The question calls for a yes-no response. But an open-ended question such as "What would you be doing today if you were a man?" is not so personal. It does not sound as threatening to the respondent. In response to an open-ended question, the source often reveals more than he or she realizes or intends to.

A sportswriter who was interviewing a pro scout at a college football game wanted to know whom the scout was there to see. When the scout diplomatically declined to be specific, the reporter tried another approach. He asked a series of questions:

- "What kind of qualities does a pro scout look for in an athlete?"
- "Do you think any of the players here today have those talents?"
- "Whom would you put into that category?"

The reporter worked from the general to the specific until he had the information he wanted. Open-ended questions are less direct and less threatening. They are more exploratory and more flexible. However, if you want to know a person's biographical data, don't ask "Can you tell me about yourself?"

Closed-Ended Questions

Eventually the reporter needs to close in on a subject, to pin down details, to get the respondent to be specific. **Closed-ended questions** are designed to elicit specific responses.

Instead of asking the mayor, "What did you think of the conference in Washington, D.C.?" you ask, "What did you learn in the session 'Funds You May Not Know Are Available'?" Instead of asking a previous employee to appraise the chancellor-designate's managerial abilities, you ask, "How well does she listen to the people who work for her?" "Do the people who work for her have specific job duties?" "Does she explain her decisions?"

A vague question invites a vague answer. By asking a specific question, you are more likely to get a specific answer. You are also communicating to your source that you have done your homework and that you are looking for precise details.

Knowing exactly when to ask a closed-ended question or when to be less specific is not something you can plan ahead of time. The type of information you are seeking and the chemistry between the interviewer and the source are the determining factors. You must make on-the-spot decisions. The important thing is to keep rephrasing the question until the source answers it adequately.

Establishing a Rapport

Tad Bartimus, former AP reporter, has interviewed hundreds of people, beginning with former President Harry S. Truman while working for her hometown weekly at age 14. She approached the ex-president and said, "Excuse me, sir, but I'm from the local paper. Could you please talk to me?"

"Well, young lady, what would you like to know?" Truman responded.

Years later, Bartimus recalled, "For the first time in my life, I was struck dumb. What *did* I want to know? What *was* I supposed to ask him? How do you *do* this interviewing stuff, anyway?"

Bartimus knows the answers to those questions now. One piece of advice she offered her colleagues in an article for *AP World* was to share and care. Bartimus urges reporters to reveal themselves as people. "A little empathy goes a long way to defuse [the] fear and hostility that is so pervasive against the press," she says.

Rapport—the relationship between the reporter and the source—is crucial to the success of the interview. The relationship is sometimes relaxed, sometimes strained. Often it is somewhere in between. The type of relationship you try to establish with your source is determined by the kind of story you are doing. Several approaches are possible.

Interview Approaches

For most news stories and personality profiles, the reporter has more to gain if the subject is at ease. Often that can be accomplished by starting off with small talk. Ask about a trophy, the plants or an engraved pen. Bring up something humorous you have found during your research. Ask about something you know the source will want to talk about. In other interviews, if you think the subject might be skeptical about your knowledge of the field, open with a question that demonstrates your knowledge.

Reporters who can show sources what they have in common also have more success getting information. When Janet Chusmir was a reporter for the *Miami Herald*, she was assigned to interview the parents of Bernardine Dohrn. Dohrn was a suspect in an anti-war protest bombing and a fugitive. Many reporters, including some from the *Herald*, had tried to talk to the parents. None had succeeded.

Chusmir went to their home and knocked on the door. She identified herself and told them why she was there. They said they didn't want to talk. She said she understood because she was a parent, too. She asked for a glass of water. They complied with her request. She edged into the house and sat down to drink the water. While she sat there, they chatted about, among other things, why the parents didn't want to be interviewed. Before she left, she had enough information for a story. Although the request for water bought the reporter some time, it was her ability to talk to them sympathetically parent-to-parent that made her successful.

On another occasion, Chusmir was among a group of reporters who showed up expecting to witness kidnappers return a mother's child. The kidnappers never showed up. The police slipped the mother into the back seat of a police car and edged through the crowd. As the car went by her, Chusmir tapped on the window. The mother rolled it down slightly. "I hope you find your child," Chusmir said. The woman told her to call. Chusmir did and got an exclusive story.

One of the mistakes reporters make is not being empathetic, Chusmir says. "I genuinely feel for these people. I think sources can sense that."

Rapport also depends on where you conduct the interview. Many persons, especially those unaccustomed to being interviewed, feel more comfortable in their workplace. Go to them. Talk to the

"I try never to go to an interview as a hostile antagonist. I am merely a reporter asking questions, with no ax to grind. I am a person with a family, a home, an unbalanced checkbook, a weight problem and a car that goes 'thonka-thonka-thonka' when it's cold. Unless my interview subject is Ivana Trump or Meryl Streep or Richard Nixon, my life is probably, at least in one way or two ways, similar to the person of whom I'm asking the questions."
—Tad Bartimus, former AP regional reporter

Masson vs. Malcolm: A Cautionary Tale

The "fabricated quotes" case of Masson vs. Malcolm is a bad soap opera. The lead characters are writer Janet Malcolm, the defendant, and psychoanalyst Jeffrey Masson, the plaintiff.

Here is the main scenario:

Masson became disillusioned with Freudian psychology when he was serving as projects director of the Sigmund Freud Archives in London. He was fired for advancing his controversial theories about Freud in 1981. Malcolm wanted to write about the situation. She established a rapport with him and taped more than 40 hours worth of interviews. But she said she did not tape-record all of their conversations, especially those that occurred when they were walking or traveling in her car.

Malcolm wrote about Masson for *The New Yorker* in 1983. Book publisher Alfred A. Knopf later published a book from that material. The placement of quotation marks around certain statements in these works provoked a dispute between subject and author. Malcom wrote that Masson said his superiors at the Sigmund Freud Archives considered him "an intellectual gigolo—you get your pleasure from him, but you don't take him out in public." Masson said he never said that. A tape recording shows that he said, "I was, in a sense, much too junior within the hierarchy of analysis for these important training analysts to be caught dead with me."

Did he call himself an "intellectual gigolo" or not? It is a catchy phrase. Masson claimed that quote and others were fabricated. He sued *The New Yorker*, Knopf and Malcolm for libel.

In 1989, the Ninth Circuit Court of Appeals ruled in favor of the defendants. The court said that an author may "under certain circumstances, fictionalize quotations to some extent." Because Masson had conceded that he was a public figure, he had to prove "actual malice"—knowledge of falsity or reckless disregard (see Chapter 21).

The court said:

Malice will not be inferred from evidence showing that the quoted language does not contain the exact words used by the plaintiff provided that the fabricated quotations are either *"rational interpretations of ambiguous"* remarks made by the public figure . . . or do not *"alter the substantive content"* of unambiguous remarks actually made by the public figure. (Italics added.)

In 1991 the Supreme Court overturned the Ninth Circuit's decision, rejecting the lower court's "rational interpretation" standard. The Court said that "quotation marks indicate that the author is not interpreting the speaker's ambiguous statement, but is attempting to convey what the speaker said."

The Court said:

Were we to assess quotations under a rational interpretation standard, we would give journalists the freedom to place statements in their subjects' mouths without fear of liability. By eliminating any method of distinguishing between the statements of the subject and the interpretation of the author, we would diminish to a great degree the trustworthiness of the printed word and eliminate the real meaning of quotations. Not only public figures but the press doubtless would suffer under such a rule.

The Court clearly was trying to protect the sanctity of quotation marks, but the Court also made it clear that not every change in a quotation is going to lead to a lawsuit. To some extent, some reporters do clean up quotes. Some reporters correct errors in grammar. Some delete "uh" or "um" without using ellipsis points. Those changes will not get a reporter into trouble. The change in words has to result in a *material change* in the meaning of a statement for actual malice to be present. But courts are going to look hard at cases where a

Masson vs. Malcolm: A Cautionary Tale (continued)

writer has put words in a speaker's mouth.

The Supreme Court remanded the case. In 1992, the Ninth Circuit let Knopf off the hook, saying, in effect, that Knopf relied on *The New Yorker* in concluding that Malcolm's manuscript was accurate.

In June 1993, a jury heard the case. It found two fabricated quotes libelous—the "intellectual gigolo" quote was not one of them. Here are the two quotes:

Malcolm quoted Masson as describing his plans for Maresfield Gardens, the home of the Freud Archives, which he hoped to occupy after the death of Anna Freud, Sigmund's child: "I would have renovated it, opened it up, brought it to life. Maresfield Gardens would have been a center of scholarship, but it would also have been a place of *sex, women, fun.* (Italics added.) It would have been like the change in *The Wizard of Oz*, from black-and-white into color." He said on tape of his meeting with a London analyst: ". . . we were going to pass women on to each other, and we were going to have a great time together when I lived in the Freud house. We'd have great parties and . . . we were going to live it up."

The second quotation involved the placement of the sentence, "Well, he had the wrong man." Masson is recounting being fired by the director of the archives. The director says Masson is upsetting Anna Freud and it might kill her. Malcolm quotes Masson talking to the director:

"What have I done? You're doing it. You're firing me. What am I supposed to do—be grateful to you?" "You could be silent about it. . . ." "Why should I do that?" "Because it is the honorable thing to do." "Well, he had the wrong man."

Masson seems to be calling himself dishonorable. On the tape, the conversation, starting with the director, says:

"You could be silent about it." . . . "Why?" . . . "Because it's the honorable thing to do and you will save face. And who knows? If you never speak about it and you quietly and humbly accept our judgment, who knows that in a few years if we don't bring you back?" Well, he had the wrong man.

While agreeing the two quotes were libelous, the jury deadlocked on damages. The judge ordered a retrial on all issues—liability as well as damages. But another defendant dropped by the wayside. The jurors did not think *The New Yorker* deliberately published false quotes, so the judge dismissed the case against the magazine.

In November 1994, a jury decided in favor of defendant Malcolm.

Then, in August 1995, Malcolm recovered a lost notebook containing her notes on some of the contested conversations. Masson stated that this new evidence did not disprove his accusations, and he would not rule out an appeal of the November 1994 verdict.

The soap opera may or may not be over, but the moral is clear. Material changes in quotations are perilous. They can lead to long court cases and expensive attorney fees even if ultimately there is no liability for damages.

business person in the office, to the athlete in the locker room, to the conductor in the concert hall. In some cases, though, you may get a better interview elsewhere if the source cannot relax at the workplace or is frequently interrupted. Reporters have talked to politicians during car rides between campaign appearances. They've gone sailing with business people and hunting with athletes. One student reporter doing a feature on a police chief spent a weekend with the chief, who was painting his home. To do a profile, which requires more than one interview, vary the location. New surroundings can make a difference.

Scott Kraft of the Associated Press once did a story on a couple who for more than two years drove the streets of Los Angeles looking for the man who had raped their 12-year-old daughter. The search was successful.

"When I knocked on their door in May, I wanted them to know that I would be careful and honest, and I wanted them to tell me everything, even though it would probably be difficult," he wrote in *Editor & Publisher*.

Kraft conducted interviews in three locations. The first was in the family's living room. The second was in a car as they revisited the places where the family searched. The third was by phone. Kraft said the mother talked more candidly on the phone after her children had gone to school.

There are times when the reporter would rather have the source edgy, nervous or even scared. When you are doing an investigation, you may want the key characters to feel uneasy. You may pretend you know more than you actually do. You want them to know that the material you have is substantive and serious. Seymour Hersh, a Pulitzer Prize-winning investigative reporter, uses this tactic. *Time* magazine once quoted a government official commenting on Hersh: "He wheedles, cajoles, pleads, threatens, asks a leading question, uses little tidbits as if he knew the whole story. When he finishes you feel like a wet rag."

In some cases, however, it is better even in an investigation to take a low-key approach. Let the source relax. Talk around the subject but gradually bring the discussion to the key issues. The surprise element may work to your favor.

So may the sympathetic approach. When the source is speaking, you may nod or punctuate the source's responses with comments such as "That's interesting." Sources who think you are sympathetic are more likely to volunteer information. That was the key to Chusmir's success. Researchers have found, for instance, that a simple "mm-hmmm" affects the length of the answer interviewers get.

Other Practical Considerations

Where you sit in relation to the person you are interviewing can be important. Unless you deliberately are trying to make those interviewed feel uncomfortable, do not sit directly in front of them. Permit your sources to establish eye contact if and when they wish.

Some people are even more disturbed by the way a reporter takes notes. A tape recorder ensures accuracy of quotes, but it makes many speakers self-conscious or nervous. If you have permission to use a tape recorder, place it in an inconspicuous spot and ignore it except to make sure it is working properly. Writing notes longhand may interfere with your ability to digest what is being said. But not taking any notes at all is risky. Only a few reporters can leave an interview and accurately write down what was said. Certainly no one can do it and reproduce direct quotes verbatim. You should learn shorthand or develop a note-taking system of your own.

Ensuring Accuracy

Accuracy is a major problem in all interviews. Both the question and the answer may be ambiguous. You may not understand what is said. You may record it incorrectly. You may not know the context of the remarks. Your biases may interfere with the message.

Figures stated during an interview must be double-checked. The mere statement of a statistic, even by a reliable source, does not ensure accuracy.

Knowing the background of your sources, having a comfortable relationship with them and keeping good notes are important elements of accuracy. All those were missing when a journalism student, two weeks into an internship at a major daily, interviewed the public information officer for a sheriff's department about criminal activity in and around a shelter for battered women. The reporter had never met the source, whom she interviewed by phone. She took notes on her interview with the deputy and others in whatever notebook happened to be nearby. She didn't record the time, date or even the source. There were no notes showing context, just fragments of quotes, scrawled in nearly illegible handwriting.

After the story was published, the developer of the shelter sued. Questioned by attorneys, the deputy swore that the reporter misunderstood him and used some of his comments out of context. In several cases, he contended, she completed her fragmentary notes by putting her own words in his mouth. He testified that most reporters come to see him to get acquainted. Many call back to check his quotes on sensitive or complex stories. She did neither.

When the court ordered the reporter to produce and explain her notes, she had trouble reconstructing them. She had to admit on several occasions that she wasn't sure what the fragments meant.

The accuracy of your story is only as good as your notes. Make sure they are complete and in order.

You have no control over some of the things that may affect the accuracy of the answers you receive in an interview. In 1946 two researchers conducted an experiment in which a group of people were asked, "Do you think there are too many Jews holding government offices and jobs?" The interviewers were divided into four groups: Jewish in appearance with a Jewish name; Jewish in appearance; non-Jewish in appearance; and non-Jewish in appearance with a non-Jewish name. Ten percent more people answered yes to the non-Jewish-appearing interviewer than did so to the Jewish-appearing interviewer with a Jewish name. Some respondents tailored their answer to what they believed the interviewer wanted to hear.

Some possibilities for making errors or introducing bias are unavoidable, but others are not. To ensure the most accurate and complete reporting possible, you should use all the techniques available to obtain a good interview, including observing, understanding what you hear and asking follow-up questions. Let's examine these and other techniques.

Observing

"Today one has the impression that the interviewer is not listening to what you say, nor does he think it important, because he believes that the tape recorder hears everything. But he's wrong; it doesn't hear the beating of the heart, which is the most important part of the interview."

— Gabriel Garcia Marquez,
Colombian writer and
Nobel laureate

Some reporters look but do not see. The detail they miss may be the difference between a routine story and one that is a delight to read. Your powers of observation may enable you to discover a story beyond your source's words. Is the subject nervous? What kinds of questions are striking home? The mayor may deny that he is going to fire the police chief, but if you notice the chief's personnel file sitting on an adjacent worktable, you may have reason to continue the investigation.

People communicate some messages nonverbally. Researchers have been able to correlate some gestures with meanings. For instance, folded arms often signal unapproachability; crossed ankles often signal tension. Many nonverbal messages, however, may not be the same for all ethnic and cultural groups. Reporters should read more about the subject.

Understanding

Understanding what you see is crucial to the news-gathering process. So is understanding what you hear. It is not enough merely to record what is being said; you must also digest it. The reporter who was investigating job discrimination was listening but not understanding. Her sources were telling her about incidents of discrimination, but all she heard were their denials.

Sometimes what you don't hear may be the message. The reporter who was trying to find out if the mayor was going to fire the police chief asked several questions about the chief's performance. What struck the reporter during the interview was the mayor's lack of enthusiasm for the chief. That unintentional tip kept the reporter working on the story until he confirmed it.

The *Miami Herald*'s Chusmir listens, too. Once when she was interviewing Joan Fontaine, the actress, Chusmir mentioned that she had a daughter about the same age as Fontaine's. Fontaine asked, "Is she jealous of you?" Listening closely, Chusmir correctly deduced that Fontaine was revealing a problem of jealousy in the family, and the interview took an unexpected turn.

Asking Follow-up Questions

If you understand what the source is saying, you can ask meaningful follow-up questions. There is nothing worse than briefing your city editor on the interview and having the editor ask you, "Well, did you ask . . ." Having to say no is embarrassing.

Even if you go into an interview armed with a list of questions, the most important probably will be the ones you ask in response to an answer. A reporter who was doing a story on bidding procedures was interviewing the mayor. The reporter asked how bid specifications were written. In the course of his reply, the mayor mentioned that the president of a construction firm had assured him the last bid specifications were adequate. The alert reporter picked up on the statement:

"When did you talk to him?"
"About three weeks ago," the mayor said.
"That's before the specifications were published, wasn't it?"
"Yes, we asked him to look them over for us."
"Did he find anything wrong with the way they were written?"
"Oh, he changed a few minor things. Nothing important."
"Did officials of any other construction firms see the bid specifications before they were advertised?"
"No, he was the only one."

Gradually, on the basis of one offhand comment by the mayor, the reporter was able to piece together a solid story on the questionable relationship between the city and the construction firm.

Other Techniques

Although most questions are designed to get information, some are asked as a delaying tactic. A reporter who is taking notes may fall behind. Emily Yoffe, a senior editor of *Texas Monthly*, will say, "Hold on a second—let me get that" or "Say that again." Other questions are intended to encourage a longer response. "Go on with that" or "Tell me more about that" encourages the speaker to add more detail.

You don't have to be stalling for time to say you don't understand. Don't be embarrassed to admit you haven't grasped something. It is better to admit to one person you don't understand than to advertise your ignorance in newsprint or on the airwaves in front of thousands. Once you have written the story, check with your sources. Check the facts. Check the concepts. Catch your errors before publication. You'll impress your editors, you will serve your readers better, your newspaper will have more credibility, and your sources will be happy to talk to you the next time.

Another device for making the source talk on is not a question at all; it is a pause. You are signaling the source that you expect more. But the lack of a response from you is much more ambiguous than

Reporters should do research after an interview to ascertain specific figures when a source provides an estimate. For example, if a shop owner says he runs one of 20 pizza parlors in town, check with the city business-license office to get the exact number.

Interviewing Checklist

I. Before the interview
   A. Know the subject
      1. Seek specific information
      2. Research the subject
      3. List the questions
   B. Know the person
      1. Know salient biographical information
      2. Know person's expertise regarding subject matter
   C. Set up the interview
      1. Set the time
         a. At interviewee's convenience—but suggest a time
         b. Length of time needed
         c. Possible return visits
      2. Set the place
         a. Interviewee's turf, or
         b. Neutral turf
   D. Discuss arrangements
      1. Will you bring a tape recorder?
      2. Will you bring a photographer?
      3. Will you let interviewee check accuracy of quotes?

II. During the interview
   A. When you arrive
      1. Control the seating arrangement
      2. Place tape recorder at optimum spot
      3. Warm up person briefly with small talk
      4. Set the ground rules
         a. Put everything on the record
         b. Make everything attributable
   B. The interview itself
      1. Use good interview techniques
         a. Ask open-ended questions
         b. Allow the person to think and to speak; pause
         c. Don't be threatening in voice or manner
         d. Control the flow but be flexible
      2. Take good notes
         a. Be unobtrusive
         b. Be thorough
      3. Use the tape recorder
         a. Assume it's not working
         b. Note digital counter at important parts
   C. Before you leave
      1. Ask if there's anything interviewee wants to say
      2. Check facts—spellings, dates, statistics, quotes
      3. Set time for rechecking facts, quotes
      4. Discuss when and where interview might appear
      5. Ask if interviewee wants extra copies

III. After the interview
   A. Organize your notes—immediately
   B. Craft a proper lead
   C. Write a coherent story
   D. Check accuracy with interviewee

"Tell me more about that." It may indicate that you were skeptical of what was just said, that you didn't understand, that the answer was inadequate or several other possibilities. The source will be forced to react. The only problem with this, says the AP's special correspondent Saul Pett, "is that it invites the dull to be dull at greater length."

Many dull interviews become interesting after they end. There are two things you should always do when you finish your questions: Check key facts, figures and quotes and then put away your pen but keep your ears open. You are not breaching any ethical rule if you continue to ask questions after you have put away your pen or turned off the tape recorder. That's when some sources loosen up.

Before you leave, ask if there's anything you forgot to ask. Put the burden on the source. You are also doing your subject a favor by giving the person a chance to contribute to the direction of the interview. You may have missed some important signals during the conversation, and now the source can be more explicit about what he or she wanted to say. Sometimes this technique leads to entirely new subjects.

Quickly review your notes and check facts, especially dates, numbers, quotes, spellings and titles. Besides helping you get it right, it shows the source you are careful. If necessary, arrange a time when you can call to check other parts of the story or clear up questions you may have as you are writing.

As a matter of courtesy, tell the source when the story might appear. You may even offer to send along an extra copy of the article when it's completed.

Remember that although the interview may be over, your relationship to the source is not. When you have the story written, call the source and confirm the information. Better to discover your inaccuracies before you print than after.

Suggested Readings

Biagi, Shirley. *Interviews That Work*. Belmont, Ca.: Wadsworth Publishing Co., 1992. A complete guide to interviewing techniques. The instruction is interspersed with interviews of journalists describing their techniques.

Burgoon, Judee K. and Saine, Thomas J. *The Unspoken Dialogue: An Introduction to Nonverbal Communication*. Boston: Houghton Mifflin, 1978. An excellent look at the subject for readers who are not acquainted with the field.

Gottlieb, Martin. "Dangerous Liaisons." *Columbia Journalism Review*, July/Aug. 1989: 21-35. In this excellent debate over whether interviewers betray sources, Gottlieb interviews several authors.

Harrington, Walt. *American Profiles*. Columbia, Mo.: University of Missouri Press, 1992. Fifteen excellent profiles and the author's explanation of how and why he does what he does.

Malcolm, Janet. *The Journalist and the Murderer*. New York: Knopf, 1990. Using the Joe McGinnis-Jeffrey MacDonald case, the author accuses all journalists of being "confidence men" who betray their sources.

Metzler, Ken. *Creative Interviewing*. Englewood Cliffs, N.J.: Prentice-Hall, 1977. An invaluable in-depth look at problems of interviewing.

Exercises

1. Learn to gather background on your sources. Write a memo of up to two pages about your state's senior U.S. senator. Concentrate on those details that will allow you to focus on how the senator views the pro-life versus pro-choice issue. Indicate the sources of your information. Do an electronic database search on the senator.

2. List five open-ended questions you would ask the senator.

3. List five closed-ended questions you would ask.

4. Interview a student also enrolled in this reporting class. Write a two- to three-page story. Be sure to focus on one aspect of the student's life. Ask your classmate to read the story and to mark errors of fact and perception. The instructor will read your story and the critique.

5. Your instructor will give you a news item. Prepare a list of questions you would ask to do a follow-up interview. As each question is read aloud in class, cross it off your list. See if you can come up with the most original and appropriate questions.

QUOTES AND
ATTRIBUTION

In this chapter
you will learn:

1. What is worth quoting
   directly.

2. How and when to
   attribute direct and
   indirect quotes.

3. How to handle both
   on- and off-the-record
   information.

*A*nd you can quote me on that."

Many people who say these words don't expect to be quoted. They mean only that they are sure of what they are saying and are not afraid or ashamed to say it. Nonetheless, these are sweet words to a reporter.

Direct quotes add color and credibility to your story. By using direct quotes, you are telling readers you are putting them directly in touch with the speaker. Like a letter, direct quotes are personal. Quotation marks signal the reader that something special is coming. Direct quotes provide a story with a change of pace, a breath of air. They also loosen up a clump of dense type.

Not everything people say should be put into direct quotes. You need to learn what to quote directly, when to use partial quotes and when to paraphrase. You also must learn how and how often to attribute quotations and other information. Like a researcher, you must know when information must be tied to a source. However, attributing a remark or some information does not excuse you from a possible libel suit. And, of course, you want to be fair.

Being fair sometimes is difficult when sources do not want to be quoted. For that reason you also must learn how to deal with off-the-record quotes and background information.

What to Quote Directly

Use direct quotes when:

- *Someone says something unique.*
- *Someone says something uniquely.*
- *Someone important says something important.*

Crisp, succinct, meaningful quotes spice up any story. But you can overdo a good thing. You need direct quotes in your stories, and you also need to develop your skill in recognizing what is worth quoting. Let's look at the basic guidelines.

Unique Material

When you can say, "Ah, I never heard that before," you can be quite sure your readers also would like to know exactly what the speaker said. Instead of quoting someone at length, look for the kernel. Sometimes it is something surprising, something neither you nor your readers would expect that person to say. For example, when Pat Williams, general manager of the Orlando Magic, spoke about the team's bad record, he said: "We can't win at home. We can't win on the road. As general manager, I just can't figure out where else to play." When singer Dolly Parton was asked how she felt about dumb blond jokes, she replied: "I'm not offended at all because I know I'm not a dumb blond. I also know I'm not a blond."

Striking statements like these should be quoted, but there is no reason to place simple, factual material inside quotation marks. Here is a segment of copy from a story about the similarities in the careers of a father and his son that needed no quotes at all:

> "My son was born on campus," says the elder Denney, 208 Westridge Drive, a professor in regional and community affairs.
>
> "In fact, he was born in the same hospital that I met my wife," he says, explaining he was in Noyes Hospital with a fractured spine when she was a student nurse.
>
> Since that time, he has earned his bachelor's degree "technically in agriculture with a major in biological science and conservation."

Although the quoted material is informative, it contains nothing particularly interesting, surprising, disturbing, new or even different. It should be written:

> Denney, of 208 Westridge Drive, is a professor in regional and community affairs. While hospitalized in Noyes Hospital with a fractured spine, he met a student nurse who became his wife. Eight years later, his son was born at the same hospital.
>
> The son has since earned a bachelor's degree in agriculture with a major in biological science and conservation.

The first version has 72 words; the second, with 60 words, is tighter and better.

A direct quotation should say something significant. Also, a direct quotation should not simply repeat what has been said indirectly. It should move the story forward. In a story that detailed the forced resignation of a Hong Kong businessman for remarks he made about Chinese Premier Li Peng in a Hong Kong magazine, reporter Steven Mufson of *The Washington Post* used this quotation:

> "If that sort of thing can happen to a businessman like Jimmy Lai, then for ordinary journalists, things can be a lot worse," said Fong So, editor of a monthly called *The 90s Decade*. "People are going to be very cautious about what they say, especially about the Chinese leadership."

The quotation is useful, it is informative, and it moves the story forward.

Sometimes spoken material is unique not because of individual remarks that are surprising or new, but because of extended dialogue that can tell the story more effectively than writers can in their own words. The writer of the following story made excellent use of dialogue:

"I often quote myself. It adds spice to my conversation."
— George Bernard Shaw, playwright

Avoid quotes that provide statistics. You are better off paraphrasing and attributing your source. Save quotes for reaction and interpretation.

Lou Provancha pushed his wire-rimmed glasses up on his nose and leaned toward the man in the wheelchair.

"What is today, Jake?" he asked.

Jake twisted slightly and stared at the floor.

"Jake," Provancha said, "Jake, look up here."

A long silence filled the tiny, cluttered room on the sixth floor of the University Medical Center.

Provancha, a licensed practical nurse at the hospital, glanced at the reporter. "Jake was in a coma a week ago," he explained. "He couldn't talk."

Provancha pointed to a wooden board propped up on the table beside him.

"Jake, what is today? What does it say here? What is this word? I've got my finger pointed right at it."

Jake squinted at the word. With a sudden effort, like a man heaving a bag of cement mix onto a truck bed, he said: "Tuesday."

Provancha grinned. It was a small victory for both of them.

The shaggy-haired nurse was coaxing his patient step-by-step back into the world he had known before a car accident pitched him into a two-month-long coma, with its resulting disorientation and memory loss.

Here's another example of how dialogue can move the story along and "show" rather than "tell" about the characters in the story. The story is about the restoration of old cars. A father is passing on a rare technique to his son:

When the lead is smooth and the irregularities filled to his satisfaction, he reaches for his file.

"How long has it been since you've done this?" his son asks.

"It's been at least 20 years."

"How do you tin it so it won't melt and all run off on the floor?"

"Very carefully."

Before the lesson is finished, a customer and two other shop workers have joined the group watching Larry at work. This is a skill few people know.

"I don't like the way this lead melts," he says.

"That's what it does when there's not enough tin?" his son asks.

"Tin helps it stick."

"Why do you pull the file instead of pushing it?"

"So I can see better."

"I would already have the fiberglass on and be done by now."

"I know, but anything worthwhile you have to work for."

The Unique Expression

When you can say, "Ah, I never heard it said *that* way before," you know you have something quotable. Be on the lookout for the clever, the colorful, the colloquial. For example, an elderly man talking about his organic garden said, "It's hard to tell people to watch what they eat. You eat health, you know."

A professor lecturing on graphic design said, "When you think it looks like a mistake, it is." The same professor once was explaining that elements in a design should not call attention to themselves: "You don't walk up to a beautiful painting in someone's home and say, 'That's a beautiful frame.' "

Sometimes something said uniquely is a colloquialism. Colloquialisms can add color and life to your copy. For example, a person from Louisiana may say: "I was just fixing to leave when the phone rang." A person from an area in Pennsylvania "makes the light out" when turning off the lights. And people in and around Fort Wayne, Ind., "redd up" the dishes after a meal, meaning that they wash them and put them where they belong.

Important Quotes by Important People

If citizen Joe Smith says, "Something must be done about this teachers' strike," you may or may not consider it worth quoting. But if the mayor says, "Something must be done about this teachers' strike," many papers would print the quote. Generally reporters quote public officials or known personalities in their news stories (though not everything the famous say is worth quoting). Remember, prominence is an important property of news.

Quoting sources that readers are likely to know lends authority, credibility and interest to your story. Presumably, a meteorologist knows something about the weather, a doctor about health, a chemistry professor about chemicals. However, it is unlikely that a television star knows a great deal about cameras, even if he or she makes commercials about cameras.

Accuracy

The first obligation of any reporter is to be accurate. Accuracy in direct quotations is paramount. Before there can be any discussion of whether or how to use direct quotations, reporters must acquire the skill of getting the exact words of the source.

It's not easy.

Scribbled notes from interviews, press conferences, meetings, etc., are often difficult to decipher and interpret. A study by Adrienne Leher, a professor of linguistics at the University of Arizona, shows only 13 of 98 quotations taken from Arizona newspapers proved to be verbatim when compared to recordings. Only twice, however, were the nonverbatim quotes considered "incompatible with what was intended."

A column by Bill Hosokawa of the *Rocky Mountain News* notes the following examples of changes in a quotation from Bronco quarterback John Elway:

The *Rocky Mountain News:* "We came out of the gate slow. I said, 'Hey, come on, man, we've got to get going here . . . You're going to be attending my funeral if you don't.' "

The *Denver Post:* "I just said, 'Hey, come on man. We gotta get

Figure 6.1.
Quotations from an expert provide evidence that your story is accurate. This fireman is giving a firsthand account of the rescue efforts following the bombing of a federal office building in Oklahoma City on April 19, 1995.

going here . . . We gotta put some points on the board. You're going to be attending my funeral if you don't.' "

A second *Denver Post* story: "In case you didn't notice it, we really came out of the blocks slow. I just said, 'Hey, come on, let's get going. You're going to attend my funeral if you don't.' "

So, does it matter whether Elway said they were slow coming out of the gate or out of the blocks? Perhaps not. But one thing's for sure, he said one or the other. One is correct, and the other is not.

Your passion for accuracy should compel you to get and record the exact words. Only then can you decide which words to put between quotation marks.

Verification

When someone important says something important, but perhaps false, just putting the material in quotes does not relieve you of the responsibility for the inaccuracies. Citizens, officials and candidates for office often say things that may be partially true or altogether untrue and perhaps even libelous. Quotations, like any other information you gather, need verification.

During the time of Sen. Joseph McCarthy, many newspapers, in the interest of strict objectivity, day after day quoted the Wisconsin senator's charges and countercharges. (It should be pointed out that some publishers did this because they agreed with his stance and because his remarks sold newspapers.) Few papers thought it was their responsibility to quote others who were pointing out the obvious errors and inconsistencies in the demagogue's remarks. Today, however, in the interest of balance, fairness and objectivity, many papers leave out, correct or point out the errors in some quotations. This may be done in the article itself or in an accompanying story.

If candidate Billy Joe Harkness says that his opponent Jimbo McGown is a member of the Ku Klux Klan, you should check before you print the charge. Good reporters don't stop looking and checking just because someone gives them some information. Look for yourself. Prisoners may have an altogether different account of a riot from the one the prison officials give you. Your story will not be complete unless you talk to all sides.

> *"When you see yourself quoted in print and you're sorry you said it, it suddenly becomes a misquotation."*
> —*Dr. Laurence J. Peter,* author of Peter's Quotations *and* The Peter Principle

Problems in Direct Quotations

By now you realize that although you should use direct quotations, they present many challenges and problems. On the following pages you'll find advice about:

- Paraphrasing quotes
- Using partial quotes
- Capturing dialect or accents
- Mix-matching questions and answers
- Correcting quotes
- Removing redundancies
- Deleting obscenity, profanity and vulgarity
- Avoiding made-up quotes
- Subjecting direct quotes to prepublication review

Paraphrasing Quotes

While some quotations need verification, others need clarification. Do not quote someone unless you are sure of what that person means. The reason (or excuse), "But that's what the man said," is not sufficient to use the quote. It is much better to skip a quotation altogether than to confuse the reader.

The best way to avoid confusing and unclear quotes or needlessly long and wordy quotes is to **paraphrase**. It is the meaning of the speaker that you must convey to the reader. As a reporter you must have confidence that at times you are able to convey that meaning in fewer words and in better language than the speaker did. You can save your editors a lot of work if you shorten quotes. Digesting, condensing and clarifying quotes take more effort than simply recording them word for word. You will not impress anyone with long quota-

> *"The surest way to make a monkey of a man is to quote him"*
> —*Robert Benchley,* humorist

tions. On the contrary, you may be guilty of some lazy writing. Here is a quote that could be cut drastically:

> "When I first started singing lessons I assumed I would be a public school teacher and maybe, if I was good enough, a voice teacher," he said. "When I graduated from the university, I still thought I would be a teacher, and I wanted to teach."

A rewrite conveys the meaning more succinctly:

> When he first started singing lessons, and even after he graduated from the university, he wanted to be a public school voice teacher.

Using Partial Quotes

It is also much better to paraphrase or to use full quotes than to use fragmentary or partial quotes. Some editors would have you avoid "orphan quotes" almost altogether. Here is an example of the overuse of partial quotes:

> The mayor said citizens should "turn off" unnecessary lights and "turn down" thermostats "to 65 degrees."

The sentence would be better with no quotation marks at all.

If it is a particular phrase that has special significance or meaning, a partial quote may be justifiable. President Bill Clinton's campaign was famous for the phrase "the economy, stupid." Anyone using that phrase to indicate the focus and strategy of the Clinton campaign certainly would have put quotation marks around it.

Sometimes you may want to put just one word in quotation marks to indicate that this was the precise word the speaker used. *USA Today* reported that Clinton said in his State of the Union address that it was "imperative" that Congress pass health and welfare reform simultaneously. You put a word or a phrase inside quotation marks if it is too strong or unusual to use in a paraphrase.

When you do use partial quotes, do not put quotation marks around something the speaker could not have said. Suppose a speaker told a student audience at a university, "I am pleased and thrilled with your attendance here tonight." It would be incorrect to write:

> The speaker said she was "pleased and thrilled with the students' attendance."

Partial quotes often contain an *ellipsis*—three spaced periods—to tell the reader that some of the words of the quote are missing. For example:

```
"I have come here tonight . . . and I have crossed state lines
. . . to conspire against the government."
```

This practice at times may be justifiable, but you should not keep the reader guessing and wondering what is missing. Sometimes the actual meaning of the speaker can even be distorted by dropping certain words. If a critic writes about a three-act play, "A great hit—except for the first three acts," an ad that picks up only the first part of that quote is guilty of misrepresentation. A journalist using the technique to distort the message is no less guilty.

Capturing Dialect or Accent

Using colorful or colloquial expressions helps the writer capture a person in a particular environment. The same is true when you write the way people talk:

"Are you gonna go?" he asked.
"No, I ain't goin'," she replied.

In everyday speech hardly anyone enunciates perfectly. To do so would sound affected. In fiction, therefore, it is common to use spellings that match speech. But when conversation is written down in newspaper reporting, readers expect correct, full spellings. Not only is correct spelling easier to read, it is also less difficult to write. Capturing dialect is difficult, as these passages from a story about a Hollywood actress illustrate:

"Boy, it's hot out theah," she started, "I could sure use a nice cold beer. How about it, uh? Wanta go get a couple beers?"

It seems strange that if she says, "theah," she wouldn't also say "beeah." Or perhaps she said, "How 'bout it, uh?" And if she said "wanta," maybe she also said "geta."

In another passage, the author has the actress speaking "straight" English:

"Would you believe I used to dress like that all the time? Dates didn't want to be seen with me. I was always being asked to change clothes before going out."

Then later in the story, she reverts to less formal speech:

"I'm tired of pickin' up checks. I've never been ta college, so I'd like to take a coupla classes. I wanta take law so I can find out who's stealing the country. And I wanta take geology. The San Andreas Fault is my hobby, y'know? I think man can beat out nature."

First the actress wanted "a couple beers." Then she wanted to take "a coupla classes." In the same passage she is tired of "pickin' " up checks, but she wants to find out who's "stealing" the country. It is unlikely she is that inconsistent in her speech.

The writer of this story tried to show us something of the character of the actress. If he wanted to convey her speech patterns, he should either have been consistent or simply reported that she talked the same off the set as on it.

Sometimes when a newspaper attempts to quote someone saying something uniquely it betrays a bias. During the 1960 presidential election campaign, some Northern newspapers delighted in quoting Alabama Gov. George Wallace exactly, even trying to reproduce his Southern drawl. But some of these same newspapers did not try to reproduce the Boston accent of John F. Kennedy or of his brothers.

However, you should not make everyone's speech the same. Reporter Barbara King laments "our frequent inability to write other than insipid speech," and "our tendency to homogenize the day-to-day speech patterns of the heterogeneous people we write about." She acknowledges that writers worry about exposing to ridicule the immigrant's halting or perhaps unconventional speech while the broker's speech appears flawless.

But King calls the argument specious. Of course, people should not be exposed to ridicule through their speech. "The point here," she says, "is simply that when the writer's intention in writing dialects, quaint expressions, nonconventional grammar, flowery or showy speech, or the Queen's English is to make a person human, that intention is not only acceptable, it's desirable."

The only way you can make people human is to *listen* to them. King says reporters and writers usually hear but rarely listen. She advises reporters to "listen for expressions, turns of phrase, idiosyncratic talk" and to work it into their stories.

USA Today reporter James Cox did that when he wrote about multimillionaire Rose Blumkin and her Mrs. B's Warehouse in Omaha, Neb. Cox wrote that the 95-year-old proprietor rues the day she hired her grandsons, Ron and Irv Blumkin, to help her manage her furniture business, especially after she began to feel as if they were trying to go over her head.

"They don't have no character. They don't have no feelings," says Mrs. B. in her thick Russian accent. "They told me I am too old, too cranky. . . . They don't know nothing. What I got in my finger they don't got in their whole heads."

Mrs. B. is wonderful with customers but has no use for the hired help. "He's a dummy, my salesman. A stupe."

Says salesman Jerry Pearson, "She's hell on the help but great with customers. She closes like a bear trap."

Reporter Cox was listening that day, and he worked those quotes into his story with great effect.

Mix-Matching Questions and Answers

Writers have other problems with quotes. They often agonize over whether they may use answers from one question to answer another question. Later on in an interview or in a trial, a person may say something that answers better or more fully a question posed earlier.

In the preceding Cox quotations of Mrs. B., notice the ellipsis in the quote about her sons. Mrs. B. probably did not say those words sequentially. The words after the ellipsis may have been said hours after the previous quote.

The only questions you must ask yourself in situations like this are: Am I being fair? Am I distorting the meaning? Am I putting quotes together that change what the speaker intended to say?

Sentences that logically go together, that logically enhance one another, and that are clearly sequential can and often should be placed together.

Correcting Quotes

The quotes from Mrs. B. bring up another and perhaps the most perplexing problem tied to proper handling of direct quotations. The Russian immigrant uses incorrect grammar. When do you, or should you, correct grammatical errors in a direct quotation? Should you expect people in news conferences or during informal interviews to speak perfect English?

Although quotation marks mean you are capturing the exact language of a speaker, it is accepted practice at many newspapers to correct mistakes in grammar and to convey a person's remarks in complete sentences. None of us regularly speaks in perfect, grammatical sentences. But if we were instead writing down our remarks, presumably we would write in grammatically correct English.

Reporters and editors differ widely on when or even whether to do this. A reporter for the *Rocky Mountain News* quoted an attorney as saying, "Her and John gave each other things they needed and couldn't get anyplace else." The reporter said the quote was accurate, but on second thought, said it might have been better to correct the grammar in the written account.

City editor Bob Reuteman of the *Rocky Mountain News* said the paper has no written policy on correcting grammatical errors in direct quotations. Rather, he said, these matters are handled on a case-by-case basis. Columnist and reader-advocate Bob Hosokawa wrote, "Because there are so many variables involved, I suppose that's the logical way to go. In this and in other similar cases, a cosmetic correction or paraphrasing would have been merciful. A bit of accuracy in reporting can be sacrificed in the interest of promoting proper English."

Some would let public figures be embarrassed by quoting them using incorrect grammar. Columnist James Kilpatrick asks, "When we

put a statement (of a public figure) in direct quotation marks, must it be exactly what was said? My own answer is yes. On any issue of critical substance, we ought not to alter a single word."

Yet, in another matter in a different column, Kilpatrick writes, "It is all very well to *tidy up a subject's syntax* (italics added) and to eliminate the ahs, ers and you-knows, but direct quotation marks are a reporter's iron-clad, honor-bound guarantee that something was actually said."

Jean Otto of the *Rocky Mountain News* writes: "A quotation that contains errors of grammar or syntax, particularly if spoken, may be corrected by a reporter or editor without dropping the quotes. Few of us speak in the same impeccable English with which we write. So unless there is a reason to illustrate a person's flawed use of language, most reporters clean up a spoken quote as a simple courtesy."

Otto cites an example of a person "who claims to be highly educated and seeks some kind of public favor." If that person is a "destroyer of language, his or her words may be printed as spoken, usually followed by sic in brackets to note that the peculiarity in the quotation is literally correct." (*Sic*, Latin for "thus," indicates that a statement was originally spoken or written exactly as quoted.)

And if you think there is some agreement on the subject of correcting grammar in direct quotations, read what the *Associated Press Stylebook and Libel Manual* says:

> Never alter quotations even to correct minor grammatical errors or word usage. Casual minor tongue slips may be removed by using ellipses but even that should be done with extreme caution. If there is a question about a quote, either don't use it or ask the speaker to clarify.

Correcting quotations is even more difficult for radio and television reporters. That's why they don't worry about it as much. Writers and editors for print might remember that the quotation they use may have been heard by millions of people on radio or television. Changing the quote even slightly might make viewers and listeners question the credibility of print reports. They might also ask why print writers feel the need to act as press agents who wish to make their subjects look good.

That applies to celebrities of all kinds (actors, sports figures), but it might also apply to registered political candidates and elected officials. At least, some argue, news agencies should have some consistency. If a reporter quotes a farmer using incorrect grammar, then should the same be done for the mayor or for a college professor?

A letter in *The Washington Post* criticized the newspaper for quoting exactly a mother of 14 children who was annoyed at Mayor Marion Barry's advice to stop having babies. The quote read: "And your job is to open up all those houses that's boarded up." The writer then accused the *Post* of regularly stringing together quotes of the president to make him appear articulate. The writer concluded: "I don't care whether the *Post* polishes quotes or not. I simply think that everyone—black or white, rich or poor, president or welfare mother—deserves equal treatment."

That's good advice.

Removing Redundancies

Another question you must deal with as a reporter is whether to remove redundancies and other irrelevant material by using ellipses. Again, there is no agreement in the industry. News editor Allan M. Siegal of *The New York Times* said in an article in the *Washington Journalism Review* that although cleaning up quotes is "a form of lie," omitting words and even sentences from quotes without indicating the omission by an ellipsis is acceptable. Siegal says the *Times* does not use ellipses because they distract the reader and "because typographically they make the paper look like chicken pox." Nor does the *Times* use brackets inside quotation marks.

By contrast, *The Washington Post* uses ellipses and brackets.

For most reporters and editors, the answer to the problem of correcting quotes is to take out the quotation marks and to paraphrase. However, David K. Shipler of *The New York Times* says that when you paraphrase, you lose a lot. The value of the quotes, he says, lies in their richness and uniqueness.

Without question, you should know the policy of your news organization regarding the use of direct quotations. But equally without question, that policy should be that you place inside quotation marks only the exact words of the speaker. Make that your personal policy, and you can't go wrong.

Deleting Obscenity, Profanity and Vulgarity

Many news organizations never allow *some* things people say to be printed or broadcast—even if they are said uniquely. Certain words or phrases are deemed offensive when they are used for emphasis rather than in the context of a serious discussion. **Obscenities** (words usually referring to sexual parts or functions), **profanities** (words referring to the deity or to beings people regard as divine) and **vulgarities** (excretory matters) are usually deleted or bleeped unless they are essential to the story. Even on major newspapers, policy often demands that an obscenity, for example, may be used only with the approval of a top editor.

Of course, there are legitimate reasons to use proper terms for sex-related terms in health stories and in some crime stories, including child molestation stories. Unlike in the past, newspapers now routinely use words such as "intercourse," "oral sex," "orgasm" and "penis." In 1993, when Virginia manicurist Lorena Bobbitt cut off her husband's penis, few newspapers hesitated to tell us exactly what happened.

Obviously, words such as "God" and "Jesus Christ" used in discussions of religion have always been acceptable to most people.

Nevertheless, the rules are different for words when used as what some call "swear" words in direct quotation. Some papers follow the *AP Stylebook* rule that says: "If a full quote that contains profanity, obscenity or vulgarity cannot be dropped but there is no compelling reason for the offensive language, replace letters of an offensive word with a hyphen. The word *damn*, for example, would become *d---* or ----.''

Regarding obscenities, profanities and vulgarities, the *AP Stylebook* says, "Do not use them in stories unless they are part of direct quotations and there is a compelling reason for them." AP style also recommends flagging the story on top with a warning that the story contains language that is offensive to some.

Nevertheless, in recent years the news business has become a little saltier, a little "racier and more streetwise," writes Rita Ciolli of *Newsday*. She quotes Don Fry, of the Poynter Institute in St. Petersburg, Fla.: "There is a lot less priggishness." Fry attributes this change to entertainment programming, especially that of cable TV.

News is more likely to reflect the sensibilities of its audience, David Bartlett, president of the Radio-Television News Directors Association, told Ciolli: "And that audience generally speaking has become more tolerant of language that once would have been considered out of bounds in polite society."

In broadcasting, of course, the FCC can still fine a broadcaster or suspend a license for indecency. Though that's unlikely, audiences are quick to let a station know that it has gone too far. When National Public Radio allowed the use of the four-letter "f-word" 10 times in its "All Things Considered" report on criminal John Gotti, complaints were so numerous and vocal that NPR adopted stricter guidelines. Now there are more bleeps and more warnings of bad language to come.

Yet, Bartlett says, "Words that entered the language as genuine industrial-strength swearwords are part of fairly normal parlance and tend to show up in print and television news programs. 'Pissed-off' used to be a lot heavier and a lot dirtier than it is today."

Ciolli quotes her editor at *Newsday*, Anthony Marro: "We try not to be casual or gratuitous in the use of vulgarities. Sometimes, in context, to show the extent of anger, terror, frustration or reflect the bitterness of a debate we will use it."

That sounds like a policy you can live with.

Avoiding Made-up Quotes

Fabricating a direct quote, even from general things that a source has said or from what the source might say if given the chance, is never a good idea. Even seasoned reporters are sometimes tempted to put quotation marks around words that their sources "meant to say," or to clarify or simplify a quote. The journalist reasons that it's more important to have a clear and concise quote for the reader than to be a slave to the verbose and unclear words of the source. Bad reasoning. Better to paraphrase.

A much worse idea is fabricating a quote that makes a source look bad or is defamatory or perhaps even libelous. That's what free-lancer Janet Malcolm was sued for doing to Dr. Jeffrey M. Masson, a renowned psychiatrist, in an article in *The New Yorker* in December 1983 (see pages 111-112).

In his dissenting opinion in Masson vs. *The New Yorker* Magazine in 1989, Judge Alex Kozinski of the 9th U.S. Circuit Court of Appeals acknowledged that the courts have a grave responsibility under the First Amendment to safeguard freedom of the press, but the right to alter quotations deliberately is not included in that right. "To invoke the right to deliberately distort what someone else has said in print is to assert the right to lie in public."

In 1991, in Masson vs. *The New Yorker* Magazine the Supreme Court rejected the lower court's "rational interpretation" standard for placing statements in quotation marks but ruled that suits can proceed to trial only if the altered quote "results in a material change in the meaning conveyed by the statement."

Had the court decided otherwise, said William Woo, editor of the *St. Louis Post-Dispatch*, "that any innocent digression was potentially actionable, the use of direct quotes would largely disappear from American journalism, thus detracting significantly from the richness of description and portrayal of events."

Woo and other professionals doubted the decision would have any significant effect on journalists or journalism. Said Woo, "Reporters are expected to be scrupulous in the use of quotations and to use paraphrases when full and accurate quotations cannot be obtained."

The message is clear. Making up quotes may not be libelous, but it is unacceptable journalism.

Practicing Prepublication Review

A decade ago, you would not have had a city editor tell you to check the accuracy of your direct quotations with your source. Today, though, it is standard practice on many newspapers. Steve Weinberg, a Missouri School of Journalism professor and former head of the Investigative Reporters and Editors, calls it PPR, prepublication review, and he says, "I have practiced PPR as a newspaper staff writer, a magazine free-lancer and a book author. Never have I regretted my practice. What I do regret is failing to do it during the first decade of my career because of mindless adherence to tradition."

Weinberg states candidly that it is not sensitivity to the feelings of his sources that is his primary motivator. Rather, he insists that PPR loosens the tongues of tight-lipped sources and gets them on the record for making their statements. PPR extends also to checking the facts. Professionals insist PPR does not compromise their stand or make them surrender control over their stories.

Journalist Phillip Weiss offers another reason why more journalists are practicing prepublication review. "The press's quiet acceptance of quote approval surely owes something to the fact that reporters are an influential elite and are themselves often the subjects of interviews," he writes. "They have had a taste of their own medicine and they don't like it."

Another reason for PPR is that it serves as a defense against libel. Jurors are less likely to find "reckless disregard for the truth" in an article that has been reviewed by the source.

You need to know the policy of your news organization, and someday, you may want to help develop a policy that not just allows but demands prepublication review.

Attributing Direct and Indirect Quotes

Now that you've learned some of the complexities of using direct quotations, let's take a look at when and how to attribute them to a source.

When to Attribute

You should almost always attribute direct quotes, with some exceptions. When the *Rocky Mountain News* attributed a quote from a 7-year-old who witnessed a gang shooting, reader advocate Bill Hosokawa took the paper to task. He did the same when the paper attributed a quote to a store clerk in which she said she saw a homicide suspect with the victim.

You should also have a good reason to allow a paragraph of direct quotations to stand without an attribution. Nevertheless, if you are quoting from a speech, an interview or a press conference and no one else is mentioned in the story, it may be excessive to put an attribution in every paragraph.

Ordinarily you should attribute indirect quotes. That is, you should usually have a source for the information you write, and when you do, attribute it to that source. The source can be a person or a written document.

However, there are exceptions. You do not have to attribute information to a source if one or more of the following is true:

- The information is a matter of public record.
- It is generally known.
- It is available from several sources.

"We, as journalists, know far more about the effect of the printed word than any citizen off the street who talks to us for a story, and that knowledge carries a responsibility with it. If someone is likely to get his head blown off because we run his name, we shouldn't run it without good reason."
— Bob Reuteman,
City Editor,
Rocky Mountain News,
quoted by Bill Hosokawa

- You are a witness.
- It is easily verifiable.
- It makes no assumptions.
- It contains no opinions.
- It is noncontroversial.

If you are a witness to damages or injuries, do not name yourself as a source in the story. Attribute this information to the police or to other authorities. But if you are on the scene of an accident and can see that three people were involved, you do not have to write: " 'Three people were involved in the accident,' Officer Osbord said." If you are unsure of the information or if there are conclusions or generalities involved, your editor probably will want you to attribute the information to an official or witness. Avoid, however, attributing factual statements to "officials" or "authorities" or "sources." "Such constructions," writes journalist Jack Hart, "suggest that we are controlled by form and that we have forgotten about function."

Hart makes a plea for common sense regarding attributions. "Let's save them for direct quotations or paraphrased quotes laced with opinion," he writes. "Or for assertions likely to be especially sensitive. Or controversial." He says we should attribute only "if it matters."

This is good advice for the veteran. Nevertheless, though it is possible to attribute too often and though you do not always need to attribute, when you have doubts, go with the attribution.

That goes for attributing anonymous sources, too. Even though you should seldom use them (see pages 139-143), you must attribute them. Try to preserve your credibility by giving as much information as you can about the sources without revealing their names. For example, you may report "a source close to the chancellor said." For the second reference to the same source, use "the anonymous source said." Sometimes, as in stories about crime victims, you may have to change someone's name and follow it with "not her real name" in parentheses.

How to Attribute

In composition and creative writing classes, you may have been told to avoid repeating the same word. You probably picked up your thesaurus to look for a synonym for the word "say," a colorless word. Without much research you may have found 100 or more substitutes. None of them is wrong. Indeed, writers may search long for the exact word they need to convey a particular nuance of meaning. For example:

A presidential candidate *announces* the choice of a running mate.
An arrested man *divulges* the names of his accomplices.
A judge *pronounces* sentence.

At other times, in the interest of precise and lively writing, you may write:

> "I'll get you for that," she *whispered*.
> "I object," he *shouted*.

Nevertheless, reporters and editors prefer forms of the verb "to say" in most instances, even if they are repeated throughout a story. And there are good reasons for doing so. "Said" is unobtrusive. Rather than appearing tiresome and repetitious, it hides in the news columns and calls no attention to itself. "Said" is also neutral. It has no connotations. To use the word "said" is to be objective.

Some of the synonyms for "said" sound innocent enough—but be careful. If you report a city official "claimed" or "maintained" or "contended," you are implying that you do not quite believe what the official said. The word "said" is the solution to your problem. If you have evidence that what the official is saying is incorrect, you should include the correct information or evidence in your story.

In some newspaper accounts of labor negotiations, company officials always "ask," while labor leaders always "demand." "Demanding" something sounds harsh and unreasonable, whereas "asking" for something is calm and reasonable. A reporter who uses these words in this context is taking an editorial stand—consciously or unconsciously.

Other words you may be tempted to use as a substitute for "say" are simply unacceptable because they represent improper usage. For example:

> "You don't really mean that," he *winked*.
>
> "Of course I do," she *grinned*.
>
> "But what if someone heard you say that?" he *frowned*.
>
> "Oh, you are a fool," she *laughed*.

You cannot "wink" a word. It is difficult, if not impossible, to "grin," "frown" or "laugh" words. But you may want to say this:

> "Not again," he *said, moaning*.
>
> "I'm afraid so," she *said with a grin*.

This usage is correct, but often it is not necessary or even helpful to add words like "moaning" or phrases like "with a grin." Sometimes, though, such words and phrases are needed to convey the meaning of the speaker.

Learning the correct words for attribution is the first step. Here are some other guidelines you should follow when attributing information:

- *If a direct quote is more than one sentence long, place the attribution at the end of the first sentence.* For example:

```
"The car overturned at least three times," the police officer
said. "None of the four passengers was hurt. Luckily, the car
did not explode into flames."
```

That one attribution is adequate. It would be redundant to write:

```
"The car overturned at least three times," the police officer
said. "None of the four passengers was hurt," he added.
"Luckily, the car did not explode into flames," he continued.
```

Nor should you write:

```
"The car overturned at least three times. None of the four
passengers was hurt. Luckily, the car did not explode into
flames," the police officer said.
```

Although you should not keep the reader wondering who is being quoted, in most cases you should avoid placing the attribution at the beginning of a quote. Do not write:

```
The police officer said: "The car overturned at least three
times. None of the four passengers was hurt. Luckily, the car
did not explode into flames."
```

However, if direct quotes from two different speakers follow one another, you should start the second with the attribution to avoid confusion:

```
    "The driver must have not seen the curve," an eyewitness
said. "Once the car left the road, all I saw was a cloud of
dust."
    The police officer said: "The car overturned at least three
times. None of the four passengers was hurt. Luckily, the car
did not explode into flames."
```

Notice that when an attribution precedes a direct quotation that is more than one sentence long, wire-service style requires that a colon follow the attribution.

▮ *Do not follow a fragment of a quote with a continuing complete sentence of quotation.* Avoid constructions like this one:

```
The mayor said the time had come "to turn off some lights. We
all must do something to conserve electricity."
```

The correct form is to separate partial quotes and complete quotes:

```
The time has come "to turn off some lights," the mayor said.
"We all must do something to conserve electricity."
```

He said, she said: Punctuating direct quotations

"Always put the comma inside quotation marks," she said.

Then she added, "The same goes for the period."

"Does the same rule apply for the question mark?" he asked.

"Only if the entire statement is a question," she replied, "and never add a comma after a question mark. Also, be sure to lowercase the first word of a continuing quote that follows an attribution and a comma.

"However, you must capitalize the first word of a new sentence after an attribution," she continued. "Do not forget to open and close the sentence with quotation marks."

"Why are there no quotation marks after the word 'comma' at the end of the fourth paragraph?" he asked.

"Because the same person is speaking at the beginning of the next paragraph," she said. "Notice that the new paragraph does open with quotation marks. Note, too, that a quote inside of a quotation needs a single quotation mark, as around the word 'comma' above."

■ *The first time you attribute a direct or indirect quote, identify the speaker fully.* How fully depends on how well the speaker is known to the readers. In Springfield, Ill., it is sufficient to identify the mayor simply as Mayor Ossie Langfelder. But if a story in the *Chicago Tribune* referred to the mayor of Springfield, the first reference would have to be "Ossie Langfelder, mayor of Springfield"—unless, of course, the dateline for the story was Springfield.

■ *Do not attribute direct quotes to more than one person, as in the following:*

"Flames were shooting out everywhere," witnesses said. "Then electrical wires began falling, and voices were heard screaming."

All you have to do is eliminate the quotation marks, if indeed any witness made the statements.

Whatever you do, do not make up a source. Never attribute a statement to "a witness" unless your source is indeed that witness. At times you may ask a witness to confirm what you have seen, but never invent quotes for anonymous witnesses. Inventing witnesses and making up quotes is dishonest, inaccurate and inexcusable.

■ *In stories covering past news events, use the past tense in attributions, and use it throughout the story.* However, stories that do not report on news events, such as features, may be more effective if the attributions are consistently given in the present tense. In a feature story such as a personality profile, when it is safe to assume that what the person once said, he or she would still say, you may use the present tense. For example, when you write, " 'I like being mayor,' she says," you are indicating that she still enjoys it.

■ *Ordinarily, place the noun or pronoun before the verb in attributions:*

"Everything is under control," the sheriff said.

If you must identify a person by including a long title, it is better to begin the attribution with the verb:

"I enjoy the challenge," says Jack Berry, associate dean for graduate studies and research.

Handling On- and Off-the-Record Information

Until you are a source in a story involving controversy, you may not understand why people sometimes don't want to talk to reporters at all or why they don't want their names in the paper. Your job would be easy if all of your sources wished to be "on the record."

Using a Source Who Does Not Wish to Be Named

Sometimes a speaker or source may not want to be quoted at all—directly or indirectly. Reporter Diana Dawson tells this story of her experience while working in Memphis:

> I had been investigating the Memphis, Tenn., mental health system for about a month with Mike Mansur, *Press-Scimitar* medical writer, when we stumbled upon two doctors who were fed up with the system. Both worked with the state hospital in Bolivar, Tenn., on a consultant basis. And both were appalled by what they'd observed.
>
> "You can't use our names or identify us in any way whatsoever," said one of the doctors. "We have to maintain a working relationship with the staff there. It's important for the patients that we are able to go in, work with the docs and catch some of the things that are going wrong."
>
> The consultants told stories of a state hospital that served all of western Tennessee but had no certified psychiatrists. Some doctors had been treated for drug and alcohol problems. The one considered the most skilled had killed himself. There were extremely few doctors for the number of patients.
>
> With that, we checked the state hospital personnel files and found that there were, indeed, no certified psychiatrists. We sat down with the medical chief and a staffing chart to determine the staff-patient ratios. We picked up a copy of the psychiatrist's autopsy report.
>
> As our investigation continued, one of the sources led us to the records we needed to prove that the patients who were taken to the city hospital emergency room with mental problems were often released within a matter of hours. They were released even if they had proven themselves dangerous to the public.
>
> The seven-part series that resulted won Tennessee's UPI grand prize for public service.

And well it should have. Here's how the first of that series began:

> Human warehousing—the stashing away of society's insane stepchildren — theoretically ended in 1977.
>
> But today, mental health professionals—including the superintendent of the Gothic asylum called Western Mental Health Institute in Bolivar—say the state psychiatric hospital's level of staffing remains suited only to human storage.
>
> "This place is staffed for custodial care," said Dr. William Jennings, superintendent of Western.
>
> Half the clinical staff consists of psychiatric technicians who have a high school education or less. As darkness falls on Bolivar, the technicians often become responsible for entire wards.
>
> Western's more than 500 patients are seen by a staff of only six licensed physicians, which includes the superintendent and one doctor who has been on sick leave for more than two months.
>
> The six physicians, each responsible for care of between 25 and 93 patients, work as many as 96 hours a week. The licensed doctors also are responsible for every move made by the eight unlicensed doctors, who have medical degrees but have not passed their state board examinations.

That is the kind of reporting that often results from talking to sources who refuse to be named. You must learn to use sound profes-

"I think there are more anonymous sources per capita in Washington than there are anywhere else in the world. Nobody has a name in Washington."

—Joann Byrd,
**Washington Post
ombudsman and
former editor of
the Everett
(Wash.) Herald,
quoted in the
American Journalism
Review**

sional judgment in handling them. If you agree to accept their information, you must honor their requests to remain off the record. Breaching that confidence destroys trust and credibility. But it is your obligation to take that information elsewhere to confirm it and get it on the record.

Guidelines for Citing Sources

Bob Woodward and Carl Bernstein, who as *Washington Post* reporters helped uncover the Watergate scandal that eventually led to the resignation of President Richard M. Nixon, were criticized for citing "high-level sources" without identifying them. Even though Woodward and Bernstein say they did not use this technique unless two independent sources had given them the same information, anonymous sources should be used rarely.

Three reasons for avoiding anonymous sources:

1. You damage your credibility.

2. Your source may be lying or floating a trial balloon.

3. You may be sued if you then name your source.

Not naming sources is dangerous for three important reasons. First, such information lacks credibility and makes the reporter and the newspaper suspect. Second, the source may be lying. He or she may be out to discredit someone or may be floating a trial balloon to test public reaction on some issue or event. Skilled diplomats and politicians know how to use reporters to take the temperature of public opinion. If the public reacts negatively, the sources will not proceed with whatever plans they leaked to the press. In such cases the press has been used—and it has become less credible.

The third reason that not naming sources is dangerous is that once you have promised anonymity to a source, you may not change your mind without risking a breach of contract suit. In 1991 the Supreme Court ruled 5-4 in Cohen vs. Cowles Media Co. that the First Amendment does not prevent news sources from suing the press for breach of contract when the press makes confidential sources public.

That's why papers such as the *Miami Herald* have a policy that only a senior editor has authority to commit the paper to a pledge of confidentiality.

Some reporters make these distinctions regarding sources and attribution:

Off the record: You may not use the information.

Not for attribution: You may use the information but may not attribute it.

Background: You may use it with a general title for a source (for example, "a White House aide said").

Deep background: You may use the information, but you may not indicate any source.

By no means is there agreement on these terms. For most people "off the record" means not for attribution. For columnist Richard Reeves, it means that you cannot use the information in any way. For James Kilpatrick, "off the record" is not for quotation, and not for attribution means the same thing. Kilpatrick also thinks there is no difference between background and deep background. Seymour Hersh, author and former reporter for *The New York Times*, says the terms are different for everyone.

Miles Beller, a reporter for the *Los Angeles Herald-Examiner*, agrees. Writing in *Editor & Publisher*, Beller says:

> Universally misunderstood and misread by journalists of every stripe, "off the record" suffers from more crude interpretations than does John Cleland's "Fanny Hill." For some reporters, [it means] "don't quote me." Others take it to mean "use the information but peg it to a 'high ranking official,' 'a government spokesman,' 'a well-placed Western diplomat' or any other such 'fill-in-the-blank sources.'" Still others believe that the phrase has lost even the slightest vestige of meaning and should be taken as seriously as Have-a-Nice-Day slogans emblazoned on T-shirts.

> *"On one of Kissinger's (then Secretary of State Henry Kissinger) sojourns, humorist Art Buchwald attributed information to a 'high U.S. official with wavy hair, horn-rimmed glasses and a German accent.'"*
> —*Alicia C. Shepard,* American Journalism Review

Because there is little agreement among journalists, sources may be equally vague about the terms. Your obligation is to make sure you and your sources understand each other. Set the ground rules ahead of time. Clarify your terms.

Also be sure you know the policy of your paper in these matters. For example, many newspapers do not allow reporters to use unidentified sources unless an editor knows the source and approves the usage. Other news organizations such as the Associated Press will not carry opinions, whether positive or negative, that are expressed by an unidentified source. The news agency will cite statements of fact without attribution, but only if the story makes it clear that the person providing this material would do so only on the condition of anonymity. *The New York Times* has a policy of not allowing direct quotations of pejorative remarks by an unidentified source.

Again, know the policy of your paper.

In addition, you should be careful not to allow a speaker suddenly to claim something is off the record. Mike Feinsilber of the Associated Press tells this story about David Gergen, at the time director of communications for President Ronald Reagan (and later for President Bill Clinton). One day Gergen "forgot the ground rules."

> Tradition in Washington, and elsewhere, is that a public official cannot go off the record after he has said his piece. And that's the rule that Gergen forgot.
>
> One day last week, he was addressing 150 advertising executives attending the annual conference of the American Association of Advertising Agencies. It was late in the afternoon; the scene was a meeting room in a Washington hotel.
>
> In his half-hour speech, Gergen spoke with somewhat more candor

than administration officials—especially those who brief reporters regularly—usually display.

Then during a question-and-answer session, one of the advertising executives asked about the administration's efforts to reverse antinuclear sentiment among college students in Europe. He started to answer, then interrupted himself.

"This is all off the record, isn't it?" he asked.

From the back of the room, I shouted, "No."

"Who are you with?"

"The Associated Press."

"Well, can we put this on background (not for attribution)?"

"Nope."

Gergen wound up his remarks quickly. . . .

The AP was the only news organization there. And it was on the record.

Nevertheless, if a city manager or police chief wishes to have a background session with you, unless it is against newspaper policy, you should not refuse. Often these officials are trying to be as open as they can under certain circumstances. Without such background sessions the task of reporting complex issues intelligently is nearly impossible. But you must be aware that you are hearing only one point of view and that the information may be self-serving.

Miles Beller gives this example:

Several years ago a woman phoned this reporter and "wanted to go off the record" in regard to a Los Angeles official's "secret ownership of a Las Vegas radio station" and other questionable holdings tied to this public servant. Funny thing though, the caller plumb forgot to mention that she was working for another candidate. This bit of minutia probably just slipped her mind, what with her man trailing so badly and the election a few weeks away.

Some sources make a habit of saying everything is off the record and of giving commonplace information in background sessions. Although you should not quote a source who asks to remain off the record, you may use information if one or more of the following is true:

- The information is a matter of public record.
- It is generally known.
- It is available from several sources.
- You are a witness.

So as not to lose credibility with your source, it's a good idea to make it clear that you plan to use the information because of one or more of the preceding reasons.

Knowing when and how to attribute background information is an art you will have to give continuing, special care and attention to as a reporter. Remember these two important points:

1. When possible, set the ground rules with your sources ahead of time.
2. Know your newspaper's policy in these matters.

Suggested Readings

Beller, Miles. "For and Off the Record." *Editor & Publisher*, Jan. 2, 1982, p. 56. Argues cogently against overuse of off-the-record information.

Callihan, E.L. *Grammar for Journalists*. Revised Edition. Radnor, Pa.: Chilton Book Company, 1979. Contains a good section on how to punctuate, attribute and handle quotations.

Davenport, Lucinda D. "News Story Quotes: Verbatim?" Paper delivered at the annual convention of the Mass Communication and Society Division, Association for Education in Journalism and Mass Communication, Norman, Okla., 1986. Discusses what students are taught from leading journalism texts about quoting verbatim.

Gibson, Martin L. "Red. Attribution Sometimes Best Left Out." *Missouri Press News*, January 1989, p. 18. Argues against attributing innocuous information.

Hale, F. Dennis. "Support Drops for Media and Free Expression." *Editor & Publisher*, Sept. 21, 1991, p. 60. Discusses the Masson and Cohen cases and others.

Hart, Jack. "Giving Credit when Credit Isn't Due." *Editor & Publisher*, Sept. 11, 1993, p. 2. Warns against useless attribution.

King, Barbara. "There's Real Power in Common Speech." *Ottaway News Extra*, No. 137, Winter 1989, pp. 8, 16. An excellent discussion of using real quotes from real people.

Leslie, Jacques. "The Anonymous Source, Second Thoughts on 'Deep Throat.'" *Washington Journalism Review*, September 1986, pp. 33-35. A superb treatment of a complicated problem.

Leslie, Jacques. "The Pros and Cons of Cleaning Up Quotes." *Washington Journalism Review*, May 1986, pp. 44-46. Shows that there are no easy answers and no agreement on how to handle direct quotations.

Stein, M.L. "9th Circuit: It's OK to Make Up Quotes." *Editor & Publisher*, Aug. 12, 1989, pp. 16, 30. Reactions from the press and lawyers to the court decision allowing quotes that are not verbatim.

Weinberg, Steve. "Thou Shalt Not Concoct Thy Quote." *Fineline*, July/August 1991, pp. 3-4. Presents reasons for allowing sources to review quotations before publication.

Weiss, Philip. "Who Gets Quote Approval?" *Columbia Journalism Review*, May/June 1991, pp. 52-54. Discusses the growing practice of allowing sources to check quotations before publication.

Exercises

1. Rewrite the following story, paying special attention to the use of quotations and attribution. Note the sensitive nature of some of the quotations. Paraphrase when necessary.

   Christopher O'Reilly is a remarkably happy young man, despite a bout with meningitis eight years ago that has left him paralyzed and brain-damaged.

   "I am happy," O'Reilly commented, as he puffed a cigarette.

   He has much to be happy about. Physical therapy has hastened his recovery since the day he awoke from a 10-week-long coma. He has lived to celebrate his 26th birthday.

   "I had a helluva birthday," he said, "I seen several friends. I had big cake," he added slowly.

   He lives in a house with his mother and stepfather in the rolling, green countryside near Springfield.

   O'Reilly's withered legs are curled beneath him now, and his right arm is mostly paralyzed, but he can do pull-ups with his left arm. He can see and hear.

   "When he came back, he wasn't worth a damn," his mother said. "The hack doctors told me he would be a vegetable all his life," she claimed.

   "He couldn't talk; he could only blink. And he drooled a lot," she smiled.

   Now, Chris is able to respond in incomplete sentences to questions and can carry on slow communication. "He don't talk good, but he talks," his mother commented.

   It all began when he stole a neighbor's Rototiller. His probation was revoked, and he found himself in the medium-security prison in Springfield. Then came "inadequate medical treatment" in the prison system. O'Reilly's family argued that he received punishment beyond what the Eighth Amendment of the U.S. Constitution calls "cruel and unusual."

"Those prison officials were vicious," they said.

As a result, he was awarded $250,000 from the state, the largest legal settlement in federal court in 10 years. "That sounds like a lot of money. But it really isn't, you know, when you consider what happened and when you consider the worth of a human life, and the way they treated him and all, we thought we should get at least a million," his mother remarked.

O'Reilly contracted the infection of the brain after sleeping "on the concrete floor" of a confinement cell, his mother maintained. He had been placed in solitary confinement because he would not clean his cell. The disease went undiagnosed for eight days, leaving him paralyzed and brain-damaged, she said.

Now O'Reilly likes watching television. "I like TV," he grinned. "And smoking."

His mother said she "never gives up hope" that "one day" her son will "come out of it."

2. Here is part of a speech by Professor Richard L. Weaver II of the Department of Interpersonal and Public Communication at Bowling Green State University. It was delivered at the International Student Leadership Conference, Bowling Green, Ohio. Assume the speech was given at your university and that you are writing for your school paper. Indicate the direct quotations you would use and why you would use them.

So I want to take a few moments this afternoon and look at this twofold problem that leaders face—building the proper foundation (your credibility) and motivating others. And did you know that the two are closely related? Your ability to motivate others is, according to the research, dependent *mostly* upon your credibility.

Let's just look briefly at what goes into credibility. Credibility is really the attitude others hold toward you at any given time. Sure, it has to do with the house *you* build, but as a leader you must realize that much more important than the house itself is the view that others have of the house that you build. Want to motivate others? Get your house in order first.

This might be a good self-test. Let me give you the top five components of credibility. You are all past, present, and/or future leaders. How do *you* measure up?

According to the research in the speech-communication discipline, the most important and first component of credibility is good, old-fashioned, *sociability*. Are you the kind of person others think of as friendly, cheerful,

good natured, warm, and pleasant? If not, why not? I've always thought that a sociable outlook had to do with the way one comes at life. Are you generally an optimist rather than a pessimist? Now, I know that most of you are optimists, but did you know that recent studies showed that those who look on the bright side tend to do better on achievement tests, have more job success, live longer, and have better health? The attitude of helplessness, typical of pessimists, is associated with the weakening of the immune system's resistance to tumors and infection. Pessimists, according to these studies, tend to neglect themselves and tend to smoke and drink more than optimists. You see, there are actually substantial benefits for:

Expecting things, in general, to work out well for you.

Expecting your best effort to be successful.

And, when looking at new situations, seeing potentials rather than roadblocks.

Beliefs in limits create limited people. Being sociable comes from an outlook on life. And such an outlook is contagious! Other people perceive it, and, what's more, they notice it quickly! If they like the outlook, they *do* respond!

The second characteristic of credibility is *competence*. There is no substitute for knowledge. You have to come off as knowing what you are doing. I'm not saying that you have to be the most intelligent, well-trained, informed, expert in your area. But I want you to know right up front, others appreciate those who have done their homework, who know what they are talking about, and who seem to have a grip on what needs to be known. You have to understand that good leaders don't waste other people's time!

The third characteristic of credibility is *extroversion*. Now, this does not mean that all leaders are bold and verbal, talkative and assertive, or animated and dynamic. But I will tell you this: it sure helps! Extroversion often comes across as enthusiasm. Knowledge is power, but enthusiasm pulls the switch! Think of the *extroverted* teachers you have had, and you often think of the *enthusiastic* teachers you have had. Why? Because the traits are similar. When a teacher says to you, "Fabulous job," or "I love it," these are bold, verbal qualities of extroversion. When teachers are highly nonverbal, using gestures, touch, and movement in front of the classroom, these are the animated and dynamic characteristics of both enthusiasm and extroversion. Just remember, the level of excitement in an organization often rises to the level of enthusiasm of the leader.

The fourth characteristic of credibility is *composure*. Credible people are often perceived as poised, in control, and self-confident. This quality helps keep the extroversion in perspective because a leader who is self-assured without being bombastic or overbearing instills confidence in others. Are you cool under pressure? Can you retain composure when you are threatened or when your leadership ability is under attack? Composure means being able to remain relaxed, calm, and cool in trying circumstances.

The fifth characteristic of credibility is *character*. Are you someone others view as virtuous (courageous), honest, unselfish, sympathetic, and trustworthy? In my experience, I have always related character with commitment and commitment with passion. How much do *you* care? There is no great success without great commitment. There is character in commitment. You look at successful people in *any* field, and you'll find they're not necessarily the best and the brightest or the fastest and strongest—they are, instead, the ones with the most commitment. Have you ever heard the acronym *WIT*?— Whatever It Takes! Successful people are willing to do whatever it takes to succeed. Are you one who sees difficulties in every opportunity or opportunities in every difficulty?

3. Attend a meeting, a press conference or a speech and tape-record it. While there, write down the quotes you would use if you were writing the story for your local newspaper. Then listen to the tape and check the accuracy of the quotations.

4. Interview at least two reporters, asking them about their policies on handling sources regarding the following:
   a. Off the record
   b. Not for attribution
   c. Background
   d. Deep background
   Write an essay of at least 200 words on the subject.

5. Check a library's computer database for sources of articles about journalists' use of anonymous sources. Read at least four articles and write a 200-word report on your findings.

6. Engage a classmate in a half-hour interview about his or her life. In your story, use as many direct quotes as you think are fitting. Then check the accuracy of your quotations with your classmate.

SOURCES AND SEARCHES

*In this chapter
you will learn:*

1. *The main sources of
   information available on
   computer.*
2. *How computers assist
   with data analysis.*
3. *The importance of more
   traditional sources of
   information.*

*W*hen Elliot Grossman of the Allentown (Pa.) Morning Call tried to document abuses of parking privileges by local police officers, he sifted through thousands of paper records to prepare his story. Grossman discovered that over the years a scam had allowed hundreds of police officers to park their private cars almost anywhere simply by signing the backs of the tickets and sending them to the Allentown Parking Authority. Any excuse, it seemed, would suffice for one of Allentown's finest.

Some data on parking tickets was available on computer, but the Parking Authority refused to release the computer tapes necessary for a quick analysis. So Grossman, with the help of a news clerk and reporting interns, decided to do it the hard way. He set out to build his own database to document the extent of the problem.

For two weeks, Grossman and his helpers sat at laptop computers in the offices of the Parking Authority and entered data on the type of violation, location of the vehicle, date and time of violation and license plate number. In many cases, other notations were made on the officer's badge number or the reason the officer was parked at the location. The result was a body of information that allowed Grossman to confirm his suspicions that many of the tickets were dismissed without good reason.

What had begun as a rule allowing the cancellation of tickets for officers on official business had grown into a local scandal, and Grossman was able to expose it.

Grossman's experience is one example of many that show how the best reporters in our business have embraced the considerable capability of personal computer technology. Once the domain of investigative reporters, computer skills are now vital in all areas of the news business. Today, no reporter who hopes to succeed in the profession can afford to be without skills in searching internal and external computer databases and building his or her own databases and spreadsheets. These skills, in addition to more traditional library search skills, are among the essential tools of today's working journalist. Like the carpenter who must know how to use a hammer and saw, the journalist must know how to use words and computers.

Fine-tuning computer skills is the topic of entire books and college courses. In this chapter, however, you will be introduced to the most common computer-assisted techniques employed by reporters and editors.

Using Computers

Reporters and editors of today have a wealth of information available at their fingertips. To access it, they merely have to become comfortable with using computers. In addition to making raw data available, computers help reporters organize and analyze information.

Sources of Computer Information

From the news library in your local office to national databases of published newspaper, magazine and broadcast stories, the amount of on-line information is staggering.

Primary sources of computerized information include:

- The news library maintained by your own publication or broadcast station (often called the **morgue**).
- The public information utilities (CompuServe, America Online, Prodigy, Delphi and others).
- The Internet, an international communications network that is an incredible, if difficult to navigate, source of information.
- The commercial database services (Dialog, Lexis/Nexis, VuText and others).
- Government databases (city, county, state and federal).
- Special-interest-group databases (those created by organizations with a cause).
- CD-ROMs.
- Self-constructed databases (such as the one created by Elliot Grossman) and spreadsheets.

Let's explore the usefulness of each in more detail.

Primary sources of computerized information

- *The morgue.*
- *The public information utilities.*
- *The Internet.*
- *The commercial database services.*
- *Government databases.*
- *Special-interest-group databases.*
- *CD-ROMs.*
- *Self-constructed databases.*

Your News Library: The Place to Start

Computer databases are a 20th-century marvel that good reporters and editors have learned to cherish. Before they were available, doing research for a story was a laborious process that involved a trip to the newspaper, magazine or broadcast station library to sift through hundreds or even thousands of tattered, yellowed clippings. Too often, clippings disappeared, were misfiled or were misplaced, making such research a hit-and-miss proposition. Despite those shortcomings, the library was considered a valuable asset. Reporters were routinely admonished, "When you are assigned to a story, first check the morgue to see what's already been written about the subject."

You will still hear that advice in news rooms today, but most of today's news libraries are computerized, which virtually ensures that an item will not disappear and will be easier to locate. Typically, you can do a check of the computerized library from your own computer, which makes it easier than ever to do good background work on a story. Your ability to search the library is limited only by your skill with search techniques.

News libraries are what computer experts call *full-text databases*, which means that all words in the database have been indexed and are searchable. Such capability gives you incredible flexibility in structuring searches using what is known as *Boolean search commands*. Boolean operators such as AND, OR and NOT allow you to structure the search to find material most closely related to the subject being researched. For example, if you are interested in finding articles on

South African President Nelson Mandela's visits to the United States, you might issue this command on the search line:

```
Mandela AND United ADJ States
```

The computer would then search for all articles containing the word "Mandela" that also contained the words "United" and "States" adjacent to each other. In this case, AND and ADJ (for adjacent) are the Boolean operators used. Such a search would produce all articles on Mandela and the United States, but would exclude any articles involving Mandela and the United Arab Emirates, despite the presence of the word "United." (It's not adjacent to the word "States.")

The result of such a search in most cases would be a report from the computer telling you how many articles match your search criteria:

```
Search found 27 articles. Would you like to see them or
further narrow your search?
```

At this point, you would have the option of further limiting the search (by date, for example) or reading all 27 articles.

It is important to remember that computers aren't really very smart. In our sample search, an article on Mandela's visit to Miami that did not contain the words "United States" would not have been found. Therefore, it is important to understand the limitations as well as the power of computer-assisted database searching. Good reporters quickly learn to take into account such possibilities and learn to recast their searches in other ways.

There are other limitations. Most library databases do not allow you to see photos, nor can you see articles as they appeared in the newspaper or magazine. Nor do most current systems permit you to hear how a broadcast story was used on the air. Instead, you have access only to a text-based version of what appeared. That limits your ability to learn how the story was displayed in the newspaper or magazine or read on the air.

Some newer library computer systems overcome these disadvantages by allowing you to call graphical reproductions of the printed page to the screen. You can view photographs, charts and maps in the same way. In broadcast applications, more and more libraries permit storage of digital video and sound clips. As such systems proliferate, the shortcomings of present computer libraries will disappear. Despite current limitations, few veteran reporters would be willing to return to the days of tattered yellow clippings. They know that computerization has made the library a more reliable source of background information.

Thus, the best reporters of today do what good reporters have always done: Check the morgue first. They simply do it with computers.

```
1/9/68      (Item 13 from file: 484)
DIALOG(R)File 484:Newspaper & Periodical Abstr.
(c) 1995 UMI. All rts. reserv.

05401961                    95501384
Hugh and Dee Dee
Overholser, Geneva
Washington Post (WP) Sec C, p 6, col 5  Jul 2, 1995  ISSN: 0190-8286
ARTICLE TYPE:    Commentary
ARTICLE LENGTH:  Medium  (6-18 col inches)
AVAILABILITY:    UMIACH  CATALOG NO.:  60208.00

    Geneva  Overholser  comments  on scandals involving actor Hugh Grant and
former  White  House  press  secretary Dee Dee Myers, who were arrested for
having  sex  with a prostitute and drunk driving, respectively, and how the
media should handle such stories.

DESCRIPTORS:     Journalistic ethics; News media; Scandals; Arrests; Drunk
                 driving; Prostitution; Public figures
NAMED PERSON:    Grant, Hugh; Myers, Dee Dee
         ------------------------------------------------------------------

1/9/69      (Item 14 from file: 484)
DIALOG(R)File 484:Newspaper & Periodical Abstr.
(c) 1995 UMI. All rts. reserv.

05401915                    95501338
Media dilemma:  Publish or more might perish
Palmer, Thomas C Jr
Boston Globe (BG) p 1, col 1  Jul 1, 1995  ISSN: 0743-1791
ARTICLE TYPE:    News
ARTICLE LENGTH:  Long  (18+ col inches)
AVAILABILITY:    UMIACH  CATALOG NO.:  60494.00

    As  executives  at  the  New York Times and Washington Post contemplated
publishing  the  Unabomber  terrorist's  lengthy manuscript in an effort to
prevent  other  victims  from  perishing,  press  observers said newspapers
rarely  face  such  potentially  life-and-death questions, and there are no
firm rules to guide them.

DESCRIPTORS:     Serial murders; Journalistic ethics; Bombings; Terrorism;
                 Corporate responsibility; Bomb scares; Publishing;
                 Newspapers
COMPANY NAME:    Washington Post Co; New York Times Co
         ------------------------------------------------------------------

1/9/70      (Item 15 from file: 484)
DIALOG(R)File 484:Newspaper & Periodical Abstr.
(c) 1995 UMI. All rts. reserv.

05393821                    95493121
ABC said to give prime deal for Jackson interview

Gunther, Marc
Boston Globe (BG) p 1, col 3  Jun 28, 1995  ISSN: 0743-1791
ARTICLE TYPE:    News
ARTICLE LENGTH:  Medium  (6-18 col inches)
AVAILABILITY:    UMIACH  CATALOG NO.:  60494.00

    The  behind-the-scenes  deal  that  got Diane Sawyer of ABC's "PrimeTime
Live"  an interview with Michael Jackson, and his wife, Lisa Marie Presley,
is examined.

DESCRIPTORS:     Journalistic ethics; Television programs
```

Figure 7.1.
A Dialog search on journalistic ethics reveals several recent citations on the subject in major newspapers.

The Public Information Utilities

Some might consider it strange to think of CompuServe, America Online, Prodigy, The Microsoft Network, eWorld and Delphi as useful sources of information for reporters. Don't tell that to reporters who have used them.

The PIUs, which we introduced in Chapter 2, are accessible to anyone with a computer and modem. Designed as services for the general public, they contain forums for discussions on topics ranging from genealogy to stamp collecting to sports. Forum participants exchange messages on every conceivable topic. Some even write computer software that facilitates the pursuit of their passion, and they frequently make that software available to others interested in the topic.

Such forums provide fertile information to reporters attempting to research a story. If you are assigned to do a story on genealogy and know nothing about the subject, what better way to gauge the pulse of those passionate about the subject than by tapping into their discussions? By logging on to one of the public information utilities, you can do just that.

Or, if you are seeking to interview those who participated in World War II's Battle of the Bulge, try posting a request for names on one of these services. Chances are you will be inundated with names and telephone numbers of individuals or various veterans' groups that would be delighted to help.

The popularity of such services among those with computers is almost impossible to overstate. What people like about the public information utilities is that they do what radio talk shows do—give people a forum in which to exchange ideas with those who share similar interests. Writing in *Editor & Publisher*, Barry Hollander, a journalism professor at the University of Georgia, contrasts the skyrocketing popularity of talk radio with the continuing decline of newspaper circulation:

Newspapers used to be an important part of what bound communities together, a common forum for ideas and discussion. But as communities fragmented along racial and demographic lines, newspapers have done a better job of chronicling the decline than offering ways to offset the trend.

A sense of connection is needed. Newspapers, and [their] electronic editions in particular, offer one opportunity to bring people together in ways similar to talk radio.

Over the years, newspapers, magazines and broadcast stations have attempted to connect with their readers and listeners by doing people-on-the-street interviews. Interviewing people at random seldom produces good results because often those interviewed know nothing about the topic or don't care. By tapping into the forums on the public information utilities or on the Internet (which we shall discuss later in this chapter), you are assured of finding knowledgeable, conversant people to interview.

But the public information utilities are much more than a good source of people to interview. Most have news from various newspapers and wire services, and information on subjects as diverse as travel and where to attend college. Most also have the full text of an encyclopedia on line. Some contain photos as well.

The largest and most useful of these services almost certainly is CompuServe, but it is also the most expensive. For a monthly fee, you can join any of them, but CompuServe adds charges for each minute you are connected to the service. Prodigy and America Online rely primarily on monthly fees for their income, although there are extra charges for heavy electronic mail usage or access to special portions of the service. Prodigy, for example, carries Access Atlanta, an electronic information service prepared by the staff of the *Atlanta Journal and Constitution*. There is an additional charge for monthly access to that service.

Other newspapers, including the *San Jose Mercury News* and the *Chicago Tribune*, and magazines, including *Time*, have allied with America Online. The *St. Louis Post-Dispatch* has opted to work with Delphi. Still others, like the *Kansas City Star*, have chosen to create their own public information utilities. The *Star*'s service, called StarNet, is designed to complement the daily newspaper and the *Star*'s popular audio service, StarTouch. Broadcast stations are exploring similar possibilities.

All of these initiatives represent efforts to expand services and to explore ways to reconnect with the public. With their huge amounts of easily accessible material, they are also useful sources of information for reporters and editors.

The Internet: Information Superhighway

When the administration of President Bill Clinton entered office, it did so with a promise to create an information superhighway on which the public could exchange information and ideas in a way never before possible.

What many soon came to realize was that construction of the information superhighway was already under way. It is known as the Internet, a creation of the federal government and universities in the United States. The Internet has now spread worldwide, and it offers most of the advantages envisioned by the Clinton administration.

The Internet is not a single computer network but rather a series of interconnected networks throughout the world. And, while commercial content initially was banned, more than half of the Internet's users are now estimated to be employees at companies throughout the world. The presence of advertising on the Internet, while sparking controversy, has gradually come to be accepted.

Like the public information utilities, forums for exchange of ideas and information are the Internet's most popular item. But the Internet's forums are far more comprehensive than those on the public information utilities. You can find forums on the Internet on topics as diverse as journalism in the Baltic countries and the French film industry.

But the Internet also serves as a significant source of easily accessible information in literally thousands of databases. You can access the databases of many federal and state agencies, which increasingly are making information available through the Internet. These include such useful items as the U.S. census, agricultural crop data and huge amounts of weather and climate data.

Access to the Internet in the past was limited largely to universi-

ber of job opportunities. He describes what attracted him to a nontraditional news job upon leaving college:

"The line between journalist and reader will blur as technology evolves. The amount of information available will be staggering. Traditional news sources will be challenged by anyone who has access to a computer, a television or even a telephone.

"To be a journalist in the new media, you must think of news as information. You must be able to present information over different media, whether it be a computer, a television, a telephone or a newspaper. But most importantly, you must not forget what you learned in your journalism classes: Present reliable, well-written information in an easy-to-read format—or the reader will go elsewhere."

ties, government agencies and large corporations. In recent years, however, many companies have started selling Internet access to individuals and smaller companies in the United States. This has made it possible for newspapers, magazines and broadcast stations to provide Internet access for reporters in their news rooms.

Some of the limitations of the Internet also have been overcome. Because the Internet is a collection of many different types of computer systems, it was not designed with ease of use in mind. This often led to frustration as users tried to grapple with many different ways of accessing information.

More recently, programs such as Gopher, developed at the University of Minnesota and named for that school's sports mascot, have simplified Internet access. Increasingly popular are programs that provide a *graphical user interface* to the Internet. These include Mosaic and Netscape. Such programs provide a consistent user interface to all Internet sites that conform to standards. Collectively, they form the World Wide Web.

The Internet is a powerful tool for reporters and editors willing to invest time in learning to use it. Further, it is becoming a popular publishing mechanism. More and more newspapers and magazines are creating Internet sites and posting material there, often as a means of attracting consumers to their more profitable traditional products.

The Internet also serves as an excellent medium for transmitting photos and even audio and video clips. It's possible to tap into the Louvre's Internet site and see paintings from that famous collection in full color. Programs such as Mosaic and Netscape make it easier to access such archives.

Many observers of the media industry believe that in the future much news and information will be consumed through an information appliance in the home capable of giving the consumer a choice of full-text, full-motion video and audio. Imagine a computer capable of providing television, and the possibilities become clear. On one device you could read the text of a presidential address or see it being delivered. On that same device, you might later watch a movie or order your groceries.

That's the information superhighway envisioned by so many, and the Internet is its forerunner. The wise journalist is in touch with what's possible today while waiting for the full potential of this powerful new medium to develop.

The Commercial Database Services

When newspapers and magazines entered the computer era in the early 1970s, publishers were quick to realize the potential value of saving and reselling previously published information. Newspapers and magazines quickly began selling access to their archives by establishing alliances with companies founded for that purpose.

Unlike the public information utilities and the Internet, the commercial database services rely totally upon revenue derived from retrieval of previously published information. There are no discussion forums for users.

Mead Data Central's Lexis/Nexis service has become the most popular of those services. It provides full-text retrieval of information published by hundreds of newspapers and magazines. Nexis, the news-retrieval service, is paired with and often sold with Lexis, which provides full-text data on court decisions at both the federal and state levels. Both are extremely useful sources of information for reporters and editors.

Another popular commercial service is Dialog, which has a larger magazine database than Nexis but contains the full text of fewer newspapers. Dialog began as an index service that provided citations and brief abstracts of published material but required the researcher to retrieve the magazine or newspaper itself to read the full text.

Increasingly, Dialog databases are full-text, which makes them more useful to journalists. Reporters and editors working on deadline seldom have time to visit the public library to find a magazine. But if the material is readily accessible by computer and modem in full-text format, the time required to conduct a search and retrieve a document is manageable.

VuText is another popular commercial service. It contains the full text of newspapers from throughout the country and is owned by Knight-Ridder, one of the nation's most respected newspaper publishing companies.

In all cases, access to these services is expensive because connect-time charges are imposed. For that reason, newspapers and magazines often limit access to the news librarian, who conducts searches at the request of reporters and editors. The justification for this practice is that librarians, who presumably are better trained in search techniques, will be more efficient in the use of precious connect time. More and more newspapers, however, are making direct access available to reporters and editors on the theory that database searching has become an essential tool of the journalist's trade. Each reporter is then monitored for excessive use of connect time.

On many topics, searching your own news library will not be sufficient. If U.S. Rep. Pat Schroeder is making her first appearance in your community and you have been assigned to cover her, your morgue probably won't help; little will have been written about her in your city. It probably will be much more useful to read recent articles published in Schroeder's home state of Colorado. By doing so, you will be armed with questions to ask about recent events of interest to her. In such situations, the national commercial databases are invaluable.

The growth of commercial databases is a great asset to reporters, who easily can see what has been written about a subject in other newspapers. But there are some potential problems if you use excerpts from those stories:

- *Copyright laws must be obeyed. Take care not to use too much material without obtaining permission. The fair-use provision of copyright law is vague and confusing about how much is too much. In general, the quoted material must be a small portion of the original work.*
- *Not all articles that appeared in a newspaper can be found in a database. Wire service and market reports, death notices, box scores, social announcements and items written by free-lancers often are excluded.*
- *Searching for informatioin with Boolean commands has obvious limi-*

tations. Some sports stories, for example, never mention the sport but assume the reader will recognize the team names and make the association. As a result, if you search for all stories on soccer, there's no guarantee you'll find them all.

- *It may have been published, but that doesn't mean it is accurate. History is littered with incidents of newspapers quoting each other's inaccuracies.*
- *You seldom have a good idea whether the reporter who wrote an account has any real knowledge of the subject matter. If you lift information from that reporter without such knowledge, you may introduce an inaccuracy.*
- *Databases aren't infallible. The information in them is entered by humans, who are susceptible to mistakes. Some material is even deliberately misleading. Databases occasionally are doctored in an attempt to prove a position or promote a cause.*

Government Databases

For years, government agencies have maintained large databases of information as a means of managing the public's business. They cover almost every conceivable service that government offers, from airplane registration and maintenance records to census data to local court records. They are maintained not only by the federal and state governments, but also by even the smallest of city and county agencies.

Because most of these databases were begun many years ago, they often reside on large mainframe computers or on dedicated minicomputers. Data are stored in various file formats, and it often is difficult to access the information. Independent analyses of the data once were impossible because they were controlled by government agencies. Further, few newspapers had the resources or the computers on which to do independent analyses.

After the introduction of personal computers in the early 1980s, reporters began finding ways to interpret mainframe data. A breakthrough technology involved the purchase of nine-track mainframe data tapes from government agencies and subsequent analysis on personal computers equipped with nine-track drives. Several Pulitzer Prizes were won using this technique, and soon the National Institute for Computer-Assisted Reporting was established at the University of Missouri to spread word about the technique. Suddenly, reporters had the technology at their disposal to make better use of existing open-records laws, both state and federal.

Among the reporters taking advantage of the technology is Penny Loeb. When she worked for *New York Newsday*, she used a computer analysis of tax and property records to reveal an astounding story: The City of New York owed $275 million to taxpayers as a result of overpayments on real estate, water and sewer taxes. To get that story, Loeb had to analyze millions of computer records. Doing that by hand would have consumed a lifetime, but with the assistance of a computer, Loeb accomplished the task in a matter of weeks.

Still, Loeb cautions against expecting instant stories:

> Don't just go get a computer tape and expect a great story. You need a tip that there is a problem that computerized data can confirm. Or you may have seen a problem occur repeatedly, such as sentencing discrimination. The computer can quantify the scope.

Analyses of this type usually are done with *relational database programs*. Relational database programs, unlike simpler *flat-file databases*, permit the user to compare one set of data to another. A classic example would be to compare a database of a state's licensed school bus drivers to another database of the state's drunken driving convictions. The result would be a list of school bus drivers guilty of such offenses.

After the introduction of this technology, investigative reporters were the first to use it. But once such databases are placed in easily accessible computer form, you can use them in your day-to-day work just as easily. For example, you might want to analyze federal records on airplane maintenance to produce a story on the safety record of a particular airline. If the records are maintained in an easily accessible format, the next time an airplane crashes it will be possible to call up the complete maintenance record of the aircraft merely by entering the plane's registration number. Such information can be extremely useful, even in a deadline situation.

Another common use of computers has been to compare bank records on home mortgages to census data. By tracking how many mortgages are issued to homeowners in predominantly black or Hispanic areas, reporters have been able to document the practice of redlining, through which banks make it virtually impossible for minorities to obtain loans.

Again, such records are useful even after the investigation is complete. Access to driver's license records, census data, bank records and other forms of data can be used daily to produce news stories, charts, maps and other graphic devices. Numbers can be useful in helping to tell a story. They can be particularly effective if used as the basis for charts to illustrate the impact of the numbers.

Special-Interest Databases

Numerous special-interest groups have discovered the usefulness of placing information in computerized databases, and they are eager to make journalists aware of the existence of that information. Some of that material may be quite useful; indeed, it may be unobtainable from other sources. But just as journalists must be wary of press releases issued by organizations promoting a cause, they must be equally wary of information in such databases. It is important to remember that organizations of this type will promote their perspective on a topic, often without any concern for balancing the information with opposing views.

CD-ROMs As a Source of Information

During the past few years massive amounts of information stored on compact disks have become a terrific new source of information. Encyclopedias, dictionaries, census data and thousands of other titles are available on CD-ROMs, which serve as an efficient and inexpensive way to store vast amounts of information. One such title is the *CIA World Fact Book*, which lists detailed information on each nation in the world. CD-ROM titles can be quick and effective references for the journalist on deadline.

Self-Constructed Databases

Like Elliot Grossman, reporters occasionally find that the data they want cannot be obtained from government agencies or private businesses. Despite open-records laws at the federal and state levels, public officials often find ways to stall or avoid giving reporters what they want and need. Further, some things just aren't available in databases.

Like Grossman, reporters who find themselves in that predicament sometimes resort to analyzing data after entering it by hand. That's a time-consuming process, but it can be effective. If your knowledge of computer programs is limited, consult with computer experts in your news organization. They will be able to recommend an appropriate tool.

If much of what you are indexing contains textual material, you will need a *free-form database*. A popular program of that type among reporters is AskSam, which has been adopted by many of the nation's leading investigative reporters. AskSam makes it easy to construct a database of quotations, notes or similar material. Many database programs do not handle such material so easily.

If you need to create a simple list of names, addresses and telephone numbers, a flat-file database might be best. Relational database comparisons, as we have discussed, require more sophisticated programs such as Microsoft's FoxPro or Borland's Quattro Pro.

Many reporters also are turning to *spreadsheets* to help them sort through the complexity of government or corporate financial data. A business reporter might use a spreadsheet program to spot trends in the allocation of resources or changes in sources of income. After you have collected data covering several years, a spreadsheet program, which can easily create graphs from the data, makes it easy to notice trends that otherwise might go undetected.

Similarly, the government reporter might use a spreadsheet to spot changes in allocations to various city, county, state or federal departments or agencies.

New uses of computers in the coverage of news are being tried daily. Today's best reporters keep abreast of technology for that reason.

How Computers Assist in Data Analysis

Earlier in this chapter, we described how some reporters have used computers to produce extraordinary stories. Let's examine one such use in more detail as described by John Ullmann, former assistant managing editor of the *Star Tribune* in Minneapolis-St. Paul and now a consultant to that newspaper. Computers, Ullmann says, have helped to elevate the quality of journalism practiced at the *Star Tribune*.

As an example, he cites an investigation by reporters Tom Hamburger and Joe Rigert that uncovered abuses in minority contracting programs. The use of computers made it possible for them to achieve an unusual depth. Instead of simply citing a litany of problems in contracting programs, computers enabled the reporters to find patterns, provide context and indict an entire system rather than just individuals and companies within that system.

Hamburger and Rigert found that front firms for big contractors had captured more than 25 percent of the $179 million awarded to Minnesota companies supposedly controlled by women and minorities in the early 1980s. They also found that two-thirds of the money earmarked for highway-construction companies run by women actually went to firms owned by female relatives of well-established male contractors.

Ullmann details how the computer helped:

Background information. Through a database search conducted by the newspaper's library staff, Hamburger and Rigert obtained articles on abuses and investigations involving similar programs in other states. They also got information on states that appeared to be running model operations. From this search, they were able to determine that reporters and government specialists had completed few investigations of minority contracting programs. A legislative database gave the reporters a comprehensive history of federal votes and committee hearings on the subject and identified key critics of the program.

Organization and retrieval. In their newspaper's computer system, the reporters established a filing system with an index of subjects and lists of documents and sources. By referring to their subject-matter index, which was cross-referenced to documents and interviews, they were able to manage the large volumes of information they collected, establish a chronology of events, prepare for interviews and organize for the writing phase. They also were able to use the computer's search function to pick out references to specific companies or individuals.

Polling and tabulation. Working with the newspaper's poll division, Hamburger and Rigert devised a census survey of all minority contractors certified in Minneapolis. The results were placed in a computer to speed up the tabulation of findings and provide breakdowns of responses from various groups. The survey found that women and minority contractors thought competition from front companies was hurting their businesses and that the government wasn't helping. The poll, in effect, confirmed what Hamburger and Rigert already had learned.

While reporting on the crash near Reno, Nev., of a plane chartered by Minnesotans, Rigert also showed how effectively computers can be used on deadline. A database search revealed that the type of plane that had crashed, a Lockheed-Electra, had the worst fatal-accident rate of any aircraft in common use.

With the report, other data from the search and information obtained on the telephone, Rigert was able to report in the next edition that 10 percent of Electras had been involved in fatal crashes, that the airplanes had the worst fatal-accident rate on record and that Electras had a history of mechanical problems. He also was able to produce a chart of each fatal crash dating back to 1959. The chart included the cause of each crash and the number of fatalities.

Yet another example: Also in Minneapolis, a challenger in the political race for prosecuting attorney accused the incumbent of being a weak plea bargainer. Under plea bargaining, a person charged with crimes agrees to plead guilty to a lesser offense than the one with which he or she was originally charged. The state thus saves the time and expense of a trial and the accused often draws a lighter sentence. The Minneapolis incumbent, of course, disagreed with his opponent. *Star Tribune* reporter Eric Black decided to reduce the rhetoric to statistics to see which candidate was correct.

Black found a state agency that maintained highly detailed statistics on criminal justice matters. But before he sought the data for which he was looking, he interviewed both candidates. He asked the challenger, "If you're right about your opponent's weak plea bargaining, how would that show up statistically and with whom would it be reasonable to compare him?" Black asked the incumbent, "If you're right and you have a strong record on plea bargaining, how would that show up statistically?"

Plea bargaining can be complicated, and the story that eventually was written contained caveats about the risks of a statistical approach in such a complex area. But Black was able to devise a valid plan of measurement that both candidates agreed in advance would be a fair measure of the incumbent's record.

The analysis showed that in comparison with prosecuting attorneys in neighboring counties, the incumbent's record was strong.

Black found other interesting material in the statistics that shed considerable light on the overall performance of Minnesota's judges and prosecutors. In fact, half of the defendants who came into the criminal justice system facing prison terms were able to avoid incarceration because of plea bargaining or leniency of judges. The chief justice of the Supreme Court, the chairman of the state Sentencing Guidelines Commission and legislators were disturbed by the article's findings.

Both stories appeared on Page One of the *Star Tribune*. The first allowed readers to go beyond the campaign rhetoric. The second allowed them to pierce the veil surrounding the criminal justice system.

The key, though, is the reporter's ability to learn how to make technology work in his or her favor. Black's study may have been useless had he not managed to get the candidates to agree on a valid means of measurement.

Such inventive uses of the computer are not limited to Minneapolis, of course. Although large metropolitan newspapers have been leaders in the field, smaller newspapers are beginning to realize the importance of tapping into the wealth of information available through databases. The reporter who fails to learn what databases can do soon will be outclassed.

Traditional Sources of Information

As critical as the use of computers may be in modern journalism, more traditional sources of information—reference books, dictionaries, encyclopedias—still play an important role in the production of the daily news product. Good reporters and editors make a habit of checking every verifiable fact. Sometimes those facts are checked through the use of computer databases; more often they are checked in books. Here is a list of 20 commonly used references:

1. *City directories.* These can be found in most cities. They provide the same information as the telephone directory but also may provide information on the occupations of citizens and the owners or managers of businesses. Useful street indexes provide information on the names of next-door neighbors.
2. *Local and area telephone directories.* Used for verifying the spelling of names and addresses. These usually are reliable, but they are not infallible.
3. *Maps* of the city, county, state, nation and world. Local maps usually are posted in the news room. Others may be found in atlases.
4. *State manuals.* Each state government publishes a directory that provides useful information on various government agencies. These directories sometimes list the salaries of all state employees.
5. *Bartlett's Familiar Quotations* (Little, Brown).
6. *Congressional Directory* (Government Printing Office). Provides profiles of members of Congress.
7. *Congressional Record* (Government Printing Office). Complete proceedings of the U.S. House and Senate.
8. *Current Biography* (Wilson). Profiles of prominent persons, published monthly.
9. *Dictionary of American Biography* (Scribner's).
10. *Facts on File* (Facts on File Inc.). Weekly compilation of news from metropolitan newspapers.
11. *Guinness Book of World Records* (Guinness Superlatives). World records listed in countless categories.
12. *National Trade and Professional Associations of the United States* (Columbia Books, Washington, D.C.).
13. *Readers' Guide to Periodical Literature* (Wilson). Index to magazine articles on a host of subjects.
14. *Statistical Abstract of the United States* (Government Printing Of-

fice). Digest of data collected and published by all federal agencies.

15. *Webster's Biographical Dictionary* (Merriam).
16. *Webster's New World Dictionary of the American Language*, Second College Edition. Primary reference dictionary recommended by both the Associated Press and United Press International.
17. *Webster's Third New International Dictionary*. Unabridged dictionary recommended by AP and UPI.
18. *Who's Who* (St. Martin's). World listings.
19. *Who's Who in America* (Marquis). Biennial publication.
20. *World Almanac and Book of Facts* (Newspaper Enterprise Association). Published annually.

These useful publications, and many others like them, enable reporters to verify data and to avoid the unnecessary embarrassment caused by errors in print.

Finding the Story

Computer databases, reference books, CD-ROMs and similar resource materials not only serve as excellent sources of background material for journalists, but also serve as sources of ideas for stories.

Not every story is dumped into a reporter's lap. Editors provide some ideas; readers provide others. Most ideas, though, are the result of an active imagination, a lively curiosity and a little help from friends. Journalists soon learn how stories written for other publications can be recast for their own. They get in the habit of carrying a little notebook to jot down ideas when something somebody says strikes a responsive chord.

But even for good journalists, the wellspring of ideas sometimes dries up. Bank these 10 sources of story ideas, good for any time and any place, for the day that happens to you:

Ten sources of story ideas:

1. *Other people.*
2. *Other publications.*
3. *News releases.*
4. *A social services directory.*
5. *Government reports.*
6. *Stories in your own newspaper.*
7. *Advertisements.*
8. *Wire copy.*
9. *Local news briefs.*
10. *You.*

■ *Other people.* As a journalist you meet many persons. What are they talking about when they aren't talking business? What have they heard lately? Journalists have to listen, even when it means eavesdropping while having a cup of coffee. What interests people? There is no better source of story ideas than the people you meet while you are off duty. They are, after all, your readers.

■ *Other publications.* Stories are recycled across the country. Read other newspapers, magazines, books, pamphlets and the magazines and newsletters of businesses and organizations.

Not all stories will work in every community. You have to know your readership. A story about urban renewal, for example, would attract more attention in New York than in Helena, Mont. The problems of water supply in the West could not be adapted to make a story on the East Coast. But a story about the federal government's hot-lunch program probably could be done equally well in New York, Kansas and California.

When you are reading other publications for ideas, remember

that you should not duplicate a story. You are looking for ideas. Think of a new angle.

▪ *News releases*. Some news releases from public relations people are used, but many of them are not. Yet they can be a valuable source of story ideas. News that one company has posted increased profits may be worth one or two paragraphs; news that several companies in your community are prospering may be a front-page story. A handout stating that an employee received a 40-year pin may be worth a follow-up.

▪ *A social services directory*. Many cities and counties have a composite listing of all agencies providing social services. Look beyond the pages. There are stories of people serving—or not serving—residents. Each of those agencies and their clients is a story.

▪ *Government reports*. Flowing from Washington like floodwaters are pages and pages of statistics. Behind every statistic, however, is a person. And every person can be a story. The census reports, for instance, list not only the number of people in a community but also their income and education, how many cars they own, whether they rent or own a house. They tell much more, too. Find out what, and you have a treasure chest of stories.

▪ *Stories in your own newspaper*. Many a stream has yielded gold nuggets after the first wave of miners has left. Newspapers sometimes play hit-and-run journalism. Ask yourself if the human-interest angle has been reported adequately. When your newspaper is concentrating on the election winners, maybe you can get an interesting story by talking to the losers and their supporters. After the story of the two-car accident has been written, perhaps there is a feature on the victims whose lives have been changed. And when the unemployment statistics are reported in your paper, remember that behind each of those numbers is a person without a job.

News stories are not the only source of ideas. Read the records column: Can you spot a trend developing in the police report section or in the birth or divorce listings? Is the divorce rate up? Have several crimes been committed in one neighborhood?

▪ *Advertisements*. In advertisements, particularly the classifieds, you may find everything from a come-on for an illegal massage parlor to an auction notice from a family losing its home. Be attentive to local radio and TV commercials, too. And look through the yellow pages. Your fingers might walk right up to a story.

▪ *Wire copy*. Browse through the copy available from your wire services. Are there stories that can be localized? When a story comes across the wires describing the increase in the rate of inflation, you should ask how the people in your community will be affected. Or if a foundation reports that Johnny cannot read, you should talk to your local education officials. Can the Johnnys in your community read any better than the national average?

▪ *Local news briefs*. Usually reports of local happenings are phoned in; sometimes they are brought in, written longhand on a piece of scratch paper. News of an upcoming family reunion may or may not be printed, but the enterprising reporter who notices in the information that five generations will attend the reunion probably has a story that will receive substantial play in the paper. A note that the

Westside Neighborhood Association is planning its annual fundraiser may result in a feature on how the neighbors plan to raise funds to upgrade recreational facilities in their area.

The local news brief as a source of stories is often overlooked. A city editor once received a call from a man who said he thought the paper might be interested in a story about his daughter coming to visit. The city editor tried to brush him off. Just before the man hung up, the editor heard, "I haven't seen her in 32 years. I thought she was dead."

■ *You*. In the final analysis, you are the one who must be alert enough to look and listen to what is going on around you. Ask yourself why, as in, "Why do people act the way they do?" Ask yourself what, as in, "What are people thinking about? What are their fears, their anxieties?" Ask yourself when, as in, "When that happened, what else was going on?" And wonder about things, as in, "I wonder if that's true in my town."

Reporters who are attuned to people rather than institutions will find the world around them a rich source of human-interest stories. Do not tune out.

Suggested Readings

Berkman, Robert. *Find It Online*. Summit, Pa.: Blue Ridge, 1994. Basic information on the use of commercial databases.

Brand, Stewart. *The Media Lab: Inventing the Future at MIT*. New York: Viking, 1987. An examination of Nicholas Negroponte's Media Lab.

Burnham, David. *The Rise of the Computer State: The Threat to Our Freedoms, Our Ethics and Our Democratic Process*. New York: Random House, 1983. A treatise on the threat to privacy posed by the government's increasing reliance on databases.

Dizard, Wilson Jr. *Old Media, New Media: Mass Communications in the Information Age*. New York: Longman, 1994. An interesting perspective, probably the best written yet, on the movement of society into the Information Age and the impact of that on existing media.

IRE Journal. This monthly magazine is available from Investigative Reporters and Editors, Columbia, Mo. It offers regular articles on the use of computers in the news-gathering process.

Exercises

1. Choose any story in your local newspaper, and tell how that story could have been improved with a database search.

2. If you were interested in determining where Apple Computers Inc. is located and the name of its president, where would you look? What other sources of information might be available?

3. Write a one-page biographical sketch of each of your two U.S. senators based on information you retrieve from your library or a database.

4. Using the Internet, which is readily available at most colleges and universities, find information on the following:
   a. The census of Rhode Island in 1990.
   b. The size of Rwanda in land area.
   c. The latest grant awards by the U.S. Department of Education.
   d. The names of universities in Norway that provide outside access via the Internet.
   e. The name of an Internet site that contains the complete works of Shakespeare.
   f. The name of an Internet site that contains federal campaign contribution data.

OBITUARIES

C*huck Ward, publisher of the* Olean (N.Y.) Times Herald, *once told his readers about the time his editor asked whether they should do a special obituary on the father of one of their employees.*

"My response was that unless the father (or any relative) of an employee met the criteria for a glorified obituary, the obituary should be treated as 99 percent of our obituaries are. . . ."

He then recounted that when he went to the visitation that evening, the line extended 50 yards outside the mortuary. He returned in an hour, and the line was still long. That got Ward thinking about his question earlier in the day, "What did he do?"

"All he did, apparently, was live a wonderful, loving life with a splendid family. During the course of that life, he must have touched the lives of countless people in our community. And they all were there to say goodbye."

Ward discovered what so many other journalists still haven't—that people don't have to be public figures to deserve well-reported obituaries. Too many obituaries read as if they were written by a computer program—efficient but lifeless. This persists despite readership surveys that show that about 50 percent of readers look at obituaries, a much higher percentage than look at most other features.

And obituaries are read critically. If the deceased was an Odd Fellow, you'd better not say he was an Elk. If she belonged to the Shiloh Baptist Church, count on a phone call if you say it was Bethany Baptist. Michael Davies, then editor of the Kansas City (Mo.) Star and Times, once told of a call from an owner of a funeral home. The caller was complaining about inaccuracies in obituaries. Skeptical, Davies checked all the next day's obits. He was shocked to find an error of some kind in nearly every one. "If we can't get obits right, how can we expect readers to believe the Page One stories?" he asked. For many people an obituary is the only story the paper ever carries about them. You are summing up a life in a few paragraphs. That's important work.

Despite this importance, many newspapers do not publish a news obituary unless the person who dies is well-known. At many papers the advertising department handles obituaries as paid notices. Many metropolitan papers have adopted this policy because to publish obits on everyone who died in the area would require a substantial amount of space. At papers where obits are handled as advertising, the skill and creativity a reporter brings to the reporting and writing of the story are missing.

Some large papers, such as the Philadelphia Daily News, the Cincinnati Enquirer, the Detroit News and the Des Moines Register, and some small papers, such as the Guntersville (Ala.) Advertiser-Gleam and the Columbia Missourian, take obituaries seriously. Ron Liebau, metro editor of the Enquirer, told the Gannetteer, "For reporters who shrug them off, I tell them they probably don't have anything more important to do."

Jim Nicholson of the Daily News, *who writes obituaries full time, won the American Society of Newspaper Editors Distinguished Writing Award. Readers want to know, he said, "How did someone live a good life? How did they get through this world?"*

Even if you work at a paper where most obituaries are paid notices or are published as death notices that are written from forms filled out by the family, when a prominent person dies, the news department will want a story. Knowing how to report and write an obit is important to you because you may make your first impression on an editor by the way you handle the assignment. The editor will examine your work critically. Is the information correct? Is it complete? Did you check additional sources? Did you follow newspaper style? Did you follow newspaper policy? This chapter examines such questions.

> *"I don't write about death. I write about life."*
>
> *—Michael Best,*
> The Detroit News

Basic Obituary Information and Style

An obituary is a news story. You should apply the same standards to crafting a lead and building the body of an obituary as you do to other stories.

Crafting a Lead

You begin by answering the same questions you would in any news story: who (Michael Kelly, 57, of 1234 West St.), what (died), where (at Regional Hospital), when (Tuesday night), why (heart attack) and how (suffered while jogging). With this information, you are ready to start the story.

The fact that Kelly died of a heart attack suffered while jogging may well be the lead, but the reporter does not know this until the rest of the information essential to every obituary is gathered. You also must know:

- Time and place of funeral services.
- Time and burial place.
- Visitation time (if any).
- Survivors.
- Date and place of birth.
- Achievements.
- Occupation.
- Memberships.

Any of these items can yield the nugget that will appear in the lead. However, if none of these categories yields notable information, the obituary probably will start like this:

> *5 safeguards for obit writers*
>
> 1. *Confirm spellings of names.*
> 2. *Check the addresses. If a telephone book or city directory lists a different address, contact the mortuary about the discrepancy.*
> 3. *Check the birthdate against the age, noting whether the person's birthday was before or after the date of death.*
> 4. *Verify with the mortuary or family any obituary phoned or faxed to the newspaper.*
> 5. *Check your newspaper's library for stories about the deceased, but be sure you don't pull stories about someone with the same name.*

```
Michael Kelly, 57, of 1234 West St., died Tuesday night at
Regional Hospital.
```

Another standard approach could be used later in the news cycle:

```
Funeral services for Michael Kelly, 57, of 1234 West St.,
will be at 2 p.m. Thursday at St. Catherine's Roman Catholic
Church.
```

However, good reporters often find distinguishing characteristics of a person's life. It may be volunteer service, an unusual or important job, service in public office or even just having a name of historical significance. Whatever distinguishes a person can be the lead of the obituary. These leads demonstrate the techniques:

Byran MacGregor, a TV and radio journalist whose pro-U.S. recording "The Americans" got wide airplay in the 1970s, died Tuesday of pneumonia. He was 46.

Randy Shilts, 42, one of the nation's first openly gay reporters, died of AIDS at his Guerneville, Calif., home Feb. 17. He tested positive for HIV in 1985 and announced in 1993 that he had AIDS.

Ted Hawkins, the versatile bluesman who spent years singing for spare change at Los Angeles' Venice Beach, died Sunday of a stroke. He was 58.

Writing approaches can be as varied for obituaries as for any other news story. For instance, the following story emphasizes the personal reactions of those who knew the deceased:

Few persons knew her name, but nearly everyone knew her face.

For 43 years, Mary Jones, the city's cheerful cashier, made paying your utility bills a little easier.

Tuesday morning after she failed to report to work, two fellow employees found her dead in her home at 432 East St., where she apparently suffered a heart attack. She was 66.

By Tuesday afternoon, employees had placed a simple sign on the counter where Miss Jones had worked.

"We regret to inform you that your favorite cashier, Mary Jones, died this morning. We all miss her."

"She had a smile and a quip for everybody who came in here," said June Foster, a bookkeeper in the office.

"She even made people who were mad about their bills go away laughing."

Building the Story Body

Most of the obituary information is provided by the mortuary on a standard form. When the obituary is written straight from the form, this is usually what results:

Michael Kelly, 57, of 1234 West St., died Tuesday night at Regional Hospital.

Kelly collapsed while jogging and died apparently of a heart attack.

Services will be at 2 p.m. Thursday at St. Catherine's Roman Catholic Church. The Rev. Sherman Mitchell will officiate. Burial will be at Glendale Memorial Gardens in Springfield.

Friends may visit at the Fenton Funeral Chapel from 7 to 9 p.m. Wednesday.

Born Dec. 20, 1935, in Boston to Nathan and Sarah Kelly, Kelly was a member of St. Catherine's Roman Catholic Church and a U.S. Navy veteran of the Korean War. He had been an independent insurance agent for the last 25 years.

He married Pauline Virginia Hatfield in Boston on May 5, 1954.

Survivors include his wife; a son, Kevin of Charlotte, N.C., and a daughter, Mary, who is a student at the University of North Carolina at Chapel Hill.

Also surviving are a brother, John of Milwaukee, Wis. and a sister, Margaret Carter, Asheville, N.C.

The Kelly obituary is a dry biography, not a story of his life. There is no hint of his impact on friends, family or community. Good reporting produces stories of life, such as this one:

Jyles Robert Whittler, a World War I veteran and son of a former slave, died Monday at Truman Veterans Hospital. He was 100.

Mr. Whittler helped build the Missouri United Methodist Church in Springfield and served as its janitor for 55 years.

In 1986, the church's basement social hall was christened the Jyles Whittler Fellowship Hall in his honor.

"He's a legend in Springfield and rightfully so," said his friend Roy Smith. "He labored hard and lived well. He's in heaven."

The more traditional biographical information, along with information about visitation and funeral services, appears later in the story.

Here is another example built on good reporting:

Ila Watson Portwood died Sunday at the Candlelight Care Center of complications stemming from a stroke she suffered about two weeks earlier. She was 89.

She was born on Aug. 30, 1908, in Boone County. She graduated from Howard-Payne School in Howard County and attended the University of Michigan.

She was the former owner and operator of the Gem Drug Company. She and her late husband, Carl, started as employees in 1929 and bought the business in 1956. They retired in 1975 and sold the company to Harold Earnest.

"She was a total lady," Earnest said. "I've never seen her mistreat anyone. Just the sweetest lady anyone can meet."

Mrs. Portwood volunteered from 1974 to 1980 at the Cancer Research Center's Women's Cancer Control Program and was named volunteer of the year in 1977.

"She was a people person," said Rosetta Miller, program coordinator. "Her caring personalized her commitment to the staff and patients. . . ."

Whittler and Portwood are ordinary people whose lives affected people. An obituary should celebrate that life rather than merely note the death.

Because much of the information in any obituary comes directly from the family, it generally is accurate. But you still should check the spelling of all names, addresses and the deceased's age against the birth date. You should also never print an obituary based on information obtained by phone from someone purporting to be a funeral home representative. Too many newspapers have been the victims of hoaxes. Always call the funeral home to confirm the call.

Choosing Your Words

Avoid much of the language found on mortuary forms and in obituaries prepared by morticians. The phrasing often is more fitting for a eulogy than a newspaper story.

Because of the sensitivity of the subject matter, euphemisms have crept into the vocabulary of obituary writers. "Loved ones," "passed away," "our dearly beloved brother and father," "the departed" and "remains" may be fine for eulogies, but such terms are out of place in a news story.

Watch your language, too, when you report the cause and circumstances of a death. Unless the doctor is at fault, a person usually dies not "as a result of an operation" but "following" or "after" one. Also, a person dies "unexpectedly" but not "suddenly." All deaths are sudden. Note, too, that a person dies "apparently of a heart attack" but not of "an apparent heart attack." And a person dies of injuries "suffered," not "received."

Be careful with religious terms. Catholics "celebrate" Mass; Reform Jews usually worship in "temples," Orthodox and Conservative Jews in "synagogues." An Episcopal priest who heads a parish is a "rector," not a "pastor." Followers of Islam are called "Muslims."

Consult your wire service stylebook when you have a question.

The stylebook prescribes usage in another instance, too. A man is survived by his wife, not his widow, and a woman is survived by her husband, not her widower. In fact, you will need to consult your local stylebook often when you are writing an obit. Do you use titles such as Mr. and Mrs.? Do you mention divorced spouses, deceased spouses or live-in companions? Do you identify pallbearers? Do you say when memorial contributions are requested?

Once you have checked the spelling and corrected the language, it is time to begin gathering additional information.

Sources of Information

As with any news story, an obituary is more complete when the information comes from several sources. Common sources for obits in-

NAME OF FUNERAL HOME: _____

PHONE: _____

PERSON TO CONTACT: _____

NAME OF DECEASED: _____

ADDRESS: _____

_____

OCCUPATION: _____

_____

AGE: _____

CAUSE OF DEATH: _____

_____

DATE AND PLACE OF DEATH: _____

_____

TIME AND PLACE OF FUNERAL SERVICES: _____

_____

CONDUCTED BY: _____

BURIAL: _____

TIME AND PLACE FOR VISITATION: _____

_____

BIOGRAPHICAL INFORMATION: _____

_____

_____

_____

_____

SURVIVORS: _____

_____

_____

_____

_____

Figure 8.1.
A mortuary form provides basic information. It's not always accurate or complete.
Check it against other sources.

clude mortuary forms, death notices and news stories in the newspaper, the newspaper's library and interviews with family and friends of the deceased.

Mortuary Forms

For many newspapers the standard form from the mortuary mentioned previously is the primary source of information. The mortuary can be of further help if you need more information. Does your city editor want a picture of the deceased? Call the mortuary. It usually can obtain one quickly from the family. Is there some conflicting or unclear information on the form? Call the mortuary.

But writing obituaries from the mortuary's information alone is a clerk's work. As a reporter you should go beyond the form. Sometimes, what the obituary form doesn't tell you is as important as what it does say.

For the writer of the following obit, the first clue that the death notice was unusual was the age. The deceased was 12. That alone was enough for the reporter to start asking questions. The result was an obituary that moved from the records column to the front page:

Sandra Ann Hill, 12, lost her lifetime struggle against a mysterious muscle ailment Wednesday night. The day she died was the first day she had ever been admitted as a hospital inpatient.

Although they knew it was coming, the end came suddenly for Sandra's family and school friends, said her father, Lester, of 1912 Jackson St.

Just last Friday, she attended special classes at the Parkdale School. "She loved it there," Hill said. "Like at recess, when the sixth graders would come in and read to her. She always wanted to be the center of attention."

"Bright as a silver dollar" was the way one of Sandra's early teachers described her. In fact, no one will ever know. Sandra couldn't talk.

"We didn't know what she knew or didn't know," her father said. Sandra's only communication with the world around her came in the form of smiles and frowns—her symbols for yes and no.

"There were times when I'd come around the corner and kind of stick my head around and say 'boo,'" her father recalled. "She smiled. She liked that."

The care and attention Sandra demanded makes the loss particularly hard for her family to accept, Hill said. "I can't really put it into words. You cope with it the best you can, keep her comfortable and happy. We always took her with us."

Sandra came down with bronchitis Friday. Complications forced her to be admitted Wednesday to Lincoln County Hospital, where she died later that night.

Sandra's fight for life was uphill all the way. It started simply enough when she was four months old. Her mother, Bonnie, noticed she "wasn't holding up her head" like her other children.

Although her ailment was never firmly diagnosed, doctors found Sandra's muscles held only half the tissues and fibers in a normal child's body. The diagnosis: a type of cerebral palsy. The prognosis: Sandra had little chance to live past the age of 2. Medical knowledge offered little help.

Sandra was born in Springfield on Jan. 15, 1984. She is survived by her parents; one brother, Michael Eugene Hill; one sister, Terrie Lynn Hill, both of the home; and her grandparents, Gordon Hill of Seale, Ala., and Mrs. Carrie Harris of Phoenix, Ariz.

Services will be at 3:30 p.m. today at the Memorial Funeral Chapel with the Rev. Jack Gleason conducting. Burial will follow at the Memorial Park Cemetery.

The family will receive friends at the Memorial Funeral Home until time for the service.

The reporter who wrote this obituary obviously did a great deal of research beyond what was on the mortuary form. Because the girl was not a public figure, the reporter could not consult a reference work such as *Who's Who in America* or a national publication. But the reporter did have access to the newspaper library and could interview the girl's family and friends. These are the sources that can help make interesting copy.

One way to irritate the source and fail to get interesting copy is to ask people who are grieving, "How do you feel?" It's a question asked often by reporters at the scene of a disaster when people are waiting to hear about their relatives or friends. As one editor commented, "How the hell should they feel? Newspapers are not in the business of measuring the degree of grief. . . ."

The Newspaper

Another good source is the paid funeral notices in the newspaper. One that appeared in the *St. Paul* (Minn.) *Pioneer Press* mentioned that there would be a party after the funeral. With the permission of the family, the reporter attended. His story began:

The ladies sat in a circle of lawn chairs in the neatly clipped backyard, between the pea patch on the right and the tomatoes and cucumbers on the left, sipping their gentle scotches and bourbons and beers, while the mosquitoes buzzed around their ears, and the evening slowly faded without pain into the night.

The story goes on to describe how the deceased had asked that her friends gather to remember the good times rather than mourn her passing.

A reporter in Columbus, Ind., spotted another good story when he realized that an obituary notice from a funeral home was for the city's "broom man." The resulting story, which appeared on Page One, began this way:

For instance, if you are writing a story of a banker, Colon says, you need to know some banking history.

"You want to know if he or she survived the Crash of '29. Did the people who worked with him or her jump out of the building? What did that person do to get where he or she is now? Did the person sell apples on street corners? Was he or she part of the WPA program?

"A reporter from Mars couldn't write a good obit. Here's why. You have to have a frame of reference to start with. That way you will find other avenues that will lead you to other interesting places. You have to know a bit about the Crash of '29 to talk to other people about it."

Colon brings a broad frame of reference to his work. He reported for the *Herald* for three years, then was an editor at the Voice of America for two years. He earned his master's degree, taught journalism and directed a program to train professional journalists in management techniques with a multicultural perspective. He returned to the *Herald* in 1993.

You probably knew him.

Notice of his death Christmas Day almost seemed to fade among the others published Thursday. Ernest W. Ferrenburg, 75, of 1210 California died at 2:50 p.m. Wednesday at Bartholomew County Hospital, the notice said.

"Nobody knew him by his name. He was just the old broom salesman," said one of his six daughters, Irene Michaelis of Greenwood.

Workers and shoppers probably can recall seeing Ferrenburg standing on a street corner downtown on Washington Street, holding a generous stock of brooms of various shapes and sizes. The thin white cane he carried told passersby he had lost his sight. That happened in a gun accident when he was 19.

The story ends this way:

Ferrenburg never considered himself handicapped.

"I can hear birds sing. I can hear little children," Mrs.

Michaelis said her father replied when asked whether he would rather see than hear. "I'd rather be blind anytime than deaf."

Hartford Courant reporter Leonard Bernstein wrote about another remarkable life after the obituary notice had already been published. It began this way:

For as long as anyone can remember, David Lowery had two dreams: to buy his own home and raise his own children.

For 23 years, he worked—often two jobs at a time—and finally, on Sept. 1, 1983, he bought a house in Hartford.

Within nine months, the second dream was fulfilled: On June 11, Lowery became a single father, bringing home two brothers from Massachusetts who had been seeking a family for two years.

And then it ended.

On July 8, a cool Sunday evening, Lowery was driving his new family home from church in Middletown when he pulled

to the side of I-91 and told the boys he was sick. The 10-year-old flagged down a passing car; the 13-year-old climbed in to go for help.

Seven hours later, David Lowery, 44, was dead of a cerebral hemorrhage.

His death did not make the headlines. No famous people spoke at the funeral.

But David Lowery—a Big Brother for 14 years in Hartford, a member of Shiloh Baptist Church in Middletown where he sang and formed a youth choir, a regular visitor to people whom others had forgotten—was loved by many, and they still mourn.

Each of the last two stories could have been run as a combination obituary and death story if someone had pursued the obituary information when it came to the city room.

The Newspaper Library

In the newspaper library, you may find an interview with the deceased, an interesting feature story or clips indicating activities not included on the obituary form. In an interview or feature story the person may have made a statement about a philosophy of life that would be appropriate to include in the obituary. The subject also may have indicated his or her goals in life, against which later accomplishments can be measured. You can find the names of friends and co-workers in the clips as well. These persons are often the source of rich anecdotes and comments about the deceased.

A reporter assigned to do the obituary of a local man, Harold Riback, hit pay dirt in the newspaper morgue. There he found the names of two associates, Pauline Yost and Viva Spiers, from whom he was able to secure some interesting details:

When Harold Riback was a student at the university, he drove a salvage truck to St. Louis at night for his father's business. He always took his books so he could study when he stopped to rest.

"Even when he was young, he was very ambitious," said Pauline Yost, the secretary for the Boone County Democratic party, while reminiscing about Riback, 66, who died Monday morning at Boone County Hospital.

"When he agreed to a project, you didn't have just a name, you had a completely involved person," said Viva Spiers, the Sixth Ward Democratic committeewoman.

Those same files also yielded another interesting quote from Riback himself:

Mr. Riback once said, "I've always had a strong community commitment. My dad used to say, 'Whenever you've enjoyed the fruits of the harvest, you have to save a little bit of the seed for the next year's crop.' When you benefit from the community, you have to give it back. This philosophy has had a strong bearing on my life."

That is the type of statement a newspaper obtains if it has a regular program of interviewing public figures for their obituaries in advance of their death. Because most newspapers do not, looking through the library and interviewing friends and relatives are the next best thing.

Your newspaper's files are not the only source for information on people who have state or national reputations. You or your librarian should also search electronic databases for stories that have appeared in other publications.

Interviewing Family and Friends

Papers treat public figures in more detail not only because they are newsworthy but also because reporters know more about them. Even though private citizens usually are less newsworthy, many good stories about them are never written because the reporter did not—or was afraid to—do the reporting. The fear is usually unfounded. William

"People are drawn to the obit page because they want to know the secret. They want to know, 'How did someone live a good life? How did they get through this world?'"
—*Jim Nicholson,* Philadelphia Daily News

Marcia Puglisi of Bethpage, Was Teacher

Marcia Z. Puglisi of Bethpage, former teacher and claims examiner, died of emphysema Wednesday at Mid-Island Hospital, Bethpage. She was 63.

Mrs. Puglisi grew up in Boston and New York City and had lived in Bethpage 42 years. She was a 1952 graduate of then-Hofstra College with a bachelor's degree in history and in 1966 was awarded a two-year fellowship to Hofstra for her master's degree in early education.

Mrs. Puglisi worked in Nassau County's day-care program, was a substitute teacher in the Island Trees school district and other local elementary schools and then for seven years worked as a claims examiner for the state Department of La-bor in Hempstead. Illness forced her to retire from there about 10 years ago.

She painted and sculpted, pursued her interests in the arts and literature, and enjoyed crossword puzzles and bargain hunting.

Mrs. Puglisi is survived by her husband of 44 years, Vincent, a professor of biology at Nassau Community College; a daughter, Diana of Port Washington; a son, Austin of Tucson, Ariz.; her mother, Olga Jones, and sister, Patricia Alden, both of Lee, Mass.; and a brother, Bruce Jones of Princeton, N.J.

A service is scheduled for 11:30 a.m. today at the William E. Law Funeral Home, Massapequa, with burial in Calverton National Cemetery.

— Schaeffer

PUGLISI—Marcia Z., of Bethpage, on December 28, 1994. Beloved Wife of Vincent for 44 years. Loving Mother of Diana and Austin. Dear Daughter of Olga Jones. Devoted Sister of Bruce Jones and Patricia Alden. Reposing at William E. Law Funeral Home, 1 Jerusalem Ave., Massapequa, N.Y. Religious Services Friday 11:30 AM, Rabbi Sam Kehati officating. Interment Calverton National Cemetery. Visiting hours Thursday 2-5 & 7-9:30 PM.

Figure 8.2.
Paid death notices are a useful source of facts as well as names of people who can be contacted for confirmation and additional information about the deceased. Compare the information in this death notice and obituary.

Buchanan, who has written many obituaries for the *Boston Globe*, said his calls are almost always welcomed: "The person I called appreciated that someone cared enough to want to know more about a loved one."

That's true even in the worst of circumstances, such as a suicide. Karen Ball, a former reporter for the *Columbia Missourian*, learned that lesson when she was assigned to do a story on Robert Somers, a university professor who had committed suicide. Ball didn't look forward to calling Mrs. Somers. First, Ball talked to students, Somers' colleagues and university staff members. She even obtained a copy of his resume.

"By knowing a lot about him—where he'd studied, what his interests were and where he worked—I knew that I could go into an interview with a bereaved relative and at least have something to talk about," she says.

Ball approached Mrs. Somers in person and explained that her husband was respected and liked. Mrs. Somers agreed to talk. To get her to elaborate on his personality and what he was like away from school, Ball prodded her with questions about their children, where they had lived before and other family matters. She also talked to Somers' mother. Ball told her some of the positive things that students and faculty had said about her son. That helped the mother deal with her sorrow and helped Ball write her story. It began:

Miko Somers sat at her kitchen table folding and unfolding her youngest daughter's bib as she talked about her husband.

"He could never do anything halfway," Mrs. Somers says. "He set such a high standard for himself. Whatever he did had to be the very best, and he pushed himself to make it that way."

Today Mrs. Somers buries her husband. Monday, Robert Somers, 40, her husband for 17 years, the father of their four daughters and an associate professor in the University's history department, took his life by driving his car head-on into a tree.

Newspaper Policy

Newspaper policy often dictates what will—and will not—be included in an obituary. Those newspapers that do have written policies may prescribe how to handle everything from addresses to suicides.

Some newspapers, for instance, prohibit a statement such as "In lieu of flowers, the family requests donations be made to the county humane society." This prohibition is in response to lobbying from florists.

Because of threats to the safety of property and the individuals involved, in some cities even information essential to the obituary no longer appears in the paper. Some newspapers specifically tell reporters not to include the address. Criminals have used information taken from the obituary columns to prey on survivors. Knowing the time of the funeral and the address of the deceased makes it easy to plan a break-in at the empty residence during the services. Therefore, this information also may be withheld.

Two other kinds of information newspapers may have restrictive policies on are the cause of death and potentially embarrassing information.

Cause of Death

If the person who dies is not a public figure and the family does not wish to divulge the cause of death, some newspapers will comply. That is questionable news judgment. The reader wants to know what caused the death. A reporter should call the mortuary, the family, the attending physician and the appropriate medical officer. Only if none of these sources will talk should the newspaper leave out the cause of death. The *Des Moines* (Iowa) *Register, Cincinnati Enquirer* and *Detroit News,* among others, require obituaries to include the cause of death.

A death certificate must be filed for each death, but obtaining it often takes days, and some states do not make the cause of death public record. Even if the state lists the cause of death and the reporter has timely access to the death certificate, the information is often vague.

Policy options

- *Run an obituary that ignores any embarrassing information and, if necessary, leave out the cause of death. If circumstances surrounding the death warrant a news story, run it separate from the obituary.*
- *Insist on including embarrassing details and the cause of death in the obituary.*
- *Insist on including embarrassing details and the cause of death in the obituary only for public figures.*
- *Put a limit on how far back in the person's life to use derogatory information such as a conviction.*
- *Print everything newsworthy that is learned about public figures but not about private figures.*
- *Print everything thought newsworthy about public and private figures.*
- *Decide each case as it comes up.*

"*This disease [AIDS]
will be the end of many
of us, but not nearly all,
and the dead will be
commemorated and
will struggle on with the
living, and we are not
going away. We won't
die secret deaths any-
more.*"

— *Prior Walter,
character in the play
"Angels in America"*

"*People are a lot more
open than they were,
but I think that they're
still not open enough
when it comes to AIDS.
It's been my experience
that nobody will admit
it unless they are in the
arts. If somebody in
business dies of AIDS,
we may never know
about it.*"

— *Irvin Horowitz,
obituary writer,
The New York Times*

If the death is caused by cancer or a heart attack or is the result of an accident, most families do not object to including the cause in the obituary. But if the cause is cirrhosis of the liver brought on by heavy drinking, many families do object, and many papers do not insist on printing the cause.

If the deceased was a public figure or a young person, most newspapers insist on the cause of death.

If the death is the result of suicide or foul play, reporters can obtain the information from the police or the medical examiner. Some newspapers include suicide as a cause of death in the obituary, others print it in a separate news story, and still others ignore it altogether. This is one way to report it:

> Services for Gary O'Neal, 34, a local carpenters' union officer, will be at 9 a.m. Thursday in the First Baptist Church.
> Coroner Mike Pardee ruled that Mr. O'Neal died Tuesday of a self-inflicted gunshot wound.

Embarrassing Information

Another newspaper policy affecting obituaries concerns embarrassing information. When the *St. Louis Post-Dispatch* reported in an obituary that the deceased had been disbarred and that he had been a key witness in a bribe scandal involving a well-known politician 13 years earlier, several callers complained.

The Reader's Advocate defended the decision to include that history in the obituary:

> One who called to complain about the obit told me it reminded her of the quotation from Shakespeare's "Julius Caesar," about how the good a man does is often buried with him and forgotten.
> Yes, I said, and the first part of that quotation could be paraphrased to say that the news a man makes often lives after him.

When author W. Somerset Maugham died, the *New York Times* reported that he was a homosexual even though the subject generally had not been discussed in public before. When public figures die, newspapers sometimes make the first public mention of drinking problems in their obituaries. Acquired immune deficiency syndrome (AIDS) is the latest cause of death to trouble editors. The death of actor Rock Hudson brought AIDS to the attention of many who had never heard of the disease before. Many newspapers agonized over whether to say that Hudson had AIDS. As other public figures died of AIDS, it became almost routine to report the cause of death. Because society still regards AIDS negatively, some spokespeople go out of their way to give the cause of death to make certain people don't think it was AIDS.

The more AIDS or any other disease is reported as a cause of death, the more accepted it will become. Cancer once had a similar stigma. Geneva Overholser, then editor of the *Des Moines Register*, has said that citizens didn't know the extent of the AIDS crisis because it wasn't included as a cause of death in obituaries. In Boise, Idaho, the newspaper reported that several people requested before they died that AIDS be listed as the cause. They did this to make people more aware of the disease. One professor who has studied AIDS coverage suggests that obituary writers ought not to soften the language or use euphemisms when reporting AIDS-related deaths; should refer to AIDS patients, rather than victims; and should try to reach the family for information and confirmation.

The crucial factor in determining the extent to which you should report details of an individual's private life is whether the deceased was a public or private person. A **public figure** is one who has been in the public eye. A participant in civic or social activities, a person who spoke out at public meetings or through the mass media, a performer, an author, a speaker—these all may be public figures. **Public officials,** individuals who have been elected or appointed to public office, are generally treated like public figures.

Whether the subject is a public figure or private citizen, the decisions newspapers must make when dealing with the obituary are sensitive and complicated. It is the reporter's obligation to be aware of the newspaper's policy. In the absence of a clear policy statement, the reporter should consult the city editor.

Suggested Readings

Casella, Peter A. "Media Mistakes Can Be Devastating." *The Bulletin*, ASNE, Sept.–Oct. 1986, p. 40. Casella, a journalist, tells about the time the broadcast media mistakenly reported that his wife had been killed in a helicopter crash.

Dalton, Laura. "Remembrance of Things Past." *Gannetteer*, Gannett Publishing Co., December 1993, pp. 10–11. Describes how various Gannett newspaper reporters handle obituaries.

Hart, Jack and Johnson, Janis. "A Clash Between the Public's Right to Know and a Family's Need for Privacy." *The Quill*, May 1979, pp. 19–24. An account of the backlash against a newspaper that printed a syndicated story of how the daughter of a locally prominent family had died a big-city prostitute.

Hipple, John and Wells, Richard. "Media Can Reduce Risks in Suicide Stories." *E&P*, Oct. 14, 1989, p. 72. A counselor who specializes in treating suicidal young people and a journalist combine to offer suggestions on handling stories involving suicide.

"The Obituarist's Art," *The Economist*, The Economist Newspaper, Ltd., Dec. 24, 1994/Jan. 6, 1995, p. 64. A history of how British newspapers treat obituaries, tracing the changes in attitudes and language.

Randolph, Eleanor, "AIDS and Obituaries," *Chicago Tribune*, Sept. 24, 1989. A round-up of how various newspapers handle AIDS as a cause of death.

"Why Do We Handle Obits in Such Deadly Fashion?" *The Bulletin*, ASNE, July–Aug. 1982, pp. 7–13. Various editors describe their attitudes toward obituaries and tell about their experiences handling obits.

Exercises

1. Which elements are missing from the following obituary information?

   a. John Peterson died Saturday at Springfield Hospital. Funeral services will be at 1:30 p.m. Tuesday. Friends may call at the Restwell Funeral Home, 2560 Walnut St., from 6 to 9 p.m. Monday. The Rev. William Thomas will officiate at services in the First Baptist Church. Burial will be at City Cemetery.

   b. Richard G. Tindall, Springfield, a retired U.S. Army brigadier general, died at his daughter's home in Summit, N.J. Graveside services will be at 2 p.m. July 3 at Arlington National Cemetery in Arlington, Va.

2. Write a lead for an obituary from the following information:

   Martha Sattiewhite, born July 2, 1974, to Don and Mattie Sattiewhite, in Springfield. Martha was killed in a car accident June 30, 1995. Funeral services will be July 2. She was president of her Springfield High School senior class and of the sophomore class at the University of Oklahoma.

3. An obituary notice comes from a local funeral home. It contains the basic information, but under achievements it lists only "former member of Lion's Club." Your city editor tells you to find out more about the deceased. Whom would you call and why?

4. If George Thomas, private citizen, committed suicide while alone in his home, would you include that in his obituary? Why or why not?

5. A few newspapers write obituaries of notable people in advance because of the short time they have after the death. Some of them even interview the subject. Write a two-page advance obituary of one of the following: Benjamin Chavis, Henry Cisneros, Abe Rosenthal, Mother Theresa, Madonna. At the end, list your sources.

American Heart Association

Missouri Affiliate, Inc., 105 E. Ash, P.O. Box Q
Columbia, Missouri 65205, 314/442-3193

FOR IMMEDIATE RELEASE

NEWS RELEASE

CONTACT: Melanie Harris
          314-443-1511

HEART-HEALTHY FOODS CAN SAVE YOU DOLLARS

You could be paying more for fatty, high-cholesterol, calorie-heavy foods than you are for heart-healthy and nutritious foods, according to the American Heart Association.

"Foods which claim the biggest portion of your grocery dollar are often actually those highest in cholesterol and saturated fat," notes Ann Cohen, Registered Dietician, and volunteer for the American Heart Association, Missouri Affiliate. These foods can contribute to high blood cholesterol levels and increase your risk of developing cardiovascular disease."

The AHA advises consumers to eat a well-balanced diet that includes selections from all major food groups. Choose lean meat, fish and poultry in moderate portions, low-fat or non-fat dairy products, polyunsaturated margarines and vegetable oils, whole grains, fruits, vegetables and nuts.

America's food stores are supplying consumers' demands for this variety of healthy foods. You'll most likely find them in your favorite grocery store.

Saving food dollars is based on many factors: what foods you buy, where you live and shop, how much time you have to cook food and how you plan your meals.

The American Heart Association offers these tips to help you save food dollars:

* Make a shopping list and plan your weekly meals. You should first

-more-

NEWS RELEASES

*R*eporters do not go out and dig up all the stories they write. Many stories come to them. They are mailed, e-mailed, telephoned, faxed or hand-delivered by people who want to get something in the paper. They come from people or offices with different titles: public relations departments, public information offices, community relations bureaus, press agents, press secretaries, publicity offices. The people who write them call their stories **news releases** or press releases; other journalists are more apt to call them handouts.

Because good publicity is so important, private individuals, corporations and government agencies spend a great deal of money to obtain it. Much of the money goes for the salaries of skilled and experienced personnel, many of whom have worked in the news business. Part of their job is to write news releases that the news media will use.

You may very well want to be among those people. You may be seeking a career in public relations or advertising, but your journalism department wisely has you begin by studying news and news writing. Only by studying news and how news organizations handle news will you be successful in public relations or in offices of public information. Knowing how reporters are taught to deal with news releases will help you write better releases if that ever is your job. Of course, studying news also helps you enormously in the advertising world.

Skilled public relations or public information practitioners know how to write news, and they apply all the principles of good news writing in their news releases. A good news release meets the criteria of a good news story.

Nevertheless, as two of the best PR professionals, Carole Howard, formerly of Reader's Digest, and Wilma Mathews, formerly with AT&T, tell us, news releases are never intended to take the place of reporters. News releases, they write in On Deadline: Managing Media Relations, simply acquaint an editor with the basic facts of potential stories. Those who write news releases come to accept that their carefully crafted sentences will be checked and rewritten by reporters.

As a reporter, you must recognize that news releases are both a help and hindrance to a newspaper. They help because without them, newspapers would need many more reporters. They are a hindrance because they sometimes contain incomplete or even incorrect information. Because they are intended to promote the interests and favorable reputation of the individuals and organizations that disseminate them, news releases, by their very nature, are not objective.

Nevertheless, wise editors do not discard news releases without reading them. These editors often give them to reporters, often the newest ones, as sources for stories.

When your editor hands you a news release, you are expected to know what to do with it. You must be able to recognize the news in the release, applying all that you have learned about news values. The release may lead you to a good story. Your resourcefulness may improve your chances of being assigned to bigger things.

Types of News Releases

After you have read a number of news releases, you will notice that generally they fall into three categories:

1. Announcements of coming events or of personnel matters—hiring, promoting, retiring and the like.
2. Information regarding a cause.
3. Information that is meant to build someone's or some organization's image.

Recognizing the types and purposes of news releases (and that some are hybrids and serve more than one purpose) will help you know how to rewrite them.

Announcements

Organizations use the news media to tell their members and the public about coming events. For example:

> The Camera Club will have a special meeting at Wyatt's Cafeteria at 7 p.m. on Wednesday, March 20. Marvin Miller will present a slide program on "Yellowstone in Winter." All interested persons are invited to attend.

Although the release promotes the Camera Club, it also serves as a public-service announcement. Newspapers that print such announcements are serving their readers. Here is another example:

> The first reception of the new season of the Springfield Art League will be on Sunday, Sept. 8, 3 to 5 p.m. in the Fine Arts Building.
> Included in the exhibition will be paintings, serigraphs, sculpture, batiks, weaving, pottery, jewelry, all created by Art League members, who throughout the summer have been preparing works for this opening exhibit of the season.
> The event also will feature local member-artists' State Fair entries, thus giving all who could not get to the fair the opportunity to see these works.
> The exhibition continues to Friday, Sept. 13. All gallery events and exhibitions are free.

Other news release announcements concern appointments, promotions, hiring and retiring. The announcement of an appointment may read like this:

> James McAlester, internationally known rural sociologist at Springfield University, has been appointed to the board of directors of Bread for the World, according to William Coburn, executive director of the humanitarian organization.
> McAlester attended his first board meeting Jan. 22 in New York City. He has been on the university faculty since 1985. Prior to that, he served as the Ford Foundation representative in India for 17 years.
> The 19,000-member Bread for the World organization is a "broad-based interdenominational movement of Christian citizens who advocate government policies that address the basic causes of hunger in the world," says Coburn.

Tips for writers of news releases

1. Follow an accepted journalistic style of writing. *Use AP style.*
2. Go easy on length. *Hold it to two double-spaced, typewritten pages.*
3. Avoid breaks. *Don't hyphenate words at the ends of lines, and don't split a sentence at the bottom of a page.*
4. Write clearly. *Avoid corporate jargon, legalese or other alien language.*
5. Remember the pyramid. *But don't put all the w's in the lead.*
6. Beware of adjectives. *Especially avoid superlatives.*
7. Make it local.
8. Attribute news to a person. *Not to a company or organization.*
9. Indent the paragraphs.

—Carole Howard and Wilma Mathews,
On Deadline: Managing Media Relations

The occasion for this release is the appointment of McAlester. But the release also describes the purpose of the Bread for the World organization. By educating readers regarding the organization's purpose, the writer hoped to promote its cause.

Companies often send releases when an employee has been promoted. For example:

> James B. Withers Jr. was named senior vice president in charge of sales of the J.B. Withers Company, it was announced Tuesday.
>
> Withers, who has been with the company in the sales division for two years, will head a sales force of 23 people.
>
> "We are sure Jim can do the job," James B. Withers Sr., company president, said. "He brings youth, intelligence and enthusiasm to the job. We're pleased he has decided to stay with the company."
>
> Founded in 1936, the J.B. Withers Company is the country's second-largest manufacturer of dog and cat collars.

A release like this one is an attempt by the company to get its name before the public and to create employee goodwill. Written in the form of an announcement, it is an attempt at free publicity.

Cause-Promoting Releases

The second category of news releases seeks to further a cause. Some of these releases come from worthwhile causes in need of funds or of volunteers. For example, the letter reprinted here is from a county chairman of the American Heart Association to the editor of a newspaper. It is not written in the form of a release, but its effect is meant to be the same:

> The alumnae and collegiate members of the Alpha Phi Sorority have just completed their annual Alpha Phi "Helping Hearts" lollipop sale. This year Valerie Knight, project chairwoman, led sorority members to achieve record-breaking sales. The lollipop sale is a national project of the Alpha Phi Sorority.
>
> Sunday, March 5, Valerie Knight presented a check for $1,800 to the American Heart Association, Shelby County Unit. The contribution was presented during a reception at the Alpha Phi house. This contribution is an important part of the annual fund-raising campaign of the American Heart Association.
>
> I wish to extend special thanks to the members of Alpha Phi and in particular to Valerie Knight for this outstanding project. In addition, I wish to thank the many merchants who participated in the project by selling lollipops in their businesses.

Heads of organizations such as this attempt to alert the public to their messages in any way they can. Any release, notice or letter they can get printed without paying for it leaves money for the cause that they represent. Sometimes the cause is a local private college:

> Libbi Given, director of the Adelphos College community campaign, has named 17 division chairpersons for the fund drive that will begin Sept. 21.

The division heads met Sept. 9 to organize for the campaign, which has a $100,000 goal, an increase of $22,000 over last year's local gift support.

The college has developed a four-year gift support plan to raise $8.5 million. Included in the amount is $4.5 million in Annual Fund gifts to provide assistance with the operating expenses of the college, as it plans almost to double its endowment base and existing on- and off-campus facilities.

Again, the cause is a good one. The college needs money, and to raise money it must publicize its fund drive.

Image-Building Releases

Another kind of news release serves to build up someone's or some organization's image. Politicians seek to be elected or to be re-elected. They desire as much *free* publicity as they can get. For example:

James M. Merlin, honorary chairman of the board and director of Merlin Corporation, has been named honorary chairman of the Finance Committee, which will seek city-wide financial support for the campaign to elect Hong Xiang as Springfield's next mayor.

Merlin, a well-known civic leader and philanthropist, termed the election of Xiang "one of the most important and far-reaching decisions the voters of Springfield will make in a long time. The city's financial crisis can only be solved through the kind of economic leadership Xiang has demonstrated the past 10 years as 1st Ward councilperson."

The appointment of Merlin as honorary chairman serves only to promote the image of the candidate. The quote is self-serving.

Organizations and government agencies at all levels often try to build their public image. Many of them have local mayors proclaim a day or a week of recognition, as in the following:

Mayor Juanita Williams has proclaimed Saturday, May 11, as Fire Service Recognition Day. The Springfield Fire Department in conjunction with the University Fire Service Training Division is sponsoring a demonstration of the fire apparatus and equipment at the Springfield Fire Training Center. The displays are from 10 a.m. to 5 p.m. at 700 Bear Blvd. All citizens are urged to attend the display or visit their neighborhood fire station on May 6.

Our PRODUCT is your SAFETY.

If an editor hands you a release such as this, he or she probably has decided that it is worth using in some form. The rest is up to you.

Handling the News Release

Regardless of the type of news release, be sure to read the information that appears on the top. Figure 9.1 is an example.

Although all of that information may be useful to you, many news releases leave unanswered questions. You probably will want to

"If you don't understand good journalistic style and format (who, what, when, where and why) for writing a press release, you harm your company and yourself."
— *G.A. Marken, President of Marken Communications Inc. Public Relations Quarterly*

"Promotions into high office are newsworthy not just to the business, financial or trade press, but also to the person's hometown papers, alumni magazines and professional society journals. Notices of service anniversaries, training courses completed, retirements and honors received are welcome at various publications; the trick is to match the medium with the message. Some of these items, depending on visual appeal, could interest television as well."
— *Carole Howard and Wilma Mathews, On Deadline: Managing Media Relations*

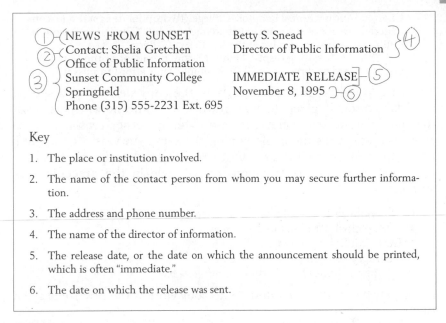

Figure 9.1.
The information at the top of a news release can provide ideas and sources that will enhance your story.

contact people other than the director of information or even the contact person if you have serious doubts about some of the data given. But for routine accuracy checks, the persons listed on the release can do the job. They may lead you to other helpful sources, too. Sometimes you may have sources of your own. And sometimes you may uncover the real story only from people who are neither connected to nor recommended by the director of information.

You may have to consult your editor regarding the release date. As a courtesy, most newspapers honor release dates. However, sometimes a morning or evening paper will publish the release early because waiting until the following day would render the information useless. Also, once a release is public knowledge, editors feel justified in publishing whatever information it contains, even prior to the suggested release date. A release date is broken for all when it is broken by one.

Rewriting the Announcement Release

Sometimes directors of information want nothing more than a listing on the record or calendar page of a newspaper. Here is an example:

FOR THE CALENDAR
Elisabeth Bertke, quiltmaker and designer from Salem, Massachusetts, will discuss her work at 7:00 o'clock P.M. Tues., February 7, in

Charters Auditorium, Hampton College. Two quilts designed and constructed by Bertke are included in the exhibit "The New American Quilt," currently on display at the Smith Art Gallery.

"This is an exciting display," Betty Martin, president of the Smith Art Gallery board of directors, said. "You simply can't afford to miss it."

This simple release may go directly to the copy desk or to a special calendar editor. If given to you, rewrite it. Some newspapers insist that you rewrite every news release if for no other reason than to avoid the embarrassment of running the same story as a competing newspaper. For some it is a matter of integrity and professionalism.

First, note all the violations of AP style in the preceding example:

- "Massachusetts" should be abbreviated *Mass.*
- "7:00 o'clock P.M." should be *7 p.m.*
- Tues. should be spelled out *Tuesday.*
- "February" should be abbreviated *Feb.*
- A hyphen should be inserted in *quilt-maker.*

Avoid relying on the copy desk to do your work if the rewrite is given to you.

You should check the other points as well. Confirm the spelling of Bertke's name, and see if there is an apostrophe in Charters Auditorium. The Smith Gallery may or may not be on the Hampton campus. Ask how long the exhibit will be at the gallery. Are quilts made by local people included in the exhibit? Perhaps your questions will lead to a feature story on local quilt-making.

In your rewrite, you will drop the quotation of Betty Martin. But you may insert better, less self-serving and less promotional quotes.

Here is another example:

Mr. Richard G. Henderson has been selected as the Outstanding Biology Teacher of Nevada of the year by the National Association of Biology Teachers. He was previously selected as Nevada Science Educator of the year.

As an outstanding representative of good high-school biology teaching Henderson will receive a certificate and a series 50 binocular microscope with an engraved citation. Henderson has been teaching at Hickman High School since 1980.

The story is far from earthshaking, but the honor is statewide. On large newspapers the release may not get much play. A small community newspaper, however, will use it and perhaps enlarge upon it.

A first reading of the release tells you it is wordy and that it leaves many questions unanswered. Henderson may be an interesting fellow, but the release tells us little about him. You should approach this release in the same way you approach any news release: Finish the reporting, and then rewrite it. News style demands a new lead to the release:

A Hickman High School science teacher has been named Outstanding Biology Teacher of the year by the National Association of
Biology Teachers.

Richard G. Henderson, a Hickman teacher since 1980, will receive a
certificate and a series 50 binocular microscope with an engraved citation.

Previously selected as Nevada Science Educator of the year, Henderson . . .

Here the story runs out of information. You need to ask the following questions:

- Age?
- Degrees from where?
- Local address?
- Spouse, family?
- Annual award? One teacher selected from each state?
- Any previous Hickman winners? Any from local high schools?
- Year he received Nevada Science Educator award?
- Nominated for the award by whom?
- Date and place of bestowal? Public ceremony?
- Value of series 50 binocular microscope?

Then call Henderson and find out how he feels about the award. Talk
to the principal, to fellow teachers and to some of Henderson's students. Good quotations will spice up your story.

Rewriting the Cause Release

Newspapers generally cooperate with causes that are community-
oriented. News releases like the following get attention:

A free tax clinic for low-income persons and senior citizens will be
held on Feb. 9 and 10 in Springfield.

The clinic is sponsored by the Central State Counties' Human Development Corporation with the Accounting Department of the Springfield University College of Business.

Senior and graduate accounting students under the direct supervision
of accounting faculty members will work with each taxpayer to help
that taxpayer complete accurately his or her tax return.

The Human Development Corporation encourages persons especially to use the clinic who may be eligible for senior citizens' credits or
other credits.

This is the fifth year the clinic has operated in Shelby County. Last
year more than 275 persons in the eight counties served were assisted.

For information regarding the location of the clinics and to make an
appointment, contact the Shelby County Human Development Corporation, 600 E. Broadway, Room 103, Springfield, 555-8376.

Again, you need more information. To begin with, you need to know
more about the Human Development Corporation. A background
paragraph on its origins, where it gets its money and its other areas of
concern will put the story into context.

The release is unclear about who is eligible. What must your income be? How old must you be? Also, you must find out the exact locations of the clinics.

Once you have all your questions answered, dig for some human interest. Talk to a participating faculty member and to students who have helped before and will help again. Then talk to some people who have been helped in the past and to some who will come for help. Obviously, you must talk to those in charge of the joint effort.

Because efforts like these are in the public interest, newspapers will give them space. They will be more critical with releases that are merely self-serving.

Rewriting the Image-Building Release

The following is a typical release from a politician:

> Sen. John C. Smith said today that nearly $400,000 in grants have been given final approval by two departments of the state government for interlocking improvements in Springfield and Lincoln County.
>
> Smith said, "This is something I have been working for this past year. It is a chance to show that state agencies are interested in communities. It also demonstrates that two agencies can work together to produce a coordinated, workable solution to improve a blighted area in Springfield."
>
> The grants, Smith said, come from the State Bureau of Outdoor Recreation—$247,000 for purchasing Baltimore and Ohio railroad rights of way and developing a strip park, and the Department of Housing and Urban Development—$150,000 for planning the Flat Branch area. The second grant also stipulates that part of the money be used to coordinate the two projects, the B&O strip park, and the Flat Branch redevelopment.
>
> "I think residents of Springfield and Lincoln County will have a chance to help out in the planning of these two facilities. I hope this means the entire community will express opinions and come to a conclusion that will see these projects become a reality in the next two years."

The first four words of the release indicate who is being served by the release. A Springfield reporter might write the lead this way to serve the reader:

> Springfield and Lincoln County will receive nearly $400,000 in state grants to fund the B&O strip park and the Flat Branch redevelopment project, Sen. John C. Smith said today.

The second paragraph of the release is a long and newsless quote from the senator. Probably he did not say those words at all; they were likely written by his press agent. You should eliminate them, or if you want a quote from the senator, call him and talk to him yourself.

The second paragraph of the story should indicate the source of the funding:

> The grants come from two state agencies. The State Bureau of Outdoor Recreation granted $247,000 for purchasing the Baltimore &

Ohio Railroad rights of way and for developing a strip park, and the Department of Housing and Urban Development granted $150,000 for planning the Flat Branch area. The second grant also stipulates that part of the money be used to coordinate the two projects.

Smith's last quote could be handled this way:

> Smith said he hoped Springfield and Lincoln County residents will have a chance to help plan the two facilities. "I hope this means the entire community will express opinions and come to a conclusion that will see these projects become a reality in the next two years."

Like many news releases of this kind, this announcement would trigger other news stories in the local papers. This story would call for local reactions from city and county officials and from local residents. The editor might assign several stories on the matter.

Releases from organizations can also be self-serving—and sometimes misleading. Suppose you were given the news release shown in Figure 9.2 (page 192) to rewrite.

Your first task is to read the release carefully. The lead cleverly suggests that dogcatchers make as much money as teachers do, although it speaks only of starting salaries. The more you read the release, the more uncomfortable you should feel with it. No one can blame teachers for wanting more money, but there are other factors to consider. What about working conditions? Teachers in Springfield's schools certainly don't have to put their lives on the line the way police officers and firefighters do. Most people do not want to spend their lives chasing stray dogs. Besides, the list of salaries in the release does not support the lead that says the starting salary of dogcatchers is higher than the starting salary of teachers.

The fact that teachers work for a little more than nine months a year is down in the fourth paragraph. The release fails to mention a two-week break over Christmas and a week off in the spring semester. Most firefighters get two weeks off per year.

Is the release trying to suggest that because teachers actually spend more than 40 hours a week working, they should not have to work more than 9 1/4 months? Not all teachers spend all their lives going to summer school. You probably know several who have summer jobs or who take long vacations.

Before you turn in a rewrite of the release, you have a lot of checking to do.

One reporter began by calling the city of Springfield's personnel office. When asked about the $21,676 starting salary of a firefighter, the personnel officer replied: "You wouldn't begin at that salary. Everyone is hired at $20,644 for a trial period of at least six months. If you work out OK, you might jump up to $21,676. Again, there are a lot of considerations besides the college degree."

Further checking revealed that the news release did indeed contain inaccurate information about the starting salaries of firefighters.

NEWS RELEASE
Springfield Community Teachers Association
Lillian A. Briggs, President
Contact: Tom Monnin, SCTA Salary Committee Chairman
Phone: 555-6794 (Central High School)
          555-2975 (home)
For Immediate Release

Springfield—Dogcatchers in Springfield make a higher starting salary than Springfield teachers, as discovered in a recent survey by the Springfield Community Teachers Association. According to their research, a new teacher in the Springfield public school system makes $20,700, while a firefighter starts at $21,676 or $976 more than a new teacher. "This is a shameful situation for an educational community," said Tom Monnin, Springfield SCTA Salary Committee chairman.

The statistics gathered by the Springfield SCTA Salary Committee indicate that police with a bachelor's degree make $23,327. This is a $2,627 gap in starting salaries for public employees with comparable education. Following is a comparison of starting salaries of some Springfield city employees and of public school teachers for the school year:

Occupation	Starting Salary
Police officer with bachelor's degree	$23,327
Firefighter with bachelor's degree	21,676
Meter reader	15,789
Animal control officer	16,576
Bus operator	15,038
Teacher with bachelor's degree	20,700

"Springfield teachers do not think city employees are overpaid but that teachers are underpaid," Monnin said.

Even though teachers work under a 9 1/4-month contract, the work week is not 40 hours. When the hours for preparing and grading, attending sports events, musical concerts, dances, other after-school activities and PTA meetings are considered, a teacher's work week is much longer than 40 hours. Summer break is used by many teachers for advanced preparation at the university, at their own expense.

The Springfield SCTA Salary Committee will present the salary proposal at the next meeting of the Springfield Board of Education.

The Springfield SCTA represents approximately 523 members in the public school system.

Figure 9.2.
A news release from the Springfield Community Teachers Association.

The reporter knew she was on to something. Comparing starting salaries was one thing. But how much could a person eventually earn in a position?

The reporter then asked about the starting salary for a police officer. "Yes," the director of personnel said, "$23,327 is the beginning salary for a police officer with a B.S. degree."

The reporter then asked whether anyone could get hired at that salary if he or she had a B.S. degree.

"Most people wouldn't stand a chance of being hired," he said. "We have more than 100 applicants for every position, so we can be quite choosy. Unless a person has had some real experience as a police officer, I don't think he would make it."

Further questioning revealed that a top salary for a police officer was $31,841 after six years of service.

The reporter then called a high-school teacher. She asked her if she had to put in more than 40 hours a week at her job.

"Oh, yes," she said. "I teach a section of English composition, and I have a lot of papers to grade. I used to spend a lot of evenings preparing for classes, but once you've taught a course, it gets easier. And then I have to go to all those football games and basketball games."

The reporter then found out that she was indeed required to attend, but only because she was in charge of the cheerleaders. When the reporter expressed sympathy, the teacher replied, "No, I really don't mind. After all, I get $1,200 a year extra for being in charge of the cheerleaders."

The reporter then learned from someone at the Springfield Schools' personnel office that quite a few teachers received compensation for after-school activities—coaching, directing plays and musical activities, advising the staffs of the school newspaper and senior yearbook, and chaperoning dances. Teachers sponsoring class and club activities could earn from $250 to $1,200; a sponsor of the pep squad could earn up to $1,200. The top teacher's salary without any of these extras was $41,400.

Now the reporter was ready to call Tom Monnin, the man whose name was on the release, for additional information. She asked if it was fair to compare a new teacher's salary with a new firefighter's salary when the top pay for a firefighter was $28,881 and the top teacher's salary was $41,400. Monnin explained that it took 17 years for a teacher with a master's degree plus 75 hours to reach that top salary. A teacher with a bachelor's degree could make $28,980 after 11 years of teaching. When the reporter asked about summers off and other vacations, Monnin replied, "I figure I work a 60-hour week. That means I work $51\frac{3}{4}$ 40-hour weeks a year."

Monnin acknowledged that many teachers got paid extra for extracurricular activities. "But not all of them do," he said. "And there are many activities we do feel the responsibility to attend."

When asked about the argument that teachers do not have to

Take special care when news releases cite studies, polls or surveys. Check the source of the figures for accuracy and possible bias. If you can't confirm the figures and their reliability, don't use them.

put their lives on the line the way police and fire officials and even dogcatchers do, Monnin replied:

"It's debatable who has to put their lives on the line. We're not as bad off as some schools, but we often have to restrain students physically."

Only now was the reporter ready to write the story. Here's what she wrote:

The Springfield Community Teachers Association said Tuesday that new firefighters earn more than new teachers.

What the teachers did not say was that a teacher eventually can earn nearly $1,200 more a year than a firefighter can.

The SCTA statement was included with a survey that lists starting teachers' salaries at $20,700. Other figures listed as starting salaries are: police officer with a bachelor's degree, $23,327; animal control officer, $16,576; meter reader, $15,789; bus operator, $15,038.

"This is a shameful situation for an educational community," said Tom Monnin, the SCTA Salary Committee chairman. "Springfield teachers do not think city employees are overpaid but that teachers are underpaid."

The association officers said that even though teachers work under a $9\frac{1}{4}$-month contract, extracurricular activities extend the workweek beyond 40 hours. Summer break, they said, is used for advanced study at the teachers' own expense.

"I figure I work a 60-hour week," Monnin said in an interview. "That means I work $51\frac{3}{4}$ 40-hour weeks a year."

Some extracurricular activities, such as coaching, directing plays and supervising cheerleaders, earn extra compensation.

Teachers are not compelled to attend after-school functions, but "we do feel the responsibility to attend," Monnin said.

Teachers also feel compelled to continue their education. Top pay for a teacher with only a bachelor's degree is $28,980 after 11 years of teaching. A teacher with a master's degree plus 75 hours of classes can earn $41,400 after 17 years of teaching.

A police officer with a bachelor's degree can reach a top salary of $31,841 after six years of police work. But a person with a bachelor's degree and no police work experience is not likely to be hired, said Phil James, the Springfield director of personnel. James also said all firefighters are hired at $20,644. If a person has a bachelor's degree and stays on, he or she could make $21,676 after a six-month trial period.

Top pay for a dogcatcher is $22,626. "I sure wish I got summers off like those teachers," Tom Merell, an animal control officer, said. "I got nothing against teachers. But most of them make more money than I'll ever make. . . . Besides, students don't bite many teachers."

The SCTA Salary Committee will present its salary proposal at the next meeting of the Springfield Board of Education.

The reporter did with this news release what you should do with many of them. She was not satisfied with the way it was written, nor with the information it contained. By asking some important questions, she was able to put together an informative and more ac-

How to handle a news release

1. *Read the information that appears on the top of the release form.*
2. *Check the news style. Ask questions about missing information. Verify any spellings or information you have doubts about.*
3. *Take for granted that you are to do a rewrite. Fill in missing information. Tighten the copy.*
4. *Watch for self-serving quotations and information. Look for news, and write it.*
5. *Look for other possible news stories—local angles, reactions and the like—that can be triggered by the release.*

curate story. Without saying that the news release was dishonest or misleading, the reporter corrected or clarified some of the information contained in it. The plight of the teacher is told clearly and objectively, but it is placed in a much better perspective than was found in the news release.

Like many news releases, this one was the basis for a story the newspaper otherwise would not have had. That is why editors pay attention to them and why reporters look for the real story.

Suggested Readings

Howard, Carole and Mathews, Wilma. *On Deadline: Managing Media Relations*. Second Edition. Prospect Heights, Ill.: Waveland Press, 1994. A practical book on how organizations should deal with the news media.

Tucker, Kerry, Derelian, Doris and Rouner, Donna. *Public Relations Writing: An Issue-Driven Behavioral Approach*. Second Edition. Englewood Cliffs, N.J.: Prentice Hall, 1994. A practical writing guide

for public relations practitioners that puts writing in the context of the issues and goals of an organization.

Wilcox, Dennis L. and Nolte, Lawrence W. *Public Relations Writing and Media Techniques*. New York: HarperCollins, 1990. Emphasizes writing, producing and distributing a variety of public relations materials.

Exercises

1. Read each of the following news releases. First, correct all departures from Associated Press style rules. Second, indicate the type of news release it is. Third, list questions you would have if you were to rewrite it, including the facts you would check and the sources you would turn to for the answers.

a. NEWS RELEASE

The 1996 Sheep Knowledge awards will be made on the basis of a comprehensive test over knowledge in the book, Raising Sheep the Modern Way, by Paula Simmons. Information concerning availability of this book may be obtained from libraries, bookstores, or university agriculture departments.

The test will be developed, administered, and scored by nationally known livestock specialists. The contest is being announced early to give students adequate time for preparation. The test will be given in Springfield at 8:00 P.M. on September 5. The contest will be open to any person who is not yet eighteen, on that day.

The four top winners will receive trophies and divide ten commercial ewes as follows: First -4 ewes, Second -3 ewes, Third -2 ewes, Fourth -1 ewe.

b. NEWS RELEASE

Plaza Frontenac will be filled with floral displays from 10:00 A.M. to 9:00 P.M. on Friday October 31 and 10:00 A.M. to 4:00 P.M. on Saturday November 1 as the East Central District of the Federated Garden Clubs of America, Inc. presents "Challenge," a flower show of artistic flower arrangements and outstanding horticultural specimens on both levels of the plaza.

Hundreds of entries, including table settings, arrangements featuring fresh flowers, evergreens and dried plants will offer decorating ideas for special occasions. Educational exhibits on state birds, the propagation and growing of African violets, and a patio garden of perennials designed by Doug and Cindy Gilberg of Gilberg Perennial Farms.

General co-chairmen for the event are Wilma Stortz and Kay Schaefer. In 1989 the group staged a major flower show at Plaza Frontenac and won a national award.

The show is free and open to the public. Plaza Frontenac is located on the corner of South Main and Hamilton. Shopping hours are 10:00 A.M. to 9:00 P.M. Monday through Friday.

c. NEWS RELEASE

The teaching faculty, administration and staff

of The South Shore Country Day School formally began the school year Friday, August 30, with an all day workshop on curriculum planning.

This year, the School will be involved in a year long task of self evaluation. All aspects of the School's curriculum and student life will be considered and a new five year, long range plan for the curriculum will be written. The School's last major plan was constructed in 1992.

The evaluation process is designed to keep curriculum consistent with the School's educational philosophy and statement of mission. It will identify problems, strengths, and opportunities for expansion. At various stages of the process, all constituencies of the School will have an opportunity to express concerns and opinions. By the end of the school year, a new plan will be ready for integration and implementation by the School's administration.

William R. Lopez, Chairman of the School's Board of Trustees, spoke to the faculty about the upcoming project and the need to change. "We will attempt to make the current school better; we will not be creating a new school," he said.

Thomas B. Lang, the School's headmaster, emphasized the importance of total faculty participation in the formulation and execution of the mission statement. "We're all in this together." Lang said. "Curriculum is the sum of all the parts. No one teaches in a vacuum."

Among topics discussed at the workshop were: the importance of academic excellence; student social service; a need for diversity within the student body; the importance of educating the whole child; providing increased opportunity for students to participate in a variety of academic and nonacademic projects; and the ethical considerations in the School.

2. Assume you are a reporter for the Springfield paper. Your instructor will be your news source for any questions you have. Rewrite each of the following releases:

a. NEWS RELEASE

Nearly 11,000 seat belt violation warnings were issued to motorists by the State Highway Patrol during the first month the new seat belt law was in effect.

Colonel Howard J. Hoffman, Superintendent of the State Highway Patrol, reported today that 10,908 warnings were issued to motorists in passenger vehicles for not wearing their seat belts as required by State Law.

Colonel Hoffman also noted that during this same reporting period, 50 persons were killed in traffic accidents investigated by the Highway Pa-

trol. Only two of the persons killed in these mishaps were found to be wearing seat belts.

"The value of wearing a seat belt cannot be overemphasized," Hoffman said. "We don't know how many of these investigated traffic deaths could have been avoided by the use of seat belts. It is known, however, that seat belts have saved lives and prevented serious injuries to others. We will continue to vigorously enforce the State seat belt law and hopefully more and more motorists will make it a habit to buckle their seat belts."

b. NEWS RELEASE

The Better Business Bureau serving the tri-state area has launched a fund-raising drive to finance the installation of a 24-hour computerized telephone service called Tel-Tips.

James C. Schmitt, President, said Tel-Tips is a unique consumer information and education system designed to give quick useful information about specific goods and services. Consumers would be provided with a number to call and the system will put the caller in contact with a selected pre-recorded message.

A goal of $20,000 has been established to finance installation of Tel-Tips and the physical expansion of the BBB's office.

"Despite efficient telephone communications and computer system, we expect to lose nearly 24,000 calls this year," said Schmitt. "Our operators are trained to limit time given to each caller to avoid losing callers, while at the same time attempting to provide complete information."

The Bureau is unable to respond to inquiries before and after business hours and on weekends, times many customers need BBB services.

Tel-Tips is a computerized information center that allows 114 consumer tip messages to be made instantly available to callers. This system answers incoming calls with a pre-recorded message and instructs the caller to dial the number of the message he or she wants to hear. This unit operates automatically with the use of a Touch-Tone telephone, 12 hours a day. A rotary dial telephone may be used during regular business hours with the assistance of an operator.

c. NEWS RELEASE

"Chest Pains," a film in the HEALTHSCOPE series produced by the American College of Physicians, will be shown from 7–8:30 p.m., Wednesday, Oct. 22, at St. Mary's Health Center. Springfield internist, Dr. Harold Kanagawa, will host a question-and-answer period following the film.

Although most people assume that chest pains signify a heart attack, the public is less aware that other conditions—hiatal hernia, ulcers, viral infections of the heart's membranes—can also cause pains that require prompt diagnosis and appropriate medical treatment. Designed to help increase awareness of these symptoms and their possible significance, "Chest Pains" features an internist and actual patients as they work together to resolve underlying medical problems.

Through a human-interest style of presentation, each 25-minute documentary encourages people to take an increased responsibility for their own well-being by establishing healthy habits and assuming a more active role in disease prevention.

The HEALTHSCOPE series is produced under an educational grant from the Upjohn Company of Kalamazoo, Mich. Other films in the series cover "Aches, Pains and Arthritis," "Diabetes," and "Abdominal Discomfort."

Dr. Kanagawa, a specialist in internal medicine, is one of 50,000 members of the American College of Physicians. Founded in 1915, the College is the largest medical specialty society in the United States. It represents doctors of internal medicine, related non-surgical specialists, and physicians-in-training.

To register or for more information, contact the Women's Life Center.

3. Your professor will give you a local news release. Using local sources and resources, report and rewrite the story.

SPEECHES, NEWS CONFERENCES AND MEETINGS

Y*ou can be quite sure that in your first year or so of general-assignment reporting you will be assigned to cover many speeches, news conferences and meetings. They are sometimes routine, sometimes of great importance. Communities often elect and re-elect their leaders on the basis of their performance at these events. Communities are rallied to causes and nations to wars by speeches, news conferences and meetings.*

For example, before President Lyndon B. Johnson's televised address on the Gulf of Tonkin incident in 1964, a Harris Survey showed that less than half of the electorate approved of the president's Vietnam policy. After his address, a second poll indicated that 70 percent approved. Before President Richard M. Nixon addressed the nation to attempt to justify the invasion of Cambodia in 1970, a Harris Survey showed that only 7 percent of the public supported the decision. Following Nixon's television address, more than 50 percent approved of the president's action. More recently, a USA Today/CNN/Gallup poll showed that President Bill Clinton's news conference regarding his troubles with the Whitewater real estate deal raised his approval rating of how he was handling Whitewater from 39 percent to 50 percent.

Some argue that it was President John F. Kennedy's display of intelligence and wit at news conferences that got him elected and earned him respect as president. President Nixon, however, had little flair for give and take, and less love for reporters. Consequently, his performance at news conferences added little to his popularity. President Ronald Reagan felt at home in front of cameras, and although he disliked news conferences, his televised speeches helped boost his image tremendously. President Clinton's town meetings helped him get to the White House.

Because speeches, news conferences and meetings are similar, all three are examined in this chapter. But the distinguishing characteristics of these three forms should be kept in mind as well.

A speech *is a public talk. Someone stands and speaks to an audience in person or on radio or television. Regardless of the medium, the nature of a speech is the same: It is a one-way communication; the speaker speaks, and the audience listens.*

Speakers usually are invited and sometimes paid to address an audience. That is not the case with those who hold a **news conference.** *People "call" a news conference. They do not send invitations to the general public, but they do alert members of the various news media. The media respond because of the importance of the person calling the news conference and because the person may have something newsworthy to say. The person holding the news conference often begins with an opening statement and then usually accepts questions from reporters. A news conference is meant to be a two-way communication.*

Unlike speeches and news conferences, meetings *are not held with an audience in mind, even though an audience may be present and al-*

lowed to participate. A meeting is primarily for communication among the members of a group or organization, whether a local parent-teacher association or the Congress of the United States. If reporters are permitted to witness a meeting, they are there to report to the public what is of interest and importance. This task of the news media is especially important if the meeting is of a governmental body that deals with the public's money collected through taxes.

You can be sure that you will spend a great deal of your time as a reporter covering speeches, news conferences and meetings. For that reason you will want to learn all you can about covering them well.

Preparation

The professional reporter knows that preparation makes covering a story much easier. In all cases, reporters should do their homework. You prepare for the speech, news conference or meeting story in much the same way. Because these events are usually planned and announced in advance, you have time for thorough preparation. Let's begin with a speech story.

Preparing for the Speech Story

Not every speech you are assigned to cover will demand a great deal of research. Many speakers and speeches will be dry and routine. The person giving it will be someone you know or someone you have covered before. At other times you may be given an assignment on short notice and may be forced to find background information after you have heard the speech. But never take the speaker or the topic for granted. A failure to get enough background on the speaker and on the speech nearly guarantees failure at writing a comprehensive speech story.

When one reporter was assigned to cover a speech by Kenneth Clark, she presumed that this was the Kenneth Clark who had done so much on culture and civilization on public television. When she called the information service at the public library, she discovered two famous Kenneth Clarks. One, Kenneth Mackenzie Clark, was indeed an expert on civilization and the arts. The other, Kenneth Bancroft Clark, was a psychiatrist and author, most famous for writing *Dark Ghetto*, the study of the effects of the ghetto on Harlem children. It was the psychiatrist who was giving the speech.

The first step in your research is to get the right person. Middle initials are important; sometimes even they are not enough. Sometimes checking the address is not enough. One reporter wrote about the wrong person because he did not know that a father and son shared the same name at the same address.

Think technical thoughts

Preparing to cover speeches, news conferences and meetings presents many technical questions for the television journalist. Here are three things to keep in mind:

■ Think visuals. *What will your backdrop be? Will there be signs, photos, samples, logos or flipcharts to help tell the story?*

■ Think sound. *Will there be one microphone or a multi-box for you to insert your mike, or will you be free to set up your own microphone?*

■ Think light. *Will the event take place outdoors or in a well-lit room, or must you bring your own lighting? How far is the* camera throw *(the distance from the event to your camera)? Will there be a camera platform or a set space, or will you be free to set up your camera anywhere?*

Before doing research on the speaker, contact the group sponsoring the speech and ask for the topic. You might find you need some reading to prepare you to understand the subject better. If you are lucky, you may get a copy of the speech ahead of time. Also check your newspaper library to see what your paper has done on the speaker. If you have access to a data bank, use it. If the assignment calls for it, visit your local library and check the references noted on pages 162-163 in Chapter 7.

If the speech is important enough, you might want to contact the speaker ahead of time for a brief interview. If he or she is from out of town, you might plan for a meeting at the airport. You might also arrange ahead of time to interview the speaker after the speech. You may have some questions and some points to clarify.

Again, not every speech will demand this much effort. But even the most routine speech assignment needs preparation. It may seem obvious, for instance, that the reason Gene Martin, the director of the local library, is addressing the state Writer's Guild is to tell members how to use the library to write better stories. Not so. Gene Martin also is a successful "true confessions" writer. He has been published dozens of times in such magazines as *True Confessions, True Romance* and others. He may be addressing the guild on how he does it.

Sooner or later you may be called on to cover speeches of major political candidates, perhaps even of the president of the United States. For this task, too, you need background—lots of it. It demands that you read the news and that you know what is going on. You *must* keep up with current events.

Preparing for the News Conference Story

Preparing for a news conference is like preparing for speeches. You need to know the up-to-date background of the person giving the news conference, and you must learn why the news conference is being held.

Often the person holding the news conference has an announcement or an opening statement. Unless that statement is leaked to the press, you will not know its content ahead of time. But you can do some educated guessing. Check out any rumors. Call the person's associates, friends or secretary. The more prepared you are, the better chance you have of coming away with a coherent, readable story.

A problem you will encounter at news conferences is that every reporter there has a line of questions to pursue. Your editor may want certain information, and other editors may want something else. You will not have time to think out your questions once you are there: The job of recording the responses to other reporters' questions will keep you too busy.

It may be impossible, as well, to arrange an interview before or after the news conference. If the person holding the news conference wanted to grant individual reporters interviews, he or she probably would not have called the news conference. But you can give it a try. You never know, and you may end up with some exclusive information.

Preparing for the Meeting Story

You never know just what to expect at a meeting, either. But again, you must do your best to prepare for it. Who are the people holding the meeting? What kind of an organization is it? Who are the key figures? Again, the morgue is your first stop.

Contact some of the key figures. See if you can find out what the meeting is about. Perhaps the president or the secretary has a written agenda for the meeting. If you know the main subject to be discussed at the meeting, you will be able to study and investigate the issues before arriving. Knowing what to expect and being familiar with the issues will make covering the meeting much easier.

A reporter with a regular **beat**—an assigned area of responsibility—usually covers the meetings of more important organizations and of groups like the city council, the school board or the county board. (Beat reporting is discussed in detail in Chapter 14.) A beat reporter has a continuing familiarity with the organization and with the issues involved. Often the meetings of important organizations are preceded by an *advance*—a report outlining the subjects and issues to be dealt with in the upcoming meeting.

In summary, then, to cover speeches, news conferences and meetings well, you must arm yourself with information concerning the people involved and the issues to be discussed. Do your homework.

Covering Speeches, News Conferences and Meetings

The story is often told of the reporter who prepared well for a speech assignment, contacted the speaker, got a copy of the speech, wrote the story and spent the evening in a bar. He didn't know until after the speech story was handed in that the speech had been canceled.

And then there's the yarn about the reporter who was assigned to cover a meeting and came back to tell the city editor there was no story.

"Why not?" the city editor asked.

"Because the meeting was canceled."

"Why was that?"

"Well," replied the young reporter, "when the meeting started, some of the board members got in this big argument. Finally, three of them walked out. The president then canceled the meeting because there was no quorum."

The reporter had been sent to cover a meeting. But the canceled meeting and the circumstances surrounding its cancellation

---

To achieve total coverage, of content and event, you must remember to:

- *Get the content correct. Tape recorders can be helpful, but always take good notes. Quote people exactly and in context.*
- *Note the background, personal characteristics and mannerisms of the main participants.*
- *Cover the event. Look around the edges—at the audience (size, reactions) and sometimes at what is happening outside the building.*
- *Get there early, position yourself and hang around afterward.*

probably were of more interest to readers than the meeting itself would have been.

Preparing to cover events is only the beginning. Knowing what to do when you get there is the next step. Remember this: Covering the *content* of a speech, news conference or meeting often is only half of the job—and sometimes the less important half. You must cover the entire *event*—the time, place, circumstances, number of people involved and possible consequences of what was said or of the actions taken.

Getting the Content Correct

You may find a tape recorder useful in covering the content of speeches, news conferences and meetings. Tape recorders often scare newspaper people, but they need not. As with anything else, you must practice using a tape recorder. You must use it again and again to become completely familiar with its idiosyncracies. In other words, learning to operate tape recorders is not enough. You need to be comfortable with the one you are using. For example, you must be sure just how sensitive the microphone is. It is sound you want, and sound you must get.

The most frequent complaint you may hear about tape recorders is that it takes too long to listen to the entire recording. You may have to listen to a whole speech again just to find a certain quote that you want to check. But you may avoid this problem if you have a tape recorder with a digital counter. At any point in a speech or a meeting when something of importance is said, you need only to note the number on the counter. Finding it later will then be no problem.

But there is one thing you *must* do even when you tape-record an event: You must take notes in exactly the same way that you would if you were not tape-recording. The truth of the matter is, you may *not* be. Malfunctions can occur with the best machines at the most inopportune times.

So, with or without a tape recorder, you must become a proficient note taker. Many veteran reporters wish they had taken a shorthand or speed-writing course early in their careers. You may find it useful to buy a speed-writing manual and become used to certain symbols. Every reporter sooner or later adopts or creates some shortcuts in note taking. You will have to do the same. Learn to abbreviate whenever you can (*wh* for *which*, *th* for *that*, *bk* for *book*, *st* for *street*, *bldg* for *building*, etc.). Make up signs (*w/* for *with*, *w/o* for *without*, *acc/* for *according to*).

You may be one of those fortunate people with a fantastic memory. Some reporters develop an incredible knack of re-creating whole conversations with complete accuracy without taking a note. But you may be one of those who takes reams of notes. If you are, take them as neatly as you can. Many of us cannot read our own handwriting at times—a nuisance, particularly when a proper name is involved.

Taking notes is most crucial when you wish to record direct

Sidebar

Using the tape recorder

Be familiar with the machine. *Practice using it. Make sure you understand its peculiarities. Check its sound capabilities.*

Set it where you can see it's working. *If it has a digital counter, note the number when you hear a quote you want.*

Take notes as if it might not be working. *After all, it might not be.*

You need to develop your own shortcuts in note taking. Clear note taking is essential—but the notes need only be clear to you. That means you must develop a consistent habit, or you won't remember what your shortcuts mean when you get to writing the story.

quotes. As you learned in Chapter 6, putting someone's words in quotation marks means only one thing: You are quoting the person word for word, exactly as the person spoke. Speeches, news conferences and meetings all demand that you be able to record direct quotes. Your stories will be lifeless and lack credibility without them. A speech story, for example, should contain many direct quotes.

Whether covering a speech, news conference or meeting, you must be careful to quote people in context. For example, if a speaker gives supportive evidence for an argument, you would be unfair not to report it. Quotes can be misleading if you carelessly or deliberately juxtapose them. Combining quotes with no indication that something was said in between them can lead to inaccuracies and to charges of unfairness. Suppose, for example, someone said:

> "Cutting down fuel costs can be an easy thing. If you have easy access to wood, you should invest in a good wood-burning stove. With little effort, you can cut your fuel bills in half."

If a reporter omitted the middle sentence of that quote, the speaker would be made to look ridiculous:

> "Cutting down fuel costs can be an easy thing. With little effort, you can cut your fuel bills in half."

But there is more to the speaker than the words he or she is saying. Quoting the speaker at length or printing a speech in its entirety may at times be justified. But when you quote a whole speech, you are recording it, not reporting it. The overall content of the speech may or may not be news. Sometimes the news may be what a speaker left unsaid. You must decide what is newsworthy.

Describing the Participants

In addition to listening to what a speaker says, you must watch for other things. A tape recording misses the facial expressions and the gestures of a speaker. These sometimes are more important than the words themselves.

For example, you may have heard the story of how Soviet Premier Nikita Khrushchev pounded the table with his shoe in the United Nations General Assembly on Sept. 20, 1960. But you probably are unsure about what he was saying or what he was protesting. Similarly, you may remember from your American history class the setting of President Franklin D. Roosevelt's fireside chats, but you probably don't remember the content.

Simply recording the words of a speaker (or of the person holding a news conference or participating at a meeting) does not indicate volume and tone of voice, inflections, pauses, emphases, and reactions to and from those in attendance. You may note that a speaker very deliberately winked while reading a sentence. Or you may notice an unmistakable sarcasm in the speaker's voice.

ON THE JOB

Departing from the Text

After receiving a master's in journalism, Barry Murov worked as an associate editor of a Washington, D.C., newsletter, where he covered federal job programs. Then after working for the *St. Louis Business Journal* for six years, first as a reporter, then as managing editor, Murov became editor of *St. Louis* magazine. Now he's employed by Fleishman-Hillard, Inc., an international public relations firm.

Murov has written and edited dozens of stories covering speeches, meetings and news conferences. Here are some tips he has for you:

Regardless of who the speaker is or where the speech is taking place, you always must note the speaker's background. A person's words often must be measured against that individual's background. For example, if an ex-Communist is speaking on communism, this fact may have a bearing on what is said. If a former CIA agent speaks about corruption in the CIA, the message would not be adequately reported if the person's background were not mentioned.

Sometimes purely physical facts about the speaker are essential to the story. A blind person pleading for funds to educate the blind, a one-armed veteran speaking about the hell of war, a gray-haired person speaking about care for the elderly—these speakers must be described physically for the story to be complete, accurate and understandable.

You also should note what the person who introduces a speaker says. This may help you understand the significance of the speaker and the importance of what he or she has to say.

Covering the Event

At all these events keep an eye on the audience and on what's happening around the edges. You need to measure the mood of the audience by noting the tone of the questions. Are they sharply worded? Is there much laughter or applause? Perhaps members of the

> "Always ask for a copy of the speech ahead of time," Murov says. "Even when you are lucky enough to get a copy, don't assume that the speaker will stick to the text."
>
> As a consultant for Fortune 500 corporations, Murov knows that "many executives tend to tinker with their speeches, even making significant changes, up until the final minute."
>
> Murov says you should follow along in the text during a speech to note where the actual presentation differs. "You don't want your story to include a statement from the text that the speaker deleted. Also, you may find the real news nugget buried in the speech."
>
> Don't leave a meeting or news conference immediately. "Go up to the spokesperson or the leader of the meeting and ask a question that hasn't been covered during the actual event.
>
> "That can benefit you in two ways: One, you will have something extra for your readers. Two, it helps you build a relationship with the spokesperson that may pay off in the future."

Figure 10.1.
Public figures may call news conferences to announce recent events or plans. Here the lawyer of Dr. Jack Kevorkian presents his perspective on the release of his client from jail after an assisted suicide. The reporters have an opportunity to find out more information by preparing in advance, asking questions and being observant during the conference.

audience boo. Does the speaker or the person holding the news conference or the person presiding over the meeting remain calm and in control at all times? Is there a casual bantering or joking with the audience? Is the audience stacked with supporters or detractors?

Sometimes the real action is taking place outside in the form of a picket line or protest of some kind. Sometimes it is right in front of you.

In the 1960s, civil rights and anti-war activists made many a speech and meeting interesting and newsworthy. When John Howard Griffin, author of *Black Like Me*, spoke in a college auditorium in Milwaukee, the audience and reporters noted the number of police officers who were continually clearing the aisles of the crowded hall. Not too unusual—just enforcing the fire code, the officers said. But some were puzzled by the fact that Griffin left immediately after his speech without giving the audience any chance for questions and discussion. It was all the more surprising because Griffin is a warm and generous man, and he had an urgent anti-racist message he wished to share.

One enterprising reporter found out someone had threatened Griffin's life. Though Griffin insisted on delivering the speech, police whisked him away immediately after he finished. Obviously, this, rather than anything Griffin said that night, was the lead for the story.

Most speeches do not involve threats on the speaker's life. But don't overlook the obvious. For example, you should note the size of the audience. Reporting a "full house" means little unless you indicate the house capacity. One way to estimate attendance is to count how many people are sitting in a row or in a typical section. Then you simply multiply that number by the number of rows or sections in the hall. Use good judgment and common sense to adjust for some sections being more crowded than others.

Arriving, Positioning Yourself and Staying On

Most reporters arrive early. At some events they have special seating, but you should probably not count on it unless you know for sure. At a speech, for example, sitting in the first row is not necessarily the best thing to do. Perhaps you should be in a position that enables you to see the reaction of the audience. If there is a question-and-answer period, you may want to be able to see the questioner. And you certainly want to be in a good position to ask questions yourself.

At a news conference the position you're in may help you get the attention of the person holding the conference. You should have your questions prepared, but preparing them is not enough. You have seen presidential news conferences on television, and you know how difficult it is to get the president's attention. Though on a smaller scale, any news conference presents the reporter with the same difficulties. You have seen how difficult it is for reporters to follow up on their own questions. At some news conferences you will not be called on twice.

But you must do more than try to get your own questions answered. You must listen to others' questions and be able to recognize the making of a good story. Too often a good question is dropped without follow-up because reporters are not listening carefully or are too intent on pursuing their own questions. Listen for what is newsworthy and pursue it. Sticking with an important subject will make the job of writing the story easier. Remember, when the news conference is finished, you will have a story to write. Piecing together notes on dozens of unrelated topics can be difficult, if not impossible.

At a meeting you should be in a position to see and hear the main participants. Ordinarily, a board or council will sit facing the audience. Before the meeting starts you should know which members are sitting where. You may want to assign each participant a number so that you do not have to write the person's name each time he or she speaks. You also can draw a sketch of where they are sitting. In this way you will be able to quote someone by number, even if you do not know their name until later. Know who the officers are. The president or the secretary may have some handouts before the meeting. After a meeting, sometimes the secretary can help you fill in missing words or information.

As a general rule, when the speech, news conference or meeting is over, do not rush off (unless you are on deadline). Hang around. Some of the best stories happen afterward. You should have some questions to ask. You may want some clarifications, or you may arrange to interview a key spokesperson. Listen for reactions from those in attendance. If you are covering a night meeting for an afternoon paper, you may be able to raise some questions and answer others that were not brought up or clarified at the meeting.

Structuring and Writing Your Story

Writing the lead for the speech, news conference or meeting story is no different from writing a lead for any story. All of the qualities of the lead discussed in Chapter 3 are important here as well.

You must be careful not to emphasize something about the event that is of great interest or curiosity but that does not lead into the rest of your story. It is tempting, for example, to lead with a striking quote. But rarely does a speaker or someone holding a news conference highlight the content or the main point in a single, quotable sentence. As always, there are exceptions. As a lead for one of Dr. Martin Luther King Jr.'s most famous addresses, a good reporter might have begun with, "I have a dream."

Because of the nature of the inverted pyramid news story, rarely should you follow the chronology of the event you are covering. But the flow of your story may demand some attention to chronology. If you pay no attention to chronology, you may distort, or cause readers to misinterpret, the meaning of the event.

Writing the Speech Story

Although you may not be called upon to cover a speech of the president of the United States, you can learn a lot about how to write a speech story from the way the pros handle an important address. Let's study how several reporters and their papers covered President Bill Clinton's 1995 State of the Union address.

Here's the way Judy Keen began her story on the front page of *USA Today*:

> President Clinton pleaded for an end to "partisanship, pettiness and pride" in his State of the Union address Tuesday.
>
> "We hear you," he told voters who gave Republicans control of Congress last November. "We will work together to earn your trust."

Keen then shifted her focus to a speech that followed Clinton's:

> New Jersey Gov. Christine Whitman hit similar notes in the GOP response: "We accept your mandate. President Clinton, you must accept it as well. Put the principles of smaller, more effective government into action."

Back to Clinton:

> Clinton voiced broad themes and offered three proposals: an unspecified minimum-wage hike, an effort to combat teen pregnancies and a registry to identify illegal immigrants when they apply for jobs.

Notice how Keen organized her coverage of a speech that was long and covered a lot of topics. In her brief, 365-word front-page story, she also broke the coverage into two parts. She wrote that Clinton promised fresh approaches to government and the economy and grouped her reporting under those two heads.

Keen did not just cover the content of the evening's events. She also noted the length of Clinton's speech (80 minutes) and some reactions. When Clinton said, "We have to change the way the government works. Let's make it smaller, less costly and smarter—leaner, not meaner," Keen reported:

> House Speaker Newt Gingrich leapt up to lead the ovation. Clinton is the first Democrat to address a GOP Congress since Harry Truman in 1948.

Like many other newspapers, *USA Today* did not limit the cov-

Figure 10.2.
Here's how the Cleveland Plain Dealer *covered the 1995 State of the Union address. Note the sidebar about the Republican response and the reference to the analysis inside. Full coverage of this major event requires several news stories.*

erage of the president's address to just one story. Judy Keen had a longer story (665 words) on page 4 that included reactions from other politicians. In both stories, Keen used direct quotations effectively, both from the president and from those reacting to the president. You must do the same to give real flavor and context to your story. Again, obtaining a copy of the speech is most helpful.

The *Los Angeles Times* printed a front-page story by Doyle McManus and Paul Richter that ran for 1,267 words.

The lead paragraphs differed noticeably from *USA Today*'s:

If one purpose of President Clinton's State of the Union Address was to seize the political initiative despite Republican control of Congress, the president could claim a measure of success Wednesday: For the first time in months, GOP leaders were responding to his proposals instead of the other way around.

The article then cited public reaction to the speech:

The first wave of public opinion polls showed a generally positive public response to Clinton's call for a leaner but still activist government. A *CNN/USA Today* poll found that the speech increased approval of Clinton's positions to 83 percent among those who watched the address, although analysts said that the boost is likely to be temporary.

The report contained much more than just a report of what the president said. The same was also true of a story by John Aloysius Farrell in the *Boston Globe*. Note how different Farrell's lead is from the other two:

President Clinton returned to the centrist "New Democrat" themes of his 1992 campaign in his State of the Union speech last night, asking Americans to join in a "new covenant" of civic responsibility and calling for national action against the problems of teen pregnancy, welfare, swollen government and shrinking middle-class incomes.

The *Globe* also ran a piece by Bob Hohler that analyzed and interpreted the speech. It began:

An uneasy peace befell the House last night as President Clinton appealed for bipartisan progress from a bitterly divided Congress.

As the first Democratic president in 40 years to stand before a Republican-controlled Congress, Clinton repeatedly stirred rousing applause from a shrunken corps of House and Senate Democrats and stony silence from the majority ranks of the GOP.

The *Globe* also ran an Associated Press story that began:

President Clinton showcased his national service program and the U.S. military operation in Haiti by inviting AmeriCorps workers and a Marine to sit with his wife during the State of the Union speech.

Again, few speeches you cover will have the significance of a State of the Union address. Nevertheless, remember that there are many ways to write and organize the coverage of a speech. Sometimes it's better to break up the coverage into several stories. Note, too, how informed reporters must be to cover a speech of this importance.

Remember, too, to look for the news. The news may not be what the speaker begins with or even what the speaker spends the most time on. What happened at the speech and what happened after the speech may be more newsworthy.

Writing the News Conference Story

Writing the news conference story may be a bit more challenging than writing the speech story. Because you will come to the conference with different questions in mind than your fellow reporters, you may come away with a different story. At least your lead may be different from those of other reporters.

A news conference often covers a gamut of topics. Often it begins with a statement from the person who called the conference.

For example, when the mayor of Springfield holds a news conference to announce her candidacy for a second term, you can be sure that she will begin with a statement to that effect. Although her candidacy might be news to some people, you may want to ask her questions about the location of a new landfill that the city is rumored to be planning. Most citizens will admit the need for landfills, but their location is always controversial. And then there's that tip you heard about the possibility of the city manager resigning to take a job in a large city.

Other reporters will come with other questions. Will there be further cuts in the city budget? Will the cuts mean that some city employees will lose their jobs? Whatever happened to the plans to expand the city jail?

After you come away from a news conference that covered many topics, you have the job of organizing the material in some logical, coherent order. Usually you will treat the most newsworthy subject first and deal with the other subjects in the order of their importance. Rarely would you report on them in the chronological order in which they were discussed.

Suppose you decided the location of the landfill was the most important item of the news conference—especially if the mayor revealed the location for the first time. You may begin your story this way:

> The city will construct its new landfill near the intersection of State Route 53 and Route E, four miles north of Springfield, Mayor Juanita Williams said today.
>
> "After nearly a year of discussion and the best advice we could obtain, we are certain the Route E location is best for all concerned," Williams said at a news conference.
>
> The mayor admitted there would be continued opposition to the site by citizens living in the general area, especially those in the Valley High Trailer Court. "No location will please everyone," Williams said.
>
> Williams called the news conference to make the expected announcement of her candidacy for a second term.

Now you have to find a way to treat the other topics of the conference. You may want to list them first in a series of bullets in this way:

```
In other matters, Williams said:
▪ City Manager Diane Lusby will not be resigning to take an-
  other post.
▪ Budget constraints will not permit any new construction on
  the city jail this year.
▪ Budget cuts will not cost any city employees their jobs.
  However, positions vacated by retiring personnel will not
  be filled.
```

After this list, you will either come back to your lead, giving more background and citing citizens or other city officials on the subject, or go on to treat, one at a time, the matters you listed. Pay particular attention to making proper transitions from paragraph to paragraph so that your story is coherent. "On other subjects, the mayor said . . . " "The mayor defended her position on . . . " "Again she stressed . . . "

If one of the subjects is of special interest, you may want to write a *sidebar*, a shorter piece to go with your main story. For this story, you may want to do a sidebar on the mayor's candidacy, her record, her possible opponents, and so on.

With a longer or more complicated story, you may want to make a summary list of all the main topics covered and place them in a box or sidebar.

Remember, your job is to give readers the news, as simply and clearly as possible. Remember, too, to cover the event as well as the content. Perhaps only three reporters turned up for the news conference, or perhaps some pickets protested the mayor's remarks about a local abortion clinic. Sometimes what happens at a news conference is more newsworthy than anything the person holding the conference says. What happens there might well be the lead of your main story, or you may want to place it in a sidebar.

Writing the Meeting Story

Readers also want you to take their place at the meeting you are covering. Let's look at a simple meeting story—in this case a meeting of a local school board:

The decision of three national corporations to protest a formula used to compute their property taxes is causing more than $264,000 to be withheld from the Walnut School District's operating budget for the 1995–96 school year.

Superintendent Max Schmidt said at Monday's school board meeting that International Business Machines Corp., ACR Corp. and Xerox are protesting that the method used in computing their 1994 property taxes was no longer valid. Nine California counties are involved in similar disputes.

The taxes, totaling $264, 688, are being held in escrow by the county until the matter is resolved. Some or all of the money eventually may be returned to the district, but the administration cannot determine when or how much.

"If we take a quarter million dollars out of our program at this time, it could have a devastating effect," Schmidt said. "Once you've built that money into your budget and you lost it, you've lost a major source of income."

Mike Harper, the county prosecuting attorney, and Larry Woods, the school district attorney, advised board members to take a "wait-and-see attitude," Schmidt said. He said that one alternative would be to challenge the corporations in court. A final decision will be made later.

The board also delayed action on repayment of $80,000

to IBM in a separate tax dispute. The corporation claims the district owes it for overpaid 1992 property taxes. The county commission has ruled the claim is legitimate and must be repaid.

A possible source of additional income, however, could be House Bill 1002, Schmidt said. If passed, this appropriations bill would provide an additional $46 million for state education, approximately $250,000 of which could go to the Walnut School District.

Charles Campbell, the district architect, said plans for the area's new vocational technical school to be built on the Rock Bridge High School campus will be given to contractors in February. Bids will be presented at the March 13 board meeting.

The board voted to have classes on Presidents Day, Feb. 20, to make up for time missed because of the teachers' strike.

The issue of the meeting was money problems—a subject that concerns every taxpayer. The writer jumped right into the subject in the lead and then in the second paragraph gave us the who, when and where. The reporter then dealt with specifics, naming names and citing figures, and quoted the key person at the meeting. In the last two paragraphs the writer dealt with other matters discussed in the meeting.

The issues discussed at a meeting are not your only considerations in covering a meeting story. Remember, too, to cover the event. Who was there? Who represented the public? Did anyone have reactions after the meeting was over?

Reporter Jennifer Galloway of the *Columbia Missourian* began her meeting story in this way:

Even though they are footing the bill, only one of Boone County's residents cared enough to attend a Tuesday night hearing on the county's 1994 budget.

With an audience of one

citizen plus two reporters, County Auditor June Pitchford presented her official report on the $21 million budget to the Boone County Commission in a silent City Council Chambers.

Even when covering routine, boring events, you are allowed to use your imagination. In addition to getting all the facts, your job is also to be interesting, to get people to read the story. Remember, one of the criteria of news is that it be unusual. Another is that it be interesting.

Finally, you are always expected to write well—even for a common event like a speech, news conference or meeting.

Suggested Readings

Biography and Genealogy Master Index. Detroit, Mich.: Gale Research Co., 1981 to present. A compilation of a large number of biographical directories with names of people whose biographies have been written. Indicates which date and volume of those reference books to consult for the actual biography.

Biography Index. New York: H.W. Wilson Co., 1946 to date. Helps you locate biographical articles that have appeared in 2,000 periodicals and journals, as well as in biographical books and chapters from collective biographies.

"Current Biography." Bronx, N.Y.: The H.W. Wilson Co., 1940 to present. Monthly publication about people in the news, including a photo of each. Excellent source for people not yet or perhaps never included in more formal biographical sources.

Exercises

1. Journalist Bill Moyers is coming to town to speak on the current U.S. president's relationship with the press. Prepare to cover the speech. Record the steps you will take to prepare for the speech and the information you have gathered on Moyers.

2. You learn that actor Robert Redford is holding a news conference before speaking to a local group about environmental issues. You also learn that Redford is personally and actively involved in these issues. Using appropriate data banks, gather and record background information on Redford.

3. Find out when the Faculty Council or similar faculty representative group is having its next meeting. Record the steps you take to prepare for the meeting and the information you gather as you prepare. Then cover the meeting and write the story.

4. The following speech by Nelson Mandela, President of South Africa, took place in Pretoria, South Africa, on May 10, 1994. Write a speech story that concentrates on the content of Mandela's speech.

Glory and Hope
Let there be work, bread, water and salt for all

Your majesties, your royal highnesses, distinguished guests, comrades and friends: Today, all of us do, by our presence here, and by our celebrations in other parts of our country and the world, confer glory and hope to newborn liberty.

Out of the experience of an extraordinary human disaster that lasted too long must be born a society of which all humanity will be proud.

Our daily deeds as ordinary South Africans must produce an actual South African reality that will reinforce humanity's belief in justice, strengthen its confidence in the nobility of the human soul and sustain all our hopes for a glorious life for all.

All this we owe both to ourselves and to the peoples of the world who are so well represented here today.

To my compatriots, I have no hesitation in saying that each one of us is as intimately attached to the soil of this beautiful country as are the famous jacaranda trees of Pretoria and the mimosa trees of the bushveld.

Each time one of us touches the soil of this land, we feel a sense of personal renewal. The national mood changes as the seasons change.

We are moved by a sense of joy and exhilaration when the grass turns green and the flowers bloom.

That spiritual and physical oneness we all share with this common homeland explains the depth of the pain we all carried in our hearts as we saw our country tear itself apart in terrible conflict, and as we saw it spurned, outlawed and isolated by the peoples of the world, precisely because it has become the universal base of the pernicious ideology and practice of racism and racial oppression.

We, the people of South Africa, feel fulfilled that humanity has taken us back into its bosom, that we, who were outlaws not so long ago, have today been given the rare privilege to be host to the nations of the world on our own soil.

We thank all our distinguished international guests for having come to take possession with the people of our country of what is, after all, a common victory for justice, for peace, for human dignity.

We trust that you will continue to stand by us as we tackle the challenges of building peace, prosperity, nonsexism, nonracialism and democracy.

We deeply appreciate the role that the masses of our people and their democratic, religious, women, youth, business, traditional and other leaders have played to bring about this conclusion. Not least among them is my Second Deputy President, the Honorable F. W. de Klerk.

We would also like to pay tribute to our security forces, in all their ranks, for the distinguished role they have played in securing our first democratic elections and the transition to democracy, from bloodthirsty forces which still refuse to see the light.

The time for the healing of the wounds has come.

The moment to bridge the chasms that divide us has come.

The time to build is upon us.

We have, at last, achieved our political emancipation. We pledge ourselves to liberate all our people from the continuing bondage of poverty, deprivation, suffering, gender and other discrimination.

We succeeded to take our last steps to freedom in conditions of relative peace. We commit ourselves to the construction of a complete, just and lasting peace.

We have triumphed in the effort to implant hope in the breasts of the millions of our people. We enter into a covenant that we shall build the society in which all South Africans, both black and white, will be able to walk tall, without any fear in their hearts, assured of their inalienable right to human dignity—a rainbow nation at peace with itself and the world.

As a token of its commitment to the renewal of our country, the new Interim Government of National Unity will, as a matter of urgency, address the issue of amnesty for various categories of our people who are currently serving terms of imprisonment.

We dedicate this day to all the heroes and heroines in this country and the rest of the world who sacrificed in many ways and surrendered their lives so that we could be free.

Their dreams have become reality. Freedom is their reward.

We are both humbled and elevated by the honor and privilege that you, the people of South Africa, have bestowed on us, as the first President of a united, democratic, nonracial and nonsexist South Africa, to lead our country out of the valley of darkness.

We understand it still that there is no easy road to freedom.

We know it well that none of us acting alone can achieve success.

We must therefore act together as a united people, for national reconciliation, for nation building, for the birth of a new world.

Let there be justice for all.

Let there be peace for all.

Let there be work, bread, water and salt for all.

Let each know that for each the body, the mind and the soul have been freed to fulfill themselves.

Never, never and never again shall it be that this beautiful land will again experience the oppression of one by another and suffer the indignity of being the skunk of the world.

The sun shall never set on so glorious a human achievement!

Let freedom reign. God bless Africa!

5. Prepare for, cover and write:

a. A speech story.

b. A news conference story.

c. A meeting story.

Then compare your stories to those appearing in the local paper.

ACCIDENTS, FIRES AND DISASTERS

*W*hen Paul Pringle of Copley News Service was assigned to write the story of a major earthquake in the metropolitan Los Angeles area, the mood was easy to capture:

It started as a nightmare, a spasm of terror in the dark, a bad dream shared by millions. Something unreal.

But it was real. At 4:31 this morning, nature wrenched a slumbering Los Angeles to the wakeful experience the city fears most: a major earthquake.

"It was a bomb," said Erik Pearson, 27, whose apartment building in the San Fernando Valley community of Northridge collapsed, killing at least nine. Pearson and his wife escaped by scaling fire hoses from the third floor.

"It went off under the building," he said. "It lifted it off the ground, and the next thing we knew we went through the floor." . . .

Pringle quickly captures the mood he wants to convey as he leads his readers into the story of a tragedy affecting millions. Ironically, as Pringle found out, disaster stories are among the easiest to write. The news is dramatic and compelling, everyone is riveted to the television screen or newspaper for more information, and the quotes are dramatic.

Gathering that news in the first place is more problematic. As a reporter, you may encounter situations in which your personal safety is at risk. More likely, you will encounter situations in which the authorities go to extremes to keep you and others away from the scene, making it more difficult to do your job. Both terrestrial and cellular telephone service may be interrupted, and public officials may be unreachable or too busy to talk. Even worse, those public officials, even if available, probably don't have a good idea of the extent of the tragedy. Like you, they will be scrambling to gather information anywhere they can get it. That may include such unusual sources as electronic mail and Internet news groups, which proved of great value to those trying to locate missing relatives after a large earthquake in the Los Angeles area. Assembling a clear, coherent story at a disaster scene is like putting together pieces of a complex puzzle; it may take hours, even days, to accomplish.

In such instances, the media perform a public service by getting information to the public rapidly. The broadcast media take the lead by warning the public of any lingering danger and putting the story into perspective as best they can, given limited access to information. In doing so, they help minimize public panic. Citizens are warned to stay away from the most dangerous areas, which in turn helps police officers, firefighters and other emergency workers deal with the situation most effectively. Then it is the turn of the print media, which try to provide more detail and explore more thoroughly the causes of the event. In doing so, they apply the critical tests of relevance, usefulness and interest in deciding what to print from the confusing mass of information available. Arguably, in such trying circumstances, the media perform at their highest level.

Coverage of accidents, fires and disasters is a staple of news reporting, but not every individual is cut out to report this type of news. In-

evitably, accident coverage equates with coverage of human tragedy. It's tough enough to cover an apartment fire and watch as the charred remains of children are removed. It's even tougher to do it on a regular basis. Reporters who regularly cover such stories see more than their share of death and dying, blood and dismemberment. That weighs heavily on even the toughest of individuals, and some otherwise terrific reporters discover that they just cannot handle continued exposure to tragedy. When the job calls for it, however, the reporter must set aside those feelings of human compassion long enough to report the news. Only then is there time to weep.

In most cases of this sort, it is helpful to remember that there's nothing you can do to help. Police and fire officials are trained in rescue and disaster-relief efforts; almost certainly, you are not. On rare occasions, however, the reporter can become a part of the story. Does the television videographer photograph a man threatening to set himself on fire or does that videographer try to stop him? Does the newspaper photographer try to stop a woman from jumping off a bridge to her death or does he photograph the plunge? You are told by your editors, quite appropriately, not to become part of the story. On the other hand, isn't the saving of a life more important? Such incidents place the reporter, photographer or videographer in an ethical dilemma. We'll explore ethical issues further in Chapter 22.

But even if this type of coverage is not your style, there's a good chance that sooner or later you will have to do it. Most beginning reporters are assigned shifts on general assignment, and it is during such shifts that you are likely to be dispatched to the scene of an accident, fire or disaster. When that occurs, think clearly and set aside your emotions. Keep in mind that you have a duty to your readers, listeners or viewers to keep them informed.

There is good reason for media interest in such events. For many years, surveys of news consumers have shown that accidents, fires and disasters rank with crime and government news near the top of items of reader interest. Those studies confirm what editors know intuitively: When people hear sirens, they want to know what happened, and more important, whether their relatives, friends or acquaintances were involved. The job of the news media is to get that information to them as quickly and accurately as possible.

The media also cover these events in their capacity as watchdog for the public over government agencies. If the police are slow in responding to an accident, is it because there are not enough officers or because they are poorly supervised? Did someone die needlessly because police, fire or ambulance personnel were slow, poorly trained or inefficient? To ask these questions on behalf of the public, reporters must observe public officials as they perform their duties.

In news rooms throughout the country, editors and reporters stay tuned to the police and fire radio frequencies on monitors provided for that purpose. When they hear something out of the ordinary, reporters, photographers and camera crews are dispatched to the scene.

Editors have varying ideas about which accident, fire and disaster stories are worth reporting at all and which are worth developing into major articles. Perhaps the most important factor in that decision is the size of the city and its newspaper. An apartment fire in which nobody was hurt may be routine in New York City and merit only one or two paragraphs in the newspaper or 10 seconds of a newscast. But in Cedar City, Utah, a similar fire may be unusual enough to warrant more extensive coverage.

As a beginning reporter you almost certainly will be assigned to cover an accident or fire. You even may become part of a team of reporters and photographers assigned to cover a disaster. Consequently, you need to know what to expect and how to get the information you need.

In some ways covering accidents, fires and disasters is the simplest form of reporting. The subject matter lends itself to the classic inverted pyramid writing style. But you also can produce far more interesting accounts of the pain and suffering—and often the remarkable strength—of people who have encountered crises.

As a reporter assigned to cover an accident, fire or disaster, you must report the effects of the event on the victims. Only then can you write a story that tells the event in terms of the human experience. This chapter addresses the reporting of both the event and its personal aftermaths.

Covering the Scene

Whether you are assigned to cover an accident, fire or disaster, many of the facts and all of the color are gathered at the scene. By being there, you will have a better picture of what happened. Too many reporters, however, cover accidents and fires as purely passive observers. You must observe. But you also must actively solicit information from those who are there. Many of them, including those directly involved, you may never be able to find again. With that advice in mind, let us turn to the techniques you should employ to secure that information at each of the scenes you will cover.

The Scene of an Accident

When dispatched to the scene of an accident, you first must concentrate on gathering the facts. Move as quickly as possible to collect this information:

1. The names, ages, addresses and conditions of the victims.
2. Accounts of witnesses or police reconstructions of what happened.
3. When the accident occurred.
4. Where it occurred.
5. Why or how it happened or who was at fault, as determined by officials in charge of the investigation.

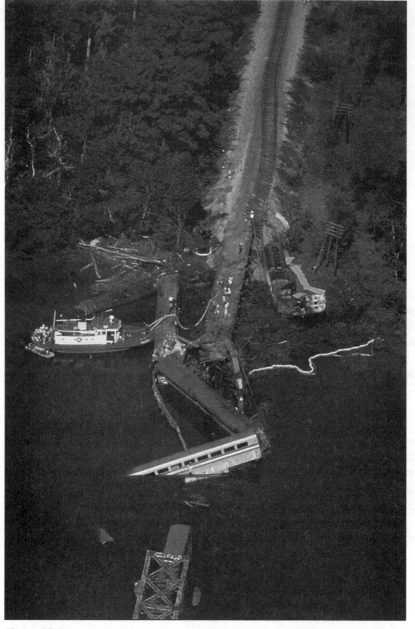

Figure 11.1.
These photographs had tremendous impact on readers and served to attract them to the accompanying stories about a train derailment in Alabama (above) and a fire resulting from the Los Angeles-area earthquake of Jan. 17, 1994 (right).

If that list sounds familiar, it should. You could simplify it to read "who, what, when, where and why." As in any news story, that information is essential. You must gather such information as quickly as possible after being assigned to the story. If the accident has just taken place, a visit to the scene is essential. Just as important is knowing what to do when you get there. These suggestions will help:

What to do at the scene of an accident:

- *Question the person in charge of the investigation.*
- *Try to find and interview witnesses.*
- *Try to find friends or relatives of the victims.*
- *If possible, interview the victims.*
- *Talk with others at the scene.*
- *Be sensitive to victims and their families.*

Question the person in charge of the investigation. This individual will attempt to gather much of the same information you want. A police officer, for example, needs to know who was involved, what happened, when it happened and who was at fault. If you are able to establish a good relationship with the investigator, you may be able to secure much of the information you need from this one source, though single-source stories usually are inadequate.

Remember that the spellings of names, addresses and similar facts must be verified later. Any veteran reporter can tell you that police officers and other public officials are notoriously bad spellers and often make errors in recording the names of the victims. To avoid such errors, call relatives of the victims or consult the city directory, telephone book or other sources to check your information.

Try to find and interview witnesses. Police and other investigators may lead you directly to the best witnesses. The most accurate account of what happened usually comes from witnesses, and the investigators will try to find them. You should, too. A good way to do that is to watch the investigators. Listen in as they interview a witness, or corner the witness after they are finished. If there is time, of course, try to find your own witnesses. You cannot and should not always rely on investigators to do your work for you.

Try to find friends or relatives of the victims. These sources are helpful in piecing together information about the victims. Through them you often get tips about even better stories.

If possible, interview the victims. Survivors of an accident may be badly shaken, but if they are able to talk, they can provide first-hand details that an official report never could. Make every attempt to interview those involved.

Talk with others at the scene. If someone has died at the scene of the accident, an ambulance paramedic or the medical examiner may be able to give you some indication of what caused the death. At the least you can learn where the bodies or the injured will be taken. That may help, because later the mortician or hospital officials may be able to provide information you need for your story.

Be sensitive to victims and their families. You have a job to do, and you must do it. That does not mean, however, that you can be insensitive to those involved in an accident.

Of course, your deadline will have a major impact on the amount of information you are able to gather. If you must meet a deadline soon after arriving at the scene, you probably will be forced to stick to the basics of who, what, when, where, why and how. Thus it is important to gather that information first. Then, if you have time, you can concentrate on more detailed and vivid information to make the story highly readable.

The following account of a tractor-trailer accident was produced in a race against the clock by the staff of an afternoon newspaper:

A truck driver was killed and a woman was injured this morning when a tractor-trailer believed to be hauling gasoline overturned and exploded on Interstate 70, turning the highway into a conflagration.

Both lanes of I-70 were backed up for miles after an eastbound car glanced off a pickup truck, hurdled the concrete median and collided with a tanker truck heading west.

The explosion was immediate, witnesses said. Residents along Texas Avenue reported the initial fireball reached the north side of the street, which is about 300 yards from the scene of the accident. A wooded area was scorched, but no houses were damaged.

Police evacuated the 600 block of Texas Avenue for fear that the fire would spread, but residents were returning to their homes at 12:35 p.m., about an hour after the collision. Authorities also unsuccessfully attempted to hold back the onlookers who gravitated to a nearby shopping center parking lot to view the blaze.

Police did not identify the driver of the truck, which was owned by a Tulsa, Okla., firm named Transport Delivery Co.

"Apparently it was gasoline," said Steve Paulsell, chief of the County Fire Protection District. "That's what it smelled like." Other officials reported the truck may have been hauling fuel oil or diesel fuel.

For an afternoon newspaper with an early afternoon deadline, such a story presents major problems, particularly when it occurs, as this one did, at about 11:30 a.m. Four reporters were dispatched to the scene; all of them called in information to a writer back at the office. There was little time to interview eyewitnesses. Because of the pressing deadline, the reporters were forced to gather most of their information from fire and police officials at the scene.

Writers for the morning newspaper, by comparison, had plenty of time to gather rich detail to tell the story in human terms. Much of the breaking news value was diminished by the next morning because of intense coverage by the afternoon newspaper, radio and television. It was time to tell the story of a hero:

Witnesses credited an off-duty fireman with saving a woman's life Monday following a spectacular four-vehicle collision on Interstate 70 just east of its intersection with Business Loop 70.

The driver of a gasoline truck involved in the fiery crash was not so lucky. Bill Borgmeyer, 62, of Jefferson City died in the cab of his rig, which jackknifed, overturned and exploded in flames when he swerved in a futile attempt to avoid hitting a car driven by Leta Hanes, 33, of Nelson, Mo.

Mrs. Hanes, who was thrown from her auto by the impact, was lying unconscious within 10 feet of the blazing fuel when firefighter Richard Walden arrived at the crash scene.

"I knew what was going on," Walden recalled, "and I knew I had to get her away from there." Despite the intense heat, Walden dragged the woman to safety.

"She had some scrapes, a cut on her knee and was beat around a little bit," Walden said, "Other than that, she was fine."

Mrs. Hanes was taken to Boone Hospital Center, where she was reported in satisfactory condition Monday night.

Smoke billowing from the accident scene reportedly was visible 30 miles away. Westbound interstate traffic was backed up as far as five miles. Several city streets became snarled for several hours when traffic was diverted to Business Loop 70. The eastbound lane of I-70 was reopened about 2 p.m.; the westbound lane was not reopened until 3 p.m. . . .

The story added detail and eyewitness accounts from several other people:

"It was a big red fireball," said Don Morgan of Clear Spring, Mo., who was driving about 100 yards behind the Borgmeyer rig when the crash occurred. "It exploded right away, as soon as it rolled over on its side."

Doug McConnell, 23, was in the kitchen of his nearby home at 606 Texas Ave. when the house shook.

"I heard a boom, and all of a sudden there was fire," he said. "It looked like a firecracker or something."

The richness of detail in the second account and the eyewitness descriptions of what happened make the story more interesting. The importance of adding such detail is apparent.

The Scene of a Fire

Accidents and fires present similar problems for the reporter, but at a fire of any size you can expect more confusion than at the scene of an accident. One major difference, then, is that the officer in charge will be busier. At the scene of an accident the damage has been done and the authorities usually are free to concentrate on their investigation. At a fire the officer in charge is busy directing firefighters and probably will be unable to talk with you. The investigation will not even begin until the fire is extinguished. In many cases the cause of the fire will not be known for hours, days or weeks. In fact, it may never be known. Seldom is that the case in an accident, except perhaps for air accidents.

Another problem is that you may not have access to the immediate area of the fire. Barriers often are erected to keep the public—and representatives of the news media—from coming too close to a burning structure. The obvious reason is safety, but such barriers may hamper your reporting. You may not be able to come close enough to firefighters to learn about the problems they are having or to obtain the quotes you need to improve your story.

These problems usually make covering a fire more difficult than covering an accident. Despite the difficulties, you cover a fire in much the same way, interviewing officials and witnesses at the scene. You also should try to interview the property owner. Moreover, because the official investigation will not have begun, you must conduct your own. When covering any fire, you must learn:

- The location of the fire.
- The names, ages and addresses of those killed, injured or missing.
- The name of the building's owner or, in the case of a grass fire or forest fire, the name of the landowner.
- The value of the building and its contents or the value of the land.
- Whether the building and contents were insured for fire damage. (Open land seldom is.)
- The time the fire started, who reported it and how many firefighters and pieces of equipment were called to the scene.
- What caused the fire, if known.

As in any story, the basics are who, what, when, where, why and how. But the nature of the fire will raise other questions that must be answered. Of primary importance is whether life is endangered. If not, the amount of property damage becomes the major emphasis of the story. Was arson involved? Was the building insured for its full value? Was there an earlier fire there? Did the building comply with the fire codes? Were any rare or extremely valuable objects inside? Were there explosives inside that complicated fighting the fire and posed an even greater threat than the fire itself?

Your job is to answer these questions for the newspaper's readers. You will be able to obtain some of that information later on from

DATE	TIME	ADDRESS

PAGE   OF   **CASUALTY REPORT**   FD-500

CHANGE 2 ☐ (74)
DELETE 3 ☐

INCIDENT NO.	EXP
8 0 9 0 5 1 3	
1 2 3   7 8   9

NAME	AGE	Time of Injury	MONTH	DAY	YEAR
S A N D O Z A M A N U E L R	3 2	0 9 4 5	0 2	0 8	9 6
LAST, FIRST MIDDLE	33 34 35 36		39 40		45

HOME ADDRESS
307 Banning Ave., Apt. 3   TELEPHONE   555-9088

46 SEX	47 CASUALTY TYPE	48 SEVERITY	49 AFFILIATION
1 ☒ Male	1 ☒ Fire Casualty	1 ☒ Injury	1 ☐ Fire Service
2 ☐ Female	2 ☐ Action Casualty	2 ☐ Death	2 ☐ Other Emergency Personnel
	3 ☐ EMS Casualty		3 ☒ Civilian

FAMILIARITY WITH STRUCTURE	LOCATION AT IGNITION	CONDITION BEFORE INJURY
Occupant 50	Unknown 51	Unknown 52

CONDITION PREVENTING ESCAPE	ACTIVITY AT TIME OF INJURY	CAUSE OF INJURY
N/A 53	Leaving building 54	Falling debris 55

NATURE OF INJURY	PART OF BODY INJURED	DISPOSITION
Broken leg 56	Leg 57	Hospitalized 58

REMARKS:
Occupant was leaving burning structure when burning eave fell and struck his leg.

By #31   Ambulance to General   Hospital

NAME	AGE	Time of Injury	MONTH	DAY	YEAR
LAST, FIRST MIDDLE	33 34 35 36		39 40		45

HOME ADDRESS   TELEPHONE

46 SEX	47 CASUALTY TYPE	48 SEVERITY	49 AFFILIATION
1 ☐ Male	1 ☐ Fire Casualty	1 ☐ Injury	1 ☐ Fire Service
2 ☐ Female	2 ☐ Action Casualty	2 ☐ Death	2 ☐ Other Emergency Personnel
	3 ☐ EMS Casualty		3 ☐ Civilian

FAMILIARITY WITH STRUCTURE	LOCATION AT IGNITION	CONDITION BEFORE INJURY
50	51	52

CONDITION PREVENTING ESCAPE	ACTIVITY AT TIME OF INJURY	CAUSE OF INJURY
53	54	55

NATURE OF INJURY	PART OF BODY INJURED	DISPOSITION
56	57	58

REMARKS:

By   Ambulance to   Hospital

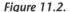
Supervisor*
*Injury reports for fire personnel,
Immediate supervisor to sign here.

SIGNATURE of person completing form/DATE
John R. Sanders.

Printed in U.S.A.

Figure 11.2.
This casualty report is typical of the types of reports available to reporters at most fire stations.

the official fire reports if they are ready before your story deadline (see Figure 11.2). But most of it will come from interviews conducted at the scene with the best available sources. Finding your sources may not be easy, but you can begin by looking for the highest-ranking fire official. Larger departments may even have a designated press officer whose job is to deal with you and other reporters.

Another important source in covering fire stories is the fire marshal, whose job is to determine the cause of the fire and, if arson is involved, to bring charges against the arsonist. You should make every effort to talk with the fire marshal at the scene, if he or she is available. In most cases, though, the marshal will be the primary source of a second-day story.

As in covering any **spot news story**—a story in which news is breaking quickly—deadlines will determine how much you can do at the scene of a fire. If your deadline is hours away, you can concentrate on the event and those connected with it. You will have time to find the little boy whose puppy was killed in the fire or interview the firefighter who first entered the building. But if you have only minutes until your deadline, you may have to press the fire official in charge for as much information as possible. You may have to coax from that person every tidbit, even making a nuisance of yourself, to gather the information you need. Through it all, you can expect confusion. There is little order to be found in the chaos of a fire.

The Scene of a Disaster

Disasters present special problems for reporters. Even the investigators may have difficulty determining where to begin. For example, when tornadoes slice through cities, efforts may be concentrated on finding those trapped in the rubble of buildings. No one may know for certain who is trapped or where they are, or, in fact, whether anyone is trapped at all.

The confusion at the scene of a disaster makes your job more difficult. Officials often are caught up in the turmoil of the moment and overestimate the number of people killed or the amount of damage. In some instances you may find yourself in the unusual position of being ahead of the investigators. You may be in a better position to determine the death toll or estimate the damage. At least you will be able to make an informed judgment about the accuracy of what you are told. American newspaper history is filled with incidents of reporters' quoting inflated estimates of deaths and damage. Failure to make informed judgments about the accuracy of those estimates leaves your newspaper open to charges of irresponsibility.

In addition to confusion you may well encounter hazards to your personal safety as a reporter at the scene of a disaster. After a tornado, for example, electric wires may lie on the ground for hours until repair crews are able to reach them. At the scene of an earthquake you may be frighteningly close to a wall about to collapse. Or, in the aftermath of that earthquake, decaying bodies may present serious health hazards.

Some guidance may be provided by your company's disaster plan. The *San Francisco Chronicle* maintains an earthquake disaster plan, and the *Miami Herald* has one for hurricanes. But no plan can prepare you for what you are likely to encounter at a disaster scene.

As you go about your work, you must avoid all the hazards present; you will be of little value to your newspaper in a hospital bed. Further, what little information you can learn by being that close probably is not worth the risk. Nevertheless, there will be times when you will be forced into dangerous situations.

Fortunately, when disasters strike, you may not have to shoulder the entire reporting load. In such cases editors usually mobilize their reporting staffs to gather as much information as quickly as possible. You probably will be assigned a specific responsibility, such as interviewing witnesses or survivors. You may then be asked to write a human-interest feature or a *sidebar*, a secondary story that runs with the major one and captures the personal side of an event. Other reporters may focus on the damage involved and compile lists of the dead and injured.

Completing the Reporting

In reporting almost any account of an accident, fire or disaster, your work at the scene will be merely the beginning. When you return to the office and sort through your notes, you probably will find that many questions remain unanswered. You must check with other sources.

> *"The news is no longer the news. . . . It's all about luridness. Body bags will be seen at 7:00, chasing ambulance at 8:00, victim's family at 9:00."*
> — **Oliver Stone,**
> *film director*

Sources to Check

When a disaster occurs, the follow-up stories often are as dramatic, important and significant as the story of the event itself. When the space shuttle Challenger exploded in January 1986, reporters began prying into records of the National Aeronautics and Space Administration and found massive evidence of inadequate concern for safety. The defective hard-rubber seals blamed for the explosion of the shuttle shortly after takeoff had been a cause of concern to safety experts for years. But even though the seals were known to be susceptible to failure in cold weather, NASA officials authorized launch of the shuttle in near-freezing conditions. Good secondary reporting led to a major story that prompted an investigation by a presidential panel.

An industrial accident should prompt calls to company executives or a corporate safety officer and may require you to check with local, state and federal regulatory agencies. If a worker is severely burned by a toxic chemical, you may have to call the federal government's Occupational Safety and Health Administration to learn what safety precautions are mandated for the use of the chemical. Only then will you be able to determine if there is reason to suspect the company—or the worker—of violating OSHA restrictions designed to ensure safety in the workplace.

Detail Important in Disaster Stories

Editors agree almost universally that when a disaster occurs, it is a time for a newspaper to pull out all the stops. Dozens of reporters and photographers may be dispatched to gather as much detail as possible. It then falls on one or two reporters back at the office to mold it all into an article that makes sense.

What follows is the main story from the *Chicago Tribune* on the day following an airplane crash in 1994. As you read the story, notice its richness of detail and the staggering number of sources it includes. Note also the second-day lead approach that followed extensive radio and television coverage of the event.

CHICAGO-BOUND PLANE CRASHES; 68 ARE KILLED

By Flynn McRoberts and George Papajohn
Tribune Staff Writers

The blustery weather that raked Chicago and Northwest Indiana on Monday will be examined closely as federal safety investigators try Tuesday to determine what caused an American Eagle turboprop to plummet from the sky, killing all 68 people aboard.

Flight 4184, a twin-engine Super ATR-72, was bound from Indianapolis to O'Hare International Airport at about 4 p.m. Monday when it plunged into a farm field about 25 miles southeast of Gary near Interstate Highway 65 and Indiana Highway 110 near Roselawn, Ind.

Twenty-one of the passengers were bound for Chicago and the other 43 passengers were connecting to other flights at O'Hare, airline officials said.

The tragedy followed by less than two months the 132 deaths in the crash of a USAir jet bound from Chicago to Pittsburgh, an accident that remains under investigation.

"It looked like there was no wing on the left-hand side" of the American Eagle plane, said Larry Midkiff, a 20-year-old construction worker who was driving home to Roselawn when he saw the plane in a steep descent. "I'm not sure because it might have been the angle of the aircraft."

Midkiff said he saw smoke streaming from the plane.

"It was coming down real steep, real hard, nose down," he said. "It wasn't coming down like it was trying to make an emergency landing. . . . It kind of dipped down behind some trees. Then it made a big puff of black smoke."

Farmer Norman Prohosky was tinkering with a grain truck in his shop when he said he heard "a real loud shrieking noise."

"It sounded to me like one of those dirt bikes that's real loud," said Prohosky, 68. Then there was "kind of a boom when it hit—something like an explosion."

That's when an employee, Robert Hilton, who was working on the other side of the shop, yelled: "Come out real quick. We had a plane crash right out here."

By the time Prohosky got out of the door, Hilton was standing and pointing to a plume of smoke about three-quarters of a mile to the east. "All we seen was a bunch of smoke, but no fire," he said. Hilton told Prohosky that the plane was coming in at "a 45-degree angle just as it hit the ground."

Jeff Hill, a reporter for Rensselaer radio stations WRIN-AM and WLQI-FM, was among the first on the scene.

"There really wasn't much to see until you got right to the point of impact," he said.

"When we started tripping over body parts, frankly, that was

Detail Important in Disaster Stories (continued)

when the decision was made to secure the area until daybreak or weather break," Hill said.

A deputy coroner at the crash scene said the plane appeared to have hit at a sharp angle, creating a crater three feet deep. Wreckage and debris were strewn over a three-quarter-mile radius, witnesses said.

A team of experts from the National Transportation Safety Board in Washington planned to fly to the crash scene Monday night to begin an investigation. They were to join Jim Hall, the agency's chairman, who had departed from Chicago for the accident scene earlier.

The investigators are expected to examine the plane's engines, avionics systems and structures, air traffic control procedures and weather conditions.

"I don't know what fool would be flying in that (expletive)," said Nick Kucki, owner of the nearby Lake Village Airport, referring to the weather. He said his small field 10 miles north of the crash site was closed by rain squalls at the time.

However, scheduled airlines routinely fly in windy, rainy weather, and passenger planes are designed to navigate safely through rough meterological conditions.

Shawn McCauley, 17, had a good view of the weather on another airfield in the area, the Griffith-Merrillville Airport in Griffith, Ind.

"It was raining like hell, coming down almost horizontal," said McCauley, who fuels planes. The wind picked up at around 2 p.m., he said.

Two hours later, at Gary, the National Weather Service reported northeast winds at 13 miles an hour, gusting up to 30 mph. The temperature was 44 degrees.

"In the general area, there were fairly strong wind shears between, I would estimate, 6,000 and 9,000 feet, strong northeast winds at about 40 knots (46 mph) around 6,000 or 7,000 feet and southwest at 40 knots at 9,000 feet," said Richard Koeneman, a Weather Service forecaster in Romeoville, Ill.

However, the shears were much different than those that sometimes accompany thunderstorms and are closer to the ground.

Those are "extremely variable . . . very transient and short-lived," he said. "This was a more steady state. It persisted over a period of several hours. . . . This wasn't a particularly surprising thing. This is a fairly typical wind shear associated with strong low-pressure situations.

"This kind of event, I imagine, was well-known by the controllers," Koeneman added.

The plane was put into service by American Eagle last March and had logged 1,300 flying hours and 1,670 takeoffs and landings, airline officials said.

It had departed at 2:56 p.m. CST from Indianapolis carrying 64 passengers, two flight attendants and a pilot and copilot.

Early Tuesday, the crew members were identified as:

—Pilot Orlando Aguiar, 29. He had logged 4,638 flight hours in his seven years with American Eagle.

—Copilot Jeffrey Gagliano, 30. He had logged 3,862 hours in his five years of service.

—Flight attendant Sandi Modaff, 27, who joined American Eagle in 1988.

—Flight attendant Amanda Holberg, 23, who joined the company Oct. 6.

All were based in Chicago.

Before the crash, the plane had been holding at 10,000 feet

Detail Important in Disaster Stories (continued)

and was cleared to descend to 8,000 at about 4 p.m., when it disappeared from controllers' radar screens, the Federal Aviation Administration said.

At 4:20 p.m., the FAA was notified of the crash by Indiana State Police.

At Indianapolis International Airport, stunned survivors of crash victims were ushered by airport personnel into Crossroads, a restaurant in the main terminal. One man sat briefly at a table outside the restaurant, his face buried in his hands. As more people with loved ones on the flight arrived, they were met by police, who kept reporters and photographers away.

At O'Hare, Scott Fisher of Bloomington, Ill., talked about his trip from Indianapolis to O'Hare on the plane scheduled next after Flight 4184.

"The guy next to me and I were talking during the whole flight about the USAir crash," he said. "The guy's brother-in-law died in that crash. You're taking a chance every time you're up in the air."

After getting off his plane, Fisher called a limo driver who had been waiting for his arrival.

"He said, 'We thought you were dead,'" Fisher said. "I feel like this is my lucky day. I'm in shock.

"I called my wife and she was hysterical. All she knew was that I was on an American (Eagle) flight from Indy. She just screamed when she heard my voice."

A temporary morgue was being prepared at North Newton High School near Morocco, Ind., about 5 miles south of the crash site. Classes were canceled Tuesday for the school's 900 students.

Officials were bracing for the task of body recovery and identification.

"This is out of our league,"

said Deputy Coroner Steve Stitz. "This is bigger than any one agency can handle."

American Airlines was sending a 30-member inspection team to the crash site from offices in Chicago and Dallas.

(Tribune reporters Gary Washburn, Terry Wilson, Jerry Thomas, Andrew Gottesman, Andy Backover, Jerry Crimmins, John O'Brien, Sue Ellen Christian, Steve Rhodes, Larry Hartstein, Kristina Marlow and Ken Armstrong also contributed to this report.)

Without a doubt, there are rough spots in the writing of that story and obvious gaps in the reporters' knowledge about what happened. One might argue that the story is too long and that some of the material could have been used more effectively in sidebars, or related stories. Yet others would argue that story length is seldom a major problem with disaster stories; people in the area affected will read them thoroughly, regardless of length.

For certain publications, a more concise approach is necessary. Let's take a look at how *USA Today* handled coverage of the same event for its national audience:

68 DIE IN INDIANA CRASH
By Jerry Bonkowski and Gary Fields

ROSELAWN, Ind.—All 68 people aboard an American Eagle flight were killed Monday when it crashed in a soybean field during a rainstorm.

Dan Savka of Roselawn came on the scene shortly after the crash: "I thought at first it was a brushfire."

Michael Schwanke of WLQI radio says, "Debris was so scattered you really couldn't tell if there was an airplane."

Don Zochert, FAA spokesman, says the plane dropped from radar at 4 p.m. CST.

Detail Important in Disaster Stories (continued)

Patrick Henry of American Eagle says the flight was due in Chicago at 3:15 p.m. CST, but its takeoff had been delayed.

Forty-three passengers were to get connecting flights in Chicago, according to Simmons Airlines, the American Eagle carrier that serves Chicago.

Henry says it's too early to speculate about the cause.

"People are talking about weather . . . but hundreds of aircraft fly in weather worse than here," Henry says.

National Transportation Safety Board teams were dispatched to the scene.

American Eagle canceled plans to celebrate its 10th anniversary today.

The NTSB, prompted by two crashes last winter, is already studying why commuter airlines crash twice as often as major carriers.

In typical fashion, *USA Today* chose to keep its story short and to the point. It was accompanied by a graphic showing how the plane might have nosedived to earth. Which approach, that of the *Chicago Tribune* or *USA Today*, is better? The *Tribune*, with knowledge that there would be high local interest in the story, chose to lead with a rather lengthy account. *USA Today*, with its much more diverse national audience, chose to keep the story short. Arguably, the approach of each newspaper was best for its audience.

When events of this type occur, editors seldom worry about readers' or viewers' levels of interest in the story. The challenge, then, is to make the account as useful and relevant as possible to the audience being reached. Editors and reporters do so by listing the names of those killed and survivors, trying to determine the cause of the tragedy and helping readers make sense of a confusing situation.

A source checklist for accidents, fires and disasters

- *Civilian witnesses*
  - *Victims of personal injury, if they are able to be interviewed*
  - *People who were involved but escaped injury*
  - *Victims of property damage, including property owners, tenants and employees*
  - *Neighbors and passersby*
- *Relatives and neighbors of victims*
- *Rescue workers (firefighters, police, EMS workers, hospital personnel, etc.)*
- *Government regulatory agencies (local, state and federal)*

Airplane crashes require a check with the National Transportation Safety Board, part of the Federal Aviation Administration, which investigates all of them, regardless of their severity. NTSB investigators usually cooperate with reporters by revealing likely causes of crashes. Try to get such information because investigations routinely last several months, and by then the cause of the crash may have little news value.

When you cover a drowning you may want to check with local authorities to find out if swimming is permitted where the drowning occurred. State water-patrol officials may help when you are reporting boating accidents.

In our well-regulated society there are government regulatory agencies at all levels that can provide details to help you focus on the problem. City agencies that deal with such matters can be found at city hall; similar county agencies probably will be located at the courthouse or county office building. State regulatory agencies are located in your state capital; regional offices of federal agencies usually are located in a nearby large city. Take advantage of their expertise.

This also is the time to call relatives of victims and to verify information gathered at the scene that can be checked with other sources. The nature and extent of such checks is dictated by the circumstances.

Reporting the Effects on People

Too often, the news media provide blanket coverage of a major accident, fire or disaster, only to drop the story in a matter of days. But the human suffering from such an event often cannot be assessed until months afterward. Some months after a series of fires blamed on an arsonist resulted in the loss of several businesses and gained national attention, reporter Jill Young Miller decided to see what had become of the people and companies affected:

Anne Moore remembers all too well the call that shook her from her sleep last spring and summoned her to the corner of 10th Street and Broadway. A silver bowl and a faded floor plan are her only mementos of the D&M Sound Systems Inc. store that flames destroyed May 27.

D&M President Moore keeps both treasures in her new store at 700 Fay St. She and other local entrepreneurs have spent the past several months piecing together their businesses, destroyed during the city's arson plague last spring.

No one has been charged with setting the Stephens Endowment Building fire that devastated D&M, the Columbia Art League, the French Room Hairdressing Salon, Spinning Wheel Realty, The Copy Center and Orlanco Financial Corp. Nor has the culprit been identified in the 10 other blazes investigators say were deliberately set last spring.

An intergovernment arson task force folded in July after arson charges were filed against two men in unrelated fires—one in Rocheport and the other at the former Brown Derby Liquors, 120 S. Ninth St. Those two fires preceded the rash of blazes that struck fear into the business community for six weeks.

Orlanco, which owned the turn-of-the-century building housing the businesses, has not decided whether to rebuild or to sell the property. Orlanco President Chris Kelly, Moore's brother, says several people have offered to buy the property, which he declined to tag with a value.

"It's worth quite a bit," he says, considering the property is "right in the very core of the retail district."

Options for the land include retail stores, offices or a combination of both, Kelly says. "We think it can be made into the dominant corner in downtown Columbia."

In the meantime, all of the businesses but The Copy Center have found new quarters.

There was not nearly enough insurance to replace what was lost, says Mildred Grissum, who owned the business at 14 N. 10th St. for five years. Grissum, now a secretary in the U.S. Department of Commerce's local office, harbors no hope of reopening her business. "At my age, I wasn't ready to start again."

Columbia Fire Chief Girard Wren estimates damages from last spring's spate of fires at $5 million. . . .

ON THE JOB

Disasters Don't Just Disappear

In December 1993, a year and a half after leaving journalism school, Lisa Arthur found herself covering the rebuilding of South Dade county for *The Miami Herald*. Hurricane Andrew had struck the area on Aug. 24, 1992, and the trail of destruction was still visible 18 months later.

The experience taught Arthur that some of the most important stories in disaster reporting come months after the initial crisis.

"When I arrived, there were still hundreds of people living in trailers, and pockets of the landscape still resembled a bombed-out Beirut," she says. "People were still suffering a great psychological trauma, and they looked to the local media to deliver the message that all was not well yet. They still needed help even though the memory of the hurricane had begun to fade for people not directly affected."

Arthur has this advice for reporters covering the long-term aftermath of any disaster. First, focus on the ordinary people and the small battles they are fighting to get their homes and lives repaired. There are still people in South Dade today who are living in trailers because contractors ripped them off or they didn't have insurance. This is fertile ground for stories that are important and can sometimes make a difference. Second, follow the money trail. Tens of millions of federal dollars flow into devastated areas. Track the money and make sure it trickles down to the people who need it. Third, look for heroes. Arthur stumbled upon a Pittsburgh philanthropist who had been quietly pumping millions of recovery dollars into South Dade. His deeds went unnoticed for two years. Arthur's story about him wound up on the front page of the *Herald*.

Too often, reporters fail to produce such retrospective articles, perhaps because of the press of newer, more timely events. Those who avoid that temptation can find good articles that not only will please editors but also will interest readers.

Complete Coverage of an Accident

The importance of pursuing every angle of a major story is well illustrated by the *San Jose* (Calif.) *Mercury*'s coverage of a tragedy that almost became a disaster. A small airplane with four people aboard lost power after takeoff and crashed into an elementary school parking lot. First- and second-grade students on recess were on a playground only 50 feet from the crash site.

When editors at the *Mercury* learned of the crash, they sent reporters and photographers to the scene. One concentrated on the main news story, which was to become the **lead story** for the day—the one most prominently displayed on the front page. This was the result:

A light plane crashed into an elementary school parking lot near 150 children on noontime recess in East San Jose Wednesday, killing three of the four persons aboard.

No one on the ground was injured, although the plane exploded and burned within 50 feet of first- and second-graders on the playground at Katherine Smith School, 2025 Clarice Drive.

Among the dead was the plane's pilot, Francis K. Allen, who had 13 years of flying experience—but who never before had flown the type of plane that he died in Wednesday, his daughter, Debbie Schlict, said.

Allen, 51, lived at 1398 Cerro Verde Lane, San Jose.

He was being checked out in the plane, a single-engine Bellanca, by an 18-year-old licensed instructor, who also was killed. The instructor was identified as Ralph G. Anello, 1681 The Alameda, Apt. 31, San Jose, who also served as co-pilot.

A Federal Aviation Administration spokesman said it is not uncommon for an 18-year-old to be an instructor. "As long as you're certified, there are no restrictions," he said.

The third victim was Ila Diane Cooper, 32, of 390 Bluefield Drive, San Jose.

The survivor, who scrambled clear of the wreck, is Lawrence Allen Herbst, 32, of 5870 Christ Drive, also San Jose. He was in stable condition at Alexian Brothers Hospital Wednesday night with first- and second-degree burns on his face, hands and elbows.

The plane apparently lost power on takeoff at 12:13 p.m. from Reid-Hillview Airport, circled south and plunged into the parking lot at the front of the school after a flight of only one minute.

Alerted by two playground aides, the children saw the faltering aircraft heading for them and ran, screaming, for the shelter of a nearby classroom wing, a witness said.

The craft overturned one car, and it and four other vehicles were bathed in flames as the plane's gas tank exploded.

Witnesses said it appeared the pilot may have nosed the craft into the ground at the last moment to avoid hitting the playground, which was in direct line with the plane's final course.

The youngest victim, Anello, is the son of Superior Judge Peter Anello, who is on vacation in Italy.

Mrs. Cooper, an employee at IBM, is survived by her husband, Donald, and two children.

Allen also was an employee at IBM.

The victims died of extensive burns, not crash injuries, the coroner's office reported.

Authorities said the plane had been rented from Western Aviation Flight Center Inc. at Reid-Hillview.

One of the first on the scene and one who helped lead Herbst away from the burning craft was Trellis Walker of San Jose, a special investigator for the Department of Defense.

"I arrived about 30 seconds after the plane hit," said Walker. "The man was staggering away from the plane, screaming, 'Oh, my God! Oh, my God! There are three others in there. Get them out!' "

"The engine was making so much noise that everyone heard the plane coming," said David Bess, a custodian at the school who was walking on the sidewalk beside the parking lot when the plane hit. . . .

Morbid as it may be, body counts matter when reporting disasters. So do damage totals. An earthquake that kills 14 people, injures 4,000 and causes $5 billion in damage is bigger news than one that results in no casualties and minor damage—even if both quakes register 6.5 on the Richter scale.

It is important to consider the big picture when reporting an accident, fire or disaster. How unusual an occurrence is it? If this is the city's first fatal fire in five years, you have a natural angle for your story. Similarly, if it is the fifth fatal fire of the year, you might want to emphasize that fact.

The reporter who wrote that story tells concisely what happened, reports the names, ages and addresses of the victims and quickly anticipates a question that readers are likely to ask: Isn't it unusual for an 18-year-old man to be a flight instructor? A spokesman for the FAA said it is not. The reporter then identifies the survivor of the crash, who understandably was not available for an interview, and tells the reader that the crash was caused by an apparent loss of power. He describes the scene, works in other details about those involved and quotes witnesses.

All the information except that from the FAA spokesman was gathered at the scene. The story is as complete as possible with the information available. There are other ways this story could have been written, but the plan chosen by this reporter worked well.

Colleagues, meanwhile, were working on related stories. Because the school was so near the airport, San Jose school officials had anticipated the possibility of something similar happening. This story emphasized that angle:

"Sure, we've thought something like this might happen someday," said James Smith. "But what could we possibly do to prepare for it?"

Smith, superintendent of the Evergreen School District, was at Katherine Smith School within half an hour Wednesday after a small airplane crashed into the parking lot.

"We have emergency procedures for things like this, and they were followed," he said. "In this case, they were the same procedures we would use for a fire drill. All the children were evacuated immediately to the back play yard, a great distance away from the crash."

The school staff responded immediately. As Principal Jennie Collett ordered the evacuation, custodian Dave Bess ran out to the flaming plane with a fire extinguisher.

"I saw the crash through the window (of the school office)," said school nurse Laura Everett. "I ran to the front door to see if I could help. But just as I got there, an aide came in and shouted for someone to call the Fire Department. I saw there was nobody else in the office, so I called for the Fire Department and an ambulance.

"Then I ran outside, but by that time the fire was great, and I didn't attempt to get near the plane."

The Evergreen District has only two school nurses. The other nurse rushed to Smith School as soon as she heard about the crash, Mrs. Everett said.

Editors of the *Mercury* knew that many of their readers have children of elementary school age. They knew that readers would cringe at the thought of their children playing within 50 feet of a plane crash site and would wonder if the school system's emergency procedures were adequate. The response of this school's staff could be indicative. In reporting this story the *Mercury* was fulfilling its responsibility of serving as a watchdog over a government agency—in this case, the school system.

Other sidebars in the *Mercury* that day provided profiles of two of the victims, the pilot and his young instructor, and an overview of the airport from which the plane took off. That story answered questions readers may have had about traffic and previous crashes at the airport, and about what other facilities were nearby.

Reporters for the *Mercury* continued to work on the story, and the next day this appeared:

Shortly after noon Wednesday, Mrs. Carmen Eros, a playground aide at Katherine Smith Elementary School, heard a loud grating noise, looked up and saw a plane heading straight for the kindergarten building where her grandson is a pupil.

At first, Mrs. Eros was so panicked she was unable to move and could think of nothing but her grandson, Adam. Then she heard the pupils, who were on their lunch recess, begin screaming.

"Without thinking I grabbed three little kids near me and covered their eyes so they wouldn't see," Mrs. Eros said. "Then I yelled to the other aide to get the kids to the building. The kids were crying and screaming, just like us."

Seconds later Mrs. Eros heard an explosion, stopped running and turned around.

"The plane now was heading right towards us and white smoke was coming from its tail," she said, motioning with her hands. "Then all of a sudden, the nose of the plane headed to the ground and it looked like the pilot crash-landed to avoid hitting us.

"I saw a man fly out of the plane, land on the sidewalk and roll over and over. Then I heard someone from the plane yell, 'Help the others! Help the others!'"

After hearing the explosion, the teachers ran outside and helped the aides gather the children inside the building. Mrs. Eros was dizzy and in shock, she said. As soon as the children were safe in the building, she went into the nurse's office and passed out.

Wednesday night she could not sleep at all, she said, and Thursday she was so nervous she made an appointment to see a doctor about getting some medication to relax. All day at work

Thursday, when she was on the playground, she got chills whenever she glanced at the spot where the plane crashed.

Killed in the crash were Ralph Anello, 18; F. Kempton Allen, 51; and Ila Diane Cooper, 32.

"When you see something like that, it's hard to just forget about it. I'm still shaken up. I wish I could sleep or at least relax. I hate to think how close all the children and my grandson came to disaster. Thank God nothing happened to the kids."

In an effort to determine the cause of the crash, federal inspectors tore down the engine of the Bellanca aircraft Thursday afternoon, but preliminary examination failed to disclose anything significant.

Jerry Jamison of the National Transportation Safety Board and Chuck Burns, coordinator of the Federal Aviation Administration, spent the day inspecting engine debris and the flight control system.

Burns said he did not think the plane ran out of fuel because of the fire that erupted after the crash.

It may be weeks before the final determination of why the plane crashed is made, the officials said.

In this story the writer looks at the crash through the eyes of a witness and follows up on the investigation of the crash.

That kind of reporting and writing makes stories of accidents, fires and disasters more readable and more meaningful. It allows the reader to know what it was like to be there. As in most good reporting, the human element is entwined with the news.

Suggested Readings

Benthall, Jonathan. *Disasters, Relief and the Media.* New York: I.B. Tauris, 1993. Covers the media's reporting of disaster relief.

Singer, Eleanor and Endreny, Phyllis M. *Reporting on Risk: How the Mass Media Portray Accidents, Diseases, Disasters and Other Hazards.* New York: Russell Sage Foundation, 1993. A critical look at media reporting of accidents and disasters.

Ullmann, John and Colbert, Jan, editors. *The Reporter's Handbook: An Investigator's Guide to Documents and Techniques.* New York: St. Martin's Press, 1991. A guide to using government documents to find sources of information.

Exercises

1. Find an accident story in a local newspaper. List all the obvious sources the reporter used in obtaining information for the story. List additional sources you would have checked.

2. Talk with a firefighter in your local fire department about the department's media policy at fire scenes. Based on what you learn, write instructions for your fellow reporters on what to expect at fires in your city or town.

3. Using your library or a computer database, compare the coverage of the same disaster in two daily newspapers. In your analysis, explain which story had the most effective coverage and why.

4. List all the apparent sources used by the *Chicago Tribune* in the airplane crash story that appears on pages 228-230. List at least two additional sources you would have checked.

5. Make a list of at least 10 federal agencies that may be of help in reporting accident, fire and disaster stories. Also list the telephone numbers of the agency offices nearest to you.

CRIME AND
THE COURTS

**In this chapter
you will learn:**

1. How crime news is
   covered and written.

2. How court news
   involving crime is
   covered and written.

3. How questions of taste
   and responsibility affect
   crime and court
   reporting.

*I*f anyone ever doubted the public's fascination with crime news, and
the media's seeming preoccupation with it, those doubts were dis-
pelled during the celebrated prosecution of football star and sports
commentator O. J. Simpson for the murder of his former wife and her
male friend.

The Simpson case of 1994–95 was pursued by the media as hotly
as any story since the trial 40 years earlier of Dr. Samuel Sheppard, a
Cleveland osteopath, for the murder of his wife. The Sheppard case, like
Simpson's, was accompanied by pervasive media attention that led to serious self-examination about the role of the media in covering crime and
the courts. It also led to substantive external examination, most notably
by the U.S. Supreme Court. In 1966, the court ruled that the Sheppard
case trial judge had not fulfilled his duty to protect the jury from the news
coverage that had saturated the Cleveland community. Nor, the court
ruled, had the trial judge fulfilled his duty to control disruptive influences
in the courtroom. At issue was whether Sheppard, with media attention
focused on the murder, could receive a fair trial. Properly, the Supreme
Court placed the burden on the trial court to control the environment and
refrained from limiting First Amendment freedoms of the press. Indeed,
the trial process had worked; despite massive publicity that some viewed
as prejudicial, Sheppard was acquitted.

If anything, publicity in the Simpson case was more pervasive than
in the Sheppard case. More than 100 news organizations applied for credentials to cover Simpson's trial, and many of those proposed sending
numerous reporters. To accommodate them, only 21 seats were available
to the media in the courtroom. Intense media coverage of high-profile trials is common. Today, many such trials are covered by television, and a
cable television channel, Court TV, devotes its programming exclusively
to satisfying public interest in courts and the legal system. Curious
Americans spend hours upon hours watching its telecasts. In Simpson's
case, even his arrest received massive television coverage, as cameras
aboard helicopters provided live coverage of every moment of the police
chase that eventually ended in Simpson's surrender at his California
mansion.

Again the question was raised: With such pervasive pretrial publicity, could such a famous defendant possibly receive a fair trial? It is a
question that has not been resolved adequately since Congress simultaneously drafted, and the states adopted, the First and Sixth amendments to
the U.S. Constitution. The First Amendment gives the press substantial
freedom to cover the news and publish as it sees fit; the Sixth Amendment
gives defendants a right to a fair and speedy trial. The two rights often
seem to conflict, although seldom, if ever, is a judge unable to find a solution to the problem.

While the media often are vilified for "pandering" to the public's fascination with crime, there is no doubt the public's interest is real. Even in
recent political campaigns, the crime problem has topped the list of public

concerns. Indeed, when defending intensive crime coverage, editors often argue that the public's demand for such information is legitimate. How can the public protect itself from crime, they argue, if the media don't report its existence? Detractors counter that the media do far more than increase public awareness of crime; instead, they argue, the media play to the baser instincts of the public by speculating on every gory detail of sensational murders and the love triangles that often lead to them.

The case against the media grows when, in a rush to be first, a reporter broadcasts or prints information that is both damning to the defendant and inaccurate. That happened on several occasions during the Simpson case as reporters allowed themselves to be used by the prosecution or the defense. Each side accused the other of leaking prejudicial information to the media. In 1966, the Supreme Court tried to address that problem by placing the burden of controlling what the media reported on the trial judge. In reality, the court had no choice; the First Amendment virtually prohibits any limitation of press freedom once the media obtain the information. Responsible news organizations know, however, that cases such as O.J. Simpson's may lead to further examinations by the Supreme Court. Next time, the result might not be so favorable. As a result, reporters try hard to be particularly accurate and responsible in their accounts of high-interest cases. Months after Simpson's acquittal, public interest in the case was as high as ever.

Such fascination with crime news is not new. Ever since Benjamin Day borrowed an idea from London newspapers and began publishing police court reports in his New York Sun, *crime news has played an important role in American journalism. The* Sun's *humorous accounts of drunkenness, theft and streetwalking were a hit with the citizens of New York in 1838, and they soon made that newspaper New York's largest daily. Today's media accounts of crime probably are less humorous and usually more responsible, and there can be little doubt that court reporting is more subdued. Now few editors seriously consider peddling crime news as a means of building circulation or audience size.*

This does not mean, however, that crime and court reports are any less important to today's editors than they were in making the Sun *an overnight success. Indeed, such reports are so common in the American media that a reporter's first assignment may well involve one or the other.*

Because of the emphasis on crime, almost every reporter eventually is called on to cover a crime or a court hearing. Such stories are not covered exclusively by reporters who have police and court beats. The general-assignment reporter often is dispatched to the scene of a crime or to a courtroom when beat reporters are occupied elsewhere.

The reporter who covers a crime or follows it through the courts walks squarely into the middle of the **free press-fair trial controversy**. *Because of past abuses by the press, real or perceived, in recent years judges and trial lawyers have sought to prevent the release of evidence or details of a crime that in their view may make it difficult to empanel an* *impartial jury. A judge's attempt to protect a defendant's Sixth Amendment right to an impartial jury seemingly may conflict with the reporter's responsibility to inform the public. But almost invariably that apparent conflict is resolved by the judge invoking the power to order a change of venue or to sequester the jury. A **change of venue** means that the trial is moved to a location where pretrial news coverage may have been less extensive. When a judge sequesters a jury, jurors are not allowed to go home, and permission to read newspapers, listen to radio or watch television during the trial is limited or denied. Jurors are housed in a hotel at public expense.*

The media are vital in transmitting crime and court news. The public wants to have such news, editors are eager to provide it, and judges and lawyers often are determined to limit it. As a reporter who almost certainly will cover crime and the courts, you must know how to meet the expectations of the public and your editors without trampling on the rights of the accused.

Gathering and Writing Crime News

The last thing Tom Wicker expected to write on Nov. 22, 1963, was a crime story. Wicker, then White House correspondent for the *New York Times*, was accompanying President John F. Kennedy on a goodwill visit to Texas. Kennedy was trying to re-establish good relations with the southern wing of the Democratic Party, and Wicker expected little more than to cover a few speeches and to interview some of the key figures.

The rest is history. An assassin's bullet hit Kennedy as his motorcade passed through Dallas' Dealey Plaza. Soon afterward the president died at Parkland Hospital, and Wicker found himself asking some of the same questions any reporter who covers a murder must ask. How many times was the victim hit? From where were the shots fired? What kind of weapon was used? What is the name of the accused? The list of such questions was endless, and more than 30 years later, many of them still have not been answered to everyone's satisfaction. Wicker later wrote:

> At first no one knew what happened, or how, or where, much less why. Gradually, bits and pieces began to fall together, and within two hours a reasonably coherent version of the story began to be possible. Even now, however, I know no reporter who was there who has a clear and orderly picture of that surrealistic afternoon; it is still a matter of bits and pieces thrown hastily into something like a whole.

The example, of course, is an extreme one. Few reporters are likely to cover a presidential assassination. But the incident illustrates how difficult it is to piece together an account of a crime, even when, as in this case, there are thousands of witnesses.

Sources of Information

Most information about crimes comes from three major sources:

- Police officials and their reports.
- The victim or victims.
- The witness or witnesses.

The circumstances of the crime may determine which of these three sources is most important, which should be checked first or whether they should be checked at all. If the victim is available, as a reporter you should make every effort to get an interview. But if the victim and witnesses are unavailable, the police and their report become primary sources.

When your editor assigns you to a crime story is important. If you are dispatched to the scene of the crime as it happens or soon afterward, you probably will interview the victim and witnesses first. The police report can wait. But if you are assigned to write about a crime that occurred the night before, the police report is the starting point.

Police and Police Reports

A police officer investigating a crime covers much of the same ground you do. The officer is interested in who was involved, what happened, when, where, why and how. Those details are needed to complete the official report of the incident, and you need them for your story.

When you write about crime, the police report always should be checked. It is often the source of such basic information as:

- A description of what happened.
- The location of the incident.
- The name, age and address of the victim.
- The name, age and address of the suspect, if any.
- The offense police believe the suspect has committed.
- The extent of injuries, if any.
- The names, ages and addresses of the witnesses.

The reporter who arrives at the scene of a crime as it takes place or immediately afterward has the advantage of being able to gather much of that information firsthand. When timely coverage is impossible, however, the police report allows the reporter to catch up quickly. The names of those with knowledge of the incident usually appear on the report, and the reporter uses that information to learn the story. See Figure 12.1 for an example of a police report.

Reporters sometimes write crime stories from the police report alone. In the case of routine stories, some editors view such reporting as sufficient. Good newspapers, however, demand more because police reports frequently are inaccurate. Most experienced reporters have read reports in which the names of those involved are mis-

BURGLARY

1. OFFENSE: Burglary
2. CASE #: 32701
3. OCCURRED AT (ADDRESS): 308 Maple St.
4. DATE/TIME OCCURRED: 0100 - 0800
5. DATE/TIME REPORTED: 0830
6. DATE/TIME REPORT WRITTEN: 0945 - 11 March

	RAC	SEX	DOB	ADDRESS	HOME PHONE	BUS PHONE
7. PERSON REPORTING: Linda L. Mellotti	W	F	9-11-45	308 Maple St.	372-1124	372-9988
8. OWNER OF BUILDING: VICTIM						
9. WITNESS: NONE						
10. VICTIM (FIRM OR INDIVIDUAL)						

11. RESIDENCE ☒ NONRESIDENCE ☐ | 12. FORCE ☒ NO FORCE ☐ | 13. DAY ☐ NIGHT ☒ UNKNOWN ☐ | 14. TYPE OF BUSINESS: | 15. POINT OF ENTRY: Back door | 16. HOW WAS ENTRY GAINED: Glass broken to unlock door

17. TYPE OF LOCK OR STRUCTURE DEFEATED: Type A | 18. DAMAGE CAUSED BY ENTRY: Broken window glass | 19. WHO SECURED BLDG: Occupant | TIME/DATE:

STOLEN PROP	20. QUAN	21. TYPE	22. BRAND	23. SERIAL #	24. PHYSICAL DESCRIPTION	25. VALUE	26. DATE ENTERED	BY	27. DATE CLEARED	BY
A	1	Console	GE	Unknown	TV set	$300				

28. SUSPECT NAME	RAC	SEX	DOB	ADDRESS	HOME PHONE	BUS PHONE
NONE						

HT | WT. | EYES | HAIR | BUILD | FACIAL HAIR | HAT | COAT | SHIRT | TROUSERS | SHOES

UNUSUAL IDENTIFIERS | MARKS SCARS & TATTOOS | PHOTO OBTAINED

SUSPECT VEHICLE COLOR | YEAR | MAKE | MODEL | STYLE | VIN | LIC YR | LIC STATE | LIC TYPE | LIC NUMBER

29. INVESTIGATING OFFICER | DEPT | 30. APPROVED BY | 31. EVIDENCE COLLECTED BY | 32. PHOTOGRAPHY BY | 33. REASSIGNED TO | BY

34. NARRATIVE:

Victim works night shift at Milan Hospital. Residence entered while she was working. TV set only item known missing.

WORK SHEET

Figure 12.1.
This burglary report is typical of the type of reports available to reporters at most police stations.

spelled, ages are wrongly stated and other basic information is inaccurate. Sometimes such errors are a result of sloppy reporting by the investigating officer or mistakes in transcribing notes into a formal report. Occasionally the officer may lie in an attempt to cover up shortcomings in the investigation or misconduct at the scene of the crime. Whatever the reason, good reporters do their own reporting and do not depend solely on a police officer's account.

Robert Snyder, a former history professor at Princeton University, studied U.S. crime reporting while a research fellow at the Gannett Center for Media Studies in New York. He was alarmed by what he found. Crime stories, he discovered, still rely heavily on one police source. That, Snyder insists, is a dangerous and seemingly irresponsible practice because one of journalism's founding principles is that a story's credibility is built on the number of sources used. Thus, while the quality of other kinds of reporting has advanced significantly thanks to innovative techniques or editors' insistence on plain old hard work, crime reporting lags behind. Indeed, it clings too often to the single-source practices of the 19th century.

The Victim

The difficulty of obtaining information about a crime often is caused by the confusion that accompanies such events. The victim may be unavailable for interviews. Even if the victim is available, the trauma of the event may have prompted enough hysteria to preclude reconstruction of the event.

That does not mean, however, that the victim's words necessarily are useless. One young reporter sent to cover a bank robbery returned to the office and announced to her editor, "I couldn't get a thing from the teller. As the cops took her away, she just kept mumbling, 'That big black gun! That big black gun!'" The editor smiled, leaned back in his chair and said, "That's your lead." He realized that the shocked teller's repetition of that phrase said more about the terror of the moment than the reporter could have conveyed in several paragraphs.

Not always, of course, is the victim's account of the story incoherent. One young reporter discovered that fact his first day on the job while filling in for the ailing police-beat reporter. In checking through a pile of incident reports, the reporter noticed that the police had captured a man armed with a rifle who had forced a cab driver to drive around town for an hour at gunpoint. The reporter called the cab driver, who by then was off duty, and produced an interesting story about a quick-thinking cabbie who worked his way out of a sticky situation.

"I just kept flippin' the button on the microphone (of the cab's two-way radio)," the driver said.

The cab company dispatcher grew curious and asked the driver if his cab was still occupied.

divisive trial of a black man acquitted of shooting to death a white police officer in what he said was self-defense.

Once, as coroners removed a charred body from a San Diego dumpster, Grimaldi was on the scene. He later was the first to report that the death was probably the work of a serial killer. He wrote about police corruption, including the chief's use of city-owned video equipment to tape a TV show on bass fishing.

"There's no better way to learn how to report and write than covering crime," Grimaldi says. "It is the quickest way to explore any community. There's humor and pathos, politics and social issues. Every rookie reporter should spend some time covering crime."

From the *Tribune*, Grimaldi went to the *Orange County Register* in 1989 as a general-assignment reporter. Crime stories taught Grimaldi reporting techniques he used for an investigation of medical deaths, rapes and drug-dealing at the California Institution for Women in Frontera. The Frontera stories won numerous national prizes.

In 1994, Grimaldi was named the *Register's* bureau chief in Washington, where he still relies on the reporting foundation first built on the police beat.

"I told him it was. He must have realized I was nervous and called the police."

Moments later, a police officer spotted the cab. The man with the rifle jumped from the back seat and fled, but the police officer caught him. The story itself was not important, but the account of the quick-witted cabbie and an alert dispatcher made it interesting. In most cases the victim's account adds immeasurably to a crime story.

Witnesses

Frequently the account of a witness is more accurate and vivid than the account of the victim. And frequently a witness will be available for an interview when a victim is not. If the victim has been taken to a hospital or is huddled with the police giving them details of what happened, you are effectively cut off from a major source.

Witnesses, like police officers and the victim, can provide vivid detail and direct quotes to make the story more readable. In addition, witnesses can provide a new view of what happened. Only after interviewing them can you determine if that view will be a useful addition to your story.

Conflicting accounts of an incident sometimes surface when you interview several sources. Such conflicts may be difficult, if not impossible, to resolve. A victim, for example, may describe an incident one way and a witness another. Presumably the victim is in the best position to know what really happened, but, because of the stress the victim encountered, the account of the witness may be more accurate. In contrast, a cool-headed victim is certainly more reliable than a distressed witness. Seldom can the reporter resolve conflicting reports, so the best solution in this case may be to acknowledge the conflict and to publish both versions of the story.

Other Possible Sources

Although police reports, victims and witnesses are the most important sources, crime reporting does not depend solely on them. In most cases there are other sources, perhaps including relatives, friends, and neighbors of the victim; the victim's doctor; the medical examiner; the prosecuting attorney; and the suspect's lawyer. A good reporter quickly pieces together an account of the crime and uses that information to determine the best sources of information.

Writing the Story

There is no magic formula for writing crime news. Solid reporting techniques pay off just as they do in other types of reporting. Then it is a matter of writing the story as the facts demand.

Sometimes the events of a crime are most effectively told in chronological order, particularly when the story is complex (this story approach is discussed in more detail in Chapter 17). More often a traditional inverted pyramid style is best. How much time the reporter has to file the story also influences the approach. Let's take a look at how the newspaper accounts of two crimes were developed over time and why different writing styles seemed appropriate for each.

The Chronologically Ordered Story

Gathering facts from the many sources available and sorting through conflicting information can be time-consuming tasks. Sometimes the reporter may have to write the story before all the facts are gathered. The result is a bare-bones account written to meet a deadline. Such circumstances often lead to crime stories written like this:

A Highway Patrol marksman shot and killed a Kansas man in a rural area south of Springfield this morning after the victim threatened to blow off the head of his apparent hostage.

A hitchhiker reportedly told police earlier this morning that his "ride" had plans to rob a service station on Interstate 70. That tip apparently followed an earlier report of a van leaving a station at the Millersburg exit of I-70 without paying for gasoline.

An ensuing hour-long chase ended at 9:30 a.m. in an isolated meadow in the Pierpont area when Capt. N.E. Tinnin fired a single shot into the stomach of the suspect, identified as Jim Phipps of Kansas City, Kan.

Phipps, armed with a sawed-off shotgun, and his "hostage," identified as Anthony Curtis Lilly, 17, also of Kansas City, Kan., eluded police by fleeing into a rugged, wooded area at the end of Bennett Lane, a dead-end gravel road off Route 163.

Tinnin said he fired the shot with a .253-caliber sniper rifle when it appeared Phipps was going to shoot Lilly. Two troopers' efforts to persuade Phipps to throw down his weapon and surrender were unsuccessful, Tinnin said.

Note that even in this bare-bones account, the available facts of this particular story dictate a chronological approach after a summary lead.

The reporter who produced that story for an afternoon newspaper did a good job of collecting information following a puzzling incident. Still, several words and phrases (the *apparent* hostage, a hitchhiker *reportedly* told police, a tip *apparently* followed) provide tip-offs that the series of events was not entirely clear.

With more time to learn the full story, a reporter for the city's morning newspaper resolved many of those conflicts. As a result, readers got a more complete account of what occurred:

James Phipps and Anthony Lilly, a pair of 17-year-olds from Kansas City, Kan., were heading west on Interstate 70 at 7:30 a.m. Friday, returning from a trip to Arkansas.

Within the next hour and a half, Phipps had used a sawed-off shotgun stolen in Arkansas to take Lilly hostage, and, after holding that shotgun to Lilly's head, was shot and killed by a Highway Patrol captain on the edge of a rugged wooded area south of Springfield.

As the episode ended, local officials had only begun to piece together a bizarre tragedy that involved a high-speed chase, airplane and helicopter surveillance, a march through a wooded ravine and the evacuation of several frightened citizens from their country homes.

As police reconstructed the incident, Phipps and Lilly decided to stop for gas at the Millersburg exit east of Springfield at about 7:30 a.m. With them in the van was Robert Paul Hudson Jr., a San Francisco-bound hitchhiker.

Hudson was not present at the shooting. He had fled Lilly's van at the Millersburg exit after he suspected trouble.

The trouble began when Lilly and Phipps openly plotted to steal some gasoline at Millersburg, Hudson told police. He said the pair had agreed to display the shotgun if trouble arose with station attendants.

Hudson said he persuaded Phipps to drop him off before they stopped for gas. He then caught a ride to Springfield and told his driver of the robbery plans he had overheard. After dropping Hudson off near the Providence Road exit, the driver called Springfield police, who picked up Hudson.

Meanwhile, Phipps and Lilly put $5.90 worth of gas in the van and drove off without paying. The station attendant notified authorities.

As he approached Springfield, Phipps turned onto U.S. 63 South, where he was spotted by Highway Patrol troopers Tom Halford and Greg Overfelt. They began a high-speed chase, which ended on a dead-end gravel road near Pierpont.

During the chase, which included a U-turn near Ashland, Phipps bumped the Highway Patrol car twice, forcing Halford to run into the highway's median.

Upon reaching the dead end, the suspects abandoned the van and ran into a nearby barn. At that point, Phipps, who Highway Patrol officers said was wanted in Kansas for escaping from a detention center, turned the shotgun on Lilly.

When Halford and Overfelt tried to talk with Phipps from outside the barn, they were met with obscenities. Phipps threatened to "blow (Lilly's) head off," and vowed not to be captured alive.

Phipps then left the barn and walked into a wooded area, pressing the gun against Lilly's head. Halford and Overfelt followed at a safe distance but were close enough to speak with Phipps.

While other officers from the Highway Patrol, the Lincoln County Sheriff's Department and Springfield police arrived at the scene, residents in the area were warned to evacuate their homes. A Highway Patrol plane and helicopter flew low over the woods, following the suspects and the troopers through the woods.

The four walked through a deep and densely wooded ravine. Upon seeing a partially constructed house in a nearby clearing, Phipps demanded of officers waiting in the clearing that his van be driven around to the house, at which time he would release his hostage.

Halford said, "They disappeared up over the ridge. I heard some shouting (Phipps' demands), and then I heard the shot."

After entering the clearing from the woods, Phipps apparently had been briefly confused by the officers on either side of him and had lowered his gun for a moment.

That was long enough for Highway Patrol Capt. N.E. Tinnin to shoot Phipps in the abdomen with a high-powered rifle. It was about 8:45 a.m. Phipps was taken to Boone County Hospital, where he soon died.

The story is as complete as possible under the circumstances. The reporter who wrote it decided to describe the chain of events in chronological order both because of the complexity of the story and because the drama of the actual events is most vividly communicated in a chronological story form.

The story is also made effective by its wealth of detail, including the names of the troopers involved, details of the chase and much, much more. The reporter had to talk with many witnesses to piece together this account. The hard work paid off, however, in the form of an informative, readable story.

Notice how the third paragraph sets the scene and provides a transition into the chronological account. Such attention to the details of good writing helps the reader understand the story with a minimum of effort.

The Sidebar Story

If a number of people witnessed or were affected by a crime, the main story may be supplemented by a sidebar story that deals with the personal impact of the crime. The writer of the preceding chronological account also decided to write a separate story on nearby residents, who had little to add to the main story but became a part of the situation nonetheless:

In the grass at the edge of a woods near Pierpont Friday afternoon, the only remaining signs of James Phipps were a six-inch circle of blood, a doctor's syringe, a blood-stained button and the imprints in the mud where Phipps fell after he was shot by a Highway Patrol officer.

Elsewhere in the area, it was a quiet, sunny, spring day in a countryside dotted by farms and houses. But inside some of those houses, dwellers still were shaken by the morning's events that had forced a police order for them to evacuate their homes.

Mrs. James G. Thorne lives on Cheavens Road across the clearing from where Phipps was shot. Mrs. Thorne had not heard the evacuation notice, so when she saw area officers crouching with guns at the end of her driveway, she decided to investigate.

"I was the surprise they weren't expecting," she told a Highway Patrol officer Friday afternoon. "I walked out just before the excitement."

When the officers saw Mrs. Thorne "they were obviously very upset and shouted for me to get out of here," she said. "I was here alone and asked them how I was supposed to leave. All they said was 'Just get out of here!'"

Down the road, Clarence Stallman had been warned of the situation by officers and noticed the circling airplane and helicopter. "I said, 'Are they headed this way soon?' and they said, 'They're here,'" said Stallman.

After Stallman notified his neighbors, he picked up Mrs. Thorne at her home and left the area just before the shooting.

On the next street over, Ronald Nichols had no intention of running.

"I didn't know what was happening," Nichols said. "The wife was scared to death and didn't know what to do. I grabbed my gun and looked for them."

Another neighbor, Mrs. Charles Emmons, first was alerted by the sound of the surveillance plane. "The plane was flying so low I thought it was going to come into the house," she said. "I was frightened. This is something you think will never happen to you."

Then Mrs. Emmons flashed a relieved smile. "It's been quite a morning," she said.

The Inverted Pyramid Account

The techniques of writing in chronological order and separating the accounts of witnesses from the main story worked well in the preceding case. More often, however, crime stories are written in the classic pyramid style because of time and space considerations:

ber took
bson's
t, then
chase

Simpson,
aid a man
sk entered
5 p.m. The
tol and de-
pson empty
cash register
ry bag.
yed but man-
a silent alarm
e counter.
ordered Simpson
room in the rear
g at 411 Fourth

Officer J.O. Holton, responding to the alarm, arrived at the store as the suspect left the building and fled south on foot.

Holton chased the man south on Fourth Street until he turned west into an alley near the corner of Olson Street. Holton said he followed the suspect for about four blocks until he lost sight of him.

Simpson said receipts showed that $1,056 was missing from the cash register. He described the robber as about 5 feet 11 inches with a bandage on his right thumb. He was wearing blue jeans and a black leather coat.

Police have no suspects.

ccount is adequate and can be written directly from rt. An enterprising reporter can add much to a story of king the time to interview the clerk and police officer. ing this story for the first edition, the reporter found the police officer. He had little to add. Then the reacted the clerk, who had plenty to say. This was the

"I'm tired of being robbed, and I'm afraid of being shot," says Robert Simpson. "So I told the owner I quit."

Simpson, 42, of 206 Fourth St. quit his job as night clerk at Gibson's Liquor Store today after being robbed for the fourth time in three weeks Friday night.

Simpson said a man wearing a red ski mask entered the store at 411 Fourth St. at about 7:35 p.m. and demanded money. Simpson emptied $1,056 into a grocery bag the robber carried and was ordered into a storage room at the rear of the building.

"He said he'd blow off my head if I didn't cooperate, so I did exactly what he told me," Simpson said. "But I managed to set off the alarm button under the counter while I was emptying the cash register."

Officer J.O. Holton responded to the alarm and arrived as the robber left the store but lost him as he fled through nearby alleys on foot.

"We keep asking the cops to set up a stakeout, but they don't do anything," Simpson said. "I know they've got a lot of problems, but that place is always getting hit."

Police records revealed that Gibson's was robbed of $502 Sept. 10, $732 Sept. 14 and $221 Sept. 24. Simpson was the clerk each time.

"This may have been the same guy who robbed me last time," Simpson said, "but I can't be sure because of that mask. Last time he had a different one."

Police Chief Ralph Marshall said he has ordered patrol cars to check the vicinity of the liquor store more often and is considering the owner's request for a stakeout.

"That's just great," Simpson said. "But they can let someone else be the goat. I quit."

Simpson described the robber as a heavy man about 5 feet 11 inches tall. He was wearing blue jeans and a black leather jacket and had a bandage on his right thumb.

Police have no suspects.

Annual crime statistics are a common source of stories. Reporters must take care when reporting them, however, if they involve small numbers. It is dramatic to say, "Murders increased by 300 percent in 1995," but it is misleading if the increase was from one murder to three.

To provide a more accurate picture, reporters can perform the equivalent of adding apples and oranges. "Unlike" items can be added, subtracted, multiplied and divided, if they are grouped in a category that makes them "like" items.

For example, you can group murders, rapes, assaults and armed robberies in the category of "violent crimes." That way, you can add murders to rapes to assaults to armed robberies. This can be useful if an individual category such as murder isn't large enough to provide much insight (as in many small towns). However, the larger category must be logical and meaningful.

The reporter took the time to get a good interview, and the direct quotes add to the appeal of the story. The reporter also recognized and brought out the best angle: the personal fear and frustration experienced by people in high-crime areas. The result is a much more imaginative use of the basic inverted pyramid formula and a much more interesting story.

The clerk, in the course of his remarks, supplied an important tip about repeated robberies at the store. Two weeks later, police arrested a man as he tried to rob the store. The earlier report was used for background, and a complete story resulted.

Television and Crime

If newspapers seem to cover a lot of crime, television seems almost obsessed with it. The Chicago Council on Urban Affairs paid for a 10-week study of local television news in that city. The major finding: Chicago's three network affiliates devote 60 percent of their newscasts to crime. For a story on TV crime coverage, the *St. Louis Post-Dispatch* monitored the late-night news for a week and discovered that 24 percent was about crime. Wrote the *Post-Dispatch's* Harry Levins:

—Network crime coverage has jumped, too. The Washington-based Center for Media and Public Affairs reports that last year the network news shows doubled their coverage of crime—and tripled their coverage of murder—from the year before.

—In Miami, several hotels have erased that city's Fox affiliate, WSVN, from their cable systems. The reason: WSVN programs eight hours of news a day, heavily spiced with blood and gore. The hotels say WSVN is scaring their guests.

Levins added that crime stories take advantage of television's prominent characteristics. Producers, anchors and other broadcast professionals he quoted all confirmed that television stations use crime stories to compete with each other in attracting larger audiences. His conclusion was that crime news suits television well because:

It is a visual medium. "Crime scenes teem with visuals: flashing lights on emergency vehicles . . . wide-eyed witnesses . . . weeping relatives. . . ."

It favors action. In television, few things are worse than "a talking head"—an anchor reading a story, a politician answering questions.

It craves immediacy. The amount of local news on television has risen sharply in the last 15 years—partly because viewers want more news, partly because news makes money. To keep each newscast fresh, sta-

tions need new news—and they can usually find something fresh and violent.

It demands brevity. "TV demands brevity; on television news, 60 seconds is a long time. Stories must be brief, and most murders can be reported briefly: good guys, bad guys, dead guys, and back to you, Steve."

It lacks full-coverage resources. Few television stations come close to matching the number of reporters at a metropolitan newspaper. As a result, few television reporters cover specialized "beats."

For these reasons, television is unlikely to reduce its emphasis on crime. Crime has tremendous viewer appeal, and in a competitive, market-driven economy, it sells.

Court Organization and Procedure

When a suspect is apprehended and charged with a crime, the reporter's job is not finished. Indeed, it has only begun. Because the public wants and needs to know whether the suspect is guilty and, if so, what punishment is imposed, the media devote much time and space to court coverage of criminal charges.

At first glance reporting court news appears to be simple. You listen to the judicial proceeding, ask a few questions afterward and write a story. It may be that simple if you have a thorough knowledge of criminal law and court procedure. If not, it can be extremely confusing. No journalism textbook or class can prepare you to deal with all the intricacies of criminal law. That is a subject better suited for law schools. You should learn the basics of law, court organization and procedure, however. With this foundation you will be prepared to cover court proceedings with at least some understanding of what is happening. This knowledge can be supplemented by asking questions of the judge and attorneys involved.

Court Organization

In the United States there are two primary court systems, federal and state. Each state has a unique system, but there are many similarities. The average citizen has the most contact with the city or municipal courts, which have jurisdiction over traffic or other minor offenses involving city ordinances. News from these courts is handled as a matter of record in many newspapers.

Cases involving violations of state statutes usually are handled in the state trial courts that can be found in most counties. These courts of general jurisdiction (often called *circuit* or *superior courts*) handle cases ranging from domestic relations matters to murder. General jurisdiction is an important designation. It means these courts can and do try more cases of more varieties than any other type of court, including federal district (trial) courts. These courts handle civil cases, such as contractual disputes, as well as the **criminal** cases that are the primary focus of news reporters.

Federal district courts have jurisdiction over cases involving violations of federal crime statutes, interpretation of the U.S. Constitution, civil rights, election disputes, commerce and antitrust matters, postal regulations, federal tax laws and similar issues. Federal trial courts also have jurisdiction in actions between citizens of different states when the amount in controversy exceeds $50,000.

Many courts handle both civil *and* criminal *cases. Media coverage often focuses on criminal cases, although civil actions, lawsuits involving disputes of one type or another, often provide excellent sources of stories.*

Court Procedure

Crimes are categorized under state statutes according to their seriousness. The two primary categories of crimes are **misdemeanors** and **felonies**. Under modern statutes, the distinction between felonies and misdemeanors involves whether the offense is punishable by imprisonment in a state penitentiary or a county jail. Thus, most state statutes describe a misdemeanor as an offense punishable by a fine or a county jail term not to exceed one year or both. Felonies are punishable by a fine, a prison sentence of more than one year or death.

Pretrial Proceedings in Criminal Cases

A person arrested in connection with a crime usually is taken to a police station for fingerprinting, photographing and perhaps a sobriety test or a lineup. Statements may be taken and used in evidence only if the person arrested has been informed of and waives what police and lawyers call *Miranda rights*, so named because the requirement was imposed in a Supreme Court case involving a defendant named Miranda. They include the right to have an attorney (either hired by the defendant or appointed by the court if the defendant is indigent) and the right to remain silent. Usually within 24 hours a charge must be filed or the person must be released. The time limit may vary from state to state, but all have some limitation to prevent unreasonable detention.

Initial Appearance

If, after consulting with police and reviewing the evidence, the *prosecuting* (or *state* or *circuit*) *attorney* decides to file charges, the defendant usually is brought before a judge and is informed of the charges and reminded of the Miranda rights. *Bail* usually is set at this time.

If the charge is a misdemeanor and the defendant pleads guilty, the case usually is disposed of immediately, and a sentence is imposed or a fine is levied. If the plea is not guilty, a trial date usually is set.

If the crime is a felony, the defendant does not enter a plea. The judge will set a date for a *preliminary hearing*, unless the defendant waives the right to such a hearing. If the defendant waives this hearing, he or she is bound over to the general jurisdiction trial court. The process of being bound over means simply that the records of the case will be sent to the trial court.

A preliminary hearing in felony cases usually is held before a magistrate or lower-level judge in state court systems. The prosecutor presents evidence to try to convince the judge there is *probable cause* to believe that a crime has been committed and that the defendant committed it.

The defendant has the right to cross-examine the state's witnesses and the defendant may present evidence, but this normally is not done. Thus, because stories about preliminary hearings often are one-sided, care must be exercised in writing a story that is well balanced. If the judge does find that there is probable cause, the prosecuting attorney then must file what is called an *information* within a short period of time (usually 10 days) after the judge has ordered the defendant bound over for trial. This information must be based on the judge's findings of probable cause.

Under most state constitutions, it is possible to bring a person accused in a felony case to trial in one of two ways. One is the pre-

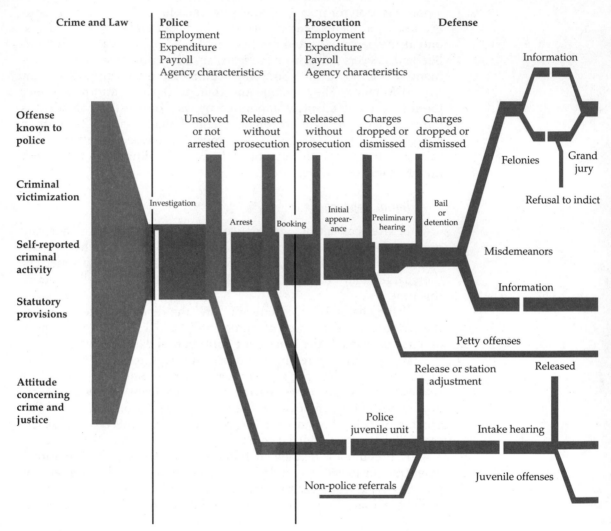

Figure 12.2.
This chart shows how cases proceed through the U.S. criminal justice system.

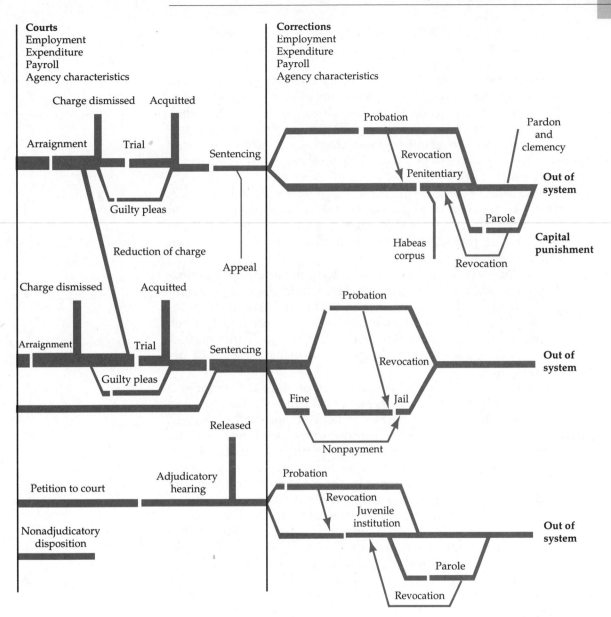

Courts
Employment
Expenditure
Payroll
Agency characteristics

Corrections
Employment
Expenditure
Payroll
Agency characteristics

Charge dismissed   Acquitted

Probation

Pardon and clemency

Arraignment   Trial

Sentencing

Revocation

Out of system

Guilty pleas

Penitentiary

Reduction of charge

Parole

Appeal

Capital punishment

Habeas corpus

Revocation

Charge dismissed   Acquitted

Probation

Arraignment   Trial

Sentencing

Revocation

Out of system

Guilty pleas

Fine   Jail

Nonpayment

Released

Adjudicatory hearing

Probation

Petition to court

Revocation
Juvenile institution

Out of system

Nonadjudicatory disposition

Parole

Revocation

liminary hearing; the other is a *grand jury indictment*. In federal courts, the U.S. Constitution requires indictment by a grand jury in felony cases instead of a preliminary hearing.

Grand jury hearings are secret. Jurors and witnesses are sworn not to reveal information about what takes place in the grand jury room, and potential defendants are not allowed to be present when testimony is given concerning them. The prosecuting attorney presents evidence to the grand jury, which must determine whether there is probable cause to prosecute. The prosecutor acts as adviser to the grand jury.

A grand jury returns a *true bill* when probable cause is found. A *no true bill* is returned if no probable cause is found. When a grand jury finds probable cause, an indictment is signed by the grand jury foreman and the prosecuting attorney. It then is presented in open court to a trial judge.

If the defendant is not already in custody, the judge orders an arrest warrant issued for the accused. *Arraignment* in the trial court follows. This is the first formal presentation of the information or the indictment to the defendant. The arraignment is conducted in open court, and the defendant enters a plea to the charge. Three pleas—guilty, not guilty and not guilty by reason of mental disease or defect—are possible.

A process known as *plea bargaining* sometimes is used at this point. Under this process, a defendant may change a plea from not guilty to guilty in return for a lighter sentence than may be imposed if a jury returns a guilty verdict. Typically, in such circumstances the defendant pleads guilty to a lesser charge than the one outstanding. A defendant charged with premeditated or first-degree murder, for example, may plead guilty to a reduced charge of manslaughter. The prosecutor often is willing to go along with such an arrangement if the time and expense of a trial can be saved and if justice is served.

If a guilty plea is entered, the judge may impose a sentence immediately, or a presentencing investigation of the defendant's background may be ordered to help the judge set punishment. Many jurisdictions require presentencing investigations, at least in felony cases. If sentencing is delayed for that purpose, a sentencing date usually is set to allow ample time for completion of the report. If a not-guilty plea is entered, the judge sets a trial date. Most jurisdictions have statutes or court rules requiring speedy trials in criminal cases and setting time limits from the date of the charge being filed to the date of the trial.

As the prosecutor and defense attorney prepare for trial, *motions* may be filed for disclosure of evidence, suppression of evidence and similar rulings. Journalists will have a special interest if a defense attorney files a motion for a change of venue, which allows the trial to be conducted in a county other than the one in which the crime occurred. Requests for venue changes often result from pretrial stories in the local media that may prejudice potential jurors. This was the case when the Los Angeles police officers accused of beating Rodney King were tried in Simi Valley.

The Trial

The trial starts as a jury, usually made up of 12 members and at least one alternate, is selected from a group of citizens called for jury duty. During the selection process (called *voir dire*) the prosecutor and defense attorney question the prospective jurors to identify jurors that each side hopes will be sympathetic to its position. In the federal system the judge often asks questions, but the prosecutor and defense attorneys may suggest questions for the judge to ask potential jurors.

Each attorney is allowed to eliminate a certain number of individuals from consideration as jurors without having to state a reason. Thus, a prospective juror believed to be prejudiced against the attorney's view can be dismissed. Elimination of a prospective juror for cause (if, for example, he or she is related to the accused) also is permitted. An unlimited number of challenges for cause is allowed each attorney. Once 12 jurors and one or more alternates are chosen and sworn, the prosecutor makes an *opening statement*. The opening statement outlines how the prosecutor, acting on behalf of the state, expects to prove each of the elements of the crime. The defense attorney may follow with an outline of the defense or may wait until after the prosecution has introduced its evidence. The defense also may waive an opening statement.

To establish what happened and to link the defendant to the crime, witnesses for the state are called to the stand. During this procedure the prosecutor asks questions, and the witness responds. The defense attorney then has an opportunity to *cross-examine* the witness. Frequently, one attorney will object to questions posed by the other, and the judge must rule on the objection. When the defense attorney finishes cross-examination, the prosecutor conducts *re-direct examination* to try to clarify points for the jury that may have become confused during cross-examination and to bolster the credibility of a witness whose credibility may have been damaged on cross-examination. Then the defense attorney may conduct another cross-examination, and the prosecutor may conduct another re-direct examination. This process can continue until both sides have exhausted all questions they want to ask the witness. After all the prosecution witnesses have testified and the state rests its case, the defense almost always makes a *motion for acquittal*, in which it argues that the state has failed to prove its case beyond a reasonable doubt. Almost as routinely as such motions are made, they are denied. A basic tenet of criminal law in the United States is that the prosecution must prove the defendant guilty. The defendant is not required to prove anything or to testify.

The defense then calls witnesses to support its case, and the prosecutor is allowed to cross-examine them. Finally, when all witnesses have testified, the defense rests. The prosecutor then calls *rebuttal witnesses* in an attempt to discredit testimony of the defense witnesses. The defense then has the right to present even more witnesses, called *surrebuttal witnesses*. After the various rebuttal witnesses have testified, the judge presents to the jury instructions—what verdicts it can return and points of law that are key to the case. The prosecutor then makes his or her closing argument, usually an impassioned plea for a guilty verdict addressed directly to the jury. The defense attorney's closing argument follows, and the prosecutor is allowed a final rebuttal. In the federal system, closing arguments precede jury instructions. The jury then retires to deliberate. Because unanimous verdicts are required for acquittal or conviction in a criminal trial, deliberations often are protracted. If the jury fails to reach a unanimous verdict (*a hung jury*) after a reasonable period of time, the judge may order a *mistrial*, in which event the entire case will be retried from the beginning of jury selection.

If a verdict is reached, the jury returns to the courtroom, where the verdict is read. In some states juries are permitted to recommend sentences when guilty verdicts are reached. Sometimes a second stage of trial occurs when the jury must decide, for example, whether to recommend life imprisonment or death. But the final decision always is made by the judge unless a crime carries a mandatory sentence. Sentencing may be done immediately, but more likely a presentencing report will be ordered and a sentencing date set.

The defense often files a motion asking that a guilty verdict be set aside. Such motions usually are denied. A motion for a new trial usually brings similar results. However, in most jurisdictions a motion for a new trial and a denial are prerequisites to the filing of an appeal. Appeals often follow guilty verdicts, so a verdict seldom is final in that sense. Except in extreme circumstances involving serious crimes, judges often permit the defendant to be released on bail pending the outcome of appeals.

Writing Court Stories

Throughout the court procedure, a reporter has opportunities to write stories. The extent to which the reporter does so, of course, depends on the importance of the case and the amount of local interest in it. In a major case the filing of every motion may prompt a story; in other cases only the verdict may be important. As in any type of reporting, news value is the determining factor.

Also, as in any form of reporting, accuracy is important. Perhaps no other area of writing requires as much caution as the reporting of crime and court news. The potential for libel is great.

Avoiding Libelous Statements

Libel is damage to a person's reputation caused by a written statement that brings the person into hatred, contempt or ridicule, or that injures his or her business or occupational pursuits (see Chapter 21). Reporters must be extremely careful about what they write.

One of the greatest dangers is the possibility of writing that someone is charged with a crime more serious than is the case. After checking clippings in the newspaper library, for example, one reporter wrote:

The rape trial of John L. Duncan, 25, of 3925 Oak St. has been set for Dec. 10 in Jefferson County Circuit Court.

Duncan is charged in connection with the June 6 rape of a Melton High School girl near Fletcher Park.

Duncan had been charged with rape following his arrest, but the prosecutor later determined the evidence was insufficient to win a rape conviction. The charge had been reduced to assault, and the newspaper had to print a correction.

In any story involving arrests, caution flags must be raised. You must have a sound working knowledge of libel law and what you can and cannot write about an incident. The reporter who writes the following, for example, is asking for trouble:

```
John R. Milton, 35, of 206 East St. was arrested Monday on a
charge of assaulting a police officer.
```

Only a prosecutor, not a police officer, may file charges. In many cases, a police officer may arrest a person with the intent of asking the prosecutor to file a certain charge. Then, when the prosecutor examines the evidence, the evidence may warrant only a lesser charge. For that reason, most newspaper editors prefer to print the name of an arrested person only after the charge has been filed. Unfortunately, deadline constraints sometimes make that impossible, and many newspapers publish the names of those arrested before the charge is filed. A decision to publish a name in such circumstances requires extreme caution. If an individual were arrested in connection with a rape and the newspaper printed that information, only to learn later that the prosecutor had filed a charge of assault, a libel suit could result. Many states, however, give journalists a qualified privilege to write fair and accurate news stories based on police reports. Once the charge is filed, the lead should be written like this:

```
John R. Milton, 35, of 206 East St. was charged Monday with
assaulting a police officer.
    Prosecutor Steve Scott said . . .
```

By writing the lead this way, the reporter shows that Milton not only has been arrested but also has been charged with a crime by the prosecutor. Carelessness leads not only to libel suits but also to attacks on a suspect's reputation.

Reporters who cover court news encounter many such pitfalls. They are not trained as attorneys, and it takes time to develop a sound working knowledge of legal proceedings. The only recourse is to ask as many questions as necessary when a point of law is not clear. It is far better to display ignorance of the law openly than to commit a serious error that harms the reputation of the accused and opens the newspaper to costly libel litigation.

However, it is also important to know that anything said in open court is fair game for reporters. If, in an opening statement, a prosecutor says the defendant is "nothing but scum, a smut peddler bent on polluting the mind of every child in the city," then by all means report it in context in your story. But if a spectator makes that same statement in the hallway during a recess, you probably would not report it. Courts do not extend the qualified privilege to report court proceedings beyond the context of the official proceeding.

Continuing Coverage of the Prosecution

With the preceding points in mind, let's trace a criminal case from the time of arrest through the trial to show how a newspaper might report each step. Here is a typical first story:

An unemployed carpenter was arrested today and charged with the Aug. 6 murder of Springfield resident Anne Compton.

Lester L. Rivers, 32, of 209 E. Dillow Lane was charged with first-degree murder, Prosecuting Attorney Mel Singleton said.

Chief of Detectives E.L. Hall said Rivers was arrested on a warrant after a three-month investigation by a team of three detectives. He declined to comment on what led investigators to Rivers.

Miss Compton's body was found in the Peabody River by two fishermen on the morning of Aug. 7. She had been beaten to death with a blunt instrument, according to Dr. Ronald R. Miller, the county medical examiner.

This straightforward account of the arrest was filed on deadline. Later, the reporter would interview neighbors about Rivers' personality and write an improved story for other editions. This bare-bones story, however, provides a glimpse of several key points in covering arrest stories.

Notice that the reporter carefully chose the words "arrested and charged with" rather than "arrested for," a phrase that may carry a connotation of guilt.

Another important element of all crime and court coverage is the **tie-back** sentence. This sentence relates a story to events covered in a previous story—in this case, the report of the crime itself. It is important to state clearly—and near the beginning of the story—which crime is involved and to provide enough information about it so that the reader recognizes it. Clarification of the crime is important even in major stories with ready identification in the community. This story does that by recounting when and where Miss Compton's body was found and by whom. It also tells that she died after being hit with a blunt instrument.

The following morning the suspect was taken to Magistrate Court for his initial court appearance. Here is a part of the story that resulted:

Lester L. Rivers appeared in Magistrate Court today charged with first-degree murder in connection with the Aug. 6 beating death of Springfield resident Anne Compton.

Judge Howard D. Robbins scheduled a preliminary hearing for Nov. 10 and set bail at $10,000.

Robbins assigned Public Defender Ogden Ball to represent Rivers, 32, of 209 E. Dillow Lane.

Rivers said nothing during the 10-minute session as the judge informed him of his right to remain silent and his right to an attorney. Ball asked Robbins to set the bail at a "reasonable amount for a man who is unemployed." Rivers is a carpenter who was fired from his last job in June.

Despite the seriousness of the charge, it is essential that Rivers be free to help prepare his defense, Ball said.

Police have said nothing about a possible connection between Rivers and Miss Compton, whose body was found in the Peabody River by two fishermen on the morning of Aug. 7. She had been beaten to death.

The reporter clearly outlined the exact charge and reported on key points of the brief hearing. Again, the link to the crime is important to inform the reader of which murder is involved.

Next came the preliminary hearing, where the first evidence linking the defendant to the crime was revealed:

Lester L. Rivers will be tried in Jefferson County Circuit Court for the Aug. 6 murder of Springfield resident Anne Compton.

Magistrate Judge Howard D. Robbins ruled today that there is probable cause to believe that a crime was committed and probable cause that Rivers did it. Rivers was bound over for trial in Circuit Court.

Rivers, 32, of 209 E. Dillow Lane is being held in Jefferson County Jail. He has been unable to post bail of $10,000.

At today's preliminary hearing, Medical Examiner Ronald R. Miller testified that a tire tool recovered from Rivers' car at the time of his arrest "could have been used in the beating death of Miss Compton." Her body was found floating in the Peabody River Aug. 7.

James L. Mullaney, a lab technician for the FBI crime laboratory in Washington, D.C., testified that "traces of blood on the tire tool matched Miss Compton's blood type."

In reporting such testimony, the reporter was careful to use direct quotes and not to overstate the facts. The medical examiner testified that the tire tool *could have been used* in the murder. If he said it *was used*, a stronger lead would have been needed.

Defense attorneys usually use such hearings to learn about the evidence against their clients and do not present any witnesses. This apparently was the motive here, because neither the police nor the prosecutor had made a public statement on evidence in the case. They probably were being careful not to release prejudicial information that could be grounds for a new trial.

The prosecutor then filed an *information*, as state law required. The defendant was arraigned in Circuit Court, and the result was a routine story that began as follows:

> Circuit Judge John L. Lee refused today to reduce the bail of Lester L. Rivers, who is charged with first-degree murder in the Aug. 6 death of Springfield resident Anne Compton.
>
> Rivers pleaded not guilty.
>
> Repeating a request he made earlier in Magistrate Court, Public Defender Ogden Ball urged that Rivers' bail be reduced from $10,000 so he could be freed to assist in preparing his defense.

The not-guilty plea was expected, so the reporter concentrated on a more interesting aspect of the hearing—the renewed request for reduced bail. Finally, after a series of motions was reported routinely, the trial began:

> Jury selection began today in the first-degree murder trial of Lester L. Rivers, who is charged with the Aug. 6 beating death of Springfield resident Anne Compton.
>
> Public Defender Ogden Ball, Rivers' attorney, and Prosecuting Attorney Mel Singleton both expect jury selection to be complete by 5 p.m.
>
> The selection process started after court convened at 10 a.m. The only incident occurred just before the lunch break as Singleton was questioning prospec-
>
> tive juror Jerome B. Tinker, 33, of 408 Woodland Terrace.
>
> "I went to school with that guy," said Tinker, pointing to Rivers, who was seated in the courtroom. "He wouldn't hurt nobody."
>
> Singleton immediately asked that Tinker be removed from the jury panel, and Circuit Judge John L. Lee agreed.
>
> Rivers smiled as Tinker made his statement, but otherwise sat quietly, occasionally conferring with Ball.

The testimony is about to begin, so the reporter set the stage here, describing the courtroom scene. Jury selection often is routine and becomes newsworthy only in important or interesting cases.

Trial coverage can be tedious, but when the case is an interesting one, the stories are easy to write. The reporter picks the most interesting testimony for leads as the trial progresses:

A service station owner testi-fied today that Lester L. Rivers offered a ride to Springfield resident Anne Compton less than an hour before she was beaten to death Aug. 6.

Ralph R. Eagle, the station owner, was a witness at the first-degree murder trial of Rivers in Jefferson County Circuit Court.

"I told her I'd call a cab," Eagle testified, "but Rivers offered her a ride to her boyfriend's house." Miss Compton had gone to the service station after her car broke down nearby.

Under cross-examination, Public Defender Ogden Ball, Rivers' attorney questioned whether Rivers was the man who offered the ride.

"If it wasn't him, it was his twin brother," Eagle said.

"Then you're not really sure it was Mr. Rivers, are you?" Ball asked.

"I sure am," Eagle replied.

"You think you're sure, Mr. Eagle, but you really didn't get a good look at him, did you?"

"I sold him some gas and got a good look at him when I took the money."

"But it was night, wasn't it, Mr. Eagle?" Ball asked.

"That place doesn't have the best lighting in the world, but I saw him all right."

The reporter focused on the key testimony of the trial by capturing it in the words of the participants. Good note-taking ability becomes important here, because trial coverage is greatly enhanced with direct quotation of key exchanges. Long exchanges may necessitate the use of the question-and-answer format:

Ball: In fact, a lot of the lights above those gas pumps are out, aren't they, Mr. Eagle?

Eagle: Yes, but I stood right by him.

Q. I have no doubt you thought you saw Mr. Rivers, but there's always the possibility it could have been someone else. Isn't that true?

A. No, it looked just like him.

Q. It appeared to be him, but it may not have been because you really couldn't see him that well, could you?

A. Well, it was kind of dark out there.

Finally, there is the verdict story, which usually is one of the easiest to write:

Lester L. Rivers was found guilty of first-degree murder today in the Aug. 6 beating death of Springfield resident Anne Compton.

Rivers stood motionless in Jefferson County Circuit Court as the jury foreman returned the verdict. Judge John L. Lee set sentencing for Dec. 10.

Rivers, 32, of 209 E. Dillow Lane could be sentenced to death in the electric chair or life imprisonment in the State Penitentiary.

Public Defender Ogden Ball, Rivers' attorney, said he will appeal.

After the verdict was announced, Mr. and Mrs. Lilborn O. Compton, the victim's parents, were escorted from the courtroom by friends. Both refused to talk with reporters.

Many other types of stories could have been written about such a trial. Lengthy jury deliberations, for example, might prompt stories about the anxiety of the defendant and attorneys and their speculations about the cause of the delay.

Covering court news requires care and good reporting. As in any kind of reporting, you must be well-prepared. If you understand the language of the courts and how they are organized, your job is simplified.

Taste and Responsibility

Some of the darkest moments in the history of the American press have involved coverage of crime and the courts. Certainly the sensational treatment of crime news was a hallmark of the yellow journalism era at the turn of the century. In the late 1890s, for example, William Randolph Hearst's *New York Journal* scored a major success in building circulation with its reports of the "Guldensuppe mystery." The torso of a man was found in the East River, and Hearst's *Journal* printed every gory detail as one part of the body after another was found in various boroughs of New York. Few would charge that the press of today is that tasteless, but much of the criticism newspapers receive still is centered on crime reporting.

> "[On] Independence Day, we celebrate our various freedoms: freedom of speech, freedom of religion and, of course, freedom of the press to ram this O.J. Simpson story down our throats 24 hours a day."
>
> —Jay Leno,
> talk show host

The Free Press-Fair Trial Controversy

Criticism of the press and its coverage of crime often is traced to the 1954 murder trial of Dr. Samuel Sheppard in Cleveland. Sheppard was accused of murdering his wife. News coverage in the Cleveland newspapers, which included front-page editorials, was intense. In 1966, the Supreme Court said the trial judge did not fulfill his duty to protect the jury from the news coverage that saturated the community and to control disruptive influences in the courtroom.

That case more than any other ignited what is known as the free press-fair trial controversy. It is a controversy that rages today, as evidenced by the O.J. Simpson case. On numerous occasions, Judge Lance Ito threatened to end television coverage of court proceedings to protect Simpson's rights. Lawyers charged that the media ignored the Sixth Amendment right of the accused to an impartial jury, and the media countered with charges that lawyers ignored the First Amendment.

Editors realize that coverage of a crime can make it difficult to empanel an impartial jury, but they argue that courts have available many remedies other than restricting the flow of information. In the Sheppard case, for example, the Supreme Court justices said a change of venue, which moves the trial to a location where publicity is not as intense, could have been ordered. Other remedies suggested by the court in such cases are to continue (delay) the trial, to grant a new trial or to head off possible outside influences during the trial by sequestering the jury. Editors also argue that acquittals have been won in some of the most publicized cases in recent years.

Despite the remedies the Supreme Court offered in the Sheppard case, trial judges continued to be concerned about empaneling impartial juries. Judges issued hundreds of gag orders in the wake of the Sheppard case. Finally, in 1976, in the landmark case of Nebraska Press Association vs. Stuart, the Supreme Court ruled that a gag order was an unconstitutional prior restraint that violated the First Amendment to the Constitution. The justices did not go so far as to rule that all gag orders are invalid. But in each case, the trial judge has to prove that an order restraining publication would protect the rights of the accused and that there are no other alternatives that would be less damaging to First Amendment rights.

That, of course, did not end the concerns of trial judges. Rather than issue gag orders restricting the press from reporting court proceedings, some attempted to close their courtrooms. In the first such case to reach the Supreme Court, Gannett vs. DePasquale, the press and public suffered a severe but temporary blow. On July 2, 1979, in a highly controversial decision, the justices said, "We hold that mem-

Figure 12.3.
No modern trial more dramatically illustrates the free press-fair trial controversy than the murder trial of O.J. Simpson. A team of defense attorneys, including Robert Shapiro and Johnnie Cochran, shown here, thrived on the intense media coverage. But many questioned the fairness of the proceedings, not only to the defendant, but also to the families of the victims, to the long-sequestered jurors and to the citizens of Los Angeles, who were paying for this real-life soap opera.

bers of the public have no constitutional right under the Sixth and Fourteenth amendments to attend criminal trials." The case itself had involved only a pretrial hearing.

As a result of the decision and the confusion that followed, the Supreme Court of Virginia sanctioned the closing of an entire criminal trial. The accused was acquitted during the second day of the secret trial. The U.S. Supreme Court agreed to hear the appeal of the trial judge's action in a case known as Richmond Newspapers vs. Virginia. On July 2, 1980, the court said that under the First Amendment "the trial of a criminal case must be open to the public." Only a court finding of an "overriding interest," which was not defined, would be grounds for closing a criminal trial.

In Massachusetts, a judge excluded the public and press from the entire trial of a man accused of raping three teen-agers. A Massachusetts law provided for the mandatory closing of trials involving specific sex offenses against minors. The U.S. Supreme Court held in 1982 in Globe Newspaper Co. vs. Superior Court that the mandatory closure law violated the First Amendment right of access to criminal trials established in the Richmond Newspapers case. The justices ruled that when a state attempts to deny the right of access in an effort to inhibit the disclosure of sensitive information, it must show that the denial "is necessitated by a compelling governmental interest." The court indicated in the opinion that in some cases *in-camera* proceedings for youthful witnesses may be appropriate. In-camera proceedings are those that take place in a judge's chambers outside the view of the press and public.

In *Press-Enterprise* vs. Riverside County Superior Court, the Supreme Court ruled in 1984 that a court order closing the jury-selection process in a rape-murder case was invalid. The court ruled that jury selection has been a public process with exceptions only for good cause. In a second *Press-Enterprise* vs. Riverside County Superior Court case, the Supreme Court said in 1986 that preliminary hearings should be open to the public unless there is a "substantial probability" that the resulting publicity would prevent a fair trial and there are no "reasonable alternatives to closure." In 1993, the Supreme Court continued its emphasis on the importance of open court proceedings. It struck down a Puerto Rican law that said preliminary hearings "shall be held privately" unless the defendant requests a public preliminary hearing.

These cases appeared to uphold the right of the press and public to have access to criminal proceedings. Judges, however, have a duty to protect the rights of the accused, and similar situations may arise in the future. The Supreme Court of the State of Washington, in Federated Publications vs. Swedberg, held in 1981 that press access to pretrial hearings may be conditioned on the agreement of reporters to abide by voluntary press-bar guidelines that exist in some states. The decision involved a preliminary hearing in a Bellingham, Wash., murder case tied to the "Hillside strangler" murders in the Los Angeles area. The state Supreme Court ruled that the lower court order was "a good-faith attempt to accommodate the interests of both defendant and press." The lower court had required reporters covering the hearing to sign a document in which the reporters agreed to abide by press-bar guidelines. The state Supreme Court said the document should be taken as a moral commitment on the part of the reporters, not as a legally enforceable document.

The U.S. Supreme Court in 1982 refused to hear an appeal of that case. Fortunately, many states have statutes to the effect that "the setting of every court shall be public, and every person may freely attend the same." When such statutes are in place, the closed courtroom controversy appears to be moot. In states that have no such statute, the result seems to be:

1. That a criminal trial must be open unless there is an "overriding interest" that requires some part of it to be closed.
2. That judges must find some overriding interest before closing pretrial hearings.

One effect of the Washington decision is that many media groups are withdrawing from state press-bar agreements in the few states that have such guidelines. Their reasoning is that the voluntary guidelines in effect could become mandatory.

In September 1994, the U.S. Judicial Conference ended its three-year experiment on cameras in federal courts by banning cameras. However, 47 states do allow cameras in at least some state courtrooms. Only Indiana, Mississippi, South Dakota and the District of Columbia ban courtroom cameras.

The fact remains that there are many ways for judges to protect the rights of the accused without trampling on the right of the press and public to attend trials and pretrial hearings. Indeed, most editors are sensitive to the rights of the accused. Most exercise self-restraint when publishing or broadcasting information about a crime. Most have attempted to establish written policy on such matters, though others insist that individual cases must be judged on their merits.

Reporters and editors must share with judges the burden of protecting the rights of the accused. They also must ensure that certain groups within our society are not treated unfairly, either by the courts or in the media. In his study of crime reporting at the Gannett Center for Media Studies, Robert Snyder discovered that minorities tend to be covered by the media mainly in the context of crime news. Crime reporting is a staple of urban news, and urban areas are where minorities are concentrated. In large cities such as New York and Los Angeles, some areas of the city often make news only because of crime. As it is reported now, Snyder says, crime is almost always a conversation about race. He concludes that if the media are to change that perception, they must cover minorities more broadly and sympathetically.

The real story of crime, Snyder says, should be the "breaking down of communities and the real weakening of the social structure."

Many editors are concerned about the way minorities are portrayed in crime stories. Many newspapers and broadcast stations, in fact, studiously avoid gratuitous mentions of race. Their reporters are allowed to mention the race of a suspect only as part of complete identification of a fugitive. For many years, it was common to read or hear references to a "six-foot-tall black man" wanted for a crime. Today, such a description would be considered unacceptable. There are too many men who fit that description, and the racial reference merely reinforces the stereotype of blacks as criminals. If, however, a complete description of a fugitive might help lead to an arrest, it is appropriate to mention race as a part of that description. Only when race becomes the central theme of a story should it be emphasized.

Similarly, most editors consider a person's sexual orientation off limits unless the story focuses on heterosexuality or homosexuality. Increasingly, though, gays and lesbians are willing to talk openly about their sexual orientation as a means of advancing the cause of gay rights. Such issues cannot and should not be ignored by the media. But tastefully handling crime news involving homosexual murders often proves to be difficult. This was never more true than in the sensational murder trial of Milwaukee's Jeffrey Dahmer, convicted of sexually molesting young boys and men, killing them and eating parts of their bodies. In such cases, the press walks a fine line between responsibly informing the public and pandering to its seemingly insatiable appetite for sensational crime news.

Issues of Taste and Ethics

Some of the major issues involving taste and ethics in crime and court reporting are these:

When should the media reveal details of how a murder or another crime was committed?

When should the media reveal details about sex crimes or print the names of sex-crime victims?

When should the media reveal a suspect's confession or even the fact that the suspect has confessed?

When should the media reveal a defendant's prior criminal record?

When should the media reveal the names of juveniles charged with crimes?

None of these questions can be answered to everyone's satisfaction, and it is doubtful whether rules can be established to apply in all such situations. There have been charges that when the media reveal details of a murder, some people employ the techniques outlined to commit more murders. This charge is directed more frequently at television, but newspapers have not been immune.

As with the Dahmer case, the reporting of sex crimes often

causes controversy. Most editors think of their publications as family newspapers or broadcasts and are properly hesitant about reporting the lurid details of sex crimes. What began as an interesting murder case in one college town turned into grist for the scandal mill. A college professor murdered one of his students who had asked for after-hours tutoring. When police unraveled the morbid tale of the professor, a homosexual necrophiliac, knowing what to write for the family newspaper became a major problem for the reporter. The newspaper provided information to the public on what had happened but deliberately avoided sensationalism. Even during the trial, specifics were avoided in favor of testimony that revealed the nature of the case in general terms:

> "He lived in a world of fantasies," the doctor said. "He spent much of his time daydreaming about homosexual, necrophilic, homicidal, suicidal and cannibalistic fantasies."

To have been more specific would have been revolting to many of the newspaper's readers.

A related problem is the question of how to handle rape reports. Too often, rapes are not reported to police because victims are unwilling to appear in court to testify against the suspects. Defense attorneys sometimes use such occasions to attack the victim's morals and imply that she consented to sexual relations. Many victims decline to press charges because of fear that their names will be made public in newspapers and on radio and television. There is, after all, still a lingering tendency to attach a social stigma to the rape victim, despite increasing public awareness of the nature of the crime.

In some states, "rape shield" statutes have been passed to prohibit a defendant's attorney from delving into the rape victim's prior sexual activity unless some connection can be shown with the circumstances of the rape charged.

Many editors will not publish or broadcast details of a suspect's confession in an effort to protect the suspect's rights. Revealing such information blocks the way for a fair trial perhaps more easily than anything else the media can do. Some newspapers and broadcast stations, however, continue to reveal assertions by police or prosecutors that a confession has been signed. Many question whether such information isn't just as prejudicial as the confession statement itself.

Occasionally, the question arises of whether to suppress an unsolicited confession. After a youth was charged with a series of robberies and was certified to stand trial as an adult, a newspaper reporter phoned the youthful defendant, who was free on bail, for an interview. The result was interesting:

> Ricketts said he and two others took money from the service station "because we was broke at the time and needed the money, and we was ignorant."
>
> He said they had "no idea we'd ever get caught. It wasn't worth it."

The defendant went on to admit to two other robberies in what amounted to a confession to the newspaper and its readers. The editor, who would not have printed a simple statement by police that the defendant had confessed to the crime, printed this one. Why? The editor reasoned that information about a confession to police amounts to secondhand, hearsay information. The confession to a reporter, however, was firsthand information obtained by the newspaper directly from the accused.

Lawyers also view as prejudicial the publication of a defendant's prior criminal record. Even if authorities refuse to divulge that information, much of it may be in the morgue. Should it be published? Most editors believe it should, particularly if a prior conviction was for a similar offense. Most attorneys disagree.

Whether to use the names of juveniles charged with crimes is a troublesome issue as well. Most states prohibit law enforcement officers and court officials from releasing the names of juveniles. The reasoning of those who oppose releasing juveniles' names is that the publicity marks them for life as criminals. Those who hold this view argue that there is ample opportunity for these individuals to change their ways and become good citizens—if the media do not stamp them as criminals. Others argue that juveniles who commit serious offenses, such as rape and armed robbery, should be treated as adults.

Questions such as these elicit divergent views from editors, some of whom regularly seek the advice of their lawyers. Little guidance for the reporter can be offered here. Because the decision to publish or not to publish is the editor's, not the reporter's, consultation is necessary. Each case must be decided on its merits.

Suggested Readings

Buchanan, Edna. *Never Let Them See You Cry.* New York: Random House, 1992. An excellent description of covering crime in Miami.

Buchanan, Edna. *The Corpse Had a Familiar Face.* New York: Random House, 1987. The first of two books by one of America's best crime reporters.

Carter, T. Barton, Franklin, Marc A. and Wright, Jay B. *The First Amendment and the Fourth Estate.* Waterbury, N.Y.: The Foundation Press, 1994. A good explanation of the law of the press.

Nelson, Harold L., Teeter, Dwight L. Jr. and LeDuc, Don R. *Law of Mass Communication.* Waterbury, N.Y.: The Foundation Press, 1989. An excellent compilation of law as it affects the working reporter.

Exercises

1. Cover a session of your local municipal court. Write a story based on the most interesting case of the day.

2. You have just been named managing editor of a newspaper. Write a policy for your staff on withholding the names of rape and sexual-assault victims.

3. Find a court story in a local newspaper. Deter-

mine what sources the reporter used in the story, and tell how the story could have been improved.

4. Using archives or databases, compare the coverage of the O.J. Simpson case in the *Los Angeles Times*, your local newspaper and *USA Today*. What are the differences in coverage?

Which newspaper's coverage is better? Explain why.

5. Reread the story about the slaying of a fugitive by a Highway Patrol officer on pages 247-248. List the sources used by the newspaper to develop the story. List at least two additional sources the reporter might have used.

FOLLOWS

*D*etails of the first Watergate story on June 17, 1972, were phoned in by Alfred E. Lewis, a Washington Post *police reporter for 35 years. The first front-page Watergate story carried his byline. It was the work of eight reporters, one named Bob Woodward. The same paper carried a story by Carl Bernstein about the suspects. As Woodward and Bernstein wrote later in* All the President's Men, *city editor Barry Sussman asked them to return to the office that Sunday morning to "follow up." Thus began one of the most intensely followed events in the history of newspapers. By reporting it, Woodward and Bernstein led the* Washington Post *to a Pulitzer Prize and became millionaires.*

Six months after his daughter had been murdered in Boston by a former boyfriend, Washington Post *reporter George Lardner Jr. decided to find out what really happened. His follow-up story, "The Stalking of Kristin," won a 1993 Pulitzer Prize. "Here I was, a big-deal reporter," Lardner told Harry Rosenthall of the Associated Press. "I had only the faintest idea of what happened. I wrote it to bring attention to the problem of battered women. The more attention, the better."*

What follows a news story may be as important or interesting as the original story. After people ask what happened, they usually ask, what happened next? Because newspapers cannot wait to go to press until a story is complete, follow-up stories (or simply, follows) are common.

A **follow** *may tell readers what happened next, or it may catch up with or complete a story broken by another paper. It may keep readers posted about a story that is breaking or continuing. Or a follow may deal with something that happened months ago and report developments since then.*

Follows are part of every news medium and are the major portion of most news magazines. Some papers and magazines offer regular columns or sections of follows. Sometimes they are the most looked-for and the most read items a publication has to offer.

Because you will be assigned to follow stories, you must learn the proper techniques for writing them.

The Second-Cycle Story

Even the best newspapers sometimes get scooped on a story. The same is true of broadcast news operations, radio or television. Competition is not a thing of the past. Newspapers try to get stories before they appear on television and vice versa. Also competing are vigorous suburban dailies and weeklies, weekly news magazines, and newspapers from other areas, including the national newspapers the *New York Times*, the *Wall Street Journal* and *USA Today*.

Sometimes one medium gets the story first because of when the news breaks. In rare cities that still have competing morning and afternoon papers, an afternoon paper will have news that occurred after the morning paper has gone to press and vice versa. A news organization should never use exactly the same story as its competitor, but neither can it ignore a story that is newsworthy.

A second-cycle story provides a fresh slant. By writing such a story, reporters allow readers and listeners to catch up with or follow a story that has already broken. To give a fresh slant to second-cycle stories, reporters can:

▪ Supply information not available when the first story was written.
▪ Use enterprise to uncover information not contained in the original.
▪ Supply fresh details, color and background, even when nothing of substance is new.
▪ Respond to the news of the first story with analysis, possible developments or the reactions of people whom the news would affect.
▪ Gather local reactions to a national or international story.

Let's look at each of these approaches.

Supplying Previously Unavailable Information

When you are asked to do a rewrite of a story appearing in a competing news medium, you are expected to make your story as dissimilar as possible without distorting the facts. Study the story carefully. Verify all the information yourself. Then discover whether you can add any new information or report any developments since your competitor wrote the story. For example, here is a part of a morning newspaper's story:

> Police called to a northside residence Wednesday found the body of a teen-age boy lying between a toolshed and a garage.
>
> Police said the victim had been tentatively identified as a 14-year-old Springfield youth. However, authorities withheld his name until relatives could make a positive identification.
>
> Lt. Richard Moses and Dr. Erwin Busiek, the medical examiner, said the victim had received several large wounds, one in his head and another on his chest. Authorities said a large rock was found near the body, but they had not determined if he had been beaten, stabbed or shot to death.
>
> An autopsy was scheduled for later Wednesday at St. John's Hospital.

A reporter rewriting the story for the afternoon paper called the police station and found that more information had become available. His story began:

> A 14-year-old boy, whose body was found Wednesday near a northside residence, has been identified as Maurice Comstock of Springfield, police said.
>
> Dr. Erwin Busiek, the medical examiner, said Comstock died from a skull fracture. A large rock near the body could have been the murder weapon, police said.

The second reporter was able to identify the victim and to give the cause of death. In this case the new information was readily available from routine sources.

"The trouble with daily journalism is that you get so involved with 'Who hit John?' that you never really know why John had his chin out in the first place."
—Chalmers Roberts,
Newsweek

Uncovering New Information

Many times you may have to do some digging to find additional information. An enterprising reporter sometimes wins bigger play with a recycled story than with the original. For example, when one newspaper reported that a man had been arrested on a driving-while-intoxicated charge, a reporter from the competing newspaper asked the police a few questions and looked at police records. What was at first a routine item on the records page became a front-page story, which began this way:

> For the third time in the last six months, James Wiley, of 403 W. Third St., has been arrested on a driving-while-intoxicated charge.
>
> Springfield police said Wiley, whose driver's license had been suspended, was using his brother-in-law's license last night.

You show enterprise when, through your own initiative, you uncover previously unknown information or add up known information to come up with a new result.

Supplying Details, Color and Background

When a story appears to cover all bases and no new developments have occurred, you still can dig for more details. Here is an example of how a reporter who followed a story made it worth reading a second time. The story first appeared like this:

> A 20-year-old Mercer County man drowned while swimming with friends yesterday afternoon at Finger Lakes State Park.
>
> Arthur James Frazier, of 164 Crescent Meadows Trailer Court, drowned at about 5:10 p.m., said Maj. Jim White of the Mercer County Sheriff's Department.
>
> Frazier's body was recovered about seven hours later by divers and a rescue squad from the Mercer County Volunteer Fire Protection District.
>
> White said Frazier swam across the lake with Stanley Shenski, 20, of Springfield, and apparently tired on his way back.
>
> Shenski said he attempted to carry the youth after he became tired but said Frazier struggled away from him and went under about 15 feet from shore. Shenski and other friends dived for Frazier but could not find him.

Here is the second-cycle story:

> Just 20 feet from life.
>
> "I got him within 20 feet of shore. Then he said he could make it. But he couldn't. When I got back to him, he pulled me under."
>
> A dejected Stanley Shenski, 20, of Springfield, was on the verge of tears. Perhaps it was anger, frustration—how could it happen that a good, strong swimmer could not swim just 20 more feet?
>
> Yet, his friend Arthur James Frazier, 20, of 164 Crescent Meadows Trailer Park, had drowned at Finger Lakes State Park. His body was recovered early this morning.
>
> "He told me he was tired, so we rested a while before swim-

ming back," Shenski said. "It was only 50 feet across."

Shenski was also angry about something else. Other swimmers, as many as 10 or 12 of them, were enjoying the lake that sunny Thursday afternoon. Shenski said he and Frazier did a lot of shouting for help.

But apparently no one heard them.

By interviewing the survivor and digging for details, the reporter was able to keep the story on the front page. The more engaging lead sets the scene before telling the story.

Here is another example of how a reporter recycled a news story into a news feature. The morning paper's account began like this:

Charles W. Moreland of Jacksonville, Fla., has been appointed administrator of Myron Barnes State Cancer Hospital by Dr. Whitney Cole, director of the State Division of Health.

Moreland, 54, succeeds Warren Mills, who retired last week after nine years as director. At a news conference, Cole praised Mills for "outstanding leadership" and cited the multimillion-dollar building program completed during Mills' tenure as an example of his achievements.

A reporter for the competing afternoon paper wrote it this way:

At 5:30 this morning, employees at Myron Barnes State Cancer Hospital caught their first bleary-eyed glimpse of the hospital's new administrator—he was roaming the halls.

But Charles W. Moreland's motive for the early morning stroll wasn't secret. He didn't expect to find someone taking one too many coffee breaks. Instead, he says, "I just wanted to meet the people who work here."

The 54-year-old Moreland will meet a host of people in the next few days. He was named administrator of Myron Barnes by Dr. Whitney Cole, health director in the State Department of Social Services.

Moreland succeeds Warren Mills, 67, who retired after nine years as administrator.

The writer of the second story chose to tell us something more than the news of the naming of a new administrator. We learn something *about* the new administrator. By doing this, the reporter tempted even those who had read the morning paper's version to look at the story again.

Here's another example. First, the morning paper's version:

Susan Teller, Fourth Ward councilwoman since 1983, announced her resignation, effective Sept. 1, at Monday night's City Council meeting.

Ms. Teller will move with her three daughters, Melanie, Betty and Diana, to Ann Arbor, Mich., to work for the University of Michigan as an instructor in city planning. She said she would remain with the council through August to help choose a new city manager and to formulate the new city budget.

"I'd like to stay with the city manager search, since I've been through it before," she said.

Ms. Teller was a council member when Jim Thompson was chosen in 1990 as Springfield's city manager.

The story of the same resignation appeared this way in the city's competing afternoon newspaper:

Fourth Ward Councilwoman Susan Teller, in her characteristically quiet way, waited her turn when it came time for general comments by Springfield City Council members at the end of last night's meeting.

Then she said, "At the end of the summer, I will be moving to Ann Arbor, Mich., to become an instructor in city planning at the University of Michigan."

Just like that. No dramatics. Teller was resigning the council seat she had been elected to three times and had held 7½ years.

She had kept her decision to herself. Even Afua Noyes, the Sixth Ward representative who is her closest friend on the council, learned the news only last weekend.

Mayor Juanita Williams, clearly unprepared, said, "This is a surprise," and then mustered her wits for a short tribute to Teller, although she noted there would be time for more comments later.

"Susan has demonstrated an outstanding ability to take care of her constituents' needs," Williams said.

Teller said she would continue to serve on the council through August, giving her a hand in the selection of the new city manager and in the preparation of next year's city budget.

The morning newspaper carried a straight news lead. The writer of the follow wrote a more reflective feature lead. Then she allowed the council member herself to tell the news by means of a direct quote. The third paragraph continues the feature style with its use of sentence fragments. The reporter had nothing new to report, but she recycled the story in an entertaining and informative manner.

Responding with Analysis, Possible Developments and Reactions

Although a news medium can choose to recycle the same information as its competitor, it has several other choices, some of them better.

Lead with an analytical approach:

```
The resignation of councilmember Susan Teller gives the
conservatives an opportunity for the first time in six years
to control the City Council.
```

Lead with possible developments:

```
John James, the conservative candidate defeated by Susan
Teller in the 1988 elections, appears to be the favorite to
replace her.
```

"The first report always leaves some details hanging. You can't do that to your readers. They want to know: Did the person die? Was the armed robber ever caught, or is the robber still on the loose? Did the store close as a result of the fire? What effects did the closing have on the neighborhood?"

—*Alison Boggs,*
reporter for the
(Spokane, Wash.)
Spokesman-Review

Lead with reaction:

> Mayor Juanita Williams said she was stunned to learn that
> Councilwoman Susan Teller would be leaving the council in
> August.

Often news media follow or recycle their own stories in the three ways mentioned above. For example, after stories about the impending baseball strike of 1994, the Associated Press moved the following story that discusses the possible economic impact of the strike on the city of St. Louis:

> ST. LOUIS (AP)—Cardinals fans may be more adversely affected by a baseball strike than they know. If their team is worth a lot in entertainment value, it is also worth a lot in taxes.
>
> If a baseball strike starts Friday and wipes out the remainder of the season, the city will lose millions in revenue, including $4,180 in Ozzie Smith's earnings tax alone.
>
> Losses would crop up not only from the players but also from the earnings tax on thousands of other stadium workers idled by a strike.
>
> In addition, the city would lose its 5 percent tax on the hotel rooms normally occupied by visiting teams and fans and a 6.6 percent sales tax on the sales of everything from peanuts to pennants. . . .

The story goes on to estimate what percentage of the crowds are from out of town and how much each out-of-town patron spends in St. Louis for a baseball game. It details how much the city would stand to lose, and who would be most affected by the strike in addition to the players and the owners:

> A strike would idle 500 ushers, 100 cleaners, 100 parking attendants and 30 security officers, including some off-duty police officers. Dozens of other miscellaneous workers, including medical workers, elevator operators, announcers and scoreboard operators, also would be idled, as would 700 to 750 concessions workers.

All of these possible developments and consequences of the baseball strike indeed came to pass. Because of solid reporting, readers had a better understanding of the impact of the strike on the city.

After the strike began, the Associated Press followed the strike by sending out a daily graphic on what each day of the strike was costing the best-paid baseball player. Remember, a well-done graphic can contain a great deal of information in little space. It will also get more reader attention and retention (See Figure 13.1).

Gathering Local Reactions to a Non-Local Story

Often a newspaper follows a national or international story by seeking local reactions. Remember, proximity is one of the characteristics of news. How has a declining or low inflation rate affected the

---

Leads for a follow

- *An analytical approach*
- *Possible developments*
- *Reaction*

A little research into accident statistics can produce a compelling follow story. For example, after reporting a late-breaking fatal auto accident, check police records to see how many fatalities have occurred at that intersection or on that stretch of road. Or, in the case of a crime, find out the frequency of that type of crime.

Strike losses

Players who would lose the most in salary during each day of the strike.

	1994 salary*	Daily loss	52-day loss
① Bobby Bonilla New York Mets	$5,700,000	$31,148	$1,619,672
② Jack McDowell Chicago White Sox	$5,300,000	$28,692	$1,506,011
③ Roberto Alomar Toronto Blue Jays	$5,000,000	$27,322	$1,420,765
Roger Clemens Boston Red Sox	$5,000,000	$27,322	$1,420,765
⑤ Cal Ripken Jr. Baltimore Orioles	$4,800,000	$26,230	$1,363,934
Minimum salary	$109,000	$596	$30,973

*Salaries listed do not include prorated shares of signing bonuses or other guaranteed income, or incentives bonuses earned, or money lost because of lost opportunities for incentive bonuses.

Source: AP research   **AP**/C. Sanderson

Figure 13.1.
This graphic is an effective follow to the news of the 1994-1995 baseball strike. It keeps the reader involved in the story by presenting an analysis of the impact on players' salaries.

buying habits of local consumers? How have cuts in Medicare affected a local nursing home?

A wire story about a cold snap in Brazil and a possible rise in coffee prices caused a reporter from a small college town to call local groceries and local coffee houses. His efforts produced an interesting and useful story:

Students who guzzle coffee to cram for that nasty econ test might do well to go coffee shopping the day they settle in for another semester.

An untimely freeze in Brazil has caused coffee prices to double in two weeks. "And prices will probably go up again," says Jill Jameson, manager of Just Right Grocery.

Two weeks ago a 13-ounce can of coffee cost $2.50. Today it's $4.99. Gourmet coffee went up $1.50 in one day.

"If I order coffee today at prices listed, tomorrow the warehouse will not honor those prices," Jameson says. "Frankly, I think the public is getting royally screwed. The recent freeze should have nothing to do with the coffee that has been sitting around in warehouses."

Apparently, Colombia and other coffee-producing countries have had no problems, but the freeze in Brazil allows everyone to raise prices.

Other local groceries were either not aware of the rise in coffee prices or they were forbidden to talk about them. Al Hayes, manager of Best Grocery, said he could not discuss product prices with anyone without permission from headquarters in Springfield. Amy

Allards, manager of Value Grocery, thought coffee prices had risen 10 percent in recent weeks. She was surprised to find the lowest price of a 13-ounce can was now $3.99.

There's some good news though. At Lokota Coffee House the price of a cup of coffee has not increased. Don't buy the beans by the pound, though. They've gone up $2 a pound.

This follow brings the story home. It shows the community how local people are affected by an event.

The Developing Story

As events unfold, a newspaper reports the latest developments to its readers. Often there is a story on the following day, and sometimes a story continues to develop over weeks or months.

The *developing story* begins with the new information in the lead. In the second or third paragraph you write a *tie-back* to the previous story. A tie-back, you may recall, is a brief review of the previous story. Remember, some readers may not have read the previous story, and you must fill them in. But be careful not to become bogged down in too many details in the tie-back paragraph. If you spend too much on it, the reader is likely to forget what the present story is about. After this background, you need a good transition back to the new information. For example, when negotiations with North Korea over inspection of its nuclear facilities seemed to be moving forward, the *New York Times* News Service ran this developing story:

Lead	SEOUL, South Korea—South Korea formally offered Monday to supply North Korea with modern nuclear power plants if the North opens its nuclear program to inspection.
Tie-back *Transition*	The offer, made in a modestly conciliatory speech by President Kim Young Sam, comes two days after the United States and North Korea agreed to measures to settle the nuclear issue, and could be a step toward realizing that goal.
Return to story	Kim's speech, his first substantive remarks on relations with the North since the death last month of its longtime leader, Kim Il Sung, outlined his vision for reunification of the Korean peninsula.
	The tone of the speech, in which he calls for the two countries to "immediately stop slandering each other," and the offer of light-water nuclear reactors, could help pave the way for the two Koreas to resume their dialogue.

Most developing stories are of three kinds. They may:

- Follow the natural course of events.
- Affect the course of events through enterprising reporting.
- Both follow and affect the course of events.

The usual organization of the developing story:

1. *New lead*
2. *Tie-back*
3. *Transition*
4. *Return to story*

morgue showed we had written precious little about it. I proposed a series and eventually got the go-ahead. In the meantime I followed up with some individual stories: a study of successful people with learning disabilities, a piece on adults with attention deficit disorder, etc."

To produce the series, I attended a week-long conference sponsored by the National Center for Learning Disabilities and interviewed leaders in the field. I spent another month interviewing, reading and researching. The three-part series ran with multiple sidebars, photographs and charts. Response was overwhelming—more than 700 phone calls in three days.

"We're still not through following up. The paper is making its first venture into civic, or public, journalism by sponsoring a learning disabilities seminar, featuring a dozen local experts.

"And I've got a list of at least a half-dozen more spin-off stories I plan to pursue on the subject."

Following the Course of Events

Some follows result from events taking their natural course. For example, in stories of trials or weather disasters, all the reporter has to do is keep up with them. A delay of 16½ months in the completion of the Denver airport provided many occasions for reporting new developments.

In the following sequence of stories a community was about to lose its city manager. Its newspaper kept its citizens informed about the developments. Note especially the leads and tiebacks in the stories following the initial story. The initial story began:

Springfield City Manager Jim Thompson has applied for a job as city manager of Peoria, Ill.

The Peoria Chronicle said Thursday Thompson is among 12 finalists for the city manager's job there.

Peoria's Mayor Ron Myer declined to say whether that's so. Myer did say, however, that there were 87 applicants for the job.

Two weeks later:

Lead — Springfield city Manager Jim Thompson still is in the running fro the job of city manager in Peoria, Ill.

Tie-back — Thompson, city manager here for 5½ years, was one of 87 applicants for the job in Peoria. City officials there and Thompson here refuse to discuss the matter.

Transition — But the *Peoria Chronicle* has reported that Thompson is now among five finalists for the position.

Return to story — The finalists were asked to submit names of references by today. The council may narrow the field further before flying candidates to Peoria for interviews later this month.

Three weeks later:

Lead — Though not the front-runner, Springfield City Manager Jim Thompson has survived another screening for the city manager's job in Peoria, Ill.

Tie-back — The Peoria City Council, in a closed session Thursday, named Thompson as one of three finalists for the position. One of 87 initial applicants, Thompson earlier survived two other screening steps. He should learn within a month whether the job is his.

Transition — But Thompson is not first in line.
The *Peoria Chronicle* said that Thompson's remaining rivals are Glen Yale, 56, Peoria's acting city manager, and Gerald R. Dale, 45, city manager of Vallejo, Calif.

Return to story — Yale is considered the front-runner.

Three weeks later:

Lead	In a surprising turnabout, Springfield City Manager Jim Thompson reportedly has emerged the front-runner for the city manager's job in Peoria, Ill.
Tie-back	Thompson, now one of two finalists, was considered second choice after Glen Yale, Peoria's acting city manager. The Peoria City Council eliminated Gerald R. Dale as a contender.
Transition	The job may now go to Thompson.
Return to story	At a closed meeting Thursday night, the council's consensus was 4 to 3 in favor of Thompson, according to the *Peoria Chronicle*. The final selection should come within two or three days.

Three days later:

Lead	Weeks of speculation ended last night when Springfield City Manager Jim Thompson announced he has resigned to take the city manager's job in Peoria, Ill.
Tie-back	Thompson, Springfield's city manager for the past 5½ years, was chosen from among 87 applicants for the job. His top contender was Glen Yale, Peoria's acting city manager, who until recent days was considered the front-runner.
Transition	Thompson's announcement came in the middle of the Springfield City Council meeting.
Return to story	His resignation is effective July 1, and he will begin work in Peoria July 5. The job will mean an $8,150 raise for Thompson.

In each instance the lead gives the new information, the tie-back puts the story into context, and the transition moves the story back to support the lead.

To write the developing story, you must establish reliable sources and consult with them regularly. Don't count on the people involved to keep you informed. Look for others with a stake in the story. In this case the reporter needed sources in Springfield and in Peoria. No source should be ignored, even if it is another newspaper. It is better, though, to do your own reporting in order to be sure your story is right.

Using Enterprise

Good reporters do more than keep up with events as they happen. Some stories would die unless reporters found information on their own initiative that otherwise would not be known. Reporters sometimes make the story happen.

When a reporter for the *Providence Journal-Bulletin* received a tip that an important state official's son would be appointed to a spe-

Figure 13.2.
The news media are inevitably involved in the developing story of an election. For example, journalists' questions influence the issues that candidates address during the live broadcasting of public debates.

cial police unit despite his lengthy criminal record, the story opened the door to evidence of widespread corruption in the state court administration. By employing a strategy of using "short-term stories to chip away at the opposition," a team of reporters found evidence of theft of court funds and a subsequent cover-up, a secret court bank account, rampant patronage hiring, the assignment of legal work to business partners, the use of court employees for private businesses, attempts to meddle in traffic cases of friends and relatives and more.

As a result, the chief justice of the Rhode Island Supreme Court resigned during impeachment proceedings. He was convicted of three misdemeanors and was facing a trial on felony charges. The chief court administrator resigned and was also facing felony charges. The legislature convened special hearings on the state courts. Court officials were forced to repay more than $40,000 in misspent funds.

One story led to one follow after another. And the newspaper won a top award from the Investigative Reporters and Editors association.

Good reporters are enterprising; they are full of energy and initiative. They are curious, inquisitive and skeptical. They ask the readers' questions: Why? What next? How does this affect me? What is this going to cost me? Virtually every news event has unanswered questions. Answer them.

Following and Affecting the Course of Events

Many times a developing story will both keep up with events as they happen and affect the course of events through enterprising reporting. Such was the case, for example, in the *St. Louis Post-Dispatch* coverage of an embezzling scandal in the St. Louis police court office. Eight workers, including at least two supervisors, several clerks and at least one janitor, were charged with skimming money from city traffic-ticket money.

Here are a few excerpts from some of the stories from that continuing coverage:

August 8, 1991
Course of events

After secretly sifting through garbage of the clerks who collect traffic fines at Kiel Auditorium, police on Wednesday nabbed eight city employees suspected of skimming cash from ticket money. . . .

(St. Louis Circuit Attorney George) Peach was vague about how much money the city workers had taken. "You could probably buy an expensive foreign car with it," he said.

Enterprise

Later, he described the amount variously as "many thousands" and "$15,000 to $20,000." . . .

Aug. 9, 1991
Course of events

Police used a hidden video camera to snare at least some of the eight people charged Thursday with skimming cash from city traffic-ticket money, sources said. . . .

Aug. 13, 1991
Course of events

A new procedure for handling fines on parking tickets began Monday at the St. Louis police court office in Kiel Auditorium. Protests from court workers who knew the new system was coming led to charges that eight of them were skimming money from traffic fines. . . .

Aug. 17, 1991
Course of events

A local political group is urging Mayor Vincent C. Schoemehl Jr. to fire city court clerk-administrator Joseph P. Roddy, eight of whose employees are charged in a ticket-skimming scheme.

Roddy has not been accused of any wrongdoing in the case. . . .

Enterprise

In 1989, the Schoemehl administration gave Roddy a $3,240 bonus in addition to his $46,150 annual salary. (Spokeswoman for Schoemehl Marie) Boykin said then that the bonus was in recognition of increased revenue taken in by the city courts under Roddy's administration. . . .

Jan. 12, 1992
Enterprise

Parking ticket revenue in St. Louis has jumped sharply since August, when eight employees of the city's Traffic Violation Bureau were arrested on charges of skimming cash.

City administrators conceded that stopping thefts is a factor. But they cited changes in the collection system that also boosted revenue. . . .

Enterprise

Revenue reports from the court and the city treasurer's office show that average monthly ticket revenue from parking meters was $44,901 higher from August through December 1991 than it had been during the previous seven months. That is an average increase of 53 percent.

May 25, 1994
Course of events

State Auditor Margaret Kelly has criticized the St. Louis municipal court for failing to seek restitution from clerks who stole as much as $300,000 in traffic- and parking-ticket money.

Kelly said in an audit released Tuesday that court officials never tried to make a precise accounting of how much was stolen. . . .

July 24, 1994
Course of events

Kiel Auditorium downtown was where motorists waited in interminably slow lines to pay city parking and traffic tickets. Nobody wanted to be there—except perhaps the clerks behind the counter who took your cash.

Enterprise

They were stealing it. At least that's what one employee told a new supervisor. The supervisor called the police in July 1991. . . .

Course of events

It is believed to be the largest theft from the city in modern times. In court records, city officials said the loss was at least $150,000 to $300,000 over two years.

Enterprise

Privately, police now say the original estimate was way low. The thefts apparently had gone on much longer than two years, they say. The clerks who were caught admitted they had learned how to steal from clerks who had been there before them.

Based upon what the thieves admitted, at least $1 million, maybe even $2 million was stolen, police estimate.

Fortunately, the city paid an insurance company to bond the traffic bureau clerks. If any money was stolen, the insurance company would pay up to $200,000.

So how much did the insurance company pay?

Nothing.

And how much did the city ask the insurance company to pay?

Nothing.

In fact, in the three years since the arrests, the city has never even filed an insurance claim.

Why? "Because we couldn't determine exactly how much money was stolen," said Thomas J. Ray, an attorney for the city.

One clue that should have helped officials with arithmetic was Jeanette Dale's confession.

Dale, who had worked for the city since 1978, admitted that every working day for the two years before she was caught in 1991 she stole $500 to $1,000 in cash.

If Dale's confession is to be believed, she alone stole at least $250,000 and as much as $500,000. . . .

As city clerk, Joe Roddy ran the traffic violations bureau for more than 10 years. . . .

Roddy insists there was simple explanation why the city never filed an insurance claim to recover the stolen money.

"The city was self-insured so we didn't pursue it," he said..

Roddy was wrong.

Since 1987—four years before the arrests in August 1991—records show the city has paid more than $3,700 to the Fidelity and Deposit Company of Maryland, which bonds the traffic bureau clerks.

July 27, 1994
Course of events

The mayor and the comptroller, responding to *Post-Dispatch* disclosures—and public outrage—say they will do whatever it takes to try to recover money stolen in the city's largest theft in modern times. . . .

July 28, 1994
Course of events

The city has seized $10,000 from one of the clerks who admitted stealing hundreds of thousands of dollars in traffic fines three years ago, City Hall announced Wednesday.

For the past year, the $10,000 was sitting in a local bank, waiting for the city to pick it up. But the city, apparently unaware of the freeze order, didn't seek its release.

Enterprise

In June 1993, a judge ordered Dale's bank account frozen so that the money could be returned to the city. . . .

The city's lawyers say they can't explain why it took them a year to find the money.

July 31, 1994
Enterprise

While St. Louis traffic court clerks were looting hundreds of thousands of dollars, City Hall was giving their boss, Joe Roddy, a bonus of thousands of dollars for doing a good job, records show.

Roddy, 74, retired last year as city courts clerk, two years after the scandal.

There was no effort to get Roddy to return his bonus of $5,015, after six of his clerks were arrested for stealing, city officials say.

Aug. 10, 1994
Course of events

After doing nothing for nearly three years, the city is suing the six former traffic court-clerks accused of looting hundred of thousands of dollars from the motorist fines.

The city is also suing the bonding company it paid to insure the honesty of the clerks.

The *Post-Dispatch* followed this story for three years, and they might not be finished with it yet. Reporters received some of the information from city officials and others. However, it was the enterprising follow-ups of the reporters that kept the story alive and the readers reading.

The Update

A third type of follow is the *update*. After a story about a person or a situation has been published, a later look may result in another story, possibly of major significance. Newspapers often have been criticized for hit-and-run reporting, for arousing the curiosity or the ire of citizens and then dropping the matter. Because of that criticism and because of reader interest, some newspapers have begun regular sections of update stories.

A good example of a simple update began with this routine story:

> "*Writing a story is like reading 'Little Red Riding Hood' to my daughter. Sometimes I read it to her in one sitting. Other times I read it in stages over several nights. Either way the story always ends, and she feels all is well. But as writers and editors, we sometimes leave Little Red Riding Hood out in the woods: We forget to end the story. And that frustrates readers.*"
>
> *—Dan Potter,*
> *former editor, now marketing manager of* The *(Independence, Mo.)* Examiner

The Springfield police will continue spot-checks, which have helped reduce the number of Springfield vehicles without city license stickers.

The spot-checks, like Tuesday's of 300 vehicles, 17 of which were cited for failure to possess a city sticker, have helped enforce the city's vehicle tax law, Police Maj. Bill Smith said. The checks are not aimed at catching any particular violation but are general inspections of the car and its driver.

At about the time of the spot-checks "the lines seem to start forming" at the city cashier's window, said W.J. McGee of the city business license office, but there are still many vehicle owners who neglect the vehicle-tax law because "it's still too hard to enforce."

McGee said about 16,000 stickers were sold in September 1995, but that now there may be 5,000 vehicles in the city without stickers. The permits are valid for a year, from October to October, and can be bought at any time.

A week later a check on the sale of city stickers resulted in the following update story:

If the response to last week's vehicle spot-checks by Springfield police is any indication, the average Springfield citizen's sense of civic responsibility may need an occasional nudge.

The nudge this time came in the form of news that motorists without the required $10 city-tax stickers were prime targets of vehicle inspectors. That bit of information brought a deluge of sticker buyers to the city cashier's office.

Police Maj. Bill Smith said the spot-checks were not directed specifically against any particular violation. Still, their effect on sticker purchases has been marked. Seventeen drivers were cited for sticker violation in last Tuesday's check of 300 cars.

"When it came out in the paper, we had them lined up" to buy stickers, a city cashier said Monday. "All three (cashiers) sell maybe 10 to 20 stickers on a normal day," she said, "but last Thursday and Friday definitely were not normal. I would guess I alone had at least 100 the first day."

The lead of the update story refers immediately to the news of the week before. The quote in the fourth paragraph talks about the effects of the newspaper story. An enterprising reporter suspected that the first story might cause some motorists to buy stickers. He was right.

If the story has not come to the readers' attention for a long period of time, you must help by giving more background information on the original story. Nearly a year after a series of articles about a missing girl, for example, a reporter wrote this update:

Mary Dorset never arrived at work that Saturday, Aug. 7, 1993.

Her sister Betty found her apartment open, her unfed cat outside the front door. All her clothing was there. Even her shoes were in the apartment. Betty said she must have left bare-footed.

Mary Dorset, who was 23 when she disappeared, was living in Springfield after dropping out as an education major at the university.

In the 13 months since her disappearance, police have traced dozens of separate leads in trying to locate her. Nothing has been successful.

Maj. Will Rivera of the Springfield police, the man who led the search for Mary Dorset, says the case has been a puzzling one from the start.

"It's peculiar we couldn't trace her movements better than we did," Rivera says. "People who should have known something didn't know at all. It was just strange."

The story then reviewed the leads police had followed in trying to find Mary Dorset. The piece concluded:

Yet Rivera says he is not ready to give up. "I haven't closed the case out yet. I'm still hunting her. I'm not going to

quit on her yet.

"It gnaws at you," he says. "Her picture is still hanging in there on the bulletin board."

Although the story is not a happy one, readers have had a question answered that may have bothered them from time to time: Did they ever find Mary Dorset?

Other good examples of updates are stories measuring a politician's campaign promises against his or her performance one or two years later, or those checking whether a law has been effective in correcting the abuses the legislators intended it to correct. Sometimes an update has nostalgic appeal: Whatever happened to . . . ?

If a story is worth writing in the first place, it probably is worth following—a day, a week, a month, a year later. Readers are interested. It's up to you to satisfy that interest.

Suggested Readings

Bernstein, Carl and Woodward, Bob. *All the President's Men*. New York: Simon and Schuster, 1974. Perhaps the most famous and best-written example of follow-up reporting ever done.

Bernstein, Carl and Woodward, Bob. *The Final Days*. New York: Simon and Schuster, 1976. More of the same.

Gruley, Bryan. *Paper Losses*. New York: Grove Press, 1993. Gruley wrote this follow-up history while on a 16-month leave as a reporter of the *Detroit News*. It chronicles the 25-year struggle between the *Detroit News* and the *Detroit Free-Press* to its present government-sanctioned joint-operating agreement.

Exercises

1. The morning paper has run this story:

   A 7-year-old Springfield girl was molested Tuesday evening near the intersection of Broadway and Rockhill Road.

   Springfield police said that at about 5:30 p.m. a man grabbed the girl by the throat and pushed her into a ravine, where he then molested her.

   Police estimate the man was alone with the victim for only about one or two minutes. The victim was fighting her assailant the whole time they were alone, said Sgt. Jack Phillip of the Springfield Police Department.

   The molester apparently was scared off when two friends the girl had been playing with began calling for her, he said.

   The assailant is described as a white male

   with a scar above his right eye, about 6 feet tall. He was last seen wearing an orange short-sleeved shirt with black jeans.

   Phillip said there is no suspect in the case and that there have been no similar incidents in the area recently.

   You learn that a second minor, an 8-year-old boy, has told police that he had been molested by a person with the same description the day before the incident with the 7-year-old, and in the same vicinity.

   That's all the information available. Write the story.

2. An earlier edition of your newspaper ran this story:

Springfield police described the 36-year-old victim of an apparent pistol whipping and robbery as bloodied and in "a daze with his head split wide open" when he was picked up Friday morning at the corner of Tenth Street and Broadway.

Police responded to a call after a citizen reported a man was "walking around downtown disoriented and possibly injured."

The victim, whose name is being withheld by police, related to officials that he had been approached by three men and robbed of his wallet and wristwatch. Police report that a small-caliber handgun was employed in the robbery and used to strike the victim several times about the head.

He was taken to the Springfield Hospital emergency room and treated for cuts, scrapes and lacerations about the face and cranium. He was released Friday morning.

Springfield Police Sgt. Jack Cron said an investigation of the armed robbery is under way, but as yet it hasn't turned up many sordid details. He blamed the lack of detailed information concerning the identities of the assailants on the severely intoxicated condition of the victim at the time of the assault.

"He had a blood-alcohol count of .43 percent," Cron said, "and according to the Missouri State Highway Patrol a count of .35 percent to .50 percent can kill you."

Cron said the department has learned that the victim drank in a downtown bar until closing and evidently was attacked shortly thereafter.

Your professor will play the role of any persons you need to investigate the story further. Get the information and write a follow to the story.

3. You are told to write a follow to this story:

WASHINGTON (AP)—Physicians need to act more aggressively on the initial complaints of women—especially younger women—who find lumps in their breasts, a study of breast cancer malpractice claims and lawsuits indicates.

The study of the Physician Insurers Association of America found that in 69 percent of cases where claims were paid because breast cancer diagnosis was delayed, the patient had discovered the lump.

"The physician needs to be impressed by such findings and order follow-up studies," said the report.

"This study indicates that self-discovery often may be ignored, especially in younger women where the incidence of malignancy is thought to be less than in older women" and is more difficult to detect, the study said.

The study reviewed 2,373 paid claims reported by 21 member companies of the association.

Discuss a possible follow-up story, and list the sources you would contact to write it.

4. A competing news medium has reported this story:

The state attorney general Thursday alerted citizens that letters sent by a man soliciting money for his totally disabled wife prey upon the people's sympathy as well as upon their pocketbooks.

About 10,000 letters requesting from $200 to $1,000 each have been mailed by an Oregon man requesting a "loan" so he can build a "small but comfortable" home. The man explains that he refused to put his wife in a nursing home and that her needs have kept him from working for the past five years.

The letters claim that the lender will earn 10 percent interest and be paid back within 10 years.

Attorney General William Turner said complaints registered at the Oregon attorney general's office claim the wife's health is falsely represented. Reports indicate that she has worked as a hotel maid, is capable of driving a car and even delivered the letters to the post office to be mailed.

Fund-raising efforts for private individuals usually are organized through a local church, business or other organization. He advises checking whether any of these efforts are under way before making any donations.

Describe at least three different ways to recycle this story and the steps you would take for each.

5. Find a copy of your local paper that is at least six months old. Look for a story that is worthy of

an update, do the necessary reporting and write a follow-up story.

6. Read a current issue of your local newspaper. Find a national report or international story that you can localize. Report and write a story.

7. Find a story in a current newspaper that is obviously a follow-up story. Do a computer search to find any previous stories on that subject in any newspaper. Then write a follow-up story of your own.

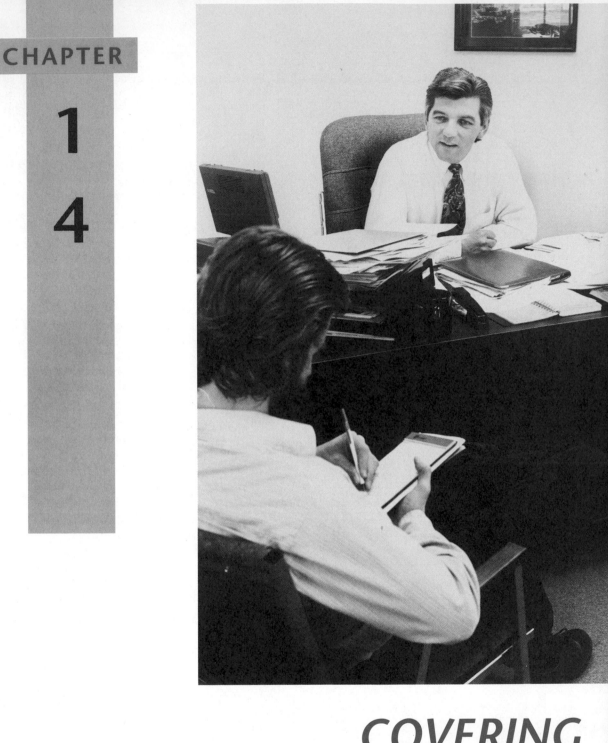

COVERING
A BEAT

*J*ust a few years out of journalism school, Susan Drumheller is already a seasoned beat reporter. She has covered local government and now education for the Idaho bureau of the Spokane (Wash). Spokesman-Review. So when a colleague, a rookie on the police beat, came across a lawsuit alleging sexual abuse by a teacher in the local district, Susan knew how to turn an incomplete and one-sided set of facts into a story that was relevant and interesting to her community.

She used everyday reporting techniques to tap sources developed over months of diligent cultivation. She used investigative techniques to dig out local and state records of teacher hiring, qualification and discipline. She used computer skills to check some public databases. She even persuaded the newspaper attorney to file suit seeking to open closed court proceedings. And she followed some guidelines she has relied on since school (see pages 304-305).

Susan Drumheller didn't dream up her guidelines. She didn't invent the techniques that allow her to follow her nose and her conscience in pursuit of good stories. She is following in the traditions of the most important job at any newspaper, the job of beat reporting.

Reporters such as Susan are the eyes and ears of their communities. They are the surrogates for their readers, keeping track of government, education, police, business and other powerful institutions that shape those readers' lives. When an education reporter, for instance, isn't tracking down an accused teacher, she may be exploring the influence of Christian fundamentalists on sex education (a critically important topic in the age of AIDS) or describing the travails of the high school marching band, a quarter of whose members play the flute.

The principles of good reporting apply to the coverage of any beat, though the beats themselves are changing as journalists change their definitions of the news that is most important to audiences. Susan's beats, education and local government, and the other traditional assignments, such as police and business, have been joined by religion, health, science and others.

The same principles also apply to specialized publications, including those aimed at particular ethnic groups, industries or professions. A reporter for Women's Wear Daily may cover designers. A reporter for Diario las Americas in Miami may cover Cuban exile politics. But each is doing the same job as Susan Drumheller—discovering and writing news that's relevant and useful to the publication's readers.

Many news organizations are responding to audience interests by creating teams of reporters to cover interrelated topics instead of institutions. One such team may write about issues of home and family life. Another may cover the arts and popular culture. Another team may focus on the problems and opportunities of urban living. Other teams or individual reporters may be responsible for such relevant but nontraditional topics as commuting, day care and aging, or the village center of modern America, the malls.

Editors and audiences expect reporters on these new beats, like those in more traditional assignments, to provide information and understanding that will help readers improve the quality of their lives. That's important work. It's rewarding work. But it's not easy.

Principles for Reporters on a Beat

Whether the beat you cover is the public library or the Pentagon, the county courthouse or the White House, the principles of covering it are the same. If you want to succeed as a reporter on that beat, you must be prepared, alert, persistent, there and wary.

That checklist will help you win the trust of your sources, keep up with important developments on your beat and avoid the trap of writing for your sources instead of your readers. Let's take a closer look at what each of those rules means in practice.

The successful beat reporter is

- *prepared.*
- *alert.*
- *persistent.*
- *there.*
- *wary.*

Be Prepared

Where should preparation begin? For you, it has already begun. To work effectively, any journalist needs a basic understanding of the workings of society and its various governments. You need to know at least the rudiments of psychology, economics and history. That is why the best education for a journalist is a broad-based one, providing exposure to the widest possible sampling of human knowledge. But that exposure will not be enough when you face an important source on your first beat. You will need more specific information, which you can acquire by familiarizing yourself with written accounts or records or by talking to sources.

Reading for Background

In preparing to cover a beat, any beat, your first stop should be the newspaper library (see Chapter 7). Many newspaper libraries now have computer access not only to material that has appeared in that newspaper but also to worldwide networks of information on virtually any topic. You can often access the contents of major newspapers, magazines, research publications and other reference libraries without regard to physical distance. Use the computer as a tool to acquire background and to understand the context of local events and issues.

In your local research, make notes of what appear to be continuing issues, questions left dangling in previous stories or ideas for stories to come. Go back several years in your preparation. History may not repeat itself, but a knowledge of it helps you assess the significance of current events and provides clues to what you can expect in the future.

The library is only the start of your preparation. You must become familiar with the laws governing the institution you cover. If a governmental organization is your beat, find the state statutes or the city charter that created the agencies you will be covering. Learn what the powers, the duties and the limitations are of each official. You may be surprised to discover that someone is failing to do all that the law requires. Someone else may be doing more than the law allows.

Look at your state's open meetings and open record laws, too. Every state has such laws, though they vary widely in scope and effectiveness. Knowing what information is open to the public by law can be a valuable tool for a reporter dealing with officials who may find it more convenient to govern privately.

Talking to Sources

Now you're ready to start talking to people. Your first interviews should be conducted in the news room with your predecessor on the beat, your city editor and any veterans who can shed some light on the kinds of things that rarely appear in statute books or even newspaper stories. Who have been good sources in the past? Who will lie to you? Who drinks to excess? Who seems to be living extravagantly? Whose friends are big land developers? Who wants to run for national office? Who has been hired, fired or promoted? Who has moved to a competing company? Remember that you are hearing gossip, filtered through the biases of those relating it. Be a little skeptical.

Some understanding of the workings of your own news room won't hurt, either. Has your predecessor on the beat been promoted, or transferred because he or she was unsatisfactory? Will an introduction from your predecessor help you or hurt you with your sources? And what are your city editor's expectations? Is your assignment to report virtually every activity of government, or will you have time to do some investigative work and analysis? Trying to live up to your boss' expectations is easier if you know in advance what they are.

Only after gaining as much background as possible are you ready to face the people you will be covering. A quick handshake and a superficial question or two may be all you have time for in the first encounter, but within a week you should arrange for sit-down conversations with your most important sources. These are get-acquainted sessions. You are trying to get to know the sources, but don't forget that they need to know you, too, if they are going to respect and trust you.

You may have noticed that the preparation for covering a beat is similar to the preparation for an interview or for a single-story assignment. The important difference is that preparing for a beat is more detailed and requires more time and work. Instead of just preparing for a short-term task, you are laying the foundation for an important part of your career. A beat assignment nearly always lasts at least six

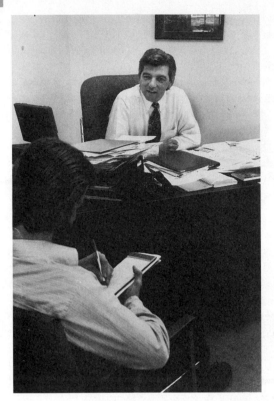

Figure 14.1.
In your first encounter with sources on a new beat, you should establish a friendly, professional relationship.

months and often two years or more. That understanding helps shape your first round of meetings with sources.

A story may emerge from those first interviews, but their purpose is much broader. You are trying to establish a relationship, trying to convert strangers into helpful partners in news gathering. To do that, you should demonstrate an interest in the sources as people as well as officials. Ask about their families, their interests, their philosophy, their goals. Make clear with your questions that you are interested rather than ignorant. (Don't ask if the source is married. You should already know that. Say, "I understand your daughter is in law school. Is she going into politics, too?" Similarly, don't ask if your source has any hobbies. Find that out beforehand. Say, "So you collect pornographic comic books. Sure takes your mind off the budget, doesn't it?")

And be prepared to give something of yourself. If you both like to fish, or you both went to Vassar, or you both have children about the same age, seize on those ties. All of us feel comfortable with people who have something in common with us. This is the time, too, to let your sources know that you know something about their work and that you're interested in it.

Was she elected as a reformer? Ask about the opposition she is encountering. Has he complained that he lacks the statutory power to do a satisfactory job? Ask if he's lobbying to change the law. Has the industry become more competitive? Ask about her strategies for meeting the challenge. Is it budget time? Let him know you're aware of the problems with last year's budget. Nothing does so much to create a warm reporter-source relationship as the reporter's demonstrated knowledge of and interest in the beat.

Solid preparation will help you avoid asking stupid questions. More important, it will help you make sure you ask the right questions. And because you have taken the trouble to get to know your sources, you are more likely to come away with responsive answers to the questions you ask.

Be Alert

On his way to lunch, Nik Deogun, then a young reporter for the *Atlanta Business Chronicle*, drove at least once a week past the old Sears building, a huge derelict purchased by the city in what the mayor proclaimed "the deal of the century." He began to wonder how renovation was proceeding. Then, as he worked on another story, he heard gossip that the project was running over budget. He began to devote a few spare minutes here and there to re-examining the city's great deal. His story for the *Chronicle* began:

> After only three years, the city of Atlanta is considering refinancing what it called at the time the "deal of the century."

The $10 million set aside for renovation was about $4 million too little, he reported. The great deal had become a huge bust. A reporter's curiosity paid off for the public.

Important stories are seldom labeled as such. In many cases the people involved may not realize the significance of what they are doing. Probably more often they realize it but hope nobody else will. The motivation for secrecy may be dishonesty, the desire to protect an image or a conviction that the public will misunderstand.

If your beat is a government agency, you will find that many public officials and public employees think they know more about what is good for the public than the public does. The theory of democratic government is that an informed citizenry can make decisions or elect representatives to make those decisions in its own best interests. If you are the reporter assigned to city hall, the school board or the courthouse, you carry a heavy responsibility for helping your readers put that theory into practice. To discharge that responsibility, you must probe beneath the surface of events in search of the "whys" and "hows" that lead to understanding.

When you are presented with a news release or hear an announcement or cover a vote, ask yourself these questions before passing the event off in a few paragraphs:

> *Who will benefit from this, and who will be hurt?* If the tentative answer to the first part suggests private interests, or the answer to the second part is the public, some digging is in order.
>
> *How important is this?* An event that is likely to affect many people for good or ill usually deserves more explanation than one affecting only a handful.
>
> *Who is for this, and who is against it?* Answers to these questions often are obvious or at least easy to figure out. When you know them, the answers to the first two questions usually become clearer.
>
> *How much will this activity cost, and who will pay?* An architect's design for renovating downtown may look less attractive when the price tag is attached. The chamber of commerce's drive to lure new industry may require taxpayers to pay for new roads, sewers, fire protection, even schools and other services for an increased population.

Once you have asked the questions and gotten answers, the story may turn out to be about no more than it appeared to be on the surface. But if you don't ask them, you—and your readers—may find out too late that more was there than met the eye. The answers allow you to judge that most important element of news value—impact.

Be Persistent

Persistence means two things to a reporter on a beat. First, it means that when you ask a question, you cannot give up until you get an answer. Second, it means that you must keep track of slow-developing projects or problems.

Insisting on a Responsive Answer

One of the most common faults of beginning reporters is that they give up too easily. They settle for answers that are unresponsive to their questions, or they return to the news room not sure they understand what they were told. In either case the result is an incomplete, confusing story.

"Why is it that our fourth-graders score below average on these reading tests?" you ask the school superintendent.

He may reply, "Let me first conceptualize the parameters of the socioeconomic context for you."

The real answer probably is, "I only wish I knew."

Your job is to cut through the jargon and the evasions in search of substance. Often that is not an easy task. Many experts, or people who want to be regarded as experts, are so caught up in the technical language of their special field that they find it almost impossible to

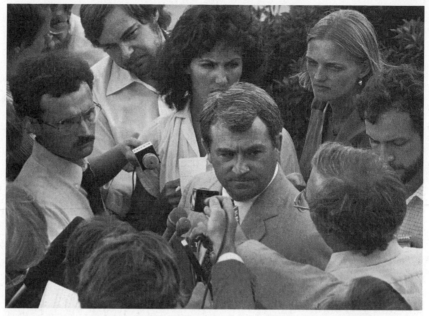

Figure 14.2.
People with newsworthy information are often unwilling sources, especially when the news reflects negatively on them. This politician, who has just been indicted by a grand jury, is clearly not eager to speak with the persistent beat reporters who are pursuing his story.

communicate clearly. Many others seek refuge in gobbledygook or resort to evasion when they don't know an answer or find the answer embarrassing. Educators and lawyers are particularly adept at such tactics.

Listen politely for a few minutes while the school superintendent conceptualizes his parameters. Then, when he finishes or pauses for breath, lead him back toward where you want to go. One way is to say, "It sounds to me as if you're saying . . ." and rephrase what he has told you in plain English. At those times when you simply are in the dark—and that may be often—just confess your puzzlement and ask for a translation. And keep coming back to the point: "But how does all that affect reading scores?" "How can the problem be solved?" "What are you doing about it?"

The techniques you have learned for preparing for interviews and conducting them will help you. Your preparation for the beat will help, too. Probably most helpful, though, are the questions you keep asking yourself rather than your source: "Does that make sense to me?" "Can I make it make sense to my readers?" Don't quit until the answer is yes. You should not be obnoxious, but you do have to be persistent.

Following Up Slow Developments

Persistence is also required when you are following the course of slow-developing events. Gardeners do not sit and watch a seed germinate. Their eyes would glaze over long before any change was apparent. Gardeners do, however, check every few days, looking for the green shoots that indicate the process is taking place as it should. If the shoots are late, they dig in to investigate.

Beat reporting works much the same way. A downtown redevelopment plan, say, or a revision in a school's curriculum is announced. The story covers the plans and the hoped-for benefits. The seed is planted. If it is planted on your beat, make a note to yourself to check on it in a week or two. And a week or two after that. And a month after that. Start a file of reminders so you won't forget. Such a file often is called a **tickler** because it serves to tickle your memory.

Like seeds, important projects of government or business take time to develop. Often what happens during the long, out-of-public-view development is more important than the announcements at the occasional news conferences or the promises of the promotional brochures. Compromises are made. Original plans turn out to be impractical or politically unpalatable. Consultants are hired. Contracts are signed. Public money is spent. The public interest may be served, or it may not.

Sometimes the story is that nothing is happening. At other times the story may be that the wrong things are happening. Consulting contracts may go to cronies of the mayor. Redevelopment may enhance the property values of big downtown landowners. Curriculum revisions may be shaped by some influential pressure groups.

Even if nothing improper is taking place, the persistent reporter will give the readers an occasional update. At stake, after all, is the public's money and welfare.

Be There

In beat reporting there is no substitute for personal contact. Trying to do it by telephone just won't work. The only way to cover a beat is to be there—every day, if possible. Joking with the secretaries, talking politics with council members and lawyers, worrying over the budget or trading gossip with the professional staff—you must make yourself a part of the community you are covering.

The payoff for this kind of cultivation? Here's Susan Drumheller again:

> When I covered City Hall, I got to know the people there really well. They knew my face. They gave me tips. I treated them fair.
>
> The fun stories had to do with the elected or prominent officials, who would do stupid things. One of my favorites was the elementary school principal who illegally passed a school bus with its stop-arm down as he rushed to work. The bus driver only recognized him because

ON THE JOB

Where the Action Is

Lewis Diuguid is associate editor of the *Kansas City Star*, but he hasn't forgotten the lessons he learned nearly 20 years ago, covering a suburban beat fresh out of journalism s chool:

> Reporters should strive to build drama into their copy, think about how people looked, sounded and even smelled when they were doing their reporting. Of course, that means that reporters will have to go out to meet with people for stories instead of trying to handcuff the news by telephone.
>
> The best beat reporters get personal with their sources. Newsmakers place great stock in getting to know the people who write about them. If they feel comfortable with a reporter

they will gossip, talk, and tell more. Getting personal doesn't involve anything close to pillow talk or sacrificing your liver to drinking at all hours for better stories.

But it does require that reporters share information about themselves with sources. What do you like to do in your spare time? What are your hobbies? Do you have a family? What are your kids' names? Share pictures that you have of them. Reporters do not have to do this the first day they get on a beat, but it is important to gradually warm up to sources so that they will share more with you.

Journalism has to be something a person would do for free. The check is for putting up with hassles associated with getting stories into the paper.

Journalists of color should never shy away from covering stories involving minorities, especially when their backgrounds and educations give them in-depth knowledge of issues related to those communities. White readers are just as happy to see stories about minorities as minorities are. Because of the push for diversity in industry, whites are looking for ways to better understand our multicultural world.

his daughter was in the car, and she usually rode that bus. That came from a tip. . . .

Not only does a beat reporter have to have a reputation among the people he or she covers as being fair, but you also need a reputation for pursuing controversial and hard stories.

Remember that the sources who are most important to you probably are in great demand by others, too. They have jobs to do. Maneuver to get as much of their time as you need, but don't demand too much. Do your homework first. Don't expect a school superintendent to explain basic concepts of education. You can learn that information from an aide or from reading. What you need to learn from the superintendent is how he or she intends to apply those concepts, or why they seem to be inapplicable here. Find out what a "Class I felony" is before asking the police chief why they are increasing. You will get the time you need more readily if busy sources know their time will not be wasted.

There are other simple techniques you can use to build and maintain good relationships with the people on your beat. Here are some of them:

Do a favor when you can. As a reporter you spend much of your time asking other people to do favors for you—giving you their time, sharing information they need not share, looking up records and figures. If a source needs a favor in return, don't refuse unless it would be unethical. The favors asked usually are small things, such as getting a daughter's engagement picture or a club announcement in the paper, procuring a print of a picture taken with the governor to decorate the official's wall, bringing in a few copies of a favorable feature you wrote.

Don't shun good news. One ill-founded but common complaint is that news media report nothing but bad news. Admittedly, there is usually no story when people are doing what they are supposed to do. Sometimes there should be, if they do their duty uncommonly well or have done it for a very long time or do it under the burden of some handicap. Sources like these "good news" stories and so do readers.

Protect your sources. Many people in government—politicians and bureaucrats alike—are willing to tell a reporter things they are not willing to have their names attached to in print or otherwise. The same is true of people in private business, who may fear reprisals from their employer, co-workers or competitors. Sometimes such would-be anonymous sources are trying to use you to enhance their own positions. You have to protect yourself and your readers against that possibility. Confer with an editor if you have doubts. Most papers are properly wary of relying on unnamed sources. Sometimes, though, the requests for anonymity are valid, necessary to protect the source's career. Once you have agreed to protect a source, you must do it. Don't tell anyone but your editor. An inability to keep your mouth shut can cost you more than a source. It can cost you your reputation. (The protection of sources has legal as well as ethical implications. So-called **shield laws** in some states offer limited exemptions for journalists from legal requirements to disclose sources—see Chapter 21. But there are no blanket exemptions. In one effort to resolve such problems, some news organizations try to negotiate written agreements obligating a source to come forward if continued secrecy might cost a reporter a jail term or the newspaper a loss in a lawsuit.)

Above all, be accurate. Inaccurate reporting leads first to loss of respect from sources, then to loss of the sources themselves and finally to loss of the job. If you are a good, tough reporter, not all your contacts on your beat will love you. But if you are an accurate reporter, they will respect you.

To build good relationships on your beat

- *Do a favor when you can.*
- *Don't shun good news.*
- *Protect your sources.*
- *Be accurate.*

The best way to assure accuracy is to check and double-check. Many of the stories you will write are likely to be complicated. You will be expected to digest budgets, master plans, legal opinions and complicated discussions, and to translate these into language your readers can understand. When in doubt, ask somebody. If you are unclear about the city manager's explanation of the budget before the council, arrange a meeting afterward and go over it. If a company's brief in a legal case has you confused, call the lawyer who wrote it. If the new master land-use plan strikes you as vague, consult with the planner. If you are writing a story on a subject you feel tentative about, arrange to read it back to the sources when it is complete. Not all experts relish being asked to translate their jargon into English, so in some cases you will have to insist, politely. The best persuader is the assurance that it is far better for your sources to take a few minutes to explain now than to see themselves misrepresented in print.

Remember, beat reporting is a lot like gardening. Both require you to be in the field every day, cultivating. And in both the amount of the harvest is directly proportional to the amount of labor invested.

Be Wary

The point of all this effort—the preparation, perceptiveness, persistence and personal contact—is to keep your readers informed. That is an obvious statement, but it needs to be made because every reporter on a beat is under pressures that can obscure the readers' importance. You must be wary of this problem.

You will have little to do with 99.9 percent of your readers. They will not write you notes when you have done a story they like or call you when they dislike what you have written. They will not offer to buy you a cup of coffee or lunch, or stop you in the hall to urge you to see things their way. But your sources will.

If you write that city council members are thinking about raising the property-tax rate, you probably will hear complaints from council members about premature disclosure. If you write that the police department is wracked by dissension, expect a less-than-friendly reaction from the chief. If you write that the CEO of a major business is looking for a new job, the chances are that he or she will deny it even though the story is true.

All sources have points of view, programs to sell, careers to advance, opponents to undercut. It is likely and legitimate that they will try to persuade you of the merit of their viewpoint, try to sell their programs through the columns of your newspaper, try to shape the news to help their careers.

Be wary of sources' efforts to use you. You can lose the critical distance a reporter must maintain from those being covered. When that happens, you start thinking like a participant rather than an observer. You begin writing for your sources rather than your audience. This is a real danger. No one can spend as much time as a reporter on a beat does with sources or devote as much effort to understanding them without becoming sympathetic. You may forget that you are writing for the outsiders when you associate so closely with the insiders.

Many veteran police reporters, for example, begin thinking like those they cover, some of them even adopting the common police officer's suspicion of journalists. The police reporter for one big-city radio station first took to carrying a gun, then quit reporting altogether to do public relations work for the sheriff's department.

One eastern newspaper had a veteran reporter covering the courts for years. A tall, dignified man with an impressive potbelly, he was called "Judge" by many of his sources, including some who were judges. He knew more law than some prosecutors and more about courthouse politics than many politicians. The trouble was that he thought, and wrote, more like a lawyer than a reporter. When he used the first-person plural pronoun in conversation, he often was referring to the attorney general's office instead of to himself and his colleagues on the paper. His writing was full of writs, dicta and other untranslated language of the law. It had become his language. Like too many diligent reporters assigned a beat, he had become part of the beat rather than an observer of it.

Covering the Most Important Local Beats

Your political science courses will introduce you to the structure of government, but from a reporter's viewpoint, function is usually even more important than structure. You must learn who holds the real power, who has the most influence on the power holders and who are the most likely sources of accurate information. The specifics vary from city to city, but there are some general principles that will help you in covering any form of state or local institution.

Writing for Readers

What does it mean to write for your readers instead of your sources? It means that you must follow several important guidelines:

Translate. The language of bureaucrats, educators, scientists or lawyers is not the same language most people speak. You need to learn the jargon of your sources, but you also need to learn how to translate it into standard English for your readers. The city planning consultant might say, "Preliminarily, the concept appeared to permit attainment of all our criteria; but, when we cost it out, we have to question its economic viability." Your lead could translate that to:

> The proposed plan for downtown redevelopment looks good on paper, but it may cost too much, the city's planning consultant said today.

Make your writing human. In big government and big business, humanity often gets lost in numbers. Your readers want and need to know the impact of those numbers on real people. How many people will be displaced by a new highway? And who are they? Who will be affected by a school closing or a welfare cut? When a police report announced that burglaries were up by 35 percent in the last two months, an enterprising reporter told the story through the eyes of a victim. It began this way:

> Viola Patterson picked her way through the shattered glass from her front door, passed the table where her television used to sit, and stopped before the cabinet that had held her family silver.
>
> She wept.
>
> Mrs. Patterson, 72, is one of the more than 75 people victimized by burglars in the last two months.

Think of the public pocketbook. If the tax rate is going up 14 cents, how much will it cost the average homeowner? If employees of a firm are seeking a 10 percent raise, how much will that cost the employer? How much of that increase will be passed on to customers? If garbage collection fees are about to be increased, how do they compare to fees in comparable cities?

The city manager proposed "adjusting" the price of electricity to lower the cost to industrial customers and raise rates to private homes. The city hall reporter did a quick survey of comparable cities around the state. Then she wrote:

> City residents, who already pay more for their electricity than residents of eight similar-sized cities around the state, would be charged an average of $4 per month more under a proposal announced Tuesday by City Manager Barry Kovac.
>
> Industrial users, whose rate now is about average among the nine cities, would enjoy the second-lowest rate under Kovac's proposal.
>
> Kovac defended his plan as "equitable and necessary to ensure continued economic growth for the city."

Get out of the office. City council votes are important, but far more people will have personal contact with government in the form of a police officer, a clerk or a bus driver than with a council member. Go to where government meets its constituents. Ride a bus. Visit a classroom. Patrol with a police officer. Not only will you get a reader's-eye view of your beat, but you may also find some unexpected stories.

Ask the reader's questions. "Why?" "How much will it cost me?" "What will I get out of it?" You are the public's ombudsman.

Remember, a good beat reporter has to be prepared, be alert, be persistent and be there. If you keep in mind, too, whom you are writing for, you'll keep the customers—and the editors—satisfied.

Crucial factors and practical principles for beat reporters

- *Power: Information is power.*
- *Money: The budget is the blueprint.*
- *Politics: Distributing power and money is politics.*

Information is power. The holder of information may be a professional administrator—the city manager, school superintendent, police chief or court clerk—or it may be an elected official—the mayor, chair of the county commission or chair of the school board. The job title is unimportant. Find the person who knows in detail how any organization really works, where the money goes and how decisions are made. Get to know that person because he or she will be the most important person on your beat.

The budget is the blueprint. This principle is a corollary of the first. Just as detailed knowledge of how an organization works is the key to controlling that organization, a budget is the blueprint for the organization's activities. The budget tells where the money comes from and where it goes. It tells how many people are on the payroll and how much they are paid. It tells what programs are planned for the year and how much they will cost. Over several years' time, the budget tells where the budget makers' priorities are, what they see as their organization's role in the community.

So, find copies of the last two or three years' budgets for your beat. Try to decipher them. Learn all you can from your predecessor and from newspaper clips. Then find the architect who drew up this blueprint—the budget director or the clerk or the assistant superintendent—and get a translation. Ask all the questions you can think of. Write down the answers.

When budget-making time arrives, follow every step. Attend every public hearing and every private discussion session you can. In those dollar figures are some of the most important stories you will write—stories of how much your readers will be paying for schools and roads and garbage pickup, stories of what they will get for your money. You'll find a guide to understanding budgets at the end of this chapter.

Distributing power and money is politics. While looking for your beat's power centers and unraveling its budget mysteries, you will be absorbing as well the most interesting part of beat reporting—politics.

At any organizational level in any form, power and money go hand-in-hand with politics. Politics provides the mechanisms through which limited resources are allocated among many competing groups. Neither elections nor political parties are necessary for politics. You will have to learn to spot more subtle forms of political maneuvering.

If you are covering city hall, for example, pay close attention as the city budget is being drafted. You may find the mayor's pet project being written in by the city manager. Nobody elects the city manager, but it is good politics for him or her to keep the mayor happy. Are the builders influential in town? If so, you will probably find plenty of road and sewer projects in the budget. Are the city employees unionized? Look for healthy wage and benefit increases if they are. Is there a vocal retirees' organization? That may account for the proposed senior citizens' center. None of those projects is necessarily bad just because it is political. But you and your readers ought to know who is getting what and why.

Now suppose an election is coming up, and the builders' campaign contributions will be heavy. A councilman who is running for mayor switches his vote from money for parks to money for new roads. Has a deal been made? Has a vote been sold? That's politics, too. Some digging is in order.

Power, money and politics are the crucial factors to watch in any beat reporting. With this in mind, let's take a closer look at the most important local beats.

City and County Government

Most medium-sized cities have council-manager governments. The mayor and council members hire a professional administrator to manage the day-to-day affairs of the city. The manager, in turn, hires the police and fire chiefs, the public works director and other department heads. Under the city charter the council is supposed to make policy and leave its implementation to the manager. Council members usually are forbidden to meddle in the affairs of any department.

Some small towns and a decreasing number of big cities have governments in which the mayor serves as chief administrator. Chicago under the late boss Richard Daley was probably the best-known example. Whatever the structure, you will have a range of good sources to draw on.

Subordinate administrators. They know details of budgets, planning and zoning, and personnel matters. They are seldom in the spotlight, so many of them welcome a reporter's attention so long as the reporter does not get them into trouble. Many are bright and ambitious, willing to second-guess their superiors and gossip about politics, again providing you can assure them that the risk is low.

Council members. Politicians, as a rule, love to talk. What they say is not always believable, and you have to be wary of their attempts to use you, but they will talk. Like most of us, politicians are more likely to tell someone else's secret or expose the other guy's deal. So ask one council member about the political forces behind another member's pet project while asking the other about the first's mayoral ambitions. That way you probably will learn all there is to know.

Pressure groups. You can get an expert view of the city's land-use policies from land developers and a different view from conservationists. The manager or the personnel director will tell one side of the labor-management story. The head of the employees' union tells the other. How about the school board's record in hiring minorities? Get to know the head of the NAACP or of the Urban League chapter. Public officials respond to pressure. As a reporter you need to understand those pressures and who applies them.

Public citizens. Consumer advocate Ralph Nader made the term *pub-*

ON THE JOB

Being Fair to Both Sources and Readers

As a beat reporter for the *Spokane* (Wash.) *Spokesman-Review*, Susan Drumheller is covering education now. Previous beats have included police and local government. It's demanding work, but she loves it.

Here are some guidelines she tries to follow in her reporting:

- "I figure using investigative techniques—while at the same time being scrupulously fair—is part of beat reporting."
- Never write one-source stories or take

Sources for the city or county government beat

- *Subordinate administrators*
- *Council members*
- *Pressure groups*
- *Public citizens*
- *Opponents*

one person's word for anything.

■ Be persistent.

■ "Be fair and accurate. That will win respect among sources and readers. Run corrections when you make a mistake; it increases credibility with sources, even if some people think corrections make the paper look bad."

■ Use documentation whenever possible.

■ Be wary of agendas. Keep an open mind.

■ "An ethics rule I stick to: I identify myself. Sometimes not until people ask. But I never misrepresent myself, even though it can work against me."

■ The most important: "Be true to yourself. Don't get sucked into writing a sensational story just because your editor got overzealous in writing the budget line. Write the truth, or as close an approximation as you can get."

■ And in the words of a former journalism school instructor, "Dress like a bum, get treated like a bum."

lic citizens popular, but every town has people—lawyers, homemakers, business executives, retirees—who serve on charter commissions, head bond campaigns, work in elections and advise behind the scenes. Such people can be sources of sound background information and useful assessments of officeholders.

Opponents. The best way to find out the weaknesses of any person or program is to talk with an opponent. Seek out the board member who wants to fire the school superintendent. Look up the police captain demoted by the new chief. Chat with the leader of the opposition to the new hospital. There are at least two sides to every public question and every public figure. Your job is to explore them all.

Once you have found the sources, keep looking, listening and asking for tips, for explanations, for reactions, for stories. The fun is just starting.

Covering a city is very much like covering a county government. In both cases you deal with politicians, with administrators, with budgets, with problems. The similarities may be obscured by differences in structure and style, however.

Cities are more likely to have professional administrators, for example. The administration of county governments is more likely to be in the hands of elected commissioners, supervisors or judges. Counties, too, are more likely to have a multitude of elected officials, from the sheriff to the recorder of deeds. City governments are more likely to be bureaucracies. One way to generalize about the differences is to say that city governments often are more efficient and county governments are more responsive.

These differences frequently mean, for a reporter, that county government is easier to cover. More elected officials mean more politicians. That, in turn, can mean more talkative sources, more open conflict, more points at which constituents and reporters alike can gain access to the governmental structure.

The principles and the problems of reporting are the same. The budget remains the blueprint whether it is drafted by a professional administrator or an elected officeholder. Knowledge is power whether it is the city manager or the elected county clerk who knows where the money goes. Politics is politics.

The Schools

No institution is more important to any community than its schools. None is worse covered. And none is more demanding of or rewarding to a reporter. The issues that arise on the school beat are among the most important in our society. If it is your beat, be prepared to write about racial tensions, drug abuse, obscenity versus free speech, religious conflict, crime, labor-management disputes, politics, sex—and yes, education.

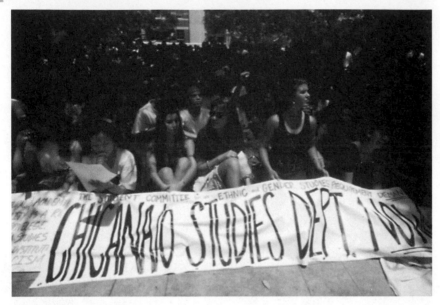

Figure 14.3.
News about education meets the tests of relevance, usefulness and interest because it affects so many readers personally. All California taxpayers have a stake in the state's response to the demand of these UCLA students for a Chicano studies department.

You've met Susan Drumheller, who covers the schools in northern Idaho. "If most beat reporters are like me, they're under a lot of pressure to produce daily and weekend pieces," she says. Most beat reporters, in fact, are a lot like Drumheller. For them, and for you, she has a few tips for keeping up with the issues and the special language of education.

"One good way is to subscribe to *Education Week* and other trade newsletters or magazines." When outcomes-based education loomed as an issue nationally, Drumheller subscribed to the state's anti-OBE newsletter. "That way I know the lingo and I know what the activists are up to." When AIDS brought sex education to the forefront, she subscribed to Boise's gay and lesbian newspaper for a perspective she wouldn't otherwise get. "And I need to subscribe to Idaho Family Forum (related to Focus on the Family and Christian Coalition) newsletter to keep up with them."

She adds, "Oh, yeah—I also get student newspapers for story ideas."

The process of learning and teaching can be obscured by the furor arising from the more dramatic issues. Even when everyone else seems to have forgotten, though, you must not forget that all those are only side issues. The most important part of the school beat is what goes on in the classroom.

Whether those classrooms hold kindergarteners or college students, the principles for covering education remain the same. For the most part, so do the issues. When the schools are private rather than public, you have fewer rights of access.

The classroom is not an easy place to cover. You may have trouble getting into one. Administrators frequently turn down such requests on the grounds that a reporter's presence would be disruptive. It would, at first. But a good teacher and an unobtrusive reporter can overcome that drawback easily. Many papers, at the start of the school year, assign a reporter to an elementary school classroom. He or she visits frequently, gets to know the teacher and pupils, becomes part of the furniture. And that reporter captures for readers much of the sight and sound and feeling of education.

There are other ways, too, of letting readers in on how well—or how badly—the schools are doing their job. Every school system administers some kind of standard tests designed to measure how well its students compare either with a set standard or with other students. The results of such tests are or ought to be public information. Insist on learning about them. Test scores are an inadequate measure of school quality, but they are good indicators. When you base a story on them, be sure you understand what is really being compared and what factors outside the schools may affect the scores. Find out what decisions are made on the basis of standardized test scores. For example, do schools whose students' average scores are relatively low get additions to their faculty? Do they get special education teachers?

Be alert to other indicators of school quality. You can find out how many graduates of your school system go to college, how many win scholarships and what colleges they attend. You can find out how your school system measures up to the standards of the state department of education. Does it hold the highest classification? If not, why not? National organizations of teachers, librarians and administrators also publish standards they think schools should meet. How close do your schools come?

In education, as in anything, you get what you pay for. How does the pay of teachers in your district compare with similar-sized districts? How does the tax rate compare? What is the turnover among teachers?

You also should get to know as many teachers, administrators and students as possible. You can learn to pick out the teachers who really care about children and learning. One way to do that is to encourage them to talk about their jobs. A good teacher's warmth will come through.

One reason schools are covered poorly is that the beat often does not produce the obvious, easy stories of politics, personalities and conflict that the city hall or police beats yield. School board meetings usually produce a spark only when a side issue intrudes. Most school board members are more comfortable talking about issues other than education itself, which often is left to the professionals.

The politics and the budgets of schools are very much like those of other institutions. The uniquely important things about the school are the classroom and what happens inside it. Your reporting will suffer if you forget that fact. So will your readers.

The Police Beat

The police beat probably produces more good, readable stories per hour of reporter time than any other beat. It also produces some of the worst, laziest reporting and generates many of our most serious legal and ethical problems. It is the beat many cub reporters start on and the beat many veterans stay on until they have become almost part of the force. It offers great frustration and great opportunity. All these contradictions arise from the nature of police work and of reporting.

If you are going to be a police reporter—and nearly every reporter is, at least briefly—the first thing you have to understand is what police officers are and what they do. We hire police officers to protect us from each other. We require them to deal every day with the dregs of society. Abuse and danger are parts of the job, as is boredom. We pay police officers mediocre wages and accord them little status. We ask them to be brave but compassionate, stern but tolerant. What we get very often is less what we ask for than what we should expect. Police work seldom attracts saints. Police officers are frequently cynical, often prejudiced, occasionally dishonest.

When you walk into a police station as a reporter for the first time, expect to be met with some suspicion, even hostility. Young reporters often are perceived by police as being radical, unkempt, anti-authority. How closely does that description fit you or your classmates? And how many of you are pro-cop?

Police departments are quasi-military organizations, with strict chains of command and strong discipline. Their members are sworn to uphold the status quo. The reasons that police and young reporters are mutually suspicious should be clear by now.

Then how do you cover these people? You do so by using the same tricks of the trade you ply at city hall or in the schools. You should:

> *Educate yourself in police lore.* Take a course in law enforcement, if you can, or take a course in constitutional law. You also might read Joseph Wambaugh's novels for a realistic portrait of the police.
>
> *Try to fit in.* Get a haircut, dress conservatively and learn the language. Remember that police officers, like the rest of us, usually are quicker to trust people who look and act the way they do.
>
> *Lend a sympathetic ear.* You enjoy talking about yourself to some-

How to cover the cops

- *Educate yourself in police lore.*
- *Try to fit in.*
- *Lend a sympathetic ear.*
- *Encourage gossip.*
- *Talk with other police-watchers.*

body who seems to be interested; so do most police officers. They know they have a tough job, and they like to be appreciated. Open your mind, and try to understand points of view with which you may disagree strongly.

Encourage gossip. Police officers may gossip even more than reporters do. Encourage such talk over a cup of coffee at the station, while tagging along in a patrol car or over a beer after the shift. The stories will be one-sided and exaggerated, but you may learn a lot. Those war stories are fascinating, besides. Just don't print anything you haven't verified.

Talk with other police-watchers. Lawyers can be good sources, especially the prosecutors and public defenders who associate every day with the police. Other law enforcement sources are good, too. Sheriff's deputies, for example, may be eager to talk about dishonesty or inefficiency in the city police department, and city police may be eager to reciprocate.

One important reason for all this work is that little of the information you need and want as a police reporter is material you are entitled to under public records laws. By law you are entitled to see only the arrest sheet (also called the *arrest log*, or the **blotter**). This record tells you only the identity of the person arrested, the charge and when the arrest took place. You are *not* entitled by law to see the arrest report or to interview the officers involved.

Writing a story depends on securing more than the bare-bones information. Finding out details depends on the good will you have generated with the desk sergeant, the shift commander and the officers on the case. The dangers—of being unfair, of damaging your and your paper's or broadcast station's reputation—are ever-present. Good reporting requires that you know what the dangers are and how to try to avoid them.

The greatest danger arises from the one-sidedness and frequent inaccuracy of police reports. At best, the reports represent the officer's viewpoint. Particularly in cases involving violence, danger, confusion or possible repercussions, there may be plausible viewpoints different from that of the police officer. Conflicting interpretations of the same situation lead many times to the dropping of charges.

To protect yourself, and to be fair to the accused, always be skeptical. Attribute any accusatory statement to the officer who made it. If the room for doubt is great enough, talk to the accused, his or her relatives or lawyer, and any witnesses you can find. The result is almost sure to be a fairer, more complete story.

Sometimes the story is that the police officers themselves are misbehaving—for example, when television showed a bystander's videotape of white police beating a black motorist named Rodney King. Other abuses are less famous. When the *Bakersfield Californian* received three letters in the same week alleging police brutality, reporter Tom Maurer decided to take a closer look. Over the next year, in his spare time and after hours, he examined records of lawsuits and police reports, interviewed victims and officers and studied medical files, including autopsy reports.

He learned that more than 20 police officers had been sued at least three times each for brutality, more than 80 suits in five years. He also learned that internal police disciplinary procedures weren't working. Only 3 percent of the more than 80 complaints were found valid by the department, compared with nearly 20 percent statewide. The results were not dramatic. No reform campaign was launched. Three officers, however, were forced to retire. Maurer's only reward was the knowledge of a job well done.

Before Edna Buchanan turned to writing crime novels, she was one of the best-known police reporters in America. She won the Pulitzer Prize for general news reporting. Here are a couple of samples from her work:

> Bad things happen to the husbands of the Widow Elkin.
>
> Someone murdered husband No. 4, Cecil Elkin, apparently smashing his head with a frying pan as he watched "Family Feud" on TV.
>
> Husband No. 3, Samuel Smilich, drowned in a weedy South Dade canal.
>
> Husband No. 2, Lawrence Myers, cannot be found, though Metro-Dade homicide detectives, the FBI and the Air Force have searched for him.
>
> Husband No. 1, Wayne Wise, was divorced about 25 years ago. He is alive and well. . . .

And this:

> "My baby was trapped in a dead body," Charles Griffith said Saturday from the Dade County jail cell where he was stripped naked and charged with first-degree murder.
>
> "I didn't go to the hospital thinking I was going to kill my daughter," said Griffith, 25. "I told the nurse to go call the po-lice, I think, before it happened. It is almost like a dream."
>
> At 10:50 p.m. Friday, Griffith, a projectionist in a porno movie house, fired two bullets into the heart of his comatose 3-year-old daughter, Joy, as she lay in her crib in the special care nursery at Miami Children's Hospital. . . .

In the letter nominating Buchanan, who covered the police beat for the *Miami Herald* for 16 years, her editors made a comment to the Pulitzer Board that sums up the importance and the attraction of the police beat: "In truth, Edna Buchanan doesn't write about cops. She writes about people."

The Courts

One way to begin trying to understand the American judicial system is to think of it as a kind of game. The opposing players in a criminal case are the state, which is the accuser, and the defendant, who is the accused. In a civil case the opponents are the plaintiff and the defendant. Each player is represented by a lawyer, who does everything possible to win for his or her client. The judge referees the contest, insisting that all players abide by the rules. At the end, the judge (sometimes with a jury) decides who won.

Such an irreverent description grossly oversimplifies a system that, because of its independence and usual honesty, stands second only to a free press in protecting the liberty of Americans. But it may help in demystifying a system that also can overawe a beginning reporter.

There is a great deal in courts and the law to inspire awe. Black-robed judges and learned attorneys speak a language full of Latin phrases and highly specialized terms. Written motions, arguments and decisions are laden with convoluted sentences and references unintelligible to the uninitiated. A court can protect your money or your freedom or deprive you of them.

You can hardly cover the courts aggressively while standing awestruck, though, so here are some tips that may help restore your working skepticism:

A skeptic's guide to the courts

- *Never trust a lawyer unless you know him or her very well.*
- *A judge's word may be law, but it isn't gospel.*
- *Truth and justice do not always prevail.*

Never trust a lawyer unless you know him or her very well. Although most lawyers are honest, all lawyers are advocates. Consequently, everything they write or say must be interpreted as being designed to help the client and hurt the opponent. That is true whether the lawyer represents the defense or prosecution in a criminal case or represents either side in a civil lawsuit. Bar association codes or ethics forbid it, but many lawyers will try to use reporters to win some advantage. Be suspicious.

A judge's word may be law, but it isn't gospel. Not every judge is a legal scholar. Most judges are, or have been, politicians. All judges are human. They are subject to error, capable of prejudice. Some are even dishonest. Otto Kerner was a judge of a federal appeals court when he was convicted of corruption that occurred while he was governor of Illinois. Abe Fortas was a justice of the U.S. Supreme Court, a close adviser of President Lyndon B. Johnson, and Johnson's nominee for chief justice when a reporter disclosed he was receiving regular payments from a man convicted of violating federal law. Fortas resigned from the court.

Truth and justice do not always prevail. Prosecutors sometimes conceal evidence favorable to the defense. Defense lawyers sometimes seize on technicalities or rely on witnesses they know to be unreliable in order to win acquittals. Judges sometimes misinterpret the rules or ignore them. Innocent people do go to jail, and guilty ones go free. Courts are no more perfect than are newspapers. The two combined can produce frightening scenes, such as the one in Cleveland in 1954 when the newspapers screamed for blood, and a political judge denied Dr. Sam Sheppard the most basic rights before convicting him of murdering his wife. The Supreme Court decision overturning that conviction became a landmark in spelling out proper trial procedures. In other cases, the press had helped correct miscarriages of justice. Reporter Gene Miller has won two Pulitzer Prizes for winning freedom for persons wrongfully imprisoned after unjust murder convictions.

The judicial system is not exempt from honest and critical reporting. And the sources of that reporting—just as in city hall or the police station—are records and people. First, a few words about court records, where to find them and how to use them.

Court Records

Whenever a case is filed in court—whether it is a criminal charge or a civil lawsuit—the court clerk assigns it a number. It also has a title. In the case of a criminal charge, the title will be State vs. Joe Doakes, or something similar. (The "vs." is short for "versus," the Latin word meaning "against.") A civil case—a lawsuit seeking damages, for example—could be Joe Doakes vs. John Doe. Doakes would be the plaintiff, the party filing the suit. Doe would be the defendant. In order to secure the records from the clerk, you must know the case number or its title, which lawyers also call the "style" of the case.

We saw in Chapter 12, on crime and the courts, how criminal cases work their way through the court system. You can follow those cases, of course, by checking the file. At least in the more important criminal cases, however, you usually keep track by checking with the prosecutor and defense lawyers.

Once a civil suit has been filed, the defense files a reply. The plaintiff may file a motion seeking information. The defense may file a motion to dismiss the suit, which the plaintiff will answer. The judge rules on each motion. You can follow it all by checking the file regularly. Except in rare cases, all motions and information filed with the court become public records. Often information from lawsuits can provide you with interesting insights into the otherwise private affairs of prominent persons or businesses.

Many lawsuits never go to trial before judge or jury. It is common procedure for lawyers to struggle for advantage over a period of months, filing motions and countermotions to gain the best position or to sound out the other side's strength. Then, after a trial date has been set, one side or the other will propose a settlement, which is negotiated. The case is dropped. One reason for that course of action is that the details of an out-of-court settlement need not be made public, unlike the outcome of a trial.

Human Sources

If a case goes to trial, you cover civil and criminal proceedings in much the same way. You must listen to testimony and, during breaks, corner lawyers for each side to seek explanation and elaboration, while filling in the background from court records and your morgue. Your personal contacts are important sources of information during this process.

Lawyers. The best sources on the court beat are likely to be lawyers. Every courthouse reporter needs to win the confidence and goodwill of the prosecutor and his or her staff. Not only can they keep you abreast of developments in criminal prosecution, they often can—because assistant prosecutors generally are young, political and ambitious—keep you tuned in to all sorts of interesting and useful courthouse gossip. They are good sources for tips on who the best and worst judges are, which local officials may be on the take, which defense lawyers are less than upright. Like all gossip, such tips need careful handling and thorough checking. But the raw material is often there.

Lawyers in private practice can be grouped, from a reporter's viewpoint, into two classes—those who will talk and those who won't. The former class usually includes young lawyers, politically ambitious lawyers and criminal defense lawyers, all of whom often find publicity helpful. Cultivate them. Lawyers have egos only slightly smaller than those of reporters. Feed those egos. Encourage them to talk about themselves, their triumphs, their ambitions. You will reap story possibilities, background information and gossip to trade with other sources.

Judges. Don't ignore judges as sources, either. Some are so conscious of their dignity and their images that they have no time for reporters. Remember, though, that most judges in most states are elected to their jobs. That makes them politicians, and it is a rare politician who slams the door on a friendly reporter. Even many federal judges, who are appointed by the president, have done a stint in politics and still have their taste for newspaper ink. Judges' egos may be even bigger than reporters'. Treat every judge accordingly.

Other court functionaries. Many other court functionaries can be helpful sources. Police officers and sheriff's deputies or U.S. marshals assigned to court duty often are underworked and glad of a chance to talk about whatever they know, which may turn out to be good backstage stuff. The bailiffs who shout for order in court and help the judge on with a robe may be retired police officers or small-time politicians and also talkative. And secretaries, as everywhere, are good to know and even better to have know you.

Human sources in court

▮ *Lawyers*
▮ *Judges*
▮ *Other court functionaries*

You cover the courts, then, as you cover any other beat. You learn the language, figure out the records and develop your sources.

Religion

More Americans attend religious services than attend college football games. More Americans are active in religion than in politics. Overwhelming majorities of Americans say that religion is important in their lives. However, you'd never guess any of those realities from reading or viewing most news reports in print or on television. The typical newspaper offers a weekly Religion page, usually published on Saturday, when circulation and readership are low. The typical television news coverage of religion is even less, often nonexistent.

There are some signs that journalism is waking up. Some papers, large and small, are expanding religion reporting beyond the weekly page. Some have expanded their definitions of the subject to include broader issues of spirituality and ethics. Others are recognizing the role of religion beyond formal worship. That's not surprising. Just consider the stories:

In *social issues*, religion plays a role in the continuing debate over sex education, AIDS research and treatment, abortion, the role of women in the church and in secular life, and an almost-endless variety of other policy questions.

Look for religion stories in
- *Social issues*
- *Politics*
- *Law*
- *International affairs*
- *Everyday life*

In *politics*, religion has become a key to campaigning and to governing. Presidents from both major political parties proclaim themselves born-again Christians. Candidates at all levels solicit the support of the religious right or, in fewer cases, make the most of their independence from it. In campaigns throughout the country, well-organized and well-financed religious organizations, usually conservative in their theology and their politics, exert influence even beyond their numbers. In major cities, candidates court Jewish and Muslim support.

In *law*, constitutional questions continue to cloud the relationship of church and state. A teacher, fired for refusing to honor a legally required moment of silent meditation in the classroom, files suit. Federal law enforcement agents raid a religious compound in Texas. The Branch Davidians choose death in the ensuing fire rather than surrender.

In *international affairs*, a tenuous truce between Catholics and Protestants in Northern Ireland follows an even more momentous agreement to work toward peace between Jews and Muslims in the Middle East. However, religion compounds ethnic differences in vicious civil wars in central Europe and central Africa. Muslim fundamentalists join the Roman Catholic church in weakening worldwide efforts at population control.

In *everyday life*, religion-based charities assume increasing importance as the American economy leaves behind growing numbers of the unskilled and uneducated. The "Religion Calendar" for just one week in a Midwestern college town includes activities that range from the African Methodist Episcopal women's group to the pagan Wiccan circle to meditation practice at the Zen Center.

So how does a reporter prepare to cover such a range of issues, personalities and events?

First, prepare. Read as widely as you can. The best-informed coverage of religion and related issues can be found in such magazines as *Christianity Today*, the *National Catholic Reporter*, *Christian Century*, *Cross Currents*, *Worldview* and other publications you'll find indexed at your local public or university library.

For theological expertise and local comment on major stories about religion, consult faculty members at the nearest Religious Studies department or seminary. But beware their possible biases. Get to know your local religious activists, in the clergy and outside. Who are the rebels and the questioners? Who are the powers behind the pulpit quietly raising money, directing spending and guiding policy?

Remember that religion is also big business. Public records and computer databases can help you trace property ownership and finances. Religious organizations often own commercial property, housing, parking lots, educational facilities. Typically, they pay no taxes, but their economic impact can be great. It isn't always positive either. Churches have been found to be slumlords.

Religious organizations pay no income taxes, either. But they are required to file federal tax forms called 990 forms to maintain their tax-exempt status. These Internal Revenue Service forms are the only income tax forms that are public by law. You'll find readers interested in the finances as well as in the good works of religion.

In addition to ignorance, other obstacles impede effective coverage of religion. Many reporters and editors are reluctant to subject religious leaders and institutions to the same scrutiny as their counterparts in business or politics. Remember that religious leaders are human. They are often good, sometimes devious, occasionally corrupt. Be respectful, but remember that a member of the clergy who demands deferential treatment just might be hiding something behind that ecclesiastical smile.

Another special problem in covering religion is the emotional intensity with which many people hold to their beliefs. If you do serious reporting, you will not be able to avoid arousing somebody's wrath. You can avoid arousing it needlessly, however, by doing your homework.

Do not confuse a Southern Baptist with an American Baptist, or a Lutheran of the Missouri Synod with a Lutheran of the Evangelical Lutheran Church of America. You will not get very far interviewing a Jesuit if you ask him what denomination he belongs to. But not every Roman Catholic priest is a Jesuit. Don't attribute the same beliefs to Orthodox, Conservative and Reform Jews. And remember that Jews and Christians, though they dominate American religious life, are only a fraction of the world's religious believers.

Some stories about religion are uplifting. They tell of selfless service to the poor, the sick, the forgotten and abandoned. They illustrate values other than money or power. They describe the courage of people who put lives and property on the line for human rights or in opposition to war. Others are not so uplifting. Parishes run up huge debts. Parochial schools hire badly trained, poorly paid teachers. Blacks are refused admission. Women are refused ordination.

Stained-glass windows are no barrier to politics. Religious issues, such as abortion, homosexuality and capital punishment, are often also political issues. Churches may use their economic clout to combat injustice or to support it. Belief can be blind.

Whatever side of religion it explores, a good story about religion will wind up on the front page along with the best of the city hall or medical stories. The techniques for getting those stories are no different, either.

Science, Medicine and the Environment

If you start work on a small or medium-size newspaper, you may find that nobody is assigned full time to cover science, medicine or environmental issues. You may have a chance to stake out one or more of these interesting and important areas for yourself. On big papers such beats usually are covered by specialists, perhaps with some academic training in the area and certainly with several years of experience. Big paper or small, you will need some basic courses in the physical and biological sciences. And you will need an introduction to the special problems and sources encountered in this area.

On these beats there will be fewer meetings to attend or offices to visit than on a city hall or school beat. More of the stories here are likely to be generated by your own enterprise or by applying the local touch to a national story. You can find out what a new pesticide ban will mean to local farmers, for instance. Or you can determine whether local doctors are using a new arthritis treatment, or what a researcher at the state university is learning about the effects of alcohol on rats.

Where can you look for story ideas? Specialized publications are good places to start. Read the *Journal of the American Medical Association*, the *New England Journal of Medicine* and *Medical World*. New developments and issues in medicine are covered in news stories. *Scientific American* and *Science News* are informed but readable sources of ideas in all the sciences. For environmental issues, read *Natural History* magazine. Your state's conservation department may put out a publication. Get on the mailing lists of the National Wildlife Federation, the Sierra Club, the Audubon Society and Friends of the Earth.

Nearly every community has human sources, too. In medicine, these include members of the local medical association, the administrator of the hospital and public health officials. In the sciences, look for local school or college faculty, employees of government agencies such as extension or research centers, even interested amateurs such as those in astronomy societies. In the area of the environment, there usually is no shortage of advocacy groups or of industries that want to defend their interests. State and federal regulatory and research agencies are helpful, too.

The special problems posed by scientific beats begin with the language your sources use. It is a language full of Latin phrases, technical terms and numbers. You will have to learn enough of it both to ask intelligent questions and to translate the answers for your readers.

A good medical dictionary and science dictionary are invaluable. Use them and continue asking for explanations until you are sure you understand.

Another problem may be convincing scientists and physicians to talk to you in any language. Many of them have had little contact with reporters. Much of the contact they have had probably has been unpleasant, either because it arose from some controversy or because the reporter was unprepared. Reluctant sources are much more likely to cooperate if you demonstrate that you have done your homework, so you have at least some idea of what they are talking about. Promise to check your story with the sources. Accuracy is as much your goal as theirs.

In medicine a concern for privacy may deter some sources from talking freely. A physician's allegiance is, and should be, to the patient. As a reporter you have no legal right to know a patient's condition or ailment. That is true even if the patient is a public official. In fact, most information about a person's medical history and condition is protected by law from disclosure by governmental record keepers. When the mayor goes to the hospital, then, and you want to know why, your only tools are your persuasiveness and the goodwill you have built up with hospital officials, the attending physician or the mayor's family.

Sources also may be guarded in comments about their work. Most researchers in medicine and science are cautious in making any claims about the significance or certainty of their work. Some are not so cautious. You must be. Check and double-check, with the researcher involved and others knowledgeable in the field, before describing any development as "important" or "dramatic" or "frightening." Overstatement will damage your credibility with sources and readers.

Sometimes a researcher will be reluctant to discuss his or her work until it has been published in a professional journal or reported at a convention. Such presentation may be more important to the scientist than any newspaper publicity. Funding and fame are high stakes for research scientists. Many, justifiably afraid of having unscrupulous fellow researchers claim credit for their work, maintain secrecy until a study is complete. An agreement to give you first notice when he or she is ready to go public may be the best you can do in this circumstance.

Despite difficulties, the coverage of science, medicine or the environment offers great challenges and rewards. The challenge is discovering and explaining developments and issues that are important to your readers. The rewards, as in all other areas of reporting, can be prizes, pay raises or—most important—recognition by your sources and peers of a job well done. The key to success in covering these beats is the same as for any other beat: Be prepared, be alert, be persistent, be there and be wary.

Making Sense of Budgets

Because the budget is the blueprint that guides the operation of any organization, a reporter must learn to read it, just as a carpenter must learn to read an architect's blueprint. In either case, that isn't as difficult as it appears at first glance.

In many cases today, you'll be able to get the budget (and other financial information as well) for your city or school district on computer disk or tape. Then you or a computer-literate colleague can create your own spreadsheet and perform analyses that not long ago were only in the power of the institution's budget director. This is another way the computer has become an essential news room tool. However, with a computer or without, first you need to know the basics of budgeting.

Every budget, whether it's your personal budget or the budget of the U.S. government, has two basic parts—revenues (income) and expenditures (outgo). Commercial enterprises earn their income primarily from sales, and not-for-profit organizations depend heavily on

GENERAL FUND—SUMMARY

Purpose

The General Fund is used to finance and account for a large portion of the current operation expenditures and capital outlays of city government. The General Fund is one of the largest and most important of the city's funds because most governmental programs (Police, Fire, Public Works, Parks and Recreation, and so on) are generally financed wholly or partially from it. The General Fund has a greater number and variety of revenue sources than any other fund, and its resources normally finance a wider range of activities.

Appropriations

	Actual Fiscal Year 1995	Budget Fiscal Year 1996	Revised Fiscal Year 1996	Adopted Fiscal Year 1997
Personnel services	$ 9,500,353	$11,306,619	$11,245,394	$12,212,336
Materials and supplies	1,490,573	1,787,220	1,794,362	1,986,551
Training and schools	93,942	150,517	170,475	219,455
Utilities	606,125	649,606	652,094	722,785
Services	1,618,525	1,865,283	1,933,300	2,254,983
Insurance and miscellaneous	1,792,366	1,556,911	1,783,700	1,614,265
Total operating	15,101,884	17,316,156	17,579,325	19,010,375
Capital additions	561,145	1,123,543	875,238	460,143
Total operating and capital	15,663,029	18,439,699	18,454,563	19,470,518
Contingency	——	200,000	200,000	100,000
Total	$15,663,029	$18,639,699	$18,654,563	$19,570,518

Figure 14.4.
The summary page of a typical city budget.

contributions from public funding and private donors. Government revenues come from sources like taxes, fees and service charges, and payments from other agencies (such as state aid to schools). The budget usually shows, in dollar figures and percentages, the sources of the organization's money. Expenditures go for such things as staff salaries, purchase of supplies, payment of utility bills, construction and maintenance of facilities, and insurance. Expenditures usually are listed either by line or by program. The difference is this: A *line item budget* shows a separate line for each expenditure, such as "Salary of police chief—$50,000." A *program budget* provides less detail but shows more clearly what each activity of the agency costs; for example, "Burglary prevention program—$250,000."

Now let's see what kinds of stories budgets may yield and where to look for those stories. Take a minute to scan Figure 14.4, a sum-

Department Expenditures

	Actual Fiscal Year 1995	Budget Fiscal Year 1996	Revised Fiscal Year 1996	Adopted Fiscal Year 1997
City Council	$ 75,144	$ 105,207	$ 90,457	$ 84,235
City Clerk	61,281	70,778	74,444	91,867
City Manager	155,992	181,219	179,125	192,900
Municipal Court	164,631	196,389	175,019	181,462
Personnel	143,366	197,844	186,247	203,020
Law Department	198,296	266,819	248,170	288,550
Planning & Community Development	295,509	377,126	360,272	405,870
Finance Department	893,344	940,450	983,342	1,212,234
Fire Department	2,837,744	3,421,112	3,257,356	3,694,333
Police Department	3,300,472	4,007,593	4,139,085	4,375,336
Health	1,033,188	1,179,243	1,157,607	1,293,362
Community Services	50,882	74,952	74,758	78,673
Energy Management	——	——	54,925	66,191
Public Works	2,838,605	3,374,152	3,381,044	3,509,979
Parks and Recreation	1,218,221	1,367,143	1,400,334	1,337,682
Communications & Info. Services	532,153	730,129	742,835	715,324
City General	1,864,200	1,949,543	1,949,543	1,739,500
Total Department Expenditures	15,663,028	18,439,699	18,454,563	19,470,518
Contingency	——	200,000	200,000	100,000
Total	$15,663,028	$18,639,699	$18,654,563	$19,570,518

Figure 14.4.
Continued.

mary page from the annual budget of a small city. You can apply the skills of reading a city's annual budget to similar accounting documents on other beats, for example, annual reports of businesses and not-for-profit organizations.

The most important budget stories usually deal with changes, trends and comparisons. Budget figures change, of course, every year. As costs increase, so do budgets. But look in our sample budget at the line for the Parks and Recreation Department. There's a decrease between Fiscal Year (FY) 1996 and 1997. Why? The summary page doesn't tell you, so you'll have to look behind it, at the detail pages. There, you'll discover that the drop results from a proposal by the city staff to halt funding of a summer employment program for teenagers. That's a story.

Another change that may be newsworthy is the sharp increase in the Police Department budget. You'd better find out the reasons for that, too. In this case, the detail pages of the budget show that most of the increase is going to pay for an administrative reorganization that is adding several new positions at the top of the department. The patrol division is actually being reduced. Another story.

Look again at that Police Department line. Follow it back to FY 1995 and you'll see that the increase last year was even bigger. In two years, the budget for police has increased by nearly one-third. That's an interesting trend. The same pattern holds true for the Fire Department as well. Some more checking is in order. With copies of previous budgets, you can see how far back the growth trend runs. You can also get from the departments the statistics on crimes and fires. Are the budget makers responding to a demonstrated need for more protection, or is something else at work behind the scenes?

More generally, you can trace patterns in the growth of city services and city taxes, and you can compare those with changes in population. Are the rates of change comparable? Is population growth outstripping growth in services? Are residents paying more per capita for city services than five or 10 years ago? More good story possibilities.

Another kind of comparison can be useful to your readers, too. How does your city government compare in cost and services with the governments of comparable cities? A few phone calls can add perspective to budget figures. Some professional organizations have recommended levels of service, such as number of police or firefighters per 1,000 inhabitants, that can help you help your readers assess how well they're being governed.

The same guidelines can be applied to the analysis of any budget. The numbers will be different, as will the department names, but the structures will be much the same. Whether you're covering the school board or the statehouse, look for changes, trends and comparisons.

Another document that is vital to understanding the finances of local government is the annual financial report. The financial report may be a few pages long or it may be a book. In any case, its purpose is relatively simple. As its name suggests, the report is an explanation of the organization's financial status at the end of a fiscal year, which often is not the same as the end of the calendar year. Here you will find an accounting of all the income the organization received during the year from taxes, fees, state and federal grants, and other sources. You'll also find status reports on all the organization's operating funds, such as its capital improvement fund, its debt-service fund and its general fund.

Making sense of the financial report, like the budget, isn't as hard as it may look. For one thing, usually the financial officer includes a narrative that highlights the most important points, at least from his or her viewpoint. But you should dig beyond the narrative and examine the numbers for yourself. The single most important section of the report is the statement of revenues, expenditures and changes in fund balance, which provides important measures of the organization's financial health. Depending on the comprehensiveness of the statement, you may have to refer to the budget document as well. You can check:

- Revenues actually received compared with budgeted revenues.
- Actual spending compared with budgeted spending.
- Actual spending compared with actual revenue.
- Changes in fund balances available for spending in years to come.

Look, for example, at Figure 14.5. This combined statement gives a picture of a city in good financial health. How can you tell? Look first at the bottom line. All of the end-of-year fund balances are positive. (Negative balances, or deficits, are shown in parentheses.) Now look at the totals in the far right-hand columns. They show an increase of more than $5 million in total funds available at the end of FY 1996 as compared with FY 1995. That seems a phenomenal increase, more than 50 percent. Better look more closely.

Run your eyes up those "total" columns. The explanation for the increase is about halfway up. In 1996, you see, the city sold general obligation bonds and received $6.8 million in extra income. Those bonds, of course, will have to be repaid over a period of years. In fact, then, the city has taken on a major new obligation rather than having reaped a windfall. If that hasn't already been reported, it should be now.

This statement also shows you what is happening from one year to the next in each of the city's major revenue sources. Sales tax revenue is up dramatically, while property tax revenue is down. That's good news for owners of homes and businesses. It suggests that the tax rate on real estate has been reduced. It also suggests that economic activity has picked up significantly. With a little more reporting, you may be onto another good story or two.

There are other clues that may lead to other stories. As in these

All Governmental Fund Types and Expendable Trust Funds for the Year Ended September 30, 1996

	Governmental Fund Types		
	General Fund	Special Revenue Funds	Debt Service Funds
REVENUES			
General property taxes	$ 663,932	$ 530,713	$192,104
Sales tax	3,967,138	3,367,510	——
Other local taxes	3,138,904	228,718	——
Licenses and permits	253,287	5,146	——
Fines	378,207	——	——
Fees and service charges	244,356	——	——
Special assessments authorized	——	——	——
Intragovernmental	4,139,690	——	——
Revenue from other governmental units	796,292	1,164,482	——
Building rentals	——	——	——
Interest	1,314,130	196,612	6,228
Miscellaneous	53,548	———	———
TOTAL REVENUES	14,949,484	5,493,181	198,332
EXPENDITURES			
Current:			
Policy development and administration	2,328,546	291,493	——
Public safety	8,403,851	——	——
Transportation	2,387,534	——	——
Health and environment	1,617,146	——	——
Personal development	1,915,376	622,065	——
Public buildings	——	——	——
Miscellaneous non-programmed activities:			
Interest expense	273,195	——	——
Other	34,975	——	——
Capital outlay	——	——	——
Debt service:			
Redemption of serial bonds	——	——	175,000
Interest	——	——	278,488
Fiscal agent fees	———	———	758
TOTAL EXPENDITURES	16,960,623	913,558	454,246
EXCESS (DEFICIENCY) OF REVENUES OVER EXPENDITURES	(2,011,139)	4,579,623	(255,914)

Figure 14.5.
A combined statement of revenues, expenditures and changes in fund balance.

Governmental Fund Types		Fiduciary Fund Type	Total (Memorandum only)	
Capital Projects Fund	Special Assessment Funds	Expendable Trust Funds	1996	1995
$ —	$ —	$ —	$ 1,386,749	$ 1,961,851
—	—	—	7,334,648	4,967,691
—	—	—	3,367,622	2,923,775
—	—	—	258,433	247,608
—	—	—	378,207	346,224
—	—	1,129,784	1,374,140	328,185
—	490,159	—	490,159	359,862
—	—	—	4,139,690	3,911,418
154,919	—	901,815	3,017,508	3,087,431
—	—	172,766	172,766	175,479
23,282	—	88,428	1,628,680	1,869,874
29,226	—	—	82,774	97,593
207,427	490,159	2,292,793	23,631,376	20,276,991
—	—	3,338	2,623,377	2,285,509
—	—	—	8,403,851	6,998,232
—	—	—	2,387,534	1,996,520
—	—	1,080,811	2,697,957	1,652,809
—	—	—	2,537,441	2,084,648
—	—	371,942	371,942	336,204
—	—	—	273,195	486,031
—	—	—	34,975	4,296
1,287,520	2,357,784	—	3,645,304	1,990,648
—	—	—	175,000	155,000
—	—	—	278,488	32,435
—	—	—	758	285
1,287,520	2,357,784	1,456,091	23,429,822	18,022,617
(1,080,093)	(1,867,625)	836,702	201,554	2,254,374

	Governmental Fund Types		
	General Fund	Special Revenue Funds	Debt Service Funds
OTHER FINANCING SOURCES (USES):			
Proceeds of general obligation bonds	—	—	—
Operating transfers from other funds	3,011,358	62,974	266,711
Operating transfers to other funds	(1,292,723)	(3,348,303)	—
TOTAL OTHER FINANCING SOURCES (USES)	1,718,635	(3,285,329)	266,711
EXCESS (DEFICIENCY) OF REVENUES AND OTHER FINANCING SOURCES OVER EXPENDITURES AND OTHER FINANCING USES	(292,504)	1,294,294	10,797
FUND BALANCES BEGINNING OF YEAR	4,195,912	3,004,533	43,645
Equity transfer to Recreation Services Fund	—	—	—
Contribution to Water & Electric Utility Fund	—	—	—
Contribution to Sanitary Sewer Utility Fund	—	—	—
Contribution to Regional Airport Fund	(200,000)	—	—
Contribution to Public Transportation Fund	—	—	—
Contribution to Parking Facilities Fund	—	—	—
Contribution to Recreation Services Fund	—	(152,000)	—
FUND BALANCES, END OF YEAR	$ 3,703,408	$4,146,827	$ 54,442

Figure 14.5.
Continued.

Governmental Fund Types		Fiduciary Fund Type	Total (Memorandum only)	
Capital Projects Fund	Special Assessment Funds	Expendable Trust Funds	1996	1995
5,681,633	1,134,261	—	6,815,894	—
415,038	469,865	—	4,225,946	3,466,261
—	(99,667)	(527,506)	(5,268,199)	(4,401,847)
6,096,671	1,504,459	(527,506)	5,773,641	(935,586)
5,016,578	(363,166)	309,196	5,975,195	1,318,788
628,856	781,248	514,378	9,168,572	8,489,184
—	—	(1,532)	(1,532)	(292,958)
—	—	—	—	(30,395)
—	—	—	—	(71,367)
—	—	—	(200,000)	(160,191)
—	—	—	—	(4,000)
—	—	—	—	(15,489)
—	—	—	(152,000)	(65,000)
$5,645,434	$ 418,082	$ 822,042	$14,790,235	$ 9,168,572

examples, they'll require more reporting and more explanation than reporters can pull from the numbers by themselves. Document in hand, head for the budget office. The guidelines offered here should help you shape your questions and understand the answers. With financial statements, as with budgets, look for changes, trends and comparisons. And always look hard at those numbers in parentheses.

Suggested Readings

Royko, Mike. *Boss.* New York: New American Library, 1971. A classic, brilliantly written study of urban machine politics.

Weinberg, Steve, ed. *The Reporter's Handbook*, Third Edition. New York: St. Martin's Press, 1996. The first comprehensive guide to using public records and documents, written by members of Investigative Reporters and Editors. A must for serious reporters. See also the readings at the end of the Investigative Reporting chapter. They'll be useful in beat reporting, too.

Exercises

1. You've been assigned to cover city government. Do some background reading in your local newspaper and the other sources described in this chapter. Then write a memo describing what you expect to be the most important issues on your new beat and whom you expect to be your most important human sources.

2. In the library or in a computer database, look up three recent national or international stories about a religious issue. Write a memo explaining how you would localize each story for your city. Include possible sources.

3. Look at the section of the budget document on page 321 headed "Department Expenditures." From the figures listed there, propose at least two story ideas. Suggest possible sources for the stories.

4. Get a copy of your city or town's current budget and come up with 10 questions a reporter should ask about the changes, patterns and trends the budget suggests.

5. Using Nexis or another public computer database, examine how two or three major newspapers cover a national beat, such as Congress or a federal agency. What similarities and differences do you see between that work and local coverage? The topics will be different, but what about sources? Do you see any different focus on reader interests?

6. Analyze a local news story about science, medicine or the environment. Identify the sources. If you were reporting this story, what other sources would you consult? What specific questions would you try to get answered?

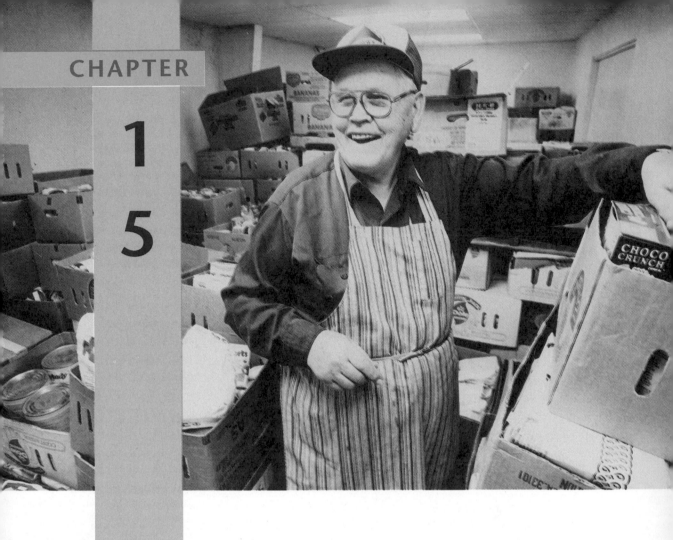

BUSINESS AND CONSUMER NEWS

*E*very story is a business story. A year after Reggie Lewis, captain of the Boston Celtics basketball team, died of a heart attack, the Wall Street Journal *ran an unusually long story detailing the fiscal decisions that may have contributed to his death.*

Protecting the reputation of a local hero was one motive for keeping drug use quiet, according to the Journal, *but there was also a lot of money involved. More than $15 million in insurance coverage of Lewis' contract was at stake. If doctors proved that Lewis' heart disease was caused by drugs, the insurance company wouldn't have to pay. Furthermore, the team's parent company, the Celtics Limited Partnership, was in the midst of a $30 million transaction that would have allowed it to buy a television station. A drug-related scandal, it was felt, could drive leery bankers away.*

The Lewis family and his team collected on the policy. In the fiscal year ending June 30, 1994, the partnership posted record earnings, boosted in part by $5.6 million in proceeds from Reggie Lewis' life insurance. Therein lies the business story.

Sports is obviously big business, but if you look closely, virtually every aspect of life is about business. Everything that is not run by the government is run by some kind of private enterprise. If you open your mind to business journalism, it is much less challenging to find stories than it is to narrow your focus.

Business stories are showing up all over the newspaper. There was a time when business was sandwiched between the comics and the classifieds, but now stories about Federal Reserve interest rates routinely make the front page. Why? Because readers want to know where interest rates are headed before they buy a car or invest in a house or stocks.

Page One stories have included one on the impact of the Republican-controlled Congress, on America's pocketbooks and one on how low unemployment drives up wages. For whatever reason, people are more interested in money matters today than they have been in the past, which causes a "chicken or egg" debate among business journalists: Does increased coverage of financial affairs create interest, or does increased interest inspire coverage?

Maybe it's neither. Maybe journalists are finally recognizing the basic tenet: Every story is a business story.

Consider day care, for example. Two decades ago, day care wasn't even a commonly used term. Today, as more and more children are born into two wage-earner families, it is commonplace. But what happens if there aren't enough day-care centers in your community? If parents can't find a safe, nurturing place, they may choose not to work. If the price of day care jumps or the quality declines, it has a huge impact on thousands of workers.

And what if the government mandates that child-care workers should receive health insurance and sick days? What does that do to the price and availability of day care?

You see? Any story can be a business story.

Yet most business desks of the past limited themselves to movements in stock prices or the consumer price index. This put many readers to sleep and ignored the majority of the potential audience.

Stock prices are still valid, of course. Many investors and business people consult their daily newspapers for just those numbers. But today, more newspapers are making the effort to explain the numbers. As in other sections of the paper, they are focusing on what those numbers mean to the reader. Business journalists are also cutting out a lot of the jargon that often confused potential readers. Instead, they are explaining things in common-sense language that most people understand. As a result, readership—and the amount of ink publishers are willing to give business news—are on the rise.

So are stories about how to spend, save and invest money. Consumer stories, which include everything from how to save money on car repairs to how to invest an inheritance, are common.

The number of jobs in business journalism is also growing. Many newspapers have "Business Monday" sections, as well as special sections that focus on specific issues, like real estate or automobiles. There are dozens of magazines devoted to personal finance, consumer news and even the business of sports. Radio and television are also expanding their coverage. CNN and CNBC, for example, devote hours of air time to consumer and economic news. There also is a broad selection of trade publications that focus on specific industries. But to get a job on the business desk, you need to understand basic business terminology and basic math. You also need to learn how to read financial statements, which is surprisingly easy. Beyond that, you need the skills of any journalist: perseverance, curiosity and an ability to ask questions and get answers.

Preparing to Cover Business News

The range of business stories can be as broad as the range of business itself. A business story may be about promotions and retirements. It may concentrate on a company's potential profits, of interest to investors and potential investors in that company. It can be a story about a new kind of instant camera that would interest not just shareholders of the company but potential buyers as well. It may deal with a drought in Kansas that affects the price farmers in Michigan will get for their wheat and the price homemakers in Florida will pay for English muffins.

These stories have obvious local angles. Sometimes, though, the local angle is not that obvious. The story about a decision by the Federal Reserve Board's Open Market Committee to expand or tighten the money supply may seem far removed from your audience. But that decision can affect your readers' ability to get a loan for a new car or house and the rate they pay for that loan. Or it can affect them in how

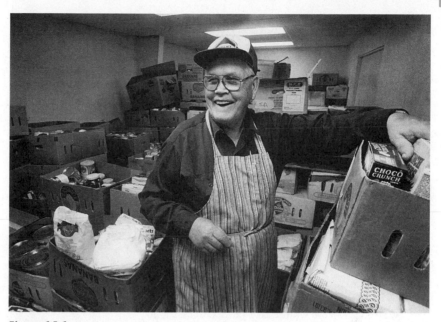

Figure 15.1.
Virtually every news story is a business news story. From this food bank worker, a reporter could learn a lot about the local economy, such as who is donating food and how many people are in need.

it adds to or subtracts from inflation. News of a sizable trade deficit for the United States may weaken the value of the dollar and increase the price of a Sony TV, a Volkswagen or a bottle of Cutty Sark Scotch whisky. It takes skill, but a good business journalist can make these seemingly esoteric stories clear and relevant to the audience.

Although many major corporate and economic decisions that affect us all are made in Washington, New York, Chicago and a few other major metropolitan centers, those cities do not have a monopoly on the creation and coverage of business news. Even in towns of a few thousand residents, businesses will be opening or closing, manufacturing plants will be increasing or decreasing production, hiring or firing employees. And those residents will be spending money for houses or cars, ski trips or Harris tweeds, or socking it away in the town's banks or savings and loan associations. There is a business story in every such development.

Business stories can be as bright and as interesting as any story in any other section of the paper. That is demonstrated regularly in such publications as the *Wall Street Journal*, the *New York Times*, the *Chicago Tribune*, *Business Week* and *Fortune* magazine. And it is becoming more common in small papers across the country. Here, for example, is the beginning of a *York Daily Record* story about a drive to increase financial regulation of cemeteries:

When Miriam Speck buried her husband Kenneth on Feb. 26, it was a sad day made sadder by the poor condition of the cemetery.

Her husband's grave at Suburban Memorial Gardens had been dug that morning, and fresh, soggy equipment tracks were still visible near the grave when the family gathered around it.

"We literally stood there with mud gushing up over our shoes," said Speck's daughter Donna Sharp. Her mother sat in the only chair provided for the service. It, too, was sinking down in the mud.

It was a lousy way to say good-bye to a husband and father. But the unnecessary grief was not over. It would drag on several more weeks, only to be punctuated by one final—and expensive—indignity.

During weekly visits to Kenneth's grave, Speck and her daughter noticed it was not being maintained. The ground over the grave had sunk about a foot and water was standing in it. The fill-in dirt was still piled off to the side.

So, two months after the burial, when the ground had thawed, mother and daughter took matters into their own hands. On a beautiful spring day they took a shovel to the cemetery to finish filling the grave themselves.

"It was horrible," Sharp recalled. "It was terrible."

While the two women were standing around the grave, the cemetery's caretaker drove up, Sharp said. He explained to them the bitter history of the cemetery, how the former owner, Don Snyder, had died last year leaving virtually no money to run it, and how the new owner was taking over.

The women were pleased that someone would be rescuing the cemetery, which is on Bull Road in Conewago Township. But their joy turned to anger once again when they found out the bronze grave marker the Specks had bought for $450 in 1977 was nowhere to be found.

Not only that, if her mother wanted a marker for her husband's grave, she would have to buy one—for the second time—from the new owner.

Sadly, Snyder had died owing more than $350,000 in personal debt that was secured by the cemetery. He had also failed to set aside funds to cover purchases of vaults and grave markers he had sold to people before they were needed. Similar situations around the state have led the state legislature to consider greater regulation of cemeteries and funeral homes.

How to Report Business Stories

What separates a business story from a soccer story—or, for that matter, a soccer story from a story about atomic particles—is the knowledge and language required to ask the right questions, to recognize the newsworthy answers and to write the story in a way that the reader without specialized knowledge will understand. A reporter who understands the subject can explain what the jargon means.

For example, the term "prime rate" by itself may be meaningless to a majority of newspaper readers. If the reporter explains that the prime rate is a benchmark interest rate banks quote to their cus-

"Money is the source of all power, the source of all evil"—and thus the source of good stories.

Deogun thinks his generalist background, both in liberal arts and in journalism, has prepared him well. Business writers need to understand the social and political context in which their subjects operate.

"I use here the same reporting skills you'd use on any beat," he adds. "If tomorrow I had to go cover fly-fishing, I wouldn't know diddley. But I'd learn. You read a lot and ask people questions."

Too much specialization in a field such as business can even be a handicap. The *Journal* serves an audience more involved in business than the audiences of most daily papers or broadcast outlets, but a reporter's job still includes a great deal of translating from the jargon of the specialist into everyday English.

A business reporter, Deogun understands, must be able to speak the technical language without falling into the trap of also writing it. "Most of your readers don't know that much about business," he observed.

Clear thinking and clear writing remain essential.

tomers and that it is a somewhat negotiable figure, readers can see that an increase of one percentage point in the prime rate could result in a higher rate of interest on a car loan or home mortgage.

But beware of writing in such simplistic terms that you tell your readers nothing useful. Besides failing your readers, you will damage respect for your newspaper in the business community. The *Wall Street Journal* avoids both traps by shunning jargon as much as possible and explaining any technical terms essential to the story. In one story, for example, the *Journal* explained the terms "Federal Open Market Committee," "federal funds rate," "M1," "M2" and "free-reserve position." The sophisticated reader might know what those terms mean, but no doubt many of the paper's readers would not.

Former presidential economic adviser Gardner Ackley once said he would like to see two things in people covering economics and business news: first, that they had taken a course in economics, and second, that they had passed it. Financial journalist Louis Rukeyser urges newspapers to enlarge their "coverage of the nation's economic scene: reporting, analysis and commentary of the highest order, adequately and prominently displayed. . . ."

A 1994 study by the First Amendment Center of the Freedom Forum called "The Headline vs. The Bottom Line: Mutual Distrust Between Business and the News Media" confirmed what business people and business journalists alike have long suspected: Neither trusts the other.

"Journalists and business executives are not just adversaries," the authors say. "Their relationship is too often characterized by lying and unfair treatment."

That conclusion was based on the fact that 38 percent of journalists responding to the questionnaire disagreed with the statement "Business journalists always treat their subjects fairly." And 69 percent of the business people responding disagreed with the statement "Business people are always candid and truthful with reporters."

The study sheds light on business journalists' biggest challenge: how to get information from someone who does not legally have to tell you anything. It often takes much more clever reporting skills to coax a story out of a business source than it does out of a government official. After all, almost all government information is open to the public. Many business records are not.

As John Seigenthaler, founder of the First Amendment Center, pointed out, "There is a feeling [among business executives] that the profit motive simply isn't understood as being as American as apple pie by numbers of journalists."

Among journalists, on the other hand, "There's a strong sense that business executives malinger, are not responsible and for the most part misrepresent and even more often refuse to communicate," he said.

The mistrust that many business people have of the press can make it difficult to cover stories adequately, even when it would be in their interest to see that the story is told. Or, if executives are willing to talk, they may become angry if the reporter quotes an opposing point of view or points out a wart on the corporate visage.

The best antidote a reporter can use against this animosity is to report fairly and accurately what a business is doing and saying. By always being fair, you usually can win the trust and confidence of business people, even if they reserve admiration for someone who can squeeze a few more cents of per-share profits out of the third quarter.

Because business executives tend to be cautious when it comes to talking with reporters, it may help you to dress more like a business manager than a social protester. That does not mean that you have to think like a manager, but appearances do count, and business people, like reporters, plumbers, generals and linebackers, feel more comfortable with their own kind.

The more you can demonstrate that you understand their business, the more likely you are to generate the trust that will draw out the information you seek. "Understanding" is not synonymous with "sympathy," but ignorance usually means a reporter is apt to misinterpret what is said.

Although public relations people often are helpful in providing background information and directing you to the executives who can provide other comment and information, you should try to get to know as many company officials as you can. Sometimes you can do this best through a "harmless" background interview, one not generated by a crisis but intended simply to learn about what the company is doing. Perhaps you can arrange to have lunch, to see what the officials are thinking about and to give them a chance to see you are probably not the demon they may have thought you to be.

Always remember that a company, government agency or pressure group may be trying to use you to plant stories that serve some special interest. Companies want a story to make them look promising to investors with the hope of driving up the price of the stock or to make them attractive merger partners. If you are suspicious, do some more digging; talk to competitors and analysts, and ask detailed questions. Just because a company or some other group is pushing a story does not mean you have to write it. The best place for some interview notes is the wastebasket.

Business journalists also are particularly challenged by conflict of interest issues, since they often write stories—some of which are unfavorable—about advertisers. Business editors across the country have become increasingly concerned as advertisers threaten to pull advertising over unfavorable coverage. A story on how to deal with car salesmen in the *San Jose Mercury News* inspired area car dealers to stage an advertising boycott that cost the paper $200,000 worth of ads a week.

Real estate agents and grocers, both traditionally large advertis-

> *"We need more bright young journalists educated and trained, able and willing to operate on that broad frontier where politics and economics meet—and confuse each other."*
> —*Louis Rukeyser, financial journalist*

ers, have worked together to pressure other newspapers. While newspapers make a show of not caving in to such pressures, advertiser threats can produce a chilling effect in the news room.

It is challenging to cover business. To do so effectively, a business reporter should be all the things any good reporter is—honest, fair, alert to possible new stories and to new angles on old stories. Business writing can be rewarding, both financially (because specialists usually earn premium pay) and intellectually.

Where to Find Business News

The starting point in writing a business story is similar to the first step in reporting any story—understanding the subject you're writing about. For the business reporter, that almost always means some basic research into the subject. For openers, check your paper's library to learn what's been written locally about your topic or company.

Then turn to your computer. If you're at a publication that subscribes to an on-line service, there is a broad spectrum of databases that provide lists and summaries of stories published on a broad range of subjects. The truly adept can plumb raw data, including actual stock market transactions, to track the impact of announcements, mergers and promotions on stock. But even people who are intimidated by the Internet can access annual reports, stock analyses, press releases and other announcements using simple computer searches.

Of growing importance are computer searches of databases that provide lists and summaries of stories published on a range of topics. Newsearch, Standard & Poor's, Predicasts, Dow Jones and Disclosure Inc. are some of the companies providing these data. Reuters, Dow Jones and Bloomberg Business News also provide background information on companies and securities, historical prices and real-time news on business and economic issues. Likewise, Business Wire, PR Newswire, Knight-Ridder/Tribune Business News, all major newspapers and magazines and the Associated Press all provide on-line business information.

If your publication doesn't subscribe to an on-line service or if you can't find what you're looking for in cyberspace, it's time to move to paper information sources. The good business reporter knows how to use the *Reader's Guide to Periodical Literature*, the *Business Periodicals Index*, the *New York Times Index*, the *Wall Street Journal Index* and perhaps the *National Newspaper Index* (which indexes the *Times*, the *Journal*, the *Los Angeles Times* and the *Washington Post*). These indexes will tell you where to find stories about your business or industry.

Another valuable secondary source for business reporters is *Predicasts' F & S Index of Corporations and Industries*, considered by many the best index for company and industry information. Predicasts indexes a broad range of business, financial and industrial periodicals, plus a few reports by brokerage houses. For information on foreign companies, see *Predicasts' F & S Index International*. The *Public Affairs Information Service Bulletin* is a less inclusive index from the areas of economics, social conditions, public administration and international relations.

Records and Reports

Here are some good sources of information that you will find invaluable when writing business stories. Remember, many of these can be accessed through various on-line databases, which means you can decide on a question, log on and have the information you need right away.

Corporate data. Basic information on corporations can be found in three directories published annually. Your university or public library probably has all three. *Dun & Bradstreet's Million Dollar Directory* includes almost 40,000 U.S. companies worth $1 million or more. It lists officers and directors, products or services, sales, number of employees and addresses and telephone numbers. The *Middle Market Directory* profiles companies worth $500,000 to $999,999. The three-volume *Standard & Poor's Register of Corporations, Directors and Executives* provides similar information for some 36,000 U.S. and Canadian companies. Volume 2 lists executives and directors with brief biographies. The third directory is the *Thomas Register of American Manufacturers* and the *Thomas Register Catalog File*. The 11 volumes are more comprehensive than the other two directories.

Investment data. To get specific information about the financial performance of a company or an industry, check reports prepared by Standard & Poor's (especially valuable is S&P's Compustat Services, Inc.), Moody's, Dun & Bradstreet or Value Line Investment Survey. These reports also discuss company prospects and major trends. Also helpful are annual corporate scoreboards prepared by *Fortune*, *Business Week* and *Forbes* magazines. *Business Week* uses S&P's Compustat to prepare its scoreboard. You would be wise to purchase and file these issues for future reference.

Financial ratios. To assess a company's financial picture and management, you should compare your subject's financial ratios with the averages for other firms in the same industry. Industry ratios and averages can be found in reports prepared by Dun & Bradstreet, Moody's and S&P's Compustat and in a number of trade journals.

Company filings. For years, the Securities and Exchange Commission operated under the guiding principle that companies should make available a maximum amount of information so that stockholders could make the most informed decision regarding management's performance. The SEC preferred to keep out of corporate affairs and let the stockholders provide necessary discipline. Much of that information was made public through SEC filings. In recent years, the SEC has required less information, but corpo-

---

Records and reports to use as sources

▪ *Corporate data*
▪ *Investment data*
▪ *Financial data*
▪ *Company filings*
▪ *Trade press*
▪ *Newsletters*
▪ *Directories*
▪ *Court records*
▪ *Local regulators*

Where to look for publicly held companies' SEC filings

13-D. *Lists owners of more than 5 percent of the voting stock. Filed within 10 business days. Must report increases and decreases of holdings.*

13-F. *Quarterly report of ownership by institutional investors. Includes holders of less than 5 percent of the company.*

8-K. *Report of significant incident.*

10-Q. *Quarterly financial statement.*

10-K. *Annual financial statement. Includes number of employees, lists of major real estate and equipment holdings, significant legal proceedings. Many other important documents, such as labor contracts, are listed by reference and can be acquired through the company, Freedom of Information Act request or private service.*

Proxy statement. *Contains information on executive salaries, director information, shareholder voting issues.*

Annual report to shareholders. *May lack much of the data found in the 10-K.*

Securities registration statement/prospectus. *Submitted when new stock is to be issued; usually contains same information as 10K and proxy, but is more up to date.*

rate filings remain a valuable source of information for reporters. You should start with the annual report, which will give you an attractively packaged overview of the company's operations and finances. The 10-K, a more detailed document required by the SEC, also will give you the number of employees, a list of major real estate and equipment holdings, and any significant legal proceedings. Many other important documents, such as labor contracts, are listed by reference and can be acquired through the company, Freedom of Information Act request or private service such as Disclosure Inc. The proxy statement, which goes to shareholders before the annual meeting or other important meetings, provides an outline of issues to be voted on, as well as executive salaries and information on the company's directors. The proxy also sometimes contains leads about the company's business dealings. Interesting nuggets are found under mundane headings like "other matters" or "legal proceedings." Always read anything pertaining to lawsuits. That can, in turn, lead you to public documents regarding a particular suit.

Many companies are quite willing to send you their annual report, 10-K and proxy statement. They may even send you the other documents outlined above. To keep up with SEC filings, you may want to follow the SEC News Digest at your local library. To obtain specific filings, you can contact an organization such as Disclosure Inc., which, for a fee, will provide copies of reports filed with the SEC by public companies.

Trade press. Beyond the newspapers and magazines you all know and read is another segment of journalism known as the **trade press**. In these journals and house organs you will find grocers talking with grocers, undertakers talking with undertakers and bankers talking with bankers. You will learn the important issues in a field, how an industry markets its products and services, and what legislation it fears and favors. Interested in health care and physicians? Try *Medical Economics*, where investigative reporter Jessica Mitford predicts you will find "many a crass and wonderfully quotable appeal to the avarice of the practitioners of the healing arts." When Chris Welles wrote a piece on the health hazards of modern cosmetics, much of his best information came from trade magazines. He found the specific periodicals by looking in the *Drug & Cosmetics Periodicals Index* and the *F & S Index of Corporations and Industries*.

A number of trade publications are independent and objective. Among them are *Advertising Age, Aviation Week & Space Technology, Institutional Investor, Oil & Gas Journal, American Banker, Medical World News* and *Variety*. Many more, however, are virtual industry public relations organs. Even these can be valuable for learning about current issues, marketing and lobbying strategies and even market shares. To find trade publications, consult the *Standard Periodical Directory, Ulrich's International Periodicals Directory, Standard Rate & Data Service: Business Publication Rates and Data*, and *Gale Directory of Publications and Broadcast Media*.

Newsletters. Newsletters have become an important source of inside information in recent years. Some are purely ideological, but others can be valuable. Among the best are *Energy Daily, Nucleonics Week, Education Daily, Higher Education Daily* and the *Washington Report on Medicine.* To find newsletters, consult *The Newsletter Yearbook Directory.*

Directories. Directories can be an invaluable tool in seeking information on companies, organizations or individuals. You can use them to learn who makes a certain product, to identify company officers or directors, or to find an expert source for an interview. Basic directories include *Who's Who, Directory of Directories, Guide to American Directories, Consultants and Consulting Organizations Directory, Directory of Special Libraries & Information Centers, Research Centers Directory, Consumer Sourcebook, Statistical Sources,* and *Directory of Industrial Data Sources.* To contact companies by phone or mail, look in the *National Directory of Addresses and Telephone Numbers,* published by Concord Reference Books Inc.

Court records. Most companies disclose only information required by the SEC. But when a corporation sues or is sued, an extensive amount of material becomes available. Likewise, criminal action against principals in a firm can provide the leads to a good story, as reporters at the *Denver Post* learned:

> Owen Taranta, a former financial officer of MiniScribe Corp., testified yesterday that the company's former chairman, Q.T. Wiles, directed an illegal scheme to cover a $15 million inventory hole.
>
> Wiles, 75, is charged with three counts of fraud in connection with the 1990 bankruptcy of the Longmont disk drive company.
>
> Taranta, of Scottsdale, Ariz., testified that company officials "shipped air" in 1987 and 1988 in order to create a paper trail that would cover MiniScribe's inventory shortfalls. Taranta said the idea for the cover-up came during an Oct. 14, 1987, meeting among company officials at which Wiles approved the scheme.
>
> But H. Alan Dill, Wiles' attorney, repeatedly attacked the credibility of Taranta, who was offered immunity by the federal government for his testimony.
>
> Dill questioned whether Taranta, a Certified Public Accountant, had ever bragged about his role in the inventory scheme, which Taranta denied. Dill also reiterated that Taranta participated with other company officials in 1987 when bricks were packed into boxes instead of disk drives to create false shipping records.

> Stephen Keating, the reporter, said later that the court testimony offered details that he had been unable to obtain. "They put bricks into boxes to inflate inventory. But until the testimony, no one really knew what was happening."

It is important to check court testimony and records of all levels, including those of bankruptcy and divorce court.

Local regulators. Frequently businesses want to enlarge their facilities or expand into new markets. To do so, a business may seek funds from an industrial revenue bond authority, which helps the company obtain large sums of money at below-market rates. Or when an institution such as a hospital wants to expand its services, often it must make a case for the expansion before a regional or local agency. In either case, documents filed to support the requests may be revealing and may put into the public record information that previously was unobtainable.

Others. The preceding items are certainly not exhaustive. Other relevant materials may be found at local tax and record-keeping offices, as well as in filings with the Federal Trade Commission, the Federal Communications Commission, the Food and Drug Administration, the Interstate Commerce Commission, the Labor Department and various state agencies. *Crain's Chicago Business* used Census Bureau figures as the basis of a story on retail sales trends. The U.S. Government Manual lists and describes government agencies, including their functions and programs. And a number of private firms specialize in economic analysis, such as the WEFA Group and Data Resources Inc. In writing about the benefits OPEC could reap from the oil company mergers, the *Wall Street Journal* cited figures generated by WEFA.

Don't overlook documents and testimony from congressional hearings. Chris Welles drew much of the best material for his book on the ending of fixed brokerage commissions, *The Last Days of the Club*, from the 29 volumes of hearings and reports that came out of several years of investigations by two congressional subcommittees. The best indication of the vast array of materials available is found in the preface to *Empire*, the extensive examination of the Howard Hughes empire by Donald L. Barlett and James B. Steele. They cite as their sources:

> thousands of Hughes' handwritten and dictated memoranda, family letters, CIA memoranda, FBI reports, contracts with nearly a dozen departments and agencies of the federal government, loan agreements, corporate charters, census reports, college records, federal income-tax returns, Oral History transcripts, partnership agreements, autopsy reports, birth and death records, marriage license applications, divorce records, naturalization petitions, bankruptcy records, corporation annual reports, stock offering circulars, real estate assessment records, notary public commissions, applications for pilot certificates, powers of attorney, minutes of board meetings of Hughes' companies, police records, transcripts of Securities and Exchange Commission proceedings, annual assessment work affidavits, transcripts of Civil Aeronautics Board proceedings, the daily logs of Hughes' activities, hearings and reports of committees of the House of Representatives and Senate, transcripts of Federal Communications Commission proceedings, wills, estates records, grand jury testimony, trial transcripts, civil and criminal court records.

Human sources on the business beat

- *Company officials*
- *Analysts*
- *Academic experts*
- *Associations*
- *Chamber of commerce officials*
- *Former employees*
- *Labor leaders*

Human Sources

Who are the people you should talk to on the business beat? Here are some who are important sources of information:

Company officials. Although many public relations people can be helpful, the most valuable information probably will come from the head of the corporation or its divisions. Chief executive officers are powerful people, either out front or behind the scenes, in your community. They are often interesting, usually well informed. Not all of them will be glad to see you, though in recent years companies and top executives have started to realize the importance of communicating their point of view to the public. Don't automatically assume the public relations person is trying to block your path. Many people working in corporate communications are truly professional, and providing information to journalists is part of their job. Remember, though, that they are paid to make the company look good, so they will likely point you in the direction of the company's viewpoint. Public relations professionals aren't objective, but that doesn't mean that the information they provide is untrue. Instead, you should assume that it is being packaged to show the company in its best light.

Analysts. To learn what the experts think about specific companies, many business reporters contact securities analysts. Analysts can be valuable if they are not overused and if you get information on the company from other sources as well. Don't assume that analysts are all-knowing, infallible seers. Remember, too, that a broker is selling stock and is not the same as an analyst. When it wrote about the possibility that broadcasting and entertainment companies could become takeover targets, the *Wall Street Journal* strengthened its story with a quote from an analyst with Donaldson Lufkin & Jenrette Securities. To find the appropriate analyst, consult *Investment Decisions Directory of Wall Street Research*, also called *Nelson's Directory*, which is a must for any business department's library.

Other analysts and researchers, frequently economists, are employed by banks, trade groups, chambers of commerce and local businesses. They often are willing to talk because the exposure is good for their organizations.

Academic experts. Your college or university will have faculty members with training and experience in varying areas of business and economics. Often they are good sources of local reaction to national developments or analysis of economic trends. They are usually happy to cooperate. Many university public information offices prepare lists of their nationally or regionally known experts and their phone numbers. The lists are available for the asking.

Associations. Although trade associations clearly represent the interests of their members, they can provide expert commentary on current issues or give explanations from the perspective of the industry. When *The New York Times* reported on the revival of the moving industry, the Household Goods Carriers Bureau, a major trade group, proved to be an important source. *The Wall Street Journal* found the National Association of Realtors a valuable source for a story on housing costs. To find trade associations, look in the *Encyclopedia of Associations* or the *National Trade and Professional Associations of the United States.*

Chamber of Commerce officials. Their bias is clearly pro-business, and they will seldom make an on-the-record negative comment about business, but they usually know who is who and what is what in the business community. The chamber may be involved in such projects as downtown revitalization and industry recruiting.

Former employees. The best business reporters say that frequently their most valuable sources are former employees of the company they're profiling. Writes Welles, "Nobody knows more about a corporation than someone who has actually worked there." He warns, "Many, probably most, have axes to grind, especially if they were fired; indeed, the more willing they are to talk, the more biased they are likely to be." The good reporter will show care in using materials thus gained.

Labor leaders. For the other side of many business stories and for pieces on working conditions, upcoming contracts and politics, get to know local union officials. The workings, legal and otherwise, of unions make good stories, too.

Others. Don't overlook the value of a company's customers, suppliers and competitors. You also may want to consult with local bankers, legislators, legislative staff members, law enforcement agencies and regulators, board members, oversight committee members and the like.

Announcements and Meetings

The source of much business news, and the *starting point* for many good stories, is the announcement by a company of a new product or the firm's reaction to some action by a government agency. Such announcements should be treated like any news release. The same standards apply to judging newsworthiness, and the same reporting techniques come into play.

The news may come in a news conference, which may be called to respond to a general situation such as a strike or takeover attempt. Or it may be called to try to add some glitter to a corporate announcement the company feels will be ignored if done by news releases alone. You can almost tell how newsworthy something is going to be by the amount of paraphernalia on hand in the news conference room. The more charts, graphs, enlarged photos, projectors and screens in the room, the more likely you are to be dazzled instead of enlightened. They should not be ignored, however, because you can never be sure in advance that something newsworthy will *not* be said.

If you work in a city where one or more corporations are based, you may have the opportunity to cover an annual meeting, which invariably produces some news. Although some are more lively and more newsworthy than others, all say something about the state of the company's business and provide an opportunity for shareholders to ask management questions about the company's performance. The time leading up to the annual meeting also can produce drama, as key players jockey for position. Here, for example, is a story from the

Columbia (Mo.) *Daily Tribune* about managerial maneuverings at a local company:

Tomorrow morning, about 270 stockholders will vote to settle a vicious feud over one of Columbia's crown jewel companies. The dispute became a civil war this year, with friends of 20 years taking sides against each other, co-founder of the company against co-founder, former mentor against student, even brother against brother.

At stake is control of Analytical Bio-Chemistry Laboratories Inc., better known as ABC Labs. The company's shareholders will meet tomorrow at the Holiday Inn Executive Center to choose six directors to the nine-member board.

Those elected will control the future of a firm whose sales last year reached $21 million, up from $7 million four years ago. Also at stake is the livelihood of some 370 employees of the environmental testing firm, about half of whom are highly skilled scientists and technicians.

The battle has very little to do with business and everything to do with personality conflicts, hurt feelings and control. There is little dispute between the groups over the future of the firm, the general philosophy for growth or the business opportunities available for the rapidly growing company. Instead, the battle is over who will sit in the board seats and call the shots.

Reporter Enterprise

As in other areas of journalism, often the best business news stories are generated by a reporter's own initiative, sparked by a hunch or a tip passed along by an editor, a shareholder or a disgruntled employee or customer. Sometimes, a self-promoting source can lead to a good story. When the president of a commodity options firm called the *Boston Globe* to suggest a story on her company, reporter Susan Trausch was dispatched. It was a new company and headed by a woman. But the reporter quickly became suspicious of some things she saw and was told. The investigation that followed produced a series on abuses in an unregulated industry and won several national prizes. The original caller got her name in the paper, all right, but hardly as she had expected.

In other cases a news release may raise questions that turn into stories. For example, a routine announcement of an executive appointment may lead a curious reporter to a story about the financial problems that produced the changes in leadership. A stockholder's question may result in a story about a new trend in corporate financing or a shift in emphasis on operations within the company. Sometimes, an offhand comment at lunch about what one executive has heard about another company will lead to a front-page story after you do some digging. Or a former employee's call that a company is quietly laying off workers may produce a story about the firm's declining fortunes.

Most major business stories are developed by using a combina-

Figure 15.2.
Trade shows bring news of consumer and business products that will be marketed in the coming selling season. Bill Gates, head of Microsoft, drew a large crowd at his news conference at a computer exposition.

tion of human and documentary sources. The techniques are no different from those of covering city hall, sports or science.

Looking at the Numbers

Although most reporters find accounting about as appealing as quantum physics or microbiology, an understanding of the numbers business generates is essential to any intelligent analysis of a company or industry. The most complete summary of the financial picture of a business is found in the annual report and the 10-K.

An annual report may be viewed as a statement of the image a company wants to project. Some companies print their reports on the highest-quality paper and fill them with big, bright color pictures; others try to project an image of dignity. Occasionally an annual report's presentation will reflect the financial health or illness of a company. The 1980 Chrysler Corp. report remains a classic; the company reported a net loss of $1.7 billion in a black-and-white report that was 32 pages long, on plain paper stock and without a single photograph. The next year it reported a loss of "only" $475 million in a report on heavier paper, and with 16 color pictures of its best-selling products. In 1982 Chrysler touted a profit of $170 million in a splashy, multicolored report that included a color portrait of then-chairman Lee Iacocca.

More than 100 million copies of annual reports are pumped out each year at a cost of $1 to $6 each. They can be a valuable tool, but you should realize that they are not written to be read like a magazine. Rather, annual reports should be approached by sections with specific goals in mind. Accountants suggest that readers skim sections and move from point to point. They note that it is less like reading than a process of digging out information.

Most veteran reporters start with the auditor's report, which is generally located near the back of the annual report, together with basic financial data, explanations of footnotes and supplementary financial information. The basic auditor's report, ranging from one long paragraph to three or four paragraphs, states that the material conforms to generally accepted auditing standards and that it fairly presents the financial condition of the company.

Until recently, an auditor's report longer than two paragraphs indicated trouble. Now, however, reporters must read the entire report closely because auditors tuck warnings of trouble in the middle of the standard language they use in all reports.

Next, move on to the footnotes, where the seeds of many fascinating stories may be germinating among the innocuous prose and numbers that follow and supplement the company's basic financial data. Then, flip back to the front of the annual report and find the report from the chairman or chairwoman. It is usually addressed "To our shareholders" and should give an overview of the company's performance.

Warren Buffett, chairman of Berkshire Hathaway Inc., is legendary for his straightforward assessment of company performance. Buffett's letters to shareholders can run to 20 pages, include references to investment guru Ben Graham, Adam Smith and Karl Marx, and offer lessons in investment theory. His letters have been compiled and make fascinating reading.

Next, take a few minutes to examine the company's operating divisions to get an idea of its different products. You should look for areas that will help the company in the future. Perhaps a new product has been developed or another company has been acquired that will boost profits.

After that you're ready to look at the numbers. Here are a few things to watch for:

Balance sheet. This is a snapshot of the company on one day, generally the last day of the fiscal year. The left side of the balance sheet lists the assets, or what the company owns. On the right side are the liabilities, or what the company owes, and the shareholders' equity, or the dollar value of what stockholders own. The two sides must balance, so the balance sheet can be summarized as assets equal liabilities plus shareholders' equity. The balance sheet shows how the year in question compares with the previous year. Reporters should note any significant changes worth exploring for a possible story.

Highlights of an annual report

- *Balance sheet*
- *Income statement*
- *Return on sales*
- *Return on equity*
- *Dividends*

Income statement. This report, also referred to as an *earnings statement* or *statement of profit and loss*, answers the key question: How much money did the company make for the year? Look first at net sales or operating revenues and determine if they went up or down. If they increased, did they increase faster than last year and faster than the rate of inflation? If sales lagged behind inflation, the company could have serious problems.

Return on sales. Company management and financial analysts calculate a number of ratios to gain better insights into the financial health of an organization. One important test of earnings is the relation of net income to sales, which is obtained by dividing net income by sales. This will tell you how much profit after taxes was produced by each dollar of sales. Reporters should remember that percentages can vary widely by industry.

Return on equity. This ratio, which shows how effectively a company's invested capital is working, is obtained by dividing net income minus preferred dividends by the common stockholders' equity for the previous year. The 1994 *Business Week* 1000 composite return on equity was 12.8 percent, a jump from 10.4 percent the preceding year.

Dividends. These are declared quarterly and generally are prominently noted in the annual report. Dividends are an inducement to shareholders to invest in the company. Because companies want to see dividends rise each quarter, they sometimes go so far as to change their accounting or pension assumptions so enough funds will be available to increase dividends. Other companies, such as Berkshire Hathaway Inc., declare no dividends because they prefer to reinvest profits internally.

Now that you have an idea of how to examine an annual report and its numbers, it is time for some important words of caution. First, the numbers in an annual report, though certified by an auditor and presented in accordance with Securities and Exchange Commission regulations, are not definite because they are a function of the accounting assumptions used in their preparation. That leads to the second and third points: Look at a company's numbers in the context of both its industry and several years' performance. To understand how well a firm is performing, examine the numbers along with those of other firms in the same industry. For example, the debt-equity ratios of utilities are much higher than those of most manufacturing companies, such as auto manufacturers. Look at how the company has performed for the last five to 10 years. Then you will discern trends, instead of basing your conclusions on a year's performance, which may be atypical.

The next caution: Don't think reading this section or passing an accounting course makes you qualified to analyze a company's finances. Rather, use the knowledge gained in this chapter to reach some preliminary conclusions that you should pursue with the experts and then with company officials. Only the best reporters are qualified to draw conclusions from company financial data and then only after years of study and practice.

A Business Mini-Glossary

A few important terms for business reporting:

Bonds. Governments and corporations issue bonds to raise capital. The bonds pay interest at a stated rate and are redeemable on a predetermined maturity date.

Constant dollars. Because of inflation, $10 doesn't buy in 1995 what it did in 1975. Constant dollars take inflation into account by figuring their value compared with a base period.

Consumer Price Index. A measure of the relative price of goods and services, the CPI is based on the net change compared with a base period. An index of 115 means the price has increased 15 percent since the base period. Thus, to report the significance of a rise or drop in the CPI, you need to know the base year.

Dow Jones Industrial Index. This is the principal daily measure of stock prices. It is based on the combined value of 30 major stocks. It reached 4,000 for the first time on Feb. 22, 1995.

IRA. Individual Retirement Accounts. These are savings accounts whose earnings (as well as some contributions) are tax-free until withdrawal. They usually can't be accessed until retirement.

Mutual funds. These are collections of bonds, stocks and other securities managed by investment companies. Individuals buy shares in them much as they buy shares of bonds, but mutual funds provide more diversity.

Stocks. A share of stock represents a piece of a company. The price varies from day to day.

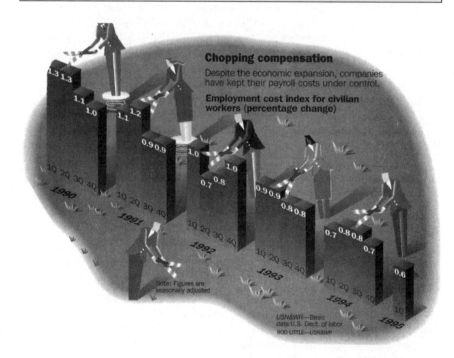

Chopping compensation

Despite the economic expansion, companies have kept their payroll costs under control.

Employment cost index for civilian workers (percentage change)

Note: Figures are seasonally adjusted

USN&WR—Basic data:U.S. Dept. of labor.
ROD LITTLE—USN&WR

Figure 15.3.
Consider preparing an information graphic when you want to present financial data to your readers in a way that will be easy to understand and remember.

Consumer News

The phrase "consumer news" is in its broadest sense arbitrary and redundant. All news is, directly or indirectly, about consumers. And many business stories could just as easily be called consumer stories. A story about the stock market may affect or be of interest to "consumers" of stocks and bonds even though those items aren't "consumed" in the same sense as corn flakes. A story about the price of crude oil affects consumers of gasoline and many other products refined from crude oil. A story about a drought that may drive up the price of wheat has an impact on consumers of hamburger buns. And a story that beef prices are increasing affects the consumer of the hamburger that goes with the bun. The person who has purchased the newspaper in which your stories run is a consumer of newspapers.

Consumer news deals with events or ideas that affect readers in their role as buyers of goods and services in the marketplace. Although news of that kind has existed for as long as there have been newspapers and was spread by word of mouth long before that, its development as a conscious area of coverage generally began in the mid-1960s with the rise of vocal consumer groups. The consumer movement was helped along immeasurably by Ralph Nader's book *Unsafe at Any Speed*, an attack on the Chevrolet Corvair. General Motors Corp.'s subsequent attempts to spy on him and the ensuing publicity when the matter went before Congress also generated interest.

In many ways consumerism is as much a political as an economic movement. The wave of federal, state and local regulations promulgated in the 1960s and '70s attests to that fact. Such legislation has affected producers of goods not only in the area of safety, but also in the realms of finance, labeling and pricing.

The media have played such a major role in publicizing crusaders such as Nader and their causes that in many respects the consumer movement is a creature of the media. Those who espouse consumer causes recognize the power public exposure can bring them. What this means to you as a reporter is that although consumer groups may be friendlier than business people, they too will try to use you to their advantage.

Where to Find Consumer News

Sources of consumer news fall into three general categories: government agencies, quasi-public consumer groups and private businesses. Let's consider each of these groups.

Government Agencies

Many municipalities, especially large cities, have a public consumer advocate who reports to the mayor and calls public attention to problems that affect consumers. Most county prosecuting attorneys' offices also have someone—or even a whole department—to challenge business practices of questionable legality. Cases of consumer fraud—in which people pay for something they do not receive or pay for something of a certain quality and receive something less—are handled by these offices.

At the state level, most states have a consumer affairs office to investigate consumer problems and to order or recommend solutions. In addition, state attorneys general investigate and prosecute cases of consumer fraud. Most states also have regulatory commissions that represent the public in a variety of areas. The most common commissions regulate insurance rates and practices, rates and levels of service of utilities and transportation companies, and practices of banks and savings and loan associations.

At the federal level, the government regulatory agencies involved in consumer affairs have the power to make rules and to enforce them. Among these are:

- The Federal Trade Commission, which oversees matters related to advertising and product safety.
- The Food and Drug Administration, which watches over prices and safety rules for drugs, foods and a variety of other health-related items.
- The Securities and Exchange Commission, which oversees the registration of securities for corporations and regulates the exchange, or trading, of those securities.
- The Interstate Commerce Commission, which regulates prices and levels of service provided by surface-transportation companies in interstate commerce.
- The Federal Power Commission, which regulates the rates and levels of service provided by interstate energy companies.

Virtually every other federal cabinet office or agency deals with some form of consumer protection, ranging from banking and finance to education to housing to highway and vehicle safety. These agencies are useful to reporters in several ways. First, they are good sources of background information and data of almost every conceivable form. Second, they are good sources of "hard" information such as the results of investigations, cautionary orders and the status of legislation affecting their area of expertise. Also, public information officers of these offices, regulatory agencies and even members of Congress usually are accessible and helpful in ferreting out information for reporters. You may have to make several calls to Washington to get plugged into the right office, but many federal agencies have regional offices in major cities.

Sources of consumer news
- *Government agencies*
- *Quasi-public consumer groups*
- *Private businesses*

Consumer Groups

Nongovernment consumer groups are composed of private citizens who have organized to represent the consumer's interest. They, too, are often good sources of background information or comment.

Common Cause, which lobbies for federal and state legislation, and Consumers Union, which publishes the popular *Consumer Reports*, are general in nature. Many states have public interest research groups. Other organizations are specialists, such as the Sierra Club, which concentrates on environmental matters. Still other groups may be more local in scope. They may try to enact such legislation as returnable-bottle ordinances or to fight what they perceive as discrimination in the way housing loans are made by banks and savings and loan associations.

These groups, through their ability to attract the attention of the media and to find sympathetic ears in Washington and the state capi-

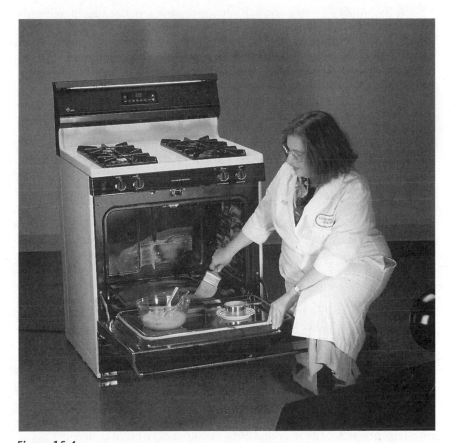

Figure 15.4.
Stories about Consumers Union's laboratory tests help your audience make informed buying decisions.

tals, have a greater impact on legislation and news coverage than their numbers would suggest. It is always a good idea to try to determine just who a particular group represents and how broad its support is, especially in cases where the group has not already established its legitimacy. The group may be an association with many members or merely a self-appointed committee with little or no general support. One person, under the guise of an association or committee, can rent a hotel meeting room and call a news conference to say almost anything. Such is the nature of the media that in most cases at least one reporter will attend the news conference and write something about it. The broader a group's support, the greater the impact of its statement. If *Consumer Reports* says an auto model is dangerous, that judgment is national news. If an individual says the same thing, nobody pays any attention.

Private Businesses

Virtually all large corporations and many smaller ones have public relations departments. They try to present their company in the most favorable light and to mask the scars as well as possible when the company is attacked from the outside, whether by the press, the government or a consumer group.

Because of the successes of the consumer movement, a number of companies have taken the offensive and have instituted programs they deem to be in the public interest. We see oil companies telling drivers how to economize on gasoline, the electric utility telling homeowners how to keep their electric bills at a minimum, banks suggesting ways to manage money better, and the telephone company pointing out the times it is least expensive to make long-distance calls.

Corporate public relations people can be valuable sources for a variety of stories by providing background information or comments and reactions to events affecting their company. Also, they may help a reporter place an event in perspective, as it affects a company or industry, for example. Sometimes they are good primary sources for feature stories about products or personalities.

How to Report Consumer Stories

Consumer stories may be "exposés," bringing to light a practice relating to consumers that is dangerous or that increases the price of a product or service. Research for such stories can be simple and inexpensive to conduct, and the findings may arouse intense reader interest. The project can be something as simple as buying hamburger at every supermarket in town to see if all purchases weigh what they are marked. Or it may be something that takes more time and work, such as surveying auto repair shops to see how much unnecessary repair work is done or how much necessary repair work is not diagnosed. Deborah Diamond of *Ladies Home Journal* took a VCR that had been rigged to need minor repairs to three different repair shops. She came back with three vastly different diagnoses and a wide range of repair costs. Only one of the repair shops identified and repaired the actual problem, which led to a story on how to protect yourself from this type of fraud.

Consumer stories also may be informational, intended to help readers make wiser or less expensive purchases. For example, if beef prices are rising, you may suggest protein substitutes that will be more healthful and less expensive. Or you may want to discuss the advantages and disadvantages of buying a late-model used car instead of a new one. Or you can point out the advantages and disadvantages of buying term life insurance instead of whole life insurance.

Other consumer stories may be cautionary, warning readers of impending price increases for products, quality problems with products or questionable practices of business or consumer groups. Such stories can have great impact. The Knight-Ridder chain's revelation that the Firestone radial tires suspected of repeated failures had not passed some of the company's own quality tests helped force a recall that cost the company millions of dollars. Ralph Nader's exposé of the Corvair led to the discontinuance of the model. Sometimes newspapers, magazines and broadcast outlets act as surrogates for consumers. One example of this is the "Action Line" kind of question-and-answer column published in many newspapers. A column like this has the power of the paper behind questions to companies and thus often is more successful than an individual in reaching satisfactory settlements on questions of refunds, undelivered purchases and other consumer complaints. The past few years have seen an explosion in television programs in which reporters go undercover with hidden cameras and act like consumers. Such stories have revealed such diverse scandals as what really happens in a day-care center after the parents leave and where the septic tank company actually dumps sewage. There are also dozens of magazines and books that focus on consumer news, from stories on what to look for when building a new house to how to select a good nursing home.

Consumer stories can be dangerous, though. It was a consumer story about how to get the best deal from a used car salesman that led to the massive advertising boycott at the *San Jose Mercury News*. A consumer story led to a lawsuit against the *Denver Post* when it published a story about a dry cleaner that consistently lost customers' clothes.

Consumer and business news stories can provide valuable services not only to readers who are consumers but to readers who are producers and financiers and regulators as well. But they must be carefully reported and compellingly written.

One especially valuable source of information for consumer stories is the *Consumer Sourcebook*, published by Gale Research Co. The two-volume book describes more than 135 federal and 800 state and local agencies and bureaus that provide aid or information dealing with consumers.

Suggested Readings

Barlett, Donald L. and Steele, James B. *Empire: The Life, Legend and Madness of Howard Hughes*. New York: Norton Press, 1979. A massive study of Hughes' empire showing diversity of documentary sources authors used in their research.

Goodman, Jordan and Bloch, Sonny. *The Dictionary of Finance and Investment Terms*. Chicago: Dearborn Financial Publishing, Inc., 1994. A necessary desk reference book for any financial writer.

MacDougall, A. Kent. *Ninety Seconds to Tell It All: Big Business and the News Media*. Homewood, Ill.: Dow Jones-Irwin, 1981. An examination of the business-press relationship.

Mitford, Jessica. *Poison Penmanship: The Gentle Art of Muckraking*. New York: Vintage Books, 1957. A classic introduction on sources, especially the trade press. Includes 17 investigative pieces with commentary on the reporting techniques.

Schmertz, Herbert. *Good-bye to the Low Profile: The Art of Creative Confrontation*. Boston: Little, Brown, 1986. Mobil executive touts the merits of public relations hardball.

Weinberg, Steve. *The Reporter's Handbook: An Investigator's Guide to Documents and Techniques*, Third Edition. New York: St. Martin's Press, 1996. See Chapter 11, "Business," for a close look at the records and documents available.

Exercises

1. Find five stories in the local newspaper that ran outside of the business section and explain how they could have been turned into business stories.

2. Invite an accounting professor to take the class through the New York Stock Exchange's "Understanding Wall Street" or Merrill Lynch's "How to Read a Financial Report."

3. Sign up for a stock market game. There are several across the country that allow students to invest play money in real stocks. Then follow your portfolio's progress in the *Wall Street Journal*.

4. Send away for a prospectus on a mutual fund and study its investment rationale. Or send away for a prospectus on a stock offering and study its price-earnings ratio, yield, dividends and other value indicators. Have a local stockbroker explain the stock's value.

5. Use Nexis to find the 10-K report on a publicly traded company with a local operation.

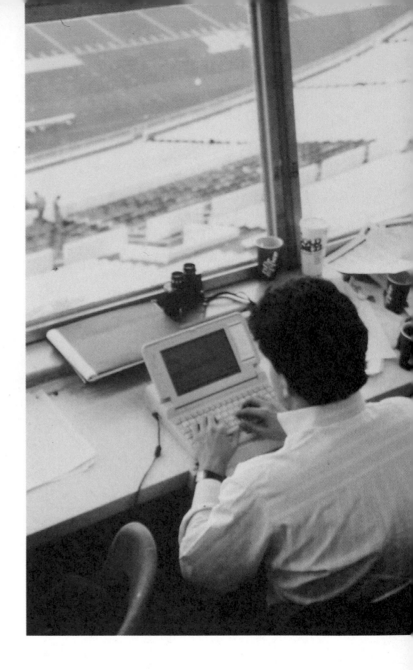

SPORTS

*T*urn on your television set. Every channel seems to carry sports. College football. Professional basketball. Auto racing. Soccer. Golf. There's color, sound, instant replay. Hours of talk before and after the actual games. Entire networks devoted to nothing but sports.

What's a writer to do? How can you give readers something they haven't already seen and heard? How can a broadcast reporter make news of a game shown live on a competing station? In the competition for time and attention that is at least as fierce as anything played in cleats or sneakers, how can you stay in the game?

Peter St. Onge, an award-winning young columnist for the Anniston (Ala) Star, has a couple of answers:

- "Look for the story that isn't easy to find, the one that others aren't writing."
- "Look for the human angle. The best sports stories aren't usually about sports; they're about the people who play sports."

Kathy Brady Tulumello, sports editor of the Phoenix Gazette, speaks of her current position in the same terms as she describes her previous beats, including police and local government (see page 358). She advocates sharing with readers news that the reporter finds interesting.

It turns out, you see, that good sports reporting is just good reporting, focused on sports. Good sports writing is good writing, period. That's so because sports, even if it is the toy department of life, is part of life. For the truly fanatical, sports seems to be life. For the more balanced fans, the same elements that make the rest of life interesting give sports its fascination.

Sports has struggle, passion, competition, heroes, villains, fun—and one attraction that's often missing in the rest of life. At the end of a game, you always know who has won and who has lost. In a world of ambiguity, there is satisfaction in certainty. All of that explains why millions of people in countries around the world want to read about sports, even the games they've seen. You don't have to be a child, after all, to head for the toy department.

Covering the Sports Beat

A good sports reporter is a good reporter. That's not always obvious, especially to beginners, because of the love of sports that lures them to the field in the first place. Most sports reporters were sports fans before they were journalists. That's not typical of other specialties. Reporters who cover government seldom attend city council meetings for fun. Medical reporters don't usually spend their days off observing operations. (Instead, they may watch a sports event.) Here's Kathy Tulumello's prescription for turning a fan into a reporter:

> Reporters need a firm foundation in police, courts and basic
> governmental reporting to develop the methodical and skeptical

approach needed to cover anything. Even a part-time stint as a copy editor can make you aware of space limitations and the detail and documentation demanded by good editors. And with new technology, don't let yourself fall behind in database reporting, online services, etc.

As a sports reporter and writer, you will likely find your workplace organized in much the same way as the news department. Typically, in the sports department of a newspaper, there will be reporters, copy editors and an editor. The difference is likely to be the scale. On small papers, the sports editor may double as writer and may even take the photographs, too. On mid-sized papers, the sports reporters usually don't specialize as the news reporters may. One day you may be covering high school swimming; the next, football or a visiting rodeo.

In broadcasting, at small and medium-sized stations, a "sports department" is likely to consist of just one person—serving as writer, photographer and sports anchor at various times of day or night. The big crews, the "guys in the truck" you hear mentioned on ESPN, are at the network level. At most local stations, you'll be expected to report, to write, to photograph and to deliver your work on camera. Sometimes, when time pressure is great or the game is big, you'll go on the air live, summarizing a game that has just ended or that may even be in progress. Then your skills at ad-libbing will be tested, a challenge print reporters don't face.

One more thing: Don't confuse sports reporters with play-by-play announcers. The latter may be reporters in a literal sense, but they usually aren't journalists. Their skill is in instant description, not the behind-the-scenes digging or the after-the-fact analysis expected of print or broadcast reporters. Often they are hired by the teams they follow or the sponsors they serve instead of by the station carrying their work.

When you're a beginning reporter, the principles that follow apply to any medium and any sport.

In Chapter 14, we discussed the techniques employed by successful reporters. Review them. They apply to coverage of sports as well as to politics or education or science. Now we will see how they can help you meet the special challenges of reporting sports.

Being Prepared

Before you even thought about sports reporting, the chances are that you were reading, watching and playing sports. In that sense, at least, preparing to be a sports reporter is easier than preparing to cover city hall. But there is more to preparation than immersing yourself in sports. Competition pushes people to their limits, bringing out their best and worst. So you need to know some psychology. Sports has played a major role in the struggles of blacks and women for equality. So you need to know some sociology and history. Sports, professional and amateur, is big business. So you need a background

in economics. Some of our greatest writers have portrayed life through sports. So you need to explore literature.

This paragraph by Grantland Rice, for example, may be the most famous lead ever written for a newspaper story:

> Outlined against a blue-gray October sky, the Four Horse-men rode again. In dramatic lore, they are known as Famine, Pestilence, Destruction and Death. These are only aliases. Their real names are Stuhldreher, Miller, Crowley and Layden. They formed the crest of the Sound Bend cyclone before which another fighting Army football team was swept over the precipice at the Polo Grounds yesterday afternoon as 55,000 spectators peered down on the bewildering panorama spread on the green plain below.

Grantland Rice, the most famous American sportswriter in the first half of this century, graduated Phi Beta Kappa from Vanderbilt University, where he majored in Latin and Greek. His prose may have been overblown by today's standards, but he wrote some memorable poetry, too. And he knew who the Four Horsemen of the Apocalypse were.

Being Alert

"It's the writer's responsibility to come up with a different approach," says Peter St. Onge. In his own words, this is how he does it:

> When my editor sent me to a PGA golf tournament, I sat at the most popular spectator hole—one that some pros could drive—and wrote about why the fans loved it. When my editor wanted a Super Bowl preview story, I went around town trying to find someone who truly believed Buffalo would beat Dallas (I didn't find anyone, which made the story even better). When a minor-league baseball player from town got called up to the big leagues, I talked to his high school coach, college coach and best friend and asked them about the moment they got the phone call from the player—and what their thoughts were.

Let's take a quick look at the story that resulted from one of those different approaches. If you read sports, you've read the story of the rookie getting summoned to the big leagues. Often, the story is one long cliché, from the obligatory "aw shucks" quote of the athlete to the recitation of statistics. The different approach yields a different and better story. Here's St. Onge's opening:

> The best friend got the call on Wednesday, just before midnight, the phone's jangle jarring him from sleep.
>
> "He called me about two minutes after he got out of his coach's office," Mark Adams remembers. "He said, 'You wanted me to call you when I got called up.'
>
> "Then he said, 'I'm there.'"
>
> The Red Sox. The big leagues. How many times had they talked about this moment? At college, on road trips, on the lake with fishing poles in their hands? They had both been star players, both good enough for a chance at professional baseball. But only one had the opportunity.
>
> Once, Tim VanEgmond had

said that he was nervous about being called up, that when he finally stepped on a major-league mound, he might feel more loneliness than anything.

"I told Tim not to worry," the best friend says. "I told him, 'You're not just playing for you. You're also playing for me.'"

After recounting the reactions and recollections of the two coaches, St. Onge summarizes both the story and the relationships:

Today, they will all be thinking of him, for all their own reasons. The best friend, the junior college coach and the college coach will try to find satellite dishes somewhere and lock onto a Boston or Milwaukee station.

But even if they can't, that's OK. The phone will ring again soon, and it will be Tim Van-Egmond, the one they saw grow up, the one they grew up with. He'll give them all the real details then. He always does. It's their moment, too.

This is a story that entertains while it informs. It shows readers something of the character of an athlete and the nature of friendship. Now here are a few tips to help you be alert to stories that get beyond the cliché:

Look for the losers. Losing may not—as football coaches and other philosophers like to assert—build character, but it certainly bares character. Winners are likely to be full of confidence, champagne and clichés. Losers are likely to be full of self-doubt, second-guessing and surliness. Winners' dressing rooms are magnets for sportswriters, but you usually can tell your readers more about the game and those who play it by seeking out the losers.

Look for the bench warmers. If you follow the reporting crowd, you'll end up in front of your local version of Cal Ripken Jr. or Steffi Graf every time. Head in the other direction. Talk to the would-be football player who has spent four years practicing but never gets into a game. Talk to the woman who dreams of being a professional golfer but is not yet good enough. Talk to the baseball player who is growing old in the minor leagues. If you do, you may find people who both love their sport more and understand it better than do the stars. You may find less press agentry and more humanity.

Look beyond the crowds. Some of the best, and most important, sports stories draw neither crowds of reporters nor crowds of fans. The recent and rapid growth of women's sports is one example. Under the pressure of federal law—the "Title IX" you read and hear about—the traditional male dominance of facilities and money in school and college athletics is giving way slowly to equal treatment for women. From junior high schools to major universities, women's teams now compete in virtually every sport except football. With better coaching, and more incentive, the quality of performance is increasing, too. The results of this revolution are likely to be felt far beyond the playing fields, just as the earlier admission of blacks to athletic equality advanced blacks' standing in other areas. Male-run sports depart-

Looking beyond the cliché

- *Look for the losers.*
- *Look for the bench warmers.*
- *Look beyond the crowds.*

ments, like male-run athletic departments, can no longer overlook women athletes.

The so-called "minor" sports and "participant" sports are other largely untapped sources of good stories. More Americans watch birds than play football. More hunt or fish than play basketball. More watch stock-car races than watch track meets. But those and similar sports are usually covered—if at all—by the newest or least talented reporter on the staff. Get out of the press box. Drop by a bowling alley, a skeet-shooting range, the local college's Frisbee-throwing tournament. Anywhere you find people competing—against each other, against nature, against their own limits—you can find good stories.

Being Persistent

It was a big story. A sports agent had told another newspaper that he had given money to and arranged travel for a star college basketball player before and during the player's senior season. The agent saw it as no big deal. He had done the same for players at universities across the country as he tried to win their allegiance for life in the professional leagues. But for the university his allegations, if true, could mean at least embarrassment and at most the forfeiting of NCAA tournament games in which the player had participated.

It was a big problem. The agent had been willing, even eager, to talk to reporters at the metropolitan newspaper that broke the story. He was available to other reporters at other papers with which he was familiar. But he had no time for student reporters at the newspaper of the university most involved. His attitude was discouraging for the reporters, frustrating for their editors and baffling for their readers.

The reporters refused to give up. They got the agent's home phone number, in a city across the continent, from the reporter who had discovered his role. They left message after message. While they waited for his call, they worked at the story from the edges by talking to people less directly involved but more accessible. The player himself, of course, was unavailable to any reporters. Finally, after a week of reading other versions of the story they wanted, the student reporters got a payoff for their persistence. The agent called. Using what they had gleaned from other interviews and previous stories, the students were able to write a story that offered readers a few new tidbits:

Nate Cebrun on Thursday described prospective agents' year-long courtship of former university basketball player Jevon Crudup as an "out-of-control bidding war."

Cebrun, a self-described middleman, said his dealings with Crudup and his mother, Mary, probably netted them only about $5,000 in cash and other gifts. But sports agents

Michael Harrison and Raul Bey must have spent even more money on Crudup, Cebrun said.

"I saw Jevon's mother at Missouri's game against Arizona in tournament action. And I know she wasn't able to afford that with the money she makes," Cebrun said in a phone interview from his Las Vegas home. "But if I were a betting man, I'd almost guarantee Harrison paid for her to go to L.A."

In this case, the reward for persistence was catching up on an important story. In other cases, the reward may be a story that otherwise wouldn't be done at all. That was the case several years ago when two young reporters for the *Lexington* (Ky.) *Herald-Leader* spent seven months pursuing suspicions that basketball players at the state university were receiving under-the-table cash from boosters in violation of NCAA rules. The story that resulted led to the ouster of the university's coach and athletic director and contributed to a continuing reform movement in college athletics. It also won honors rarely earned by sports reporters, including a Pulitzer Prize.

The most important reward of persistence, though, is the loyalty of readers who feel well-served.

Being There and Developing Contacts

Being there, of course, is half the fun of sports reporting. You're there at the big games, matches and meets. You're there in the locker rooms, on team buses and planes, with an inside view of athletics and athletes that few fans ever get. And you should be there, most of the time. If you are to answer your readers' questions, if you are to provide insight and anecdote, you must be there, most of the time.

Sometimes you should try being where the fans are. Plunk down $10 (of the newspaper's money) for an end-zone seat and write about a football game from the average fan's point of view. Cover a baseball game from the bleachers. Cold hot dogs and warm beer are as much a part of the event as is a double play. Watch one of those weekend sports shows on television and compare the way a track meet or a fishing trip is presented to the way it is in person. Join a city league softball team or a bowling league for a different kind of inside view.

A sports reporter must develop and cherish sources just as a city hall reporter must. You look for the same kinds of sources on both beats. Players, coaches and administrators—like city council members and city managers—are obvious sources. Go beyond them. Trainers and equipment managers have insiders' views and sometimes lack the fierce protectiveness that often keeps players, for example, from talking candidly. Alumni can be excellent sources for high school and college sports stories. If a coach is about to be fired or a new fund drive

Figure 16.1.
The press box may provide a good vantage point for announcing the play-by-play, but covering the sports beat in depth means being there with the athletes.

is being planned, important alumni are sure to be involved. You can find out who they are by checking with the alumni association or by examining the list of major contributors that every college proudly compiles. The business managers and secretaries who handle the money can be invaluable for much-needed but seldom-done stories about the finances of sport at all levels. Former players sometimes will talk more candidly than those who are still involved in a program. As on any beat, look for people who may be disgruntled—a fired assistant coach, a benched star, a big contributor to a losing team. And when you find good sources, cherish them. Keep in contact, flatter them, protect them. They are your lifeline.

Unfortunately, being where a reporter needs to be isn't always easy or pleasant. Just ask Lisa Olson. A young reporter for the *Boston Herald*, Olson was doing her job, interviewing a New England Patriot football player in the locker room, when several other players began harassing her. At least one player made sexually suggestive comments and gestures while he stood nude beside her. After a complaint, and after much national publicity, players and the team owner were fined and reprimanded by the National Football League. Many other women, and some men, have found themselves victims of harassment by athletes, coaches or fans. Life in the toy department isn't always fun. Sports reporters, especially women, may find their professionalism tested in ways—and in surroundings—seldom encountered by colleagues on beats that usually are considered more serious.

Being Wary and Digging for the Real Story

It is even harder for a sports reporter than it is for a political or police reporter to maintain a critical distance from the beat. The most obvious reason is that most of the people who become sports reporters do so because they are sports fans. To be a fan is precisely the opposite of being a dispassionate, critical observer. In addition, athletics—especially big-time athletics—is glamorous and exciting. The sports reporter associates daily with the stars and the coaches whom others, including cynical city hall reporters and hard-bitten managing editors, pay to admire at a distance. Finally, sports figures ranging from high school coaches to owners of professional baseball teams deliberately and persistently seek to buy the favor of the reporters who cover their sports.

We are taught from childhood that it is disgraceful to bite the hand that feeds you. Professional teams and many college teams routinely feed reporters. (One Missouri newspaper created a minor furor when it disclosed that a lobbyist in the state capital took political reporters to St. Louis for baseball games. But it creates no furor at all for the same baseball team to give free admission, free food and free beer to the reporters covering those games.) Major-league baseball teams even pay reporters to serve as official scorers for the game. In one embarrassing incident, the reporter-scorer made a controversial decision that preserved a no-hit game for a hometown pitcher. His story of the game made little mention of his official role. The reporter for the opposition paper wrote that if it had been *his* turn to be scorer, he would have ruled the other way.

Sports journalism used to be even more parasitic toward the teams it covered than is the case now. At one time, reporters routinely traveled with a team at the team's expense. Good newspapers pay their own way today.

Even today, however, many reporters find it rewarding monetarily as well as psychologically to stay in favor with the teams and athletes they cover. Many teams pay reporters to write promotional pieces for game programs. And writing personality profiles or "inside" accounts for the dozens of sports magazines can be a profitable sideline.

Most sports reporters, and the editors who permit such activities, argue that they are not corrupted by what they are given. Most surely are not. But temptation is there for those who would succumb. Beyond that, any writer who takes more than information from those he or she covers is also likely to receive pressure, however subtle, from the givers.

Every sports reporter is given a great deal by high school and college coaches or publicity agents, who feed reporters sheets of statistics, arrange interviews, provide space on the team bus or plane, and allow access to practice fields and locker rooms. And what do they want in return? They expect nothing more than an unbroken series of favorable stories. Too often, they get just that. Only the names have been changed in this excerpt from a metropolitan newspaper:

> The State U. troops reported today to begin three weeks' tune-up before the Fighting Beagles invade Western State.
>
> Offensive commander Pug Stanley had some thoughts available Thursday before some 90-odd players arrived.
>
> "We really made some strides this year," Stanley declared. . . . Charlie Walker, he said, is no longer feeling his way around at quarterback. The Beagle pass catchers are hardly old men, but the top four targets are two juniors and two sophomores rather than two sophomores and two freshmen.
>
> State U.'s heaviest artillery is located behind Charlie Walker. Beagle runners ranged from good to outstanding a year ago. Most are back, with a season's more experience.
>
> "Our runners keep on getting better," commented their attack boss. "Our backfield has to be our biggest plus. We're going to burn some people with it this year."

The story did not mention that State U., which had managed only a 6-5 record the previous year against weak opposition, was universally picked to finish in the second division of its second-rate conference. That's not only bad writing, but bad reporting.

Anywhere athletics is taken seriously, from the high schools of Texas to the stadiums of the National Football League, athletes and coaches are used to being given special treatment. Many think of themselves as being somehow different from and better than ordinary people. Many fans agree. Good reporters, though, regard sports as a beat, not a love affair.

Those sports reporters maintain their distance from the people they cover, just as reporters on other beats do, by keeping their readers in mind. Readers want to know who won, and how. But they also want to know about other sides of sports, sides that may require some digging to expose. Readers' questions about sports financing and the story behind the story too often go unanswered.

> *Money.* Accountants have become as essential to sports as athletes and trainers. Readers have a legitimate interest in everything from ticket prices to the impact of money on the actual contests.
>
> *The Real "Why."* When a key player is traded, as much as when a city manager is fired, readers want to know why. When athletes leave school without graduating, find out why. When the public is asked to pay for the expansion of a stadium, tell the public why. One of the attractions of sports is that when the contest is over, the spectators can see who won and how. Often that is not true of struggles in government or business. The "whys" of sports, however, frequently are as hard to discover as they are in any other area.
>
> *The Real "Who."* Sports figures often appear to their fans, and sometimes to reporters, to be larger than life. In fact, athletics is an intensely human activity. Its participants have greater physical

"Slowly, but ever so surely, is vanishing the notion that the sports department's job is to cover the games and perpetuate the image that sports are pure, its participants are All-American boys, and its pages [are] places simply to report the game and what was said after it was over.

"And who knows, maybe someday we'll even achieve equal status in job title. Through the years, it has always been 'reporter' on the news side, sports 'writer' in my world.

"I'm beginning to discover more sports reporters."

—**Tom Tuley,**
executive sports editor
Cincinnati Post

skills, and larger bank accounts, than most other people, but they are people. Probably the best two descriptions of what it is really like to be a major-league athlete were written by athletes—*Ball Four* by Jim Bouton and the novel *North Dallas Forty* by Pete Gent. Still, some of the best sportswriting results from the continuing effort by reporters to capture the humanity of games. Roger Kahn, in perhaps the finest baseball book ever written, *The Boys of Summer*, needed only two inches of type to capture Carl Erskine, the old Dodger pitcher, in this scene with his wife and their mentally retarded son:

> Jimmy Erskine, nine, came forward at Betty's tug. He had the flat features and pinched nostrils of Mongolism [the then-popular term for Down syndrome].
> "Say, 'Hello, Roger,'" Betty said.
> Jimmy shook his head and sniffed.
> "Come on," Carl said.
> "Hosh-uh," Jimmy said. "Hosh-uh. Hosh-uh."
> "He's proud," Carl said, beaming. "He's been practicing to say your name all week, and he's proud as he can be." The father's strong right hand found Jimmy's neck. He hugged the little boy against his hip.

As Tom Tuley observed, sports reporting is much more than covering the contests and perpetuating the myths.

Covering the Contests

A major part of any sports reporter's job, however, is covering the games, matches or meets. That task is harder than it might seem. You have the same problems you would have in covering any event, from a city council meeting to a riot. You must decide what to put in your lead, capture the most interesting and significant developments, find some good quotes, answer as many of your readers' probable questions as you can and meet your deadline. But a reporter covering a football game, for instance, has a major concern that a reporter writing about a council meeting does not have. Most of the readers of your football story already know a great deal about the game. Many were there. Others saw it on television or listened on radio. They know *what* happened. They expect you to tell them *why* and *how*.

A story like this one, though it may be easy to produce, falls far short of meeting that demand:

> Jefferson High turned two fumble recoveries into touchdowns and shut out Oakland High, 16-0, Monday night at Hickley Field.
> The Cyclones, who held Oakland to minus 32 yards rushing in the game, scored their points on consecutive possessions in the second quarter.
> The scoring started when Jefferson recovered a fumble at the Eagle 42-yard line and marched in for the score.

The reporter is adding little to what most fans already know.

The only two quotes in the story, just two paragraphs from the end, could have been pulled from a list of coaches' stock comments, suitable for all occasions:

"We didn't make the mistakes we did last week against West," said Cyclones Coach David Carlson.

Oakland Coach Lyle Wheel-er praised his defense after the game. "I thought they played real well. They were on the field the whole game."

Too many games are reported just as that one was, without probing the hows and whys. The reporter sits in the press box, has three-quarters of a story written before the game is over, breezes through each dressing room just long enough to ask, "Any comment, Coach?" and applies the finishing touches to the story on the way to the telephone or back to the office. But that is recording, not reporting.

Suppose, instead, that the reporter had done a little homework. Some digging would have revealed that this was Oakland's third loss of the season, with no victories. It would have shown that Coach Wheeler had predicted before the season a winning record, possibly a conference championship. And it would have shown that the player counted on to be the star of the team had been dropped from the squad just before the first game for "disciplinary reasons."

Suppose the reporter had gotten to know the players and supporters of the team. He or she would have learned that the black athletes and many of their parents believed the suspension of the star, who was black, was a case of racial discrimination by the white coach. And if the reporter had gotten out of the press box, there might have been more revealing comments from players and fans, some explanation of what was seen on the field. The story might have read:

From the top row of the Hickley Field Stadium, Gary Thomas watched in agony as his former teammates at Oakland High lost their third game of the season, 16-0, to arch-rival Jefferson High.

He groaned each time an Oakland ball carrier was dropped for a loss. He cursed each of Oakland's four lost fumbles.

"Cut left," he muttered as halfback David Oldham ran head-on into four Jefferson tacklers. "Hold the ball, damn it," as Oldham fumbled.

The outcome of Friday's game would have been different, Thomas believes, if he had been on the field displaying the skills that made him the leading rusher in the conference last year as a junior.

But he is spending his senior season in the stands, suspended from the team for what Coach Lyle Wheeler calls

"disciplinary reasons" after a fight with a white student in a
school restroom. Thomas thinks he was discriminated against.

"The dude just don't like blacks," he said of Wheeler.

Black and white teammates agreed as they wearily dressed
after the game that they want Thomas back in uniform.

"We ain't got a prayer without him," said Oldham, who is
white.

Linebacker Chris Pannell, who is black, added, "He's the
heart of this team. Without him, we got no heart."

Coach Wheeler, asked about the effect of Thomas' absence,
responded by praising his defense. "I thought they played real
well. They were on the field the whole game."

Jefferson ran 62 offensive plays to only 42 for Oakland.
But, had it not been for the fumbles, which put Jefferson in
easy scoring range three times, Oakland might have escaped
with a scoreless tie.

That story tells its readers not only what happened, but how it happened and at least part of why it happened. It combines solid reporting with deft writing to add something that was new and interesting
even for those who had seen or heard the game.

Notice first the form of the story. In sports writing, as elsewhere
in journalism, the inverted pyramid structure has given way in many
cases to an alternate approach. (You will learn about these alternatives in Chapter 17.) In this story the reporter starts by setting the
scene and introducing the most important character, while also providing essential information about the game. Your goals for the opening of any story about a sports event should be twofold:

Focus on the unique element. No sporting event is quite like any
other. A perceptive reporter picks out what made this game different and shares it with the reader. The unique element may be
a single play, a questionable ruling by an official, an untimely injury. Or it may be, as in this case, the missing player. Find that
unique element and you have found the key to your story. Your
lead may be a quote, the description of a scene, an analysis by
some expert observer or your own summary of the contest's high
point. Whatever opening device you choose, be sure the facts
support it. A summary or analysis based on fact is permissible in
a news story. Reliance on your own opinion is not.

Tell the reader who won. No description is so compelling and no
analysis so astute that a reader will forgive you if you forgot to
say at the start what the outcome of the event was. The basic
who, what and where must never be left out or buried in the
body of your story. The story is, after all, about the contest.

As in the story on Oakland High, the body of your story should develop the unique angle brought out in the lead. This writing technique gives a unified focus and maintains the reader's interest. In the course of the story, you should also meet three other objectives:

Describe what happened. In addition to knowing the outcome, your audience will want to read at least the highlights of *how* it was reached, if only to savor them again. Analysis and background are hollow without the solid descriptive core of what happened. In the Oakland High story, that description begins in the second and third paragraphs and resumes in the last paragraph of the excerpt.

Answer readers' questions. The story should supply the explanation—or part of it, at least— of *why* the game turned out as it did. It should tell its readers something they could not have discovered easily for themselves. The reporter of the Oakland High story accomplished that by taking the trouble to learn the background of the event, and then by seeking out the right sources. Rarely should you have to rely on your own expertise to answer the questions of why and how. Experts abound at virtually every sports event. Assistant coaches or scouts sit in the press box. The coaches and players directly involved are available after the game. Alumni, supporters, former players can be found if you will just go looking. The most important question for you to ask as a reporter is what your readers will want to know. Then try to find the answers for them.

Get the competitors into the story by using good quotes. Your audience usually wants to know what the competitors think about what they have done. When winners exult, when losers cry, put your audience in the scene. That is part of the attraction of sports. The hours spent getting to know them pay off when the athletes share with you—and your audience—what the contest was really like.

The preparation and techniques of interviewing are essentially the same in a locker room as in a politician's office, though you seldom have occasion to interview a mayor who is dressing or undressing. The reward for a good job in either situation is the same, too. You get, as in the preceding story, lively quotes that provide some insight.

Writing about Sports

Many sports journalists think of themselves more as writers than reporters. This chapter is intended to help you become a sports reporter. But good writing is an important part of any top reporter's skills, and sports offers abundant material for good writing.

Good writing is precise, conveying what the author means to say and nothing else. It is descriptive, re-creating for the reader the sights, the sounds, the smells of the event. It is suited in pace and in tone to the story—lively for an exciting game, somber for the reflections of a loser.

Remember, you produce a good game story by

- *Doing your homework before the game.*
- *Spotting the unique element and building the story on it.*
- *Telling your readers who won and how.*
- *Answering readers' questions.*
- *Getting the participants into the story.*

Consider, for example, the possibilities offered a writer by one of the most common but least valued contributors to sports—mud.

```
The ball skittered across the cleat-torn field, slithering
through the slop of mud and water.
    Two players raced after it, but their legs tangled. They
fell into the muck and slid out of bounds.
    It was a beautiful day for Cougar soccer on Friday. The
Cougars are American Midwest Conference champions after
defeating Lindenwood 3-1.
```

Or you could try a summary lead and then let an athlete do the talking:

```
What a mess.
    The Springfield cross-country team knew it would be facing
the best runners in the state on Saturday. But the team didn't
know the Class 4A state championships would turn into a
mudfest.
    "It was awesome," said Springfield junior Nathan Mechlin. "I
sank into the mud about ankle-high. It was fun. I loved it."
```

You can almost feel the mud between your toes, or in your eyes. The ball went "slithering through the slop." Two players, legs tangled, "fell into the muck." A teen-aged runner, mud-covered, exults, "It was awesome."

Good writing captures the environment and the emotions. It is based on detailed observation and full of imaginative word choices. It doesn't require elaborate settings or major-league athletes. It just requires you to use the tools of the craft.

Here's Peter St. Onge again, this time writing about a 13-year-old baseball player:

The right-hander in Joey Dinneny knows it's silly, but the left-hander in him has this little baseball dream. You know how those leftys are. . . .

He is toeing the rubber at Shea Stadium. Bottom of the ninth. Mets lead by a run. (A reminder: This is a dream.) Dinneny strikes out the first two batters on nasty right-handed curves. Big lefty up next. . . . Dinneny pauses. He takes the glove off his left hand and *puts it on his right*. He's going to pitch lefty! The crowd gasps. The batter is rattled. He strikes out swinging! Mets win!

How many of us can wish for that?

Joey Dinneny can.

Dinneny is a right-handed pitcher for the Royals of the Waterbury Koufax League. Dinneny is also a left-handed pitcher for the Royals of the Waterbury Koufax league. In official baseball terminology, this would be called "weird."

Tips on working with sports statistics

- *Perspective is vital. A 400-meter dash time of 52 seconds is poor for a collegian but outstanding for a freshman in high school.*
- *Don't repeat in a story what already is included in box scores or other statistical listings.*
- *If you have a list of figures in your story, consider presenting it in graph or chart form.*
- *Avoid using statistics you don't understand. If you don't know what earned-run averages mean, don't refer to them.*

This story is fun. From the fanciful dream sequence to the "official baseball terminology" conclusion of weirdness, the writer matches the boy's imagination with his own. He describes the dream with the same detail he brings to the reality. Note the repetition for effect, to emphasize the two-pitchers-in-one point of the piece. Note, too, the conversational tone. We're being told a story, not given a report. Too often, sports figures take themselves too seriously—too often, sports writers fall into their clichés. Good writers, whatever the topic, tell stories we want to read.

Perhaps the best contemporary sports reporter and writer is Thomas Boswell of the *Washington Post*. He has won the Best Newspaper Writing award of the American Society of Newspaper Editors. Here are a few samples of his work. First, the opening of a story about aging baseball players:

The cleanup crews come at midnight, creeping into the ghostly quarter-light of empty ballparks with their slow-sweeping brooms and languorous, sluicing hoses. All season, they remove the inanimate refuse of a game. Now, in the dwindling days of September and October, they come to collect baseball souls.

Age is the sweeper, injury his broom.

Mixed among the burst beer cups and the mustard-smeared wrappers headed for the trash heap, we find old friends who are being consigned to the dust bin of baseball's history. If a night breeze blows a back page of the Sporting News down in the stadium aisle, pick it up and squint at the one-time headline names now just fine print at the very bottom of a column of averages.

Notice the imagery, as gloomy as the subject matter. Notice the pacing, with long, complex sentences slowing the eye to match the mood of sadness. Notice the metaphor, age as the sweeper, injury the broom. But notice, too, the sharp-eyed description that must ring true to anyone who has ever seen or thought about the debris cast aside by a baseball crowd.

A little later in the same story:

"I like a look of Agony," wrote Emily Dickinson, "because I know it's true." For those with a taste for a true look, a glimpse beneath the mask, even if it be a glimpse of agony, then this is the proper

time of year. Spring training is for hope; autumn is for reality. At every stop on the late-season baseball trail, we see that look of agony, although it hides behind many expressions.

Familiarity with the classics of literature did not die with Grantland Rice. Boswell not only can find the line, he can make it work.

From another story, this one about a championship boxing match, comes a short paragraph that is equally powerful but sharply different in tone:

Figure 16.2.
Thomas Boswell of the Washington Post *sets a high standard for excellence in sports reporting and writing.*

> Boxing is about pain. It is a night out for the carnivore in us, the hidden beast who is hungry.

Later in that story, Boswell returns to the theme:

> But boxing never changes. One central truth lies at its heart and it never alters: Pain is the most powerful and tangible force in life.
>
> The threat of torture, for instance, is stronger than the threat of death. Execution can be faced, but pain is corrosive, like an acid eating at the personality.
>
> Pain, as anyone with a toothache knows, drives out all other emotions and sensations before it. Pain is priority. It may even be man's strongest and most undeniable reality.
>
> And that is why the fight game stirs us, even as it repels us.

From the poetry of aging to the brutality of pain, Boswell matches his images, his pace and his word choice to the subject matter. The principles of careful observation and clear writing cover all occasions.

There is one thing that sets a writer like Boswell apart from many lesser writers. It is his attitude toward his readers. That may be worth copying, too. After winning the ASNE award, he told an interviewer:

We vastly underestimate our audience in newspapers. In 11 years I have never had one letter from anybody saying, "What's all this highfalutin talk?" I get the most touching letters from people who seem semi-literate but who really appreciate what you're doing. I think the fact that people are capable of understanding the Bible, or sensing the emotion in Shakespeare, just proves how far they are above our expectations.

Suggested Readings

Feinstein, John. *A Season on the Brink*. New York: Macmillan, 1986. This chronicle of a year with Indiana basketball coach Bobby Knight entertains while explaining much about the high-pressure world of big-time college sports.

Flood, Curt. *The Way It Is*. New York: Trident Press, 1971. The first-person story of the baseball player whose challenge to the reserve clause revolutionized professional sports in America. Also noteworthy are the caustic comments on sports writers.

Kahn, Roger. *The Boys of Summer*. New York: New American Library, 1973. One of the best sports books ever written.

Sports Illustrated. Features the best continuing examples of how sports should be reported.

Wolff, Alexander and Keteyian, Armen. *Raw Recruits*. New York: Pocket Books, 1990. A hard look at college basketball recruiting written by two veterans of *Sports Illustrated*.

Exercises

1. You have been assigned to cover your college's men's basketball team. Write a memo describing at least five likely sources and listing at least five story ideas.

2. Now do the same for the women's basketball team. Compare facilities, funding, fan interest and actual coverage. Be prepared to discuss your findings.

3. Select a "minor" sports event, such as a wrestling meet or a volleyball game. Prepare for and cover the event. Write the story.

4. Choose one of the story ideas in Exercise 1 or 2. Report and write it.

5. Compare the coverage of a major event in your local newspaper and in *Sports Illustrated*. Which seems better written? Why?

6. Compile an inventory of the on-line sources available to fans and reporters in your area. What story possibilities does your list suggest?

ALTERNATIVES TO THE
INVERTED PYRAMID

*B*arney Calame, the deputy managing editor of the Wall Street Journal, was chatting with a group of journalists. Talking about the number of his family members who had lived long lives, Calame offered an example:

> "My grandmother, who had one leg, lost the other when she tried to flee the nursing home in a wheelchair when she was 96."
>
> He stopped. Everyone looked at him expectantly.
>
> "Well?" said one listener.
>
> "Well what?" Calame asked.
>
> "How did your grandmother lose her other leg? Why was she fleeing the nursing home?"
>
> "Grandmother decided that she didn't like living in the nursing home," Calame responded. "She took off in her wheelchair, tipped going over the curb and spilled onto the street. She developed an infection in her injured leg and later had to have it amputated."

Calame was telling stories to friends. When we tell stories, we start at the beginning, or at least close enough to the beginning so the story makes sense. The approach allows the speaker to build to the climax.

In the inverted pyramid, we get to the point as quickly as possible. That approach saves readers' and listeners' time, but it's not the best way to tell stories. If we want to engage our readers intellectually and emotionally, if we want to inform and entertain, we must use writing techniques that promise great things to come and then fulfill that promise. To that end, we should use the devices of narration: scene re-creation, anecdotes, foreshadowing and dialogue. With these devices, we reward readers.

Narration requires structures other than the inverted pyramid. Some of the structures are hybrids of the inverted pyramid and chronology structures. Others are adaptations of chronology. These structures are even suitable for breaking news stories if you are able to gather enough information to re-create scenes jammed with pertinent detail, if you are able to confirm the chronology, if you are able to capture the dialogue. These structures also support investigative reports, profiles, oddities and issue stories—all genres that allow you more time to gather and write.

If time, detail and space are available, take advantage of these devices and structures. Whether you are writing about a car accident, the Boy Scouts, the health-care system, corruption in government or the 8-year-old running the corner lemonade stand, writing the story will be easier if you know some of the alternatives to the inverted pyramid.

The Techniques of Narration

Exposition is the ordering of facts. **Narration** is the telling of a story. When we arrange facts from most to least important, we call the structure the inverted pyramid. When we use scenes, anecdotes and dialogue in chronology to build to a climax, we call the structure narration.

Storytellers don't speak in monotone. They add inflection to maintain listeners' interest. To avoid telling stories in monotone, writers re-create scenes with detail and dialogue, foreshadow the good stuff to come and tempt readers to continue reading by offering them treats in the form of anecdotes.

In exposition, the writer clearly stands between the reader and the information. The people in the story whisper to the writer, who turns and speaks to the reader. In narration, the storytellers move aside and allow readers to watch the action unfold. Ken Burns retold the history of the Civil War to millions of viewers by re-creating the scenes and dialogue. Journalists can use the same techniques.

Vivid Scenes

Gene Roberts, managing editor of the *New York Times*, tells about his first job at a daily newspaper. His publisher, who was blind, would have the newspaper read to him each morning. One day, the publisher called Roberts into his office. He complained, "Roberts, I can't see your stories. Make me see."

We should all try to make readers see, smell, feel, taste and hear. One way to do that is to re-create scenes. First, you have to be there. You need to capture the sights, the sounds and the smells that are pertinent. Alan Cowell of the *New York Times* quickly establishes a scene in his opening of a story about the Egyptian government's attempt to regulate the economy.

CAIRO—In a tangled part of town called Boulaq, all narrow streets and gimcrack homes and children beyond counting, a man called Hamid told a story the other day that said much about the problems confronting President Hosni Mubarak in the Arab world's most populous nation.

The streets are narrow and full of children, the homes are cheap. We discover these details are pertinent when we read that Hamid can no longer afford bread because it costs a quarter of his income.

To re-create scenes, you must use all your senses to gather information, and your notebook should reflect that reporting. Along with the results of interviews, your notebook should bulge with details of sight and smell, sound and touch. Gather details indiscriminately. Later, you can discard those that are not germane.

Daniel Browning of the *Post-Dispatch* provides pertinent details in a St. Louis neighborhood scene:

It's a quiet, turn-of-the-century neighborhood with ornate brick homes and solid families.

Pigeons and song birds greet the children as they head to school past a few carefully tended flower and vegetable gardens.

"We've got a good, sweet block," Wali Furqan said. "Nice, quiet kids; clean homes. . . ."

Yet two blocks to the north, on Bailey Avenue, crack dealers sell their poison, and drive-by shootings regularly shatter the peace.

Signs indicate that gangs are creeping toward the Furqans' block. Around the corner on Barrett Street, cryptic graffiti shouts a warning. It says "Blood," "B-town" and "Hitman."

Figure 17.1.
This photo accompanied a story about public reaction to the discovery of the body of Polly Klaas, a 12-year-old Petaluma, Calif., kidnapping victim. Her grandfather is shown at the search center that had been set up two months earlier, when the kidnapping occurred. What details of the scene do you think were mentioned in the story?

Children walking past flower and vegetable gardens contrast with gang signs two blocks away. The writer has removed himself to allow readers to see the scene for themselves. The writer who lacks the details to re-create the scene falls back on generalities. See what you lose by substituting "nice neighborhood" for "turn-of-the-century neighborhood with ornate brick homes and solid families." You cannot build scenes on generalities and abstractions.

Dialogue

To place people in the scene, you should also ask enough questions to get the dialogue—the conversations. "What did you say to your husband? What was his response? Then what happened? Where were you when that happened? Then what did you do?" Repeat the same questions to other participants until you are satisfied you know what happened.

Quotations move from the source to the reporter to the reader. The reader is aware that the reporter is the intermediary. News stories typically use quotations because the people are talking to reporters:

Deidra Baker, wife of the shuttle commander, described seeing husband Michael stuck inside a 2,000-ton rocket ship filled with explosive fuel.

"We were quite obviously very concerned," said Baker. "I don't think anybody's happier than the families that the safety systems worked and everybody's okay."

Dialogue is a conversation between two or more people, neither of whom normally is the reporter. This is dialogue between Cindy Martling, a rehabilitation nurse, and Mary Jo, the patient's wife, after Martling scolded the patient for feeling sorry for himself:

She wandered around a bit, then saw Mary Jo standing in the hallway. The two women went to each other and embraced. "I'm sorry," Martling said through more tears. "I didn't mean to lose control. I hope I didn't offend you."

"What you did was wonderful," Mary Jo said. "He needed to hear that. Dan is going to work through it, and we're all going to be OK."

When Edna Buchanan, noted crime reporter, worked for the *Miami Herald*, she used dialogue in re-creating a scene about a disc jockey who was assaulted while working alone one morning. At the point in the story that the disc jockey, James T., encounters his visitor, Buchanan moves from quotations, in which the source is speaking to the reporter, to dialogue:

James T. put the caller on hold. He always urges listeners to "Have a great day! You are in control of your day." He answered the door—and his day went out of control.

There stood a young man in a red shirt. James T. likes young people. Only the day before he had spoken to fifth- and sixth-graders at Sunset Elementary School and to students and parents at Arcola Junior High, hoping to inspire and motivate them.

"Can I go on the air and say something to somebody?" the man in the red shirt asked.

"I'm sorry, you can't, but if you'd like to make a dedication or want me to play something for you, I will," James T. replied.

"You mean it's Saturday morning and I can't say something on the air?"

James T. felt a twinge of alarm, since it was Wednesday morning.

"If you'd like me to say hello to someone, tell me who, and I'll do that, but you have to hurry, I have only a couple of seconds."

"C'est la Vie," the extended seven-minute, four-second version, was almost over. The man in the red shirt thought for a moment, then pulled out a gun. . . .

Dialogue is a key element in re-creating scenes. The reporter has to leave to let the action play out.

Foreshadowing

Foreshadowing is the technique of advertising what's coming. Movie makers tease you with the scenes they think will encourage you to buy a ticket. Broadcasters foreshadow to keep you from leaving during a commercial: "Coming up, there's a burglar prowling your neighborhood." Every lead foreshadows the story. The ones that not only tell but promise more good stuff to come are the most successful. Tom Koetting of the *Wichita Eagle* spent nine months observing the recovery of a doctor who had nearly lost his life in a farm accident. He produced a story of about 100,000 words. The simple lead promised great things to come: "Daniel Calliendo Jr. had not expected to meet death this calmly."

What follows is a longer opening that is packed with promises of great things to come. It was written by a college student.

Deena Borman's relationship with her roommate, Teresa, during her freshman year in college had shattered long before the wine bottle.

Weeks had gone by with Teresa drawing further and further away from Deena. Finally, after repeatedly hearing Teresa talk about suicide, Deena says, "I kept telling her how silly she was to want to die."

That made Teresa angry, so she threw a full wine bottle at Deena. It shattered against the wall and broke open the simmering conflict between them. That was when Deena tried to find out what had gone wrong with Teresa's life, and that was when Teresa told Deena that she wanted to do something to get rid of her.

And that was when Deena began to be scared of her own roommate.

The writer is promising a great story. What *is* wrong with Teresa? Does Teresa really try to hurt Deena? Does Deena really have something to be scared about? There is a promise of great things to come. Would you keep reading?

Anecdotes

The ultimate treats, **anecdotes** are stories embedded in stories. They can be happy or sad, funny or serious. Whatever their tone, they should illustrate a point. You are likely to remember the anecdotes more than anything else in the story. You probably remember the stories that your professors tell regardless of whether you remember the rest of the lecture. Long after you've forgotten this chapter, you'll probably remember the Barney Calame anecdote and some of the other examples. Facts inform. Anecdotes inform and entertain.

Befitting something so valuable, they are hard to obtain. You can't get them by asking your source, "Got any good anecdotes?" But you can get them by asking your source for examples. A source told *St. Louis Post-Dispatch* reporter Daniel Browning that if you treat people with respect, they will return the favor. The reporter asked for an example, and this is what he later wrote:

The thin menacing man at the counter one recent morning put him to the test.

"I'm trying to take your order, sir," Gretha Furqan said. "What do you want to eat?"

The man wobbled on his feet, then spat out a stream of unconnected words. "Gun" and "shoot you" bobbed among them.

The couple's 2-year-old daughter, Walidah, suddenly slipped under the counter and pushed past the man's legs. His bloodshot eyes followed the toddler.

Wali Furqan quickly stepped to the counter. He smiled broadly.

"You can't curse in the restaurant," he told the man. "Why don't you go now and come back when you're sober?"

The man looked perplexed. Wali Furqan, still smiling, repeated himself.

Finally, the man apologized and let a friend order. . . .

To get anecdotes such as this, you ask for examples. You phrase your questions to get stories: "Can you give me an example of that?" "What's the funniest thing that ever happened to you while you were standing in front of an audience?" "What's the worst case you've ever seen come into this emergency room?" "So Mary is a practical joker. What are some of the practical jokes you've seen her pull?" "Everyone tells me Rodney is always the first one they call when they need help on a project. Has he ever helped you?"

When you get the response, you can ask follow-up questions to fill in the blanks. When Furqan related the story about the drunk in his restaurant, he probably didn't describe the man as thin and menacing, he probably didn't trace his daughter moving from underneath the counter to the man and he probably didn't mention bloodshot eyes. These are typical of details the reporter gets with further questions.

All of these elements—scene re-creation, dialogue, foreshadowing and anecdotes—are the ingredients of narration. Most stories move from exposition to narration several times during a story. Now let's look at the structures in which you can use these techniques.

How to Modify the Inverted Pyramid

In Chapter 3, you saw examples of inverted pyramid stories that didn't have the news in the first paragraph. But as soon as the writer set the hook, the news lead would appear. The writer arranged the rest of the story in the traditional descending order of importance. Further modification, though, offers writers more choices. For instance, when Jane Meinhardt of the *St. Petersburg Times* wrote about an unusual burglary ring, she started with a non-news lead, went to news and then back to chronology. Let's see how it works:

Setting the scene

PALM HARBOR—They carried knapsacks and bags to tote loot. They had a screwdriver to pry open doors and windows. They used latex gloves.

They acted like professional criminals, but officials say they were teenage burglars coached and directed by a Palm Harbor woman whose son and daughter were part of her gang.

Traditional lead information

Pinellas County Sheriff's deputies arrested Rovana Sipe, two of her children and two other teens Wednesday after a series of home burglaries.

"She was the driver," said Sheriff's Sgt. Greg Tita. "She pointed out the houses. She's the one who said 'Do these.'"

Support lead

Sipe, 38, of 2333 State Road 584, was charged with two counts of being a principal in burglary. She was held Thursday in lieu of $20,000 bail.

Her daughter, Jackie Shifflet, 16, was charged with grand theft. Her son, Ryan Shifflet, 15, was charged with two counts of burglary.

Charles Ruhe, 17, of 1600 Ensley Ave., in Safety Harbor, and Charles Taylor, 16, of 348 Jeru Blvd. in Tarpon Springs, also were held on four counts of burglary each.

"They were very well-prepared to do burglaries, especially with the guidance they were given," Tita said. "We recovered thousands of dollars of stolen items. Anything that could be carried out, was."

Back to chronology

The burglary ring unraveled Tuesday, Tita said. A Palm Harbor woman saw a large, yellow car driven by a woman drop off three boys, he said. The three went to the back of her house.

They put on gloves and started to pry open a window with a screwdriver, she said. When she tapped on a window, they ran.

She called 911. As she waited for deputies, other neighbors saw the boys walk through a nearby neighborhood carrying bags.

Deputies chased the boys and caught two. The third got into a large yellow car driven by a woman.

The bags contained jewelry, a shotgun and other items deputies say were taken from another house in the neighborhood. Tita said the boys, later identified as Taylor and Ruhe, told detectives about other burglaries in Dunedin and Clearwater and who else was involved.

At Sipe's house, detectives found stolen VCRs, televisions, camcorders and other valuables. They arrested the other two teens and Sipe.

"We're very familiar with this family and its criminal history," Tita said. "We have found stolen property at the house in the past and made juvenile arrests."

This is news, but it is presented as a story rather than facts. The traditional lead isn't in the first paragraph, but it's not too deep in the story, either. And when the writer returns to the chronology, she uses a transition that signals a story to come: "The burglary ring unraveled Tuesday, Tita said." The transition has echoes of "Let me tell you how it happened." Journalists shouldn't be afraid to experiment with different story forms.

The Focus Structure

For centuries, writers have told stories by focusing on one individual or group that represents a bigger population. This approach allows the writer to make large institutions, complex issues and seven-digit numbers meaningful. Not many of us can understand—let alone explain—

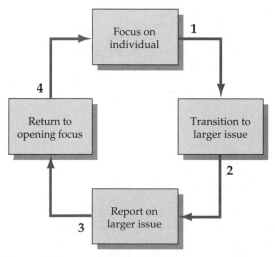

Figure 17.2.
Steps in applying the focus structure.

the marketing system for wheat, but we could if we followed a bushel of wheat from the time it was planted until a consumer picked up a loaf of bread in the supermarket. The *Wall Street Journal* knew that not many of us would be attracted to a story about the interaction between two or more pesticides. That's why one reporter told the story of an individual to tell a story of pesticide poisoning:

> Thomas Latimer used to be a vigorous, athletic man, a successful petroleum engineer with a bright future.
> Then he mowed the lawn.

Want to read on? Even though Joseph Stalin was hardly talking about literary approaches, he summed up the impact of focusing on a part of the whole when he said, "Ten million deaths are a statistic; one death is a tragedy." Think about that the next time you hear that a plane crash has killed 300 people. You probably are not emotionally touched by the crash unless you know someone who was on the plane. If you were able to write the story of the crash by focusing on a couple of the victims, you would have a better chance of emotionally involving your readers. Issues such as health care, budget deficits and sexual harassment don't have much emotional appeal. You make them relevant if you discuss the issue by focusing on someone affected by it. One writer examining sexual harassment in the Navy found a specific person through whom she could tell the story:

> When Lt. Sally Fountain telephoned a repair office aboard this aircraft carrier the other day, a male sailor answered and called to his boss, "Hey, there's a lieutenant chick on the phone for you."
>
> Minutes later, the sailor's angry supervisor hauled the young man before Lt. Fountain, a 31-year-old electronic warfare officer on EA-6B radar-jamming planes, to apologize formally for his remark. "It showed me that men on board are trying to nip that stuff in the bud," Lt. Fountain said.
>
> Old habits die hard in the Navy, which for more than two years has been battered by the Tailhook scandal and the bungled investigations into sexual assaults on dozens of women by pilots involved in the scandal. But men and women here say the supervisor's response shows that the Navy is learning from the episode and fighting to correct the behavior that gave the service such self-inflicted wounds.

Fountain is concrete; the issue of sexual harassment is abstract. Readers can identify with Fountain.

Reporters working on local stories have just as many opportunities to apply this approach as those writing national and international stories. For example, instead of keeping score on the United Way fund drive, focus on the people who will benefit—or fail to benefit—from the campaign. If the streets in your city are bad, write about the problem from the point of view of a driver. If Dutch elm disease is killing the trees in your city, concentrate on a homeowner who has lost several. The focus structure offers the writer a powerful method of reducing institutions, statistics and cosmic issues to a level readers can relate to and understand.

Advertising agencies use the technique, too. That's why instead of being solicited for money to help the poor and starving, you are asked to support one child for only pennies a day. The technique gives poverty and hunger a face. Millions starving is an abstraction; one starving child is a tragedy.

Completing the Set-Up

You've completed your reporting. You've found a person through whom you can tell your story. You have all the information about the issue. You know you are going to open with a scene or an anecdote or some other approach that will say to the reader, "I've got an interesting story to tell." Now you must finish the set-up to the story. The **set-up** consists of the transition to the theme paragraph, the theme paragraph, the so-what, the to-be-sure and foreshadowing. Let's look at each of these.

The set-up consists of
- *The transition to the theme paragraph*
- *The theme paragraph*
- *The so-what*
- *The to-be-sure*
- *Foreshadowing*

Add the Transition and Theme Paragraph

When you open with a scene or an anecdote, you must construct a transition, that *explicitly* makes the connection to the theme paragraph, also commonly called the **nut paragraph**. "Explicitly" is the key word. If you fail to help readers understand the point of the opening, however interesting it is, you risk losing them. The transition in this example is in italics:

> Anita Poore hit the rough pavement of the parking lot with a thud. She had never felt such intense, stabbing pain and could barely lift her heavy head. When she reached for the car door, a police officer stared at her and asked her husband, "Is she drunk?" A wave of nausea swept over her, and she vomited.
>
> "That's it. Get her out of here!" the officer demanded.
>
> Poore was not drunk. She avoided jail, but she faces a life sentence of pain. Now 25, she has suffered migraine headaches since she was in seventh grade.
>
> *Not that it is much comfort, but she's not alone.* Health officials estimate that Americans miss 157 million workdays a year because of migraines and spend more than $2 million a year on over-the-counter painkillers for migraine, tension and cluster headaches. Researchers haven't found a cure, but they have found methods to lessen the pain.

The transition explicitly places her among those who miss work, buy painkillers and are still waiting for a cure. What follows is the theme. Earlier in this chapter, you were introduced to Hamid, the Egyptian who couldn't afford bread when prices were increased. Here is how the writer connected Hamid to the theme paragraph (italics added):

His story reflected a much wider malaise. Since President Mubarak came to power in October 1981, when Islamic fundamentalists assassinated President Anwar el-Sadat, Egypt has confronted a deepening economic crisis that has brought soaring prices and unpredictable shortages to a fast-growing population that now exceeds 55 million.

When you have involved the reader and successfully written the explicit transition to the theme paragraph, you are ready to build the rest of the set-up.

Add Foreshadowing

Foreshadowing can be done in a single line (The killing started early and ended late.), or it can be developed as part of several paragraphs. The goal is to assure readers they will be rewarded if they continue reading. This is what Erik Larson of the *Wall Street Journal* promised the readers of his fire investigation story:

And so began what may well be the most intensive scientific investigation in the history of arson—not a whodunit, exactly, but a whatdunit. So far the inquiry has taken Seattle investigators places arson squads don't typically go, even to the Navy's weapons-testing grounds at China Lake in California. Along the way, the investigation has attracted a team of scientists who, likewise ensnared by the "Twilight Zone" nature of the mystery, volunteered time and equipment. At one point the investigators themselves torched a large building just to test a suspected fuel.

Add the So-What

The so-what tells readers explicitly why they should care. Thomas Latimer was poisoned when he mowed his lawn. So what? Hamid can't afford bread. So what? Anita Poore almost got arrested for having a migraine headache. Interesting, but so what? Reporters and editors know the so-what, or they wouldn't spend time on the story. Too often, however, they fail to tell it to readers. Latimer's story is interesting, but it's much more important when you are told why you should care. The brackets identify the so-what:

The makers of the pesticide, diazinon, and of Tagamet firmly deny that their products had anything to do with Mr. Latimer's condition. The pesticide maker says he doesn't even believe he was exposed to its product. And in fact, Mr. Latimer lost a lawsuit he filed against the companies. [Even so, the case intrigues scientists and regulators because it illustrates the need for better understanding of the complex interactions between such everyday chemicals as pesticides and prescription drugs.

Neither the Food and Drug Administration nor the Environmental Protection Agency conducts routine tests for such interactions. Indeed, the EPA doesn't even evaluate the synergy of two or more pesticides commonly used together. "We have not developed ways to test any of that," says an EPA spokesman. "We don't know how to do it." And a new congressional report says the FDA lacks both the resources and the enforcement powers to protect Americans from all kinds of poisons.]

The so-what is the impact—the relevance—to people who have no warning that two or more pesticides may interact to poison them. In other cases, the so-what may be included in the theme statement. Let's look at the migraine story again:

[1] Not that it is much comfort, but she's not alone. [2] Health officials estimate that Americans miss 157 million workdays a year because of migraines and spend more than $2 million a year on over-the-counter painkillers for migraine, tension and cluster headaches. [3] Researchers haven't found a cure, but they have found methods to lessen the pain.

The first sentence is the transition; the second is the so-what; the third is the theme, which includes foreshadowing. The so-what establishes the dimensions of the problem. When you define the so-what, you are establishing the story's impact.

Add the To-Be-Sure

To maintain an even-handed approach, writers must acknowledge that there are two or more other sides to the story. We've seen in the pesticide story that the makers of the drugs and pesticides "firmly deny that their products had anything to do with Mr. Latimer's condition." We see the technique again in an article about the impact of gambling on Tunica, Miss. Writer Jenny Deam opens with a scene in the mayor's store. The mayor says gambling is the best thing that ever happened to the town. At the front counter, a woman is asking for the $85 back she paid on furniture last week. She lost her grocery money gambling. What comes next is a combination theme and to-be-sure statement (italics added):

And so is the paradox of this tiny Mississippi Delta county, now that the casinos have come to call.

On the one hand, unemployment in a place the Rev. Jesse Jackson once called "America's Ethiopia" has dropped from nearly 24 percent to a low last fall of 5 percent. Anyone who wants a job has one with the casinos. There are more jobs than people to fill them. In a county of about 8,100 people, the number of food stamp recipients fell from 4,218 before the casinos to 2,907 now.

But there is another side. New problems never before seen.

Since the first casino opened in 1992, the number of DUI arrests has skyrocketed by 400 percent. U.S. Highway 61 leading to Memphis is constantly jammed. On a busy weekend as many as 28,000 cars head toward the nine casinos now open. The criminal court system is just as overloaded. In 1992, there were 1,500 cases filed. A year later, 2,400. As of last month there had already been 6,800 cases filed for this year.

"Well," says the mayor, "It's just like anything else in life: You got to take the evil with the good."

the scene, whether it be a breaking news scene or the office of some bureaucrat, assess your surroundings. Take mental pictures. What kind of pictures are on the desk and wall? What books do they read? Is the place clean? Always check out the bathroom and kitchen of a house. They tell more about the subject than any other rooms."

When you get the story, she advises, "Act like Columbo." See if there are holes in the story.

"Then when you get back to the office, paint that picture for me. Give me the most gripping part of the story with lots of tight detail. And then get to the point. Give me a nut graph that sums up your story and a significance graph that tells me why I should waste my precious time reading it."

It works for Reed. She has won several writing and reporting awards and gained national notice for a series in which she and a colleague revealed that the military pays more than a million dollars a month to service personnel serving prison terms.

Now that the story has been defined, Deam is ready to examine both sides of the issue.

And now that you have constructed the set-up, you are ready to enter the body of the story.

Writing the Body

Think of readers as people antsy to do something else. To maintain their interest, offer them frequent examples to support your main points. In narration, you employ the anecdotes, the scenes and the dialogue to move the story line. You mix exposition—the facts—with narration—the story line. Every few paragraphs, Erik Larson offered readers another story to keep them reading about the arson investigation. Here's just one of them:

Two firemen, William Meredith and Lt. Matthew Johnson, entered a portion of the building separated from the main body of the blaze by a fire wall. On their side, the air was warm but tolerable. On the far side, though they couldn't have known it, temperatures were estimated in excess of 5,000 degrees.

Lt. Johnson stayed below with the water hose, while Mr. Meredith climbed a stairway to hunt for open flames. Still, he felt nothing unusual.

Moments later, however, a portion of the roof elsewhere in the warehouse collapsed, rolling outward with so much force it snapped the fire wall at a height of about eight feet. Raw energy surged past the break.

"It was just staggering," Mr. Meredith recalls. "It was like a thousand little needles going through me. White-hot needles."

Mr. Meredith made his way down the steps, but couldn't find his partner. He followed the hose to its nozzle, then outside, then back in again, where he now heard the cry of a low-air alarm from a firefighter's breathing apparatus. He followed the sound to Lt. Johnson, who was alive but disoriented.

When the two men tried to exit by retracing Mr. Meredith's route, they became lost within the structure. They tried radioing for help, but got no response. Lt. Johnson, his air supply now dangerously low, lay on the floor, the coolest and safest place in a fire. Mr. Meredith sought help.

As the heat rose, he also became disoriented. At one point he saw a crack in the wall, a firetruck just outside. He squeezed through the crack and rested against the cool skin of the vehicle feeling utter relief. "It was the most vivid thing," he says.

An instant later, he realized he was still in the warehouse.

He did escape, but doesn't remember how. Medics discovered that his core temperature, a measure of heat buildup deep inside the body, had reached lethal levels. "He was baked," says Mr. Fowler, the consultant. "Just as if you stuck him in an oven at 2,000 degrees for five minutes."

That anecdote supports the point that the fires reach incredible temperatures.

The outline for the body of your story should look something like this:

    I.   Point A
        Support: Anecdote/scene/quotations/documents
    II. Point B
        Support: Anecdote/scene/quotations/documents

And so on. To support each point, you'd like to have anecdotes and scenes, including dialogue, as evidence. Sometimes you also offer good quotations or supporting documents. More complicated stories will have more complicated outlines. If you are telling the story chronologically, you may introduce flashbacks to introduce events out of sequence.

Think of your story as an interstate highway. The highway is your narrative thread. In one story, it might be chronology. In another, it may be movement from one location to another. At times, you need to exit the highway to introduce other examples and ideas. The exits should be smooth—easy off, easy on.

Writing the Ending

Stories should end, not just stop. One good technique, called a tie-back, is one of the significant differences between the inverted pyramid and the focus structure. The inverted pyramid diminishes in importance and interest so that it can be cut from the end, but the focus structure has an ending. If the story has to be shortened, the writer or editor will have to delete something other than the ending. In a profile of a retiring college administrator, a student writer opened this way:

> When Don Ruthenburg was 12, he started fixing an old car he couldn't yet drive. When he turned 16, he was driving the prettiest and fastest car in town.
> Throughout his career, Ruthenburg has demonstrated that same perseverance.
> When he came to Columbia College in 1984, the school was on academic probation and $3.8 million in debt. Now the school has received a 10-year qualified accreditation, has $2.6 million in the bank, has doubled student enrollment to 1,900 and has increased its endowment from $360,000 to over $1.8 million.

The story ends with a tie-back to the lead:

> Ruthenburg will have more free time after he retires on June 30. But he is not going to stop working.
> He plans to rebuild a Pepsi-Cola truck, which he bought from an Ohio farmer seven years ago for $1,400.
> "The tires and the back deck were all gone when I towed it down here," he says.

Another way to end is a summary, not of the last point in the story but of the story's theme itself. Here's Erik Larson concluding his arson story:

> One thing is certain, Mr. Fowler says: The arsonist is a professional, not a pyromaniac out to watch things burn. "If this guy were crazy we'd have caught him a long time ago," he says. "But this guy is a businessman."

Anecdotes, dialogue, scenes and good quotes all can end the story. What you must avoid is ending the last *section* of the story instead of wrapping up the story line.

Putting It Together

We've seen bits and pieces of narration in the focus structure. Now let's look at how a writer used narration to re-create a homicide attempt. What you are about to read is an example of the use of chronology. It appeared in the *Madison* (Wis.) *Capital Times* nine days after a bombing. Inverted pyramid news stories based on police reports appeared in the intervening days. Given the time to reconstruct the event, reporter Todd Moore used chronology to tell the kind of story that newspapers are trying to do more frequently. Here is the first half of the story:

In the dark and in the rain, no one would be likely to notice the man walking east on the railroad tracks just south of the Beltline.

In the early morning hours of Monday, May 3, 35-year-old John P. DiCristina told his wife he was going fishing. In reality he was going hunting. His target was his supervisor at the Dane County Highway Department, Robert C. Anderson.

Just hours before, DiCristina had checked into the Trail's End motel on the south side. Once there he set to work, cracking open shotgun shells and pouring the powder into a 6-inch-long piece of pipe that was closed at one end. With wires, battery and detonating device in place, he screwed the top down tight.

It was a hefty piece of work. He was by most accounts a careful and methodical man, but even he would be surprised at how well this would work. He learned how to do it from the television show "Mac-Gyver."

Walking along the darkened tracks, it wasn't far from the motel to Anderson's house, perhaps no more than three miles. On a hillside in McFarland, Anderson's only neighbors were the white oil storage tanks to the north. At night, Terminal Road would be mostly empty.

According to one supervisor at the Highway Department, DiCristina was quiet and unassertive. "You'd just about have to step onto his toes to get him to say ouch," the supervisor said. Few knew that his personal problems had grown to a point that he was now willing to act.

In the past he reportedly had thought of suicide. On this wet spring night, he was willing to risk homicide.

Sometime before dawn DiCristina slid the pipe bomb to the rear of Anderson's oversized country mailbox. Trigger set, he closed the lid and slipped away.

Anderson, in contrast to the quiet man who was trying to injure and perhaps kill him, was known as a tough—some say abusive—boss with a military demeanor that won him few friends in the rank and file of the Highway Department.

The sun couldn't have been over the ridge behind his house when Anderson stopped at his mailbox at 7:55 that very morning. On his way to work he meant to drop off some mail for the postal carrier to pick up. The post that held the mailbox was wobbly, so he placed one hand on top of it to open it.

In holding the box still, Anderson saved himself. The motion-sensitive trigger failed to complete the circuit. That would happen a little more than four hours later. Anderson drove off to work.

DiCristina didn't go to work that Monday morning. Around 12:30 p.m. his wife found him at their home in Indiana Springs. And 10 minutes later—at 12:40 p.m.—postal carrier Stanley Bengston was driving up to the Anderson home to deliver the mail.

By one investigator's account, Bengston saw the package at the back of the mailbox only an instant before an immense explosion occurred. Shrapnel tore into Bengston and his car. Once the postman came to his senses, he drove himself to get medical attention, peppered with wounds and powder burns to his face, chest, arm and hand. He is now recovering and refuses to comment.

Investigators from the county, the city of McFarland and the Postal Service set to work chasing a number of leads, uncertain of whom the target was supposed to be. Anderson had no problem reeling off a long list of those who might harbor a grudge against him. Once questioning focused on Dane County garage employees, DiCristina became nervous, especially when authorities began fingerprinting people.

The bomb went off Monday, but he skipped work. He returned Tuesday and Wednesday. Thursday he left early and had himself admitted to Parkway Hospital. The authorities picked him up Friday at 2:30 p.m. With his lawyer, Richard Auerbach, at his side he waived his rights as part of a prearranged plea with the U.S. attorney,

Kevin Potter, and the county district attorney, William Foust. It was there that he stammered out this confession:

"I would like to take responsibility for my actions. I have had great remorse since the time it happened. I acted alone. I had no help. I did this during a time of considerable confusion in my mind but I am not offering any excuses."

DiCristina went on: "I know what I did was wrong and I did in fact put a device, a homemade device, in Mr. Anderson's mailbox. I didn't have any intent to kill anybody. I guess my intent was to scare the man but I did no research before I assembled the device and I really had no idea what I was doing and it turned out to be far more powerful than I anticipated, but nonetheless I did this and I acted alone."

The confession was part of a deal that would help him avoid federal charges.

By late afternoon, DiCristina had pleaded no contest before Dane County Circuit Judge Daniel Moeser to charges of property damage by explosives and first-degree recklessly endangering safety. Shortly thereafter he was sent to Mendota Mental Health Institute for evaluation.

Behind the swift resolution of the case lay hours of agony for DiCristina and his wife, Ruth. It wasn't until Tuesday afternoon that he even asked her if she had heard about the bombing. She hadn't. But the second he brought it up, she knew what was in store. She asked him if he did it and he admitted he did. The couple subsequently decided that the only thing to do was for John to turn himself in, but only after the legal machinery had been put in motion.

Asked why her husband put

the bomb in his boss' mailbox she points to job-related stress. But investigator's reports point to a man beset by health prob-lems, marital concerns, a tough childhood and lingering depression. . . .

Many readers knew the outcome of this story, but a good story told well will attract them. This version offers richness of detail, reveals nuances, explains the "why." This type of reporting and storytelling should be used as often as possible.

Suggested Readings

Brooks, Terri. *Words' Worth: A Handbook on Writing & Selling Nonfiction*. New York: St. Martin's Press, 1989. Full of detailed advice and examples.

Clark, Roy Peter and Fry, Donald, eds. *Best Newspaper Writing: 1994*. St. Petersburg, Fla.: The Poynter Institute, 1994. Each year the winning entries in the American Society of Newspaper Editors writing contest are published in this book, which also contains interviews with the writers.

Kennedy, George, Moen, Daryl R. and Ranly, Don. *Beyond the Inverted Pyramid: Effective Writing for Newspapers, Magazines and Specialized Publications*. New York: St. Martin's Press, 1993. A book-length treatment of material found in Chapters 4 and 17 of *News Reporting and Writing*.

Sims, Norman, ed. *The Literary Journalists*. New York: Ballantine Books, 1984. With an introductory essay defining literary journalism, this book offers reprints from the best of the bunch.

Zinsser, William. *On Writing Well*, Fourth Edition. New York: HarperPerennial, 1994. An entertaining narrative on the art of writiing.

Exercises

1. Write four to eight paragraphs about how you and your classmates learned to be reporters. Pick a scene from one of your classes and re-create it. Provide the transition into the body of the story and then stop.

2. Interview a student in your reporting class. Ask questions that elicit anecdotes. Write an anecdote about the person.

3. Using a chronologic approach, write approximately eight paragraphs of a story about some aspect of your experience in the reporting class.

4. Choose a personal experience that is worth telling in a first-person story. Write two to three pages using chronology in the first person.

5. Analyze focus structure stories found on the front page of either the *Wall Street Journal* or *USA Today*. How many elements of the set-up can you identify? Find all the anecdotes. Identify any dialogue.

6. Write the first two pages of an event of your life. Try to include as many parts of the set-up as you can: scenes, dialogue, foreshadowing and the so-what statement.

SOCIAL SCIENCE
REPORTING

*R*eporters Marianne Lavelle, Marcia Coyle and Claudia MacLachlan of the National Law Journal *wanted to test a widely shared assumption: that a community's color affects the federal government's approach to pollution. They collected on computer data from more than 1,000 lawsuits, dozens of federal reports and census data. They built two of their own databases on personal computers and used spreadsheet formulas to analyze the mass of material. In eight months of work, they demonstrated proof of discrimination.*

At Gannett News Service, reporter Pamela Brogan and special projects editor Wendell Cochran wanted to find out how the U.S. Congress, after mandating employment equality, treated its own women workers. In addition to dozens of interviews, they bought a computer database listing government employees, devised their own programs to incorporate missing information and sorted the data on personal computers. They showed a glass ceiling so thick it would have been illegal, except that Congress exempted itself from the law.

"Dateline NBC" wanted to know how safe America's blood supply is in the age of AIDS. Producers Steve Eckert and Mark Hosenball, associate producer David Hinchman and correspondent Stone Phillips used the Freedom of Information Act to obtain government inspection records. They did their own analysis of a variety of computer records. In six months, they showed that safeguards were shaky, tests sometimes weren't made and public assurances of safety were misleading.

These projects and hundreds like them have two things in common. All combine old-fashioned reporting with newly acquired computer skills. And all rely on the techniques of the social sciences.

Journalists don't usually regard themselves as scientists. Many would resist the very suggestion. But the best reporting has a great deal in common with the work of political scientists, historians and sociologists. Like social scientists, these reporters frame research questions or hypotheses. They seek answers to their questions by the careful accumulation of reliable data and the use of scientific formulas and statistics to analyze the information they've gathered. They double-check their findings for reliability. Then they report clearly and carefully what they have learned.

The increasing complexity of the world around us requires the journalists of today and tomorrow to learn tools adequate to the task of understanding and explaining that world. Often the most useful tools turn out to be those developed and regularly used by social scientists.

Participant Observation

When KSTP-TV in Minneapolis was examining school bus safety, an important question was the training of the drivers. Reporters studied records and interviewed drivers, but the station wanted a firsthand look. So a producer got a job at a bus company to experience the situation from inside.

Journalists call this **undercover reporting**. Social scientists call it participant observation. Both sets of researchers use the tool for the same reasons. Participant observers get close-up pictures of their subjects, pictures not obtainable by studying statistics or by formal interviewing. Facts and feelings can be captured that otherwise would remain unknown.

Along with its unique advantages, participant observation also poses some unique problems. These problems may have no clear solutions, but you and your editors need at least to consider them before you set out to become an ambulance attendant or a migrant worker.

The Problem of Invasion of Privacy. Unless you identify yourself as a reporter, you are, in effect, spying on the lives of people who are not aware they are being observed—an ethically questionable activity (see pages 476-477). But if you do identify yourself, the advantages of the technique can be lost. Sensitivity is essential, especially when the people you write about may be embarrassed or have their jobs placed in jeopardy.

The Problem of Involvement. There are two things to watch out for here. First, do not become so involved that you change the course of the events you are observing. You may be on stage, but you are not a star performer. Second, do not assume that the people you are observing feel the same way you do. No matter how hard you work at fitting in, you remain an outsider, a visitor. The view from inside a migrant workers' camp or a psychiatric hospital is different when you know you will be there for two weeks instead of two years or a lifetime.

The Problem of Generalizing. Scientists know well the danger of generalizing on the basis of limited observation. Reporters don't always know that or sometimes forget it. Keep in mind that, although participant observation yields a detailed picture of a specific situation, it tells you nothing reliable about any other situation. Participant observation is a good tool, but it is a limited one. It usually works best as a supplement to the standard techniques of interviewing and examining documents.

Systematic Study of Records

The examples at the beginning of this chapter all relied, in various ways, on the systematic study of records. In each case, the reporters gathered information, devised a system for sorting it into useful categories and then analyzed the results to draw reliable conclusions about the problem under investigation.

Kathleen Kerr and Russ Buettner of *Newsday* faced the same sort of problem. Their goal: to discover whether New York City's

Problems of undercover reporting
∎ *Invasion of privacy*
∎ *Involvement*
∎ *Generalizing*

could do the job more effectively than I do.

"The real problem is what to do with all that data once it is in usable form."

That requires, among other skills, a grasp of simple statistics, a realization that may chill those who took up journalism—as many have—at least partly to avoid math. Jon says: "In other words, when you are faced with half a million records, where do you start? If the story idea is not firm, some simple statistical tools, including graphing, help me browse the data. Some people might call this a fishing expedition. I like to refer to this process by its social science term—*hypothesis testing.*"

And here's the payoff: "I find computer-assisted reporting very exciting. The use of computers, when combined with solid analysis skills, allows reporters to move beyond simply reacting to events. While remaining objective, we can take a more proactive role and give our readers a perspective on current issues that may not be found elsewhere."

criminal justice system discriminated against the poor. Their method: to acquire computer databases of city and state records on 27,810 prisoners, then to use their own computer to sort those cases by race and other criteria. Their findings: The poor, especially minorities, often were denied bail and forced to wait in jail for trials that often found them not guilty. No amount of traditional interviewing and observing could have produced such credible stories.

Scholars long have used such systematic study of records in their research. Its use by reporters is still limited but growing. The advantage of detailed analysis of court records, budgets, voting records and other documents is that it permits reporters and readers to draw conclusions based on solid information. The widespread availability of powerful personal computers and easy-to-use analytical programs brings the systematic study of records within the reach of any news organization.

The main obstacles to such study are shortages of time and money. Major projects for a large metropolitan daily often require months of work by one or more reporters. On small papers, especially, you may have trouble freeing yourself for even several days. And reporters' time and computer time both cost money. Editors and publishers must be convinced that the return will be worth the investment before they will approve. You probably should have at least some clues that wrongdoing, injustice or inefficiency exists before launching a systematic study.

Once you have begun a study, you should make sure that it is in fact systematic. You must either examine all the pertinent records or choose the ones you examine in such a way that they will be truly representative of the rest. Be sure you are asking the right questions and recording the information necessary to answer them. A computer can perform complicated analyses very quickly, but it cannot analyze facts that have not been fed into it. People who use computers have a word for that problem: *GIGO*, an acronym for "Garbage *In*, Garbage *Out.*"

Don't set out on a systematic study without assurances of time and money, a clear idea of what you're looking for and expert technical advice. If the expertise is unavailable at your newspaper, look to the nearest college.

Field Experiments

Instead of just asking questions about mail service, The Associated Press tested it. Letters were mailed from one bureau to another, some with ZIP codes and some without, some by air mail and some by regular first-class mail. A scientist conducting the same kind of test would call it a **field experiment**. In all such experiments researchers take some action in order to observe the effects.

Lies, Damned Lies and Statistics

Get your facts first, and then you can distort them as much as you please.
—Mark Twain

Sometimes, reporters distort the facts without even trying.

The *San Jose* (Calif.) *Mercury News* reported in the lead of a November 1993 special report that women are "10 times more likely to be represented on the Supreme Court of the United States than on the average board of directors for a company in Silicon Valley." The *Mercury News* based that statement on the fact that 22.2 percent of the justices were women, compared with 2.9 percent of Silicon Valley directors.

But there were about 135 million women in the United States; two of them were Supreme Court justices and 30 of them were Silicon Valley directors. Thus, despite the paucity of women on Silicon Valley boards, the likelihood of a woman being represented there was actually 15 times greater than on the Supreme Court.

In its effort to illustrate a point, the *Mercury News* stumbled into an error that is common in newspapers. It generalized to the entire population (all U.S. women) from figures that applied only to sub-populations (women on the Supreme Court and Silicon Valley boards). What the *Mercury News* should have said was that the "ratio of women on the Supreme Court is nearly 10 times greater than on the boards of directors of Silicon Valley companies."

The lesson from the *Mercury News* story is that even when you think you're comparing apples to apples, make sure you don't have some oranges in there. You must have the same base population for a comparison to mean anything.

Also, when reporting survey results, you can draw conclusions only from the sample population surveyed. For example, an Associated Press poll about the Major League Baseball strike of 1994–1995 questioned Americans identifying themselves as baseball fans, who constituted 26 percent of the overall population. The fact that 21 percent of the respondents blamed the players for the strike does not mean that 21 percent of Americans blamed the players—only that 21 percent of a relatively small, self-ordained group of fans did.

Moreover, the baseball survey reflected those fans' attitude at one point in time—Nov. 30–Dec. 6, 1994. Attitudes change over time, so the date a survey is taken must be included when reporting public opinion polls.

Here are some other ways statistics can deceive:

Bias can influence the credibility of a survey. For example, a 1993 national survey on sexual behavior indicated that 1 percent of 3,321 men questioned said they were gay, compared with the 10 percent commonly accepted as constituting the gay population. When reporting the survey results, *Time* magazine pointed out that people might be reluctant to discuss their sexual orientation with a "clipboard-bearing stranger."

One year does not a trend make. A large increase in the number of rapes merits a story, but it might represent a fluctuation rather than a trend. Depending on the subject matter, you need to study at least five to 10 years of data to determine whether there is a significant shift.

The way organizations compile figures can change, and that can distort comparisons. In the late 1980s, the formula for compiling AIDS cases among heterosexuals was changed. The figures skyrocketed, as did the number of media reports on the spread of AIDS to the general population. Not all the reports noted the change in compiling the statistics.

Conclusions that sound credible might not hold up under the scrutiny of cause and effect. Advocacy groups that call for less violence on television say studies show TV violence causes violence in children. They cite research at Yale showing that prolonged viewing of violent programs is associated with aggressive behavior among children. But the association could be that children who tend to be aggressive watch more violent programming, not the other way around.

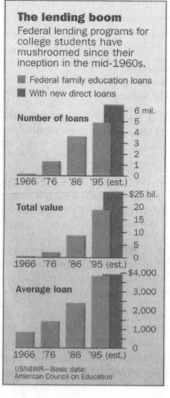

The lending boom

Federal lending programs for college students have mushroomed since their inception in the mid-1960s.

■ Federal family education loans
■ With new direct loans

Number of loans

1966 '76 '86 '95 (est.)

Total value

1966 '76 '86 '95 (est.)

Average loan

1966 '76 '86 '95 (est.)

USN&WR—Basic data: American Council on Education

Figure 18.1.
These graphs dramatically illustrate the growth of federal lending programs for college students. Three measurements of growth are presented to give a full picture.

Reporters may not think of themselves as scientists, but they conduct a great many experiments. The mailing experiment is a common one. Another frequent test is to examine the honesty of auto mechanics by taking a car in perfect condition to several shops and reporting what each finds "wrong" with it. Consumer reporters also commonly check weights and measures: Does a "pound" of hamburger really weigh a pound? Or they test for discrimination by having a black and a white reporter apply for insurance policies or mortgages.

If they are to be successful, reporters' field experiments must follow the same guidelines—and avoid the same pitfalls—that scientists' experiments must. A little scientific jargon is necessary here. It is fairly straightforward, though, and it will be useful if you ever have the opportunity to set up an experiment.

Your field experiment must have a *hypothesis*, a statement of what you expect to find. Your hypothesis must be stated clearly and simply. When it is, it will help focus your attention on the two elements of the experiment—the independent variable and the dependent variable. The *variables*, just as their name implies, are the things that change during the experiment. The *independent variable* is what you think may be a cause. You change it and observe what happens to the *dependent variable*, the effect.

Let's take an example. Suppose you think bankers in your town are discriminating against women by demanding more collateral for loans from them than from men. Form a hypothesis: "Women are forced to put up more collateral to secure loans than men are." The variables are the gender of the borrower and the amount of collateral demanded. Gender is the independent variable, the suspected cause. For your experiment, then, you will have applicants of each gender seek a bank loan. You will be looking for any change in the dependent variable—the collateral demanded.

There are two other steps you must take to assure a successful experiment. First you must *control* the experiment. Every aspect of the experiment must be carefully structured to make sure that any change you observe is caused only by the independent variable you want to test. For example, your male and female loan applicants must be as much alike as possible in the financial details they provide, the way they dress, their race and their age. Otherwise, any differences in the responses by the loan officer might be due to something other than gender, the variable you are interested in. Also, the applicants should visit the same bank or banks and speak to the same officials. Without careful control of the experiment, you may end up unable to say with certainty that you have proved or disproved your hypothesis. Then you've got no story.

The other step is called *randomization*, or *random selection*. In a small town you could run your experiment at every bank. But in a big city that would be impossible. So, if you want to be reasonably sure that the results of the experiment apply to all the banks in town, you must choose at random the ones to approach. Randomization allows you to assume that what you select—10 banks, for instance—is representative of the whole—the total number of banks in the city.

Choosing a bank or anything else, such as a name, at random simply means that you employ a method for choosing that gives every bank or every name an equal chance of being picked. The procedure for making a random selection is beyond the scope of an introductory reporting text. The Suggested Readings at the end of the chapter include several books in which you can find that and other material relating to the concepts introduced here. Much of that other material deals with statistics. Many experiments require statistical analysis to ensure that what you have found is significant. Most polls and surveys require some statistical analysis, too. Explanations of the fairly simple math involved also can be found in the books listed in Suggested Readings.

Public Opinion Polls

Public opinion polling has become an important tool of journalists. Many news organizations now go beyond reporting the findings of

---

"Average" can mean different things to different people

In reporting statistics, be certain you know the "average" involved. All of the following are averages:

Mean—*the arithmetic average, found by adding all the figures in a set of data and dividing by the number of figures. The mean of 2, 4 and 9 is 5 (2 + 4 + 9 = 15; 15 ÷ 3 = 5).*

Median—*the middle value in a set of figures. If there is no middle value because there is an even number of figures, average the two middle numbers. The median of 2, 4 and 9 is 4. The medians of 5, 7, 9 and 11 and of 3, 7, 9 and 15 both are 8 (7 + 9 = 16; 16 ÷ 2 = 8).*

Mode—*the most frequent value in a set of figures. The mode of 2, 5, 5, 5, 15 and 23 is 5.*

such national polling firms as the Gallup and Louis Harris organizations to conducting or commissioning their own surveys. Several journalism schools—including those at the universities of Alabama, Florida, North Carolina and Missouri—have developed scientific polling operations staffed by faculty and students to serve newspapers and broadcasters in their regions.

When polls are conducted properly and reported carefully, they can be both interesting and useful, telling people something they could not know otherwise and perhaps even helping to produce wiser public policies. But when they are badly done or sloppily reported, polls can be bad news for journalists and readers alike.

The chances are good that sometime in your reporting career you will want to conduct an opinion poll or at least help with one your newspaper is conducting. The Suggested Readings listed at the end of the chapter will tell you much of what you need to know for that. Even if you never work on one, you almost certainly will be called on to write about the results of polls. What follows will help you understand what you are given and help you make sure your readers understand it, too.

Requirements for Sound Polling

The Associated Press Managing Editors Association prepared a checklist of the information you should have and should share with your audience about any poll on which you are reporting. Several of those points require some explanation.

Information about a poll to be shared with your audience

- *The identity of the sponsor of the survey.*
- *The exact wording of the questions asked.*
- *A definition of the population sampled.*
- *The sample size and, where the survey design makes it relevant, the response rate.*
- *Some indication of the allowance that should be made for sampling error.*
- *Which results are based on only part of the sample (for example, probable voters, those who have heard of the candidate, or other subdivisions).*
- *When the interviews were collected.*
- *How the interviews were collected—in person, in homes, by phone, by mail, on street corners, or wherever.*

Identity of sponsor. The identity of the survey's sponsor is important to you and your readers because it gives some clues to possible bias. Most people would put more trust in a Gallup or Harris poll's report that, for instance, Smith is far ahead of Jones in the presidential campaign, than they would in a poll sponsored by the Smith for President organization.

Exact wording of questions. The exact wording of the questions is important because the answer received often depends at least in part on how the question was asked. (See Chapter 5 on interviewing for more detail.) The answer might well be different, for example, if a pollster asked, "Whom do you favor for president, Jones or Smith?" rather than "Wouldn't Jones make a better president than Smith?"

Population. In the third point on the checklist, the word "population" is another bit of jargon. Most of us use the word to mean the number of people living in the town, state or country. In science, however, **population** means the total number of people— or documents or milkweed plants or giraffes—in the group being studied. For an opinion survey the population might be all registered voters in the state, black males under 25 or female cigarette smokers. To understand what the results of a poll mean, you must know what population was studied. The word "sampled" simply refers to the procedure discussed earlier in which a small number—or **sample**—of persons is picked at random so as to be representative of the population.

Sample size and response rate. The sample size is important because—all other things being equal—the larger the sample, the more reliable the survey results should be. The response rate is especially important in surveys conducted by mail, in which a low rate of response may invalidate the poll.

Margin of error. The *sampling error* of any survey is the allowance that must be made for the possibility that the opinion of the sample may not be exactly the same as the opinion of the whole population. A simpler name for it is **margin of error**. The margin of error depends mainly on the size of the sample. For instance, all other things being equal, a sample of 400 would have a margin of error of 5 percent while a sample of 1,500 would have a margin of error of 3 percent. If, with a sample of 1,500, the poll shows Jones with 60 percent of the votes and Smith with 40 percent, you can be confident that Jones actually has between 57 and 63 percent while Smith actually has between 37 and 43 percent. The laws of probability say that the chances are 19 to 1 that the actual percentages fall in that range. Those odds make the information good enough to publish.

Which results are based on part of the sample. The existence of sampling error helps explain why it is important to know which results may be based on only part of the sample. The smaller that part, the greater the margin of error. In political polls it is always important to know whether the results include responses from all eligible voters or just those likely to vote. The opinions of the likely voters are more important than the others.

When interviews were collected. When the interviews were collected may be of critical importance in interpreting the poll, especially during campaigns when the candidates themselves and other events may cause preferences to change significantly within a few days. Think, for example, of presidential primaries. As candidates join or drop out of the race, the support for each of the other candidates changes. A week-old poll may be meaningless if something dramatic has happened since it was taken. Candidates have been known to use such outdated results to make themselves appear to be doing better than they really are, or their opponents worse. Be on guard.

How interviews were collected. When the poll is your newspaper's, the obligation remains to let your readers know how it was taken. It is also incumbent on the paper to reveal how reliable the poll is.

The Need for Caution in Interpreting Polls

Whether you are helping to conduct a survey or just reporting on one produced by someone else, you must exercise caution. You should be on guard for the following potential problems:

Potential problems with polls

- *The people interviewed must be selected in a truly random fashion if you want to generalize from their responses to the whole population.*
- *The closer the results, the harder it is to say anything definitive.*
- *Beware of polls that claim to measure opinion on sensitive, complicated issues.*

The people interviewed must be selected in a truly random fashion if you want to generalize from their responses to the whole population. If they are not, you have no assurance that the interview subjects are really representative. The old-fashioned people-in-the-street interview is practically worthless as an indicator of public opinion for this reason. The man or woman in the street probably differs in important ways from all those men and women who are not in the street when the questioner is.

Also invalid are such "polls" as the questionnaires members of Congress mail to their constituents. Only strongly opinionated—and therefore unrepresentative—people are likely to return them. For the same reason the "question-of-the-day" feature some newspapers and broadcast stations carry tells you nothing about the opinions of the great mass of people who do not respond. Even worse are the TV polls that require respondents to call a 900 number to register their opinions. Because there is a charge for such calls, these pseudo-polls produce not only misleading results but profits that encourage their use.

The closer the results, the harder it is to say anything definitive. Look again at the example of the Smith-Jones campaign. Suppose the poll showed Smith with 52 percent and Jones with 48 percent of the vote. Smith may or may not be ahead. With the 3 percent margin of error, Smith could actually have only 49 percent, and

Figure 18.2.
An exit poll of voters in key districts provides an early clue about the likely outcome of the election.

Jones could have 51 percent. All that you could report safely about those results is that the race is too close to call. Many reporters—and pollsters—are simply not careful enough when the outcome is unclear.

Beware of polls that claim to measure opinion on sensitive, complicated issues. Many questions of morality, or social issues such as race relations, do not lend themselves to simple answers. Opinions on such matters can be measured, but only by highly skilled researchers using carefully designed questions. Anything less can be dangerously oversimplified and highly misleading.

Surveying, like field experiments, systematic analysis and participant observation, can help you as a reporter solve problems you could not handle as well by other techniques. But these are only tools. How effectively they are used—or how clumsily they are misused—depends on you.

Suggested Readings

Campbell, Donald and Stanley, Julian. *Experimental and Quasi-Experimental Designs for Research.* Skokie, Ill.: Rand McNally, 1966. A classic guide to field experimentation that is also useful in providing a better understanding of scientific research.

Demers, David Pearce and Nichols, Suzanne. *Precision Journalism: A Practical Guide.* Newbury Park, Calif.: Sage Publications, 1987. A primer for students and journalists, simply written and complete with examples.

McCombs, Maxwell, Shaw, Donald L. and Grey, David. *Handbook of Reporting Methods.* Boston: Houghton Mifflin, 1976. Offers examples of real-life uses of social science methods in journalism, but does not provide enough on statistics to serve as a guide in employing the methods.

Meyer, Philip. *Precision Journalism*, Second edition. Bloomington, Ind.: Indiana University Press, 1993. A detailed introduction to surveying, conducting field experiments and using statistics to analyze the results by a reporter who pioneered the use of these methods in journalism. The theoretical justification of the techniques is included as well.

Williams, Frederick. *Reasoning with Statistics.* New York: Holt, Rinehart and Winston, 1979. A nonintimidating but sufficiently complex guide to using mathematical tools.

Exercises

1. Find a newspaper story that reports on the results of a public opinion survey. Analyze the story using the guidelines discussed in this chapter.

2. Using the technique described by Philip Meyer in *Precision Journalism* (see the Suggested Readings), design a simple survey. Write a memo outlining your plan.

3. Design a field experiment: State your hypothesis, identify the dependent and independent variables, and describe the controls you will use.

4. As a class project, carry out one of the surveys a class member designed in Exercise 2.

5. Now analyze the data you've collected in Exercise 4. SPSS or a similar software package is relatively easy to use. A computer-literate faculty member or one of the suggested readings can give you the technical help you may need. As a final step, write the story of your findings.

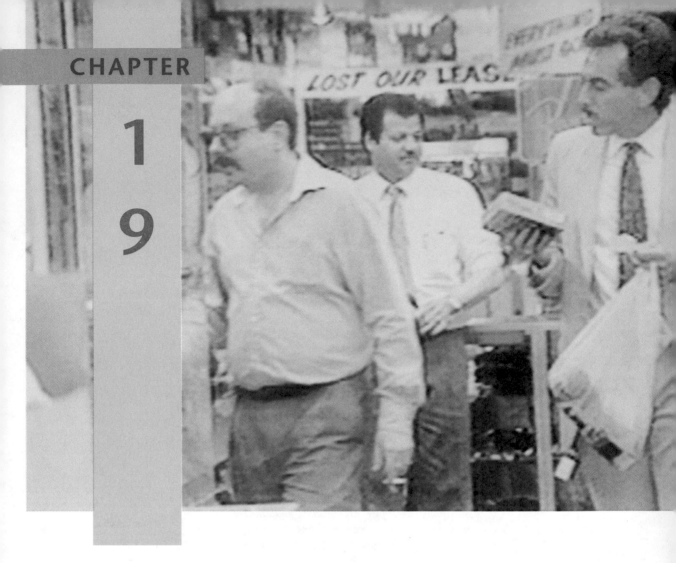

INVESTIGATIVE REPORTING

*I*n Raleigh, N.C., a young reporter fresh from journalism school brings his newly acquired computer skills to bear on topics including school performance, unregistered gun dealers and the likely impact of popular anti-crime legislation. In Orange County, Calif., a team led by another reporter just a few years older begins examining causes and effects of devastating firestorms before the embers have cooled. In Akron, Ohio, an experienced editor overcomes his own initial skepticism and directs an unprecedented dissection of the city's attitudes and actions toward race.

These examples and hundreds like them across the nation represent the new face of investigative reporting. No longer content to expose wrongdoing, no longer intent merely on putting the bad guys in jail—admirable as those goals remain—the investigative reporters of today and tomorrow are using the techniques of social science and the tool of the computer to explore the most important problems facing our society.

Investigative reporting has a rich tradition in American journalism. The fiercely partisan editors of the Revolutionary era dug for facts as well as the mud they hurled at their opponents. In the early 20th century investigative reporting flowered with the "muckrakers," a title bestowed with anger by Theodore Roosevelt and worn with pride by journalists. Lincoln Steffens explored the undersides of American cities, one by one, laying bare the corrupt combinations of businessmen and politicians that ran them. Ida Tarbell exposed the economic stranglehold of the oil monopoly. Theodore Dreiser, Upton Sinclair and Frank Norris revealed the horrors of working life in factories and meat-packing plants.

Their professional heirs today bring to the work the same commitment to exposure and reform. They use refinements of many of the same techniques: in-depth interviews, personal observation, analysis of documents. But modern muckrakers have a powerful tool their predecessors didn't dream of. The computer allows reporters today to compile and analyze masses of data, to perform complicated statistical tests, to create charts and graphs to enhance understanding. This tool, in turn, requires of reporters numeracy as well as literacy. It requires the addition of another set of skills to every serious journalist's repertoire.

The importance of computer-assisted reporting, as it is called, opens to young reporters an opportunity for early admission to this major league of journalism. If you learn computer skills along with the techniques taught in this chapter, you will be equipped for the 21st century.

The Process

Most investigations start with a hunch or a **tip** that something or someone deserves a close look. If a preliminary search bears out that expectation, a serious investigation begins. When enough information has been uncovered to prove or modify the reporter's initial hunch, it's time to analyze, organize and write the story.

Figure 19.1.
Ida Tarbell, one of the original muckrakers, helped set the pattern for investigative reporting with her expose of Standard Oil.

Beginning the Investigation

No good reporter sets out on an investigation unless there is some basis for suspicion. That basis may be a grand jury report that leaves something untold or a tip that some public official is on the take. It may be a sudden upsurge in drug overdoses or it may be long-festering problems in the schools. Without some idea of what you're looking for, investigation is too likely to turn into wild-goose chasing.

Based on the tip or suspicion, together with whatever background material you have, you form a hypothesis. Reporters hardly ever use that term, but it is a useful one, because it shows the similarity between the processes of investigative reporting and scientific investigation (see Chapter 18). In both, the *hypothesis* is the statement of what you think is true. Your hypothesis may be, "The mayor is a crook," or, "The school system is being run incompetently." It is a good idea to state clearly your hypothesis when you start an investigation. By doing so, you focus on the heart of the problem and cut down on the possibility of any misunderstanding with your editor or other reporters who may be working with you.

Once the hypothesis is stated, the reporter—like the scientist—sets out to prove or disprove it. You should be open to the possibility of disproof. Reporters—like scientists—are not advocates. They are seekers of truth. No good reporter ignores or downplays evidence just because it contradicts his or her assumptions. In journalism, as in science, the truth about a situation is often sharply different from what is expected. An open mind is an essential quality of a good investigative reporter. Remember, too, that you may have a good story even if your hypothesis is disproved.

Carrying Out the Investigation

The actual investigative work usually proceeds in two stages. The first is what Robert W. Greene, who was a legendary reporter and editor for *Newsday*, named the **sniff**. In this stage you sniff around in search of a trail worth following. If you find one, the second stage, the serious investigation, begins.

The preliminary checking should take no more than a day or two. Its purpose is not to prove the hypothesis but to find out the chances of proving it. You make that effort by talking with the most promising source or sources, skimming the most available records, consulting knowledgeable people in your news room. The two questions you are trying to answer at this stage are: (1) "Is there a story here?" and (2) "Am I going to be able to get it?" If the answer to either question is no, there is little point in pursuing the investigation.

When the answer to both questions is yes, however, the real work begins. It begins with organization. Your hypothesis tells you where you want to go. Now you must figure out how to get there. Careful organization keeps you on the right track and prevents you from overlooking anything important as you go. Many reporters take a kind of perverse pride in their illegible notebooks and cluttered desks. As an investigative reporter you may have a messy desk, but you should arrange your files of information clearly and coherently. Begin organizing by asking yourself these questions:

- Who are my most promising sources? Who is likely to give me trouble? Whom should I go to first? Second? Last?
- What records do I need? Where are they? Which are public? How can I get to the ones that are not readily accessible?
- What is the most I can hope to prove? What is the least that will still yield a story? How long should the investigation take?

Now draw up a plan of action. Experienced reporters often do this mentally. But when you are a beginner, it's a good idea to write out a plan and then to go over it with your editor. The editor may spot some holes in your planning or have something to add. And an editor is more likely to give you enough time if he or she has a clear idea of what has to be done.

Carry out your plan, allowing flexibility for the unexpected twists most investigations take. During your first round of interviews, keep asking who else you should talk to. While you are checking records, look for references to other files or other persons.

Be methodical. Many investigative reporters spend an hour or so at the end of every day adding up the score, going through their notes and searching their memories to analyze what they have learned and what they need next. Some develop elaborate, cross-indexed files of names, organizations and incidents. Others are less formal. Virtually all, however, use a code to disguise names of confidential sources so that those sources will remain secret even if the files are subpoenaed. The method you use isn't important, as long as you understand it. What is vitally important is that you have a method and use it consistently. If you fail to keep careful track of where you're going, you may go in the wrong direction, or in circles.

Doing the Work

The Raleigh, N.C., *News & Observer* is a mid-sized newspaper with a tradition of public service. So it is no surprise that the paper has embraced computer-assisted reporting as an approach to important stories that would otherwise be difficult if not impossible to do. Jon Schmid Sotomayor joined the *News & Observer* when he finished his graduate journalism program. His title was assistant database editor (see Chapter 18). His job was to locate and analyze information stored in government computers, most of it public by law but accessible only to the skilled.

With a colleague, he looked behind the numbers that seemed to show above-average performance by students in the Durham public schools. They got the state's standards for what student achievement should be in reading and math for each grade level. Then they got the school district's computer records of test scores by school, by grade and by race. By matching the two sets of numbers, the reporters produced a story with ominous overtones for their community. Two paragraphs summed up in words what the numbers meant:

> Based on a state measurement of the new end-of-grade tests, nearly 40 percent of Durham students in grades three through eight don't have the basic skills required for their grade level.
>
> And at some schools, more than three-quarters of the students fall short of required academic skills.

Sometimes skilled reporters can react to events with instant investigation. That's what James Grimaldi and several colleagues at the *Orange County* (Calif.) *Register* did as they tried to find out what had gone wrong with firefighting efforts during blazes that burned more than 700 homes and 170,000 acres.

Frustrated firefighters told of water shortages, miscommunication and bureaucratic bungling. The reporters immediately went be-

"The use of computers, when combined with solid analysis skills, allows reporters to move beyond simply reacting to events. While remaining objective, we can take a more proactive role and give our readers a perspective on current issues which may not be found elsewhere."

—*Jon Schmid Sotomayor,* Raleigh News & Observer

yond those interviews by seeking state and local documents. They collected incident reports and summaries, meeting minutes, dispatch logs, transcripts of dispatch tapes, water district telemetry readings, city council minutes, lawsuits, even the environmental-impact statement on a proposed reservoir.

They used an Excel spreadsheet program on the news room's Macintosh computers to compile and compare their data.

Then, in a series of stories over a three-month period, Grimaldi's team was able to show readers that a larger reservoir—not built because of environmental and political concerns—could have added significantly to water pressure and supplies at crucial times. They showed how antiquated communications systems hindered rather than enhanced reactions. They showed how confusion and muddled command structure kept firefighting aircraft on the ground while homes burned.

Readers were outraged. Local and state officials responded with investigations of their own and promises of quick remedial action.

You don't have to be a seasoned veteran or belong to a special-projects team to do good investigative reporting. You do need the skills of a Jon Schmid Sotomayor and the vision of a James Grimaldi.

Go to the scene of the disaster and don't let the breaking story stop you from thinking ahead. There, you will find almost all of the sources to tell you what went wrong in responding to the disaster. Though you will have to get your proof through public-record requests, you will get your leads at the scene."

—*James Grimaldi,*
Orange County Register

Getting It Right

The importance of accuracy in investigative reporting cannot be overstated. It is the most essential element in good journalism of any kind. In investigative reporting especially, inaccuracy leads to embarrassment, to ruined reputations and, sometimes, to lawsuits. The reputations ruined often are those of the careless reporter and newspaper. Most investigative stories have the effect of accusing somebody of wrongdoing or incompetence. Even if the target is a public official whose chances of suing successfully for libel are slim, fairness and decency require that you be sure of your facts before you put them in print.

The *Washington Post*, during its famous Watergate investigation, followed the policy of requiring verification from two independent sources before an allegation could be published. That is a good rule to follow. People make mistakes. They lie. Their memories fail. Documents can be misleading or confusing. Check and double-check. There is no good excuse for an error.

Writing the Story

Most investigative stories require consultation with the newspaper's lawyer before publication. As a reporter you will have little or nothing to say about the choice of your paper's lawyer. That lawyer, though, will be an important part of your investigative career. The lawyer advises on what you can print safely and what you cannot.

Most editors heed their lawyer's advice. If you are lucky, your paper's lawyer will understand and sympathize with good, aggressive journalism. If he or she does not, you may find yourself forced to argue for your story. You will be better equipped for such an argument—and few reporters go through a career without several—if you understand at least the basics of the laws of libel and privacy. Chapter 21 outlines those laws, and several good books on law for journalists are listed in the Suggested Readings at the end of the chapter.

The last step before your investigation goes public is the writing and rewriting. After days or weeks of intense reporting effort, the writing strikes some investigative reporters as a chore—necessary but unimportant. That attitude is disastrous. The best reporting in the world is wasted unless it is read. Your hard-won exposé or painstaking analysis will disappear without a trace unless the writing attracts readers and maintains their interest. Most reporters and newspapers that are serious about investigative reporting recognize this. They stress good writing almost as much as solid reporting. The *Chicago Tribune*, for example, assigns an especially skilled writer to its Pulitzer Prize-winning investigative task force as it nears the completion of each project. The writer's sole job is to present months of reporting work as clearly and dramatically as possible. Other newspapers prefer to let their reporters do their own writing.

How do you write the results of a complicated investigation? The general rule is, as simply as you can. One approach is to use a hard lead, displaying your key findings in the first few paragraphs. Another choice, often used, is to adopt one of the alternative approaches to storytelling explained in Chapter 17.

Here's an illustration of how hard and softer leads can work together to give readers important information in a form that's easy to understand and to remember. In the previous chapter, we met Jon Schmid Sotomayor of the *Raleigh News & Observer*. He and two colleagues used computer-assisted reporting to analyze the probable impact of a "three strikes and you're out" anti-crime law proposed for North Carolina. Numbers formed the backbone of the story, but people were its face. And readership was its goal.

Here's the lead of the Page One story:

> In a nation where the fear of crime tops the public worry-chart, no anti-crime plan has generated the name recognition and gutsy appeal of "Three Strikes and You're Out." It's a catchy All-America slogan with get-tough grit—lock up violent three-times losers for life. No hope of parole, ever.
>
> But what would the law mean for North Carolina?
>
> Very little.
>
> If a Three Strikes law had been at the plate in North Carolina, its batting average would be .0005—about one criminal of every 2,000 sent to prison.

Notice the conversational tone, the built-in explanation—even a definition of the key term. Notice the pacing—two complex sentences followed by two short and simple ones. Notice the directness: What would it mean? Very little. Notice the use of the same baseball metaphor adopted by proponents of the law to show its real irrelevance. Still, this is a hard-news lead. It makes the central point of the story quickly and clearly.

But the best stories usually are about people, and this one is no exception. Accompanying the hard-edged analysis were profiles of two of the career criminals at whom the law is aimed. Here's one introduction:

> John Coy Lynch says he was born under a bad sign.
>
> "It seems like trouble looks for me wherever I go," Lynch says. "Just bad luck and being in the wrong place at the wrong time—and just one of them spur-of-the-moment things."
>
> But in Lynch's case, bad luck is spelled drugs, drink, guns and knives.

The writers let their subject introduce himself, in his own words. Then, having shown readers his view of himself, they provide another perspective. In just three paragraphs, you already have a picture of a violent man who feels sorrier for himself than for anyone else.

Writing an investigative story so that it will be read takes the same attention to organization and to detail as does any good writing. Here are a few tips that apply to all types of writing but especially to investigative stories:

To write a story that will be read

▪ *Get people into the story.*
▪ *Keep it simple.*
▪ *Tell the reader what your research means.*
▪ *Organize.*
▪ *Suggest solutions.*

Get people into the story. Any investigation worth doing involves people in some way. Make them come alive with descriptive detail, the kind we learned of in John Coy Lynch's story.

Keep it simple. Look for ways to clarify and explain complicated situations. When you have a mass of information, consider spreading it over more than one story—in a series or in a main story with a sidebar. Think about how charts, graphs or lists can be used to present key facts clearly. Don't try to print everything you know. Enough to support your conclusions is sufficient; more than that is too much.

Tell the reader what your research means. A great temptation in investigative reporting is to lay out the facts and let the reader draw the conclusions. That is unfair to you and your reader. Lay out the facts, of course, but tell the reader what they add up to. A reporter who had spent weeks investigating the deplorable conditions in his state's juvenile corrections facilities wrote this lead:

> Florida treats her delinquent children as if she hated them.

If the facts are there, drawing the obvious conclusions is not editorializing. It is good and helpful writing.

Organize. Careful organization is as important in writing the investigative story as in reporting it. The job will be easier if you have been organized all along. When you are ready to write, examine your notes again. Make an outline. Pick out your best quotes and anecdotes. Some reporters, if they are writing more than one story, separate their material into individual folders, one for each story. However you do it, know what you are going to say before you start to write.

Suggest solutions. Polls have shown that readers prefer investigative stories that show how to correct the problems described in the stories. Many of today's best newspapers are satisfying readers' demands by going beyond exposure in search of solutions. Are new laws needed? Better enforcement of present laws? More resources? Better training? Remember that the early 20th-century Progressive movement of which the original muckrakers were a part produced reforms, not just good stories.

Think of writing as the climax of a process that begins with a hypothesis, tests that hypothesis through careful investigation, checks and double-checks every fact, and satisfies the concerns of newspaper editors and lawyers. Every step in that process is vital to the success of any investigative story.

The Sources

Investigative reporters—like other reporters—get their information from people or documents. The perfect source would be a person who had the pertinent documents and was eager to tell you what those documents mean. Don't count on finding the perfect source. Instead, count on having to piece together the information you need from a variety of people and records—some of the people not at all eager to talk to you and some of the records difficult to obtain and, if you do gain access to them, to understand. Let's consider human sources first.

Human Sources

Suppose you get a tip that the mayor received campaign contributions under the table from the engineering firm that just got a big city contract. Who might talk?

Enemies. A person's enemies usually are the best sources when you are trying to find out anything bad about him or her. More often than not, the enemies of a prominent person will have made it their business to find out as much as possible about that person's misdeeds and shortcomings. Frequently, they will share what they know with a friendly reporter.

Friends. Surprisingly, friends are sometimes nearly as revealing as enemies. In trying to explain and defend a friend's actions, they may tell you more than you knew before. Occasionally you may find that someone your target regards as a friend is not much of a friend after all.

Human sources for investigative reports

- *Enemies*
- *Friends*
- *Losers*
- *Victims*
- *Experts*
- *Police*
- *People in trouble*

Losers. Like enemies, losers often carry a grudge. Seek out the loser in the last election, the losing contender for the contract, the loser in a power struggle. Bad losers make good sources.

Victims. If you are investigating a failing school system, talk with its students and their parents. If your story is about nursing home abuses, talk with some patients and their relatives. The honest and hard-working employees caught in a corrupt or incompetent system are victims, too. They can give you specific examples and anecdotes. Their case histories can help you write the story.

Experts. Early in many investigations, there will be a great deal you may not understand. You may need someone to explain how the campaign finance laws could be circumvented, someone to interpret a contract, or someone to decipher a set of bid specifications. Lawyers, accountants, engineers or professors can help you understand technical jargon or complicated transactions. If they refuse to comment on your specific case, fit the facts you have into a hypothetical situation.

Police. Investigative reporters and law enforcement agents often work the same territory. If you are wise, you will make friends with carefully selected agents. They can—and frequently will—be of great help. Their files may not be gold mines, but they have investigative tools and contacts you lack. When they get to know and trust you, they will share. Most police like seeing their own and their organization's names in the paper. They know, too, that you can do some things they cannot. It takes less proof for you to be able to print that the mayor is a crook than it may take to convince a jury. Most police investigators want to corner wrongdoers any way they can. You can use that attitude to your advantage.

People in Trouble. Police use this source and so can you, although you cannot promise immunity or a lesser charge, as the police can. A classic case is the Watergate affair. Once the Nixon administration started to come unraveled, officials trying to save their careers and images began falling all over each other to give their self-serving versions of events. People will react similarly in lesser cases.

As an investigative reporter, you cultivate sources in the same ways a reporter on a beat does. You just do it more quickly. One excellent tactic is to play on their self-interest. Losers and enemies want to get the so-and-so, and thus you have a common aim. (But don't go overboard. Your words could come back to haunt you.) Friends want their buddy's side of the story to be explained. So do you. If you keep in mind that, no matter how corrupt your target may be, he or she is still a human being, it may be easier to deal sympathetically with that person's friends. That attitude may help ensure that you treat the target fairly, as well.

Experts just want to explain the problem as you present it. And you just want to understand. People in trouble want sympathy and some assurance that they still merit respect. No reporter should have trouble conveying either attitude.

Another way to win and keep sources is to protect them. Occasionally a reporter faces jail unless he or she reveals a source. Even jail is not too great a price to pay in order to keep a promise of confidentiality. More often, the threats to confidentiality are less dramatic. Other sources, or the target of the investigation, may casually ask, "Where'd you hear that?" Other reporters, over coffee or a beer, may ask the same question. Hold your tongue. The only person to whom a confidential source should ever be revealed is your editor.

Human sources pose problems as well as solving them. They may lie to you. To get at an enemy or protect a friend, to make themselves look better or someone else look worse—and sometimes just for fun—people lie to reporters. No reporter is safe and no source is above suspicion. They may use you, too, just as you are using them. The only reason most people involved on any side of a suspicious situation will talk about it is to enhance their own position. That is neither illegal nor immoral, but it can trip up a reporter who fails to take every self-serving statement with the appropriate grain of salt.

Sources may change their stories as well. People forget. Recollections and situations change. Pressures can be applied. Fear or love or ambition or greed can intrude. A source may deny tomorrow—or in court—what he or she told you today.

Finally, sources will seldom want to be identified. Even the enemies of a powerful person often are reluctant to see their names attached to their criticisms in print. So are friends. Experts, while willing to provide background information, often cite their codes of ethics when you ask them to go on the record. Stories without identifiable sources have less credibility with readers, with editors, even with colleagues.

Written Sources

Fortunately, not all sources are human. Records and documents neither lie nor change their stories, they have no axes to grind at your expense and they can be identified in print. Many useful documents are public records, available to you or any other citizen on request. Others are non-public but still may be available through your human sources.

Public Records

As the examples earlier show, a great deal can be learned about individuals and organizations through records that are available for the asking, if you know where to ask. Let's take a look at some of the most valuable public records and where they can be found.

Property Records. Many investigations center on land—who owns it, who buys it, how it is zoned, how it is taxed. You can find out all that information and more from public records. Your county

Public records as sources for investigative reports

- *Property records*
- *Corporation records*
- *Court records*
- *Campaign and conflict-of-interest reports*
- *Loan records*
- *Minutes and transcripts*

recorder's office (or its equivalent) has on file the ownership of every piece of land in the county as well as the history of past owners. Most such offices have their files cross-indexed so that you can find out the owner of the land if you know its location, or the location and size of the property if you know the owner. Those files also will tell you who holds a mortgage on the land. The city or county tax assessor's office has on file the assessed valuation of the land, the basis for property taxes. Either the assessor or the local zoning agency can tell you for what use the property is zoned. All requests for rezoning are public information, too.

Corporation Records. Every corporation must file with the secretary of state a document showing the officers and principal agent of the company. The document must be filed with every state in which the company does business. The officers listed may be only "dummies," stand-ins for the real owners. Even if that is the case, you can find out at least who the stand-ins are. But that is only the beginning. Publicly held corporations must file annual reports with the Securities and Exchange Commission in Washington. The reports list officers, major stockholders, financial statements and any business dealing with other companies owned by the corporation. Nonprofit corporations—such as foundations and charities—must file with the Internal Revenue Service an even more revealing statement, Form 990, showing how much money came in and where it went (see Figure 19.2). Similar statements must be filed with the attorneys general of many states. Corporations often are regulated by state or federal agencies as well. They file regular reports with the regulating agency. Insurance companies, for instance, are regulated by state insurance commissioners. Nursing homes are regulated by various state agencies. Broadcasters are overseen by the Federal Communications Commission, truckers by the Interstate Commerce Commission. Labor unions must file detailed statements showing assets, officers' salaries, loans and other financial information with the U.S. Department of Labor. Those statements are called "5500 Forms."

Once you have such corporation records, you must interpret them. Your public library has books that tell you how. Or your newspaper's own business experts may be willing to help.

Court Records. Few people active in politics or business go through life without some involvement in court actions. Check the offices of the state and federal court clerks for records of lawsuits. The written arguments, sworn statements and answers to questions (interrogatories) may contain valuable details or provide leads to follow. Has your target been divorced? Legal struggles over assets can be revealing. Probate court files of your target's deceased associates may tell you something you need to know.

Campaign and Conflict-of-Interest Reports. Federal—and most state—campaign laws now require political candidates to disclose, during and after each campaign, lists of who gave what to whom. Those filings can yield stories on who is supporting the candidates. They also can be used later for comparing who gets

Form **990** | **Return of Organization Exempt From Income Tax** | OMB No. 1545-0047

Under section 501(c) of the Internal Revenue Code (except black lung benefit trust or private foundation) or section 4947(a)(1) nonexempt charitable trust

1994

Department of the Treasury
Internal Revenue Service

Note: *The organization may have to use a copy of this return to satisfy state reporting requirements.*

This Form is Open to Public Inspection

A For the 1994 calendar year, OR tax year period beginning , 1994, and ending , 19

B Check if:
☐ Change of address
☐ Initial return
☐ Final return
☐ Amended return (required also for State reporting)

Please use IRS label or print or type. See Specific Instructions.

C Name of organization

Number and street (or P.O. box if mail is not delivered to street address) | Room/suite

City, town, or post office, state, and ZIP code

D Employer identification number

E State registration number

F Check ▶ ☐ if exemption application is pending

G Type of organization—▶ ☐ Exempt under section 501(c)(   ) ◀ (insert number) OR ▶ ☐ section 4947(a)(1) nonexempt charitable trust

Note: ***Section 501(c)(3) exempt organizations and 4947(a)(1) nonexempt charitable trusts MUST attach a completed Schedule A (Form 990).***

H(a) Is this a group return filed for affiliates? . . . . ☐ Yes ☐ No

(b) If "Yes," enter the number of affiliates for which this return is filed: . . ▶ ______

(c) Is this a separate return filed by an organization covered by a group ruling? ☐ Yes ☐ No

I If either box in H is checked "Yes," enter four-digit group exemption number (GEN) ▶ ______

J Accounting method: ☐ Cash ☐ Accrual ☐ Other (specify) ▶

K Check here ▶ ☐ if the organization's gross receipts are normally not more than $25,000. The organization need not file a return with the IRS; but if it received a Form 990 Package in the mail, it should file a return without financial data. **Some states require a complete return.**

Note: *Form 990-EZ may be used by organizations with gross receipts less than $100,000 and total assets less than $250,000 at end of year.*

Part I Statement of Revenue, Expenses, and Changes in Net Assets or Fund Balances

Revenue

1	Contributions, gifts, grants, and similar amounts received:				
a	Direct public support	1a			
b	Indirect public support	1b			
c	Government contributions (grants)	1c			
d	**Total** (add lines 1a through 1c) (attach schedule—see instructions) (cash $ ______ noncash $ ______)			1d	
2	Program service revenue including government fees and contracts (from Part VII, line 93)			2	
3	Membership dues and assessments (see instructions)			3	
4	Interest on savings and temporary cash investments			4	
5	Dividends and interest from securities			5	
6a	Gross rents	6a			
b	Less: rental expenses	6b			
c	Net rental income or (loss) (subtract line 6b from line 6a)			6c	
7	Other investment income (describe ▶)			7	
		(A) Securities		(B) Other	
8a	Gross amount from sale of assets other than inventory		8a		
b	Less: cost or other basis and sales expenses		8b		
c	Gain or (loss) (attach schedule)		8c		
d	Net gain or (loss) (combine line 8c, columns (A) and (B))			8d	
9	Special events and activities (attach schedule—see instructions):				
a	Gross revenue (not including $ ______ of contributions reported on line 1a)	9a			
b	Less: direct expenses other than fundraising expenses	9b			
c	Net income or (loss) from special events (subtract line 9b from line 9a)			9c	
10a	Gross sales of inventory, less returns and allowances	10a			
b	Less: cost of goods sold	10b			
c	Gross profit or (loss) from sales of inventory (attach schedule) (subtract line 10b from line 10a)			10c	
11	Other revenue (from Part VII, line 103)			11	
12	**Total revenue** (add lines 1d, 2, 3, 4, 5, 6c, 7, 8d, 9c, 10c, and 11)			12	

Expenses

13	Program services (from line 44, column (B)—see instructions)	13	
14	Management and general (from line 44, column (C)—see instructions)	14	
15	Fundraising (from line 44, column (D)—see instructions)	15	
16	Payments to affiliates (attach schedule—see instructions)	16	
17	**Total expenses** (add lines 16 and 44, column (A))	17	

Net Assets

18	Excess or (deficit) for the year (subtract line 17 from line 12)	18	
19	Net assets or fund balances at beginning of year (from line 74, column (A))	19	
20	Other changes in net assets or fund balances (attach explanation)	20	
21	Net assets or fund balances at end of year (combine lines 18, 19, and 20)	21	

For Paperwork Reduction Act Notice, see page 1 of the separate instructions. Cat. No. 11282Y Form **990** (1994)

Figure 19.2.
Form 990, which nonprofit corporations must file with the IRS, is a public record that can reveal important information.

what from which officeholder. Many states require officeholders to file statements of their business and stock holdings. These can be checked for possible conflicts of interest or used as background for profile stories.

Loan Records. Commercial lenders usually file statements showing property that has been used as security for loans. Known as Uniform Commercial Code filings, these can be found in the offices of state secretaries of state and, sometimes, in local recorder's offices.

Minutes and Transcripts. Most elected and appointed governing bodies, ranging from local planning and zoning commissions to the U.S. Congress, are required by law to keep minutes or transcripts of their meetings.

Using and Securing Public Records

The states and the federal government have laws designed to ensure access to public records. Many of those laws—including the federal *Freedom of Information Act*, which was passed to improve access to government records—have gaping loopholes and time-consuming review procedures. Still, they have been and can be useful tools when all else fails. Learn the details of the law in your state. You can get information on access laws and their interpretations by contacting the Freedom of Information Center at the University of Missouri, 20 Walter Williams Hall, Columbia, Mo. 65211.

Non-Public Records

Non-public records as sources for investigative reports

- *Investigative files*
- *Past arrests and convictions*
- *Bank records*
- *Income tax records*
- *Credit checks*

Non-public records are more difficult, but often not impossible, to obtain. To get them, you must know that they exist, where they are and how to gain access. Finding out about those things requires good human sources. You should know about a few of the most valuable non-public records.

Investigative Files. The investigative files of law enforcement agencies can be rich in information. You are likely to see them only if you have a good source in a particular agency, or one affiliated with it. If you do obtain such files, treat them cautiously. They will be full of unsubstantiated allegations, rumor and misinformation. Be wary of accepting as fact anything you have not confirmed yourself.

Past Arrests and Convictions. Records of past arrests and convictions increasingly are being removed from public scrutiny. Usually these are easier than investigative files to obtain from a friendly police or prosecuting official. And usually they are more trustworthy than raw investigative files.

Bank Records. Bank records would be helpful in many investigations, but they are among the most difficult to get. Bankers are trained to keep secrets. The government agencies that regulate banks are secretive as well. A friend in a bank is an investigative reporter's friend indeed.

Income Tax Records. Except for those made public by officeholders, income tax records are guarded carefully by their custodians, and properly so. Leaks are rare.

Credit Checks. Sometimes you can get otherwise unavailable information on a target's financial situation by arranging through your newspaper's business office for a credit check. Credit reports may reveal outstanding debts, a big bank account, major assets and business affiliations. Use that information with care. It is unofficial, and companies that provide it intend it to be confidential.

Problems with Written Sources

Even when you can obtain them, records and other written sources present problems. They are usually dull. Records give you names and numbers, not anecdotes or sparkling quotes. They are bare bones, not flesh and blood. They can be misleading and confusing. Many highly skilled lawyers and accountants spend careers interpreting the kinds of records you may find yourself attacking without their training. Misinterpreting a document is no less serious an error than misquoting a person. And it's easier to do.

Documents usually describe without explaining. You need to know the "why" of a land transaction or a loan. Records tell you only the "what."

Most investigative reporters use both human and documentary sources. People can explain what records cannot. Documents prove what good quotes cannot. You need people to lead you to documents and people to interpret what the documents mean. And you need records to substantiate what people tell you. The best investigative stories combine both types of sources.

New Tools, Traditional Goals

As you've seen, the computer is the most important new tool of investigative reporting. Once you know how to use it, the computer allows you to obtain, analyze and present information in ways that would have been impossible just a few years ago, let alone in the era of the original muckrakers. But useful as it is, the computer is only a tool. Many modern investigative reporters are guided by goals that would be easily recognized by their predecessors of a century ago.

Today's investigators, like the original muckrakers, often are not satisfied with uncovering individual instances of wrongdoing. They are inclined to want to look at organizations as a whole, at entire systems. They seek not only to expose but to explain. And in many cases they also seek to change the problems and abuses they reveal. Many, perhaps most, investigative reporters think of themselves not only as chroniclers of fact or even analysts. They see themselves as reformers.

ON THE JOB

Computers Help Define the Story

Bob Paynter and his wife, Barbara, graduated from journalism school together and started their careers in a bureau of the *Anderson* (S.C.) *Independent.* "We covered 13 counties in northeast Georgia," he recalls. Then began the nomadic life typical of many young reporters—to Jackson, Miss., and Cincinnati. A detour, also typical, into magazines ended in unemployment when the magazine folded. And then to the *Akron Beacon Journal.*

There, Bob eased into investigative work. "I kept wanting to go deeper and deeper into stories," he says. "The managing editor was inclined that way. The rest is history."

After a few years, a project looking into

statewide campaign finance led Paynter into computer-assisted reporting. "Computers help define the story: Here's what we want to do and why." Computers also led to his current assignment as project editor. "It's a great job. I've got an editor's title, but I'm still basically a reporter."

As lead reporter and editor, he directed a year-long examination of race relations in Akron that won for the *Beacon Journal* the Pulitzer Prize for public service, the highest honor in American journalism.

Like many experienced journalists, Bob regards the Pulitzer with a mix of pride and skepticism. "It's a crapshoot to win something like that. I'm real proud of the work, especially since it was a team operation. If you let it, a Pulitzer can mess up your life. Still, I'd rather it happened than it didn't happen."

The Pulitzer is yesterday's story. Within a few months, he and his staff were deep into another computer-assisted project. This one was an investigation of drug enforcement. "The *Beacon Journal* has a taste for that sort of thing," he says.

This, too, was true of the muckrakers. Today, increasingly, news organizations are involving themselves in trying to solve as well as identify the problems of their communities.

One example, which won a Pulitzer Prize for public service, was the remarkable effort by the *Akron* (Ohio) *Beacon Journal* to explore and try to close the racial divisions in that city. Bob Paynter, an experienced reporter and projects editor for the paper, explains how it all began as staff members joined millions of other Americans in pondering the Los Angeles riots of the early 1990s:

> At the time, as news people, the obvious question was: What's the situation here? After all these years of not talking about it overtly, how are the races getting along in Akron? Do we have a problem? Could a smaller version of L.A. happen in the former rubber capital of the world?
>
> Less obvious was how to get the answer. How do you approach such a potentially huge and slippery set of questions without over-simplifying, over-generalizing or over-moralizing and without putting your entire readership to sleep?
>
> Is it even worth the effort?

Paynter, who would wind up spending the next year of his life directing the project, was initially skeptical. He saw a much higher probability of embarrassing failure than of measurable success. In the end, he took on the challenge. He met it by relying on measurement.

The computer was the tool that made the measurement possible. Paynter had just completed a computer-assisted project using census data. He used those same data to show in quantifiable, graphic terms how the races lived in Akron.

The computer also was essential in analyzing the results of a citywide survey of attitudes the newspaper commissioned. The computer digested data ranging from test scores to tax rates, from crime statistics to housing values.

The computer even permitted journalists to find, using census data, neighborhoods that seemed to illustrate the overall patterns. So reporters knew where to look for the ordinary people they wanted to interview.

In short, computer-generated charts and graphs showed disparities and distances more clearly and dramatically than words alone could do. What motivated use of the tool, though, were two old-fashioned commitments. One was to understand, with brutal honesty, the realities of race in the city. The other, which sent a shiver down the spine of a journalist as steeped in the tradition of objectivity as Bob Paynter, sprang from a tradition that predates objectivity in American journalism. That's the tradition of activist journalism—the newspaper not just as observer but as catalyst, as leader.

Here's Paynter's description of how *Beacon Journal* editor Dale Allen came to lead his paper beyond objectivity:

The same frustration that had been producing those "what's the answer" questions at story meetings apparently was keeping Allen up nights as well.

His concern: Would a warts-on examination of racial realities in our community be perceived as rabble-rousing, as little more than hornet's-nest poking to no good end other than single-copy sales? Certainly we would be accused of that. But would our accusers have a point?

Then he had a novel idea:

Just because we didn't have a "solution" didn't mean there wasn't one out there—or a hundred, or even a thousand.

Why not invite the community itself to engage in the search? And so that the invitation not be a symbolic, though empty, passing of the buck, why not involve the Beacon Journal in its capacity as corporate citizen?

So the paper invited individuals and organizations to suggest solutions. *Beacon Journal* staffers brought together, across racial lines, people with shared interests. More than 140 community organizations signed up and began working to cross the racial chasm the paper's reporting had identified.

And the conclusion of the former skeptic:

That's certainly not journalism. And it's never pretended to be. But as an outgrowth of quality journalism—which at its best ought to be tackling intractable social ills—there is a certain logic to the approach for a communications company. It's one that I wouldn't mind seeing explored more fully in the future here and elsewhere.

You can make the combination of new tools and old commitments continue to yield problem-solving investigations like "A Question of Color."

The Obstacles

You have seen now why investigative reporting is important and how it can be done. The picture would not be complete, though, without a brief look at the reasons why not every newspaper or broadcast organization does investigative reporting. As a reporter you will face certain obstacles. You and your editors will have to overcome them if you are to do real investigative reporting. Good newspapers and news broadcasters do overcome such obstacles.

Obstacles to investigative reporting
- *Money*
- *Staffing*
- *Lack of courage*

Money and Staffing

The first obstacle is money. Investigative reporting is the most expensive kind of reporting. It takes time, and time is money. The Akron project took a year. *Newsday's* investigative team spent nine months on a series about heroin traffic. Two *Miami Herald* reporters spent most of their time for more than two years on an investigation of corruption in a federal housing program. Usually, the reporters doing investigations are the paper's or station's best and highest-paid. Frequently, fees for experts are involved. Lawyers charge for looking over a story and much, much more if a suit is filed. Space to publish the results costs money, too.

The second obstacle is staffing. Most newspapers and broadcast organizations, large or small, are understaffed. When a reporter is devoting time to an investigation, somebody else must be found to fill the gap. Many editors are unable or unwilling to adjust for prolonged absences by a key reporter. You may be able to get around that obstacle by doing your investigating in bits and pieces, keeping up with routine assignments all the while. That kind of part-time probing requires a high level of dedication on your part and your editor's. Such commitment is hard to sustain over long stretches of time.

Lack of Courage

The third obstacle is a lack of courage. This is the great inhibitor. Investigative reporting *means* disturbing the status quo. It means poking into dark corners, asking hard questions about controversial, sensitive affairs. Investigative reporting upsets people. If you are looking into the right things, the people who get upset are likely to be important.

Violence or the threat of violence directed toward reporters and newspapers is rare. The 1975 murder of investigative reporter Don Bolles in Phoenix was shocking partly because such things hardly ever happen. But pressure, usually applied to your editor or publisher, is common enough. It takes courage to stand up to such pressure.

The Nixon administration threatened the lucrative television licenses of the Washington Post Co. during the Watergate investigation. The federal government sued the *New York Times*, *Boston Globe* and *St. Louis Post-Dispatch* to prevent publication of the Pentagon Papers. FBI and CIA agents investigated newspapers and harassed reporters during the era of Vietnam and Watergate. Those were dramatic cases. The papers involved were big and rich, and they resisted.

Other pressures are directly economic. A newspaper's survival can be threatened. The financially weak *Miami News* ran a series of stories on grocery pricing, and grocery chains—whose ads are the lifeblood of any paper—pulled out their advertising. The *Philadelphia Inquirer*, then also unprofitable, published exposés of police corruption. The spouses of police officers picketed the paper, and sympathetic unions of mailers and delivery workers refused to distribute the paper. The cost was in the hundreds of thousands of dollars.

More common and less visible are the social pressures and social influence of editors' and publishers' peers. It is common for the top executive of a newspaper to associate socially with the political and business leaders who may be the targets of investigative reporting. It is also common for the reporters who work for those executives to be pulled off such stories.

If you find yourself on a paper lacking money or staff, you can still find ways to do investigative reporting, at least part-time, if you want to badly enough. But if you find yourself on a paper lacking courage, you have only two choices—give up or leave.

Fortunately, investigative reporting is so important and its rewards are so substantial that more reporters than ever are finding the support to do it. You can, too.

Suggested Readings

Downie, Leonard Jr. *The New Muckrakers.* New York: New Republic Book Co., 1976. Personality sketches and descriptions of how some of the best investigative reporters work.

The IRE Journal. Publication of Investigative Reporters and Editors Inc. Walter Williams Hall, University of Missouri, Columbia, Mo. 65205. Every issue has articles on investigations, guides to sources and documents, and a roundup of legal developments. Edited transcripts of IRE conferences also are available at the same address.

Rose, Louis J. *How to Investigate Your Friends and Enemies.* St. Louis: Albion Press, 1981. Very good on the nuts and bolts of investigating.

Weinberg, Steve. *The Reporters' Handbook*, Third Edition. New York: St. Martin's Press, 1996. Tells you how to get and how to use the most important records and documents.

Weinberg, Steve. *Trade Secrets of Washington Journalists.* Washington, D.C.: Acropolis Press, 1981. Excellent guide to Washington sources, written and human.

Williams, Paul. *Investigative Reporting and Editing.* Englewood Cliffs, N.J.: Prentice-Hall, 1978. This classic in the field is good on both how and why to investigate.

Exercises

1. School board member Doris Hart reported at last week's meeting of the board that major flaws, including basement flooding and electrical short circuits, have shown up in the new elementary school. She noted that this is the third straight project designed by consulting architect Louis Doolittle in which serious problems have turned up. School Superintendent Margaret Smith defended Doolittle vigorously. Later, Hart told you privately that she suspects Doolittle may be paying Smith off to keep the consulting contract, which has earned the architect more than $100,000 per year for the past five years.

   Describe how you will investigate:
   a. The sniff.
   b. Human sources. Who might talk? Where should you start? Whom will you save for last?
   c. What records might help? Where are they? What will you be looking for?
   d. What is the most you can hope to prove? What is the least that will yield a story?

2. Choose a public official in your city or town and compile the most complete profile you can using only public records.

3. Use one or more of the computer databases described in Chapter 7 to learn as much as you can about your representative in Congress. Write the most complete investigative profile you can from the databases. In a memo, explain what additional information you'd need to complete your story and where it might be found.

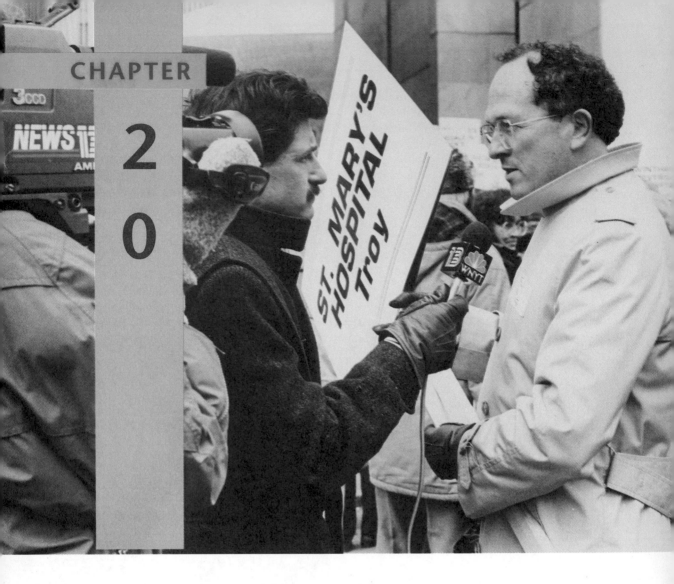

WRITING NEWS FOR
RADIO AND TELEVISION

*E*arthquake in Japan!
    The local time in Kobe, Japan, was 5:46 a.m. on Tuesday, Jan. 17, 1995. The magnitude was 7.2 on the Richter scale. More than 5,000 deaths, more than 60 missing, nearly 27,000 injured. It was an event made for broadcasting.

Not many people first learned about the 1995 Kobe quake from the newspapers. The broadcast media did what they do best: They made it possible for anxious people the world over to keep abreast of what was happening and what witnesses on the scene could say about it. Moreover, broadcasters were able to repeat what they had broadcast earlier for those who missed it the first time.

Of course, the broadcast media are not always present to record the news while it is happening. Much of the time, broadcast journalists must write and report news after it has occurred.

Writing for broadcast news is a relatively new profession. Few people heard the first radio newscasts in 1920, and few watched the first news items broadcast over experimental television in the 1920s. Today large numbers of people say that television is their major source of news. Just how many say so depends on who is taking the survey, the newspaper industry or the television industry. The same is true regarding whether newspapers or television news programs are the most credible news sources.

We do know, however, that the number of daily newspapers in this country continues to decline while the number of radio and television stations continues to grow. According to the Newspaper Association of America, the number of daily newspapers decreased from 2,042 in 1930 to 1,556 in 1994, a decrease of 486. From 1984 to 1994, dailies decreased by 145. According to the 1994 Broadcast & Cable Yearbook, from 1984 to 1994, AM stations increased in number from 4,733 to 4,948 (215); FM stations increased in number from 4,649 to 6,595 (1,946); TV stations increased in number from 1,149 to 1,516 (367).

Many, if not most, of these radio and television stations provide at least some news that is written for them by journalists working for the wire services or employed by the stations.

Selecting and writing news for television and radio is different from selecting and writing news for newspapers. The differences arise primarily from the technologies involved in print and in the electronic media. This chapter explores these differences and discusses news reporting and writing for the broadcast media.

Criteria for Selecting Broadcast News

Emphases of broadcast news

- *Timeliness*
- *Information*
- *Audio or visual impact*
- *People*

In Chapter 1, you learned the basic criteria of journalism in the 1990s: relevance, usefulness and interest. You also learned the specific criteria of news value: impact, conflict, novelty, prominence, proximity and timeliness. All of these criteria apply to the selection of print and broadcast news. However, there are four criteria of broadcast news selection that distinguish it from print news. Broadcast newswriters emphasize timeliness above all other news values; information more than explanation; news that has audio or visual impact; and people more than concepts.

Timeliness

The broadcast newswriter emphasizes one criterion of news value—timeliness—more than others. *When* something happens often determines whether a news item will be used in a newscast. The breaking story receives top priority.

Broadcast news "goes to press" many times a day. If an event is significant enough, regular programming can be interrupted. The broadcast media are the "now" media. This sense of immediacy influences everything in broadcast news, from what is reported to how it is reported. Even when television and radio air documentaries or in-depth segments, they typically try to infuse a sense of urgency, a strong feeling of the present, an emphasis on what's happening now.

Information

Timeliness often determines *why* a news item is broadcast; time, or lack of it, determines *how* it is reported. Because air time is so precious, broadcast news emphasizes the what and the where more than the why or the how. In other words, broadcasters are generally more concerned with information than with explanation. Most stories must be told in 20 to 30 seconds; rarely does a story run longer than two minutes. A minute of news read aloud is only 15 lines of copy, or about 150 words. After commercial time is subtracted, a half-hour newscast has only 22 minutes of news, which amounts to about one-half of a front page of a newspaper. Although broadcast newswriters may never assume that their audience knows anything about a story, they may often have to assume that listeners or viewers will turn to newspapers or to news magazines for further background and details.

Of course, because of the long success of "60 Minutes" and because of relatively low production costs, news magazine formats such as "Primetime Live," "20/20" and "48 Hours" continue to proliferate. They represent a somewhat different challenge to television news writers, but even in a news magazine format, the writing resembles that done for broadcast news.

Audio or Visual Impact

Another difference between broadcast and print news results from the technologies involved. Some news is selected for radio because a reporter has recorded an on-the-scene audio report. Some news is selected for television because it is visually appealing or exciting. For this reason, news of accidents or of fires that may get attention only in the records column of the newspaper may get important play on a television newscast. If a television crew returns with good pictures of an event, that event may receive more prominence in the next newscast, regardless of its significance. Of course, this is not always the case.

People

Finally, an important difference between broadcast and print news selection is that broadcasting more often attempts to tell the news through people. Broadcasting follows the "classic writing formula" as described by Rudolf Flesch in "The Art of Readable Writing": Find a problem, find a person who is dealing with the problem and tell us how he or she is doing. Broadcast journalists look for a representative person or family, someone who is affected by the story or who is a chief player. Thus, rather than using abstract concepts with no sound or visuals, broadcasting humanizes the story.

Writing Broadcast News

Good writing is good writing, and most of what you learned in Chapter 4 about writing applies also to broadcast news. However, the differences between broadcast news and print news affect how stories are written. Broadcast writing emphasizes certain characteristics that newspaper writing does not, and story structure may also vary.

Characteristics of Broadcast Newswriting

Broadcast newswriting

- *Emphasizes immediacy*
- *Has a conversational style*
- *Is tightly phrased*
- *Is clear*

Because of the emphasis on timeliness in the broadcast media, newswriters must emphasize immediacy, aim for a conversational style, and try to write very tightly and clearly. When preparing news copy for radio or television, you should do the same.

Immediacy

Broadcasting achieves a sense of *immediacy* in part by avoiding the past tense and emphasizing the present tense as much as possible. Note the use of present-tense verbs (*italicized*) in this Associated Press story:

(New York)—R-U-486 *is* illegal in the U-S—but a New York gynecologist reportedly *is using* a combination of drugs to work just like the French abortion pill. The *New York Times* *says* Dr. Richard Hausknecht *induces* abortions by *using* two drugs already on the market. He *tells* the newspaper he's used the method in more than 100 nonsurgical abortions.

Hausknecht *says* he *wants* to show that there *is* a "safe, simple, effective, legal technique for terminating pregnancies."

Medical researchers *criticize* him for using the method before clinical trials *determine* its safety and effectiveness.

But Hausknecht *insists* he *is doing* nothing illegal. And the *Times says* authorities *are inclined* to agree.

The drugs *induce* a miscarriage in two stages. Hausknecht *says* the procedure *is* available for 500 dollars.

Notice, too, that the verbs "is using" and "is doing" are the progressive form of the present tense. Broadcast writing often uses the progressive form to indicate continuing action. Of course, to be accurate, the past tense is sometimes necessary, as in the clause "he's used the method . . ." Note, however, that broadcast writers use the present perfect tense more than the past tense because, again, the present perfect indicates past action that is continuing. It's what's happening—now.

Sometimes the sense of immediacy is underscored by adding the time element. You might say, "just minutes ago," or on a morning newscast, "this morning." If there is no danger of inaccuracy or of deceit, though, references to time can be omitted. For example, if something happened yesterday, it may be reported today like this:

```
The latest rash of fires in southern California is under
control.
```

But if the past tense is used in a lead, the time element should be included:

```
The legislature sent a welfare reform bill to the governor
late last night, finishing just in time before the spring
recess.
```

The best way to avoid the past tense is to avoid yesterday's story. You can do that by bringing yesterday's story up to date. By leading with a new development or a new fact, you may be able to use the present tense. Broadcast writers need to be especially aware of the techniques of follow-up stories described in Chapter 13.

Remember, radio and television are "live." Your copy must convey that important characteristic.

Conversational Style

"Write the way you talk" is questionable advice for most kinds of writing; however, with some exceptions, it is imperative for broadcast writing. "Read your copy aloud" is good advice for most kinds of writing; for broadcast writing, that's what it's all about.

Conversational style is simple and informal. The key is to remember that you are talking to people. Tell them what just happened. Tell them what you just saw or heard. Imagine yourself going up to a friend and saying, "Guess what I just heard!"

Write so that your copy *sounds* good. Use simple, short sentences, written with transitive verbs in the active voice. People rarely use verbs in the passive voice when they talk; it usually sounds cumbersome and awkward. You don't go around saying, "Guess what I was just told by somebody."

Because casual speech contains contractions, they belong in your broadcast copy, too. Conversational style also permits the use of occasional sentence fragments and of truncated sentences. Sentences are sometimes strung together loosely with dashes and sometimes begin with the conjunction "and" or "but," as in the following example from the Associated Press:

> (Los Angeles)—A five-year plan to beef up the Los Angeles police department is hitting roadblocks.
>
> A review by the *Los Angeles Times* finds that officers are leaving the force faster than expected. And the process of hiring and training new officers is going more slowly than expected.
>
> A year ago, Mayor Richard Riordan (REER'-duhn) promised to find the money to increase the force by more than 28-hundred officers over five years. That's an increase of nearly 40 percent.
>
> But the *Times* says that the city was able to increase police ranks only about half as much as it wanted in the first year of the plan.
>
> City leaders say they'll achieve their goals by the end of the five years.

Writing in conversational style does not mean that you may use slang or colloquialism or incorrect grammar. Nor does it mean that you can use vulgar or off-color expressions. Remember that your audience includes people of all ages and sensitivities. The broadcast media have been given credit for raising the level of properly spoken English. Make your contribution.

Tight Phrasing

Although actual conversational English tends to be wordy, you must learn to write in a conversational style without being wordy. That means you must condense. Cut down on adjectives and adverbs. Eliminate the passive voice. Use strong active verbs. Make every word count. Use tight phrasing.

Keeping it short means selecting facts carefully because often you don't have time for the whole story. AP broadcast newswriter Ed Golden says that what AP's member broadcasters want most is good, tight writing that is easy to follow. Let's look at how a wire story written for newspapers can be condensed for broadcasting. Here are the opening paragraphs of a 10-paragraph story from the AP newspaper wire:

DENVER (AP)—Teachers seeking better working conditions and a greater role in school governance struck today for the first time in 25 years, setting up picket lines outside the city's 107 public schools.

Officials worked to keep classes running for the district's 63,000 students with substitute teachers, administrators and regular teachers who declined to strike.

Picket lines went up at daybreak, less than 12 hours after teachers voted to go on strike by a nearly 2-to-1 margin. Talks had broken off Saturday.

Union President Leonard Fox estimated 3,000 of the district's 3,800 teachers stayed away from class. It was not immediately clear to what extent classes were disrupted. There were no reports of violence. School Superintendent Irv Moskowitz said all schools were open and administrators were working to bring in more substitutes to staff more classes Tuesday.

"As time goes on, you'll see our programs become more efficient," Moskowitz said.

The story goes on to quote a picketing teacher and a sympathetic high-school student and ends with lots of dollar figures regarding salaries, raises and the pay package.

Now here's how the story appeared on the Associated Press broadcast wire in its entirety:

(Denver)—Denver school officials say all public schools are open today despite a strike by teachers.

Officials say the district's 63-thousand students are being taught by a combination of administrators, substitute teachers and regular teachers crossing the picket lines.

The union estimates three thousand of the district's 38-hundred teachers are on strike.

The teachers voted by nearly a two-to-one margin last night to reject a one-year contract offer.

This is the first teachers' strike in Denver in 25 years.

In the broadcast version, listeners or viewers are given the bare facts. They must turn to their newspapers for the details. Researchers have found that those who watch television news generally spend more time reading their newspaper. They may be reading, in part, to get the background.

Golden gives two other tips for turning newspaper copy into broadcast copy. First, if the newspaper story is complicated, break it down into separate stories. Second, read the newspaper version to the end before beginning to write the broadcast version. Often, he says, the best angle for the broadcast story is at the bottom of the newspaper story.

In broadcast news, tight writing is important even when there is more time. Broadcast writers waste no words, even in **documentaries**, which provide in-depth coverage of events. Here's how the famous CBS correspondent Edward R. Murrow introduced the well-known documentary on the state of migrant workers in this country:

This is an American story that begins in Florida and ends in New Jersey and New York State with the harvest. It is a 1960

```
Grapes of Wrath that begins at the Mexican border in
California and ends in Oregon and Washington. It is the story
of men and women and children who work 136 days of the year
and average 900 dollars a year. They travel in buses. They
ride trucks. They follow the sun.
```

Murrow's writing style consists of simple, declarative sentences, written in the present tense, tightly, carefully, dramatically. It is casual and conversational; most of the words have one or two syllables. It is simple but not oversimplified. It is vivid and clear.

Clarity

"Short words are best, and old words, when short, are best of all."
— *Winston Churchill*

Unlike newspaper readers, broadcast news viewers and listeners can't go back over the copy. They see or hear it only once, and their attention waxes and wanes. So you must try harder to be *clear* and *precise*. All of the emphasis on condensing and writing tightly is useless if the message is not understood. Better not to report at all than to fill air time with messages that have no meaning.

Clarity demands that you write simply, in short sentences filled with nickel-and-dime words. Don't look for synonyms. Don't be afraid to repeat words or phrases. Oral communication needs reinforcement. Avoid foreign words and phrases; do not use Latin words (*sine qua non*) or Latinisms (*somnambulist* for "sleepwalker"). Avoid phrases like "the former" and "the latter." Repeat the proper names in the story rather than using pronouns. The listener can easily forget the name of the person to whom the pronoun refers.

When you are tempted to write a dependent clause in a sentence, make it an independent clause instead. Keep the subject close to the verb. Close the gap between the doer and the activity. Look at this news item:

```
A man flagged down a Highway Patrol officer near Braden,
Tennessee, today and told him a convict was hiding in his
house. The prisoner, one of five who escaped from the Fort
Pillow Prison on Saturday, surrendered peacefully.
```

The second sentence contains 12 words between the subject, "prisoner," and the verb, "surrendered." By the time the broadcaster reaches the verb, many listeners will have forgotten what the subject was. The story is easier to understand this way:

```
A man flagged down a Highway Patrol officer near Braden,
Tennessee, today and told him a convict was hiding in his
house. The prisoner surrendered peacefully. He's one of five
who escaped from the Fort Pillow Prison on Saturday.
```

The third sentence is still a complex sentence, but it is easily understood. The complex sentence is often just that—complex—only more so in oral communication.

Clarity also requires that you resist a clever turn of phrase. Although viewers and listeners probably are intelligent enough to understand it, they simply will not have the time. A good figure of speech takes time to savor. If listeners pause to savor it (presuming they grasped it in the first place), they will not hear what follows. Clever columnists often fail as radio commentators. Too often the listener asks, "What was that?"

Of course, there are exceptions. The twist of a truism may convey a point with clarity and impact. In documentaries or commentaries the writer has more license. Even a literary allusion may be illuminating, as it was when Eric Sevareid concluded his remarks about the nation's farewell to Martin Luther King Jr.:

> So the label on his life must not be a long day's journey
> into night. It must be a long night's journey into day.

Generally, though, literary speech is undesirable in broadcast news. Even more dangerous than figures of speech are numerical figures. Don't barrage the listener or viewer with a series of numbers. If you must use statistics, break them down so that they are understandable. It is better to say, for example, that one of every six Americans smokes than to say there are 40 million smokers in the United States. You may have to say how many billion dollars a federal program will cost, but you will help listeners understand if you say that it will cost the average wage earner $73 for each of the next five years.

Remember that you are writing for the benefit of your viewers and listeners. You serve them best by emphasizing immediacy and by writing conversationally, tightly and clearly.

Story Structure

Now that you know the characteristics of broadcast writing, let's examine the story structure. Writers must craft broadcast leads somewhat different from print leads. They must also construct special introductions and conclusions to video or audio segments and synchronize their words with taped segments.

Writing the Broadcast Lead

Both newspaper and broadcast reporters must attract the attention of their audience. Much of what you learned in Chapter 17 applies to broadcast leads. However, people tend to do things when listening to radio or watching television, so when you write for broadcasting you strive to attract their attention in different ways.

listeners and be able to retain that information.

"When I begin to write, I know what my source just told me. I even know which sound bites I want to use. That helps me when I take notes and when I write my story."

As his partner drives, Lopez forms his story while it's still fresh in his mind. "By the time I reach my office, my story is pretty well scripted. All I have to do is polish it."

Lopez watches what his photographer is shooting. "Because I know what is shot, I can write to the video."

He also talks over the script with photographers and often reads rough scripts to them. "Many times they have another take on the situation that helps smooth out a story." Lopez says.

The San Antonio native always reads the story aloud beforehand. "That helps me eliminate wordiness and make the story less confusing. Some people are embarrassed to read aloud in the news room. I'm not. After all, it's my face out there."

One way to do this is by preparing your audience for what is to come. You cue the listeners to make sure they are tuned in. In effect, you are saying, "Now listen to this." You introduce the story with a general statement, something that will pique the interest of the audience, and then go to the specific. For example:

General statement   Things are far from settled for Springfield's teacher strike.

Specifics   School officials and union representatives reached no agreement yesterday. They will not meet again for at least a week.

Sometimes the lead, or **set-up**, will be a simple phrase:

Set-up   Injuries and heavy wind damage in Braddyville, Iowa.

Specifics   A tornado swept through the farming village of Braddyville, Iowa, this evening. And authorities report at least half the town was leveled. They say four persons required hospitalization.

Sometimes the opening sentence will cover a number of news items:

There were several accidents in the Springfield vicinity today.

"Cuing in" is only one method of opening a broadcast story. Other leads go immediately into the what and the who, the where and the when. In broadcast news the what is most important, followed by who did the what. The time and the place may be included in the lead, but seldom is the why or the how. If time permits, the why and the how may come later in the story, but often they are omitted.

The first words of the lead are the most important. Don't keep the listener guessing as to what the story is about. Don't begin with a dependent clause or with prepositional phrases as in this example:

With the strong backing of Governor Whitman, a second state spending-limit bill is scheduled for final Senate action today.

The opening words are meaningless without what comes later. The listener may not know what you are talking about. A better way to introduce this story is:

The Senate will vote today on whether to limit state spending--with the strong backing of Governor Whitman.

As you do in a lead for a newspaper story, be sure to "tee up," or identify, an unfamiliar name. By introducing a person, you prepare listeners for the name that they otherwise may miss. Do it this way:

```
Veteran Kansas City, Kansas, businessman and civic leader
Ivar Larson died yesterday in a nursing home at age 83.
```

Don't mislead. The opening words must set the proper tone and mood for the story. Attract attention; tease a little. Answer questions, but don't ask them. Question leads are for commercials. Lead the listener into your story.

Writing Lead-Ins and Wrap-Ups

Broadcast journalists must learn how to write a different kind of lead, called the **lead-in**, that introduces a taped excerpt from a news source or from another reporter. The functions of a lead-in are to set the scene by briefly telling the where, the when and sometimes the what, and to identify the source or reporter. The lead-in should contain something substantive. Here's an example:

```
A grand jury has decided not to charge a Springfield teen-
ager in the killing of his father. Jan Morrow reports the
panel felt the death was an accident.
```

Lead-ins should generate interest. Sometimes several sentences are used to provide background, as in the following:

```
We'll all be getting the official word this morning on how
much less our dollars bought last month. The consumer price
index for March is expected to show another sharp rise in
retail prices. The rate of inflation was one percent in
January and one-point-two percent in February. Here's more on
our inflation woes from Bill McKinney.
```

Be careful not to include in the lead-in what is in the story. Just as a headline should not be stolen word for word from a lead of a newspaper story, the lead-in should not use the opening words of the correspondent. The writer must know the contents of the taped report in order to write a proper lead-in.

After the recorded report, you may want to wrap up the story before going on to the next item. This is especially important in radio copy because there are no visuals to identify the person just heard. If the story reported by Evelyn Turner was about a meeting to settle a strike, you might wrap up her report by adding information:

```
Turner reports negotiations will resume tomorrow.
```

A wrap-up such as this gives your story an ending and clearly separates it from the next story.

Writing for Videotape

Writing for a videotaped report really begins with the selection of the subject and how it is to be videotaped. The writing continues through the editing and selection process. And always, it is done with the pictures clearly in mind.

Words and pictures must be complementary, never interfering with each other. Neither should the words and pictures ignore each other. Your first responsibility is to relate the words to the pictures. If you do not, viewers will not get the message because they will be spending their time wondering what the pictures are about.

"Writing a silence is as important as writing words. We don't rely on video enough."

—John Hart, veteran broadcaster

You can, however, stick too closely to the pictures by pointing out the obvious in a blow-by-blow account. You need to avoid both extremes and use what Russ Bensley, formerly of CBS News, calls the "hit-and-run" technique. This means that at the beginning of a scene or when a scene changes you must tell the viewer where you are or what is happening. Once you are into the scene, the script may be more general and less closely tied to the pictures. For example, if the report concerns the continuation of a hospital workers' strike and the opening scene shows picketers outside the hospital you can explain the tape by saying:

```
Union members are still picketing Mercy Hospital today as

the hospital workers' strike enters its third week.
```

Viewers now know two things that are not obvious in the tape: who is picketing and where. If the tape switches to people sitting around a table negotiating, you must again set the scene for viewers:

```
Meanwhile, hospital administrators and union leaders

are continuing their meetings--apparently without suc-

cess.
```

Once you have related the words to the pictures, you may go on to tell other details of the strike. You are expected to provide information not contained in the pictures themselves. In other words, you must not only comment on the tape but complete it as well. Part of completing it is to give the report a wrap-up or a strong ending. Don't be cute and don't be obvious, but give the story an ending. Here's one possible ending for the strike story:

```
Strikers, administrators, patients and their families

agree on one sure effect of the strike--it's a bad time to be

sick.
```

Now that you have learned some principles of writing broadcast news, you must learn how to prepare the copy.

Preparing Broadcast Copy

Preparing copy to be read by a newscaster is different from preparing it for a typesetter. Your goals are to make the copy easy for the newscaster to read and easy for the audience to understand. What follows will help you accomplish these two goals.

Format

Most broadcast news editors want triple-spaced copy. Leave two to three inches on the top of the page and one to two inches on the bottom.

For radio copy, set your computer so that you have 70 characters to a line (see Figure 20.1). Each line will average about 10 words, and

```
west broadway                                                       slug

12-30                                                               time of newscast

1-11-96                                                             date of broadcast

flanagan                                                           reporter's name




     Members of Citizens for the Preservation of West Broadway

plan to gear up their petition drive again this weekend.  The group

began circulating petitions last weekend.

     The petitions request the City Council to repeal all previous

ordinances and resolutions on the widening.  Many residents of the

West Broadway area complain that the proposed widening project will

damage its residential nature.

     Petition-drive coordinator Vera Hanson says the group is pleased

with the show of support from residents all over Springfield . . .

but it won't know exactly how many signatures it has until next week.
```

Figure 20.1.
Sample of radio copy.

the newscaster will average 15 lines per minute. Most stations require you to start each story on a separate piece of paper. That way, the order of the stories can be rearranged, or stories can be added or dropped easily. If a story goes more than one page, write "MORE" in parentheses at the bottom of the page.

Television copy is written on the right half of the page in a 40-character line (see Figure 20.2). Each line will average about six words, and the newscaster will average about 25 lines per minute. The left side of the copy is used for audio or video information. This information, which is not to be read by the newscaster, is usually typed in all caps. The copy that is read generally appears upper- and lowercase. In television copy the stories are numbered, and each story is on a separate page. If a story goes more than one page, write "MORE" in parentheses at the bottom of the page.

Do not hyphenate words, and be sure to end a page with a com-

"jorgenson" is the name of the reporter.

"six" is the time of the newscast.

"6-17" is the day of the broadcast.

"art" is the slug for the story.

"MOC:" means the person is live on camera with audio from his or her microphone.

"SOT:27" means there is sound on the tape lasting 27 seconds.

"NAT SND UNDER" means the tape sound should be kept at a low level.

"VOICE OVER" means the voice is from the anchor person in the studio speaking over the tape that is being shown.

"SUPER: BUCHANAN HIGH SCHOOL" indicates the title that should be shown over the tape.

":00-:05" indicates that the title should be shown five seconds after the report of this news item begins.

```
jorgenson          six          6-17          art


 MOC: JORGENSON                    A lesson in art and architecture paid

                               off for some Buchanan High School students

 SOT     :27                   today.  Ribbons were the prizes for winning
 NAT SND UNDER
 VOICE OVER

 SUPER: BUCHANAN HIGH SCHOOL   entries in a sketch exhibit of scenery and
        :00-:05

                               buildings in the capital city area.

                                   The Springfield art club sponsored the

                               show and called in Springfield College art

                               professor Bill Ruess to judge the artwork.

                                   Ruess says he was impressed by the

                               students' skills, especially those who tried

                               their hand at the different art media for

                               the first time.
```

Figure 20.2.
Sample of television copy.

plete sentence or, if possible, with a complete paragraph. If the next page should be missing in the middle of a broadcast, the newscaster can end, at least, with a complete sentence or paragraph.

At many stations copy is prepared for a **videoprompter**, a mechanical or electronic device that projects the copy next to the camera so the newscaster can read it while appearing to look straight into the lens. Copy for the videoprompter is often typed down a column in the middle of the page.

Date the first page of your script, and type your last name in the upper left-hand corner of every page. Stations vary regarding these directions. The local news director determines the slug for a story and its placement. Some directors insist that the slug contain the time of the broadcast. If a story continues to a second page, write under the slug "first add" or "second add," or "page 2," "page 3," and so forth.

Stations with computerized news rooms may use scripting software that alters these formats somewhat.

Names and Titles

In broadcast style, unlike that followed by newspapers, well-known names, even on first reference, are not given in full. You may say Senator Kerrey of Nebraska or Governor Merrill of New Hampshire. Middle initials should not be used unless they are a natural part of someone's name (Edward R. Murrow) or unless they are necessary to distinguish two people with the same first and last names.

Titles should always precede names so that listeners are better prepared to hear the name. When you use titles, the first name and middle initial may be omitted. For example, broadcasters would say Vice President Gore and Secretary of State Christopher. Newspapers write out names like Elmer J. "Lucky" Cantrell. In broadcast, use either the first name or the nickname, but not both.

Pronunciation

The writer's job is to help the newscaster pronounce the names of people and places correctly. To do this, you should write out difficult names phonetically in parentheses. NBC, for example, has its own reference list, and many individual stations have handbooks of their own. You may have to look up difficult names in unabridged dictionaries. If you don't find the name there, use your telephone. Call the person's office, or the consulate or embassy. If the name is of a U.S. town, try calling an operator in that town. There is no rhyme or reason to the way some people pronounce their names or to the way some names of places are pronounced. Never assume. Never try to figure it out. Find out. Here's an example of how you should write out difficult names:

First stop: Cairo for a meeting with Egyptian President
Hosni Mubarak (HAHS'-nee moo-BAH'-rahk) and then to Damascus
for a meeting with Syrian President Hafez Assad (HAH'-fez AH'-
sahd).

Perhaps most people would know how to pronounce Lima (LEE-mah), Peru, but not everyone can pronounce Lima (LIGH-mah), Ohio. You must note the difference between NEW-erk, N.J., and new-ARK, Del., both spelled Newark. And who would guess that Pago Pago is pronounced PAHNG-oh PAHNG-oh?

Abbreviations

Generally, you should *not* use abbreviations in broadcast copy. It is easier to read a word written out than to read its abbreviation. Do not abbreviate the names of states, countries, months, days of the week or military titles. There are exceptions, and when you use them, use hyphens instead of periods because the final period in the abbreviation may be misread as the end of the sentence.

You may abbreviate U-S when used as an adjective, and Dr., Mr., Mrs. and Ms.; a.m. and p.m. If initials are well known—U-N, G-O-P, F-B-I—you may use them. Hyphens are not used for acronyms such as NATO and HUD that are pronounced as one word.

Symbols and Numbers

Do *not* use symbols in broadcast copy because a newscaster can read a word more easily than he or she can remember a symbol. Such symbols as the dollar sign ($) and the percent sign (%) are never used. Don't even use the abbreviation for number (no.).

Numbers can be a problem for both the announcer and the listener. As in newspaper style, write out numbers one through nine. But write out eleven, too, because 11 might not be easily recognized as a number. Use figures for 10, and from 12 to 999. The eye can easily take in a three-digit number, but write out the words thousand, million and billion. Hence, 3,800,000 becomes three million, 800 thousand. Write out fractions (two-and-a-half million dollars) and decimal points (three-point-two-percent).

Some stations have exceptions. Figures often are used when giving the time (3:20 a.m.), sports scores (The score was 5 to 2) and statistics, market reports (The Dow Jones industrial index was up 2-point-8 points) and addresses (30-0-2 Grand Street). In common speech no one would give an address as three thousand two.

Ordinarily, you may round off big numbers. Thus 48-point-3 percent should be written "nearly half." But don't say "more than one hundred" if 104 people died in an earthquake.

Use *st*, *nd*, *rd* and *th* after dates: August 1st, September 2nd, October 3rd and November 4th. Make the year easy to pronounce: June 9th, 19-73.

Quotations and Attributions

Most broadcast newswriters rarely use quotation marks. Because it is difficult and awkward to indicate to listeners which words are being quoted, use indirect quotes or a paraphrase instead.

If it is important that listeners know the exact words of a quotation (as when the quoted words are startling, uncomplimentary or possibly libelous), the quote may be introduced by saying "in his words," "with these words," "what she called," or "he put it this way." Most writers prefer to avoid the formal "quote" and "unquote," though "quote" is used more than "unquote." Note the following example:

```
In Smith's words, quote, "There is no way to undo the harm
done."
```

If you must use a direct quotation, the attribution always should precede the quotation. Because listeners cannot see the quotation marks, they would have no way of knowing the words are a direct quote. If by chance the words were recognized as a quote, listeners would have no idea who is saying them. For the same reason, the attribution must always precede the indirect quote.

And if you must use a direct quotation, keep it short. If the quote is long and it is important to use it, you should use a tape of the person saying it. However, if you are compelled to use a quote of more than a sentence in your copy, break it up with phrases like, "Smith went on to say" or "and still quoting the senator."

Punctuation

In broadcast copy, less punctuation is good punctuation. The one exception is the comma. Commas help the newscaster pause at appropriate places. Use commas, for example, after introductory phrases referring to time and place, as in the following:

```
In Paris, three Americans on holiday met their death today
when their car overturned and caught fire.
     Last August, beef prices had reached an all-time high.
```

Sometimes three periods are used in place of the comma. Periods also take the place of the parenthesis and of the semicolon. They indicate a pause and are more easily visible. The same is true of the dash—typed as two hyphens. Note the dash in the following example:

```
    But the judge grumbled about the news coverage, and most
    prospective jurors agreed  saying the news coverage has been
    prone to overstatement, sensationalism and errors.
```

The only punctuation marks you need are the period, comma, question mark, dash, hyphen and, rarely, quotation marks. To make the words easier to read, use the hyphen in some words, even when the dictionary does not use it: anti-discrimination, co-equal, non-aggression.

Corrections

When preparing broadcast copy, do *not* use the copy-editing marks you learned for editing newspaper copy. If a word has an error in it, cross out the word and write the corrected word above it.

Note this sentence with newspaper copy editing:

```
    The Stag Brewery at Beleville, (Illinois,) soon will be phased

    out of operation, and it/s 230 workers already are lo_oking

    for new jobs.
```

Here's how you correct it for broadcasting:

```
                        Belleville, Illinois                phased
    The Stag Brewery at Beleville, Illinois, soon will be hpased

                            its                    looking
    out of operation, and it's 230 workers already are lo oking

               jobs
    for new jbos.
```

Again, your function is to make the copy easier to read. Avoid making the newscasters go up and down to find the right words, as in the following.

```
         price   gold   London
    The  pirce of glod in london at the afternoon fixing was 240

    dollars.
```

Better to correct it this way:

```
         price of gold in London
    The  pirce of glod in london at the afternoon fixing was 240

    dollars.
```

And, of course, always make your corrections neatly and clearly. Most broadcast news rooms now use computers for script writing. Where that is true, there is no excuse for copy to contain *any* handwritten corrections.

Stations may vary in their writing style and in the preparation of copy. But if you learn what is presented here, you will be well prepared. Differences will be small, and you will adapt to them easily.

Suggested Readings

Bliss, Edward Jr. and Hoyt, James L. *Writing News for Broadcast*, Third Edition. New York: Columbia University Press, 1994. A classic writing text that excels in good writing.

Block, Melvin. *Writing Broadcast News—Shorter, Sharper, Stronger.* Chicago: Bonus Books, 1989. An excellent book by a former network newswriter.

Flesch, Rudolf. *The Art of Readable Writing.* New York: Macmillan, 1986. This book explains the famous Flesch formula for assessing readability.

Stephens, Mitchell. *Broadcast News*, Third Edition. Fort Worth, TX: Harcourt Brace College, 1993. Covers all aspects of broadcast writing and the business of broadcast news.

White, Ted. *Broadcast News Writing and Reporting.* New York: St. Martin's, 1993. The best book on all aspects of broadcast newswriting.

Exercises

1. Watch a local evening television newscast. Make a simple list of the news stories. Then try to find those stories in the next morning's local newspaper and compare the coverage.

2. Check to see if the following AP stories written for broadcast follow acceptable broadcast style. Are they technically correct? Do they emphasize immediacy? Change the copy where you think necessary.

   a. (Los Angeles)—Coming soon to theaters near you—the "Hour of Power."

      T-V minister Robert Schuller (SHOO'-lur) is bringing his religious program to movie theaters in America, Australia, Europe and Hong Kong.

      Schuller started out in 1955 with a drive-in preaching service. Now, his syndicated T-V show is seen worldwide by about 20 million people.

      Recently, N-B-C bought out a European network and dropped the "Hour of Power." So Schuller decided to start transferring his shows to film and showing them in theaters.

      The first installments run in Australian theaters later this month.

      Admission will be free.

   b. (Augusta, Georgia)—Pregnant soldiers continue to serve their country, although they can't fight in wars.

      According to Army statistics compiled at Fort McPherson in Atlanta, nine percent of the 20-thousand women in U-S combat units can't be deployed because of pregnancy.

      During pregnancy, soldiers are excused from marching, overnight field assignments and overseas deployment—such as the recent missions in Haiti and the Persian Gulf.

      They get time off for doctors' appointments and six weeks of paid maternity leave.

      Critics say pregnant women in the Army raise health care costs, slow down the troops, and weaken the military's warrior spirit.

      But the Pentagon says women make good soldiers, even though they get time off for pregnancy.

   c. (Johnson Space Center, Houston)—The crew of the shuttle "Endeavour" is making the most of its extra day in space.

      The astronauts are using a powerful radar to gather information to help make more sophisticated and accurate topographical maps.

      Today, the radar scanned ocean currents near the Antarctic Circle and forests in North Carolina. As of Sunday, it had collected enough data to fill nearly 52 miles of tape.

      Scientists will later use the data to make three-D maps accurate in elevation to within six yards. The best maps now are accurate to within ten yards.

      The shuttle is scheduled to return to Earth tomorrow after eleven days in space.

d. (Los Angeles)—It's getting a little bit cheaper to fill up your gas tank.

A biweekly survey of ten-thousand gas stations reports that average gas prices were down one penny in the last two weeks. Prices have been dropping since August due to lower crude oil prices and seasonal demand.

The survey says consumers paid about a dollar-21 to about a dollar-33, depending on the grade of fuel.

Full-service fill-ups averaged about 30 cents more per gallon than self-serve.

3. Rewrite the following AP newspaper briefs in broadcast writing style. Assume the news is current and that you have time for one paragraph of four or five lines for each story.

a. ZURICH, Switzerland (AP)—Thieves have stolen seven Picasso paintings worth more than $40 million from an art gallery, police said today.

Zurich police said the break-in occurred over the weekend through the cellar of a neighboring house.

A police statement said two works, "Seated Woman," and "Christ of Montmartre" were the most valuable of the paintings stolen. Both paintings were stolen in 1991 from a Zurich gallery and were recovered the following year.

b. SEAL BEACH, Calif. (AP)—State authorities have disputed a retirement community's rules on keeping its pools and golf courses off-limits to underage users—whom it defines as being under 55.

The State Fair Employment and Housing Department filed a complaint against Leisure World after Alfred and Mary Gray objected last year to a no-access policy for younger spouses at Leisure World's recreational facilities. Mary Gray was 51 at the time.

Operators of Seal Beach Leisure World, whose 9,000 residents comprise one-third of the city's population, have decided to contest the federal Unruh Civil Rights Act cited by state officials, administrator Bill Narans said.

c. MINNEAPOLIS (AP)—Northwest Airlines announced Sunday it is cutting domestic fares up to 40 percent for holiday travelers.

Tickets must be purchased by Friday for travel between Nov. 12 and Jan. 14 in the lower 48 states and Alaska, and for travel to Canada between Nov. 24 and Jan. 14.

Discounts vary depending on travel dates and are not available on certain popular days, including Nov. 23 and Nov. 26, and Dec. 23 and Dec. 26.

With the discounted, non-refundable fares, a passenger could travel round-trip between Hartford, Conn., and San Francisco for $400 or between Minneapolis and Washington for $260 on certain days.

Major airlines historically have matched major fare sales on competitive routes.

Separately, Trans World Airlines and Southwest Airlines announced sales over the weekend.

4. Read a copy of a current newspaper. Then write a five-minute newscast. Pay special attention to lead-ins and wrap-ups. (Do not include sports material in your broadcast.)

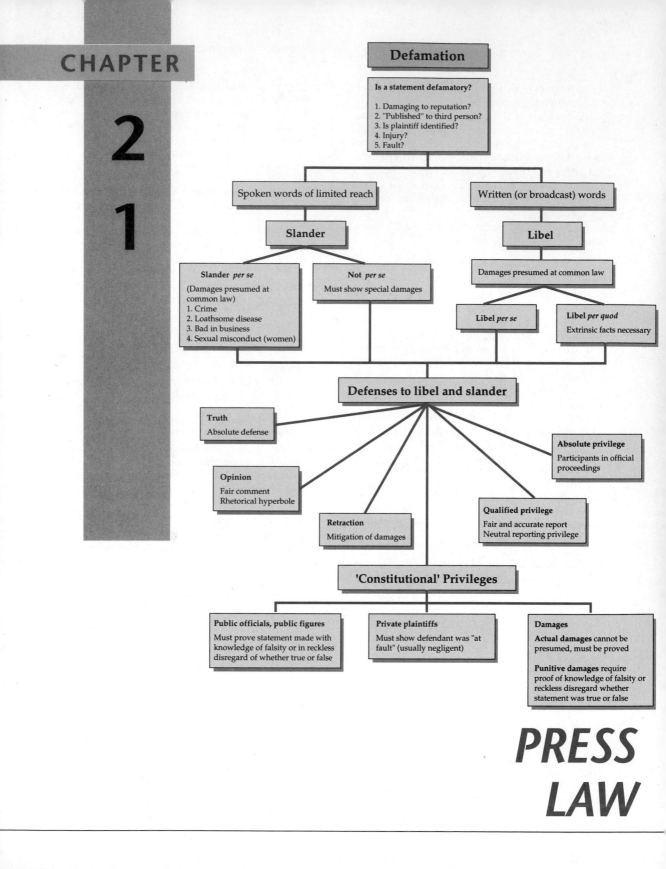

Defamation

Is a statement defamatory?

1. Damaging to reputation?
2. "Published" to third person?
3. Is plaintiff identified?
4. Injury?
5. Fault?

Spoken words of limited reach

Written (or broadcast) words

Slander

Libel

Slander *per se*

(Damages presumed at common law)
1. Crime
2. Loathsome disease
3. Bad in business
4. Sexual misconduct (women)

Not *per se*
Must show special damages

Damages presumed at common law

Libel *per se*

Libel *per quod*
Extrinsic facts necessary

Defenses to libel and slander

Truth
Absolute defense

Absolute privilege
Participants in official proceedings

Opinion
Fair comment
Rhetorical hyperbole

Retraction
Mitigation of damages

Qualified privilege
Fair and accurate report
Neutral reporting privilege

'Constitutional' Privileges

Public officials, public figures
Must prove statement made with knowledge of falsity or in reckless disregard of whether true or false

Private plaintiffs
Must show defendant was "at fault" (usually negligent)

Damages
Actual damages cannot be presumed, must be proved

Punitive damages require proof of knowledge of falsity or reckless disregard whether statement was true or false

PRESS LAW

I f you write that, I'll sue."
That threat can be intimidating to the young reporter who hears it for the first time. Those with a bit more experience will have encountered the situation many times. In either case, such a threat should not be taken lightly. It is at least possible that the person making it is both serious about the threat and accurate in insisting that your information is incorrect. If you are wrong, both you and your publication or station could suffer.

Reporters who know their stories are accurate are seldom intimidated by such threats. If what you write is true, and you can prove it, you have little to fear when threats of lawsuits are tossed about. The laws that pertain to libel, invasion of privacy and protection of sources are among the many you should know about. In an era when people increasingly turn to the courts to solve their problems, it makes sense to have an understanding of your rights as a journalist to gather and write the news. In recent years, the courts have chipped away at those rights in instances ranging from investigating prisons to covering divorce actions.

In one particularly threatening case that almost resulted in the closing of the Alton (Ill.) Telegraph, the libel judgment was for $9.2 million. The case ended in bankruptcy court, where the award was reduced to $2.1 million, still a major loss. Despite those setbacks, the press has ample opportunity to report the news as long as those reports are fair and accurate. It is important that you learn the essentials of libel and privacy and understand the basics of contempt of court.

Your Rights

The Constitution signed in Philadelphia in 1787 did not contain explicit protections of freedom of speech and of the press. Those protections were added four years later in the First Amendment, which states:

> Congress shall make no law respecting an establishment of religion, or prohibiting the free exercise thereof; or abridging the freedom of speech, or of the press; or the right of the people peaceably to assemble, and to petition the Government for a redress of grievances.

"The government's power to censor the press was abolished so the press would remain forever free to censure the government."

*—Hugo Black,
Supreme Court Justice*

Read that again: "Congress shall make no law . . . abridging the freedom of . . . the press." No other business in the United States enjoys that specific constitutional protection, unless you count religion as business.

Why should there be such protection for the press? The Supreme Court gave an eloquent answer to that question in a 1957 obscenity decision. The press is protected, the court ruled, to assure the "unfettered interchange of ideas for bringing about the political and social changes desired by the people."

The free flow of ideas is necessary in a democracy because people who govern themselves need to know about their government and those who run it, as well as about the social and economic institutions that greatly affect their day-to-day lives. Most people get that information through newspapers, radio and television.

In 1966 Congress passed the **Freedom of Information Act** to assist anyone in finding out what is happening in our federal agencies. This act, which was amended in 1974 to improve access to government records, makes it easier for you to know about government business. All 50 states have similar **open-records laws**. Though of great assistance to the press, the laws also are used by individuals and businesses to gain information previously kept secret by the government. There are other laws assuring access to government transactions. The federal government and all the states have *open-meetings laws*—often called **sunshine laws**—requiring that the public's business be conducted in public. However, all of these access laws contain exemptions keeping some meetings private.

The First Amendment, the Freedom of Information Act and sunshine laws demonstrate America's basic concern for citizen access to information needed for the "unfettered interchange of ideas." However, there are laws that reduce the scope of freedom of the press.

> *"Journalists don't believe . . . the Freedom of Information Act was created to be turned on us as an excuse to hide information."*
> *—Sarah Overstreet,*
> *columnist*

Libel

Traditionally, most of the laws limiting the absolute principle of freedom of the press have dealt with libel. These laws result from the desire of legislatures and courts to help individuals protect their reputations. This was explained by U.S. Supreme Court Justice Potter Stewart in a libel case (brackets added):

> The right of a man [or woman] to the protection of his [or her] own reputation from unjustified invasion and wrongful hurt reflects no more than our basic concept of the essential dignity and worth of every human being—a concept at the root of any decent system of ordered liberty.

Protection for reputations dates back centuries. In 17th-century England individuals were imprisoned and even disfigured for making libelous statements. One objective was to prevent criticism of the government. Another was to maintain the peace by avoiding duels. Duels are rare today, and government is freely criticized, but the desire to protect an individual's reputation is just as strong.

Two cases concerning generals, government and reputations are of special interest to journalists and help in understanding libel. These extensively covered trials were held in the winter of 1984–1985 in the same federal courthouse in Manhattan.

In one, against CBS correspondent Mike Wallace and producer George Crile, Gen. William C. Westmoreland said a 1982 report by CBS accused him, as commander of the U.S. forces in Vietnam, of participating in a "conspiracy at the highest levels of American military intelligence" to underreport enemy troop strength in 1967. The purpose of the alleged underreporting, CBS said, was to create the impression that the United States was winning the war.

The other case was based on a 1983 *Time* magazine cover story, "Verdict on the Massacre," about Israel's 1982 judicial inquiry into the massacre of several hundred civilians in two Palestinian refugee camps in Lebanon. The *Time* article was about Israeli Gen. Ariel Sharon's conversations with the Gemayel family on the day after Bashir Gemayel's assassination. *Time* said Sharon had "reportedly discussed with the Gemayels the need for the Phalangists to take revenge for the assassination of Bashir."

Libel is damage to a person's reputation caused by bringing him or her into hatred, contempt or ridicule in the eyes of a substantial and respectable group. Both generals sued. Their attorneys knew they would have to show that their clients had suffered hatred, contempt or ridicule because these statements were serious attacks on their clients' reputations and not just unpleasant comments.

Westmoreland was concerned that the CBS broadcast about a "conspiracy" to underreport enemy troop strength would cause people to believe he had deceived President Lyndon Johnson about the enemy. Sharon's concern was that the *Time* report suggested he had allowed, even encouraged, "revenge" killings of hundreds of civilians while he was in command in Lebanon.

The Westmoreland case ended before being submitted to the jury when both parties signed a joint statement announcing an out-of-court settlement on Feb. 19, 1985. The sudden and surprising end to the case has been attributed to the damaging testimony of two former subordinates, one a former classmate of Westmoreland at West Point.

In the joint statement CBS said it made no concessions and paid no money to Westmoreland. Both parties said they were satisfied "that their respective positions have been effectively placed before the public for its consideration and that continuing the legal process at this stage would serve no further purpose." Legal fees in the case amounted to an estimated $8 million to $10 million.

The Sharon case is more helpful in understanding the complexities of libel. The jury's decision was in three parts. The first part of the verdict was in answer to the question: Was the paragraph concerning Sharon defamatory? The jury said it was. This means the *Time* article had damaged Sharon's reputation and brought him into hatred, contempt or ridicule.

The second question for the jury was this: Was the paragraph concerning Sharon and revenge false? Again the jury answered affirmatively. If the answer had been "no," the case would have ended here. Truth is a complete defense for libel.

The third question for the jury: Was the paragraph published with "actual malice"—with knowledge that it was false or reckless disregard of whether it was false ("serious doubt" that it was true)?

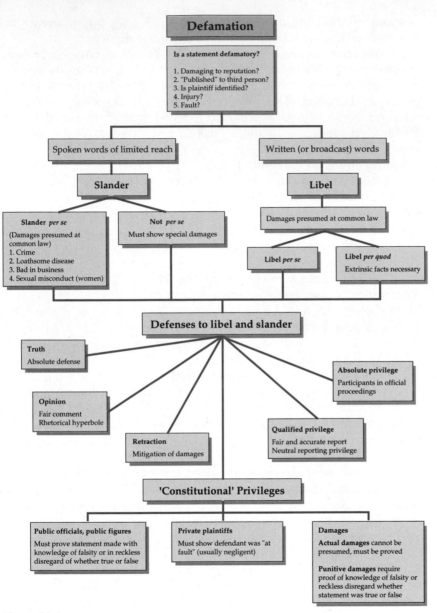

Figure 21.1.
An understanding of libel and related concepts is essential for journalists.

The jury answered "no." Thus the trial ended in favor of *Time* magazine, despite the jury ruling that the article was defamatory.

There are four categories courts use to help jurors like those in the Sharon case decide if someone's reputation has been damaged because he or she has been brought into hatred, contempt or ridicule. They are:

1. Accusing someone of a crime. (This may have been the basis in the Sharon case.)
2. Damaging a person in his or her public office, profession or occupation. (If the statements by CBS and *Time* against Westmoreland and Sharon did not accuse them of crimes, they did damage them in their profession as military men.)
3. Accusing a person of serious immorality (often accusing a woman of being unchaste). Many states have statutes that make an accusation of unchastity a cause of action in a libel suit.
4. Accusing someone of having a loathsome disease. This category was fading as an area of defamation. However, with the advent of AIDS, it may reappear.

This does not mean you never can say a person committed a crime, was unethical in business, was adulterous or had a loathsome (contagious) disease. It does mean you must be certain that what you write is true.

Libel Suit Defenses

There are three traditional defenses against libel: truth, privilege, and fair comment and criticism. Two other constitutional defenses—the actual malice and negligence tests—also help libel defendants.

Truth

Truth is the best defense against libel. However, knowing the truth is one thing; proving it is another. In April 1986, the Supreme Court ruled that a person who sues for libel must prove that the news account was false. This now sets a uniform rule for all 50 states—the burden of proof in libel cases involving matters of public concern is on the plaintiff. This decision does not, however, change the responsibility of the reporter to seek the truth in every possible way.

You cannot be certain, for example, whether a person charged with arson actually started the fire. Who told you that Joe Jones started the fire? The first source to check is the police or fire report. If a police officer or fire marshal says that Jones started a fire, you can report not that he did it but that he has been accused of doing it. You should go no further than this unless you have information you would be willing to present in court.

Be sure you report no more than what you know is true. You might, for instance, learn that Helen Greer has not paid any of her bills for two years, and the only way she can get merchandise is to pay cash when goods are delivered. Who gave you this information? If the truth is that a former employee of Ms. Greer told you, that is all the truth you have. The truth, then is, not that Helen Greer has not paid any of her bills for two years and has a bad credit rating. The only truth is that a former employee said it. Without supporting evidence for charges such as these, careful journalists will not print or broadcast the charges. If you do and your employer is sued for damaging Helen Greer's reputation, you would have to try to convince the court that the charge was true. But what if Ms. Greer presents canceled checks and calls suppliers who deny that she owes them any money? You would lose the libel suit. You must be able to prove that Helen Greer is a credit risk before you print or broadcast it, not just that she was accused of bad business practices by a former employee.

When a newspaper in Oklahoma reported that a wrestling coach had been accused of requiring a sixth-grader, who wanted to rejoin the team, to submit to a whipping by his fellow students while crawling naked through the legs of team members, the coach sued. He claimed damage to his reputation.

In cases like this, the reporter has to be certain not just that one or more participants told of the incident but also that the statements were true. In court, some participants might testify to an occurrence and others might testify the incident never took place. A jury would have to decide on the credibility of the participants.

While you must always strive for absolute truth in all of your stories, the courts will settle for what is known as **substantial truth** in most cases. This means that you must be able to prove the essential elements of all you write.

Privilege

In addition to truth, the courts traditionally have allowed another defense against libel: *privilege*. This defense applies when you are covering any of the three branches of government. The courts allow legislators, judges and government executives the *absolute privilege* to say anything—true or false—when acting in their official capacities. The rationale is that the public interest is served when an official is allowed to speak freely and fearlessly about making laws, carrying them out or punishing those who do not obey them. Similarly, a participant in a judicial proceeding, such as an attorney, court clerk or judge, is absolutely privileged to make false and even defamatory statements about another person during that proceeding.

In the executive branch it isn't always clear whose statements are privileged and when. The head of state and the major officers of executive departments of the federal and state governments are covered. However, minor officials might not enjoy the protection of absolute privilege.

As a reporter you do have a **qualified privilege,** sometimes called *neutral reporting* or *conditional privilege*, to report what public officials say. Your privilege is conditioned on your report's being full, fair and accurate coverage of the court session, the legislative session or the president's press conference, even if any one of those includes

The keys to avoiding a libel suit are rooted in professionalism and common sense. He suggests that journalists ask themselves these questions:

▮ Have I reported fully?
▮ Have I reported factually?
▮ Have I reported fairly?
▮ Have I reported in good faith?

"If you can answer those four questions in the affirmative, the law will take care of itself," he says. With the Gannett Company since 1978, Paulson has been executive editor of *Florida Today* in Melbourne, Fla., editor of the *Green Bay* (Wis.) *Press-Gazette* and managing editor of the *Bridgewater* (N.J.) *Courier-News*.

Paulson established on-line services for both *Florida Today* and Gannett Suburban Newspapers, the first of such projects for Gannett.

defamatory statements. You can quote anything the president of the United States says without fear of losing a libel suit, even if the president is not acting in an official capacity. Reporters have a qualified privilege to report unofficial statements. But there are many other levels of executives in federal, state and local government. Mayors of small towns, for instance, often hold part-time positions. Although you are conditionally privileged to report on what those officials say when they are acting in their official capacities, a problem can arise when the part-time mayor says something defamatory when not acting in an official capacity. Some jurisdictions might grant a neutral reporting privilege; some may not.

Fair Comment and Criticism

In some writing you may be commenting or criticizing rather than reporting. The courts have protected writers who comment on and criticize the public offerings of anyone in the public eye. Included in this category are actors and actresses, sports figures, public officials and other newsworthy persons. Most often, such writing occurs in reviews of plays, books or movies, or in commentary on service in hotels and restaurants.

The courts call this **fair comment and criticism.** You are protected as long as you do not misstate any of the facts on which you base your comments or criticism, or as long as you do not wrongly imply that you possess undisclosed, damaging information that forms the basis of your opinion. Merely labeling a fact as an opinion will not result in opinion protection, the U.S. Supreme Court ruled in 1990.

The Actual Malice Test

It was a small but momentous step from fair comment and criticism to the case of *New York Times* vs. Sullivan. In 1964 the U.S. Supreme Court decided that First Amendment protection was broader than just the traditional defenses of truth and privilege and that the press needed even greater freedom in coverage of public officials.

The case started with an advertisement for funds in the *New York Times* of March 29, 1960, by the Committee to Defend Martin Luther King Jr. and the Struggle for Freedom in the South. The advertisement contained factual errors concerning the police, according to Montgomery, Ala., Commissioner L.B. Sullivan. He thought the errors damaged his reputation, and he won a half-million-dollar judgment against the *New York Times* in an Alabama trial court.

The Supreme Court said it was considering the case "against the background of a profound national commitment to the principle that debate on public issues should be uninhibited, robust and wide open." Thus Justice William Brennan wrote that the Constitution requires a federal rule prohibiting a public official from recovering damages from the press for a defamatory falsehood relating to his or her official conduct, *unless* the public official can prove the press had knowledge that what was printed was false or that the story was printed with reckless disregard of whether it was false or not.

The justices thereby gave you protection to write virtually anything about officeholders or candidates unless you know that what you are writing is false or you recklessly disregard the truth of what you write. They called this the **actual malice test.**

The actual malice test was applied later in a case involving a story on CBS's "60 Minutes" about a retired Army officer. Col. Anthony Herbert contended the broadcast falsely portrayed him as a liar. He tried to prove that producer Barry Lando recklessly disregarded whether it was a false broadcast or not. Herbert asked some questions that Lando claimed were protected by the First Amendment because they inquired into his state of mind and into the editorial processes during the production of the program.

The Supreme Court said in 1979 that the "thoughts and editorial processes of the alleged defamer would be open to examination." The court pointed out that protecting the editorial process "would constitute a substantial interference with the ability of a defamation plaintiff to establish . . . malice" as required by the *New York Times* case. The press greeted the ruling with displeasure, though some attorneys noted that the inquiry into the editorial process could help journalists as much as hurt them. It could help by permitting journalists and their attorneys to demonstrate how careful they were in gathering and selecting the information printed.

Assume, for example, you are told that years ago your town's mayor had been involved in a bootlegging operation. Your source is a friend of the mayor who knew him 30 years ago in Idaho. You print the story. After it is published, you find it was not the mayor but his brother who was the bootlegger. The mayor sues. You are in trouble. You must try to convince the court that you should have been able to trust your source and that you did not act with actual malice. If the source had given you many valid stories in the past, you might be able to convince the court that you had good reason to believe what you were told. You also would have to show what else you did or failed to do before you printed the story. Did you call anyone in Idaho to check? Did you talk to the mayor? Did you try other ways to verify the information? All these questions could be asked as the court tries to decide whether you recklessly disregarded the truth.

Usually a reporter who has tried diligently to do all possible research for a story will be able to meet the actual malice test and win a libel action. The key is verification: checking the information with as many sources as possible.

The decision in the Sharon case discussed earlier in the chapter is an example of the burden of proving actual malice against the press.

The jury decided that *Time* did not know at the time the article in question was printed that its statement about Gen. Sharon was false.

In 1991, the Supreme Court decided Masson vs. *The New Yorker*, the so-called "fabricated quotes" case (see Chapter 5). Overruling a lower court's decision that journalists could fictionalize quotations by making rational interpretations of speakers' remarks, the Supreme Court protected the sanctity of quotation marks. But the court also made clear that not every deliberate change in a quotation is libelous. Only a "material change in the meaning conveyed by a statement" poses a problem.

Although Masson won the right to try his case, he lost against all defendants. Janet Malcolm, the journalist who misquoted Masson, won in 1994.

Standards Applicable to Public Figures

The actual malice protection was expanded in two cases in 1967 to include not only public officials but also *public figures*—persons in the public eye but not in public office.

The first case stemmed from a *Saturday Evening Post* article that accused Coach Wally Butts of conspiring to fix a 1962 football game between Georgia and Alabama. At the time of the article, Butts was the athletic director of the University of Georgia. The article, titled "The Story of a College Football Fix," was prefaced by a note from the editors of the *Post* stating:

> Not since the Chicago White Sox threw the 1919 World Series has there been a sports story as shocking as this one. . . . Before the University of Georgia played the University of Alabama . . . Wally Butts . . . gave (to Alabama's coach) . . . Georgia's plays, defensive patterns, all the significant secrets Georgia's football team possessed.

The *Post* reported that, because of an electronic error about a week before the game, George Burnett, an Atlanta insurance salesman, accidentally had overheard a telephone conversation between Butts and the head coach of Alabama, Paul Bryant.

Coach Butts sued Curtis Publishing Co., publishers of the *Post*, and won a verdict for $60,000 in general damages and $3 million in punitive damages. The Curtis Co. appealed the case to the Supreme Court and lost. The trial judge reduced the amount of the damages to $460,000.

The second case was decided the same day. Gen. Edwin Walker sued the Associated Press for distributing a news dispatch giving an eyewitness account by an AP staffer on the campus of the University of Mississippi in the fall of 1962. The AP reported that Gen. Walker personally had led a student charge against federal marshals during a riot on the Mississippi campus. The marshals were attempting to enforce a court decree ordering the enrollment of a black student.

Walker was a retired general at the time of the publication. He had won a $2 million libel suit in a trial court. However, the Supreme Court ruled against him.

In both cases the stories were wrong. In both, the actual malice test was applied. What was the difference between the Butts and Walker cases? The justices said the football story was in no sense "hot news." They noted that the person who said he had heard the conversation was on probation in connection with bad-check charges and that *Post* personnel had not viewed his notes before publication. The court also said, as evidence of actual malice on the part of the *Post*, that no one looked at the game films to see if the information was accurate; that a regular staffer, instead of a football expert, was assigned to the story; and that no check was made with someone knowledgeable in the sport. In short, the *Post* had not done an adequate job of reporting.

The evidence in the Walker case was considerably different. The court said the news in the Walker case required immediate dissemination because of the riot on campus. The justices noted that the AP received the information from a correspondent who was present on the campus and gave every indication of being trustworthy and competent.

In an earlier case, the Supreme Court had defined a public official as a government employee who has, or appears to the public to have, substantial responsibility for or control over the conduct of governmental affairs. In the Butts and Walker cases the court used two definitions of a public figure. The first, like Butts, is a person who has assumed a role of special prominence in the affairs of society—someone who has pervasive power and influence in a community. The second, like Walker, is a person who has thrust himself into the forefront of a particular public controversy in order to influence the resolution of the issues involved.

There are other examples of public figures. A college professor who has become involved with any public controversy ranging from grading practices to gay rights may have made himself or herself a public figure. A police officer who is the leader of the Police Association may be a public figure because of his or her power and influence.

In the 1970s the Supreme Court decided three cases that help journalists determine who is and is not a public figure. The first case involved Mrs. Russell A. Firestone, who sued for libel after *Time* magazine reported that her husband's divorce petition had been granted on grounds of extreme cruelty and adultery. Mrs. Firestone, who had married into the Firestone Tire and Rubber Co. family, claimed that those were not the grounds for the divorce. She also insisted that she was not a public figure with the burden of proving actual malice. The Supreme Court agreed. Even though she had held press conferences and hired a clipping service, the court ruled that she had not thrust herself into the forefront of a public controversy in an attempt to influence the resolution of the issues involved. The court admitted that marital difficulties of extremely wealthy individuals may be of some interest to some portion of the reading public but added that Firestone had not freely chosen to publicize private matters about her married life. The justices said she was compelled to go to court to "obtain legal release from the bonds of matrimony." They said she assumed no "special prominence in the resolution of public questions." The case was sent back to Florida for a finding of fault, and a new trial was ordered. Firestone remarried, and the case was settled out of court.

The second case involved Sen. William Proxmire of Wisconsin, who had started what he called the Golden Fleece Award. Each month he announced a winner who, in his opinion, had wasted government money. One such winner was Ronald Hutchinson, a behavioral scientist who had received federal funding for research designed to determine why animals clench their teeth. Hutchinson had published articles about his research in professional publications. In deciding that Hutchinson was not a public figure, the court ruled that he "did not thrust himself or his views into public controversy to influence others." The court admitted there may have been legitimate concerns about the way public funds were being spent but said this was not enough to make Hutchinson a public figure.

The third case concerned an individual found guilty of contempt of court in 1958 for his failure to appear before a grand jury investigating Soviet espionage in the United States. Ilya Wolston's name had been included in a list of people indicted for serving as Soviet agents in a 1974 book published by the Reader's Digest Association. Wolston had not been indicted, and he sued. The Supreme Court, in deciding that he was not a public figure, found that Wolston had played only a minor role in whatever public controversy there may have been concerning the investigation of Soviet espionage. The court added that a private individual is not automatically transformed into a public figure merely by becoming involved in or being associated with a matter that attracts public attention.

Lower courts have ruled that in other situations individuals have become public figures by the nature of their activities. These include an attorney in local practice for 32 years who had been involved in major disputes and social activities, a newspaper publisher who regularly had taken strong public stands on controversial issues, and a college dean who had attempted to influence the proposed abolition of his position.

Assume you are covering a proposal to fluoridate the water of your town. Among those you may write about are:

- The mayor (or town or county supervisor), who obviously is a public official.
- A doctor who has a private medical practice but is so concerned about the effects of fluoridation that he has made many public speeches. He has become a public figure because he had thrust himself to the forefront of the fluoridation controversy.
- A former state senator who now owns a radio station and is well-known in the community. She, too, is a public figure because of her prominence in the affairs of the city.

But how about the attorney who is handling the litigation for the individuals opposed to fluoridation? If he also is a spokesman for this group, he may be treated as a public figure. However, if he does no more than file the legal papers with the courts and leaves the press conferences and public appearances to others, he has not thrust himself to the forefront of the controversy. Do you have the same protection from a libel action when you write about him as you do with the persons you are certain are public figures or public officials?

A 1974 Supreme Court decision says the answer usually is no. In the landmark Gertz vs. Welch case, the justices said states *may give more protection* to private individuals if a newspaper or radio or television station damages their reputations than if the reputations of either public officials or public figures are damaged.

Standards Applicable to Private Citizens

Private citizens who sue for punitive, or punishment, damages must meet the same actual malice test as public officials and public figures do. Because of the Gertz case, states have been allowed to set their own standards for libel cases involving private citizens who sue only for actual damages. Roughly 20 states and the District of Columbia have adopted a *negligence test*, which requires you to use the same care in gathering facts and writing your story as any reasonable reporter would use under the same or similar circumstances. If you make every effort to be fair and answer all the questions a reasonable person may ask, you probably would pass the negligence test.

One state, New York, has adopted a *gross irresponsibility test*. Four states have established a more stringent standard that requires private citizens to prove *actual malice*. In the remaining states the matter is unsettled because of conflicting cases or cases that are still pending, or because there have been no cases to resolve the issue (see the table on page 457).

Invasion of Privacy

Libel is damage to an individual's reputation. **Invasion of privacy** is a violation of a person's right to be left alone.

As a reporter, you may be risking an invasion of privacy suit under any of the following circumstances:

- You physically intrude into a private area to get a story or picture—an act closely related to trespass.
- You publish a story or photograph about someone that is misleading and thus portray that person in a "false light."
- You disclose something about an individual's private affairs that is true but also is offensive to individuals of ordinary sensibilities.

"There are only two occasions when Americans respect privacy. . . . Those are prayer and fishing."
—Herbert Hoover, 31st president

Tests of Libel Applicable to Media Defendants

State	Test of Libel
Alabama	Unsettled
Alaska	Actual Malice
Arizona	Negligence
Arkansas	Negligence
California	Unsettled
Colorado	Actual Malice
Connecticut	Unsettled
Delaware	Negligence
District of Columbia	Negligence
Florida	Unsettled
Georgia	Unsettled
Hawaii	Negligence
Idaho	No Cases
Illinois	Negligence
Indiana	Actual Malice
Iowa	Unsettled
Kansas	Negligence
Kentucky	Negligence
Louisiana	Unsettled
Maine	No Cases
Maryland	Negligence
Massachusetts	Negligence
Michigan	Negligence
Minnesota	Negligence
Mississippi	Negligence
Missouri	Unsettled
Montana	Unsettled
Nebraska	No Cases
Nevada	No Cases
New Hampshire	Negligence
New Jersey	Actual Malice
New Mexico	Negligence
New York	Gross Irresponsibility
North Carolina	Negligence
North Dakota	No Cases
Ohio	Negligence
Oklahoma	Negligence
Oregon	Negligence
Pennsylvania	Unsettled
Rhode Island	Negligence
South Carolina	Negligence
South Dakota	No Cases
Tennessee	Negligence
Texas	Negligence
Utah	Negligence
Vermont	Negligence
Virginia	Negligence
Washington	Negligence
West Virginia	Negligence
Wisconsin	Negligence
Wyoming	No Cases

Invasion of privacy may also be claimed if someone's name or picture is used in an advertisement or for similar purposes of trade. Called *appropriation*, this does not affect you when you are performing your reporting duties.

Consent is a basic defense in invasion of privacy suits. Make sure, however, that your use of the material does not exceed the consent given.

Another basic defense in an invasion of privacy suit is that you're a reporter covering a newsworthy situation. The courts usually protect the press against invasion of privacy suits when it is reporting matters of legitimate public interest. There are exceptions, however.

> *Trespassing.* One exception arises when you invade someone's privacy by entering private property to get a story. You cannot trespass on private property to get a story or take a picture even if it is newsworthy. The courts will not protect you when you are a trespasser. Two *Life* magazine staffers lost an invasion of privacy suit because, posing as patients, they went into a man's home to get a story about a faith healer. They lost the case even though they were working with the district attorney and the state board of health. You may enter private property only when you are invited by the owner or renter.

> *Portraying in a "false light."* The court also will not protect you if you invade someone's privacy by publishing misleading information about that person. For example, a legal problem arises if a photograph or information from a true story about a careful pedestrian struck by a careless driver is used again in connection with a story, say, about careless pedestrians. The pedestrian who was hit could file a lawsuit charging libel, "false light" invasion of privacy or even both in some states.

> Some states do not recognize "false light" invasion of privacy and insist that libel is the appropriate form of suit. But "false light" suits can cover situations where a picture or story is misleading but not defamatory. Even flattering material can place a person in an unwanted, false light.

> *Causing unwanted publicity offensive to a person of ordinary sensibilities.* The third category of invasion of privacy that the courts recognize—unwanted publicity—concerns stories about incidents that, because they are true, cannot be defamatory but can be offensive to a person of ordinary sensibilities. An example is a picture published by *Sports Illustrated* in which a football fan's pants zipper was open. The fan sued for invasion of privacy but lost. Also in the area of unwanted publicity, the Supreme Court held in 1975 and again in 1989 that truthfully reporting the name of a rape victim is permitted. In 1976 and in 1979 the justices upheld the right of the press to publish the names of juveniles involved with the law because the information was truthful and of public significance.

The courts say that in order for privacy to be invaded, there must be a morbid and sensational prying into private lives. Merely be-

You may be committing invasion of privacy by

- *Trespassing on private property*
- *Portraying someone in a "false light"*
- *Publishing unwanted publicity that is offensive to a person of ordinary sensibilities.*

ing the subject of an unflattering and embarrassing article is not enough.

Protection of Sources and Notes

Another area you must know about is your ability—or inability—to protect your sources and notes. The problem may arise in various situations. A grand jury that is investigating a murder may ask you to reveal the source of a story you wrote about the murder. You may be asked to testify at a criminal or a civil trial. Or the police may obtain a warrant to search the news room, including your desk.

The conflict here is between a reporter's need to protect sources of information and the duty of every citizen to testify to help the courts determine justice. By the nature of your work as a reporter, you will be at the scene of events that are important and newsworthy. Anyone wanting the facts about an event can subpoena you to bring in all the details. Journalists usually resist. They work for their newspaper or radio or television station, not a law enforcement agency. Their ability to gather information would be compromised if the sources knew that their identities or their information would go to the police.

By 1990 some protection against testifying—**shield laws**—had been adopted by 28 states. The states are:

Alabama	Kentucky	New York
Alaska	Louisiana	North Dakota
Arizona	Maryland	Ohio
Arkansas	Michigan	Oklahoma
California	Minnesota	Oregon
Colorado	Montana	Pennsylvania
Delaware	Nebraska	Rhode Island
Georgia	Nevada	Tennessee
Illinois	New Jersey	
Indiana	New Mexico	

Congress had not acted in this area in part because journalists themselves were divided about the desirability of such legislation.

However, Congress did pass the *Privacy Protection Act* of 1980. Under that act, federal, state or local enforcement officers generally may not use a search warrant to search news rooms. Instead, they must get a subpoena for documents, which tells the reporters to hand over the material. Officers may use a warrant to search news rooms only if they suspect a reporter of being involved in a crime or if immediate action is needed to prevent bodily harm, loss of life or destruction of the material.

The difference between a *search warrant* and a *subpoena* is great. If officers can search with a warrant, they knock on the door, enter the news room, and search on their own. With a subpoena for documents, reporters are asked to turn over the material to authorities at a predetermined time and place. A subpoena does not permit officers to search the news room. In addition, it gives reporters time to challenge in court the necessity of turning over the material.

Even in states with shield laws, judges in most criminal cases involving grand juries will not allow you to keep your sources secret. In other criminal cases, courts may allow confidentiality if a three-part test is met. Supreme Court Justice Potter Stewart suggested this test in his dissent in Branzburg vs. Hayes:

> Government officials must, therefore, demonstrate that the information sought is *clearly* relevant to a *precisely* defined subject of government inquiry. . . . They must demonstrate that it is reasonable to think the witness in question has that information. . . . And they must show that there is not any means of obtaining the information less destructive of First Amendment liberties. . . .

In civil litigation you may be permitted to keep sources confidential in most cases unless the court finds that the information sought is unavailable from other sources and highly relevant to the underlying litigation or of such critical importance to the lawsuit that it goes to the heart of the plaintiff's claim.

If you are sued for libel, you will find it very difficult both to protect your sources and to win the lawsuit. The court might very well rule against you on whether a statement is true or false, if it came from a source you refuse to name.

The only Supreme Court decision to guide journalists on protection of sources is Branzburg vs. Hayes, decided in 1972. The justices said the sole issue was the obligation of reporters to respond to grand jury subpoenas as other citizens do and to answer questions relevant to the investigation of a crime. According to the court, then, reporters cannot protect their sources before a grand jury.

William Farr, now a *Los Angeles Times* reporter, spent 46 days in virtual solitary confinement in a Los Angeles jail in 1971 for refusing to disclose to a judge his source for a newspaper article about the trial of Charles Manson, the mass murderer. Myron Farber spent 40 days in a New Jersey jail and his paper, the *New York Times*, was fined $286,000 in 1978 (later reduced to $185,000) for failure to comply with subpoenas directing the paper to produce documents and materials during a murder trial.

Despite the publicity, the Farber case is of limited legal importance outside New Jersey. The precedent-setting case is U.S. vs. Nixon (1974). The Nixon case requires a showing in court of the need for tapes, documents or other materials before people not directly involved in a court case can be ordered to comply with sub-poenas.

That principle is relevancy, and it extends back to the Marie Torre case in 1958. Torre spent 10 days in jail in New York for refus-ing to disclose a confidential source the court said was relevant in a li-bel action by Judy Garland against CBS. Others have been jailed or threatened with jail by judges since John Peter Zenger, editor of the *New York Weekly Journal*, refused to reveal the name of the author of a letter in the *Journal* in 1735.

The only way to avoid such confrontation with the courts is not to promise a source you will keep his or her name confidential. Only for the most compelling reason should you get yourself into this judi-cial conflict between the First Amendment right of a free press and the Sixth Amendment right to a fair trial.

In 1991, the U.S. Supreme Court ruled in Cohen vs. Cowles Media Company that the First Amendment does not prevent a source from suing a news organization if a reporter has promised the source confidentiality but the newspaper publishes the source's name any-way.

Access to Courts

Judicial acknowledgment of the right of access to courtrooms has had a sudden, cometlike history since 1979. The Supreme Court held in 1979 that "members of the public have no constitutional right" under the Sixth Amendment to attend criminal trials. In a reversal exactly one year later, the justices held that the public and the press have a First Amendment right to attend criminal trials.

The justices said the right was not absolute, but that trial judges could close criminal trials only when there was an "overriding inter-est" to justify such closure. The basic concern of judges when they close trials is to protect the accused person under the Sixth Amend-ment right to an "impartial jury"—often translated by attorneys into "a fair trial."

In addition, the First Amendment prevents the government from conducting business—even trials—in secret. In fact, in the Richmond Newspapers case in 1980, Chief Justice Warren Burger traced the unbroken and uncontradicted history of open judicial pro-ceedings in England and the United States. He concluded that there is a "presumption of openness" in criminal trials and pointed out the im-portant role of the news media as representatives of the public.

The next question for the justices was the role of the state legis-latures in closing trials. Massachusetts had a statute mandating closure of the courtroom for specified sexual offenses involving a victim un-der 18. The Supreme Court said in 1982 that the mandatory closure statute violated the First Amendment right of access to criminal trials even though safeguarding the physical and psychological well-being of a minor was a compelling concern.

The court said it was up to the trial judge to decide on a case-by-case basis whether closure is necessary to protect the welfare of a minor victim. The trial court should weigh the minor's age, psychological maturity and understanding, the nature of the crime, the desires of the victim, and the interests of parents and relatives.

So by 1984 the Supreme Court had decided that openness in criminal trials "enhances both the basic fairness of the criminal trial and the appearance of fairness so essential to public confidence in the system."

But when does a trial actually begin? At what point does the presumption that trial proceedings should be open first apply? Is there a right of access to jury-selection proceedings? The justices said in 1984 that the process of jury selection is a matter of importance "not simply to the adversaries but to the criminal justice system." In writing the opinion, Chief Justice Burger said openness has what can be described as a "community therapeutic value" after especially violent crimes. He said seeing that the law is being enforced and the criminal justice system is functioning can provide an outlet for the public's understandable reactions and emotions.

Public proceedings vindicate the concerns of victims and the community in knowing that offenders are being brought to account for their criminal conduct "by jurors fairly and openly selected." Proceedings of jury selection could be closed, the chief justice said, only when a trial judge finds that closure preserves an "overriding interest" and is narrowly tailored to serve that interest.

Judges are using that option. For instance, when John Gotti was convicted of Mafia activities in New York, the jurors' names were kept secret. Gotti's attorneys unsuccessfully challenged the anonymity. Jurors' names in the Rodney King and Reginald Denny cases in Los Angeles were also withheld.

Finally, in 1986 the Supreme Court decided the issue of right of access to a preliminary hearing. A California court had held a 41-day closed preliminary hearing on the pretext of protecting the accused under the Sixth Amendment right to an impartial jury trial. Chief Justice Burger said the right of the accused to a "fair trial" and the public right of access "are not necessarily inconsistent." He added, "As we have repeatedly recognized, one of the important means of assuring a fair trial is that the process be open to neutral observers."

The chief justice acknowledged that some kinds of government operations "would be totally frustrated if conducted openly." A classic example is the grand jury system. However, "other proceedings plainly require public access," he said.

Finally, the chief justice said only an overriding interest found by a trial judge can overcome the presumption of openness of criminal

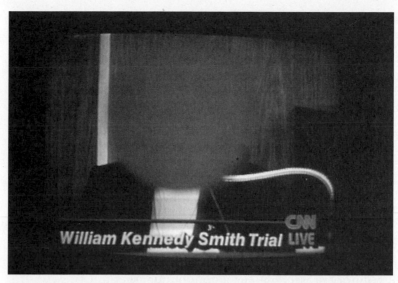

Figure 21.2.
In some court telecasts, the faces of witnesses such as minors or rape victims may be obscured to protect their privacy. This was done for the chief prosecution witness during the rape trial of William Kennedy Smith, but after he was found not guilty, Patricia Bowman decided to reveal her identity to the public.

proceedings. (See Chapter 12 for more on crime and the courts.) Today, 47 states allow cameras in at least some state courtrooms. However, cameras are not permitted in federal courts.

Copyright and Fair Use

The purpose of copyright law is to ensure compensation to authors for contributing to the common good by publishing their works. The Constitution provides for this in Article 1, Section 8, by giving Congress the power to secure "for limited times to authors and inventors the exclusive right to their respective writing and discoveries." The same section indicates that this provision is intended "to promote the progress of science and useful arts" for the benefit of the public. Copyright laws protect your work and prohibit you from using significant amounts of others' writings without permission, and, in some cases, a fee.

The most recent copyright statute went into effect Jan. 1, 1978. Key elements of this law include:

- That copyrightable works are protected from the moment they are fixed in tangible form, whether published or unpublished.
- That copyright protection begins with a work's "creation and . . .

endures for a term consisting of the life of the author and 50 years after the author's death."

■ That works for hire and anonymous and pseudonymous works are protected for 75 years from publication or 100 years from creation, whichever is shorter.

■ That there is a "fair use" limitation on the exclusive rights of copyright owners. In other words, it may be permissible to use small excerpts from a copyrighted work without permission. According to the Supreme Court, factors that govern fair use are:

1. The purpose and character of the use.
2. The nature of the copyrighted work.
3. The substantiality of the portion used in relationship to the copyrighted work as a whole.
4. The effect on the potential market for or value of the copyrighted work.

Although a work is copyrighted from the moment it is fixed in tangible form, the copyright statute says certain steps are necessary to receive statutory protection. The author or publisher must:

■ Publish or reproduce the work with the word "copyright" or the symbol ©, the name of the copyright owner and the year of publication.

■ Deposit two copies of the work with the Library of Congress within three months of publication. Failure to do so will not affect the copyright but could lead to imposition of fines.

■ Register the work at the Library of Congress by filling out the form supplied by the Copyright Office and sending the form, the specified number of copies (usually one copy with unpublished work and two copies with published work), and a $20 fee. The deposit and registration fee can be combined and usually are.

Copyright law has a special provision for broadcasters of live programs. Broadcasters need only to make a simultaneous tape of their live broadcasts in order to receive copyright protection. In short, the tape fulfills the requirement that a work be in a "fixed" form for copyright protection. Because a digitial form is a "fixed" form, editors of electronic newspapers already meet that copyright requirement.

However, some aspects of copyright law changed when the United States enacted the 100-year-old *Berne Convention*, an international copyright treaty primarily intended to dissuade foreigners from pirating American film productions. The Berne Convention went into effect in 1989. Other changes in copyright law under the Berne Convention include the following:

Placing a copyright notice on a work is no longer necessary to preserve a copyright after publication. This is in line with the Berne Convention principle that the exercise of a copyright should not be subject to formalities. But the copyright notice is still useful in that it acts as a bar to an infringer's defense of innocent infringement.

Registration is no longer a prerequisite for access to the federal courts for an infringement action. But registration is required for the copyright owner to recover statutory damages. (Without registration, the copyright owner can recover only the damages he or she can prove, court costs and "reasonable" attorney's fees.) The amount of statutory damages, generally between $500 and $20,000, is determined by the judge. However, if the infringer was not aware he or she was infringing a copyright, the court may award as little as $200. Similarly, if the infringement was willful, the court can award up to $100,000.

Copyright registration, then, remains highly advisable.

Suggested Readings

Carter, T. Barton, Franklin, Marc A. and Wright, Jay B. *The First Amendment and The Fourth Estate*, Sixth Edition. Westbury, N.Y.: Foundation Press, 1994.

Gilmour, Donald M., Barron, Jerome A., Simon, Todd F. and Terry, Herbert A. *Mass Communications Law*, Fifth Edition. New York: West, 1990.

Holsinger, Ralph and Dills, Jon Paul. *Media Law*, Third edition. New York: McGraw-Hill, 1987.

Middleton, Kent R. and Chamberlin, Bill F. *The Law of Public Communication*, Third Edition. New York: Longman, 1994.

Nelson, Harold L., Teeter, Dwight L. Jr. and Le Duc, Don R. *Law of Mass Communications*, Seventh Edition. Westbury, N.Y.: Foundation Press, 1992.

Overbeck, Wayne. *Major Principles of Media Law*. Fort Worth, Texas: Harcourt Brace, 1993.

Pember, Don R. *Mass Media Law*, Sixth Edition. Dubuque, Iowa: Brown, 1993.

Zelensky, John D. *Communications Law*. Belmont, Cal.: Wadsworth, 1993.

Exercises

1. Which defense for libel discussed in this chapter would you have used in defending *Time* magazine in the lawsuit filed by Gen. Ariel Sharon? Why?

2. The *New York Times* vs. Sullivan case was significant as a landmark decision in favor of the press. Discuss what the consequences for the press could have been if the decision had been different.

3. You are on an assignment with your photographer, who enters a house without permission and photographs the sale of illegal drugs. Discuss the issues raised by the circumstances and explain why you would or would not publish the pictures.

4. Using the Lexis database, determine how the U.S. Supreme Court has used Richmond Newspapers vs. Virginia, 448 U.S. 555 (1980), in later cases dealing with openness in criminal proceedings.

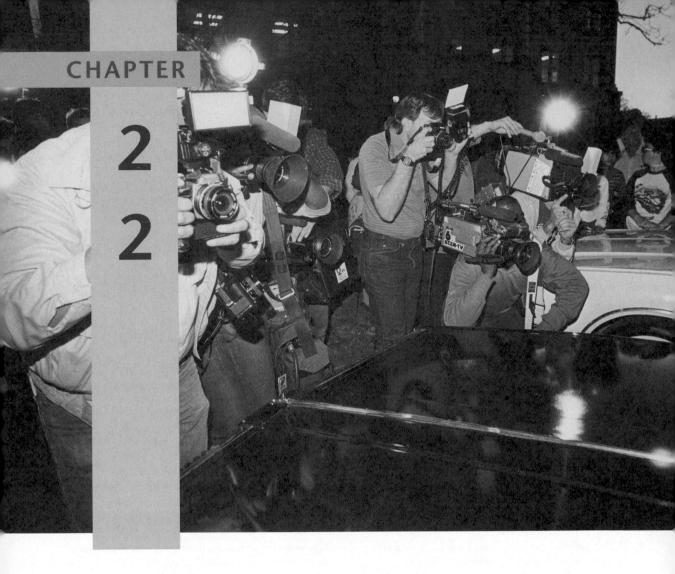

ETHICS

In this chapter you will learn:

1. Philosophical approaches that can provide answers to ethical questions.
2. A means of ethical reasoning.
3. Ethical questions of special importance to journalists.

▪ *A doctor who prescribes medicine for a patient without a proper examination would be violating a code of ethics. The doctor could lose the right to practice.*

▪ *A lawyer who deliberately misleads a client would be guilty of violating a code of ethics. The lawyer could be disbarred and kept from practicing law.*

▪ *A certified public accountant who knowingly signs a statement misrepresenting a company's financial position would be violating a code of ethics. The CPA could lose the right to practice.*

▪ *A journalist who accepts a stolen document and poses as a police investigator to get private telephone records might be violating a code of ethics. The journalist could win a Pulitzer Prize.*

The doctor, the lawyer and the accountant all have mandatory codes of ethics, prescribed and enforced by their professions. Journalism as a profession has been slow to establish a mandatory and enforced code because of a fear that it might in some way infringe upon freedom of the press.

In other professions, enforcing a code means the profession must have the power to keep people from practicing unless they have membership or a license to practice. That means also that the profession must have the power to suspend a license and to keep members from practicing if they violate the code of the profession.

For some professions, the state requires a license to practice. If as a condition of keeping that license, people may not express certain ideas, that is a form of censorship. Because journalists are not licensed by states, it is difficult to determine who is a journalist. In fact, the Supreme Court has said that it does not want to define a journalist.

Therefore, government does not keep anyone from practicing journalism, although individual news organizations have established and enforced codes of ethics that have restricted journalists from practicing journalism in their organizations. For example, some journalists who have plagiarized have been suspended or fired from their news organizations.

Because of the wide range of the First Amendment and its relatively few legal restraints, perhaps no profession has a greater need to discuss proper means of conduct. As the Commission on Freedom of the Press concluded in 1947, unless journalists set their own limits on what is acceptable and responsible, government will eventually and inevitably do it for them.

Associations of journalists such as the Society of Professional Journalists do have codes of conduct. (Of course, journalists do not have to belong to such organizations to practice journalism.) Moreover, journalism professor Jay Black surveyed 304 media organizations and found that four out of 10 newspapers and three out of 10 television stations said they relied on written codes. Larger news organizations are more likely to have them. Half of them have adopted them within the past decade, and a third or more amended them in the '90s.

Critics of journalism codes of ethics condemn them either for being hopelessly general and therefore ineffective or for being too restrictive. Some argue that strict codes might help improve journalists' credibility, but others say they merely make journalists an easier target for libel suits.

Your organization may or may not have a code of ethics. Either way, you should devise your own ethical values and principles. Your upbringing, and perhaps your religious training and your education, have already helped prepare you to do that.

Three Ethical Philosophies

Your personal ethics may derive from the way you answer one fundamental question: Does the end justify the means? Another way of asking that is, should you ever do something that is not good in itself in order to achieve a goal that is good?

If you answer no to that question, you are in some sense at least an *absolutist* or a legalist. You would then most likely subscribe to *deontological* ethics. If you answer yes to that question, you are more of a *relativist* and would subscribe to *teleological* ethics. If you answer maybe or sometimes, you would subscribe to a form of *situation ethics*.

Don't be put off by the jargon of philosophers. To understand ethical thinking better, to be able to discuss ethics and to solve ethical problems that arise on the job, you need to learn the vocabulary of ethicists.

Deontological Ethics

Deontology is the ethics of duty. According to this philosophy, it is the person's duty to do what is right. Some actions are always right; some are always wrong. There exists in nature (or for those with religious faith, in divine revelation) a fixed set of principles or laws, from which there should be no deviation. The end never justifies the means. That is why some refer to this kind of ethical philosophy as absolutism or legalism.

If it is wrong to lie, it always is wrong to lie. If a murderer comes to your door and asks where your roommates are so that he or she could murder them, if you were an absolutist, you would not lie to save their lives. It doesn't matter that your friends might be killed. The consequences are irrelevant.

An absolutist or legalist has one clear duty—to discover the rules and to follow them. An absolutist or legalistic ethical philosophy could spawn a conscientious objector who not only would refuse to take up arms but who would also refuse even to go to war as a medic. If war is absolutely wrong, it is absolutely wrong to participate in war in any way.

One such absolutist was Immanuel Kant (1724–1804). Kant proposed the categorical imperative that states that you should do only those things that you would be willing to have everyone follow

"Ethics is a system of principles, a morality or code of conduct. It is the values and rules of life recognized by an individual, group or culture seeking guidelines to human conduct and what is good or bad, right or wrong."
—*Conrad C. Fink,*
professor
Media Ethics

as a universal law. Once you make that decision, you regard it as "categorical" and without exception, and it is imperative that you do it.

Many people draw support for their absolutism or legalism from their religious beliefs. They will cite the Bible or the Koran or some other book they believe to be divinely inspired. If they themselves cannot find the answer, they will turn to their minister, priest, rabbi or guru for the answer to their ethical dilemma. The absolutist is concerned only with doing the right thing, and one need only to discover what that is.

The absolutist journalist is concerned only with whether an event is newsworthy. If it is interesting, timely, significant or important, it is to be reported, regardless of the consequences. The duty of the journalist is to report the news. Period. Walter Cronkite once said that if journalists worried about what all the possible consequences could be for reporting something, they would never report anything.

What happens when journalists have knowledge of something, some corruption in government or marital infidelity of a political candidate, and do not report it? What happens when the public learns that journalists knew and did not let the public know? What happens to public trust? The public relies on the news media to keep them informed. That is why journalists enjoy First Amendment privileges.

This philosophy was best enunciated by Charles A. Dana, who in 1868 began a 29-year career as editor of the *New York Sun*. Dana said, "Whatever God in his infinite wisdom has allowed to happen, I am not too proud to print."

The absolutists discount any criticism of the press for printing or broadcasting certain stories. Stop blaming the messenger, they say. We don't make events happen; we just report them.

When a television news producer was asked why he telecast the confession of a suspect, he replied, "Because it's news."

The deontological philosophy is attractive to many journalists because it assumes the need for full disclosure. Nothing newsworthy ever is withheld from the public. In the end, these journalists believe, publishing without fear of the consequences or without favor for one group's interests over another's is the highest ethical principle. Journalists are unethical only when they withhold the news.

"I tell the honest truth in my paper, and I leave the consequences to God."
—James Gordon Bennett, newspaper publisher, 1836

Teleological Ethics

Teleological ethics holds that what makes an act ethical is not the act itself but the consequences of the act. The end can and often does justify the means. This philosophy makes ethics more relativistic than absolutist or legalistic.

For example, stealing may not always be wrong. In some cases, it may be virtuous. A mother who steals food for her starving child would be performing a good act. A person who lies to save someone's life would be acting ethically. A person who kills to protect his or her own life is acting morally.

Involved in teleological ethics is the intention of the person performing the act. What some people would proclaim as unethical, another would do for a good purpose or a good reason. Police often work undercover. They conceal their identity as police officers in order to apprehend criminals. If in that process they must lie or even get involved in some criminal activity, so be it. Their purpose is to protect the public; their intention is to work for the good of society.

Some journalists would not hesitate to do the same. As we shall discuss later, some would require some conditions be in place before they will steal or use deceit, but they would do it nonetheless. Their purpose is to be the watchdog of government, to protect the common good, to keep the public fully informed. What they must do to accomplish these goals, they argue, is clearly ethical.

The extreme form of the end justifying the means was best expressed by the 15th century philosopher Machiavelli. In the 20th century, John Dewey reflected this philosophy with his pragmatism—whatever works is ethical.

This pragmatism often applies to business in general and to the business of journalism. If a story about a local grocery brings threats of withdrawing advertising, some editors will refrain from publishing the story. If a favorable story brings more advertising dollars, they will publish the story. They'll generally do whatever works.

Situation Ethics

When asked whether the end justifying the means, persons subscribing to situation ethics would reply that it all depends.

Antinomianism

Complete relativists or *antinomians* hold that there are no laws and only one operative principle. That principle is that every person and every ethical situation is unique, and to solve an ethical dilemma by applying principles held by others or principles that apply in other cases is unethical. The only way to be ethical is to view each situation as unique and to solve the ethical problem entirely on its own merits.

This position does not mean that antinomians have no ethics. It does not mean that they would always lie or cheat or steal. An antinomian journalist would not hesitate in some instances to pose as someone other than a journalist in an attempt to gather information. In other cases, the antinomian would not. It depends entirely on the situation because no two situations are alike.

John Merrill's Deontelics

Other relativists are not as extreme. Some ethicists shy away from absolutism and say that one must consider both the act *and* the consequences of the act. Journalism scholar and ethicist John Merrill calls such ethics *deontelics*—a word he coined combining deontological and teleological ethics. To act responsibly, journalists must consider more than just the ethics of the act; neither dare they ignore that in most cases some acts are of their very nature unethical.

For example, telling the truth is paramount for a journalist. Lying is of its very nature unethical—in most cases. According to deontelic theory, there may be a rare time when lying is justifiable for a good purpose. For example, an investigative reporter might justify lying about his or her identity as a journalist as the only way to get information for an important story.

Mixed-Rule Deontology

Similar to deontelics is what other ethicists, such as Edmund Lambeth, call *mixed-rule deontology*. Journalists have a duty to consider both the act itself and the possible consequences of the act. Though certainly not claiming to be a relativist, Lambeth sets forth certain guidelines that make some acts, usually considered unethical, ethical in certain situations. We'll see some of those guidelines and those of the Society of Professional Journalists when we discuss journalists' use of deceit.

Love of Neighbor

A third type of situation ethics is that enunciated by Joseph Fletcher, author of *Situation Ethics*. Fletcher bases his philosophy on love of neighbor as articulated in the Golden Rule and the maxim "You shall love your neighbor as yourself." He presents his ethic from a Christian perspective with roots in Judaic teaching, but one need not profess Christianity to share the conviction that all principles are relative to one absolute—love of neighbor. Indeed, many religions, as well as secular humanism, hold human values as the highest good.

Although the person who subscribes to this belief understands and accepts other ethical maxims and weighs them carefully when facing an ethical decision, he or she must be prepared to set them aside completely if love of neighbor demands it. In the broad sense, then, followers of Fletcher's form of situation ethics always place people first. In every ethical dilemma, they always do what is best for people. Sometimes, they must choose between love for one person and love for a larger community of people.

Utilitarianism

The kind of thinking that Fletcher advocates leads to another form of relativism called *utilitarianism*. Your choices are ethical if you always choose the action that is likely to bring the most happiness to the greatest number of people. This theory of John Stuart Mill and Jeremy Bentham was later modified to emphasize the greatest good rather than the greatest happiness. Some utilitarians also add the words "over a long period of time." In other words, some actions may seem wrong if one looks merely at the present situation.

For example, in February 1995 it may have seemed wrong to expose U.S. soldiers to risk and possible death by sending them to depose the military dictatorship in Haiti, but for the eventual good of that country, to stabilize U.S. borders and for the spread and preservation of democracy in this hemisphere, it may have been deemed by some to be an ethical act.

Clearly, most journalists subscribe to this ethical philosophy. Even though they know that publishing a particular story about the infidelities of a public figure may destroy the person's reputation, hurt his or her family and perhaps even lead to suicide, many journalists would decide that for the greater good, the public should have this information. Publishing it would be even more justifiable if the public official were involved in embezzlement or taking bribes.

Even though some journalists would admit that publishing pretrial publicity may endanger a defendant's right to a fair trial, they also believe that by keeping an eye on the police and the courts, all people in the long run have a better chance for a fair trial.

Critics of journalists and utilitarians say this philosophy is too easy to practice and too vague to be useful. Some journalists respond that it is the only practical philosophy in a hurry-up, deadline-focused world. They believe that the greatest good for the greatest number demands a general operating principle: When in doubt, unless some clear circumstance dictates against it, it is better to report the news. Otherwise, the public cannot rely on its news agencies. As a result, the role of the press in a democracy, and perhaps democracy itself, is abolished. Democracy, after all, also practices a form of utilitarianism—one called majority rule.

Ayn Rand's Rational Self-Interest

Ayn Rand's ethics of rational self-interest is the opposite of utilitarianism and certainly of Christianity or any form of altruism. Her "ethical egoism" would never sacrifice one's self for the good of others but would always act entirely on what best serves one's self. One is kind to others only if it serves one's rational self-interest.

Journalists who are ethical egoists do not mind using people for stories, even though the people they use may have no idea how embarrassing the story may be to them. Photographers would take pictures of dying or dead children and of their grieving parents. Broadcasters would not hesitate to telecast people committing suicide. Whatever helps them get good stories and thus advance in the profession is ethical.

Some critics accuse journalists of embracing this philosophy merely to sell newspapers or to increase their ratings. However, on many occasions journalists report stories that anger both their readers and their advertisers.

John Rawls' Veil of Ignorance

A different form of rational self-interest is manifested in the ethical philosophy of John Rawls. His "veil of ignorance" would have you treat all people the same, as if there is no difference in social or economic status. Race, gender, age, looks—behind the veil, all are equal; all are to be treated the same. If there is any unequal treatment, it must benefit the least advantaged person or persons.

Rawls argues that these considerations would make people act more in tune with their rational self-interest. People would be more likely to look out for themselves if they placed themselves in the position of others.

In our society, research indicates that wealthy white men committing the same crime as poor African Americans seldom receive the same sentence. This is especially true of those who receive the death penalty. This situation would change if courts and juries would use the veil of ignorance.

Journalists often are more likely to treat famous people—especially if they are politicians—more harshly than average citizens. If journalists placed themselves behind the veil along with the politicians, perhaps their adversarial attitude would dissipate somewhat.

Aristotle's Golden Mean

Another form of relativistic ethics in Aristotle's *Golden Mean*. It states quite simply that the best moral position is usually a moderate one that avoids either of two extremes. Aristotle does not insist that this position be squarely in the middle. Rather, he believes that by considering both extremes a person is more likely to find a rational and moral position.

Journalists have a choice ranging from running no photographs of a tragedy to running the most graphic display of violent death. If they subscribe to the ethics of the Golden Mean, they would try to run a photo that indicates the horror of the tragedy without offending the sensibilities of their audience or of the family involved.

Solving Ethical Dilemmas

Unless you are an absolutist, ethical reasoning can take many forms. You may adopt one or more of the above ethical stances, and they will be your guide in your day-to-day ethical decision making. What is paramount is that you engage in what Lambeth and others have called "principled reasoning." You must deliberate by reflecting on ethical principles—principles that will help you decide proper or moral ways to act.

Principled reasoning assumes that you are not acting ethically if you do something simply because you have been told to do it or because that's what everyone else does. You are not ethical if you report the story just to beat the competition.

For example, suppose you had received the recording of the phone call of Nicole Brown Simpson, the murdered former wife of O.J. Simpson, that made it evident that an enraged Simpson had come to his ex-wife's house to threaten and intimidate her. Clearly the tape was damaging to Simpson's case because anyone who heard it would have to admit that it indicated Simpson was capable of being out of control and, therefore, perhaps capable of murder.

Suppose another station or network had already broadcast the tape? How would you go about making a rational, ethical decision?

To help journalists and others make ethical decisions, ethicists Clifford Christians, Kim Rotzoll and Mark Fackler have adapted a model of moral reasoning devised by Dr. Ralph Potter of the Harvard Divinity School called the Potter Box.

The box has four elements:

1. *Apprising the situation.* Making a good ethical decision begins with good reporting. You need all the facts from a variety of sources. Reaching a decision without trying to know all the facts makes any ethical decision impossible.

    The fact may be simply that a competing station has broadcast the Nicole Brown Simpson tape. The Los Angeles police verify that the tape is real. What do you do?

2. *Identifying values.* What are your personal values, your news organization's values, your community's values, the nation's values? For example, you may place high value on your personal credibility and that of your news organization. Certainly, freedom of the press is a value prized by this nation.

    You value your audience's right to know, but you may value a person's right to a fair trial more. You also value your independence and not being used by the police department or by the prosecution or by the defense, as was clearly evident on all sides in the Simpson case.

3. *Appealing to ethical principles.* You need to look at the various ethical principles discussed above. The principles are not meant to be a shopping list from which you choose the one that serves your personal interest. To be ethical you may have to choose the principle or principles that are far from expedient. Even if you choose a utilitarian solution, Aristotle's mean may keep you from doing the extreme, and Kant's categorical imperative may keep you from doing it at all.

    You have a duty to your audience to present them with the news. Not broadcasting the Nicole Brown Simpson tape may result in a certain loss of credibility. This may be especially true in that another

ON THE JOB

Creating a Culture of Ethical Reporting

With a B.A. in philosophy and an M.A. in journalism, John Callan joined *People* magazine's Los Angeles bureau in 1988; then he helped form start-up news teams at Fox Television's "The Late Show," *The Orange County Business Journal,* and at Warner New Media, where he was start-up lead and editorial director of "Desert Storm," *Time* magazine's first interactive CD-ROM news disc.

Callan then moved to Hungary, where he was a founder and co-owner of the *Budapest Business Journal.* In 1993, he returned to Los Angeles, where he reorganized and redesigned *The* station has broadcast it. Perhaps Aristotle's Golden Mean would indicate that you should not broadcast the tape itself but rather present a news account of the tape. Kant's categorical imperative might indicate that to jeopardize a person's right to a fair trial is always wrong.

4. *Choosing loyalties.* You owe a certain loyalty to your news organization, yes, but you must also be loyal to your readers, listeners or viewers. And what about loyalty to your sources and to the people about whom you are reporting?

As mentioned above, you have a duty to serve your audience. Not running the tape may cause them to turn elsewhere for the news. Can you ignore altogether that another station has broadcast the recording? You must also consider loyalty to your station's owners and stockholders.

Usually there is not one clear answer to a difficult ethical dilemma. Seldom do the most reasonable and experienced news veterans agree completely. But principled reasoning at least makes an ethical decision possible.

The four steps in the box need not be followed in any particular order. Also, you need not stop the reasoning after you have touched upon the four elements. The reasoning should continue, even to another discussion of another ethical dilemma.

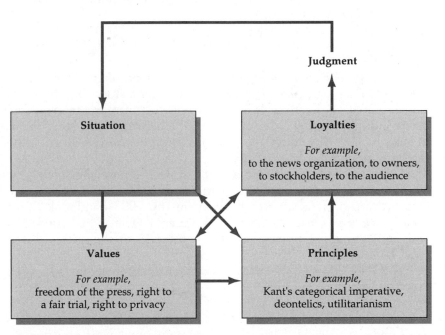

Figure 22.1.
Journalists can use the model of the Potter Box to help them analyze and resolve ethical problems.

It is this continuing ethical dialectic or dialogue that helps create ethical journalism and ethical journalists. Journalists should not just reflect society. They should present a *reasoned* reflection. Journalism should be done by people who make informed, intelligent and prudent choices.

The main objection to the Potter Box is that it takes too much time and is impractical in the deadline business of journalism. However, as you become more acquainted with ethical principles and more practiced at principled reasoning, you can make ethical decisions much more quickly and reasonably.

Although each case is different and you must always know the situation, you need not always start from the beginning. After a while you know what your values are, where your loyalties lie and which principles will most likely apply.

Ethical Problems

Journalism ethicist Ralph Barney says that journalists must always be about protecting the First Amendment, "which allows them to push the envelope for the good of society." Because of the First Amendment, society has fewer "rules" for journalists in spite of special problem areas they face. In the following sections, we will discuss some of those problem areas.

Deceit

Perhaps the most bothersome of ethical problems facing journalists involves using deceit of some kind to get a story. Deceit covers a wide range of practices. When may you lie, misrepresent yourself, use a hidden tape recorder or camera? When may you steal documents? For the absolutist, the answer is simple—never! But for the rest of us, the answer is not easy.

A group of journalists in an ethical decision-making seminar at The Poynter Institute for Media Studies devised a list of criteria to justify the use of deceit. You'll find it in the 1993 handbook *Doing Ethics in Journalism* published by The Sigma Delta Chi Foundation and The Society of Professional Journalists. *All* of the criteria listed must be present. (See box for a synopsis.)

Ethicist Edmund Lambeth has written that for deceit to be used the abuse must be in immediate need of correction and the news media must be the only means to correct it.

Obviously, police often work undercover. Many journalists do the same—especially if it is to expose police malfeasance. After all, shouldn't journalists, like other citizens, call the police when they see that the law is being broken?

Journalists use deceit most often in consumer reporting. For ex-

Ethical problems faced by journalists

- *Deceit*
- *Conflicts of interest*
- *Friendship*
- *Payola*
- *Freebies*
- *Checkbook journalism*
- *Participation in the news*
- *Invasion of privacy*
- *Withholding information*
- *Plagiarism*

"Journalists demean themselves and damage their credibility when they misrepresent themselves and their work to news sources and, in turn, to the public at large."

—Everette E. Dennis, Executive Director of The Freedom Forum Media Studies Center

---

Conditions for Journalists to Use Deceit

▪ Issue of profound public importance.
  — of vital public interest, revealing system failure at high levels
  — a preventive measure against profound harm to individuals
▪ All alternatives exhausted.
▪ Full disclosure of deception and reason for it.
▪ Full commitment to the story of everyone involved.
▪ Harm prevented outweighing any harm caused.

▪ Meaningful, collaborative and deliberative decision-making process, taking into account
  — short- and long-term consequences of deception
  — impact on credibility
  — motivations for actions
  — deceptive act in relation to their editorial mission
  — legal implications
  — consistency of reasoning and action

---

ample, the journalists who exposed a VCR repair shop that charged $200 for minor repairs (see page 353) could hardly have done so by revealing that they were journalists. Is there any way other than deceit to expose a crooked dentist who puts unnecessary crowns on people's teeth?

Conflicts of Interest

Reporting generally assumes that the reporter starts out with no point of view, that the reporter is neither out to get someone nor to get something out of the story. This basic tenet is the foundation for any and all credibility.

Ethicist Jay Black reports that most news-media ethics codes devote the bulk of their substance to determining what constitutes a conflict of interest. And well they should.

Friendship

Perhaps the most obvious, the most frequent and the most overlooked conflict of interest confronting journalists is friendship. Professor Paul Fisher, founder of the Missouri Freedom of Information Center, called friendship the greatest obstacle to the flow of information.

Because it's impossible to ascertain, no one knows whether friendship causes more stories to be reported or more stories to be killed. Either way, it sets up a powerful conflict of interest.

Sometimes reporters get too close to their sources. That's why, in some news organizations, beat reporters are shifted around.

Friendship can involve one's family, or a friend of one of the family. In smaller communities especially, editors and producers dine with members of the Chamber of Commerce, the Kiwanis, the Kings Daughters, the Country Club. Sometimes a story involves a close acquaintance of a co-worker, or a member of one's church.

If you ever find yourself covering a story that involves a personal acquaintance, ask your supervisor to assign the story to someone else.

Payola

No one would condone accepting payment for writing a story other than from one's employer. The *Honolulu Advertiser* suspended a free-lance columnist when it learned he had accepted $500 to write an article favorable to the dairy industry. The *Kansas City Star* fired a veteran outdoors writer for mentioning the name of a van he had received for free.

News organizations frown upon reporters doing promotional work for people they cover. For example, Lou Dobbs, managing editor of Cable News Network business news, was reprimanded by CNN for making promotional videos for Wall Street firms.

Other conflicts of interest are not so obvious. The *San Jose Mercury News* prohibits its business news reporters and editors from owning stock in local companies.

Will news agencies prohibit journalists from accepting speakers' fees? Will Congress attempt to legislate full disclosure of journalists' income and associations? Ken Auletta quotes Rep. Robert G. Torricelli of New Jersey in *The New Yorker* magazine:

"What startles many people is to hear television commentators make paid speeches to interest groups and then see them on television commenting on those issues. It's kind of a direct conflict of interest. If it happened in government, it would not be permitted."

Auletta writes that ABC's Sam Donaldson attacked the Independent Insurance Agents of America for treating congressional staff to a Key West junket. That same group had paid Donaldson $30,000 to lecture to them several months earlier.

What about the reporters who spout their opinions on Sunday morning talk shows and then "objectively" report on those same matters on Monday?

Freebies

- "Whoever said there's no free lunch was obviously not a sports reporter," writes Laura Shutiak in the *Calgary Herald*. Sports reporters are not the only journalists who are wined and dined by those seeking publicity.
- "Put a movie star in a room with 100 journalists armed with knives and forks and some might say you've got a fair fight," writes Dan Cox in *Variety*. "If you're a studio chieftain, however, those are the kind of odds you like, because you know that when the day is done, your latest pic is in for a stupendously inordinate amount of 'safe' press coverage—or, as some marketing whizzes maintain, free advertising."

Cox quotes a senior VP of marketing for a film company saying, "Now it seems they have a press junket for nearly every film." Why?

As advertising costs increase, executives work harder for free advertising.

- Why did Renault launch its new model in Tanzania? Eric Bailey writes in the *Daily Telegraph* that journalists came from all over the world in waves of 15 to 20 over a three-month period, "each group moving seamlessly through the swims and safaris, barbecues and bush cocktails, 24 hours apart."

- "Forget about the free meals at ritzy restaurants," writes Paul Lomartire, television writer for the *Palm Beach Post*. "Let's talk about the giveaways." He reports that the Fox network made news by giving critics and reporters a three-suit overnight bag filled with odds and ends, plus a Polaroid camera with a "Models, Inc." logo. "Some critics, too stupid to just say no, complained to Fox that the expensive gifts compromised their ethics."

   Lomartire reports: "A precious few refuse all gifts. Many haul the stuff back to their newspapers to reward secretaries and others. Many work for papers with no policy about freebies so they keep it all." At the *Post*, he writes, all the TV loot is sold twice-yearly at employee auctions, and the money is given to charity.

- "Many travel writers have long accepted free trips in return for writing favorable stories," writes James S. Hirsch in *The Wall Street Journal*, "but now a new twist has emerged in the cozy ties between the travel industry and the trade press. International journalists attending a travel conference in Miami this week have been issued an edict: Submit published stories about the conference or forfeit your place at the table next year."

A new twist indeed. But freebies have always come with a price:

- Can reporters remain objective?
- Do reporters write stories they would otherwise not write?
- Does the public perceive the reporter who has accepted or is suspected of accepting freebies as objective?

It is this perception that bothers most news organizations the most. Some argue that the least reporters must do is disclose prominently in their stories any freebies they have accepted. As in any case of deceit, reporters must disclose how they were able to get the story and why accepting freebies was necessary. For example, small news outlets cannot afford to send their travel writers on expensive tours.

Most news organizations have rules against accepting freebies. The Scripps-Howard newspaper group says, "When the gifts exceed the limits of propriety, they should be returned." The Society of Professional Journalists says, "Nothing of value shall be accepted." Is a cup of coffee something of value? The Associated Press expects its staff members to return gifts of "nominal value." Is a baseball cap of nominal value?

President Bill Clinton's Secretary of Agriculture Mike Espy resigned because he was under investigation for accepting free tickets to sports events, travel and lodging from companies that do business with the Department of Agriculture. Should journalists resign if they accept gifts from organizations they cover?

The *Orange County* (Calif.) *Register* ethics code says reporters may accept free meals and drinks only if the meal itself or the events surrounding it are of news value. The code also allows tickets or passes to cultural and athletic events only for the purpose of covering those events.

The *San Jose* (Calif.) *Mercury-News* "will pay for meals and drinks shared with news sources, for luncheons or dinners which are covered as news events and for restaurant meals reviewed." It prohibits free tickets to sports events, movies, fairs, amusement parks and all entertainment that has a charge.

You must learn the ethics code of your news organization, and sometimes, your personal code may be more stringent than that of your organization. In that case, follow your own code. Remember, you may not think a freebie will influence your reporting. But does your audience think it might?

Checkbook Journalism

Does the audience believe your story if you have paid your source for it? Should you always report that you have a paid source? Is it ethical to pay a source for an exclusive story? Should news people be in the business of keeping other news people from getting a story?

In the O.J. Simpson case, "journalists" paid witnesses for their stories, which subsequently caused the witnesses' testimony to be tossed out of court. Are paid sources likely to have an ax to grind? Do they come forward only for financial gain?

The terrible consequence of checkbook journalism is that even legitimate news professionals may be cut off from sources who want and expect pay. Some sources have begun asking for a fee even for good news. The increase in tabloid journalism, both in print and in broadcast, have brought the opportunists out in droves. The networks say that they do not pay for interviews, but the tabloids say payments are disguised as consultant fees, writes Richard Zoglin in *Time* magazine.

He reports that the traditional stigma against checkbook journalism may be fading away. He quotes Everette Dennis, executive director of Columbia University's Freedom Forum Media Studies Center, saying: "It's hard to argue that the ordinary person shouldn't share in the benefit of what's going to be a commercial product."

Surely, good reporting would demand that you pay sources only when necessary and only if you can get other sources to corroborate your findings. You'd also better be sure that your bosses know that you're doing it.

> *"But I don't believe that paying sources is unethical, as long as it's disclosed to the reader; in some cases I think it makes for better journalism. It gives a fair share of the profits to sources who spend time and take risks."*
>
> *—John Tierney, from "Newsworthy," reprinted from The New York Times Company*

Participation in the News

In some organizations, you'd also better let your bosses know which organizations you belong to. When the *Fairfield* (Iowa) *Daily Ledger* fired two reporters who had joined a local church-sponsored pro-life group, the two reporters filed a $250,000 lawsuit charging the paper with religious discrimination and with violation of their civil rights.

The *Washington Post* issued a memo to staffers that barred any reporters who had participated in a pro-abortion rights march in Washington "from any future participation in coverage of the abortion issue." Don Kowet reported in the *Washington Times* that the same memo prohibited any "newsroom professional" from participating in such a protest.

But what about participating in a political campaign? Must a religion reporter be an atheist?

According to Kowet, Richard Harwood, *Washington Post* ombudsman at the time, told a conference of journalists: "You have every right in the world to run for office, or participate in a political activity or lobbying activity. You don't have the 'right' to work for the *Washington Post*."

Nevertheless, some worry that uninvolved journalists will be uninformed journalists, an unconnected group of elitists. The problem is compounded when editors and even news organizations are involved in community projects. May the editor join the yacht club? May the station support the United Way? Is the *New York Times*'s coverage of the Metropolitan Museum of Art influenced by its generous support of that institution? May an HIV-positive journalist report on AIDS?

Finally, should journalists demand of themselves what they demand of politicians—full disclosure of their financial investments and memberships, as well as public knowledge of their personal tastes, preferences and lifestyles?

> "If you're not involved in the community at all and you're totally neutralized, you end up not knowing enough about the community, not being able to get enough leads and so on in order to do your job."
> — *Tony Case, quoting ethicist Louis W. Hodges in* Editor & Publisher

Invasion of Privacy

Most journalists would cry out against an invasion of their own privacy. Yet many of them do argue for a vague "right to know" when they report on others, especially if those others are public officials or public figures. The head-on collision of the right to know and the right to privacy will confront you every day of your reporting lives. The Constitution mentions neither "right."

The most obvious and talked-about issue dealing with the right to privacy is naming crime victims, especially rape and abuse victims. Some states, such as Florida, have legislated against publishing rape victim's names, only to have the law struck down by a Florida District Court. The Supreme Court has held that news agencies cannot be punished for publishing lawfully obtained information or information from a public record. Meanwhile, legislators are looking for ways to close the records on rape and to punish police, hospitals, court clerks and other officials for releasing victims' names.

And so it comes down to a matter of ethics, and, as usual, there is no complete agreement. But nearly all news outlets would not publish a rape victim's name without the victim's approval. The same is true of juvenile victims of sex crimes. The obvious reasons are that the victim has suffered enough and need suffer no further shame. Even though reporting incidents of rape has risen from 10 percent of all such crimes to 20 percent, most victims will not come forward because of the stigma attached.

What you do as a reporter when a seamy tabloid prints the name is another problem entirely. If the name is public, should you go public?

A similar problem arises with publishing the names of juvenile offenders. Traditionally, news organizations have held that juveniles are juveniles and are entitled to make juvenile mistakes, even if those mistakes are crimes. Juvenile court records are, after all, sealed. Again, the courts have upheld the right to publish juvenile offenders' names on the public record. Some media critics, such as the *Fresno Bee* ombudsman Lynne Enders Glaser, have applauded the publication of the names of juvenile offenders. She wrote: "It doesn't take a rocket scientist to figure out that more and more violent crimes are being committed by young people. And in increasing numbers, *Bee* readers have challenged the law and the media to stop protecting the identity of criminals because of their age."

However, in addition to the stigma attached to the juvenile offender's name forever and the embarrassment of his or her parents and family, some are worried that in some groups a youth's notoriety will *encourage* other young people to violate the law. Others argue that shame will stop other juveniles from committing crimes.

Reporting on crime victims or juvenile crimes are just two of the myriad privacy issues you will face. Journalists are still protected when writing about public officials and public figures—most of the time. But what about the children of politicians or celebrities?

Photographers and videographers must be especially concerned with privacy. "Lead with blood" is not an uncommon dictum in TV newsrooms. But how much blood? And how often and under what circumstances do we stick cameras into people's grieving and anxious faces? When may we ask, if at all, "How did you feel when you saw your daughter go down for the last time?"

When a reporter asked President Harry Truman about how he felt when he heard that President John Kennedy was killed, Truman answered, "It's none of your damn business."

When is privacy paramount, and under what circumstances do you fail as a journalist to keep your audience informed?

Withholding Information

May you ever withhold information from the news organization for which you work? If you are writing what you hope to be a bestselling book, may you save some "news" until the book is published?

If you work as a journalist, are you ever off duty? A doctor isn't. Doctors take an oath to treat the sick. If you witness something at a friend's house or at a party, do you tell your news director about it?

One reporter was fired when his boss discovered that he attended a post-concert party of a rock band where lines of cocaine were available for the sniffing. The reporter did not include this information in his coverage of the band. His defense was that if he reported the drug abuse, he would never get interviews or close to other rock groups and he would be finished as a music critic. His defense didn't work.

If you learn that a political candidate is "sleeping around," would you withhold that information? Would you do so even if you knew that if the public had that information, the candidate would not be elected? Suppose after the election it became clear that you had had the information before the election but did not publish it? The *Portland Oregonian* apologized to its readers for not publishing reports about Sen. Bob Packwood's alleged sexual harassment charges until after he was re-elected.

However, St. Louis WKBQ General Manager Bill Viands did not apologize when a popular St. Louis weatherman committed suicide after WKBQ aired intimate messages left on the answering machine of a woman who said he had been harassing her. In a *Chicago Tribune* story by Staci D. Kraemer, WKBQ producer Courtney Landrum said, "I couldn't believe it was unethical in any way shape or form. . . ."

Leading politicians in France blamed negative reporting questioning the integrity of Prime Minister Pierre Beregovoy for driving him to take his own life. Press critics blamed the media treatment of Vince Foster, counselor to President Bill Clinton, for his suicide. His suicide note lamented that ruining people's lives was sport in our nation's capital.

Sometimes the press withholds information. In El Paso, Texas, the media held a story of the kidnapping of two boys for two days because of threats, relayed by the FBI, that the kidnappers would kill the boys if the kidnapping were publicized. The boys were eventually freed unharmed.

Sometimes the press doesn't. Sometimes it comes down to what ethicist Edmund Lambeth calls humaneness. You never do needless harm to an individual or inflict needless pain or suffering. It is better that you do the least harm possible. You certainly don't do harmful stories deliberately to harass someone or without a good reason. No one likes a mean bully.

Beware of Plagiarism!

Taking material verbatim from the newspaper library. Even when the material is from your own newspaper, it is still someone else's work. Put it in your own words or attribute it.

Using material verbatim from the wire services. Sometimes writers take Associated Press material, add a few paragraphs to give some local flavor, and publish it as their own work. Even though it is a common practice, it is not right.

Using material from other publications. Some blame electronic databases for a whole new explosion of plagiarism. Sometimes writers steal the research of others without attribution. And sometimes they use others' work without realizing it.

Using news releases verbatim. The publicists are delighted, but you should be ashamed—especially if you put your name on an article. Rewrite it, except perhaps for the direct quotations, and use them sparingly. If you use a whole release, cite its source.

Using the work of fellow reporters. If more than one reporter works on a story, if you use a byline on top, put the other names at the end of the story.

Using old stories over again. Columnists, beware! Your readers have a right to know when you are recycling your material. Some of them might catch you at it, and there goes your credibility.

—Roy Peter Clark

Plagiarism

No one wants you to use his or her work as your own. No one condones plagiarism. The problem is defining just what constitutes plagiarism. Probably you know when you do it even if no one else does.

Newspaper leaders such as the *Washington Post* and the *New York Times* knew when their staff did it and disciplined the writers. Boston University journalism Dean H. Joachim Maitre did it and was forced to resign as dean.

In the daily practice of journalism, reporters, consciously or unconsciously, deal with many situations that could involve plagiarism. Roy Peter Clark of the Poynter Institute has listed them (see sidebar).

As William A. Henry III wrote in *Time* magazine, a reporter has a First Amendment bond with the public. "Plagiarism," he writes, "imperils that bond, not because it involves theft of a wry phrase or piquant quote, but because it devalues meticulous, independent verification of fact—the bedrock of a press worth reading."

That bond is not just with the public. It's with your fellow workers and the news organization for which you work. Your personal ethics will safeguard and nurture that bond. Once it is broken, so are you.

Three final guidelines:

■ *Be free of obligations to anyone or to any interest except the truth. As scholar John Merrill has written, the primary obligation of the journalist is to be free.*

■ *Be fair. Even chidren know when you treat them unfairly or when they are being unfair. So do you.*

■ *Remember good taste. Some actions and stories may be ethical, but they may be in bad taste.*

Suggested Readings

Black, Jay, Steele, Bob and Barney, Ralph. *Doing Ethics In Journalism: A Handbook with Case Studies.* Greencastle, Ind.: The Sigma Delta Chi Foundation and The Society of Professional Journalists, 1993. A well-organized, usable handbook, containing ethics codes of various journalism societies and news organizations.

Christians, Clifford, Rotzoll, Kim and Fackler, Mark. *Media Ethics, Cases and Moral Reasoning,* Third Edition. New York: Longman, 1991. Applies the Potter Box method of principled reasoning to dozens of journalism, advertising and public relations cases.

Fletcher, Joseph. *Situation Ethics: The New Morality.* Philadelphia: Westminster Press, 1966. A classic work on Christian situation ethics.

Lambeth, Edmund B. *Committed Journalism,* Second Edition. Bloomington, Ind.: Indiana University Press, 1992. Creates an ethics code specific to the practice of journalism.

Merrill, John. *The Imperative of Freedom: A Philosophy of Journalistic Autonomy.* New York: Hastings House, 1974; Lanham, Md.:, University Press of America, 1990. Establishes freedom as the primary imperative of the journalist.

Wilkins, Lee and Patterson, Philip. *Media Ethics, Issues and Cases,* Second Edition. Dubuque, Ia.: WCB Brown and Benchmark Publications, 1994. An excellent discussion of journalism ethics with up-to-date cases.

Exercises

1. You learn that the daughter of a local bank president has been kidnapped. The family has not been contacted by the kidnappers, and police officials ask you to keep the matter secret for fear the abductors might panic and injure the child. Describe how a deontologist, a teleologist and a situation ethicist would make their decisions on how to handle the situation.

2. Would a travel writer ever be justified in accepting a free trip? Explain your answer by using various theories of situation ethics.

3. You are a photographer for a newspaper. On your way back from a track meet, you see a man who looks as if he is thinking about jumping off a bridge. You have a camera with motor-drive action, which permits you to take pictures in rapid-fire sequence. Would you:
   a. Shoot pictures from a distance?
   b. Approach the man slowly, take pictures and try to talk him out of jumping?
   c. Step out of his sight and radio to the newspaper to send police?
   d. Take some other action?
   Justify your response.

4. For at least a year, on four of five occasions, reporters on your paper have heard rumors that a rest home for the aged was negligent in their care of the elderly. Your editor asks you to get a job there as a janitor and report what you find. What would be your response?

5. A Christian minister is running for mayor of your city, which is a conservative, traditional community. You learn that he and his wife of 18 years have a son who was born just four months after they were married. Decide whether you would release that information by using the Potter Box.

6. Do a computer search of articles written in the past three years on whether journalists should publish the names of rape victims. Then write a brief summary of your findings.

Copy Editing and Proofreading Symbols

Writing and editing for today's media are done almost exclusively on computers. Only in the book industry are most manuscripts still prepared on paper. Nevertheless, at some small newspapers and magazines, editors prefer to edit on paper. For that reason, failure to learn the copy editing symbols used in manuscript preparation is a mistake. There is a good chance you will need to use those symbols at some point in your career, if only to satisfy the occasional editor who prefers doing things the old-fashioned way.

You are even more likely to use proofreading symbols, which are used on galley proofs and page proofs to correct typeset copy. While there are some similarities in the two sets of symbols, there also are differences. The chart on page 488 shows the most common copy editing symbols (used in manuscript preparation) and the chart below illustrates the most common proofreading symbols (used to correct typeset copy).

ʌ Insert at this point.	⌄⌄ Space evenly.
⊥ Push down space.	⌒ Close up entirely.
ℯ Take out letter, letters or words.	⊏ Move to left.
ꝯ Turn inverted letter.	⊐ Move to right.
(lc) Set lowercase.	⊔ Lower letter or word.
(wf) Wrong font letter.	⊓ Raise letter or word.
(ital) Reset in italic type.	(out, see copy) Words are left out.
(rom) Reset in roman (regular) type.	∥ Straighten lines.
(bf) Reset in bold face type.	¶ Start new paragraph.
○ Insert period.	(no ¶) No paragraph. Run together.
⌄ Insert comma.	(tr) Transpose letters or words.
⌃ Insert semicolon.	(?) Query; is copy right?
H Insert hyphen.	⊢ Insert dash.
∨ Insert apostrophe.	▫ Indent 1 em.
⌄⌄ Enclose in quotation marks.	▫▫ Indent 2 ems.
≡ Replace with a capital letter.	▫▫▫ Indent 3 ems.
# Insert space.	(stet) Let it stand.

Figure A.1.
Proofreading Symbols.

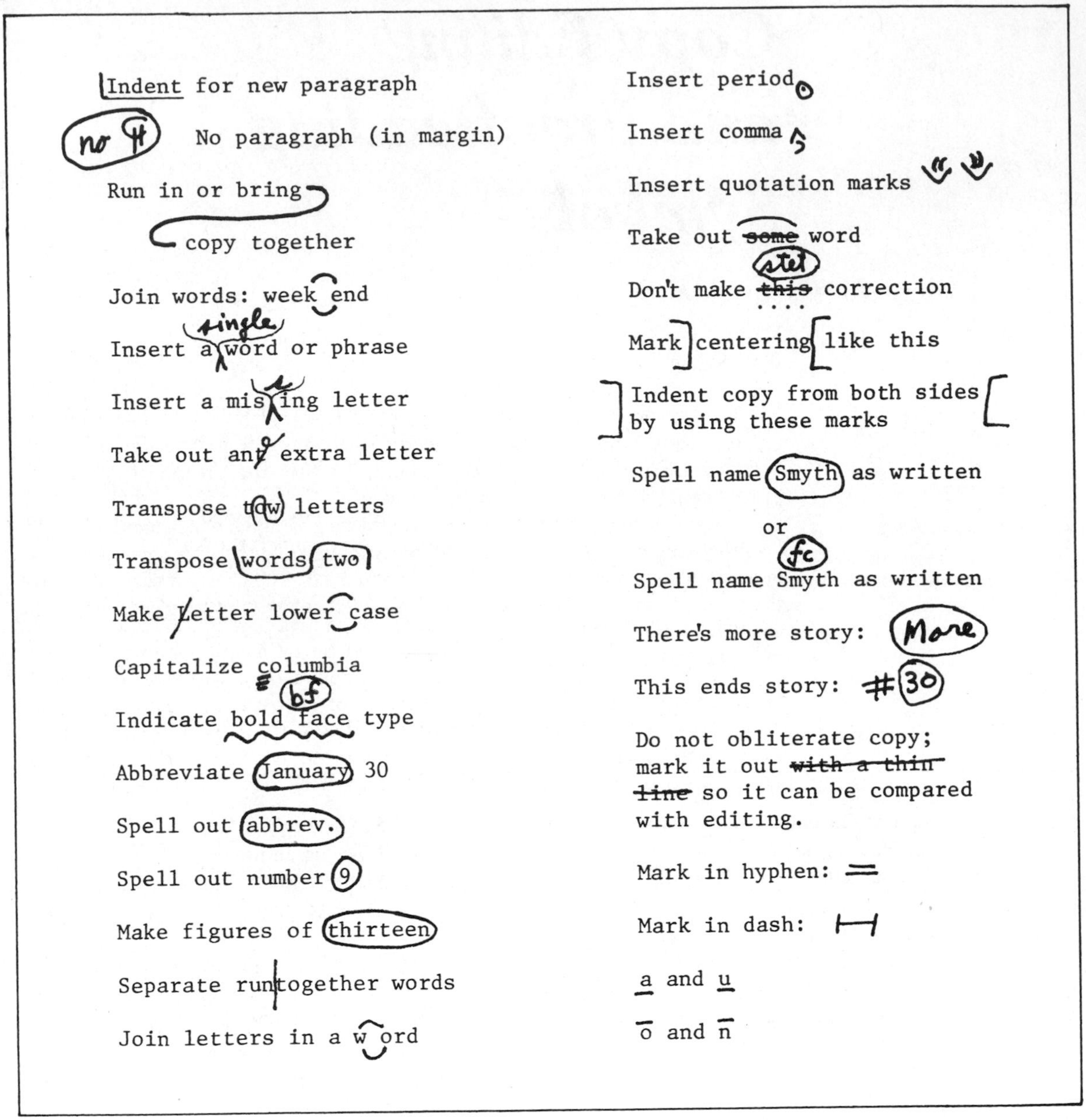

Indent for new paragraph

no ¶   No paragraph (in margin)

Run in or bring copy together

Join words: week end

Insert a *single* word or phrase

Insert a missing letter

Take out any extra letter

Transpose tow letters

Transpose words two

Make Letter lower case

Capitalize columbia

Indicate bold face type

Abbreviate January 30

Spell out abbrev.

Spell out number 9

Make figures of thirteen

Separate run together words

Join letters in a w ord

Insert period

Insert comma

Insert quotation marks

Take out some word

Don't make this correction   stet

Mark centering like this

Indent copy from both sides by using these marks

Spell name Smyth as written

or   fc

Spell name Smyth as written

There's more story: More

This ends story: # 30

Do not obliterate copy; mark it out with a thin line so it can be compared with editing.

Mark in hyphen: =

Mark in dash: ⊢—⊣

a and u

o and n

Figure A.2.
Copy Editing Symbols.

Wire Service Style

A burro is an ass. A burrow is a hole in the ground. As a journalist you are expected to know the difference.

That piece of advice could be found in one edition of *The United Press International Stylebook*, a reference manual otherwise free of wit. If nothing else, the passage serves to dispel the myth that style rules encourage bland writing and conformity in newspapers.

Instead, style rules provide needed consistency throughout the paper so that the reader can focus on content, not differences of little substance. Some readers, for example, are irritated to find *employee* in one story and *employe* in the next. Both spellings can be found in dictionaries, but observing a style rule eliminates that annoying inconsistency. Style rules help reporters and editors avoid wasting time arguing about such details as the correct spelling of *OK* (or *okay*). Even more important, style rules provide guidance in the often troublesome areas of grammar, punctuation, capitalization, abbreviation and the like.

Despite that, editors are far from unanimous in their support of style. Louis D. Boccardi of The Associated Press wrote that journalists approach style questions with varying degrees of passion: "Some don't really think it's important. Some agree that basically there should be uniformity for reading ease if nothing else. Still others are prepared to duel over a wayward lowercase." Boccardi's comment appears in the foreword of *The Associated Press Stylebook*, a book designed as a reference manual as well as a stylebook. It is almost identical to *The United Press International Stylebook*. Indeed, the two news services collaborated in writing similar versions as a service to clients who subscribe to both.

Together, the AP and UPI stylebooks are the major source of American newspaper style. Many newspapers rely on them as their only source of style. Some issue supplements listing deviations from wire service style and establishing local style rules. Some, mostly large newspapers, have their own stylebooks.

Because newspapers depend so heavily on the AP and UPI stylebooks, this appendix focuses on the rules they establish. It is designed to point out the most common violations of style so that you, as a reporter, will learn to avoid them. It would be difficult, if not impossible, for you to commit to memory all the style rules in the *AP Stylebook*. But you can learn to avoid the most common mistakes while developing the habit of referring to your stylebook when in doubt.

In this appendix style rules are categorized under the headings of Capitalization; Abbreviations and Acronyms; Punctuation and Hyphenation; Numerals; and Grammar, Spelling and Word Usage. Following an introduction to each section, a listing of the most common style rules is provided. The appendix serves as an excellent reference for beginning reporters, but it should not be considered a substitute for the more comprehensive stylebooks. The authors thank the AP and UPI for granting permission to use excerpts from their stylebooks.

Capitalization

In general, avoid unnecessary capitals. Use a capital letter only if you can justify it by one of the principles listed here.

Many words and phrases, including special cases, are listed separately in the complete stylebooks. Entries that are capitalized without further comment should be capitalized in all uses.

If there is no relevant listing in the stylebooks for a particular word or phrase, consult *Webster's New World Dictionary*. Use lowercase if the dictionary lists it as an acceptable form for the sense in which the word is being used.

As used in the stylebooks, *capitalize* means to use uppercase for the first letter of a word. If additional capital letters are needed, they are called for by an example or a phrase such as *use all caps*.

Some basic principles:

PROPER NOUNS: Capitalize nouns that constitute the unique identification for a specific person, place or thing: *John, Mary, America, Boston, England*.

Some words, such as the examples just given, are always proper nouns. Some common nouns receive proper noun status when they are used as the name of a particular entity: *General Electric, Gulf Oil*.

PROPER NAMES: Capitalize common nouns such as *party, river, street* and *west* only when they are an integral part of the full name for a person, place or thing: *Democratic Party, Mississippi River, Fleet Street, West Virginia*.

Lowercase these common nouns when they stand alone in subsequent references: *the party, the river, the street*.

Lowercase the common noun elements of names in all plural uses: *the Democratic and Republican parties, Main and State streets, lakes Erie and Ontario*.

POPULAR NAMES: Some places and events lack officially designated proper names but have popular names that are the effective equivalent: *the Combat Zone* (a section of downtown Boston), *the Main Line* (a group of Philadelphia suburbs), *the South Side* (of Chicago), *the Badlands* (of North Dakota), *the Street* (the financial community in the Wall Street area of New York).

The principle applies also to shortened versions of the proper names for one-of-a-kind events: *the Series* (for the World Series), *the Derby* (for the Kentucky Derby). This practice should not, however, be interpreted as a license to ignore the general practice of lowercasing the common noun elements of a name when they stand alone.

DERIVATIVES: Capitalize words that are derived from a proper noun and still depend on it for their meaning: *American, Christian, Christianity, English, French, Marxism, Shakespearean*.

Lowercase words that are derived from a proper noun but no longer depend on it for their meaning: *french fries, herculean, manhattan cocktail, malapropism, pasteurize, quixotic, venetian blind*.

Common Problems

Newspapers conform to the basic rule of capitalization of the English language: Proper nouns—specific persons, places and things—are capitalized; common nouns are not. That rule is simple enough, but knowing when to capitalize words in other usages may not be as obvious.

When in doubt about whether to capitalize, refer to your stylebook. If that fails to solve the problem, refer to the primary supplemental reference established by the AP and UPI—*Webster's New World Dictionary of the American Language*, Third College Edition.

TRADEMARKS: Almost every editor has received a letter that reads something like this:

> Dear Editor:
>
> We were delighted to read your April 5 article about the popularity of Frisbees in your community.
>
> Unfortunately, however, you failed to capitalize the word *Frisbee* throughout the article. Because the word *Frisbee* is a trademark of our company, it should always be capitalized.

Such warnings of trademark infringements usually are nice enough. Businesses realize there are many trademarked words, and it is difficult for editors to keep up with them all. Only when violations repeatedly occur are threats of lawsuits tossed about.

Reporters and editors try to ensure that they don't turn words that are trademarks into generic terms. Companies register such words to protect their rights to them and have every reason to expect that newspapers will honor those rights.

Newspapers, however, are not eager to provide knowingly what amounts to free advertising for products in their news columns. Thus reporters and editors are encouraged to use generic words instead of trademarks. Here are some examples of substitution:

- Use *real estate agent* or *salesperson* rather than *Realtor*, a trademark of the National Association of Real Estate Boards.
- Use *soft drink* or *cola* rather than *Coke*, a trademark of the Coca-Cola Co.
- Use *gelatin*, not *Jell-O*.
- Use *bleach*, not *Clorox*.
- Use *refrigerator*, not *Frigidaire*.

The list of such words is lengthy, and some may be real sources of confusion. It is permissible to use *jeep*, for example, when referring to an Army vehicle, but the similarly named civilian vehicle is a *Jeep*. When in doubt refer to the AP or UPI stylebooks for a list of many trademarked names.

PLURALS OF PROPER NOUNS: More confusion can result when referring to plurals of proper nouns. You would write about the *Tennessee Legislature* and the *Colorado Legislature* when each is used in the singular form. The plural, however, would be the *Tennessee and Colorado legislatures*. The same rule applies when referring to streets: *Ninth Street* and *Cherry Street*, but *Ninth and Cherry streets*.

RELIGIOUS TERMS: References to a deity often cause confusion. Style provides for the capitalization of proper names referring to a monotheistic deity, such as *God, Buddha, Allah, the Son, the Father*. However, pronouns used to refer to a deity—*he, him, thee, thou*—are lowercase.

TITLES: For the unwary reporter, titles are another source of trouble. Generally, formal titles used directly before a person's name are capitalized: *President Bill Clinton, Secretary of State Warren Christopher, Queen Elizabeth II*. When used after a person's name, the title is lowercased: *Bill Clinton, president of the United States; Warren Christopher, secretary of state; Elizabeth II, queen of England*.

Occupational titles—those more descriptive of a person's job than formal status—generally are not capitalized. Thus, you should lowercase references to *movie star Eddie Murphy, astronaut Neil Armstrong* or *outfielder José Canseco.*

DIRECT QUOTATION: Perhaps the most abused rule of capitalization deals with the first word of a direct quotation. That word should be capitalized following the source only when it:

- Starts a complete sentence.
- Is separated from the source by a comma.
- Appears in direct quotation marks.

Thus, it is permissible to write:

Correct   Clinton said, "It was a tiring trip."
Clinton said "it was a tiring trip."
Clinton said it was a tiring trip.

These constructions are incorrect:

Incorrect   Clinton said "It was a tiring trip."
Clinton said, "it was a tiring trip."
Clinton said, it was a tiring trip.

Alphabetized Listing

academic departments   Use lowercase except for words that are proper nouns or adjectives: *the department of history, the history department, the department of English, the English department.*

administration   Lowercase: *the administration, the president's administration, the governor's administration, the Clinton administration.*

AIDS   Acceptable in all references for *acquired immune deficiency syndrome,* sometimes written as acquired immunodeficiency syndrome.

air force   Capitalize when referring to U.S. forces: *the U.S. Air Force, the Air Force, Air Force regulations.* Do not use the abbreviation USAF.

Use lowercase for the forces of other nations: *the Israeli air force.*

animals   Capitalize the name of a specific animal, and use Roman numerals to show sequence: *Bowser, Whirlaway II.*

For breed names, follow the spelling and capitalization in *Webster's New World Dictionary.* For breeds not listed in the dictionary, capitalize words derived from proper nouns; use lowercase elsewhere: *basset hound, Boston terrier.*

army   Capitalize when referring to U.S. forces: *the U.S. Army, the Army, Army regulations.*

Use lowercase for the forces of other nations: *the French army.*

Bible   Capitalize, without quotation marks, when referring to the Scriptures of the Old Testament or the New Testament. Capitalize also related terms such as *the Gospels, Gospel of St. Mark, the Scriptures, the Holy Scriptures.*

Lowercase *biblical* in all uses.

Lowercase *bible* as a non-religious term: *My dictionary is my bible.*

brand names   When they are used, capitalize them.

Brand names normally should be used only if they are essential to a story.

Sometimes, however, the use of a brand name may not be essential but is acceptable because it lends an air of reality to a story: *He pulled up in a Cadillac* may be preferable to the less specific *luxury car.*

building   Never abbreviate. Capitalize the proper names of buildings, including the word *building* if it is an integral part of the proper name: *the Empire State Building*.

bureau   Capitalize when part of the formal name for an organization or agency: *the Bureau of Labor Statistics, the Newspaper Advertising Bureau*.

Lowercase when used alone or to designate a corporate subdivision: *the Washington bureau of The Associated Press*.

cabinet   Capitalize references to a specific body of advisers heading executive departments for a president, king, governor and the like: *The president-elect said he has not made his Cabinet selections*.

The capital letter distinguishes the word from the common noun meaning cupboard, which is lowercase.

Cabinet titles   Capitalize the full title when used before a name; lowercase in other uses: *Secretary of State Warren Christopher*, but Ron Brown, *secretary of commerce*.

century   Lowercase, spelling out numbers less than 10: *the first century, the 20th century*.

For proper names, follow the organization's practice: *20th Century Fox, Twentieth Century Fund, Twentieth Century Limited*.

chairman, chairwoman   Capitalize as a formal title before a name: *company Chairman Henry Ford, committee Chairwoman Anne Roberts*.

Do not capitalize as a casual, temporary position: *meeting chairman Robert Jones*.

Do not use *chairperson* unless it is an organization's formal title for an office.

chief   Capitalize as a formal title before a name: *She spoke to Police Chief William Bratton. She spoke to Chief William Bratton of the New York police*.

Lowercase when it is not a formal title: *union chief Walter Reuther*.

church   Capitalize as part of the formal name of a building, a congregation or a denomination; lowercase in other uses: *St. Mary's Church, the Roman Catholic Church, the Catholic and Episcopal churches, a Roman Catholic church, a church*.

Lowercase in phrases where *the church* is used in an institutional sense: *He believes in separation of church and state. The pope said the church opposes abortion*.

city council   Capitalize when part of a proper name: *the Boston City Council*.

Retain capitalization if the reference is to a specific council but the context does not require the city name:

BOSTON (AP)—The City Council . . .

Lowercase in other uses: *the council, the Boston and New York city councils, a city council*.

committee   Capitalize when part of a formal name: *the House Appropriations Committee*.

Do not capitalize *committee* in shortened versions of long committee names: the Special Senate Select Committee to Investigate Improper Labor-Management Practices, for example, became known as the *rackets committee*.

congress   Capitalize *U.S. Congress* and *Congress* when referring to the U.S. Senate and House of Representatives. Although *Congress* sometimes is used as a substitute for the House, it properly is reserved for reference to both the Senate and House.

Capitalize *Congress* also when referring to a foreign body that uses the term, or its equivalent in a foreign language, as part of its formal name: *the Argentine Congress, the Congress*.

Lowercase *congress* when it is used as a synonym for *convention* or in second reference to an organization that uses the word as part of its formal name: *the Congress of Racial Equality, the congress*.

constitution   Capitalize references to the U.S. *Constitution*, with or without the *U.S.* modifier: *The president said he supports the Constitution*.

When referring to constitutions of other nations or of states, capitalize only with the name of a nation or a state: *the French Constitution, the Massachusetts Constitution, the nation's constitution, the state constitution, the constitution*.

Lowercase in other uses: *the organization's constitution*.

Lowercase *constitutional* in all uses.

courthouse   Capitalize with the name of a jurisdiction: *the Cook County Courthouse, the U.S. Courthouse*. Lowercase in other uses: *the county courthouse, the courthouse, the federal courthouse*.

Court House (two words) is used in the proper names of some communities: *Appomattox Court House, Va.*

court names   Capitalize the full proper names of courts at all levels.

Retain capitalization if U.S. or a state name is dropped: *the U.S. Supreme Court, the Supreme Court; the Massachusetts Superior Court, the state Superior Court, the Superior Court, Superior Court*.

For courts identified by a numeral: *2nd District Court, 8th U.S. Circuit Court of Appeals*.

directions and regions   In general, lowercase *north, south, northeast, northern* and so on when they indicate compass direction; capitalize these words when they designate regions.

federal   Use a capital letter for the architectural style and for corporate or governmental bodies that use the word as part of their formal names: *Federal Express, the Federal Trade Commission*.

Lowercase when used as an adjective to distinguish something from state, county, city, town or private entities: *federal assistance, federal court, the federal government, a federal judge*.

Also: *federal District Court* (but *U.S. District Court* is preferred) and *federal Judge Ann Aldrich* (but *U.S. District Judge Ann Aldrich* is preferred).

federal court   Always lowercase. The preferred form for first reference is to use the proper name of the court.

Do not create non-existent entities such as *Manhattan Federal Court*. Instead, use *a federal court in Manhattan*.

food   Most food names are lowercase: *apples, cheese, peanut butter*.

Capitalize brand names and trademarks: *Roquefort cheese, Tabasco sauce*.

Most proper nouns or adjectives are capitalized when they occur in a food name: *Boston brown bread, Russian dressing, Swiss cheese, Waldorf salad*.

Lowercase is used, however, when the food does not depend on the proper noun or adjective for its meaning: *french fries, graham crackers, manhattan cocktail*.

former   Always lowercase. But retain capitalization for a formal title used immediately before a name: *former President Reagan*.

fraternal organizations and service clubs   Capitalize the proper names: *American Legion, Lions Club, Independent Order of Odd Fellows, Rotary Club*.

Capitalize also words describing membership: *He is a Legionnaire, a Lion, an Odd Fellow, an Optimist and a Rotarian*.

geographic names   Capitalize common nouns when they form an integral part of a proper name, but lowercase them when they stand alone: *Pennsylvania Avenue, the avenue; the Philippine Islands, the islands; the Mississippi River, the river.*

Lowercase common nouns that are not part of a specific proper name: *the Pacific islands, the Swiss mountains, Chekiang province.*

government   Always lowercase: *the federal government, the state government, the U.S. government.* Never abbreviate.

governmental bodies   Follow these guidelines:

FULL NAME: Capitalize the full proper names of governmental agencies, departments, and offices; *the U.S. Department of State, the Georgia Department of Human Resources, the Boston City Council, the Chicago Fire Department.*

WITHOUT JURISDICTION: Retain capitalization in referring to a specific body if the dateline or context makes the name of the nation, state, county, city or town unnecessary: *the Department of State* (in a story from Washington), *the Department of Human Resources* or *the state Department of Human Resources* (in a story from Georgia), *the City Council* (in a story from Boston), *the Fire Department* or *the City Fire Department* (in a story from Chicago).

Lowercase further condensations of the name: *the department, the council.*

FLIP-FLOPPED NAMES: Retain capital letters for the name of a governmental body if its formal name is flopped to delete the word *of: the State Department, the Human Resources Department.*

GENERIC EQUIVALENTS: If a generic term has become the equivalent of a proper name in popular use, treat it as a proper name: Use *Walpole State Prison,* for example, even though the proper name is the *Massachusetts Correctional Institution-Walpole.*

PLURALS, NON-SPECIFIC REFERENCES: All words that are capitalized when part of a proper name should be lowercased when they are used in the plural or do not refer to a specific existing body. Some examples:

All states except Nebraska have a state senate. The town does not have a fire department. The bill requires city councils to provide matching funds. The president will address the lower houses of the New York and New Jersey legislatures.

heavenly bodies   Capitalize the proper names of planets, stars, constellations and the like: *Mars, Earth, Arcturus, the Big Dipper, Aries.*

For comets, capitalize only the proper noun element of the name: *Halley's comet.*

Lowercase *sun* and *moon,* but if their Greek names are used, capitalize them: *Helios* and *Luna.*

historical periods and events   Capitalize the names of widely recognized epochs in anthropology, archaeology, geology and history: *the Bronze Age, the Dark Ages, the Middle Ages, the Pliocene Epoch.*

Capitalize also widely recognized popular names for periods and events: *the Atomic Age, the Boston Tea Party, the Civil War, the Exodus* (of the Israelites from Egypt), *the Great Depression, Prohibition.*

Lowercase *century: the 18th century.*

Capitalize only the proper nouns or adjectives in general descriptions of a period: *ancient Greece, classical Rome, the Victorian era, the fall of Rome.*

holidays and holy days   Capitalize them: *New Year's Eve, New Year's Day, Groundhog Day, Easter, Hanukkah* and so on.

house of representatives   Capitalize when referring to a specific governmental body: *the U.S. House of Representatives, the Massachusetts House of Representatives.*

Capitalize shortened references that delete the words *of Representatives: the U.S. House, the Massachusetts House.*

Retain capitalization if U.S. or the name of a state is dropped but the reference is to a specific body:

BOSTON (AP)—The House had adjourned for the year.

Lowercase plural uses: *the Massachusetts and Rhode Island houses.*

Apply the same principles to similar legislative bodies, such as *the Virginia House of Delegates.*

judge   Capitalize before a name when it is the formal title for an individual who presides in a court of law. Do not continue to use the title in second reference.

Do not use *court* as a part of the title unless confusion would result without it:

- No *court* in the title: *U.S. District Judge Ann Aldrich, District Judge Ann Aldrich, federal Judge Ann Aldrich, Judge Ann Aldrich, U.S. Circuit Judge Homer Thornberry, appellate Judge John Blair.*
- *Court* needed in the title: *Juvenile Court Judge John Jones, Criminal Court Judge John Jones, Superior Court Judge Robert Harrison, state Supreme Court Judge William Cushing.*

When the formal title *chief judge* is relevant, put the court name after the judge's name: *Chief Judge John Garrett Penn of the U.S. District Court in Washington, D.C.; Chief Judge Sam J. Ervin III of the 4th U.S. Circuit Court of Appeals.*

Do not pile up long court names before the name of a judge. Make it *Judge John Smith of Allegheny County Common Pleas Court.* Not: *Allegheny County Common Pleas Court Judge John Smith.*

Lowercase *judge* as an occupational designation in phrases such as *beauty contest judge.*

legislature   Capitalize when preceded by the name of a state: *the Kansas Legislature.*

Retain capitalization when the state name is dropped but the reference is specifically to that state's legislature:

TOPEKA, Kan. (AP)—Both houses of the Legislature adjourned today.

Capitalize *legislature* in subsequent specific references and in such constructions as: *the 100th Legislature, the state Legislature.*

Lowercase *legislature* when used generically: *No legislature has approved the amendment.*

Use *legislature* in lowercase for all plural references. The *Arkansas and Colorado legislatures are considering the amendment.*

magazine names   Capitalize the name but do not place it in quotes. Lowercase *magazine* unless it is part of the publication's formal title: *Harper's Magazine, Newsweek magazine, Time magazine.* Capitalize *the* in a magazine's name if that is the way the publication prefers to be known.

Check the masthead if in doubt.

monuments   Capitalize the popular names of monuments and similar public attractions: *Lincoln Memorial, Statue of Liberty, Washington Monument, Leaning Tower of Pisa.*

mountains   Capitalize as part of a proper name: *Appalachian Mountains, Ozark Mountains, Rocky Mountains.*

Or simply: *the Appalachians, the Ozarks, the Rockies.*

nationalities and races   Capitalize the proper names of nationalities, peoples, races, tribes and the like: *Arab, Arabic, African-American, American, Caucasian, Cherokee, Chicano, Chinese* (both singular and plural), *Eskimo* (plural *Eskimos*), *French Canadian, Gypsy* (*Gypsies*), *Hispanic, Japanese* (singular and plural), *Jew, Jewish, Latin, Negro* (*Negroes*), *Nordic, Oriental, Sioux, Swede* and so on.

Lowercase *black* (noun or adjective), *white, red, mulatto* and the like.

Lowercase derogatory terms such as *honky* and *nigger*. Use them only in direct quotes when essential to the story.

navy   Capitalize when referring to U.S. forces: *the U.S. Navy, the Navy, Navy policy.*

Lowercase when referring to the naval forces of other nations: *the British navy.*

newspaper names   Capitalize *the* in a newspaper's name if that is the way the publication prefers to be known.

Lowercase *the* before the newspaper names if a story mentions several papers, some of which use *the* as part of the name and some of which do not.

organizations and institutions   Capitalize the full names of organizations and institutions: *the American Medical Association; First Presbyterian Church; General Motors Corp.; Harvard University; Harvard University Medical School; the Procrastinators Club; the Society of Professional Journalists.*

Retain capitalization if *Co., Corp.* or a similar word is deleted from the full proper name: *General Motors.*

FLIP-FLOPPED NAMES: Retain capital letters when commonly accepted practice flops a name to delete the word *of: College of the Holy Cross, Holy Cross College; Harvard School of Dental Medicine, Harvard Dental School.*

Do not, however, flop formal names that are known to the public with the word *of: Massachusetts Institute of Technology,* for example, not *Massachusetts Technology Institute.*

planets   Capitalize the proper names of planets: *Jupiter, Mars, Mercury, Neptune, Pluto, Saturn, Uranus, Venus.*

Capitalize *earth* when used as the proper name of our planet: *The astronauts returned to Earth.*

Lowercase nouns and adjectives derived from the proper names of planets and other heavenly bodies: *martian, jovian, lunar, solar, venusian.*

plants   In general, lowercase the names of plants, but capitalize proper nouns or adjectives that occur in a name.

Some examples: *tree, fir, white fir, Douglas fir; Dutch elm, Scotch pine; clover, white clover, white Dutch clover.*

police department   In communities where this is the formal name, capitalize *police department* with or without the name of the community: *the Los Angeles Police Department, the Police Department.*

If a police agency has some other formal name such as *Division of Police,* use that name if it is the way the department is known to the public. If the story uses *police department* as a generic term for such an agency, put it in lowercase.

If a police agency with an unusual formal name is known to the public as a police department, treat *police department* as the name, capitalizing it with or without the name of the community. Use the formal name only if there is a special reason in the story.

If the proper name cannot be determined for some reason, such as the need to write about a police agency from a distance, treat *police department* as the proper name, capitalizing it with or without the name of the community.

Lowercase *police department* in plural uses: *the Los Angeles and San Francisco police departments.*

Lowercase *the department* whenever it stands alone.

political parties and philosophies Capitalize both the name of the party and the word *party* if it is customarily used as part of the organization's proper name: *the Democratic Party, the Republican Party.*

Capitalize *Communist, Conservative, Democrat, Liberal, Republican, Socialist* and so on when they refer to the activities of a specific party or to individuals who are members of it. Lowercase these words when they refer to political philosophy.

Lowercase the name of a philosophy in noun and adjective forms unless it is derivative of a proper name: *communism, communist; facism, fascist.* But: *Marxism, Marxist; Nazism, Nazi.*

pontiff Not a formal title. Always *lowercase.*

pope Capitalize when used as a formal title before a person's name; lowercase in all other uses: *Pope John Paul II spoke to the crowd. At the close of his address, the pope gave his blessing.*

presidency Always lowercase.

president Capitalize *president* only as a formal title before one or more names: *President Clinton, Presidents Ford and Carter.*

Lowercase in all other uses: *The president said today. He is running for president. Lincoln was president during the Civil War.*

religious references The basic guidelines:

DEITIES: Capitalize the proper names of monotheistic deities: *God, Allah, the Father, the Son, Jesus Christ, the Son of God, The Redeemer, the Holy Spirit.*

Lowercase pronouns referring to the deity: *he, him, his, thee, thou, who, whose, thy.*

Lowercase *gods* in referring to the deities of polytheistic religions.

Capitalize the proper names of pagan and mythological gods and goddesses: *Neptune, Thor, Venus.*

Lowercase such words as *god-awful, goddamn, godlike, godliness, godsend.*

LIFE OF CHRIST: Capitalize the names of major events in the life of Jesus Christ in references that do not use his name: *The doctrines of the Last Supper, the Crucifixion, the Resurrection and the Ascension are central to Christian belief.*

But use lowercase when the words are used with Christ's name: *The ascension of Jesus into heaven took place 40 days after his resurrection from the dead.*

Apply the principle also to events in the life of Christ's mother: *He cited the doctrine of the Immaculate Conception and the Assumption.* But: *She referred to the assumption of Mary into heaven.*

RITES: Capitalize proper names for rites that commemorate the Last Supper or signify a belief in Christ's presence: *the Lord's Supper, Holy Communion, Holy Eucharist.*

Lowercase the names of other sacraments or rites: *bar mitzvah, bat mitzvah.*

Capitalize *Benediction* and *Mass.* But: *a high Mass, a low Mass, a requiem Mass.*

OTHER WORDS: Lowercase *heaven, hell, devil, angel, cherub, an apostle, a priest* and the like.

Capitalize *Hades* and *Satan*.

seasons   Lowercase *spring, summer, fall, winter* and derivatives such as *springtime* unless part of a formal name: *Dartmouth Winter Carnival, Winter Olympics, Summer Olympics.*

senate   Capitalize all specific references to governmental legislative bodies, regardless of whether the name of the nation or state is used: *the U.S. Senate, the Senate; the Virginia Senate, the state Senate, the Senate.*

Lowercase plural uses: *the Virginia and North Carolina senates.*

The same principles apply to foreign bodies.

Lowercase references to non-governmental bodies: *The student senate at Yale.*

sentences   Capitalize the first word of every sentence, including quoted statements and direct questions: *Patrick Henry said, "I know not what course others may take, but as for me, give me liberty or give me death."*

Capitalize the first word of a quoted statement if it constitutes a sentence, even if it was part of a larger sentence in the original: *Patrick Henry said, "Give me liberty or give me death."*

In direct questions, even without quotation marks: *The story answers the question, Where does true happiness really lie?*

Social Security   Capitalize all references to the U.S. system.

Lowercase generic uses such as: *Is there a social security program in Sweden?*

state   lowercase in all *state of* constructions: *the state of Maine, the states of Maine and Vermont, New York state.*

Do not capitalize *state* when used simply as an adjective to specify a level of jurisdiction: *state Rep. William Smith, the state Transportation Department, state funds.*

Apply the same principle to phrases such as *the city of Chicago, the town of Auburn* and so on.

statehouse   Capitalize all references to a specific statehouse, with or without the name of the state: *The Massachusetts Statehouse is in Boston. The governor will visit the Statehouse today.*

Lowercase plural uses: *the Massachusetts and Rhode Island statehouses.*

subcommittee   Lowercase when used with the name of a legislative body's full committee: *a Ways and Means subcommittee.*

Capitalize when a subcommittee has a proper name of its own: *the Senate Permanent Subcommittee on Investigations.*

titles   In general, confine capitalization to formal titles used directly before an individual's name. Lowercase and spell out titles when they are not used with an individual's name: *The president issued a statement. The pope gave his blessing.*

Lowercase and spell out titles in constructions that set them off from a name by commas: *The vice president, Al Gore, attended the meeting. John Paul II, the current pope, does not plan to retire.*

ABBREVIATED TITLES: The following formal titles are capitalized and abbreviated as shown when used before a name outside quotations: *Dr., Gov., Lt. Gov., Rep., Sen.* and certain military ranks. Spell out all except *Dr.* when they are used in quotations.

All other formal titles are spelled out in all uses.

ACADEMIC TITLES: Capitalize and spell out formal titles such as *professor, dean, president, chancellor* and *chairman* when they precede a name. Lowercase elsewhere.

Lowercase modifiers such as *history* in *history Professor Oscar Handlin* and *department* in *department Chairman Jerome Wiesner.*

FORMAL TITLES: Capitalize formal titles when they are used immediately before one or more names: *Pope John Paul II, President Washington, Vice Presidents John Jones and Jane Smith.*

LEGISLATIVE TITLES: Use *Rep., Reps.,* and *Sens.* as formal titles before one or more names in regular text. Spell out and capitalize these titles before one or more names in a direct quotation. Spell out and lowercase *representative* and *senator* in other uses.

Spell out other legislative titles in all uses. Capitalize formal titles such as *assemblyman, assemblywoman, city councilor* and *delegate* when they are used before a name. Lowercase in other uses.

Add *U.S.* or *state* before a title only if necessary to avoid confusion: *U.S. Sen. Nancy Kassebaum spoke with state Sen. Joseph Carter.*

First Reference Practice. The use of a title such as *Rep.* or *Sen.* in first reference is normal in most stories. It is not mandatory, however, provided an individual's title is given later in the story.

Deletion of the title on first reference is frequently appropriate, for example, when an individual has become well-known: *Tom Eagleton endorsed President Clinton today. The former Missouri senator said he believes the president deserves another term.*

Second Reference. Do not use a legislative title before a name on second reference unless it is part of a direct quotation.

Congressman, Congresswoman, Rep. and *U.S. Rep.* are the preferred first-reference forms when a formal title is used before the name of a U.S. House member. The word *congressman* or *congresswoman,* in lowercase, may be used in subsequent references that do not use an individual's name, just as *senator* is used in references to members of the Senate.

Congressman and *Congresswoman* should appear as capitalized formal titles before a name only in direct quotation.

Organizational Titles. Capitalize titles for formal, organizational offices within a legislative body when they are used before a name: *Speaker Newt Gingrich, Majority Leader Dick Armey, Minority Leader Richard Gephardt, Democratic Whip David Bonior, Chairman Arlen Specter of the Senate Intelligence Committee.*

MILITARY TITLES: Capitalize a military rank when used as a formal title before an individual's name.

Spell out and lowercase a title when it is substitued for a name: *Gen. John J. Pershing arrived today. An aide said the general would review the troops.*

ROYAL TITLES: Capitalize *king, queen* and so on when used directly before a name.

trademark   A *trademark* is a brand, symbol, word or the like that is used by a manufacturer or dealer and protected by law to prevent a competitor from using it: *AstroTurf,* for example, is a type of artificial grass.

In general, use a generic equivalent unless the trademark name is essential to the story.

When a trademark is used, capitalize it.

Abbreviations and Acronyms

The notation *abbrev.* is used in the AP and UPI stylebooks to identify the abbreviated form that may be used for a word in some contexts.

A few universally recognized abbreviations are required in some circumstances. Some others are acceptable depending on the context. But in general, avoid alphabet soup.

Guidance on how to use a particular abbreviation or acronym is provided in entries alphabetized according to the sequence of letters in the word or phrase. Some general principles:

BEFORE A NAME: Abbreviate the following titles when used before a full name outside direct quotations: *Dr., Gov., Lt. Gov., Mr., Mrs., Ms., Rep., the Rev., Sen.* and certain military designations. Spell out all except *Dr., Mr., Mrs.* and *Ms.* when they are used before a name in direct quotations.

AFTER A NAME: Abbreviate *junior* or *senior* after an individual's name. Abbreviate *company, corporation, incorporated* and *limited* when used after the name of a corporate entity.

In some cases, an academic degree may be abbreviated after an individual's name.

WITH DATES OR NUMERALS: Use the abbreviations *A.D., B.C., a.m., p.m., No.,* and abbreviate certain months when used with the day of the month.

IN NUMBERED ADDRESSES: Abbreviate *avenue, boulevard* and *street* in numbered addresses: *He lives on Pennsylvania Avenue. He lives at 1600 Pennsylvania Ave.*

STATES AND NATIONS: The names of certain states, the *United States* and the former *Union of Soviet Socialist Republics* (but not of other nations) are abbreviated with periods in some circumstances.

ACCEPTABLE BUT NOT REQUIRED: Some organizations and government agencies are widely recognized by their initials: *CIA, FBI, GOP.*

If the entry for such an organization notes that an abbreviation is acceptable in all references or on second reference, that does not mean that its use should be automatic. Let the context determine, for example, whether to use *Federal Bureau of Investigation* or *FBI.*

AVOID AWKWARD CONSTRUCTIONS: Do not follow an organization's full name with an abbreviation or acronym in parentheses or set off by dashes. If an abbreviation or acronym would not be clear on second reference without this arrangement, do not use it.

Names not commonly known by the public should not be reduced to acronyms solely to save a few words.

SPECIAL CASES: Many abbreviations are desirable in tabulations and certain types of technical writing.

CAPS, PERIODS: Use capital letters and periods according to the listings in the stylebooks. For words not in the books, use the first-listed abbreviation in *Webster's New World Dictionary.*

If an abbreviation not listed in the stylebooks or the dictionary achieves widespread acceptance, use capital letters. Omit periods unless the result would spell an unrelated word.

Common Problems

Abbreviations save much space for newspapers in a year's time but editors use them only when readers will recognize them instantly. Newspapers are in the business of communicating to their readers. Saving space to the detriment of understanding is an intolerable offense.

There are many exceptions to the rules of abbreviation discussed in this section. They can be determined only by consulting a stylebook, and in each case the meaning of the abbreviation should be clear.

STATE NAMES: Although the U.S. Postal Service uses two-letter abbreviations for state names, they have been rejected for newspaper use because of the potential for confusion. *MS*, the post office abbreviation for *Mississippi*, could be mistaken for *Missouri* or the recently popularized courtesy title for a woman, *Ms.* Instead, the AP and UPI use the more familiar state abbreviations that have won general acceptance through the years.

State names are abbreviated only when they follow city names.

The names of eight states never are abbreviated by the AP and UPI, though some newspapers make exceptions:

Alaska	Iowa	Texas
Hawaii	Maine	Utah
Idaho	Ohio	

The most common mistakes are made when abbreviating *California* (*Calif.*, not *Cal.*), *Kansas* (*Kan.*, not *Kans.*), *Kentucky* (*Ky.*, not *Ken.*), *Nebraska* (*Neb.*, not *Nebr.*), *Pennsylvania* (*Pa.*, not *Penn.*) and *Wisconsin* (*Wis.*, not *Wisc.*).

The accepted state abbreviations are listed under the *state names* entry in the alphabetized listing that follows this section.

DATES: Confusion also can arise in abbreviating dates. Months are abbreviated only when followed by the day of the month in constructions such as *Sept. 13*. Five months are never abbreviated: *March, April, May, June* and *July*. These are easy to remember because they begin with March and are consecutive. Therefore, write *Nov. 6*, but *March 16*. Days of the week are never abbreviated in newspapers, except in tabular matter such as stock-market listings.

ADDRESSES: Street names also are a source of confusion. The words *street*, *avenue* and *boulevard* can be abbreviated, but only when preceded by a street name and number.

He lives at 311 Ninth St.
He rode down Ninth Street.

The same rule applies in abbreviating direction with an address. Write *311 S. Ninth St.* but *South Ninth Street*. Addresses with the direction northeast, southeast, southwest and northwest are abbreviated with periods:

He lives at 212 Westwinds Drive S.W. in Chicago.

OTHER ABBREVIATIONS: Generally, abbreviations of one- and two-word terms take periods, whereas abbreviations of terms consisting of three or more words do not. Thus, write *U.S.* and *U.N.*, but *FBI*, *CIA* and *mph*. An exception is made when an abbreviation without periods spells an unrelated word. Write *c.o.d.*, not *cod*, which is a kind of fish. Other exceptions are listed in the stylebooks, the most common of which is *TV* (no periods).

Alphabetized Listing

academic degrees   If mention of degrees is necessary to establish someone's credentials, the preferred form is to avoid an abbreviation and use instead a phrase such as: *John Jones, who has a doctorate in psychology.*

Use an apostrophe in *bachelor's degree, a master's,* and the like.

Use abbreviations such as *B.A., M.A., L.L.D.* and *Ph.D.* only when the need to identify many individuals by degree on first reference would make the preferred form cumbersome. Use these abbreviations only after a full name—never after just a last name.

When used after a full name, an academic abbreviation is set off by commas: *Daniel Moynihan, Ph.D., spoke.*

Do not precede a name with a courtesy title for an academic degree and follow it with the abbreviation for the degree in the same reference.

addresses   Use the abbreviations *Ave., Blvd.* and *St.* only with a numbered address: *1600 Pennsylvania Ave.* Spell them out and capitalize when part of a formal street name without a number: *Pennsylvania Avenue.* Lowercase and spell out when used alone or with more than one street name: *Massachusetts and Pennsylvania avenues.*

All other street designations (*alley, drive, road, terrace* and so on) are always spelled out. Capitalize them when part of a formal name without a number; lowercase when used alone or with two or more names.

Always use figures for an address number: *9 Morningside Circle.*

Spell out and capitalize *First* through *Ninth* when used as street names; use figures with two letters for *10th* and above: *7 Fifth Ave., 100 21st St.*

AFL-CIO   Acceptable in all references for the *American Federation of Labor and Congress of Industrial Organizations.*

AIDS   Acceptable on all references for *acquired immune deficiency syndrome,* sometimes written as acquired immunodeficiency syndrome.

aircraft names   Use a hyphen when changing from letters to figures; no hyphen when adding a letter after figures: *F-15, 747, 747B.*

AM   Acceptable in all references for the *amplitude modulation* system of radio transmission.

a.m., p.m.   Lowercase, with periods. Avoid the redundant *10 a.m. this morning.*

Amtrak   This acronym, drawn from the words *American travel by track,* may be used in all references to the *National Railroad Passenger Corp.* Do not use *AMTRAK.*

armed services   Do not use abbreviations *USA, USAF* and *USN.*

assistant   Do not abbreviate. Capitalize only when part of a formal title before a name: *Assistant Secretary of State Thomas M. Tracy.* Wherever practical, however, an appositional construction should be used: *Thomas M. Tracy, assistant secretary of state.*

association   Do not abbreviate. Capitalize as part of a proper name: *American Medical Association.*

attorney general, attorneys general   Never abbreviate. Capitalize only when used as a title before a name: *Attorney General Janet Reno.*

Bible   Do not abbreviate individual books of the Bible.

Citations listing the number of chapter(s) and verse(s) use this form: *Matthew 3:16, Luke 21:1-13, 1 Peter 2:1.*

brothers   Abbreviate as *Bros.* in formal company names: *Warner Bros.* For possessives: *Warner Bros.' profits.*

Christmas   Never abbreviate *Christmas* to *Xmas* or any other form.

CIA   Acceptable in all references for *Central Intelligence Agency*.

c.o.d.   Acceptable in all references for *cash on delivery* or *collect on delivery*. (The use of lowercase is an exception to the first listing in *Webster's New World Dictionary*.)

company, companies   Use *Co.* or *Cos.* when a business uses the word at the end of its proper name: *Ford Motor Co., American Broadcasting Cos.* But: *Aluminum Company of America*.

If *company* or *companies* appears alone in second reference, spell the word out.

The forms for possessives: *Ford Motor Co.'s profits, American Broadcasting Cos.' profits*.

Conrail   This acronym is acceptable in all references to *Consolidated Rail Corp.* (The corporation originally used *ConRail*, but later changed to *Conrail*.)

corporation   Abbreviate as *Corp.* when a company or government agency uses the word at the end of its name: *Gulf Oil Corp., the Federal Deposit Insurance Corp.*

Spell out and lowercase corporation whenever it stands alone.

The form for possessives: *Gulf Oil Corp.'s profits*.

courtesy titles   (*Note:* Many newspapers consider the AP style [UPI style varies] on this subject to be sexist and have chosen to treat courtesy titles for women as those for men are treated—by first and last name on first reference and last name only on second reference. For the same reason, other newspapers use courtesy titles for both men and women on second reference. Despite those increasingly common deviations, the AP policy is presented here; it is still the predominant policy at U.S. newspapers.)

In general, do not use the courtesy title *Miss, Mr., Mrs.* or *Ms.* with first and last names of the person: *Hillary Rodham Clinton, Jimmy Carter*.

Do not use *Mr.* in any reference unless it is combined with *Mrs.: Mr. and Mrs. John Smith*.

On sports wires, do not use courtesy titles in any reference unless needed to distinguish among people of the same last name.

On news wires, use courtesy titles for women on second reference, following the woman's preference. If the woman says she does not want a courtesy title, refer to her on second reference by last name only. Here are some guidelines:

MARRIED WOMEN: The preferred form on first reference is to identify a woman by her own first name and her husband's last name: *Mary Smith*. Use *Mrs.* on the first reference only if a woman requests that her husband's first name be used or her own first cannot be determined: *Mrs. John Smith*.

On second reference, use *Mrs.* unless a woman initially identified by her own first name prefers *Ms.: Pamela Harriman, Mrs. Harriman, Ms. Harriman*; or no title: *Pamela Harriman, Harriman*.

If a married woman is known by her maiden last name, precede it by *Miss* on second reference unless she prefers *Ms.: Diana Ross, Miss Ross, Ms. Ross*; or no title, *Diana Ross*.

UNMARRIED WOMEN: For women who have never been married, use *Miss, Ms.* or no title on second reference according to the woman's preferences.

For divorced women and widows, the normal practice is to use *Mrs.* or no title, if she prefers, on second reference. But, if a woman returns to the use of her maiden name, use *Miss, Ms.* or no title if she prefers it.

MARITAL STATUS: If a woman prefers *Ms.* or no title, do not include her marital status in a story unless it is clearly pertinent.

detective   Do not abbreviate.

district attorney   Do not abbreviate.

doctor   Use *Dr.* in first reference as a formal title before the name of an individual who holds a doctor of medicine degree: *Dr. Jonas Salk.*

The form *Dr.*, or *Drs.* in a plural construction, applies to all first-reference uses before a name, including direct quotations.

If appropriate in the context, *Dr.* also may be used on first reference before the names of individuals who hold other types of doctoral degrees. However, because the public frequently identifies *Dr.* only with physicians, care should be taken to assure that the individual's specialty is stated in first or second reference. The only exception would be a story in which the context left no doubt that the person was a dentist, psychologist, chemist, historian or the like.

In some instances it also is necessary to specify that an individual identified as *Dr.* is a physician. One frequent case is a story reporting on joint research by physicians, biologists and so on.

Do not use *Dr.* before the names of individuals who hold only honorary doctorates.

Do not continue the use of *Dr.* in subsequent references.

ERA   (1) Acceptable in all references to baseball's *earned run average.* (2) Acceptable on second reference for *Equal Rights Amendment.*

FBI   Acceptable in all references for *Federal Bureau of Investigation.*

FM   Acceptable in all references for the *frequency modulation* system of radio transmission.

ICBM, ICBMs   Acceptable on first reference for *intercontinental ballistic missile(s)*, but the term should be defined in the body of a story.

Avoid the redundant *ICBM missiles.*

incorporated   Abbreviate and capitalize as *Inc.* when used as part of a corporate name. It usually is not needed, but when it is used, do not set off with commas: *J.C. Penney Co. Inc. announced* . . .

IQ   Acceptable in all references for *intelligence quotient.*

junior, senior   Abbreviate as *Jr.* and *Sr.* only with full names of persons or animals. Do not precede by a comma: *Joseph P. Kennedy Jr.*

The notation *II* or *2nd* may be used if it is the individual's preference. Note, however, that *II* and *2nd* are not necessarily the equivalent of *junior*—they often are used by a grandson or nephew.

If necessary to distinguish between father and son in second reference, use the *elder Smith* or the *younger Smith.*

mount   Spell out in all uses, including the names of communities and of mountains: *Mount Clemens, Mich.; Mount Everest.*

mph   Acceptable in all references for *miles per hour* or *miles an hour.*

No.   Use as the abbreviation for *number* in conjunction with a figure to indicate position or rank: *No. 1 man, No. 3 choice.*

Do not use in street addresses, with this exception: *No. 10 Downing St.*, the residence of Britain's prime minister.

Do not use in the names of schools: *Public School 19.*

point   Do not abbreviate. Capitalize as part of a proper name: *Point Pleasant.*

saint   Abbreviate as *St.* in the names of saints, cities and other places: *St. Jude; St. Paul, Minn.; St. John's, Newfoundland; St. Lawrence Seaway.*

Sault Ste. Marie, Mich.; Sault Ste. Marie, Ontario   The abbreviation is *Ste.* instead of *St.* because the full name is *Sault Sainte Marie.*

state names   Follow these guidelines:

STANDING ALONE: Spell out the names of the 50 U.S. states when they stand alone in textual material. Any state name may be condensed, however, to fit typographical requirements for tabular materials.

EIGHT NOT ABBREVIATED: The names of eight states are never abbreviated in datelines or text: *Alaska, Hawaii, Idaho, Iowa, Maine, Ohio, Texas* and *Utah.*

ABBREVIATIONS REQUIRED: Use the following state abbreviations in these circumstances:

- In conjunction with the name of a city, town, village or military base in most datelines.
- In conjunction with the name of a city, county, town, village or military base in text (see examples in the punctuation that follows).
- In short-term listings of party affiliation: *D-Ala., R-Mont.*

Ala.	Md.	N.D.
Ariz.	Mass.	Okla.
Ark.	Mich.	Ore.
Calif.	Minn.	Pa.
Colo.	Miss.	R.I.
Conn.	Mo.	S.C.
Del.	Mont.	S.D.
Fla.	Neb.	Tenn.
Ga.	Nev.	Vt.
Ill.	N.H.	Va.
Ind.	N.J.	Wash.
Kan.	N.M.	W.Va.
Ky.	N.Y.	Wis.
La.	N.C.	Wyo.

TV   Acceptable as an adjective or in such constructions as *cable TV.* But do not normally use as a noun unless part of a quotation.

UFO, UFOs   Acceptable in all references for *unidentified flying objects(s).*

U.N.   Used as an adjective, but not as a noun, for *United Nations.*

U.S.   Used as an adjective, but not as a noun, for *United States.*

Punctuation and Hyphenation

Think of punctuation and hyphenation as a courtesy to your readers, designed to help them understand a story.

Inevitably, a mandate of this scope involves gray areas. For this reason, the punctuation entries in the AP and UPI stylebooks refer to guidelines rather than rules. Guidelines should not be treated casually, however.

Common Problems

PERIODS: In school you may have been taught that there are times when the period is placed outside quotation marks at the end of a sentence, as in the following example:

> Stephen Crane wrote "The Red Badge of Courage".

In newspapers, however, the period always goes inside the quotation marks:

> Stephen Crane wrote "The Red Badge of Courage." [*Note:* AP style is to designate book titles by quotation marks, but this textbook uses italics, following the style some newspapers have adopted.]

However, a period can be placed inside or outside a closing parenthesis, depending on the usage. If the parenthetical phrase is a complete sentence, the period goes inside the parenthesis. If it is not a complete sentence, it goes outside:

> Barbara bought all the dogs at the kennel (except the German shepherd).
> Barbara bought all the dogs at the kennel. (The total cost was $239.)

COMMAS: Like periods, commas always are placed inside quotation marks.

Newspapers often omit commas before conjunctions in series of items unless the omission confuses the meaning:

> The school's colors are black, gold and white.
> I had orange juice, toast, and ham and eggs for breakfast.

Newspaper style also calls for the elimination of commas between words that relate closely: *Martin Luther King Jr.*, not *Martin Luther King, Jr.*

Commas are used with appositives, adjacent nouns with the same relationship to the rest of the sentence, even before a conjunction:

> John Smith, a freshman, Ralph Jones, a sophomore, and Bill Keith, a senior, were elected.
> Milwaukee, Wis., and Melbourne, Fla., were selected as sites for the tournament.

When referring to dates, do not use commas when only the month and year are mentioned:

> President Clinton was inaugurated in January 1993 on the steps of the Capitol.

When the month and year are accompanied by an exact date, however, commas are used to set off the year.

> President Clinton was inaugurated on Jan. 20, 1993, on the steps of the Capitol.

Notice that the comma is needed after the year as well as before.

SEMICOLONS: Semicolons are used to indicate greater separation of thought and information than commas convey, but less than the separation a period implies:

> Survivors include a son, James Jones of Chicago; two sisters, Jane Thomson of Chicago and Jill Revel of Milwaukee; and several grandchildren.

Note that the semicolon is used before the final *and* in such a series.

The semicolon is rarely used in newspapers to link independent clauses when a coordinating conjunction is missing:

> His plane arrived at 10 p.m.; it was due at 9 a.m.

Despite the infrequent use of such a construction, it is permissible.

DASHES: To indicate an abrupt change, dashes are used:

We will win the game—if I can play.

They also can be used to set off a series within a phrase:

The flowers—white, yellow and red—adorned the flower box below the window.

Dashes should be used sparingly, though. When used to excess they make for difficult reading.

HYPHENS: The abused or forgotten punctuation mark in almost all writing in this country is the hyphen. Unfortunately, newspapers are among the worst offenders. Hyphens are plentiful on sports pages:

The Tigers won 14-7.

Too often, however, newspaper reporters and editors omit the necessary hyphen when two or more words function as a compound adjective:

He is an out-of-state student.

A 30-yard field goal led to the last-minute victory.

Omit the hyphen, however, in compound modifiers involving the adverb *very* or adverbs ending in *-ly: a very cold morning, an easily remembered rule*.

Increasingly, hyphens are disappearing when two words are joined to function as a noun: *makeup*, not *make-up; layout*, not *lay-out*.

Suspensive hyphenation also creates trouble for reporters, who frequently omit the hyphens. Write *a 10- to 30-year prison term*, not *a 10 to 30 year prison term* or *a 10 to 30-year prison term*. In this usage the writer refers to a 10-year prison term and a 30-year prison term. By omitting the first *year*, space is saved, yet the meaning is clear. Completion of the phrase is suspended until after the second numeral, which accounts for the term *suspensive hyphenation*.

APOSTROPHES: Apostrophes are used most often in possessives. They also are used to indicate omitted letters (*I've, rock 'n' roll, ne'er-do-well*) or omitted figures (*Spirit of '76, class of '62, the '20s*). They also are used for plurals of a single letter: *your p's and q's, the Oakland A's*.

The apostrophe is not used for plurals of numerals or multiple-letter combinations: *1920s, ABCs*.

In newspaper usage, the possessive of plural nouns and singular proper names ending with the letter *s* is formed with an apostrophe: *the girls' books, the horses' stables, Dickens' novels, Texas' schools*. The possessive of singular common nouns ending with *s* is formed with *'s*, unless the next word begins with *s: hostess's invitation, hostess' story*.

Generally, the possessive of singular nouns ending with *s* sounds such as *ce, x* and *z* should be followed by *'s: justice's verdict, Marx's theories, Butz's jokes*. There are exceptions in some cases when words not ending in *s* have an *s* sound and are followed by a word that begins with *s*. Thus, you should write *appearance' sake*, or *conscience' sake*, but you must add the *'s* in the case of *appearance's cost* or *conscience's voice*. A common error is to use the apostrophe in the possessive *its*. *It's* is the contraction of *it is; its* is the possessive form of *it*.

QUESTION MARKS AND EXCLAMATION POINTS: Question marks often are placed improperly in relation to quotation marks. The meaning dictates how a question mark is used:

Who wrote "Gone with the Wind"? [*Note:* AP style is to designate book titles by quotation marks, but this textbook uses italics, following the style some newspapers have adopted.]

He asked, "How long will it take?"

In the first example, the entire sentence, not just the quoted material, is the question posed, so the question mark belongs outside the quotation marks. In the second example, only the quoted portion of the sentence is a question, so the question mark is placed inside the quotation marks.

The question mark supersedes the comma normally used when supplying attribution for a quotation:

"Who is there?" she asked.

Similarly, an exclamation point replaces the comma in attributing a direct quotation:

"Halt!" the guard shouted.

Alphabetized Listing

ampersand (&)   Use the ampersand when it is part of a company's formal name: *Baltimore & Ohio Railroad, Newport News Shipbuilding & Dry Dock Co.*

The ampersand should not otherwise be used in place of *and.*

all-   Use a hyphen:

all-around (*not* all-round) all-out
all-clear   all-star

anti-   Hyphenate all except the following words, which have specific meanings of their own:

antibiotic	antiknock	antiphony
antibody	antimatter	antiseptic
anticlimax	antimony	antiserum
antidote	antiparticle*	antithesis
antifreeze	antipasto	antitoxin
antigen	antiperspirant	antitrust
antihistamine	antiphon	antitussive

*And similar terms in physics such as *antiproton.*

This approach has been adopted in the interests of readability and easily remembered consistency.

apostrophe (')   Follow these guidelines:

POSSESSIVES: See the *possessives* entry.

OMITTED LETTERS: *I've, it's, don't, rock 'n' roll. 'Tis the season to be jolly. He is a ne'er-do-well.*

OMITTED FIGURES: *The class of '62. The Spirit of '76. The '20s.*

PLURALS OF A SINGLE LETTER: *Mind your p's and q's. He learned the three R's and brought home a report card with four A's and two B's. The Oakland A's won the pennant.*

DO NOT USE: For plurals of numerals or multiple-letter combinations.

by In general, no hyphen. Some examples:

byline   byproduct
bypass   bystreet

By-election is an exception.

co- Retain the hyphen when forming nouns, adjectives and verbs that indicate occupation or status:

co-author   co-owner   co-signer
co-chairman   co-partner   co-star
co-defendant co-pilot   co-worker
co-host   co-respondent (in a divorce suit)

(Several are exceptions to *Webster's New World Dictionary* in the interests of consistency.) Use no hyphen in other combinations:

coed   coexist   cooperative
coeducation   coexistence   coordinate
coequal   cooperate   coordination

Cooperate, coordinate and related words are exceptions to the rule that a hyphen is used if a prefix ends in a vowel and the word that follows begins with the same vowel.

colon The most frequent use of a colon is at the end of a sentence to introduce lists, tabulations, texts and the like.

Capitalize the first word after a colon only if it is a proper noun or the start of a complete sentence: *He promised this: The company will make good all the losses.* But: *There were three considerations: expense, time and feasibility.*

INTRODUCING QUOTATIONS: Use a comma to introduce a direct quotation of one sentence that remains within a paragraph. Use a colon to introduce longer quotations within a paragraph and to end all paragraphs that introduce a paragraph of quoted material.

PLACEMENT WITH QUOTATION MARKS: Colons go outside quotation marks unless they are part of the quotation itself.

comma The following guidelines treat some of the most frequent questions about the use of commas. Additional guidelines on specialized uses are provided in separate entries.

For more detailed guidance, consult "The Comma" and "Misused and Unnecessary Commas" in the Guide to Punctuation section at the back of *Webster's New World Dictionary*.

IN A SERIES: Use commas to separate elements in a series, but do not put a comma before the conjunction in a simple series: *The flag is red, white and blue. He would nominate Tom, Dick or Harry.*

Put a comma before the concluding conjunction in a series, however, if an integral element of the series requires a conjunction: *I had orange juice, toast, and ham and eggs for breakfast.*

Use a comma also before the concluding conjunction in a complex series of phrases: *The main points to consider are whether the athletes are skillful enough to compete, whether they have the stamina to endure the training, and whether they have the proper mental attitude.*

WITH EQUAL ADJECTIVE: Use commas to separate a series of adjectives equal in rank. If the commas could be replaced by the word *and* without changing the sense, the adjectives are equal: *a thoughtful, precise manner; a dark, dangerous street.*

Use no comma when the last adjective before a noun outranks its predecessors because it is an integral element of a noun phrase, which is the equivalent of a single noun: *a cheap fur coat* (the noun phrase is *fur coat*); *the old oaken bucket; a new, blue spring bonnet.*

WITH INTRODUCTORY CLAUSES AND PHRASES: A comma normally is used to separate an introductory clause or phrase from a main clause: *When he had tired of the mad pace of New York, he moved to Dubuque.*

The comma may be omitted after short introductory phrases if no ambiguity would result: *During the night he heard many noises.*

But use the comma if its omission would slow comprehension: *On the street below, the curious gathered.*

WITH CONJUNCTIONS: When a conjunction such as *and, but* or *for* links two clauses that could stand alone as separate sentences, use a comma before the conjunction in most cases: *She was glad she had looked, for a man was approaching the house.*

As a rule of thumb, use a comma if the subject of each clause is expressly stated: *We are visiting Washington, and we also plan a side trip to Williamsburg. We visited Washington, and our senator greeted us personally.* But do not use a comma when the subject of the two clauses is the same and is not repeated in the second: *We are visiting Washington and plan to see the White House.*

The comma may be dropped if two clauses with expressly stated subjects are short. In general, however, favor use of a comma unless a particular literary effect is desired or it would distort the sense of a sentence.

INTRODUCING DIRECT QUOTES: Use a comma to introduce a complete, one-sentence quotation within a paragraph: *Wallace said, "She spent six months in Argentina and came back speaking English with a Spanish accent."* But use a colon to introduce quotations of more than one sentence.

Do not use a comma at the start of an indirect or partial quotation: *He said his victory put him "firmly on the road to a first-ballot nomination."*

BEFORE ATTRIBUTION: Use a comma instead of a period at the end of a quote that is followed by attribution: *"Rub my shoulders," Miss Cawley suggested.*

Do not use a comma, however, if the quoted statement ends with a question mark or exclamation point: *"Why should I?" he asked.*

WITH HOMETOWNS AND AGES: Use a comma to set off an individual's hometown when it is placed in apposition to a name: *Mary Richards, Minneapolis, and Maude Findlay, Tuckahoe, N.Y., were there.* However, the use of the word *of* without a comma between the individual's name and the city name generally is preferable: *Mary Richards of Minneapolis and Maude Findlay of Tuckahoe, N.Y., were there.*

If an individual's age is used, set it off by commas: *Maude Findlay, 48, Tuckahoe, N.Y., was present.* The use of the word *of* eliminates the need for a comma after the hometown if a state name is not needed: *Mary Richards, 36, of Minneapolis and Maude Findlay, 48, of Tuckahoe, N.Y., attended the party.*

IN LARGE FIGURES: Use a comma for most figures higher than 999. The major exceptions are: street addresses (*1234 Main St.*), broadcast frequencies (*1460 kilohertz*), room numbers, serial numbers, telephone numbers, and years (*1976*).

PLACEMENT WITH QUOTES: Commas always go inside quotation marks.

dash   Follow these guidelines:

ABRUPT CHANGE: Use dashes to denote an abrupt change in thought in a sentence or an emphatic pause: *We will fly to Paris in June—if I get a raise. Smith offered a plan—it was unprecedented—to raise revenues.*

SERIES WITHIN A PHRASE: When a phrase that otherwise would be set off by commas contains a series of words that must be separated by commas, use dashes to set off the full phrase: *He listed the qualities—intelligence, charm, beauty, independence—that he liked in women.*

ATTRIBUTION: Use a dash before an author's or composer's name at the end of a quotation: *"Who steals my purse steals trash."—Shakespeare.*

IN DATELINES:

NEW YORK (UPI)—The city is broke.

IN LISTS: Dashes should be used to introduce individual sections of a list. Capitalize the first word following the dash. Use periods, not semicolons, at the end of each section. Example:

Jones gave the following reasons:
—He never ordered the package.
—If he did, it didn't come.
—If it did, he sent it back.

WITH SPACES: Put a space on both sides of a dash in all uses except the start of a paragraph and sports agate summaries.

ellipsis (. . .)   In general, treat an ellipsis as a three-letter word, constructed with three periods and two spaces, as shown here.

Use an ellipsis to indicate the deletion of one or more words in condensing quotes, texts and documents. Be especially careful to avoid deletions that would distort the meaning.

ex-   Use no hyphen for words that use *ex-* in the sense of *out of*:

excommunicate   expropriate

Hyphenate when using *ex-* in the sense of *former*:

ex-convict   ex-president

Do not capitalize *ex-* when attached to a formal title before a name: *ex-President Carter.* The prefix modifies the entire term: *ex-New York Gov. Mario Cuomo*; not *New York ex Gov.*

Usually *former* is better.

exclamation point (!)   Follow these guidelines:

EMPHATIC EXPRESSIONS: Use the mark to express a high degree of surprise, incredulity or other strong emotion.

AVOID OVERUSE: Use a comma after mild interjections. End mildly exclamatory sentences with a period.

PLACEMENT WITH QUOTES: Place the mark inside quotation marks when it is part of the quoted material: *"How wonderful!" he exclaimed. "Never!" she shouted.*

Place the mark outside quotation marks when it is not part of the quoted material: *I hated reading Spenser's "Faerie Queene"!* [*Note:* AP style is to designate book titles by quotation marks, but this textbook uses italics, following the style some newspapers have adopted.]

extra-   Do not use a hyphen when *extra-* means *outside of* unless the prefix is followed by a word beginning with *a* or a capitalized word:

extralegal	extraterrestrial
extramarital	extraterritorial

But:

extra-alimentary	extra-Britannic

Follow *extra-* with a hyphen when it is part of a compound modifier describing a condition beyond the usual size, extent or degree:

extra-base hit	extra-large book
extra-dry drink	extra-mild taste

fore-   In general, no hyphen. Some examples:

forebrain	foregoing
forefather	foretooth

There are three nautical exceptions, based on long-standing practice:

fore-topgallant	fore-topsail
fore-topmast	

full-   Hyphenate when used to form compound modifiers:

full-dress	full-page
full-fledged	full-scale
full-length	

See *Webster's New World Dictionary* for the spelling of other combinations.
great-   Hyphenate *great-grandfather, great-great-grandmother* and so on.

Use *great grandfather* only if the intended meaning is that the grandfather was a great man.

hyphen   Hyphens are joiners. Use them to avoid ambiguity or to form a single idea from two or more words.

Some guidelines:

AVOID AMBIGUITY: Use a hyphen whenever ambiguity would result if it were omitted: *The president will speak to small-business men.* (*Businessmen* normally is one word. But *The president will speak to small businessmen* is unclear.)

COMPOUND MODIFIERS: When a compound modifier—two or more words that express a single concept—precedes a noun, use hyphens to link all the words in the compound except the adverb *very* and all adverbs that end in *ly: a first-quarter touchdown, a bluish-green dress, a full-time job, a well-known man, a better-qualified woman, a know-it-all attitude, a very good time, an easily remembered rule.*

Many combinations that are hyphenated before a noun are not hyphenated when they occur after a noun: *The team scored in the first quarter. The dress, a bluish green, was attractive on her. She works full time. His attitude suggested that he knew it all.*

But when a modifier that would be hyphenated before a noun occurs instead after a form of the verb *to be,* the hyphen usually must be retained to avoid confusion: *The man is well-known. The woman is quick-witted. The children are soft-spoken. The play is second-rate.*

The principle of using a hyphen to avoid confusion explains why no hyphen is required with *very* and *ly* words. Readers can expect them to modify the word that follows. But if a combination such as *little-known man* were not hyphenated, the reader could logically be expecting *little* to be followed by a noun, as in *little man*. Instead, the reader encountering *little known* would have to back up mentally and make the compound connection on his or her own.

TWO-THOUGHT COMPOUNDS: *serio-comic, socio-economic.*

COMPOUND PROPER NOUNS AND ADJECTIVES: Use a hyphen to designate dual heritage: *Italian-American, Mexican-American.*

No hyphen, however, for *French Canadian* or *Latin American.*

AVOID DUPLICATED VOWELS, TRIPLED CONSONANTS: Examples:

anti-intellectual   pre-empt

shell-like

WITH NUMERALS: Use a hyphen to separate figures in betting odds, ratios, scores, some fractions and some election returns. See examples in entries under these headings in the section on numerals.

When large numbers must be spelled out, use a hyphen to connect a word ending in *y* to another word: *twenty-one, fifty-five* and so on.

SUSPENSIVE HYPHENATION: The form: *He received a 10- to 20-year sentence in prison.*

in-   No hyphen when *in-* means "not":

inaccurate

insufferable

Often solid in other cases:

inbound   infighting

indoor   inpatient (n., adj.)

infield

A few combinations take a hyphen, however:

in-depth   in-house

in-group   in-law

Follow *Webster's New World* when in doubt.

-in   Precede with a hyphen:

break-in   walk-in

cave-in   write-in

parentheses   In general, be sparing with parentheses.

Parentheses are jarring to the reader. Because they do not appear on some news service printers, there is also the danger that material inside them may be misinterpreted.

The temptation to use parentheses is a clue that a sentence is becoming contorted. Try to write it another way. If a sentence must contain incidental material, then commas or two dashes are frequently more effective. Use these alternatives whenever possible.

There are occasions, however, when parentheses are the only effective means of inserting necessary background or reference information. The stylebooks offer guidelines.

periods   Follow these guidelines:

END OF DECLARATIVE SENTENCE: *The stylebook is finished.*

END OF A MILDLY IMPERATIVE SENTENCE: *Shut the door.*

Use an exclamation point if greater emphasis is desired: *Be careful!*

END OF SOME RHETORICAL QUESTIONS: A period is preferable if a statement is more a suggestion than a question: *Why don't we go.*

END OF AN INDIRECT QUESTION: He asked what the score was.

INITIALS: *John F. Kennedy, T.S. Eliot* (no space between *T.* and *S.*, to prevent them from being placed on two lines in typesetting).

Abbreviations using only the initials of a name do not take periods: *JFK, LBJ.*

ENUMERATIONS: After numbers or letters in enumerating elements of a summary: *1. Wash the car. 2. Clean the basement.* Or: *A. Punctuate properly. B. Write simply.*

possessives   Follow these guidelines:

PLURAL NOUNS NOT ENDING IN *s*: Add *'s: the alumni's contributions, women's rights.*

PLURAL NOUNS ENDING IN *s*: Add only an apostrophe: *the churches' needs, the girls' toys, the horses' food, the ships' wake, states' rights, the VIPs' entrance.*

NOUNS PLURAL IN FORM, SINGULAR IN MEANING: Add only an apostrophe: *mathematics' rules, measles' effects.* (But see INANIMATE OBJECTS below.)

Apply the same principle when a plural word occurs in the formal name of a singular entity: *General Motors' profits, the United States' wealth.*

NOUNS THE SAME IN SINGULAR AND PLURAL: Treat them the same as plurals, even if the meaning is singular: *one corps' location, the two deer's tracks, the lone moose's antlers.*

SINGULAR NOUNS NOT ENDING IN *s*: Add *'s: the church's needs, the girl's toys, the horse's food, the ship's route, the VIP's seat.*

Some style guides say that singular nouns ending in s sounds such as *ce, x,* and *z* may take either the apostrophe alone or *'s.* See SPECIAL EXPRESSIONS below, but otherwise, for consistency and ease in remembering a rule, always use *'s* if the word does not end in the letter *s: Butz's policies, the fox's den, the justice's verdict, Marx's theories, the prince's life, Xerox's profits.*

SINGULAR COMMON NOUNS ENDING IN *s*: Add *'s* unless the next word begins with *s: the hostess's invitation, the hostess' seat; the witness's answer, the witness' story.*

SINGULAR PROPER NAMES ENDING IN *s*: Use only an apostrophe: *Achilles' heel, Agnes' book, Ceres' rites, Descartes' theories, Dickens' novels, Euripides' dramas, Hercules' labors, Jesus' life, Jules' seat, Kansas' schools, Moses' law, Socrates' life, Tennessee Williams' plays, Xerxes' armies.*

SPECIAL EXPRESSIONS: The following exceptions to the general rule for words not ending in s apply to words that end in an s sound and are followed by a word that begins with s: *for appearance' sake, for conscience' sake, for goodness' sake.* Use *'s* otherwise: *the appearance's cost, my conscience's voice.*

PRONOUNS: Personal, interrogative and relative pronouns have separate forms for the possessive. None involves an apostrophe: *mine, ours, your, yours, his, hers, its, theirs, whose.*

Caution: If you are using an apostrophe with a pronoun, always doublecheck to be sure that the meaning calls for a contraction; *you're, it's, there's, who's.*

Follow the rules listed above in forming the possessive of other pronouns: *another's idea, others' plans, someone's guess.*

COMPOUND WORDS: Applying the rules above, add an apostrophe or *'s* to the word closest to the object possessed: *the major general's decision, the major generals' decisions, the attorney general's request, the attorneys general's request.*

Also: *anyone else's attitude, John Adams Jr.'s father, Benjamin Franklin of Pennsylvania's motion.* Whenever practical, however, recast the phrase to avoid ambiguity: *the motion by Benjamin Franklin of Pennsylvania.*

JOINT POSSESSION, INDIVIDUAL POSSESSION: Use a possessive form after only the last word if ownership is joint: *Fred and Sylvia's apartment, Fred and Sylvia's stocks.*

Use a possessive form after both words if the objects are individually owned: *Fred's and Sylvia's books.*

DESCRIPTIVE PHRASES: Do not add an apostrophe to a word ending in *s* when it is used primarily in a descriptive sense: *citizens band radio, a Cincinnati Reds infielder, a teachers collage, a Teamsters request, a writers guide.*

Memory Aid: The apostrophe usually is not used if *for* or *by* rather than *of* would be appropriate in the longer form: *a radio band for citizens, a college for teachers, a guide for writers, a request by the Teamsters.*

An *'s* is required, however, when a term involves a plural word that does not end in *s: a children's hospital, a people's republic , the Young Men's Christian Association.*

DESCRIPTIVE NAMES: Some governmental, corporate and institutional organizations with a descriptive word in their names use an apostrophe; some do not. Follow the user's practice: *Actors Equity, Diners Club, the Ladies' Home Journal, the National Governors' Conference, the Veterans Administration.* See the stylebook entries for these and similar names frequently in the news.

QUASI POSSESSIVES: Follow the rules above in composing the possessive form of words that occur in such phrases as *a day's pay, two weeks' vacation, three days' work, your money's worth.*

Frequently, however, a hyphenated form is clearer; *a two-week vacation, a three-day job.*

DOUBLE POSSESSIVE: Two conditions must apply for a double possessive—a phrase such as *a friend of John's*—to occur: (1) The word after *of* must refer to an animate object, and (2) the word before *of* must involve only a portion of the animate object's possessions.

Otherwise, do not use the possessive form on the word after of: *The friends of John Adams mourned his death.* (All the friends were involved.). *He is a friend of the college.* (Not college's, because college is inanimate.)

MEMORY AID: This construction occurs more often, and quite naturally, with the possessive forms of personal pronouns. *He is a friend of mine.*

INANIMATE OBJECTS: There is no blanket rule against creating a possessive form for an inanimate object, particularly if the object is treated in a personified sense. See some of the earlier examples, and note these: *death's call, the wind's murmur.*

In general, however, avoid excessive personalization of inanimate objects, and give preference to an *of* construction when it fits the makeup of the sentence. For example, the earlier references to *mathematics' rules* and *measles' effects* would better be phrased: *the rules of mathematics, the effects of measles.*

post-   Follow *Webster's New World Dictionary*. Hyphenate if not listed there. Some words without a hyphen:

postdate	postgraduate	postscript
postdoctoral	postnuptial	postwar
postelection	postoperative	

Some words that use a hyphen:

post-bellum   post-mortem

prefixes   See separate listings for commonly used prefixes.
Three rules are constant, although they yield some exceptions to first-listed spellings in *Webster's New World Dictionary*.

- Except for *cooperate* and *coordinate*, use a hyphen if the prefix ends in a vowel and the word that follows begins with the same vowel.
- Use a hyphen if the word that follows is capitalized.
- Use a hyphen to join doubled prefixes: *sub-subparagraph*.

pro-   Use a hyphen when coining words that denote support for something. Some examples:

pro-business	pro-peace
pro-labor	pro-war

No hyphen when *pro* is used in other senses:

produce

pronoun

profile

question mark   Follow these guidelines:

END OF A DIRECT QUESTION: *Who started the riot?*
Did he ask who started the riot? (The sentence as a whole is a direct question despite the indirect question at the end.)
You started the riot? (A question in the form of a declarative statement.)
INTERPOLATED QUESTION: *You told me—Did I hear you correctly?—that you started the riot.*
MULTIPLE QUESTIONS: Use a single question mark at the end of the full sentence:
Did you hear him say, "What right have you to ask about the riot?"
Did he plan the riot, employ assistants and give the signal to begin?
Or, to cause full stops and throw emphasis on each element, break into separate sentences: *Did he plan the riot? Employ assistants? Give the signal to begin?*
CAUTION: Do not use question marks to indicate the end of indirect questions:
He asked who started the riot. To ask why the riot started is unnecessary. I want to know what the cause of the riot was. How foolish it is to ask what caused the riot.
QUESTION-AND-ANSWER FORMAT: Do not use quotation marks. Paragraph each speaker's words:
Q. *Where did you keep it?*
A. *In a little tin box.*

PLACEMENT WITH QUOTATION MARKS: Inside or outside, depending on the meaning:

Who wrote "Gone with the Wind"? [*Note:* AP style is to designate book titles by quotation marks, but this textbook uses italics, following the style some newspapers have adopted.]

He asked, "How long will it take?"

MISCELLANEOUS: The question mark supersedes the comma that normally is used when supplying attribution for a quotation: *"Who is there?" she asked.*

quotation marks   The basic guidelines for open-quote marks (") and close-quote marks ("):

FOR DIRECT QUOTATIONS: To surround the exact words of a speaker or writer when reported in a story:

"I have no intention of staying," he replied.

"I do not object," he said, "to the tenor of the report."

Franklin said, "A penny saved is a penny earned."

A speculator said the practice is "too conservative for inflationary times."

RUNNING QUOTATIONS: If a full paragraph of quoted material is followed by a paragraph that continues the quotation, do not put close-quote marks at the end of the first paragraph. Do, however, put open-quote marks at the start of the second paragraph. Continue in this fashion for any succeeding paragraphs, using close-quote marks only at the end of the quoted material.

If a paragraph does not start with quotation marks but ends with a quotation that is continued in the next paragraph, do not use close-quote marks at the end of the introductory paragraph if the quoted material constitutes a full sentence. Use close-quote marks, however, if the quoted material does not constitute a full sentence.

DIALOGUE OR CONVERSATION: Each person's words, no matter how brief, are placed in a separate paragraph with quotation marks at the beginning and the end of each person's speech:

"Will you go?"

"Yes."

"When?"

"Thursday."

NOT IN Q-AND-A: Quotation marks are not required in formats that identify questions and answers by *Q.* and *A.*

NOT IN TEXTS: Quotation marks are not required in full texts, condensed texts or textual excerpts.

IRONY: Put quotation marks around a word or words used in an ironical sense: *The "debate" turned into a free-for-all.*

UNFAMILIAR TERMS: A word or words being introduced to readers may be placed in quotation marks on first reference:

Broadcast frequencies are measured in "kilohertz."

Do not put subsequent references to *kilohertz* in quotation marks.

AVOID UNNECESSARY FRAGMENTS: Do not use quotation marks to report a few ordinary words that a speaker or writer has used:

Wrong: *The senator said he would "go home to Michigan" if he lost the election.*

Right: *The senator said he would go home to Michigan if he lost the election.*

PARTIAL QUOTES: When a partial quote is used, do not put quotation marks around words that the speaker could not have used.

Suppose the individual said, *"I am horrified at your slovenly manners."*

Wrong: *She said she "was horrified at their slovenly manners."*
Right: *She said she was horrified at their "slovenly manners."*
Better when practical: Use the full quote.

QUOTES WITHIN QUOTES: Alternate between double quotation marks ("or") and single marks ('or'):

She said, *"I quote from his letter, 'I agree with Kipling that "the female of the species is more deadly than the male," but the phenomenon is not an unchangeable law of nature,' a remark he did not explain."*

Use three marks together if two quoted elements end at the same time: *She said, "He told me, 'I love you.'"*

PLACEMENT WITH OTHER PUNCTUATION: Follow these long-established printers' rules:

- The period and the comma always go within the quotation marks.
- The dash, the semicolon, the question mark and the exclamation point go within the quotation marks when they apply to the quoted matter only. They go outside when they apply to the whole sentence.

re- The rules in *prefixes* apply. The following examples of exceptions to first-listed spellings in *Webster's New World Dictionary* are based on the general rule that a hyphen is used if a prefix ends in a vowel and the word that follows begins with the same vowel:

re-elect	re-enlist
re-election	re-enter
re-emerge	re-entry
re-employ	re-equip
re-enact	re-establish
re-engage	re-examine

For many other words, the sense is the governing factor:

recover (regain)	resign (quit)	reform (improve)
re-cover (cover again)	re-sign (sign again)	re-form (form again)

Otherwise, follow *Webster's New World Dictionary*. Use a hyphen for words not listed there unless the hyphen would distort the sense.

semicolon In general, use the semicolon to indicate a greater separation of thought and information than a comma can convey but less than the separation that a period implies. The stylebooks offer guidelines.

suffixes See separate listings for commonly used suffixes.

Follow *Webster's New World Dictionary* for words not in this book.

If a word combination is not listed in *Webster's New World Dictionary*, use two words for the verb form; hyphenate any noun or adjective forms.

suspensive hyphenation The form: *The 5- and 6-year-olds attend morning classes.*

Numerals

A *numeral* is a figure, letter, word or group of words expressing a number.

Roman numerals use the letters *I, V, X, L, C, D* and *M*. Use Roman numerals for wars and to show personal sequence for animals and people: *World War II, Native Dancer II, King George VI, Pope John Paul II.*

Arabic numerals use the figures *1, 2, 3, 4, 5, 6, 7, 8, 9* and *0*. Use Arabic forms unless Roman numerals are specifically required.

The figures *1, 2, 10, 101*, etc. and the corresponding words—*one, two, ten, one hundred one*, etc.—are called *cardinal numbers*. The term *ordinal number* applies to *1st, 2nd, 10th, 101st, first, second, tenth, one hundred first*, etc.

Follow these guidelines in using numerals:

LARGE NUMBERS: When large numbers must be spelled out, use a hyphen to connect a word ending in *y* to another word; do not use commas between other separate words that are part of one number: *twenty; thirty; twenty-one; thirty-one; one hundred forty-three; one thousand one hundred fifty-five; one million two hundred seventy-six thousand five hundred eighty-seven.*

SENTENCE START: Spell out a numeral at the beginning of a sentence. If necessary, recast the sentence. There is one exception—a numeral that identifies a calendar year.

Wrong: *993 freshmen entered the college last year.*

Right: *Last year 993 freshmen entered the college.*

Right: *1976 was a very good year.*

CASUAL USES: Spell out casual expressions:

A thousand times no! Thanks a million. He walked a quarter of a mile.

PROPER NAMES: use words or numerals according to an organization's practice: *Twentieth Century Fund, Big Ten.*

FIGURES OR WORDS? For ordinals:

- Spell out *first* through *ninth* when they indicate sequence in time or location—*first base, the First Amendment, he was first in line.* Starting with *10th*, use figures.
- Use *1st, 2nd, 3rd, 4th*, etc. when the sequence has been assigned in forming names. The principal examples are geographic, military and political designations such as *1st Ward, 7th Fleet* and *1st Sgt.*

OTHER USES: For uses not covered by these listings: Spell out whole numbers below 10, use figures for 10 and above. Typical examples: *The woman has three sons and two daughters. He has a fleet of 10 station wagons and two buses.*

IN A SERIES: Apply the appropriate guidelines: *They had 10 dogs, six cats and 97 hamsters. They had four four-room houses, 10 three-room houses and 12 10-room houses.*

Common Problems

Whether a numeral is written out or shown in figures usually depends on usage. Because of that, reporters frequently are confused about which form is correct.

THE GENERAL RULE: Figures are used in address numbers, ages, dates, highway designations, monetary units, percentages, speeds, sports, temperatures and times. They also are used to identify aircraft and weapons by model number and following the abbreviation *No.*, as in *No. 1 man.*

EXCEPTIONS: Casual references to temperatures, other than actual thermometer readings, are written out:

The temperature at 9 p.m. was 8 degrees, a drop of four degrees since noon.

Casual numbers are written out when the numbers one through nine are used infrequently in a story:

The baker made eight pies last night.

The school will accept only three more students.

Alphabetized Listing

act numbers   Use Arabic figures and capitalize *act*: *Act 1*; *Act 2, Scene 2*. But: *the first act, the second act.*

addresses   Always use figures for an address number: *9 Morningside Circle.*

Spell out and capitalize *First* through *Ninth* when used as street names; use figures with two letters for *10th* and above: *7 Fifth Ave., 100 21st St.*

ages   Always use figures. When the context does not require *years* or *years old*, the figure is presumed to be years.

aircraft names   Use a hyphen when changing from letters to figures; no hyphen when adding a letter after figures.

Some examples for aircraft often in the news: *B-1, BAC-111, C-5A, DC-10, FH-227, F-4, Phantom II, F-86 Sabre, L-1011, MiG-21, Tu-144, 727-100C, 747, 747B, VC-10.*

amendments to the Constitution   Use *First Amendment, 10th Amendment,* and so on.

Colloquial references to the Fifth Amendment's protection against self-incrimination are best avoided, but where appropriate: *He took the Fifth seven times.*

Arabic numerals   The numerical figures *1, 2, 3, 4, 5, 6, 7, 8, 9, 10.*

In general, use Arabic forms unless denoting the sequence of wars or establishing a personal sequence for people and animals.

betting odds   Use figures and a hyphen: *The odds were 5-4. He won despite 3-2 odds against him.*

The word *to* seldom is necessary, but when it appears it should be used with hyphens in all constructions: *3-to-2 odds, odds of 3-to-2, the odds were 3-to-2.*

Celsius   Use this term rather than *centigrade* for the temperature scale that is part of the metric system.

When giving a Celsius temperature, use these forms: *40 degrees Celsius* or *40° C* (note the space and no period after the capital C) if degrees and Celsius are clear from the context.

cents   Spell out the word *cents* and lowercase, using numerals for amounts less than a dollar: *5 cents, 12 cents.* Use the *$* sign and decimal system for larger amounts: *$1.01, $2.50.*

Numerals alone, with or without a decimal point as appropriate, may be used in tabular matter.

congressional districts   Use figures and capitalize *district* when joined with a figure: *the 1st Congressional District, the 1st District.*

Lowercase *district* whenever it stands alone.

court decisions   Use figures and a hyphen: *The Supreme Court ruled 5-4, a 5-4 decision.* The word *to* is not needed, but use hyphens if it appears in quoted matter: *"the court ruled 5-to-4, the 5-to-4 decision."*

court names   For courts identified by a numeral: *2nd District Court, 8th U.S. Circuit Court of Appeals.*

dates   Always use Arabic figures, without *st, nd, rd* or *th.*

decades   Use Arabic figures to indicate decades of history. Use an apostrophe to indicate numerals that are left out; show plural by adding the letter *s*: *the 1890s, the '90s, the Gay '90s, the 1920s, the mid-1930s.*

decimal units   Use a period and numerals to indicate decimal amounts. Decimalization should not exceed two places in textual material unless there are special circumstances.

dimensions   Use figures and spell out *inches, feet, yards* and the like to indicate depth, height, length and width. Hyphenate adjectival forms before nouns.

Use an apostrophe to indicate feet and quote marks to indicate inches (5′6″) only in very technical contexts.

distances   Use figures for *10* and above, spell out *one* through *nine*: *He walked four miles.*

district   Use a figure and capitalize *district* when forming a proper name: *the 2nd District.*

dollars   Use figures and the *$* sign in all except casual references or amounts without a figure: *The book cost $4. Dad, please give me a dollar. Dollars are flowing overseas.*

For specified amounts, the word takes a singular verb: *He said $500,000 is what they want.*

For amounts of more than $1 million, use the *$* and numerals up to two decimal places. Do not link the numerals and the word by a hyphen: *He is worth $4.35 million. He is worth exactly $4,351,242. He proposed a $300 billion budget.*

The form for amounts less than $1 million: *$4, $25, $500, $1,000, $650,000.*

election returns   Use figures, with commas every three digits starting at the right and counting left. Use the word *to* (not a hyphen) in separating different totals listed together: *Bill Clinton defeated George Bush 43,682,625 to 38,117,331. Ross Perot got 19,217,213 votes.*

Use the word *votes* if there is any possibility that the figures could be confused with a ratio: Clinton *defeated* Bush *16 votes to 3 votes in Dixville Notch.*

Do not attempt to create adjectival forms such as *the 48,881,221-41,805,422 vote.*

fractions   Spell out amounts less than 1 in stories, using hyphens between the words: *two-thirds, four-fifths, seven-sixteenths.*

Use figures for precise amounts larger than *1*, converting to decimals whenever practical.

Fractions are preferred, however, in stories about stocks.

When using fractional characters, remember that most newspaper type fonts can set only ⅛, ¼, ⅜, ½, ⅝, ¾, and ⅞ as one unit; use 1½, 2⅝, etc. with no space between the figure and the fraction. Other fractions require a hyphen and individual figures, with a space between the whole number and the fraction: *1 3-16, 2 1-3, 5 9-10.*

highway designations   Use these forms, as appropriate in the context, for highways identified by number: *U.S. Highway 1, U.S. Route 1, U.S. 1, Route 1, Illinois 34, Illinois Route 34, state Route 34, Route 34, Interstate Highway 495, Interstate 495.* On second reference only for Interstate: *I-495.*

mile   Use figures for amounts under 10 in dimensions, formulas and speeds: *The farm measures 5 miles by 4 miles. The car slowed to 7 miles per hour. The new model gets 4 miles more per gallon.*

Spell out below 10 in distances: *He drove four miles.*

millions, billions   Use figures with *million* or *billion* in all except casual uses: *I'd like to make a billion dollars.* But: *The nation has 1 million citizens. I need $7 billion.*

Do not go beyond two decimals: *7.51 million persons, $2.56 billion, 7,542,500 persons, $2,565,750,000.* Decimals are preferred where practical: *1.5 million. Not: 1½ million.*

Do not mix *millions* and *billions* in the same figure: *2.6 billion.* Not: *2 billion 600 million.*

Do not drop the word *million* and *billion* in the first figure of a range: *He is worth from $2 million to $4 million.* Not: *$2 to $4 million,* unless you really mean *$2.*

Note that a hyphen is not used to join the figures and the word *million* or *billion,* even in this type of phrase: *The president submitted a $300 billion budget.*

minus sign   Use a hyphen, not a dash, but use the word *minus* if there is any danger of confusion.

Use a word, not a minus sign, to indicate temperatures below zero: *minus 10* or *5 below zero.*

No.   Use as the abbreviation for *number* in conjunction with a figure to indicate position or rank: *No. 1 man, No. 3 choice.*

Do not use in street addresses, with this exception: *No. 10 Downing St.,* the residence of Britain's prime minister.

Do not use in the names of schools: *Public School 19.*

page numbers   Use figures and capitalize *page* when used with a figure. When a letter is appended to the figure, capitalize it but do not use a hyphen; *Page 1, Page 10, Page 20A.*

One exception: *It's a Page One story.*

percentages   Use figures: *1 percent, 2.5 percent* (use decimals, not fractions), *10 percent.*

For amounts less than 1 percent, precede the decimal with a zero: *The cost of living rose 0.6 percent.*

Repeat *percent* with each individual figure: *He said 10 percent to 30 percent of the electorate may not vote.*

political divisions   Use Arabic figures and capitalize the accompanying word when used with the figure: *1st Ward, 10th Ward, 3rd Precinct, 22nd Precinct, the ward, the precinct.*

proportions   Always use figures: *2 parts powder to 6 parts water.*

ratios   Use figures and a hyphen: *the ratio was 2-to-1, a ratio of 2-to-1, a 2-1 ratio.* As illustrated, the word *to* should be omitted when the numbers precede the word *ratio.*

Always use the word *ratio* or phrase such as *a 2-1 majority* to avoid confusion with actual figures.

Roman numerals   They use letters (*I, X,* etc.) to express numbers.

Use Roman numerals for wars and to establish personal sequence for people and animals: *World War I, Native Dancer II, King George V, Pope John XXIII, John Jones I, John Jones II, John Jones III.* See the *junior, senior* entry in the section on abbreviations and acronyms.

Use Arabic numerals in all other cases.

scores   Use figures exclusively, placing a hyphen between the totals of the winning and losing teams: *The Reds defeated the Red Sox 4-3, the Giants scored a 12-6 football victory over the Cardinals, the golfer had a 5 on the first hole but finished with a 2-under-par score.*

Use a comma in this format: *Boston 6, Baltimore 5.*

sizes   Use figures: *a size 9 dress, size 40 long, 10½ B shoes, a 34½ sleeve.*

speeds   Use figures. *The car slowed to 7 miles per hour, winds of 5 to 10 miles per hour, winds of 7 to 9 knots, 10-knot winds.*

Avoid extensively hyphenated constructions such as *5-mile-per-hour winds.*

telephone numbers   Use figures. The forms: *(212) 262-4000, 262-4000, (212) MU2-0400.* If extension numbers are given: *Ext. 2, Ext. 364, Ext. 4071.*

The parentheses around the area code are based on a format that telephone companies have agreed upon for domestic and international communications.

temperatures   Use figures for all except *zero.* Use a word, not a minus sign, to indicate temperature below zero.

times   Use figures except for *noon* and *midnight.* Use a colon to separate hours from minutes: *11 a.m., 1 p.m., 3:30 p.m.*

Avoid such redundancies as *10 a.m. this morning, 10 p.m. tonight* or *10 p.m. Monday night.* Use *10 a.m. today, 10 p.m. today* or *10 p.m. Monday,* etc.

The construction *4 o'clock* is acceptable, but time listings with *a.m.* or *p.m.* are preferred.

weights   Use figures: *The baby weighed 9 pounds, 7 ounces. She had a 9-pound 7-ounce boy.*

years   Use figures, without commas: *1975.* Use an *s* without an apostrophe to indicate spans of decades or centuries: *the 1890s, the 1800s.*

Years are the lone exception to the general rule in that a figure is not used to start a sentence: *1976 was a very good year.*

Grammar, Spelling and Word Usage

This section lists common problems of grammatical usage, word selection and spelling.

a, an   Use the article *a* before constant sounds: *a historic event, a one-year term* (sounds as if it begins with the letter *w*), *a united stand* (sounds like *you*).

Use the article *an* before vowel sounds: *an energy crisis, an honorable man* (the *h* is silent), *an NBA record* (sounds as if it begins with the letter *e*), *an 1890s celebration.*

accept, except   *Accept* means to receive. *Except* means to exclude.

adverse, averse   *Adverse* means unfavorable: *He predicted adverse weather. Averse* means reluctant, opposed: *She is averse to change.*

affect, effect   *Affect,* as a verb, means to influence: *The game will affect the standings.*

Affect, as a noun, is best avoided. It occasionally is used in psychology to describe an emotion, but there is no need for it in everyday language.

Effect, as a verb, means to cause: *He will effect many changes in the company.*

Effect, as a noun, means result: *The effect was overwhelming. He miscalculated the effect of his actions. It was a law of little effect.*

aid, aide   *Aid* is assistance. An *aide* is a person who serves as an assistant.

ain't   A dialectical or substandard contraction. Use it only in quoted matter or special contexts.

allude, refer   To *allude* to something is to speak of it without specifically mentioning it.

To *refer* is to mention it directly.

allusion, illusion   *Allusion* means an indirect reference: *The allusion was to his opponent's record.*

Illusion means an unreal or false impression: *The scenic director created the illusion of choppy seas.*

among, between   The maxim that *between* introduces two items and *among* introduces more than two covers most questions about how to use these words: *The funds were divided among the elementary schools, the middle schools and the high schools.*

However, *between* is the correct word when expressing the relationships of three or more items considered one pair at a time: *Discussions are under way between the White House and the House and Senate committees.*

As with all prepositions, any pronouns that follow these words must be in the objective case: *among us, between him and her, between you and me.*

anticipate, expect   *Anticipate* means to expect and prepare for something; *expect* does not include the notion of preparation:

They expect a record crowd. They have anticipated it by adding more seats to the auditorium.

anybody, any body, anyone, any one   One word for an indefinite reference: *Anyone can do that.*

Two words when the emphasis is on singling out one element of a group: *Any one of them may speak up.*

apposition   A decision on whether to put commas around a word, phrase or clause used in apposition depends on whether it is essential to the meaning of the sentence (no commas) or not essential (use commas).

because, since   Use *because* to denote a specific cause-effect relationship: *He went because he was told.*

Since is acceptable in a casual sense when the first event in a sequence led logically to the second but was not its direct cause: *He went to the game since he had been given the tickets.*

blond, blonde   Use *blond* as a noun for males and as the adjective for all applications: *She has blond hair.*

Use *blonde* as a noun for females.

boy   Applicable until 18th birthday is reached. Use *man* or *young man* afterward.

brunet, brunette.   Use *brunet* as a noun for males and as the adjective for both sexes.

Use *brunette* as a noun for females.

burglary, larceny, robbery, theft   Legal definitions of *burglary* vary, but in general a *burglary* involves entering a building (not necessarily by breaking in) and remaining unlawfully with the intention of committing a crime.

Larceny is the legal term for the wrongful taking of property. Its non-legal equivalents are *stealing* and *theft.*

Robbery in the legal sense involves the use of violence or threat in committing larceny. In a wider sense it means to plunder or rifle and may thus be used even if a person was not present: *His house was robbed while he was away.*

Theft describes a larceny that did not involve threat, violence or plundering.

USAGE NOTE: You *rob* a person, bank, house, etc., but you *steal* the money or the jewels.

collective nouns   Nouns that denote a unit take singular verbs and pronouns: *class, committee, crowd, family, group, herd, jury, orchestra, team.*

Some usage examples: *The committee is meeting to set its agenda. The jury reached its verdict. A herd of cattle was sold.*

PLURAL IN FORM: Some words that are plural in form become collective nouns and take singular verbs when the group or quantity is regarded as a unit.

Right: *A thousand bushels is a good yield.* (A unit.)

Right: *A thousand bushels were created.* (Individual items.)

Right: *The data is sound.* (A unit.)

Right: *The data have been carefully collected.* (Individual items.)

compose, comprise, constitute   *Compose* means to create or put together. It commonly is used in both the active and passive voices: *He composed a song. The United States is composed of 50 states. The zoo is composed of many animals.*

Comprise means to contain, to include all or embrace. It is best used only in the active voice, followed by a direct object: *The United States comprises 50 states. The jury comprises five men and seven women. The zoo comprises many animals.*

Constitute, in the sense of form or make up, may be the best word if neither *compose* nor *comprise* seems to fit: *Fifty states constitute the United States. Five men and seven women constitute the jury. A collection of animals can constitute a zoo.*

Use *include* when what follows is only part of the total: *The price includes breakfast. The zoo includes lions and tigers.*

contractions   Contractions reflect informal speech and writing. *Webster's New World Dictionary* includes many entries for contractions: *aren't* for *are not*, for example.

Avoid excessive use of contractions. Contractions listed in the dictionary are acceptable, however, in informal contexts or circumstances where they reflect the way a phrase commonly appears in speech or writing.

contrasted to, contrasted with   Use *contrasted to* when the intent is to assert, without the need for elaboration, that two items have opposite characteristics. *He contrasted the appearance of the house today to its ramshackle look last year.*

Use *contrasted with* when juxtaposing two or more items to illustrate similarities and/or differences: *He contrasted the Republican platform with the Democratic platform.*

dangling modifiers   Avoid modifiers that do not refer clearly and logically to some word in the sentence.

Dangling: *Taking our seats, the game started.* (*Taking* does not refer to the subject, *game*, nor to any other word in the sentence.)

Correct: *Taking our seats, we watched the opening of the game.* (*Taking* refers to *we*, the subject of the sentence.)

either   Use it to mean *one or the other*, not *both*.

Right: *She said to use either door.*

Wrong: *There were lions on either side of the door.*

Right: *There were lions on each side of the door. There were lions on both sides of the door.*

either . . . or, neither . . . nor   The nouns that follow these words do not constitute a compound subject; they are alternate subjects and require a verb that agrees with the nearer subject:

Neither they nor he is going. Neither he nor they are going.

essential clauses, non-essential clauses   These terms are used instead of *restrictive clause* and *non-restrictive clause* to convey the distinction between the two in a more easily remembered manner.

Both types of clauses provide additional information about a word or phrase in the sentence.

The difference between them is that the essential clause cannot be eliminated without changing the meaning of the sentence—it so "restricts" the meaning of the word or phrase that its absence would lead to a substantially different interpretation of what the author meant.

The non-essential clause, however, can be eliminated without altering the basic meaning of the sentence—it does not "restrict" the meaning so significantly that its absence would radically alter the author's thought.

PUNCTUATION: An essential clause must not be set off from the rest of a sentence by commas. A non-essential clause must be set off by commas.

The presence or absence of commas provides the reader with critical information about the writer's intended meaning. Note the following examples:

- *Reporters who do not read the stylebook should not criticize their editors.* (The writer is saying that only one class of reporters, those who do not read the stylebook, should not criticize their editors. If the *who . . . stylebook* phrase were deleted, the meaning of the sentence would be changed substantially.)
- *Reporters, who do not read the stylebook, should not criticize their editors.* (The writer is saying that all reporters should not criticize their editors. If the *who . . . stylebook* phrase were deleted, this meaning would not be changed.)

USE OF WHO, THAT, WHICH: When an essential or non-essential clause refers to a human being or an animal with a name, it should be introduced by *who* or *whom*. (See the *who, whom* entry.) Do not use commas if the clause is essential to the meaning; use them if it is not.

That is the preferred pronoun to introduce essential clauses that refer to an inanimate object or an animal without a name. *Which* is the only acceptable pronoun to introduce a non-essential clause that refers to an inanimate object or an animal without a name.

The pronoun *which* occasionally may be substituted for *that* in the introduction of an essential clause that refers to an inanimate object or an animal without a name. In general, this use of *which* should appear only when *that* is used as a conjunction to introduce another clause in the same sentence: *He said Monday that the part of the army which suffered severe casualties needs reinforcement.*

essential phrases, non-essential phrases   These terms are used in this book instead of *restrictive phrase* and *non-restrictive phrase* to convey the distinction between the two in a more easily remembered manner.

The underlying concept is the one that also applies to clauses:

An *essential phrase* is a word or group of words critical to the reader's understanding of what the author had in mind.

A *non-essential phrase* provides more information about something. Although the information may be helpful to the reader's comprehension, the reader would not be misled if the information were not there.

PUNCTUATION: Do not set an essential phrase off from the rest of a sentence by commas:

- *We saw the award-winning movie "One Flew Over the Cuckoo's Nest."* (No comma, because many movies have won awards, and without the name of the movie the reader would not know which movie was meant.)
- *They ate dinner with their daughter Julie.* (Because they have more than

one daughter, the inclusion of Julie's name is critical if the reader is to know which daughter is meant.)

■ *We saw the 1976 winner in the Academy Award competition for best movie, "One Flew Over the Cuckoo's Nest."* (Only one movie won the award. The name is informative, but even without the name no other movie could be meant.)

■ *They ate dinner with their daughter Julie and her husband, David.* (Julie has only one husband. If the phrase read *and her husband David*, it would suggest that she had more than one husband.)

■ *The company chairman, Henry Ford II, spoke.* (In the context, only one person could be meant.)

■ *Indian corn, or maize, was harvested.* (*Maize* provides the reader with the name of the corn, but its absence would not change the meaning of the sentence.)

DESCRIPTIVE WORDS: Do not confuse punctuation rules for non-essential clauses with the correct punctuation when a non-essential word is used as a descriptive adjective. The distinguishing clue often is the lack of an article or pronoun:

Right: *Julie and husband David went shopping. Julie and her husband, David, went shopping.*

Right: *Company Chairman Henry Ford II made the announcement. The company chairman, Henry Ford II, made the announcement.*

every one, everyone   Two words when it means each individual item: *Every one of the clues was worthless.*

One word when used as a pronoun meaning all persons: *Everyone wants to be happy.* (Note that *everyone* takes singular verbs and pronouns.)

farther, further   *Farther* refers to physical distance: *He walked farther into the woods.*

Further refers to an extension of time or degree. *She will look further into the mystery.*

fewer, less   In general, use *fewer* for individual items, *less* for bulk or quantity.

flaunt, flout   To *flaunt* is to make an ostentatious or defiant display: *She flaunted her beauty.*

To *flout* is to show contempt for: *He flouts the law.*

flier, flyer   *Flier* is the preferred term for an aviator or a handbill.

Flyer is the proper name of some trains and buses: *the Western Flyer.*

girl   Applicable until 18th birthday is reached. Use *woman* or *young woman* afterward.

good, well   *Good* is an adjective that means something is as it should be or is better than average.

When used as an adjective, *well* means suitable, proper, healthy. When used as an adverb, *well* means in a satisfactory manner or skillfully.

Good should not be used as an adverb. It does not lose its status as an adjective in a sentence such as *I feel good.* Such a statement is the idiomatic equivalent of *I am in good health.* An alternative, *I feel well,* could be interpreted as meaning that your sense of touch was good.

hopefully   It means in a hopeful manner. Do not use it to mean it is hoped, let us hope or we hope.

Right: *It is hoped that we will complete our work in June.*

Right: *We hope that we will complete our work in June.*

Wrong as a way to express the thought in the previous two sentences: *Hopefully, we will complete our work in June.*

imply, infer   Writers or speakers *imply* in the words they use. A listener or reader *infers* something from the words.

in, into   *In* indicates location: *He was in the room.*

Into indicates motion: *She walked into the room.*

lay, lie   The action word is *lay*. It takes a direct object. *Laid* is the form for its past tense and its past participle. Its present participle is *laying.*

Lie indicates a state of reclining along a horizontal plane. It does not take a direct object. Its past tense is *lay*. Its past participle is *lain*. Its present participle is *lying.*

When *lie* means to make an untrue statement, the verb forms are *lie, lied, lying.*

like, as   Use *like* as a preposition to compare nouns and pronouns. It requires an object: *Jim blocks like a pro.*

The conjunction *as* is the correct word to introduce clauses. *Jim blocks the linebacker as he should.*

majority, plurality   *Majority* means more than half of an amount. *Plurality* means more than the next highest number.

marshal, marshaled, marshaling, Marshall   *Marshal* is the spelling for both the verb and noun: *Marilyn will marshal her forces. Erwin Rommel was a field marshal.*

Marshall is used in proper names: *George C. Marshall, John Marshall, the Marshall Islands.*

obscenities, profanities, vulgarities   Do not use them in stories unless they are part of direct quotations and there is a compelling reason for them.

Confine the offending language, in quotation marks, to a separate paragraph that can be deleted easily.

In reporting profanity that normally would use the words *damn* or *god*, lowercase god and use the following forms: *damn, damn it, goddamn it*. Do not, however, change the offending words to euphemisms. Do not, for example, change *damn it* to *darn it.*

If a full quote that contains profanity, obscenity or vulgarity cannot be dropped but there is no compelling reason for the offensive language, replace letters of an offensive word with a hyphen. The word *damn*, for example, would become *d—* or *—*.

off of   The *of* is unnecessary: *He fell off the bed.* Not: *He fell off of the bed.*

on   Do not use on before a date or day of the week when its absence would not lead to confusion: *The meeting will be held Monday. He will be inaugurated Jan. 20.*

Use *on* to avoid an awkward juxtaposition of a date and a proper name: John met *Mary on Monday.* He told *Clinton on Thursday that the bill was doomed.*

Use *on* also to avoid any suggestion that a date is the object of a transitive verb: *The House killed on Tuesday a bid to amend the crime bill. The Senate postponed on Wednesday its consideration of a bill to reduce import duties.*

over   It is not interchangeable with *more than.*

Over refers to spatial relationships: *The plane flew over the city.*

More than is used with figures: *More than 40,000 fans were in the stadium.*

people, persons   Use *person* when speaking of an individual: *One person waited for the bus.*

The word *people* is preferred to *persons* in all plural uses. For example: *Thousands of people attended the fair. What will people say? There were 17 people in the room.*

Persons should be used only when it is in a direct quote or part of a title as in Bureau of Missing Persons.

People also is a collective noun that takes a plural verb when used to refer to a single race or nation: *The American people are united.* In this sense, the plural is *peoples: The peoples of Africa speak many languages.*

principal, principle   *Principal* is a noun and adjective meaning someone or something first in rank, authority, importance or degree: *She is the school principal. He was the principal player in the trade. Money is the principal problem.*

Principle is a noun that means a fundamental truth, law, doctrine or motivating force: *They fought for the principle of self-determination.*

prior to   *Before* is less stilted for most uses. *Prior to* is appropriate, however, when a notion of requirement is involved: *The fee must be paid prior to the examination.*

reign, rein   The leather strap for a horse is a *rein*, hence figuratively: *seize the reins, give free rein to, put a check rein on.*

Reign is the period a ruler is on the throne: *The king began his reign.*

should, would   Use *should* to express an obligation: *We should help the needy.*

Use *would* to express a customary action: *In the summer we would spend hours by the seashore.*

Use *would* also in constructing a conditional past tense, but be careful:

Wrong: *If Soderholm would not have had an injured foot, Thompson would not have been in the lineup.*

Right: *If Soderholm had not had an injured foot, Thompson would not have been in the lineup.*

spelling   The basic rule when in doubt is to consult the stylebooks, followed by, if necessary, a dictionary.

Memory Aid: Noah Webster developed the following rule of thumb for the frequently vexing question of whether to double a final consonant in forming the present participle and past tense of a verb:

- If the stress in pronunciation is on the first syllable, do not double the consonant: *cancel, canceling, canceled.*
- If the stress in pronunciation is on the second syllable, double the consonant: *control, controlling, controlled; refer, referring, referred.*
- If the word is only one syllable, double a consonant unless confusion would result: *jut, jutted, jutting.* An exception, to avoid confusion with *buss*, is *bus, bused, busing.*

Here is a list of commonly misspelled words:

adviser	cave in (v.)	copter
accommodate	cave-in (n., adj.)	council
Asian flu	chauffeur	counsel
ax	cigarette	drought
baby-sit	clue	drunken
baby sitter	commitment	employee
baby-sitting	consensus	embarrass
cannot	consul	eyewitness

firefighter	kidnaping	skillful
fulfill	likable	subpoena
goodbye	machine gun	teen-age (adj.)
hanged	percent	teen-ager
harass	percentage	under way
hitchhiker	reconnaissance	vacuum
homemade	restaurant	weird
imposter	restaurateur	whiskey
judgment	rock 'n' roll	X-ray (n., v., adj.)

subjunctive mood   Use the subjunctive mood of a verb for contrary-to-fact conditions, and expressions of doubts, wishes or regrets:

If I were a rich man, I wouldn't have to work hard.

I doubt that more money would be the answer.

I wish it were possible to take back my words.

Sentences that express a contingency or hypothesis may use either the subjunctive or the indicative mood depending on the context. In general, use the subjunctive if there is little likelihood that a contingency might come true:

If I were to marry a millionaire, I wouldn't have to worry about money.

If the bill should overcome the opposition against it, it would provide extensive tax relief.

But:

If I marry a millionaire, I won't have to worry about money.

If the bill passes as expected, it will provide an immediate tax cut.

that (conjunction)   Use the conjunction *that* to introduce a dependent clause if the sentence sounds or looks awkward without it. There are no hard-and-fast rules, but in general:

- *That* usually may be omitted when a dependent clause immediately follows a form of the verb *to say*: *The president said he had signed the bill.*
- *That* should be used when a time element intervenes between the verb and the dependent clause: *The president said Monday that he had signed the bill.*
- *That* usually is necessary after some verbs. They include: *advocate, assert, contend, declare, estimate, make clear, point out, propose* and *state*.
- *That* is required before subordinate clauses beginning with conjunctions such as *after, although, because, before, in addition to, until* and *while*: *The senator said that before he would vote for the bill, it would have to be amended.*

When in doubt, include that. Omission can hurt. Inclusion never does.

that, which, who, whom (pronouns)   Use *who* and *whom* in referring to persons and to animals with a name: *John Jones is the man who helped me.* See the *who, whom* entry.

Use *that* and *which* in referring to inanimate objects and to animals without a name.

See the *essential clauses, non-essential clauses* entry for guidelines on using *that* and *which* to introduce phrases and clauses.

under way   Two words in virtually all uses: *The project is under way. The naval maneuvers are under way.*

One word only when used as an adjective before a noun in a nautical sense: *an underway flotilla.*

verbs In general, avoid awkward constructions that split infinitive forms of a verb (*to leave, to help*, etc.) or compound forms (*had left, are found out*, etc.).

Awkward: *She was ordered to immediately leave on an assignment.*

Preferred: *She was ordered to leave immediately on an assignment.*

Awkward: *There stood the wagon that we had early last autumn left by the barn.*

Preferred: *There stood the wagon that we had left by the barn early last autumn.*

Occasionally, however, a split is not awkward and is necessary to convey the meaning:

He wanted to really help his mother.

Those who lie are often found out.

How has your health been?

The budget was tentatively approved.

who, whom Use *who* and *whom* for references to human beings and to animals with a name. Use *that* and *which* for inanimate objects and animals without a name.

Who is the word when someone is the subject of a sentence, clause or phrase: *The woman who rented the room left the window open. Who is there?*

Whom is the word when someone is the object of a verb or preposition: *The woman to whom the room was rented left the window open. Whom do you wish to see?*

See the *essential clauses, non-essential clauses* entry for guidelines on how to punctuate clauses introduced by *who, whom, that* and *which*.

who's, whose *Who's* is a contraction for *who is*, not a possessive: *Who's there?*

Whose is the possessive: *I do not know whose coat it is.*

widow, widower In obituaries: A man *is survived by his wife,* or *leaves his wife*. A woman *is survived by her husband* or *leaves her husband*.

Guard against the redundant *widow of the late*. Use *wife of the late* or *widow of*.

Glossary

absolute privilege The right of legislators, judges and government executives to speak without threat of libel when acting in their official capacities.

absolutism The ethical philosophy that there is a fixed set of principles or laws from which there is no deviation. To the absolutist journalist, the end never justifies the means.

actual malice Reckless disregard of the truth. It is a condition in libel cases.

actual malice test Protection for reporters to write anything about an office-holder or candidate unless they know that the material is false or they recklessly disregard the truth.

ad An advertisement.

add A typewritten page of copy following the first page. "First add" would be the second page of typewritten copy.

advance A report dealing with the subjects and issues to be dealt with in an up-coming meeting or event.

advertising department The department of the newspaper responsible for advertisements. Most advertising departments have classified and display ad sections.

anchor One in the television studio who ties together the newscast by reading the news and providing transitions from one story to the next.

anecdotal lead A newspaper story beginning that uses humor or an interesting incident.

anecdote An informative and entertaining story within a story.

angle The focus of, or approach to, a story. The latest development in a continuing controversy, the key play in a football game, or the tragedy of a particular death in a mass disaster may serve as an angle.

antinomianism The ethical philosophy that recognizes no rules. An antinomian journalist judges every ethical situation on its own merits. Unlike the situation ethicist, the antinomian does not use love of neighbor as an absolute.

AP The Associated Press, a worldwide news-gathering cooperative owned by its subscribers.

APME Associated Press Managing Editors, an organization of managing editors and editors whose papers are members of The Associated Press.

arraignment A court proceeding at which a defendant is informed of the charge. At the proceeding, the defendant is asked to enter a plea, and bail may be set.

background Information that may be attributed to a source by title, but not by name; for example, "a White House aide said."

backgrounder Story that explains and updates the news.

beat A reporter's assigned area of responsibility. A beat may be an institution, such as the courthouse; a geographical area, such as a small town; or a subject, such as science. The term also refers to an exclusive story.

blotter An old-fashioned term for the arrest sheet that summarizes the bare facts of an arrest. Today this information is almost always kept in a computer.

books Assembled sheets of paper, usually newsprint, and carbon paper on which reporters prepare stories. Books are not used with modern computerized processes.

brightener A story, usually short, that is humorous or pleasing to the reader. It is also called a *bright*.

bureau A news-gathering office maintained by a newspaper at other than its central location. Papers may have bureaus in the next county, in the state capital, in Washington, D.C., or in foreign countries.

bureau chief The director of a newspaper's news operations in a remote site or bureau.

business department The newspaper department that handles billing, accounting and related functions.

byline A line identifying the author of a story.

chain Two or more newspapers owned by a single person or corporation. Also known as a *group*. The American chain owning the most newspapers is Gannett.

change of venue An order transferring a court proceeding to another jurisdiction for prosecution. This often occurs when a party in a case claims that local media coverage has prejudiced prospective jurors.

circulation department The department responsible for distribution of the newspaper.

city editor The individual (also known as the *metropolitan,* or *metro, editor*) in charge of the city desk, which coordinates local news-gathering operations. At some papers the desk also handles regional and state news done by its own reporters.

civil law Statutes under which an individual or a group can take action against another individual or group.

clips Stories clipped from your own or other newspapers.

closed-ended question A direct question designed to draw a specific response; for example, "Will you be a candidate?"

conditional privilege See *qualified privilege*.

contributing editor Magazine columnist who works under contract and not as an employee of the magazine.

control The process of structuring an experiment so that the only forces affecting the outcome are the variables you are observing.

copy What reporters write. A story is a piece of copy.

copy desk The desk at which final editing of stories is done, headlines are written and pages are designed.

copy editor A person who checks, polishes and corrects stories written by reporters. Usually copy editors write headlines for those stories, and sometimes they decide how to arrange stories and pictures on a page.

cover To keep abreast of significant developments on a beat or to report on a specific event. The reporter covering the police beat may be assigned to cover a murder.

criminal law Statutes under which a grand jury or an officer of the court can take action against an individual.

cub A beginning reporter.

cutline The caption that accompanies a newspaper or magazine photograph. The term dates from the days when photos were reproduced with etched zinc plates, called cuts.

database A computerized information bank, usually accessed by newspapers on a subscription basis.

deadline The time by which a reporter, editor or desk must have completed scheduled work.

deep background Information that may be used but that cannot be attributed to either a person or a position.

delayed-identification lead Opening paragraph of a story in which the "who" is identified by occupation, city, office, or any means other than by name.

dependent variable See *variable*.

desk A term used by reporters to refer to the city editor's or copy editor's position, as in, "The desk wants this story by noon."

desk assistant Entry-level position in television news rooms. Desk assistants handle routine news assignments such as monitoring wire services and listening to police scanners.

developing story One in which newsworthy events occur over several days or weeks.

dialogue A conversation between two or more people, neither of whom normally is the reporter.

dig To question or investigate thoroughly, as in, "Let's do some digging into those campaign reports."

documentary In-depth coverage of an issue or event, especially in broadcasting.

editor The top-ranking individual in the news department of a newspaper, also known as the *editor in chief*. The term may refer as well to those at any level who edit copy.

editorial department The news department of a newspaper, responsible for all content of the newspaper except advertising. At some papers this term refers to the department responsible for the editorial page only.

editorialize To inject the reporter's or the newspaper's opinion into a news story or headline. Most newspapers restrict opinion to analysis stories, columns and editorials.

editorial page editor The individual in charge of the editorial page and, at larger newspapers, the op-ed (opposite editorial) page.

executive producer The television executive with overall responsibility for the look of the television newscast.

fair comment and criticism   Opinion delivered on the performance of anyone in the public eye. Such opinion is legally protected if reporters do not misstate any of the facts on which they base their comments or criticism, and it is not malicious.

felony   Serious crime punishable by death or imprisonment.

field experiment   A research technique in which the reporter deliberately takes some action to observe the effects. For example, a perfectly tuned automobile could be taken to several repair shops to find out if the mechanics would invent problems that required fixing.

field producer   Behind-the-scenes television reporter who often does much of the field work for a network's on-camera correspondents.

follow   A story supplying further information about an item that has already been published; *folo* is an alternate spelling.

foreshadowing   A technique of teasing readers with material coming later in the story as a way of encouraging them to keep reading.

Freedom of Information Act   A law passed in 1966 to make it easier to obtain information from federal agencies. The law was amended in 1974 to improve access to government records.

free press-fair trial controversy   The conflict between a defendant's right to an impartial jury and a reporter's responsibility to inform the public.

futures file   A collection, filed according to date, of newspaper clippings, letters, notes and other information to remind editors of stories to assign.

general manager   The individual responsible for the business operations of a newspaper. Some newspaper chains award this title to the top-ranking local executive.

graf   A shortened form of *paragraph*, as in "Give me two grafs on that fire."

graphics editor   Usually, the editor responsible for all non-photographic illustrations in a newspaper, including information graphics, maps and illustrations.

handout   See *news release*.

hard lead   A lead that reports a new development or newly discovered fact. See also *soft lead*.

hard news   Coverage of the actions of government or business; or the reporting of an event, such as a crime, an accident or a speech. The time element often is important. See also *soft news*.

human-interest story   A piece valued more for its emotional impact or oddity than for its importance.

hypothesis   In investigative reporting the statement a reporter expects to be able to prove, as in, "The mayor took a bribe from that massage parlor." In an experiment the statement of what a researcher hopes to find.

immediate-identification lead   The opening paragraph of a story in which the "who" is reported by name.

independent variable   See *variable*.

indictment   A document issued by a grand jury that certifies there is sufficient evidence against a person accused of a crime to warrant holding that person for trial.

information graphic   A visual representation of data.

invasion of privacy   Violation of a person's right to be left alone.

inverted pyramid   The organization of a news story in which information is arranged in descending order of importance.

investigative reporting   The pursuit of information that has been concealed, such as evidence of wrongdoing.

IRE   Investigative Reporters and Editors, a group created to exchange information and investigative reporting techniques. IRE has its headquarters at the University of Missouri School of Journalism.

lay out (v.)   The process of preparing page drawings to indicate where stories and pictures are to be placed in the newspaper.

layout (n.)   The completed page drawing, or page dummy.

lead   (1) The first paragraph or first several paragraphs of a newspaper story (sometimes spelled *lede*); (2) the story given the best display on Page One; (3) a tip.

lead-in   An introduction to a filmed or recorded excerpt from a news source or from another reporter.

lead story   The major story displayed at the top of Page One.

libel   Damage to a person's reputation caused by a false written statement that brings the person into hatred, contempt or ridicule, or injures his or her business or occupational pursuit.

maestro   The leader of a news-gathering team. Reporters, copy editors, editors and graphic designers work with a maestro to create special reports.

managing editor   The individual with primary responsibility for day-to-day operation of the news department.

margin of error (also called sampling error)   In surveys, the range within which you can be confident of accuracy. A survey with a margin of error of 3 percent, for example, typically has a 95 percent chance of being accurate within 3 percent above or below the exact result. An allowance must be made in any survey for the possibility that the sample questioned may not be exactly like all other members of the population.

misdemeanors   Minor criminal offenses, including most traffic violations, which usually result in a fine or brief confinement in a local jail.

more   Designation used at the end of a page of copy to indicate there are one or more additional pages.

morgue   The newspaper library, where published stories, photographs and resource material are stored for reference.

multiple-element lead   The opening paragraph of a story that reports two or more newsworthy elements.

narration   The telling of a story, usually in chronological order.

negligence test   The legal standard that requires reporters to use the same care in gathering facts and writing a story as any reasonable individual would under similar circumstances.

network correspondent   A television reporter who delivers the news on camera. Network correspondents may or may not do the actual news-gathering for their stories.

new media The emerging forms of computer-delivered news.

news conference An interview session, also called a *press conference*, in which someone submits to questions from reporters.

news director The top news executive of a local television station.

news editor The supervisor of the copy desk. At some newspapers, this title is used for the person in charge of local news-gathering operations.

news release An item, also called a *handout* or *press release*, that is sent out by a group or individual seeking publicity.

news room The place, sometimes called the *city room*, where reporters and editors work.

news story A story that emphasizes the facts, often written in inverted pyramid style.

news value How important or interesting a story is.

not for attribution Information that may not be ascribed to its source.

nut paragraph A paragraph that summarizes the key element or elements of the story. Usually found in a story not written in inverted pyramid form. Also called a *nut graf*.

obscenity A word or phrase usually referring to sexual parts or functions in an offensive way.

off-camera reporter One who gathers news for television but does not report on the air.

off the record Usually means, "Don't quote me." Some sources and reporters, however, use it to mean, "Don't print this." Phrases with similar, and equally ambiguous, meanings are "not for attribution" and "for background only."

op-ed page The page opposite the editorial page, frequently reserved for columns, letters to the editor and personality profiles.

open-ended question One that permits the respondent some latitude in the answer; for example, "How did you get involved in politics?"

open meetings laws State and federal laws, often called *sunshine laws*, guaranteeing access to meetings of public officials.

open records laws State and federal laws guaranteeing access to many—but not all—kinds of government records.

page designer One who designs newspaper or magazine pages.

parallelism A technique of presenting ideas in similar grammatical forms.

paraphrase A paraphrase digests, condenses and clarifies a quotation to convey the meaning more precisely or succinctly than the way in which the speaker's words express it. Quotation marks are eliminated.

participant observation A research technique in which the reporter joins in the activity he or she wants to write about.

payola Money or gifts given in the expectation of favors from journalists.

photo editor The individual who advises editors on the use of photographs in the newspaper. The photo editor also may supervise the photography department.

piece See *story*.

plagiarism The use of any part of another's writing and passing it off as your own.

play   A shortened form of *display*. A good story may be played at the top of Page One; a weak one may be played inside.

poll   The measurement of opinion by questioning members of some small group chosen at random so as to be representative of the entire group. A poll is also referred to as a *survey* or *public opinion poll*. See also *randomization*.

population   In scientific language the whole group being studied. Depending on the study the population may be, for example, voters in St. Louis, physicians in California or all residents of the United States.

preliminary hearing   A court hearing held to determine whether there is probable cause that a defendant committed a crime and whether the defendant should be bound over for grand jury action or trial in a higher court.

press   The machine that prints the newspaper. Also a synonym for journalism, as in the phrase "freedom of the press." Sometimes used to denote print journalism, as distinguished from broadcast journalism.

press agent   A person hired to gain publicity for a client. The tactics used, often called *press agentry*, might include the staging of interviews or stunts designed to attract the attention of reporters.

press box   The section of a stadium or arena set aside for reporters.

press conference   See *news conference*.

press release   See *news release*.

privilege   A defense against libel that claims the right to repeat what government officials say or do in their official capacities.

production department   The department of the newspaper that transforms the work of the news and advertising departments into the finished product. The composing room and press room are key sections of this department.

profanity   A word or phrase contemptuously referring to the deity or to beings regarded as divine; a sacrilegious expression.

profile   A story intended to reveal the personality or character of an institution or person.

public figure   A person who has assumed a role of prominence in the affairs of society and who has persuasive power and influence in a community or who has thrust himself or herself to the forefront of a public controversy. Courts have given journalists more latitude in reporting on public figures.

public journalism   The new (or rediscovered) approach to journalism that emphasizes connections with the community rather than separation from it. Among the newspapers best known for practicing public journalism are the Wichita (Kan.) *Eagle* and the Charlotte (N.C.) *Observer*.

publisher   The top-ranking executive of a newspaper. This title often is assumed by the owner, although chains sometimes designate as publisher the top local executive.

Pulitzer Prize   The most prestigious of journalism awards. It was established by Joseph Pulitzer and is administered by Columbia University.

qualified privilege   The right to report what government officials say or do in their official capacities if the report is full, fair and accurate. Also called *conditional privilege*.

quote   As a noun, the term refers to a source's exact words, as in, "I have a great quote here." As a verb, it means to report those words inside quotation marks.

randomization   The mathematical process used to assure that every member of a population being studied has an equal chance of being chosen for questioning or observation. See also *poll*.

records column The part of the newspaper featured regularly that contains such information as routine police and fire news, births, obituaries, marriages and divorces.

reporter A person whose job it is to gather and write the news for a publication or a broadcast outlet.

rewrite To write a story again in an effort to improve it. It also means to take information over the telephone from a reporter in the field and mold it into a story.

roundup A story including a number of related events. After a storm, for example, a reporter might do a roundup of accidents, power outages and other consequences of the storm.

sample A portion of a group, or population, chosen for study as representative of the entire group.

scenic lead A lead that concentrates on a description of an environment.

second-cycle story A second version of a story already published, also called a *second-day story*. It usually has new information or a new angle.

senior editor One who edits sections of major magazines.

senior writer A title reserved for a magazine's best and most experienced reporters.

series Two or more stories on the same or related subjects, published on a predetermined schedule.

set-up In broadcasting, an introductory statement to pique the interest of listeners or viewers.

shield laws Legislation giving journalists the right to protect the identity of sources.

show producer Television news specialists who produce individual newscasts and report to the executive producer.

sidebar A secondary story intended to be run with a major story on the same topic. A story about a disaster, for example, may have a sidebar that tells what happened to a single victim.

situation ethics The philosophy that recognizes that a set of rules can be broken when circumstances dictate the community will be served better by it. For example, a journalist who believes it normally unethical to deceive a news source may be willing to conceal his or her identity to infiltrate a group operating illegally.

slug A word that identifies a story as it is processed through the newspaper plant. It is usually placed in the upper left-hand corner of each take of the story. See also *take*.

sniff The preliminary phrase of an investigation.

soft lead A lead that uses a quote, anecdote or other literary device to attract the reader. See also *hard lead*.

soft news Stories about trends, personalities or lifestyles. The time element usually is not important. See also *hard news*.

sources People or records from which a reporter gets information. The term often is used to describe persons, as opposed to documents.

spot news A timely report of an event that is unfolding at the moment.

spreadsheet Computer program adept at managing numbers. Often used for budgets.

story The term most journalists use for a newspaper article. Another synonym is *piece*, as in, "I saw your piece on the mayor." A long story may be called a *takeout* or a *blockbuster*.

stylebook A book of standard usage within newspaper text. It includes rules on grammar, punctuation, capitalization and abbreviation. The AP and UPI publish similar stylebooks that are used by most papers. (Portions of the AP and UPI stylebooks are reprinted in Appendix 2 of this book.)

substantial truth The correctness of the essential elements of a story.

summary lead The first paragraph of a news story in which the writer presents a synopsis of two or more actions rather than focusing on any one of them.

sunshine laws See *open meetings laws*.

take A page of typewritten copy for newspaper use.

30 A designation used to mark the end of a newspaper story. The symbol # is an alternate designation.

tickler A file of upcoming events kept on paper or computer at the assignment desks of most news organizations. See also *futures file*.

tie-back The sentence or sentences relating a story to events covered in a previous story. Used in follow-up or continuing stories or in parts of a series of stories. Also, the technique of referring to the opening in the ending of the story.

tip A fragment of information that may lead to a story; also called a *lead*.

transition A word, phrase, sentence or paragraph that moves the reader from one thought to the next and shows the relationship between them.

undercover reporting A technique in which a reporter pretends to be someone else in order to gain access to otherwise unobtainable information.

universal desk A copy desk that edits material for all editorial departments of a newspaper.

update A type of follow that reports on a development related to an earlier story.

UPI United Press International, a worldwide news-gathering organization that is privately owned.

variable In an experiment, one of the elements being observed. The independent variable is what is thought to be a cause; the dependent variable is the effect of that cause.

videographer A television camera operator.

videoprompter A mechanical or electronic device that projects broadcast copy next to the television camera lens so that a newscaster can read it while appearing to look straight into the lens.

vulgarity A word or phrase dealing with excretory matters in a less-than-polite way.

wrap-up The completion of commentary that comes at the end of a taped segment in broadcasting; a strong ending to a report.

Acknowledgments (cont. from p. iv)

P. 251. "Prime Time Crime: TV Coverage Heavy; Violence Easy to Cover and Gripping, Too" by Harry Levins, Aug. 14, 1994, reprinted with permission of the *St. Louis Post-Dispatch*, copyright 1994.

Pp. 284-287. Articles reprinted with permission of the *St. Louis Post-Dispatch*, copyright 1991–1995.

Pp. 381-382. Article by Jane Meinhardt, *St. Petersburg Times*, reprinted courtesy of *St. Petersburg Times*.

Pp. 387, 388. "High Heat" by Erik Larson, Copyright © Dow Jones & Co., reprinted by permission.

Pp. 389-391. "A rainy night, a grudge, a bomb" by Todd Moore, reprinted courtesy of the *Madison* (Wis.) *Capital Times*.

Illustration Credits

Chapter 1 opener, p. (xxii), Bob Daemmrich/The Image Works.

Figure 1.1, p. 6, Courtesy of New Directions for News.

Figure 1.2, p. 8, Courtesy of New Directions for News.

Photo p. 10, Courtesy of Nancy Tracewell.

Chapter 2 opener, p. 16, Jeff Greenberg/Photo Edit.

Photo p. 22, Courtesy of the *Wall Street Journal*.

Figure 2.7, pp. 28-29, Reprinted by permission of the *Seattle Times*.

Photo p. 36, Courtesy of Kabby Hong.

Photo p. 40, Courtesy of April Eaton.

Chapter 3 opener, p. 46, *The Sun*, Baltimore.

Figure 3.1, pp. 50-51, *The Sun*, Baltimore.

Photo , p. 52, Courtesy of Kelley Carpenter.

Chapter 4 opener, p. 72, Kenneth Jarecke/Contact Press Images.

Figure 4.1, p. 76; *top left* (William Raspberry), The *Washington Post* Writers Group; *top right* (Anna Quindlen), Graig Filipacchi/Gamma Liaison; *bottom* (Russell Baker) Harold Krieger, Courtesy of William Morrow & Company, Inc.; p. 77; *top* (Edna Buchanan), Pulitzer Prize Committee, Columbia Star-Telegram; *bottom* (Molly Ivins), Bob Daemmrich/Stock Boston.

Photo p. 78, Dale Blackwell/Fort Worth *Star-Telegram*.

Figure 4.2, p. 79, Les Stone/Sygma.

Chapter 5 opener, p. 96, Robert Kalman/The Image Works.

Figure 5.1, p. 101, Robert Kalman/The Image Works.

Photo p. 102, Courtesy of Karen Branch.

Figure 5.2, p. 103, J. Bryson/Sygma.

Figure 5.3, p. 105, Courtesy of CBS News, New York City.

Chapter 6 opener, p. 120, Bob Daemmrich/The Image Works.

Figure 6.1, p. 125, Bob Daemmrich/The Image Works.

Photo p. 130, Courtesy of Jo Ellen Krumm.

Chapter 7 opener, p. 148, Robert McElroy/Woodfin Camp.

Photo p. 154, Courtesy of Charles Hammer.

Chapter 8 opener, p. 166, Elise Amendola/AP Wide World Photos.

Photo p. 174, Courtesy of Yves Colon.

Figure 8.2, p. 177, Reprinted with permission from *Newsday*.

Chapter 9 opener, p. 182, Courtesy of the American Heart Association.

Photo p. 190, Courtesy of Jo Johnston.

Chapter 10 opener, p. 198, Doug Bauman/*The Oakland Press*/Sygma.

Photo p. 204, Photo by Larry Sharron, Courtesy of Barry Murov.

Figure 10.1, p. 205, Doug Bauman/ *The Oakland Press*/Sygma.

Figure 10.2, p. 209, Courtesy of *The Plain Dealer*, Cleveland.

Chapter 11 opener, p. 216, Mark Kulaw/*N.W. Florida Daily News*/Sygma.

Figure 11.1, p. 220, Mark Kulaw/*N.W. Florida Daily News*/Sygma; p. 221, Douglas A. Pizac/AP/Wide World Photos.

Photo p. 232, Courtesy of the *Miami Herald*.

Chapter 12 opener, p. 238, Faye Ellman.

Photo p. 244, Courtesy of *The Orange County Register*.

Figure 12.3, p. 265, Damian Dovarganes/AP/Wide World Photos.
Chapter 13 opener, p. 272, Peter Morgan/Reuters/Bettman.
Photo p. 280, Courtesy of Renée Stovsky.
Figure 13.2, p. 283, Bob Daemmrich/Stock, Boston.
Chapter 14 opener, p. 292, D. Ogust/The Image Works.
Figure 14.1, p. 296, D. Ogust/The Image Works.
Figure 14.2, p. 299, Bob Daemmrich/Stock, Boston.
Photo p. 300, Courtesy *Kansas City Star*.
Photo p. 306, Courtesy Susan Drumheller.
Figure 14.3, p. 308, Lester Sloan/*Newsweek*/Gamma-Liaison.
Chapter 15 opener, p. 330, Bob Daemmrich/Stock, Boston.
Figure 15.1, p. 333, Bob Daemmrich/Stock, Boston.
Photo p. 334, Courtesy Nik Deogun.
Figure 15.2, p. 345, Mantel/Sipa Press.
Figure 15.3, p. 348, Rod Little/*US News and World Report*.
Figure 15.4, p. 351, Reprinted with permission from *Consumer Reports*; Published by Consumers Union of the United States, Inc.
Chapter 16 opener, p. 356, Bob Daemmrich/Stock, Boston.
Photo p. 358, Courtesy the *Phoenix Gazette*.
Figure 16.1, p. 363, Alan Carey/The Image Works.
Figure 16.2, p. 372, *Washington Post* photo.
Chapter 17 opener, p. 374, Marc Pesetsky/Reuters/Bettmann.
Figure 17.1, p. 377, Paul Sakuma/AP/Wide World Photos.
Photo p. 386, Skip Peterson/*Dayton Daily News*.
Chapter 18 opener, p. 392, Bob Daemmrich/Stock, Boston.
Photo p. 394, Courtesy Jon Schmid Sotomeyer.
Figure 18.1, p. 395, Richard Gabe/*US News and World Report*.
Figure 18.2, p. 401, Bob Daemmrich/Stock, Boston.
Chapter 19 opener, p 404, Courtesy CBS News, New York City.
Figure 19.1, p. 406, Courtesy of the Pelletier Library, Allegheny College, Meadville, PA 16335.
Photo p. 418, Courtesy Bob Paynter.
Chapter 20 opener, p. 424, Beringer/Dratch/The Image Works.
Photo p. 432, Courtesy Russ Lopez.
Chapter 21 opener, p. 444 © 1989 by Sandra Davidson Scott.
Figure 21.1, p. 448, © 1989 by Sandra Davidson Scott.
Photo p. 450, Courtesy Ken Paulson
Figure 21.2, p. 463, Allan Tannenbaum/Sygma.
Chapter 22 opener, p. 466, Bob Daemmrich/Stock, Boston.
Photo p. 474, Courtesy John Callan.

Index